Presented To:

From:

Date:

Tree of Life
עץ חיים

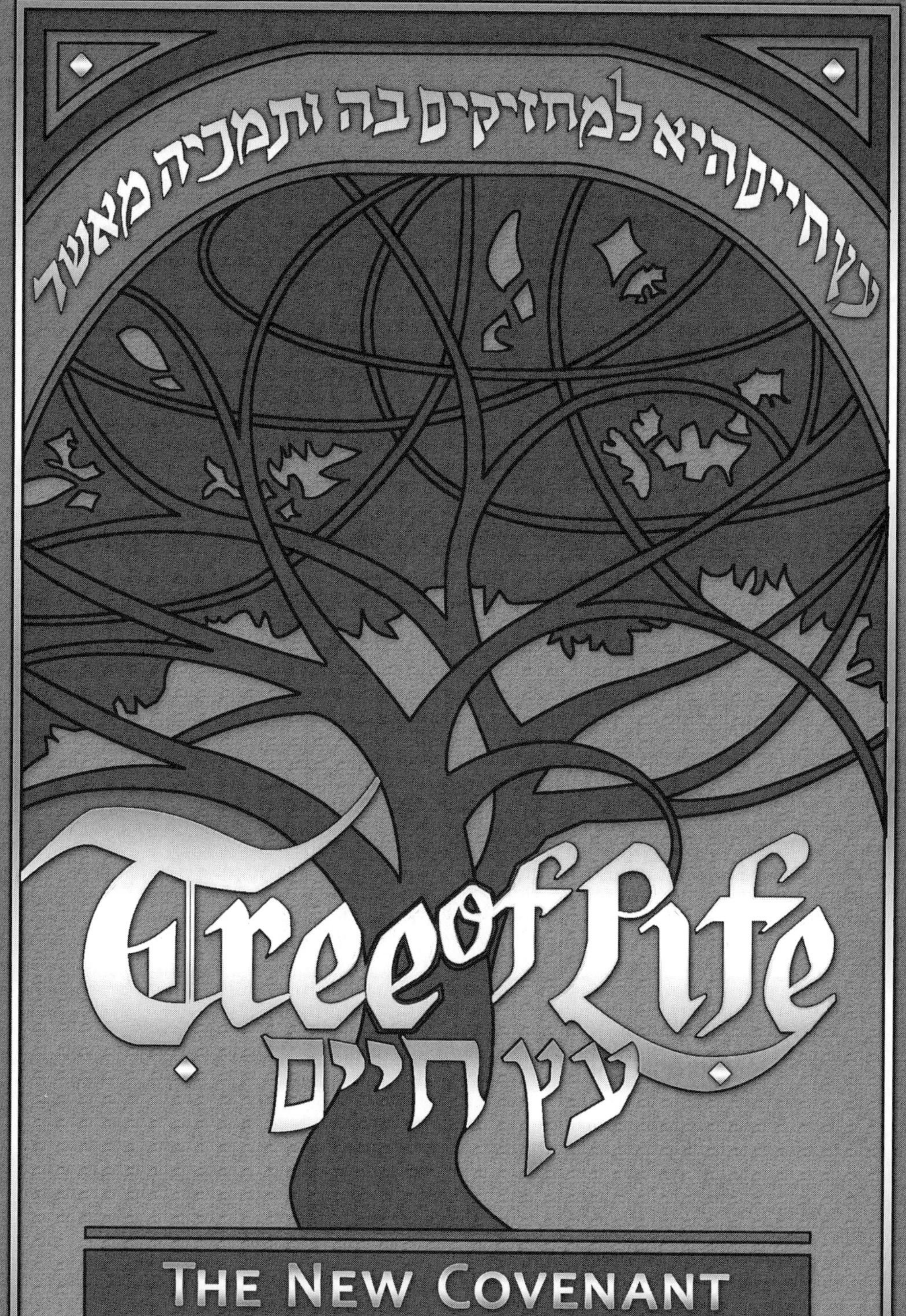
עץ חיים היא למחזיקים בה ותמכיה מאשר
Tree of Life
עץ חיים
THE NEW COVENANT

DESTINY IMAGE® PUBLISHERS, INC.

P.O. Box 310, Shippensburg, PA 17257-0310

"Speaking to the Purposes of God for This Generation and for the Generations to Come."

This book and all other Destiny Image, Revival Press, MercyPlace, Fresh Bread, Destiny Image Fiction, and Treasure House books are available at Christian bookstores and distributors worldwide.

For a U.S. bookstore near you, call 1-800-722-6774.

For more information on foreign distributors, call 717-532-3040.

Reach us on the Internet: www.destinyimage.com.

ISBN 13 TP: 978-0-7684-3815-4

ISBN 13 HC: 978-0-7684-3816-1

ISBN 13 E-book: 978-0-7684-8984-2

For Worldwide Distribution, Printed in the U.S.A.

1 2 3 4 5 6 7 8 9 10 11 / 13 12 11

Messianic Jewish Family Bible Project

Board of Directors

Dear Readers,

What a privilege to delve into God's Word in the original languages and determine its message as it applies to Messiah's community today! Our collaborative team, composed of scholars from five international Messianic Jewish organizations, works closely together. Taking a consensus building approach, the vetting team looks carefully at the underlying Greek and Hebrew, to render a translation that is accurate, readable, reverential, and true to the worldview that brings together Jewish and Gentile people in Yeshua. By the time our text has passed through these various lenses with helpful editorial suggestions, the blending produces a vibrant storyline that no single contributor could offer individually.

It is critical for each one—translators, theologians, language experts, editors, designers, artists, and you our readers—to remember that this story is not about us. The Tree of Life is God's story! The narrative comes alive in the vivid, in-the-moment drama of the pages within this Good Book. Even the tenses of Greek verbs come alive in English when the historic presents are translated in present time. As we grasp hold of it and hold it tight (Proverbs 3:18), we can appropriate His story for our own lives.

The vetting process reflects this intensely personal and intimate interaction. The end of this process is a fresh and authentic understanding that invites the reader to watch history almost as a participant standing at the scene of historic event after historic event. For example, when Yeshua tells the high priest of Israel that God will raise and seat Him at God's very own right hand (Ps. 110:1 in Mark 14:61-67), the reader, standing with Peter at the scene, can almost hear the high priest rip apart his own clothing and turn Yeshua over to the Romans for blasphemy! It's no wonder that every Messianic Jew, in the days following the resurrection, understood clearly that God had vindicated His Son, Yeshua Ben-Elohim, by seating Yeshua at His own right hand—a privilege that no one but deity could boast in and then experience!

The Tree of Life Messianic Family Bible strives to maintain the cultural flavor of the original Jewish context, so that all who enter this story might deepen their understanding and be enriched. We all can rejoice with the psalmist in singing Hinei mah tov—Behold, how good and how pleasant it is for brothers and sisters to dwell together in unity (Psalm 133:1).

It is the prayer of the theologians in our Messianic Jewish Family Bible Project that every reader may hear God's voice within the pages of His Word, and that we all might truly listen and respond. Revelation 22:17 gives each one of us the invitation to freely take the water of life—let the one who is thirsty come!

In Messiah's Service,
Tree of Life Bible
Theology Team

Biblical Text Development Team

Biblical Text Management Team

Rabbi Jeffrey E. Feinberg, M.Div., Ph.D.
Patricia K. Feinberg, M.S.T., M.A.
Etz Chaim Messianic Congregation, UMJC

Theology Vetting Team

Rabbi Jeffrey Adler, M.Div.
Sha'arey Yeshua Messianic Synagogue, IAMCS

Raymond L. Gannon, M.Div., Th.M., Ph.D., Ph.D.
Director of Messianic Jewish Studies, The King's College and Seminary

Noel S. Rabinowitz, Th.M., Ph.D.
Associate Professor of Biblical Studies, The King's College

Rich Robinson, M.Div., Ph.D.
Senior Researcher, Jews for Jesus

Rabbi Eric Tokajer, Th.B.
Brit Ahm Messianic Jewish Synaogue, IAMCS

Biblical Language Experts

Richard E. Averbeck, M.Div., Ph.D.,
Professor of Old Testament & Semitic Languages,
Trinity Evangelical Divinity School

Michael Brown, Ph.D
President, FIRE School of Ministry

Craig Keener, M.Div., Ph.D.,
Professor of New Testament, Palmer Seminary of Eastern University

Adjunct Translators

Rabbi John Fischer, Ph. D, Th. D.
The Netzer David International Yeshiva, Founder

Patrice Fischer, Ph. D
The Netzer David International Yeshiva, Co-Founder

Henri Louis Goulet, M.A., S.T.M., PhD (ABD) Candidate
University of Cape Town, South Africa

Stanley Horton, M. Div, Th. D.
Assemblies of God, Beloved Church Elder

Seth Postell, Ph.D.
Professor, Israel College of the Bible

Matthew Salathe, M.R.S. D. Min
Master of Rabbinic Studies, The Netzer David International Yeshiva

Theology Team Adviser

Daniel Juster, M. Div., M.Div., Th.D.
President, Tikkun International Ministries

Literary Editor

Rabbi Glenn Blank, M.S., Ph.D.
Beit Simcha, Director of Tikkun America

Creative Development Team

Dean Drawbaugh
Destiny Image Publishers, General Manager

Daniah Greenberg
Tree of Life Bible, Project Manager

Jacob Rogers
Marketing and Web Design, treeof lifebible.org

Buck Stephens
Tree of Life Bible, Corporate Adviser

Michael Washer
Fine Artist & Graphic Designer, mwmastersdesign.com

Board of Reference

Foundation for Leadership and Messianic Education
flamefoundation.org

International Alliance of Messianic Jewish Congregations and Synagogues
iamcs.org

Jewish Voice Ministries International
jewishvoice.org

Jews For Jesus
jewsforjesus.org

Jewish Jewels
jewishjewels.org

Messianic Daily News
messianicdailynews.com

Messianic Jewish Israel Fund
mjif.org

Messianic Jewish Alliance of America
mjaa.org

Messianic Jewish Resources International
messianicjewish.net

Promise Keepers & Road to Jerusalem
promisekeepers.org

Shivat Tzion Ministries
prophecyrevealed.com

Shoresh David Messianic Synagogues of Florida
shoreshdavid.org

Sounds of Shalom Internet Radio Station
soundsofshalom.com

Tikkun Ministries International
tikkunministries.org

Union of Messianic Jewish Congregations
umjc.org

Endorsements

"The Tree of Life Bible is a wonderful new Bible. It is Jewish in context without being strained in archaic language. It is trustworthy. It provides great art, helpful section titles and more. Jewish and Gentile people will love this Bible."

Daniel Juster, Th. D.,
Director of Tikkun International,
Author of *Jewish Roots, A Foundation of Biblical Theology,* and *Israel, the Church and the Last Days.*

"Jewish people wrestle with the question of what it means to be both Jewish and Jesus-believing. Messianic Jewish theologians engaged in Bible translating wrestle with the question of how to help readers understand the so-called Christian text in its actual Jewish context. What you have in hand is an excellent example of how that challenge has been met and resolved. You'll love it."

Dr. Jeffrey L. Seif
Zola Levitt Ministries

Table of Contents

Acknowledgments

This Messianic Jewish Family Bible Project was inspired by the lifelong experiences and calling of a group of Rabbi's wives who recognized the desperate need for an updated Messianic translation for the children of our unique synagogues.

This yearning led to a journey that was started by the initial sacrificial efforts of a fifth generation Messianic Jewish family, the Galileys, who began preparing manuscripts for a Messianic Children's Bible. While that work has yet to be completed, it helped to galvanize our community to come together to create a brand new, vetted translation that is a modern day fulfillment of Romans 3:2. May God bless Rabbi Steve, Deborah and Joshua Galiley for their contribution to the initial vision that was the forerunner to this completed work of the TLV New Covenant.

We also want to honor Dr. David Stern and Rabbi Barry Rubin in their publication of the Complete Jewish Bible. That groundbreaking work is credited with creating the common language that began building the culture of our growing Messianic community over this last decade. We pray God continues to use the CJB mightily for many decades to come.

With special thanks, we also want to acknowledge the work of Kahunapule Michael Johnson of World Outreach Ministries, the author of the HNV, the World English Bible: Messianic Edition. That labor of love produced an online version with enough Hebrew flavor to inspire us to press on when our project seemed too huge to dream of completing. Their willingness to share it free-of-charge with the entire world is a blessing only our Abba in Heaven can reward fully. We are honored to have use of their scholarship and brotherhood.

Likewise, we want to formally acknowledge all the hard work and endless scholarship that has gone into creating all of the many Bible translations our team of scholars gleaned from, including the NKJV, the NASB, the NIV, and the NET. We are truly grateful.

For all these contributions, we thank our Messiah and Lord, Yeshua. We hope to that restoring the family Bible to the heart of every home can renew our communities and impact the world around us with God's message of love through Messiah Yeshua. He truly is the author and finisher of our faith. Blessed is He who comes in the Name of the Lord!

Board of Directors
Messianic Jewish Family Bible Project

Tree of Life Bible Features

Brand New Professionally Vetted Text: With God's help, our team has assembled a brand new English translation of the New Covenant using the 27th Nestle-Aland Novum Testamentum Graece and over a dozen additional resources including every mainstream,vetted English Bible translation. Plus, we especially enjoyed learning from the work of the HNV scholars, and the work of David Stern in the Complete Jewish Bible. Our fervent hope was to render a messianic sensitive text that would be as accurate as the NASB, as reverent as the NKJV, and as readable as the NIV. We pray our effort is worthy of the great and mighty God we serve. We stand in awe of His Name.

Messianic Illustrations: In an age of visual media, having new art pieces to enjoy with our young family members is paramount. Our team collaborated about our vision to produce 24 original pieces of art for this TLV New Covenant. Our messianic artist, Michael Washer, has created new renderings in pencil of some of the world's most beloved biblical scenes. His research and diligence succeed in bringing a refreshing passion for the Jewish roots of our shared faith in Messiah *Yeshua* (Jesus). Enjoy!

Cross Referencing Footnotes: We chose to use the footnotes in this Bible to assist the reader in three important ways. First, we noted each time the New Covenant writers were pointing you to a Messianic Prophecy verse from the Tanakh (Old Covenant). These footnotes are a treasure hunt for readers who want to research the evidence of *Yeshua* through the eyewitness testimony of His followers! Next, we used some footnotes to indicate variances in the original manuscripts referenced in this work. Lastly, we include occasional footnotes that provide a better understanding about biblical units of weights and measures.

Inspiring Book Introductions: Having information that explains who the author is, who his audience is and when the book was approximately written helps the modern day reader to better understand the cultural perspective of each book of the Bible. For example, it is fascinating to learn that even *Yeshua's* own brothers, Jacob (James), and Judah (Jude), came to believe in Him after His resurrection!

Storytelling Headings: The headings are especially interesting. The "A Look into..." pages tell the unique story line of each of the Gospels. Take note that the headings in Acts follow the same historical progression of Luke. Meanwhile, the Letters' headings are road signs to the theme of each dialog between the reader and his specific audience. We believe it helps to see all these headings as landmarks within a flowing text. And, we hope they will help you easily navigate to the last place you were reading. Studying large portions of text in context may promote a more inductive small group learning style.

Unique Glossary: Instead of a concordance, we chose to provide a glossary to explain the specific vocabulary that makes this Bible so exciting. As lifelong students of God's Word, our research revealed that there are many words used in Scripture that some people tend to skip over. Or, they determine the definition of a word by interpreting it's meaning within each sentence. We chose to provide you with the definition we intended when we translated to help us determine a baseline for shared language for our readers. Taking time to learn definitions helps build a strong foundation for shared understanding. We believe the reader will find this valuable.

Hebrew Word Choices: Hebrew words often contain layers of meaning that are dependent upon the context in which the word is used. For example, most of our readers know that *shalom* technically means "peace," but it can also be a simple greeting, or, in the fullest terms, "complete restoration and wholeness." When we chose words for this messianic translation, we took careful liberty using occasional Hebrew 'transliterated' words (*in italics*) to add fuller meaning to the text. In this way, you will find their definitions in the glossary, and we were able to resist paraphrasing. Plus, you can learn Hebrew by sounding out the English letters.

Family Friendly Vocabulary: This Bible is designed for adults and youth to enjoy together. The majority of vocabulary choices are at about a current 10th grade reading level. We sought to provide a reasonable perimeter to encourage both family devotionals and advanced scholarship. We believe that the lessons in the Bible can be grasped by all ages and enjoyed across generations. We do not believe that using more advanced vocabulary would have increased the accuracy of this translation. We want everyone to feel able to read and understand this new biblical text.

Original Maps: We included two maps of the Promised Land, how it may have looked during *Yeshua's* journey in Luke and how the Land of Israel is measured today when this book is published. And, we included maps of all four of Rabbi Paul's journeys when writing his letters throughout the Middle East. Being able to look at where and how the Good News spread abroad on the same land God's people inhabit today, both Jew and Gentile alike, reaffirms the faithfulness of our Creator.

Messianic Shabbat Prayers: You will find a handful of very popular Shabbat prayers in the back of this Bible. These are most commonly used for worship time in both homes and community gatherings. Shabbat begins at sundown on Friday evening and usually includes a family meal together. Shabbat day is spent worshipping *ADONAI* in corporate gatherings, studying the Bible, praying for the sick, home fellowship meals, welcoming seekers and resting in Him. Then, just before the sun goes down that afternoon, we close Shabbat by blessing *ADONAI*.

The Lord's Prayer (in Hebrew): Finally, we chose to include "The Lord's Prayer" in Hebrew as an open invitation to all people who desire to follow the teachings of our Messiah, Yeshua. When we pray as *Yeshua* taught us, and come to our Heavenly Father in His Name, we are putting our trust in Him.

Foreword

It is a tree of life to those who grasp hold of it,
and all who hold it tight will be blessed (Proverbs 3:18).

Besorah is the Hebrew word for Gospel, and it means Good News! In this new, vetted translation of the New Covenant, you can read about this Good News four times. Matthew, Mark, Luke, and John each give their own story of the life of *Yeshua*—Jesus—whose name means salvation for Jewish and Gentile people alike.

Why read this Tree of Life Version (TLV) of the New Covenant? Because it gives families a fresh perspective of how first-century Jews came to worship the Risen Lord, *Yeshua Ben-Elohim.*[a] Reading this account will help you understand who *Yeshua* really is, so you can worship and give glory to God.

God's Promise to Abraham's Seed

For thousands of years the Jewish people have been waiting for a Messiah to come. Even learned Jewish people of *Yeshua's* day were waiting for the One *Adonai* had promised through His prophets.

During *Yeshua's* lifetime here on earth, many Jewish people did not fully understand who He was. When He was born and angels proclaimed the Good News, only a few shepherds were present. *Yeshua* grew up an average person in an average place. He was thirty years old, and still few people knew who He was. His hometown did not believe in Him, and there was little faith and no recognition. At *Yeshua's* immersion, a voice from Heaven said, "This is My Son, whom I love; with Him I am well pleased."[b] But the people did not know that *Yeshua Ben-David* was *Yeshua Ben-Elohim,*[c] because in Jewish terms it didn't make sense.

The New Covenant tell *Yeshua's* story and how people came to believe as they walked with Him, one "step of faith" at a time.

When *Yeshua* began His public ministry at a wedding in Cana, people may have thought He was some kind of "miracle worker." They understood He could do miracles, but the average Jewish person didn't associate His mighty works with His being deity—at least not during *Yeshua's* life on earth. Demons cried out; Gentiles bowed low; and the blind, the lame, and others at the margin may have seen *Yeshua* as the Prophet or even as lord—but not "Lord," as in the only Son of the only God in all the world.

As *Yeshua* grew in popularity, the religious authorities saw Him as a threat to the establishment. The more miracles He did, the more they hardened. Their reaction was to conspire to kill Him. The people, meanwhile, flocked to *Yeshua*. Miracles were happening! News was spreading! Yet the crowd followed out of self-interest, some just trying to get miracles out of *Yeshua*. Many would come and go. Even some of *Yeshua's*

a Son of God, a title for the Messiah.
b Matthew 3:17.
c *Yeshua* Son of David was *Yeshua* Son of God.

followers left when He said they must eat His flesh and drink His blood. They couldn't grasp that *Yeshua* was imparting His very life into them—the teaching was just too difficult. Only the closest remnant of His followers remained, and they continued to struggle in their budding faith.

Yeshua used Psalm 110 to ask a question of the crowd, the Pharisees, and the *Torah* scholars.[a] How could King David call his son "Lord"? No one had an answer, and it silenced the arguments against Him. But they still didn't understand who *Yeshua* was. How could David's offspring be deity?

At *Yeshua's* trial, the *kohen gadol* confronted Him about His identity. It was then that *Yeshua* joined Psalm 110 together with Daniel 7.[b] He said they would see "the Son of Man sitting at the right hand of power and coming on the clouds of heaven." Seated where? On the throne of God? At the right hand of Power? Nobody believed such a wild claim! Blasphemy was the charge, as the *kohen gadol* tore his clothes and turned *Yeshua* over to the Romans to be beaten and killed.

God in the Flesh

But the story doesn't end there! *Yeshua* had said that God would send Him back, that God would raise Him up and give Him a seat on the throne.[c] Before the resurrection, nobody could digest the idea that life after death could start right now. God in the flesh? That's beyond our imagination! The disciples couldn't even begin to think of *Yeshua* as God-in-the-flesh until He returned from the dead. Yet seeing is believing.

All of a sudden it makes sense—the virgin birth, the miracles, everything! The disciples now understood that if *Yeshua* had risen from the dead, the rest of the story would follow too—all the things Scripture said, namely that God would seat Him at His right hand and send Him back one day in the clouds with great glory. God would do that only with His equal. He wouldn't raise up an angel to send back, and He certainly wouldn't raise up some random person who claimed to have His authority. Once the Jewish people saw *Yeshua* resurrected, they could put their trust in Him. Yes, seeing is believing.

We're all like Thomas—we doubt until we can see for ourselves. When *Yeshua* rises from the dead and shows up to the disciples, Thomas is missing and doesn't believe the news. Yet when Thomas sees the risen *Yeshua*, He is the first Jew we read about saying, "My God and my Lord!"[d] *Yeshua* responds by telling him, "Blessed are the ones who have not seen and yet have believed!" Often perceived as a rebuke, this response challenges Thomas to grow in faith and encourages future believers to trust as well.

Notice the vividness of the historic present tense demonstrated here, and how it captures the reader in the scene as it unfolds. At first, this switch to the present may seem a bit unusual, until you imagine the Gospel writers reliving their story with you as an eyewitness by their side.

The Gospel accounts reveal a gradual dawning of awareness among those who come to put their trust in *Yeshua*. The day Peter says, "You are the Messiah, the Son

a Mark 12:35-37; Matthew 22:44-46; Luke 20:42-43.
b Matthew 26:64; Mark 14:62; Luke 22:69
c Matthew 26:64
d John 20:25-28

of the Living God,"[a] he doesn't fully understand that *Yeshua* is God's equal. When the disciples see *Yeshua* calming the sea, they do not see Him as God's equal. Even when *Yeshua* raises Lazarus from the dead, people do not see Him as God's equal.

In Greek, *Yeshua's* title is "Kurios"—but you, the reader, must decide whether it means "Sir," "Master," or "Lord." Only the Narrator knows for sure! Over time, we come to realize that *Yeshua* is no ordinary master. *Yeshua* is Lord—and not the kind of Lord that could be a king, or a miracle worker, or a supernatural being like an angel, or even one of the gods that other nations would worship. He is the Risen Lord, *Yeshua Ben-Elohim*.

The Tree of Life Messianic Family Bible

The Gospel accounts of this book have been certified and inspected to give a thoroughly Jewish understanding of what happened during *Yeshua's* life. Many of the largest Messianic Jewish organizations of the world have pooled their talents and reached agreement on the authenticity of the Jewish understanding of this translation. The aim of their top theologians has been to enter into a process of dialogue and writing to ensure accuracy, clarity, and reverence for God's Word. More than fifty people have worked together to make ***The Tree of Life Messianic Family Bible*** the kind of resource that moms can read to their kids, congregations can read at their services, and scholars can use as a text for study and commentary. It is our hope that Jewish people will learn, once again, that they were the first to recognize *Yeshua* as Lord and proclaim Him as *Ben-Elohim*. We hope that in this way, all Israel will be saved![b]

In fact, bringing so many Jewish and Messianic Jewish perspectives together for one project was something of a miracle already. With unanimous consent, not majority rule, the Lord is blessing our work. Rest assured that our rigorous translation and vetting process has been cross checked by respected Christian scholars. The beauty of having such a diverse team is that all involved are committed to "do no violence to the text."

Destiny Image Publishing graciously agreed to help fund the development of the manuscript under the direct guidance of the Theology Committee of this Bible project. Halleluyah!

Accuracy with Readability

Faithfulness to the original text is one key principle for this newly vetted ***Tree of Life New Covenant***. It is a new translation born out of the public domain American Standard Version of 1901, updated by a Messianic Jewish reading of the Greek text, Nestle-Aland *Novum Testamentum Graece* 27th edition. Our goal is to create a reliable and accurate text that is accessible to family members for generations to come.

For such a momentous task, we invite the *Ruach ha-Kodesh* to guide us. One great challenge is to maintain a balance between accuracy and readability. One of the unique features of this version is the vibrant, "in the moment" vividness of this text. You can "hear" Matthew, Mark, Luke, and John telling their testimonies about Messiah as we stick as close to the Greek as possible using the historic present tense of the verb. This pulls you right into their stories!

a Matthew 16:16
b cf. Romans 11:26

We have provided you with introductions to help you understand who each narrator is and a glossary to help you learn new words that give more meaning to the text. Pay special attention to the different headings that give a unique voice to each Gospel. Matthew's headings show lesson themes. Mark's headings show the signs and wonders of Yeshua's ministry. Luke's headings show the historical progression of Yeshua's journey among mankind. John's headings are more metaphorical in nature.

So the Entire World Will Know

For centuries scribes have faithfully preserved the Bible, word for word, in Hebrew, Aramaic, and Greek. If a scribe made a single mistake copying the *Torah*, the whole scroll was considered unfit for use. Before the modern printing press, scribes produced copies on animal skins, and they often illustrated Bibles with beautiful artwork.

In addition to archeological discoveries confirming its historical reliability, one of the most amazing proofs of the Bible's accuracy came out of a cave in the Judean desert, just as the modern state of Israel was born in 1948, when a Bedouin shepherd discovered the Dead Sea Scrolls. Jewish people who lived in the first century left behind scrolls of most books of the Hebrew Bible. Miraculously, the Word of God has been preserved!

With the invention of the printing press, Bibles became available to own and keep in every home. Before then, only religious leaders could pass Scripture down to people through word of mouth, memorization, and song. Mostly it was read out loud at public gatherings and worship times.

When the United States was colonized, the Bible was an integral part of daily family life. For the next 150 years, it was the mainstay of the family altar at home. With the Bible, children learned how to read, and the Bible became foundational to the moral values, laws, and culture of most Americans, both Christian and Jewish. Yet in recent generations, the prominence of the Family Bible in American life, literacy, and morality has waned. It is time for a Family Bible revolution!

Yeshua—The Tree of Life

We want the whole world to know that it is Jewish to believe in *Yeshua*, the Jewish Messiah. *Yeshua* is the Messiah for all who believe—Jew and Gentile alike. We are all one in Messiah's love.

If you are a Jew who is curious about Messiah, these New Covenant will help you, with help from the *Ruach ha-Kodesh*, to see how *Yeshua* became the Prophet like Moses, full of glory, grace, and truth. Compare what Matthew, Mark, Luke, and John say with what the Hebrew Bible says—the footnotes point the way for you. If you are already a believer in Messiah *Yeshua*, you are encouraged to share copies of these New Covenant with others. The seed of the Good News will cause salvation to sprout wherever it is read. *Yeshua* alone is able to fill an empty heart and rebuild a broken life. *Yeshua* is the Tree of Life.

The middle wall of partition is crumbling, and the Spirit of God is restoring our unity and teaching us that our diversity is our strength, not a weakness. The time to favor Zion is now.

The Good News According to Matthew

Introduction

None of the Gospels originally came with titles, but the Gospel of Matthew was most likely written by Matthew, also called Levi. He was a tax collector and one of the twelve *shlichim*. The Gospel was written some time around 70–85 C.E.

Matthew is one of the two most "Jewish" Gospels, along with John. With a first-century Jewish audience in mind and drawing richly on references to the *Tanakh*, it paints a picture of *Yeshua* as the fulfillment of the Messianic hope, the promised Messiah, and the King of Israel (whose kingdom is both future, yet begun now). In this way Matthew shows that *Yeshua's* coming, His person, and His work of atonement is the fulfillment of God's promises given in the Hebrew Bible—the promises of the God of Abraham, Isaac, and Jacob. Matthew also emphasizes *Yeshua* as the One who fulfills the *Torah*. And as a Jew, Matthew has significant things to say about the Jewish leadership of his day and their attitude toward *Yeshua*, as relevant today as in the first century. Though Jewish in its orientation, the Gospel ends with a call to make disciples of *all* nations, thereby showing the worldwide implications of Jesus' coming.

Whereas the shorter Gospel of Mark focuses on *Yeshua's* deeds, Matthew is richer in giving us *Yeshua's* teaching and in portraying *Yeshua* as the authoritative teacher of Israel. There are five teaching sections, each ending with "when *Yeshua* had finished..." Chief among these are the Sermon on the Mount, the large number of parables, and *Yeshua's* teaching on the end of the age. Matthew, along with Luke, also tells of the events surrounding *Yeshua's* virgin birth.

The breadth of Matthew's Gospel makes it suitable for Jewish people willing to study what God has promised in the *Tanakh* concerning the Messiah, and also for anyone who wants to learn something about *Yeshua*, His relation to the Hebrew Bible, and the dynamics of faith in *Yeshua* within the Jewish community.

A Look Inside Matthew

Baruch Ha-Ba! Blessed Is He
Who Comes! (21:1)
Faith Moves Mountains (21:18)
Questions about
Yeshua's Authority (21:23)
A Parable about Intentions
and Actions (21:28)
Parable of the Vineyard (21:33)

Invitation to the Wedding Feast (22:1)
A Trap about Paying Taxes (22:15)
Religious Leaders Ask
a Tricky Question (22:23)
The Greatest Mitzvot (22:34)
Yeshua Overturns the Arguments (22:41)

Seven Woes (23:1)
Holy Temple to Be Destroyed (23:37)

Signs of the End of Time (24:3)
Watching for Messiah's Return (24:32)
The Faithful Servant (24:45)

Parable of the Ten Virgins (25:1)
Parable of the Talents (25:14)
The Righteous Judge (25:31)

The Conspiracy Grows (26:1)
A Woman Anoints *Yeshua*
for Burial (26:6)
Betrayed and Sold for Silver (26:14)
"Your Will Be Done" (26:36)
Taken into Custody (26:47)
Yeshua's Trial Begins (26:59)
Peter Denies *Yeshua* (26:69)

Judah's Remorse (27:1)
"Kill the King!" (27:11)
Nailed to a Stake (27:27)
Yeshua Lays Down His Life (27:45)
The Tomb Is Sealed (27:55)
Guarding the Tomb (27:62)

The Son Is Risen! (28:1)
The Good News Cannot Be Hidden (28:9)
Authority to Make
Disciples Everywhere (28:16)

1

Forefathers of *Yeshua* the Messiah

[1]The book of the genealogy[a] of *Yeshua*
ha-Mashiach, Ben-David,[b] *Ben-Avraham*:
[2]Abraham fathered Isaac, Isaac fathered
Jacob, Jacob fathered Judah and his
brothers, [3]Judah fathered Perez and
Zerah by Tamar,[c] Perez fathered Hezron,
Hezron fathered Ram, [4]Ram fathered
Amminadab, Amminadab fathered
Nahshon, Nahshon fathered Salmon,
[5]Salmon fathered Boaz by Rahab, Boaz
fathered Obed by Ruth,[d] Obed fathered
Jesse, [6]and Jesse fathered David the
king.

David fathered Solomon by the
wife of Uriah,[e] [7]Solomon fathered
Rehoboam, Rehoboam fathered Abi-
jah, Abijah fathered Asa, [8]Asa fathered
Jehoshaphat, Jehoshaphat fathered
Joram, Joram fathered Uzziah, [9]Uzziah
fathered Jotham, Jotham fathered Ahaz,
Ahaz fathered Hezekiah, [10]Hezekiah
fathered Manasseh, Manasseh fathered
Amon, Amon fathered Josiah, [11]and
Josiah fathered Jeconiah and his broth-
ers at the time of the exile to Babylon.

[12]After the Babylonian exile Jeconiah
fathered Shealtiel, Shealtiel fathered
Zerubbabel, [13]Zerubbabel fathered
Abiud, Abiud fathered Eliakim, Eliakim
fathered Azor, [14]Azor fathered Zadok,
Zadok fathered Achim, Achim fathered
Eliud, [15]Eliud fathered Eleazar, Eleazar
fathered Matthan, Matthan fathered
Jacob, [16]and Jacob fathered Joseph the
husband of Miriam, from whom was born
Yeshua who is called the Messiah. [17]So all
the generations from Abraham to David
are fourteen generations, from David
until the Babylonian exile are fourteen
generations, and from the Babylonian
exile until the Messiah are fourteen
generations.

The Miraculous Birth of *Yeshua*

[18]Now the birth of Yeshua the Messiah happened this way. When His
mother Miriam was engaged to Joseph
but before they came together, she was
found to be pregnant through the Ruach
ha-Kodesh. [19]And Joseph her husband,
being a righteous man and not wanting to disgrace her publicly, made up his
mind to dismiss her secretly. [20]But while
he considered these things, behold, an
angel of ADONAI appeared to him in a
dream, saying, "Joseph son of David, do
not be afraid to take Miriam as your wife,
for the Child conceived in her is from the
Ruach ha-Kodesh. [21]She will give birth to
a son; and you shall call His name Yeshua,
for He will save His people from their
sins."

[22]Now all this took place to fulfill what
was spoken by ADONAI through the
prophet, saying, [23]"Behold, the virgin
shall conceive and give birth to a son,
and they shall call His name Immanuel,"
which means "God with us."[f]

[24]When Joseph woke up from his
sleep, he did as the angel of ADONAI commanded him and took Miriam as his wife.
[25]But he did not know her intimately
until she had given birth to a Son. And he
called His name Yeshua.

2

Wise Men Follow His Star

[1]Now after *Yeshua* was born in Bethlehem of Judea, in the days of King Herod,
magi from the east came to Jerusalem,
[2]saying, "Where is the One who has been
born King of the Jews? For we saw His
star in the east and have come to worship Him."[g]

a 1:1. The Greek term is *genesis*.
b 1:1. cf. 2 Sam. 7:12-16; Ps. 89:4-5(3-4); Isa. 9:5-6(6-7).
c 1:3. cf. Gen. 38:24-30.
d 1:5. cf. Ruth 4:12-17.
e 1:6. cf. 2 Sam. 12:24.
f 1:23. Isa. 7:14; 8:8, 10.
g 2:2. cf. Isa. 9:5-6(6-7); Jer. 23:5; 30:9.

Matthew 1:22-23

Now all this took place to fulfill what was spoken by ADONAI through the prophet, saying, "Behold, the virgin shall conceive and give birth to a son, and they shall call His name Immanuel," which means "God with us."

[3]When King Herod heard, he was troubled, and all Jerusalem with him. [4]And when he had called together all the ruling *kohanim* and *Torah* scholars, he began to inquire of them where the Messiah was to be born. [5]So they told him, "In Bethlehem of Judea, for so it has been written by the prophet:

[6]'And you, Bethlehem, land of Judah,
are by no means least among the rulers of Judah;
For out of you shall come a ruler
who will shepherd My people Israel.'"[a]

[7]Then Herod secretly called the magi and determined from them the exact time the star had appeared. [8]And he sent them to Bethlehem and said, "Go and search carefully for the Child. And when you have found Him, bring word back to me so that I may come and worship Him as well."

[9]After listening to the king, they went their way. And behold, the star they had seen in the east went on before them, until it came to rest over the place where the Child was. [10]When they saw the star, they rejoiced exceedingly with great gladness. [11]And when they came into the house, they saw the Child with His mother Miriam; and they fell down and worshiped Him. Then, opening their treasures, they presented to Him gifts of gold, frankincense, and myrrh.[b] [12]And having been warned in a dream not to go back to Herod, they returned to their own country by another way.

The Angel of *Adonai* Appears

[13]Now when they had gone, behold, an angel of *Adonai* appears to Joseph in a dream, saying, "Get up! Take the Child and His mother and flee to Egypt. Stay there until I tell you, for Herod is about to search for the Child, to kill Him."[c]

a 2:6. Mic. 5:1(2); cf. 2 Sam. 5:2.
b 2:11. cf. Ps. 72:10-11.
c 2:13. cf. Exod. 1:16.

[14]So he got up, took the Child and His mother during the night, and went to Egypt. [15]He stayed there until Herod's death. This was to fulfill what was spoken by *Adonai* through the prophet, saying, "Out of Egypt I called My Son."[d]

[16]Then when Herod saw that he had been tricked by the magi, he became furious. And he sent and killed all boys in Bethlehem and in all its surrounding area, from two years old and under, according to the time he had determined from the magi. [17]Then was fulfilled what was spoken through Jeremiah the prophet, saying,

[18]"A voice is heard in Ramah,
weeping and loud wailing,
Rachel sobbing for her children
and refusing to be comforted,
because they are no more."[e]

[19]But when Herod died, behold, an angel of *Adonai* appears in a dream to Joseph in Egypt, [20]saying, "Get up! Take the Child and His mother and go to the land of Israel, for those seeking the Child's life are dead."

[21]So he got up, took the Child and His mother, and went to the land of Israel. [22]But hearing that Archelaus was king of Judea in place of his father Herod, he became afraid to go there. Then after being warned in a dream, he withdrew to the region of the Galilee. [23]And he went and lived in a city called *Natzeret*,[f] to fulfill what was spoken through the prophets, that *Yeshua* shall be called a *Natzrati*.

3

John's Witness to Israel's Leaders

[1]In those days, John the Immerser came proclaiming in the wilderness of Judea, [2]"Turn away from your sins, for

d 2:15. Hos. 11:1.
e 2:18. Jer. 31:14(15).
f 2:23. From *netzer*, meaning *shoot* or *branch*; cf. Isa. 11:1.

the kingdom of heaven is near!"[a] 3For he is the one Isaiah the prophet spoke about, saying,

> "The voice of one crying in the
> wilderness,
> 'Prepare the way of ADONAI,
> and make His paths straight.'"[b]

4Now John wore clothing from camel's hair and a leather belt around his waist, and his food was locusts[c] and wild honey.
5Then Jerusalem was going out to him, and all Judea and all the region around the Jordan. 6Confessing their sins, they were being immersed by him in the Jordan River.

7But when he saw many Pharisees and Sadducees coming to his immersion, he said to them, "You brood of vipers! Who warned you to flee from the coming wrath? 8Therefore produce fruit worthy of repentance; 9and do not think that you can say to yourselves, 'We have Abraham as our father'! For I tell you that from these stones God can raise up children for Abraham. 10Already the axe is laid at the root of the trees; therefore every tree that does not produce good fruit is cut down and thrown into the fire!

11"As for me, I immerse you in water for repentance. But the One coming after me is mightier than I am; I am not worthy to carry His sandals. He will immerse you in the Ruach ha-Kodesh and fire. 12His winnowing fork is in His hand, and He shall clear His threshing floor and gather His wheat into the barn; but the chaff He shall burn up with inextinguishable fire."d

The Heavens Open at *Yeshua's Mikveh*

13Then *Yeshua* came from the Galilee to John, to be immersed by him in the Jordan. 14But John tried to prevent Him, saying, "I need to be immersed by You, and You are coming to me?"

15But *Yeshua* responded, "Let it happen now, for in this way it is fitting for us to fulfill all righteousness." So John yielded to Him.

16After being immersed, Yeshua rose up out of the water; and behold, the heavens were opened to Him, and He saw the Spirit of Gode descending like a dove and coming upon Him. 17And behold, a voice from the heavens said, "This is My Son, whom I love; with Him I am well pleased!"f

4

Overcoming Temptation with God's Word

1Then *Yeshua* was led by the *Spirit* into the wilderness to be tempted by the devil. 2After He had fasted for forty days and forty nights, He was hungry. 3And when the tempter came to Him, he said, "If You are *Ben-Elohim*, tell these stones to become bread."

4But He replied, "It is written, 'Man shall not live by bread alone, but by every word that comes from the mouth of God.'"[g]

5Then the devil took Him into the holy city and placed Him on the highest point of the Temple. 6"If You are *Ben-Elohim*," he said, "throw Yourself down. For it is written,

> 'He shall command His angels concerning you,'[h]
> and 'upon their hands they shall lift
> you up,
> so that you may not strike your foot
> against a stone.'"[i]

a 3:2. cf. Dan. 2:44.
b 3:3. Isa. 40:3.
c 3:4. cf. Lev. 11:22.
d 3:12. cf. Ps. 1:4; Jer. 7:20.
e 3:16. cf. Gen. 1:2
f 3:17. cf. Ps. 2:7; Prov. 30:4.
g 4:4. Deut. 8:3.
h 4:6. Ps. 91:11.
i 4:6. Ps. 91:12.

7 *Yeshua* said to him, "Again it is written, 'You shall not put ADONAI your God to the test.'"[a]

8 Again, the devil takes Him to a very high mountain and shows Him all the kingdoms of the world and their glory. 9 And he said to Him, "All these things I will give You, if You fall down and worship me."

10 Then *Yeshua* says to him, "Go away, satan! For it is written, 'You shall worship ADONAI your God, and Him only shall you serve.'"[b] 11 Then the devil leaves Him. And behold, angels came and began to take care of Him.

Yeshua Withdraws to Seek God

12 Now when *Yeshua* heard that John had been handed over, He withdrew to the Galilee. 13 Leaving *Natzeret*, He came and settled in Capernaum, which is by the sea in the regions of Zebulun and Naphtali. 14 This was to fulfill what was spoken through Isaiah the prophet, saying,

15 "Land of Zebulun and land of
  Naphtali,
the way of the sea, beyond the
  Jordan,
Galilee of the nations—
16 the people sitting in darkness
  have seen a great light,
and those sitting in the region and
  shadow of death,
on them a light has dawned."[c]

17 From then on, *Yeshua* began to proclaim, "Turn away from your sins, for the kingdom of heaven is near."

Raising Up Fishers of Men

18 Now as *Yeshua* was walking by the Sea of Galilee, He saw two brothers, Simon who was called Peter and Andrew his brother. They were casting a net into the sea, for they were fishermen. 19 And He said to them, "Follow Me, and I will make you fishers of men." 20 Immediately they left their nets and followed Him.

21 Going on from there, He saw two other brothers, Jacob the son of Zebedee and John his brother. They were in the boat with Zebedee their father, mending their nets, and He called them. 22 Immediately they left the boat and their father and followed Him.

23 *Yeshua* was going throughout all the Galilee, teaching in their synagogues and proclaiming the Good News of the kingdom, and healing every kind of disease and sickness among the people. 24 News about Him spread throughout all Syria. And they brought to Him all the sick—those tormented by various diseases and afflictions, those plagued by demons, the epileptics, the paralyzed—and He healed them. 25 And large crowds followed Him from the Galilee, the Decapolis, Jerusalem, Judea, and beyond the Jordan.

5

Drash on the Mountain

1 Now when *Yeshua* saw the crowds, He went up on the mountain. And after He sat down, His disciples came to Him. 2 And He opened His mouth and began to teach them, saying,

3 "Blessed are the poor in spirit,
  for theirs is the kingdom of heaven.
4 "Blessed are those who mourn,
  for they shall be comforted.
5 "Blessed are the meek,
  for they shall inherit the earth.
6 "Blessed are those who hunger and
  thirst for righteousness,
  for they shall be satisfied.
7 "Blessed are the merciful,
  for they shall be shown mercy.
8 "Blessed are the pure in heart,
  for they shall see God.
9 "Blessed are the peacemakers,
  for they shall be called sons of God.

a 4:7. Dt. 6:16.
b 4:10. Dt. 6:13.
c 4:15-16. Isa. 8:23-9:1(9:1-2).

10“Blessed are those who have
been persecuted for the sake of
righteousness,
for theirs is the kingdom of heaven.

11“Blessed are you when people revile you and persecute you and say all kinds of evil against you falsely, on account of Me.

12Rejoice and be glad, for your reward in heaven is great! For in the same way they persecuted the prophets who were before you.”[a]

Called to Be Salt and Light

13“You are the salt of the earth; but if the salt should lose its flavor, how shall it be made salty again? It is no longer good for anything, except to be thrown out and trampled under foot by men.

14“You are the light of the world. A city set on a hill cannot be hidden. 15Neither do people light a lamp and put it under a basket. Instead, they put it on a lampstand so it gives light to all in the house. 16In the same way, let your light shine before men so they may see your good works and glorify your Father in heaven.”

Filling the Law to the Fullest

17“Do not think that I came to abolish the *Torah* or the Prophets! I did not come to abolish, but to fulfill. 18Amen, I tell you, until heaven and earth pass away, not the smallest letter or serif[b] shall ever pass away from the *Torah* until all things come to pass. 19Therefore, whoever breaks one of the least of these commandments, and teaches others the same, shall be called least in the kingdom of heaven. But whoever keeps and teaches them, this one shall be called great in the kingdom of heaven. 20For I tell you that unless your righteousness exceeds that of the Pharisees and *Torah* scholars, you shall never enter the kingdom of heaven!

21“You have heard it was said to those of old, ‘You shall not murder,[c] and whoever commits murder shall be subject to judgment.’ 22But I tell you that everyone who is angry with his brother shall be subject to judgment. And whoever says to his brother, ‘*Raca*’ shall be subject to the council[d]; and whoever says, ‘You fool!’ shall be subject to fiery Gehenna.

23“Therefore if you are presenting your offering upon the altar, and there remember that your brother has something against you, 24leave your offering there before the altar and go. First be reconciled to your brother, and then come and present your offering.

25“Make friends quickly with your opponent while you are with him on the way. Otherwise, your opponent may hand you over to the judge, and the judge to the assistant, and you will be thrown into prison. 26Amen, I tell you, you will never get out of there until you have paid back the last penny![e]

27“You have heard that it was said, ‘You shall not commit adultery.’[f] 28But I tell you that everyone who looks upon a woman to lust after her has already committed adultery with her in his heart. 29And if your right eye causes you to stumble, gouge it out and throw it away! It is better for you that one part of your body should be destroyed, than that your whole body be thrown into Gehenna.[g] 30And if your right hand causes you to stumble, cut it off and throw it away! It is better for you that one part of your body should be destroyed, than that your whole body go into Gehenna.

31“It was said, ‘Whoever sends his wife away, let him give her a certificate of divorce.’[h] 32But I say to you that everyone who divorces his wife, except for sexual immorality, makes her commit adultery;

a 5:12. cf. 2 Chr. 36:16.
b 5:18. Lit. one *iota* or one horn/projection/hook; in Hebrew, one *yod* or one crown/ornament/stroke.
c 5:21. Exod. 20:13; Dt. 5:17.
d 5:22. Lit. *Sanhedrin*.
e 5:26. Lit. *quadrans*, a small Roman coin.
f 5:27. Exod. 20:13(14); Deut. 5:18.
g 5:29. cf. Isa. 66:24; for more, see Glossary.
h 5:31. Heb. *get*; cf. Deut. 24:1-4.

and whoever marries a divorced woman commits adultery.

33“Again, you have heard that it was said to those of old, ‘You shall not swear falsely, but shall carry out your oaths to ADONAI.’[a] 34But I tell you, do not swear at all—not by heaven, for it is the throne of God; 35or by the earth, for it is the footstool of His feet;[b] or by Jerusalem, for it is the city of the Great King.[c] 36And do not swear by your head, for you cannot make a single hair white or black. 37But let your word ‘Yes’ be ‘Yes’ and your ‘No,’ ‘No’—anything more than this is from the evil one.”

Overcoming Evil with Good

38“You have heard that it was said, ‘An eye for an eye, and a tooth for a tooth.’[d] 39But I tell you, do not resist an evildoer. But whoever slaps you on your right cheek, turn to him also the other. 40And the one wanting to sue you and to take your shirt, let him also have your coat. 41Whoever forces you to go one mile, go with him two. 42Give to the one who asks of you, and do not turn away from the one who wants to borrow from you.

43“You have heard that it was said, ‘You shall love your neighbor[e] and hate your enemy.’ 44But I tell you, love your enemies and pray for those who persecute you, 45so that you may be children of your Father in heaven. He causes His sun to rise on the evil and the good, and sends rain on the righteous and the unrighteous. 46For if you love those who love you, what reward do you have? Even the tax collectors do the same, don’t they? 47And if you greet only your brothers, what more are you doing than anyone else? Even the pagans do that, don’t they? 48Therefore be perfect, just as your Father in heaven is perfect.”

a 5:33. Lev. 19:12.
b 5:34-35. cf. Isa. 66:1(LXX).
c 5:35. cf. Ps. 48:3(2).
d 5:38. Exod. 21:24; Lev. 24:20; Deut. 19:21.
e 5:43. Lev. 19:18.

6

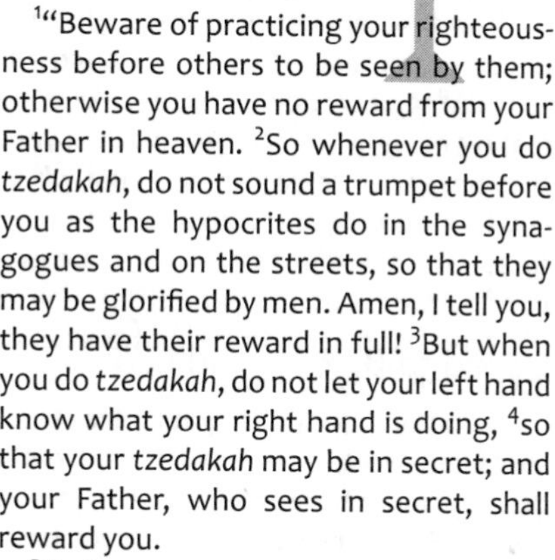

Righteous Living

1“Beware of practicing your righteousness before others to be seen by them; otherwise you have no reward from your Father in heaven. 2So whenever you do *tzedakah*, do not sound a trumpet before you as the hypocrites do in the synagogues and on the streets, so that they may be glorified by men. Amen, I tell you, they have their reward in full! 3But when you do *tzedakah*, do not let your left hand know what your right hand is doing, 4so that your *tzedakah* may be in secret; and your Father, who sees in secret, shall reward you.

5“When you pray, do not be like the hypocrites; for they love to pray standing in the synagogues and on the street corners, so that they may be seen by others. Amen, I tell you, they have their reward in full! 6But you, when you pray, go into your inner room; and when you have shut your door, pray to your Father who is in secret. And your Father, who sees in secret, shall reward you. 7And when you are praying, do not babble on and on like the pagans; for they think they will be heard because of their many words. 8Do not be like them, for your Father knows what you need before you ask Him.

9“Therefore, pray in this way:

‘Our Father in heaven,
  sanctified be Your name.
10Your kingdom come,
  Your will be done
  on earth as it is in heaven.
11Give us this day our daily bread.
12And forgive us our debts
  as we also have forgiven
  our debtors.
13And lead us not into temptation,
  but deliver us from the evil one.’[f]

f 6:13. Some mss. add: For yours is the kingdom and the power and the glory, forever. Amen.

14“For if you forgive others their transgressions, your heavenly Father will also forgive you. 15But if you do not forgive others, neither will your Father forgive your transgressions.

16“And whenever you fast, do not become sad-faced like the hypocrites, for they neglect their faces to make their fasting evident to men. Amen, I tell you, they have their reward in full! 17But when you fast, anoint your head and wash your face, 18so that your fasting won’t be evident to men, but to your Father who is in secret. And your Father, who sees in secret, will reward you.[a]

19“Do not store up for yourselves treasures on earth, where moth and rust[b] destroy and where thieves break in and steal. 20But store up for yourselves treasures in heaven, where neither moth nor rust destroys and where thieves do not break in or steal. 21For where your treasure is, there will your heart be also.

22“The eye is the lamp of the body. Therefore if your eye is good, your whole body will be full of light. 23But if your eye is bad, your body will be full of darkness. If therefore the light that is in you is darkness, how great is the darkness!

24“No one can serve two masters; for either he will hate the one and love the other, or he will stick by one and look down on the other. You cannot serve God and money.”[c]

Overcoming Worry with Trust

25“So I say to you, do not worry about your life—what you will eat or drink, or about your body, what you will wear. Isn’t life more than food and the body more than clothing?

26“Look at the birds of the air. They do not sow or reap or gather into barns; yet your Father in heaven feeds them. Are you not of more value than they? 27And which of you by worrying can add a single hour to his life?[d] 28And why do you worry about clothing? Consider the lilies of the field, how they grow. They neither toil nor spin. 29Yet I tell you that not even Solomon in all his glory clothed himself like one of these.[e] 30Now if in this way God clothes the grass—which is here today and thrown into the furnace tomorrow—will He not much more clothe you, O you of little faith?

31“Therefore do not worry, saying, ‘What will we eat?’ or ‘What will we drink?’ or ‘What will we wear?’ 32For the pagans eagerly pursue all these things; yet your Father in heaven knows that you need all these. 33But seek first the kingdom of God and His righteousness, and all these things shall be added to you. 34Therefore do not worry about tomorrow, for tomorrow will worry about itself. Each day has enough trouble of its own.”

7

Measuring Your Measure

1“Stop judging, so that you may not be judged. 2For with the judgment you judge, you will be judged; and with the measure you use, it will be measured to you.

3“Why do you look at the speck in your brother’s eye, but do not notice the beam in your own eye? 4Or how will you say to your brother, ‘Let me take the speck out of your eye,’ and look, the beam is in your own eye? 5Hypocrite, first take the beam out of your own eye, and then you will see clearly to take the speck out of your brother’s eye.

6“Do not give what is holy to dogs or throw your pearls before pigs; otherwise they will trample them under their feet, then turn and rip you to shreds.

a 6:16-18. cf. Isa. 58:3-6.
b 6:19. Lit. act of eating, devouring.
c 6:24. Lit. *mammon*, Aramaic for *wealth, property*; sometimes personified as Mammon.
d 6:27. Or a cubit to his height.
e 6:29. cf. 1 Ki. 10:4-7.

[7]"Ask, and it shall be given to you. Seek, and you shall find. Knock, and it shall be opened to you. [8]For everyone who asks receives, and the one who seeks finds, and to the one who knocks it shall be opened.

[9]"For what man among you, when his son asks him for bread, will give him a stone? [10]Or when he asks for a fish, will give him a snake? [11]If you then, being evil, know how to give good gifts to your children, how much more will your Father in heaven give good things to those who ask Him! [12]So in all things, do to others what you would want them to do to you—for this is the *Torah* and the Prophets.

[13]"Enter through the narrow gate; for the gate is wide and the way is broad that leads to destruction, and those who enter through it are many. [14]How narrow is the gate and difficult the way that leads to life, and those who find it are few."

Judging the Fruit

[15]"Watch out for false prophets,[a] who come to you in sheep's clothing but inwardly are ravenous wolves. [16]You will recognize them by their fruit. Grapes aren't gathered from thorn bushes or figs from thistles, are they? [17]Even so, every good tree produces good fruit, but the rotten tree produces bad fruit. [18]A good tree cannot produce bad fruit, nor can a rotten tree produce good fruit. [19]Every tree that does not produce good fruit is chopped down and thrown into the fire. [20]So then, you will recognize them by their fruit.

21"Not everyone who says to Me, 'Lord, Lord!' will enter the kingdom of heaven, but he who does the will of My Father in heaven. 22Many will say to Me on that day, 'Lord, Lord, didn't we prophesy in Your name, and drive out demons in Your name, and perform many miracles in Your name?' 23Then I will declare to them, 'I never knew you. Get away from Me, you workers of lawlessness!'"[b]

Building on a Firm Foundation

[24]"Therefore everyone who hears these words of Mine and does them will be like a wise man who built his house on the rock. [25]And the rain fell, and the floods came, and the winds blew and beat against that house; and yet it did not fall, for its foundation had been built on the rock. [26]Everyone who hears these words of Mine and does not act on them will be like a foolish man who built his house on the sand. [27]And the rain fell, and the floods came, and the winds blew and beat against that house; and it fell—and great was its fall."

[28]Now when *Yeshua* had finished these words, the crowds were astounded at His teaching, [29]for He was teaching them as one having authority and not as their *Torah* scholars.

8

Healing Those who Trust

[1]When He came down from the mountain, large crowds followed Him. [2]And a man with *tzara'at* came to Him and bowed down before Him, saying, "Master, if You are willing, You can make me clean."

[3]*Yeshua* stretched out His hand and touched him, saying, "I am willing. Be cleansed." Immediately his *tzara'at* was cleansed. [4]And *Yeshua* said to him, "See that you tell no one; but go show yourself to the *kohen* and offer the gift that Moses commanded, as a testimony to them."[c]

[5]Now when *Yeshua* came into Capernaum, a centurion came begging for help. [6]"Master," he said, "my servant is lying at home paralyzed, horribly tormented."

a 7:15. cf. Deut. 18:20-22; Isa. 28:7-13; Jer. 5:30-31; 6:13-15; 14:13-15; Ezek. 13; Mic. 3:5-8.

b 7:23. cf. Ps. 6:9(8).

c 8:4. cf. Lev. 14:2.

7 *Yeshua* said to him, "I'll come and heal him."

8 But the centurion said, "Master, I'm not worthy to have You come under my roof. But just say the word and my servant will be healed. 9 For I also am a man under authority, with soldiers under me. I say to this one, 'Go!' and he goes; and to another, 'Come!' and he comes; and to my servant, 'Do this!' and he does it."

10 Now when *Yeshua* heard this, He marveled and said to those who were following, "Amen, I tell you, I have not found anyone in Israel with such great faith! 11 Moreover, I tell you that many will come from the east and the west, and they will recline at table with Abraham and Isaac and Jacob in the kingdom of heaven. 12 But the sons of the kingdom will be driven out into the outer darkness; in that place will be weeping and gnashing of teeth."

13 Then *Yeshua* said to the centurion, "Go. As you have believed, let it be done for you." And the servant was healed in that same hour.

14 And when *Yeshua* came into Peter's house, He saw Peter's mother-in-law lying down, sick with a fever. 15 *Yeshua* touched her hand, and the fever left her. Then she got up and began to take care of Him.

16 When evening came, the people brought to Him many who were afflicted by demons. He forced out the spirits with a word and healed all who were sick. 17 So was fulfilled what was spoken through Isaiah the prophet, saying,

> "He Himself took our sicknesses
> and carried away our diseases."[a]

Following the Call

18 Now when *Yeshua* saw a crowd around Him, He gave orders to go to the other side of the sea. 19 Then a *Torah* scholar came to Him and said, "Teacher, I will follow You wherever You go."

20 *Yeshua* tells him, "Foxes have dens and birds of the air have nests, but the Son of Man has nowhere to lay His head."

21 Then another of the disciples said, "Master, first let me go and bury my father."

22 But *Yeshua* tells him, "Follow Me, and let the dead bury their own dead."

Master of the Storm

23 As He got into the boat, His disciples followed Him. 24 Suddenly a great storm arose on the sea, so that the boat was being covered by the waves. But *Yeshua* kept on sleeping. 25 So they came and woke Him up, saying, "Master, save us! We're perishing!"

26 He said to them, "Why are you afraid, O you of little faith?" Then He got up and rebuked the winds and the sea, and it became totally calm.

27 The men were amazed, saying, "What kind of person is this? Even the winds and the sea obey Him!"

Freedom from Demons

28 When He came to the other side, into the region of the Gadarenes, two demon-plagued men coming from the graveyard[b] met Him. They were so violent that no one could pass by that way. 29 And they screamed, "What's between You and us,[c] *Ben-Elohim*? Have You come here to torment us, before the appointed time?"

30 Now a large herd of pigs was feeding some distance away from them. 31 The demons kept begging Him, "If You drive us out, send us into the herd of pigs."

32 And He told them, "Go!" So they came out and went into the pigs, and the whole herd rushed down the cliff into the sea and drowned. 33 The herdsmen ran away, went into the town, and told everything, including what had happened to the demon-plagued men. 34 The whole town came out to meet *Yeshua*.

a 8:17. Isa. 53:4.

b 8:28. Lit. *tombs*.

c 8:29. A Hebrew idiom, lit. *What to us and you?*

And when they saw him, they begged Him to leave their region.

9

Authority to Pardon Sins

1After getting into a boat, *Yeshua* crossed over and came to His own town. 2Just then, some people brought to Him a paralyzed man lying on a cot. And seeing their faith, *Yeshua* said to the paralyzed man, "Take courage, son! Your sins are forgiven."

3Then some of the *Torah* scholars said among themselves, "This fellow blasphemes!"

4And knowing their thoughts, *Yeshua* said, "Why are you entertaining evil in your hearts? 5For which is easier, to say, 'Your sins are forgiven,' or to say, 'Get up and walk'? 6But so you may know that the Son of Man has authority on earth to pardon sins..." Then He tells the paralyzed man, "Get up, take your cot and go home." 7And he got up and went home. 8When the crowd saw it, they were afraid and glorified God, who had given such authority to men.

A Physician for Sinners

9As *Yeshua* was passing by from there, He saw a man named Matthew sitting at the tax collector's booth. He said to him, "Follow Me." And he got up and followed Him.

10Now it happened that when *Yeshua* was reclining at the table in the house, many tax collectors and sinners came and were reclining with *Yeshua* and His disciples. 11When the Pharisees saw this, they said to His disciples, "Why does this Teacher of yours eat with tax collectors and sinners?"

12But when He heard this, *Yeshua* said, "Those who are healthy have no need for a doctor, but those who are sick do. 13Now go and learn what this means: 'Mercy I desire, and not sacrifice.'[a] For I didn't come to call the righteous, but the sinful."

Teaching New Ways

14Then John's disciples came to Him, saying, "Why do we and the Pharisees fast, but Your disciples do not fast?"[b]

15And *Yeshua* said to them, "The guests of the bridegroom cannot mourn while the bridegroom is with them, can they? But the days will come when the bridegroom is taken away from them, and then they will fast.

16"And no one puts a patch of unshrunk cloth on an old garment, for the patch pulls away from the garment and a worse tear happens. 17Nor do they put new wine into old wineskins. Otherwise the skins burst, and the wine spills out and the skins are ruined. But they put new wine into fresh wineskins, and both are preserved."

Compassion in the Shepherd's Touch

18Just as He was saying these things to them, a synagogue leader came and began to bow before Him, saying, "My daughter has just died, but come lay Your hand on her and she will live." 19And *Yeshua* got up and began to follow him, with His disciples.

20Just then a woman, losing blood for twelve years,[c] came from behind and touched the *tzitzit* of His garment. 21For she kept saying to herself, "If only I touch His garment, I will be healed."

22But then *Yeshua* turned and saw her. "Take heart, daughter," He said, "your faith has made you well." That very hour the woman was healed.

23When *Yeshua* came into the synagogue leader's house and saw the flute players and the noisy crowd wailing, 24He said, "Go away, for the girl isn't dead, but

a 9:13. Hos. 6:6; Mic. 6:6-8; Zech. 10:2.
b 9:14. Some mss. add *much* or *often*.
c 9:20. cf. Lev. 15:25.

sleeping." And they began jeering at Him.
25But when the crowd had been cleared
out, He went in and took her hand, and
the girl got up. 26And news of this spread
all around that region.

27As *Yeshua* went on from there, two
blind men followed Him, crying out,
"*Ben-David*, have mercy on us!"

28When He went into the house, the
blind men came to Him. And *Yeshua* said
to them, "Do you believe that I am able
to do this?"

"Yes, Master," they said to Him.

29Then He touched their eyes, saying,
"According to your faith, let it be done
for you." 30And their eyes were opened.
And *Yeshua* warned them sternly, "See
that no one knows." 31But they went
out and spread the news about Him all
around that region.

32As they were going out, a mute man
plagued by a demon was brought to Him.
33After the demon was driven out, the
mute man started speaking. The crowds
were astounded, saying, "Never has anything like this been seen in Israel!" 34But
the Pharisees were saying, "By the prince
of demons He drives out demons."

35Now *Yeshua* was going around all
the towns and villages, teaching in their
synagogues and proclaiming the Good
News of the kingdom, and healing every
kind of disease and sickness. 36When He
saw the crowds, He felt compassion for
them, because they were harassed and
helpless, like sheep without a shepherd.[a]
37Then He said to His disciples, "The harvest is plentiful, but the workers are few.
38Therefore pray to the Lord of the harvest that He may send out workers into
His harvest field."

10

Instructions to the Twelve

1*Yeshua* summoned His twelve disciples
and gave them authority over unclean
spirits, so they could drive them out and
heal every kind of disease and sickness.
2Now these are the names of the twelve
shlichim: first, Simon, called Peter, and his
brother Andrew; Jacob the son of Zebedee and John his brother; 3Philip and
Bartholomew; Thomas and Matthew the
tax collector; Jacob, the son of Alphaeus,
and Thaddaeus; 4Simon the Zealot,[b] and
Judah the man from Kriot,[c] the one who
also betrayed Him.

5*Yeshua* sent out these twelve and
ordered them, "Do not go to the Gentiles, and do not enter into any Samaritan
town. 6But go instead to the lost sheep
of the house of Israel. 7As you go, proclaim, 'The kingdom of heaven has
come near!' 8Heal the sick, raise the
dead, cleanse those with *tzara'at*, drive
out demons. Freely you received, freely
give. 9Do not get gold or silver or copper
for your money belts, 10or a bag for the
journey, or two shirts,[d] or sandals, or a
walking stick; for the worker is entitled
to his food.

11"Whatever town or village you shall
enter, find out who in it is worthy and
stay there until you leave. 12As you come
into the house, greet it. 13If the household is worthy, let your *shalom* come
upon it. But if it's not worthy, let your
shalom return to you. 14And whoever will
not receive you or listen to your words,
as you leave that house or that town,
shake the dust off your feet. 15Amen, I tell
you, it will be more tolerable for Sodom
and Gomorrah[e] on the Day of Judgment
than for that town.

16"Behold, I am sending you out as
sheep in the midst of wolves, so be wise
as serpents and innocent as doves. 17But
beware of men, for they will hand you
over to the courts and flog[f] you in their
synagogues. 18You will be brought before

a 9:36. cf. Num. 27:17; 2 Chr. 18:16.

b 10:4. Lit. *Cananean*, Aramaic for *zealot, enthusiast*; perhaps formerly affiliated with the Jewish nationalistic Zealot party.

c 10:4. Judas Iscariot (Heb. *Yehudah Ish Kriot*, Judah, the man from Kriot); cf. Josh. 15:25.

d 10:10. Lit. *tunics* or *undershirts*.

e 10:15. cf. Gen. 19:24, 27-28.

f 10:17. cf. Dt. 25:2-3.

governors and kings because of Me, as
a witness to them and to the Gentiles.
19But when they hand you over, do not
worry about how or what you should say,
for it shall be given to you in that hour
what you should say. 20For it is not you
speaking, but the Spirit of your Father
speaking through you.

21"Brother will betray brother to
death, and a father his child; and children
will rise up against their parents and
have them put to death. 22And you will
be hated by all because of My name, but
the one who endures to the end shall be
saved. 23Whenever they persecute you
in one city, flee to the next. Amen, I tell
you, you will never finish going through
the cities of Israel before the Son of Man
comes.

24"A disciple is not above his teacher,
nor a slave above his master. 25It is
enough for the disciple to become like
his teacher, and the slave like his master.
If they have called the head of the house
beelzebul, how much more the members
of his household!

26"So do not fear them, for there
is nothing concealed that will not be
revealed and nothing hidden that will
not be made known. 27What I tell you
in the darkness, speak in the light; and
what you hear in your ear, proclaim from
the housetops! 28And do not fear those
who kill the body but cannot kill the
soul. Instead, fear the One who is able to
destroy both soul and body in Gehenna.[a]

29"Are not two sparrows sold for a
penny?[b] Yet not one of them shall fall to
the ground apart from your Father's consent. 30But even the hairs of your head
are all numbered. 31So do not fear; you
are worth more than many sparrows.

32"Therefore whoever acknowledges
Me before men, I will also acknowledge
him before My Father who is in heaven.
33But whoever denies Me before men, I
will also deny him before My Father who
is in heaven.

34"Do not think that I came to bring
shalom on the earth; I did not come to
bring *shalom*, but a sword. 35For I have
come to set

'a man against his father,
a daughter against her mother, and
a daughter-in-law against her
mother-in-law;
36and a man's enemies will be the members of his household.'[c]

37"He who loves father or mother
more than Me isn't worthy of Me, and he
who loves son or daughter more than Me
isn't worthy of Me. 38And whoever does
not take up his cross and follow after Me
isn't worthy of Me. 39He who finds his life
will lose it, and he who loses his life for
My sake will find it.

40"He who receives you receives Me,
and he who receives Me receives the
One who sent Me. 41He who receives a
prophet in the name of a prophet shall
receive a prophet's reward, and he who
receives a *tzaddik* in the name of a *tzaddik* shall receive a *tzaddik's* reward. 42And
whoever gives to one of these little ones
even a cup of cold water in the name of
a disciple, amen I tell you, he shall never
lose his reward."

11

Signs and Wonders Bear Witness

1When *Yeshua* had finished instructing
His twelve disciples, He went on from
there to teach and preach in their towns.
2Now when John heard in prison about
the works of the Messiah, he sent word
through his disciples 3and said to *Yeshua*,
"Are You the Coming One, or do we look
for another?"

a 10:28. Lit. *the Valley of Hinnom*, see Jer. 7:31; 19:5-6; 32:35; cf. Isa. 66:24.
b 10:29. Lit. *assarion*, a small Roman copper coin.
c 10:36. cf. Mic. 7:6.

[4]*Yeshua* replied, "Go report to John what you hear and see: [5]the blind see and the lame walk, those with *tzara'at* are cleansed and the deaf hear, and the dead are raised and the poor have good news proclaimed to them. [6]Blessed is the one who is not led to stumble because of Me."[a]

A Prophet Without Honor

[7]Now as they were leaving, *Yeshua* began to talk to the crowd concerning John. "What did you go out to the wilderness to see? A reed shaken by the wind? [8]No? So what did you go out to see? A man dressed in finery? Look, those who wear finery are in the palaces of kings! [9]Then what did you go out to see? A prophet? Yes, I tell you, even more than a prophet. [10]This is the one about whom it is written,

'Behold, I send My messenger
before You,
who will prepare Your way before
You.'[b]

[11]"Amen, I tell you, among those born of women, none has arisen greater than John the Immerser. Yet the least in the kingdom of heaven is greater than he. [12]From the days of John the Immerser until now, the kingdom of heaven is treated with violence, and the violent grasp hold of it. [13]For all the prophets and the *Torah* prophesied until the time of John. [14]And if you are willing to accept it, he is Elijah who is to come. [15]He who has ears, let him hear!

[16]"But to what shall I compare this generation? It's like children sitting in the marketplaces who call to one other, saying,

[17]'We played the flute for you,
but you did not dance.
We wailed,
but you did not mourn.'

[18]"For John came neither eating nor drinking, and they say, 'He has a demon!' [19]The Son of Man came eating and drinking, and they say, 'Look, a glutton and a drunkard, a friend of tax collectors and sinners!' Yet wisdom is vindicated by her deeds."[c]

[20]Then *Yeshua* began to denounce the towns where most of His miracles had happened, because they did not turn from their sins. [21]"Woe to you, Chorazin! Woe to you, Bethsaida! For if the miracles done in you had been done in Tyre and Sidon,[d] they would have turned long ago in sackcloth and ashes. [22]Nevertheless I tell you, it will be more bearable for Tyre and Sidon on the Day of Judgment than for you. [23]And you, Capernaum? Will you be lifted up to heaven? No, you will go down to *Sheol*! For if the miracles done in you had been done in Sodom, it would have remained to this day. [24]Nevertheless I tell you that it will be more bearable for the land of Sodom on the Day of Judgment than for you."

Yeshua Teaches the Ways of His Father

[25]At that time *Yeshua* said in response, "I praise You, Father, Lord of heaven and of earth, that You have hidden these things from the wise and discerning and revealed them to infants. [26]Yes, Father, for this way was pleasing to You.

[27]"All things have been handed over to Me by My Father. No one knows the Son except the Father, and no one knows the Father except the Son[e] and anyone to whom the Son chooses to reveal Him. [28]Come to Me, all who are weary and burdened, and I will give you rest. [29]Take My yoke upon you and learn from Me, for I am gentle and humble in heart, and 'you

a 11:6. cf. Isa. 35:5-6; 26:19; 29:18-19; 61:1.
b 11:10. Exod. 23:20; Mal. 3:1, 23(4:5).
c 11:19. Some mss. say *children*; cf. Lk. 7:35.
d 11:21. cf. Jer. 47:4; Ezek. 26-28.
e 11:27. cf. Ps. 2:7; Prov. 30:4.

will find rest for your souls.'[a] 30For My yoke is easy and My burden is light."

12

The Lord of *Shabbat*

1At that time *Yeshua* went through the grain fields on *Shabbat*. His disciples became hungry and began to pluck heads of grain and eat them. 2But when the Pharisees saw this, they said to Him, "Look, Your disciples are doing what is not permitted on *Shabbat*."

3But He said to them, "Haven't you read what David did when he became hungry, and those with him? 4How he entered into the house of God, and they ate the show-bread, which was not permitted for him to eat, nor for those with him, but only for the *kohanim*?[b] 5Or haven't you read in the *Torah* that on *Shabbat* the *kohanim* in the Temple break *Shabbat* and yet are innocent? 6But I tell you that something greater than the Temple is here. 7If you had known what this means, 'I desire mercy, not sacrifice,'[c] you wouldn't have condemned the innocent. 8For the Son of Man is Lord of *Shabbat*."

9Leaving from there, He went into their synagogue. 10A man with a withered hand was there. And so that they might accuse Him, they questioned *Yeshua*, saying, "Is it permitted to heal on *Shabbat*?"

11He said to them, "What man among you will not grab his sheep and lift it out, if it falls into a pit on Shabbat? 12How much more valuable then is a man than a sheep! Therefore it is permitted to do good on *Shabbat*."

13Then He said to the man, "Stretch out your hand." And he stretched it out and it was restored, as healthy as the other. 14But the Pharisees went out and plotted against Him, how they might destroy Him.

God's Chosen Servant Brings Hope

15Knowing this, *Yeshua* went away from there. And large crowds followed Him, and He healed them all. 16And He sternly warned them not to make Him known. 17This was to fulfill what was spoken through Isaiah the prophet, saying,

18"Here is My servant whom I chose,
the One I love, in whom My soul takes delight.
I will put My Spirit upon Him,
and He shall proclaim justice to the nations.
19He will not quarrel or cry out,
nor will anyone hear His voice in the streets.
20A crushed reed He will not break,
and a smoldering wick he will not snuff out,
until He brings forth justice to victory.
21And in His name the nations shall hope."[d]

Whose Power Will Rule?

22Then a demon-plagued man, who was blind and mute, was brought to *Yeshua*; and He healed him, so that he spoke and saw. 23All the crowds were astounded and saying, "This can't be *Ben-David*, can it?"

24But hearing this, the Pharisees said, "This fellow drives out demons only by beelzebul, the ruler of demons."

25Knowing their thoughts, *Yeshua* said to them, "Every kingdom divided against itself is destroyed, and every city or house divided against itself will not stand. 26If satan drives out satan, he is divided against himself; how then will his kingdom stand? 27And if I drive out demons by beelzebul, by whom do your sons drive them out? For this reason, they will be your judges. 28But if I drive out demons by the Spirit of God, then the kingdom of God has come upon you. 29Or

a 11:29. Jer. 6:16.
b 12:3-4. cf. Lev. 24:5-9; 1 Sam. 21:5-7(4-6).
c 12:7. Hos. 6:6.
d 12:18-21. Isa. 42:1-4.

how can one enter a strong man's house and carry off his property, unless he first ties up the strong man? Then he will thoroughly plunder his house. 30 He who is not with Me is against Me, and he who does not gather with Me scatters.

31 "For this reason I say to you, every sin and blasphemy will be forgiven men, but blasphemy against the *Spirit* will not be forgiven. 32 Whoever speaks a word against the Son of Man will be forgiven, but whoever speaks against the *Ruach ha-Kodesh* will not be forgiven, neither in this age nor in the one to come."

33 "Either make the tree good and its fruit good, or make the tree rotten and its fruit rotten; for the tree is known by its fruit. 34 You brood of vipers! How can you who are evil say anything good? For from the overflow of the heart the mouth speaks. 35 The good man from his good treasury brings forth good, and the evil man from his evil treasury brings forth evil. 36 But I tell you that on the Day of Judgment, men will give account for every careless word they speak. 37 For by your words you will be justified, and by your words you will be condemned."

A Sign Greater than Jonah

38 Then some of the *Torah* scholars and Pharisees answered Him, "Teacher, we want to see a sign from You."

39 But *Yeshua* replied to them, "An evil and adulterous generation clamors for a sign, yet no sign shall be given to it except the sign of Jonah the prophet. 40 For just as Jonah was in the belly of the great fish for three days and three nights,[a] so the Son of Man will be in the heart of the earth for three days and three nights. 41 The men of Nineveh will rise up at the judgment with this generation and condemn it, because they repented at the preaching of Jonah. And behold, something greater than Jonah is here. 42 The Queen of the South[b] will rise up at the judgment with this generation and condemn it, for she came from the ends of the earth to hear the wisdom of Solomon. And behold, something greater than Solomon is here.

43 "Now when an unclean spirit goes out of a man, it passes through waterless places looking for rest and doesn't find it. 44 Then it says, 'I'll go back home where I came from.' And when it comes, it finds the house vacant, swept clean, and put in order. 45 Then it goes and brings along seven other spirits more evil than itself, and they go in and live there. And that man's last condition becomes worse than the first. So also will it be for this evil generation."

Who Is *Yeshua's* Family?

46 While *Yeshua* was still speaking to the crowds, His mother and brothers were standing outside, trying to speak to Him. 47 Someone said to Him, "Look, Your mother and Your brothers are standing outside, trying to speak to You."[c]

48 But to the one telling Him this, *Yeshua* responded, "Who is My mother? And who are My brothers?" 49 Stretching out His hand toward His disciples, He said, "Here are My mother and My brothers. 50 For whoever does the will of My Father in heaven, he is My brother and sister and mother."

13

Simple Stories, Profound Truths

1 On that day after *Yeshua* left the house, He was sitting by the sea. 2 And large crowds gathered around Him; so He got into a boat and sat down, and the whole crowd stood on the shore. 3 And He told them many things in parables, saying, "Behold, a sower went out to spread some seed. 4 As he was scattering the seed, some seeds fell by the road;

a 12:40. Jonah 2:1(1:17).
b 12:42. cf. Queen of Sheba; 1 Ki. 10:1-10; 2 Chr. 9:1-12.
c 12:47. Some mss. omit this verse.

and the birds came and ate them up.
5Other seeds fell on rocky ground, where
they didn't have much soil. They sprang
up immediately, because the soil wasn't
deep. 6But when the sun came up, they
were scorched; and because they had no
roots, they withered away. 7Other seeds
fell among the thorns, and the thorns
grew and choked them out. 8But others fell on good soil and were producing
fruit. They yielded a crop—some a hundredfold, some sixty, some thirty. 9He
who has ears,[a] let him hear."

10Then the disciples came to Him and
said, "Why do You speak to them in
parables?"

11And He replied to them, "To you has
been given to know the secrets of the
kingdom of heaven, but to them it has
not been given. 12For whoever has, to
him more will be given and he will have
plenty. But whoever does not have, even
what he has will be taken away from
him. 13For this reason I speak to them in
parables,

because seeing they do not
see,
and hearing they do not hear nor do
they understand.

14"And in them the prophecy of Isaiah
is being fulfilled, which says,

'You will keep on hearing
but will never understand;
you will keep looking, but will never
see.
15For the heart of this people has
become dull,
their ears can barely
hear,
and they have shut their eyes.
Otherwise they might see with their
eyes,
hear with their ears,
and understand with their hearts.
Then they would turn back,
and I would heal them.'[b]

16"But blessed are your eyes because
they see, and your ears because they
hear. 17Amen, I tell you, many a prophet
and *tzaddik* longed to see what you are
seeing and did not see, and to hear what
you are hearing and did not hear."

Parable of the Sower Explained

18"You then, hear the parable of the
sower. 19When anyone hears the word
of the kingdom and doesn't understand
it, the evil one comes and snatches away
what was sown in his heart. This is the
one having been sown along the road.

20"The one sown on rocky ground,
this is the one who hears the word and
immediately receives it with joy. 21Yet he
has no root himself but lasts only a short
while; and when trouble or persecution
comes because of the word, immediately
he falls away.

22"But the one sown among the
thorns, this is the one who hears the
word; and the worries of the world and
the seduction of wealth choke the word,
and it becomes unfruitful.

23"Now the one sown on the good
soil, this is the one who hears the word
and understands. He indeed bears fruit,
yielding a hundredfold, some sixty, some
thirty times what was sown."

Yeshua Tells More Parables

24He presented to them another parable, saying, "The kingdom of heaven is
like a man who sowed good seed in his
field. 25But while the men were sleeping, his enemy came and sowed weeds
among the wheat and went away. 26Now
when the stalk sprouted and produced
grain, then the weeds also appeared.
27So the slaves of the landowner came
and said to him, 'Master, didn't you sow

a 13:9, 43. Some mss. add *to hear.*

b 13:14-15. Isa. 6:9-10.

good seed in your field? Then where did
the weeds come from?' [28]But he replied,
'An enemy did this.' Now the slaves say
to him, 'Do you want us, then, to go
out and gather them up?' [29]But he says,
'No, for while you are gathering up the
weeds, you may uproot the wheat with
them. [30]Let both grow together until the
harvest. At harvest time, I will tell the
reapers, "First, gather up the weeds and
tie them in bundles to burn them up; but
gather the wheat into my barn."'"

[31]He presented to them another parable, saying, "The kingdom of heaven is
like a mustard seed, which a man took
and planted in his field. [32]It's the smallest
of all seeds; yet when it's full grown, it's
greater than the other herbs. It becomes
like a tree, so that the birds of the air
come and nest in its branches."[a]

[33]He told them another parable, "The
kingdom of heaven is like *hametz*, which
a woman took and hid in three measures
of flour, until it was all leavened."

[34]All these things *Yeshua* spoke to the
crowds in parables. And apart from a parable, He wasn't speaking to them, [35]in
order to fulfill what was spoken through
the prophet, saying,

> "I will open My mouth in
> parables,
> I will utter things hidden
> since the foundation of the
> world."[b]

[36]Then He sent the crowds away and
went into the house. His disciples came
to Him, saying, "Explain to us the parable
of the weeds of the field."

[37]He answered, "The one sowing the
good seed is the Son of Man, [38]and the
field is the world. And the good seed,
these are the sons of the kingdom; and
the weeds are the sons of the evil one.
[39]The enemy who sowed them is the
devil, the harvest is the end of the age,
and the reapers are angels. [40]Therefore
just as the weeds are gathered up and
burned with fire, so shall it be at the end
of the age. [41]The Son of Man will send
forth His angels, and they will gather out
of His kingdom all stumbling blocks[c] and
those who practice lawlessness. [42]They
will throw them into the fiery furnace[d]; in
that place will be weeping and gnashing
of teeth. [43]Then the righteous will shine
forth as the sun[e] in the kingdom of their
Father. He who has ears, let him hear!

[44]"The kingdom of heaven is like a
treasure hidden in the field, which a man
found and hid. And because of his joy, he
goes out and sells all that he has and buys
that field.

[45]"Again, the kingdom of heaven is
like a merchant searching for fine pearls.
[46]Upon finding a pearl of great value,
he went out and sold all that he had and
bought it.

[47]"Again, the kingdom of heaven is
like a dragnet that was cast into the sea,
gathering things of every kind. [48]When it
was filled, they pulled it ashore; and they
sat down and gathered up the good into
containers, but threw the bad away. [49]So
it will be at the end of the age. The angels
will come forth and separate the wicked
from among the righteous [50]and throw
them into the fiery furnace;[f] in that place
will be weeping and gnashing of teeth.

[51]"Have you understood all these
things?"

They said to Him, "Yes."

[52]Then He said to them, "Therefore
every *Torah* scholar discipled for the
kingdom of heaven is like the master of a
household who brings out of his treasure
both new things and old."

Unbelief in the Hometown Synagogue

[53]Now when *Yeshua* had finished these
parables, He left that place. [54]Coming
into His hometown, He began to teach

a 13:32. Ps. 104:12 (103:12 LXX).
b 13:35. Ps. 78:2.
c 13:41. cf. 1 Cor. 1:23.
d 13:42. Dan. 3:6.
e 13:43. cf. Dan. 12:3.
f 13:50. cf. Dan. 3:6.

them in their synagogue so that they
were amazed. "Where did this fellow get
this wisdom and these mighty works?"
they said. 55"Isn't this the carpenter's
son? Isn't His mother called Miriam,
and His brothers Jacob and Joseph and
Simon and Judah? 56And His sisters,
aren't they all with us? So where does
He get all these things?" 57And they took
offense at Him.

But *Yeshua* said to them, "A prophet
is not without honor except in his hometown and in his own house." 58And He
did not do many mighty works there
because of their unbelief.

14

Yeshua's Cousin Beheaded

1At that time Herod the tetrarch heard
the report about *Yeshua*. 2He said to his
servants, "This is John the Immerser—
he has risen from the dead! Because of
this, these powers are at work in Him."
3For Herod had arrested John, bound
him, and put him in prison for the sake of
Herodias, the wife of his brother Philip,
4because John had been telling him, "It
is not permitted for you to have her."[a]
5Although Herod wanted to kill John, he
feared the crowd because they considered John a prophet.

6But when Herod's birthday celebra-
tion came, the daughter of Herodias
danced before them and pleased Herod,
7so much that he promised with an oath
to give her whatever she might ask.
8Prompted by her mother, she said,
"Give me the head of John the Immerser,
here on a platter!" 9The king became
sorrowful; but because of his oaths and
those reclining with him, he commanded
it to be given. 10And he sent and had
John beheaded in the prison. 11His head
was brought on a platter and given to
the girl, and she brought it to her mother.
12John's disciples came forth and took
the body and buried it. Then they went
and reported to *Yeshua*.

Feeding Hungry Followers

13Now when *Yeshua* heard this, He
went away from there privately by boat
to an isolated place. But when the crowds
heard, they followed Him on foot from
the towns. 14As *Yeshua* came ashore, He
saw a large crowd and felt compassion
for them and healed their sick. 15When
it became evening, the disciples came to
Him, saying, "This place is isolated, and
the hour is already late. Send the crowds
away so they can go into the villages and
buy food for themselves."

16But *Yeshua* said to them, "They don't
need to leave—you give them something to eat."

17"We have nothing here except five
loaves and two fish," they said to Him.

18"Bring them here to Me," He said.

19Ordering the crowd to recline on
the grass, He took the five loaves and
the two fish; and looking up to heaven,
He offered the *bracha*. After breaking
the loaves, He gave them to the disciples, and the disciples gave them to the
crowds. 20They all ate and were satisfied,
and the disciples picked up twelve baskets full of broken pieces left over. 21Now
those eating were about five thousand
men, besides women and children.

Testing Peter's Faith to Walk on Water

22Right away, *Yeshua* made the disciples get into the boat and go ahead of
Him to the other side, while He sent the
crowds away. 23After He had sent the
crowds away, He went up on the hillside
by Himself to pray. And when evening
came, He was there alone. 24But the boat
was already a long way[b] from land, tossed
around by the waves, for the wind was
against it. 25Now in the fourth watch[c] of
the night, *Yeshua* came to them, walking

a 14:4. cf. Lev. 18:16; 20:21.

b 14:24. Lit. *many stadia*; 1 stadion is about 600 ft.

c 14:25. Roman time, 3-6 a.m.

on the sea. 26But when the disciples saw Him walking on the sea, they were terrified, saying, "It's a ghost!" And they cried out with fear.

27But immediately, *Yeshua* spoke to them, saying, "Take courage! I am. Don't be afraid."

28Answering, Peter said to Him, "Master, if it's You, command me to come to You on the water."

29And He said, "Come!"

And Peter got out of the boat and walked on the water to go to *Yeshua*. 30But seeing the wind, he became terrified. And beginning to sink, he cried out, saying, "Master, save me!"

31Immediately *Yeshua* reached out His hand and grabbed him. And He said to him, "O you of little faith, why did you doubt?"

32When they got into the boat, the wind ceased. 33And those in the boat worshiped Him, saying, "You really are *Ben-Elohim!*"[a]

34After they had crossed over, they came to land at Gennesaret. 35And when the men of that place recognized *Yeshua*, they sent word into all the surrounding region. And they brought to Him all those who were in bad shape 36and kept begging Him that they might just touch the *tzitzit* of His garment—and all who touched it were cured.

15

Religious Leaders Quiz *Yeshua*

1Then some Pharisees and *Torah* scholars came to *Yeshua* from Jerusalem. They said, 2"Why do Your disciples transgress the tradition of the elders? For they do not do the ritual handwashing when they eat bread."

3And answering, He said to them, "Why do you also transgress the commandment of God for the sake of your tradition? 4For God said, 'Honor your father and mother'[b] and 'He who speaks evil of father or mother must be put to death.'[c] 5But you say, 'Whoever tells his father or mother, "Whatever you might have gained from me is a gift to God,"[d] 6he need not honor his father.' On account of your tradition, you made void the word of God. 7Hypocrites! Rightly did Isaiah prophesy about you, saying,

8'This people honors Me
with their lips,
but their heart is far from
Me.
9And in vain they worship Me,
teaching as doctrines the
commandments of men.'"[e]

10Then *Yeshua* called the crowd and said to them, "Hear and understand. 11It's not what goes into the mouth that makes the man unholy; but what comes out of the mouth, this makes the man unholy."[f]

12Then the disciples came and said to Him, "Do You know that the Pharisees took offense when they heard this saying?"

13But He replied, "Every plant that My heavenly Father has not planted will be uprooted. 14Leave them alone; they are blind guides of the blind. And if a blind man leads a blind man, both will fall into a pit."

15Then Peter answered and said to Him, "Explain this parable to us."

16"Are you also still lacking understanding?" *Yeshua* said. 17"Don't you grasp that whatever goes into the mouth passes into the stomach and then is ejected into the sewer? 18But the things that proceed out of the mouth come forth from the heart, and those things make the man unholy. 19For out of the heart come evil thoughts, murder, adultery, sexual immorality, theft, false

a 14:32-33. Prov. 30:4.

b 15:4. Exod. 20:12; Deut. 5:16.
c 15:4. Exod. 21:17; Lev. 20:9.
d 15:5. cf. M. Ned. 1, 9, 11.
e 15:8-9. Isa. 29:13.
f 15:11. cf. Lev. 10:10.

witness, and slander.[a] 20These are the things that make the man unholy; but to eat with unwashed hands does not make the man unholy."

A Reward for a Humble Woman

21Now *Yeshua* left from there and went away to the region of Tyre and Sidon. 22And behold, a Canaanite woman from that district came out and started shouting, "Have mercy on me, O Master, *Ben-David*! My daughter is severely tormented by a demon."

23But He did not answer her a word. And when His disciples came, they were urging Him, saying, "Send her away, because she keeps shouting at us."

24But He responded, "I was sent only to the lost sheep of the house of Israel."

25So she came and got down on her knees before Him, saying, "Master, help me!"

26And answering, He said, "It's not right to take the children's bread and throw it to the dogs."

27But she said, "Yes, Master, but even the dogs eat the crumbs that fall from their masters' table."

28Then answering, *Yeshua* said to her, "O woman, great is your faith! Let it be done for you as you wish." And her daughter was healed in that very hour.

29After *Yeshua* left there, He went along the Sea of Galilee. Then He went up on a mountainside and was sitting there. 30And large crowds came to Him, bringing with them the lame, blind, disabled, mute, and many others. And they laid them at His feet, and He healed them. 31So the crowd marveled when they saw the mute speaking, the disabled made whole, the lame walking, and the blind seeing.[b] And they praised the God of Israel.

a 15:19. cf. Jer. 17:9.
b 15:31. cf. Isa. 35:5-6.

Feeding More Hungry Followers

32*Yeshua* called His disciples and said, "I have compassion for the crowd, because they've stayed with Me for three days now and have nothing to eat. I don't want to send them away hungry, because they might pass out on the way."

33The disciples said to Him, "Where in this wasteland is enough bread to satisfy such a large crowd?"

34*Yeshua* said to them, "How many loaves do you have?"

"Seven," they said, "and a few small fish."

35After directing the crowd to recline on the ground, 36He took the seven loaves and the fish; and after giving thanks, He broke them. And He began giving them to the disciples, and the disciples to the crowds. 37And they all ate and were satisfied. And they picked up the broken pieces left over—seven baskets full. 38And those who ate were four thousand men, besides women and children. 39And after sending away the crowds, *Yeshua* got into the boat and went to the region of Magadan.

16

Religious Leaders Demand Signs

1Now the Pharisees and Sadducees came up, and testing *Yeshua*, they asked Him to show them a sign from heaven. 2But He replied to them, "When evening comes, you say, 'Fair weather coming, for the sky is red,' 3and in the morning, 'Stormy weather today, for the sky is red and gloomy.' You know how to discern the appearance of the sky, but you cannot discern the signs of the times! 4An evil and adulterous generation clamors for a sign, yet no sign will be given to it

except the sign of Jonah."[a] And leaving
them behind, He went away.
5Now when the disciples came to the
other side of the sea, they had forgotten
to take bread. 6"Watch out," *Yeshua* said
to them, "and beware of the *hametz* of
the Pharisees and Sadducees."
7And they began to discuss among
themselves, saying, "We didn't bring any
bread."
8But knowing this, *Yeshua* said, "O you
of little faith, why do you discuss among
yourselves that you have no bread? 9You
still don't get it? Don't you remember
the five loaves for the five thousand, and
how many baskets of leftovers you gathered? 10Or how about the seven loaves
for the four thousand and all the baskets
of leftovers you gathered? 11How is it
that you don't understand that I wasn't
talking to you about bread? Now beware
of the *hametz* of the Pharisees and Sadducees!" 12Then they understood that
He wasn't talking about the *hametz* in
the bread, but about the teaching of the
Pharisees and Sadducees.

The Father Reveals His Son

13When *Yeshua* came into the region of
Caesarea Philippi, He asked His disciples,
"Who do people say that the Son of Man
is?"
14They answered, "Some say John
the Immerser, others say Elijah, and still
others say Jeremiah or one of the other
prophets."
15He said, "But who do you say I am?"
16Simon Peter answered, "You are the
Messiah, the Son of the living God."
17*Yeshua* said to him, "Blessed are you,
Simon son of Jonah, because flesh and
blood did not reveal this to you, but My
Father who is in heaven! 18And I also tell
you that you are Peter, and upon this
rock I will build My community[b]; and the
gates of *Sheol* will not overpower it. 19I
will give you the keys of the kingdom of
heaven. Whatever you forbid on earth

a 16:4. cf. Jonah 2:1(1:17).
b 16:18. Greek *ekklesia*, Hebrew *kahal*.

will have been forbidden in heaven and
what you permit on earth will have been
permitted in heaven." 20Then He ordered
the disciples not to tell anyone that He
was the Messiah.

First Prediction: Death & Resurrection

21From that time on, *Yeshua* began to
show His disciples that He must go to
Jerusalem and suffer many things from
the elders and ruling *kohanim* and *Torah*
scholars, and be killed, and be raised on
the third day.
22Peter took Him aside and began to
rebuke Him, saying, "Never, Master! This
must never happen to You!"
23But He turned and said to Peter, "Get
behind Me, satan! You are a stumbling
block to Me, for you are not setting your
mind on the things of God, but the things
of men."
24Then *Yeshua* said to His disciples,
"If anyone wants to follow after Me, he
must deny himself, take up his cross, and
follow Me. 25For whoever wants to save
his life will lose it, but whoever loses his
life for My sake will find it. 26For what
will it profit a man if he gains the whole
world but forfeits his soul? Or what will
a man give in exchange for his soul? 27For
the Son of Man is about to come in the
glory of His Father with His angels, and
then 'He will repay everyone according
to his deeds.'[c] 28Amen, I tell you, there
are some standing here who will not
taste death until they see the Son of Man
coming in His kingdom."

17

Two Witnesses and a Voice from Heaven

1After six days, *Yeshua* takes with Him
Peter and Jacob and John his brother,
and brings them up a high mountain by

c 16:27. Prov. 24:12; cf. Ps. 62:13(12); Dan. 12:2.

themselves. [2]Now He was transfigured
before them; His face shone like the
sun, and His clothes became as white as
the light. [3]And behold, Moses and Elijah
appeared to them, talking with *Yeshua*.
[4]Peter responded to *Yeshua*, "Master, it's
good for us to be here! If You wish, I will
make three *sukkot* here—one for You,
and one for Moses, and one for Elijah."[a]

[5]While He was still speaking, suddenly
a bright cloud overshadowed them; and
behold, a voice from out of the cloud,
saying, "This is My Son, whom I love; with
Him I am well pleased. Listen to Him!"[b]

[6]When the disciples heard this, they
fell face down, terrified. [7]But *Yeshua*
came and touched them. "Get up,"
He said. "Stop being afraid." [8]And lifting their eyes, they saw no one except
Yeshua alone.

[9]As they were coming down from the
mountain, *Yeshua* commanded them,
saying, "Do not tell anyone about the
vision until the Son of Man is raised from
the dead."

[10]The disciples questioned Him, saying,
"Why then do the *Torah* scholars say that
Elijah must come first?"

[11]*Yeshua* replied, "Indeed, Elijah is coming and will restore all things.[c] [12]I tell you
that Elijah already came; and they didn't
recognize him, but did to him whatever
they wanted. In the same way, the Son
of Man is about to suffer at their hands."
[13]Then the disciples understood that He
was speaking to them about John the
Immerser.

See What Faith Can Do

[14]When they came to the crowd, a
man came to *Yeshua*, falling on his knees
before Him and saying, [15]"Master, have
mercy on my son, for he has seizures and
suffers badly. For he often falls into the
fire and often into the water. [16]I brought
him to Your disciples, but they couldn't
heal him."

[17]And answering, *Yeshua* said, "O faithless and twisted generation![d] How long
shall I be with you? How long shall I put
up with you? Bring him here to Me."
[18]*Yeshua* rebuked the demon and it came
out of him, and the boy was healed from
that very hour.

[19]Then the disciples came to *Yeshua* in
private and said, "Why couldn't we drive
it out?"

20And He said to them, "Because you
trust so little. Amen, I tell you, if you have
faith the size of a mustard seed, you will
say to this mountain, 'Move from here to
there,' and it will move. Nothing will be
impossible for you."(21)e

Second Prediction: Death & Resurrection

[22]Now while they were gathering in
the Galilee, *Yeshua* said to them, "The
Son of Man is about to be delivered into
the hands of men; [23]and they will kill Him,
and on the third day He will be raised."
And the disciples became greatly
distressed.

[24]When they came to Capernaum, the
collectors of the Temple tax came to
Peter and said, "Your teacher pays the
Temple tax,[f] doesn't He?"

[25]"Yes," Peter said.

Now when Peter came into the house,
Yeshua spoke to him first, saying, "What
do you think, Simon? The kings of the
earth, from whom do they collect tolls or
tax? From their sons or from strangers?"

[26]After Peter said, "From strangers,"
Yeshua said to him, "Then the sons are
free. [27]But so that we do not offend
them, go to the sea and throw out a
hook, and take the first fish that comes
up. And when you open its mouth, you'll
find a coin.[g] Take that, and give it to
them, for Me and you."

a 17:4. cf. Exod. 40:34.
b 17:5. cf. Ps. 2:7; Prov. 30:4; Isa. 9:5(6); Deut. 18:15.
c 17:10-11. cf. Mal. 3:23(4:5).

d 17:17. cf. Deut. 32:5.
e 17:21. Most manuscripts omit verse 21: *But this kind does not go out except by prayer and fasting.*
f 17:24. Greek *double drachma*, Hebrew *half-shekel*; cf. Ex. 30:13; 38:26.
g 17:27. Lit. *stater*, a silver coin worth four drachmas or one shekel; the Temple Tax for two people.

18

Childlike Humility

[1]At that hour the disciples came to *Yeshua*, saying, "Who then is greatest in the kingdom of heaven?"

[2]And He called a child to Himself, set him in the midst of them, [3]and said, "Amen, I tell you, unless you turn and become like children, you shall never enter the kingdom of heaven. [4]Whoever then shall humble himself like this child, this one is the greatest in the kingdom of heaven. [5]And whoever welcomes one such child in My name, welcomes Me.

[6]"But whoever causes one of these little ones who trust in Me to stumble, it would be better for him to have a heavy millstone hung around his neck and to be sunk in the depth of the sea! [7]Woe to the world because of snares! For snares must come, but woe to that man through whom the snare comes!

[8]"And if your hand or your foot causes you to stumble, cut it off and throw it away from you. It's better for you to enter into life crippled or lame than, having two hands or two feet, to be thrown into fiery Gehenna. [9]If your eye causes you to stumble, pluck it out and throw it away from you. It's better for you to enter into life with one eye than, having two eyes, to be thrown into fiery Gehenna.

Parable of the Lost Sheep

[10]"See that you do not despise one of these little ones, for I tell you that their angels in heaven continually see the face of My Father in heaven.(11)[a]

[12]"What do you think? If a certain man has a hundred sheep and one of them goes astray, won't he leave the ninety-nine on the mountains and go looking for the one that is straying? [13]And if he finds it, amen I tell you, he rejoices over it more than over the ninety-nine that didn't stray. [14]Even so, it's not the will of your Father in heaven that one of these little ones should be lost."

Restoring a Lost Brother

[15]"Now if your brother sins against you, go and show him his fault while you're with him alone. If he listens to you, you have won your brother. [16]But if he does not listen, take with you one or two more, so that 'by the mouth of two or three witnesses every word may stand.'[b] [17]But if he refuses to listen to them, tell it to Messiah's community. And if he refuses to listen even to Messiah's community, let him be to you as a pagan and a tax collector.

[18]"Amen, I tell you, whatever you forbid on earth will have been forbidden in heaven and what you permit on earth will have been permitted in heaven. [19]Again I say to you, that if two of you agree on earth about anything they may ask, it shall be done for them by My Father in heaven. [20]For where two or three are gathered together in My name, there I am in their midst."

Lessons about Forgiveness

[21]Then Peter came to Him and said, "Master, how often shall I forgive my brother when he sins against me? Up to seven times?"

[22]*Yeshua* said to him, "No, not up to seven times, I tell you, but seventy times seven![c] [23]Therefore, the kingdom of heaven may be compared to a king who wanted to settle accounts with his slaves. [24]When he had begun to settle up, a man was brought to him who owed him ten thousand talents.[d] [25]But since he didn't have the money to repay, his master ordered him to be sold, along with his wife and children and all that he had, and payment to be made. [26]Then the slave fell

a 18:11. Some manuscripts add verse 11: *For the Son of Man has come to save that which was lost*; cf. Lk. 19:10.

b 18:16. Deut. 19:15.

c 18:22. Lit. *seventy-seven*; cf. Gen. 4:24.

d 18:24. One talent was worth 6000 denarii, or about 16 years' wages.

on his knees and begged him, saying, 'Be patient with me, and I'll repay you everything.' 27 And the master of that slave, filled with compassion, released him and forgave him the debt.

28 "Now that slave went out and found one of his fellow slaves who owed him a hundred denarii. And he grabbed him and started choking him, saying, 'Pay back what you owe!'

29 "So his fellow slave fell down and kept begging him, saying, 'Be patient with me, and I'll pay you back.' 30 Yet he was unwilling. Instead, he went off and threw the man into prison until he paid back all he owed.

31 "So when his fellow slaves saw what had happened, they were deeply distressed. They went to their master and reported in detail all that had happened. 32 Then summoning the first slave, his master said to him, 'You wicked slave! I forgave all that debt because you pleaded with me. 33 Wasn't it necessary for you also to show mercy to your fellow slave, just as I showed mercy to you?' 34 Enraged, the master handed him over to the torturers until he paid back all he owed.

35 "So also My heavenly Father will do to you, unless each of you, from your hearts, forgives his brother."

19

Marriage and Covenant Faithfulness

1 Now when *Yeshua* had finished these words, He moved on from the Galilee and entered the region of Judea beyond the Jordan. 2 Large crowds followed Him, and He healed them there. 3 Pharisees came up to *Yeshua*, testing Him and saying, "Is it permitted for a man to divorce his wife for any reason at all?"

4 "Haven't you read?" He answered. "He who created them from the beginning 'made them male and female'[a] 5 and said, 'For this reason a man shall leave his father and mother and be joined to his wife, and the two shall become one flesh.'[b] 6 So they are no longer two, but one flesh. Therefore what God has joined together, let no man separate."

7 They said to Him, "Why then did Moses command to 'give her a certificate of divorce and put her away?'"[c]

8 *Yeshua* said to them, "Because of your hardness of heart Moses permitted you to divorce your wives, but from the beginning it was not so. 9 Now I tell you, whoever divorces his wife, except for sexual immorality, and marries another, commits adultery."[d]

10 The disciples said to Him, "If that's the case for a man and his wife, it's better not to marry!"

11 But He said to them, "Not everyone can accept this saying—only those to whom it has been given. 12 For there are eunuchs who were born that way from their mother's womb; and there are eunuchs who were made that way by men; and there are eunuchs who made themselves eunuchs for the sake of the kingdom of heaven. He who can accept this, let him accept it."

Receiving the Kingdom of Heaven

13 Then little children were brought to *Yeshua* so that He might lay hands upon them and pray. Then the disciples rebuked those who brought them.[e] 14 But *Yeshua* said, "Let the little children come to Me and do not hinder them, for the kingdom of heaven belongs to such as these." 15 After laying His hands upon them, He went on from there.

a 19:4. Gen. 1:27.
b 19:5. Gen. 5:2; 2:24.
c 19:7. Dt. 24:1, 3.
d 19:9. Some mss. add: *and whoever marries a divorced woman commits adultery.* Other mss. say: *except for sexual immorality, makes her commit adultery, and whoever marries a divorced woman commits adultery.*
e 19:13. Lit. *But the disciples rebuked them.*

Matthew 19:14

But Yeshua said, "Let the little children come to Me and do not hinder them, for the kingdom of heaven belongs to such as these."

16Now behold, one came to Him and said, "Teacher, what good shall I do to have eternal life?"

17"Why do you ask Me about what is good?" *Yeshua* said to him. "There is only One who is good; but if you want to enter into life, keep the commandments."

18"Which ones?" he said.

Yeshua said, "'Do not murder, do not commit adultery, do not steal, do not give false testimony, 19honor your father and mother,' and 'love your neighbor as yourself.'"[a]

20"All these I've kept," the young man said to Him. "What do I still lack?"

21*Yeshua* said to him, "If you wish to be perfect, go, sell what you own, and give to the poor; and you will have treasure in heaven. Then come, follow Me." 22But when the young man heard this statement, he went away grieving, for he had much property.

23Then *Yeshua* said to His disciples, "Amen, I tell you, it is hard for a rich man to enter the kingdom of heaven. 24Again I tell you, it is easier for a camel to go through the eye of a needle, than for a rich man to enter the kingdom of God."

25When the disciples heard this, they were utterly astonished and said, "Then who can be saved?"

26And looking, *Yeshua* said to them, "With men this is impossible, but with God all things are possible."[b]

27Then Peter said to Him, "Look, we've left everything to follow You! So what will we have?"

28And *Yeshua* said to them, "Amen, I tell you, when the Son of Man sits on His glorious throne in the new world,[c] you who have followed Me shall also sit on twelve thrones, judging the twelve tribes of Israel. 29And everyone who has left houses or brothers or sisters or father or mother or children or property, for My name's sake, will receive a hundred times as much, and will inherit eternal life. 30But many who are first will be last, and the last first."

20

Parable of the Day Laborers

1"For the kingdom of heaven is like the master of a household, who went out early in the morning to hire workers for his vineyard. 2Now when he had agreed with the workers for a denarius per day, he sent them into his vineyard. 3And he went out about the third hour and saw others standing in the marketplace, idle. 4And to them he said, 'You go into the vineyard too, and I'll give you whatever is right.' 5So they went. Again he went out about the sixth and ninth hour and did the same. 6And about the eleventh hour, he went out and found others standing around. And he said to them, 'Why have you been standing here idle the whole day?'

7"'Because no one hired us,' they said to him.

"He said to them, 'You go into the vineyard, too.'

8"Now when evening came, the owner of the vineyard said to his foreman, 'Call the workers and pay them their wages, beginning from the last to the first.' 9And those who had come about the eleventh hour each received a denarius. 10And when the first came, they supposed that they would receive more; yet they too received a denarius.

11"But when they received it, they began to grumble against the master of the house, 12saying, 'These last guys did one hour, and you've made them equal to us, who bore the burden and scorching heat of the day!'

13"But answering, he said to one of them, 'Friend, I'm doing you no wrong. Didn't you agree with me on a denarius? 14Take what is yours and go. But I want to give this last guy the same as you. 15Am

a 19:19. Exod. 20:12-13(12-16); Deut. 5:16-17(16-20); Lev. 19:18b.

b 19:26. cf. Gen. 18:14; Jer. 32:17.

c 19:28. Lit. *regeneration*; cf. Rom. 8:19-23; Tit. 3:5; 2 Pet. 3:13; Rev. 21:5.

I not permitted to do what I want with what belongs to me? Or is your eye evil because I am good?'

16"So the last will be first, and the first last."

Third Prediction: Death & Resurrection

17Now as *Yeshua* was going up to Jerusalem, He took the Twelve aside privately; and on the way he told them, 18"Look, we're going up to Jerusalem, and the Son of Man will be handed over to the ruling *kohanim* and *Torah* scholars. They will condemn Him to death 19and hand Him over to the Gentiles to mock, and to scourge, and to crucify. Yet on the third day, He will be raised up."[a]

Leading by Serving

20Then the mother of the sons of Zebedee came with her sons to *Yeshua*, and she was kneeling down and asking something from Him.

21"What do you want?" He said to her.

She said to Him, "Declare that these two sons of mine might sit, one on Your right and one on Your left, in Your kingdom."

22But *Yeshua* replied, "You don't know what you're asking! Are you able to drink the cup I am about to drink?"

"We are able," they say to Him.

23He said to them, "You shall indeed drink My cup. But to sit on My right and left, this isn't Mine to grant. Rather, it's for those for whom it has been prepared by My Father."

24Now when the ten heard, they became indignant with the two brothers. 25But *Yeshua* called them over and said, "You know that the rulers of the nations lord it over them, and their great ones play the tyrant over them. 26It shall not be this way among you. But whoever wants to be great among you shall be your servant, 27and whoever wants to be first among you shall be your slave— 28just as the Son of Man did not come to be served, but to serve, and to give His life as a ransom for many."

a 20:18-19. cf. Ps. 22; Isa. 52:12-53:12.

What Do You Want Me to Do for You?

29Now as they were leaving Jericho, a large crowd followed Him. 30And here two blind men sitting by the roadside, when they heard that *Yeshua* was passing by, cried out, saying, "Have mercy on us, O Master, *Ben- David*!" 31The crowd warned them to be quiet, but they cried out all the more, saying, "Have mercy on us, O Master, *Ben-David*!"[b]

32*Yeshua* stopped and called out to them. "What do you want Me to do for you?" He said.

33They said to Him, "Master, let our eyes be opened!" 34Moved with compassion, *Yeshua* touched their eyes. Instantly they regained their sight and followed Him.[c]

21

Baruch Ha-Ba! Blessed Is He Who Comes!

1Now as they drew near to Jerusalem and came to Bethphage, to the Mount of Olives, then *Yeshua* sent two disciples, 2saying to them, "Go into the village before you. Right away, you'll find a donkey tied up and a colt with her. Untie them and bring them to Me. 3If anyone says anything to you, you shall say, 'The Master needs them.' And right away he will send them."

4This happened to fulfill what was spoken through the prophet, saying,

5"Say to the daughter of
Zion,

b 20:31. cf. Isa. 61:1(LXX); Lk. 4:18.
c 20:30-34. cf. Isa. 35:5; 42:6-7.

Matthew 21:9

The crowds going before Him and those following kept shouting, saying, "Hoshia-na to Ben-David! Baruch ha-ba b'shem ADONAI! Blessed is He who comes in the name of the LORD! Hoshia-na in the highest!"

'See, your King is coming to
you,
humble and sitting on a
donkey,
a colt, the foal of a
donkey.'"[a]

6The disciples went and did as *Yeshua*
had directed them. 7They brought the
donkey and colt and put their clothing on
them, and He sat on the clothing. 8Most
of the crowd spread their clothing on the
road, and others began cutting branches
from the trees and spreading them on
the road. 9The crowds going before
Him and those following kept shouting,
saying,

"*Hoshia-na* to *Ben-David*!
Baruch ha-ba b'shem ADONAI!
Blessed is He who comes in the name
of the LORD!
Hoshia-na in the highest!"[b]

10When He entered Jerusalem, the
whole city was stirred up, saying, "Who
is this?" 11And the crowds kept saying, "This is the prophet *Yeshua*, from
Natzeret in the Galilee."
12Then *Yeshua* entered the Temple[c] and
drove out all those selling and buying in
the Temple. He overturned the tables
of the moneychangers[d] and the seats
of those selling doves.[e] 13And He said to
them, "It is written, 'My house shall be
called a house of prayer,'[f] but you are
making it 'a den of thieves'!"[g]
14The blind and lame came to Him in
the Temple, and He healed them. 15But
when the ruling *kohanim* and *Torah* scholars saw the wonders He performed, and
the children crying out in the Temple and
saying, "*Hoshia-na* to *Ben-David*," they
became indignant. 16And they said to
Him, "Do You hear what these children
are saying?" "Yes," *Yeshua* said to them.
"Haven't you ever read,

'Out of the mouth of babes and nurs-
ing toddlers
You have prepared praise for
Yourself'?"[h]

17Then He left them and went out of
the city to Bethany, and He spent the
night there.

Faith Moves Mountains

18Now early in the morning, as He
was returning to the city, He became
hungry. 19Seeing a lone fig tree by the
road, He came up to it and found nothing on it except leaves only. And He said
to it, "May no fruit ever come from you
again!" And the fig tree shriveled up at
once.
20When the disciples saw it they were
astonished. "How did the fig tree shrivel
on the spot?" they asked.
21*Yeshua* answered them, "Amen, I tell
you, if you have faith and do not doubt,
not only will you do what was done to the
fig tree, but even if you say to this mountain, 'Be taken up and thrown into the
sea,' it will happen. 22And whatever you
ask in prayer, trusting, you shall receive."

Questions about *Yeshua's* Authority

23Now when He entered the Temple,
the ruling *kohanim* and the elders of the
people came to Him while He was teaching, saying, "By what authority are You
doing these things? Who gave You this
authority?"
24*Yeshua* replied to them, "I also will
ask you one question. If you tell Me, I likewise will tell you by what authority I do
these things. 25John's immersion, where
was it from? From heaven or from men?"
They began to dialogue among themselves, saying, "If we say, 'From heaven,'

a 21:5. Isa. 62:11; Zech. 9:9(9:9 LXX); cf. Gen. 49:10-11.
b 21:9. cf. Ps. 118:25-26.
c 21:12a. Some mss. add: *of God*.
d 21:12b. cf. Deut. 14:24-26.
e 21:12c. cf. Lev. 1:14; 5:7; 12:8.
f 21:13. Isa. 56:7.
g 21:13. Jer. 7:11.
h 21:16. Ps. 8:3(2).

He will say to us, 'Then why didn't you believe him?' [26]But if we say, 'From men,' we fear the crowd, for all hold up John as a prophet." [27]So answering *Yeshua*, they said, "We don't know."

Then He said to them, "Neither am I telling you by what authority I do these things."

A Parable about Intentions and Actions

[28]"Now what do you think? A man had two sons, and he went to the first and said, 'Son, go work in the vineyard today.' [29]The son answered, 'I won't,' but afterward he had a change of heart and went. [30]The man went to the second son and said the same thing. But he answered, 'I will, sir,' and didn't go. [31]Which of the two did the will of the father?"

"The first," they said.

Yeshua said to them, "Amen, I tell you, the tax collectors and prostitutes are going ahead of you into the kingdom of God. [32]For John came to you in the way of righteousness, and you did not believe him. But the tax collectors and prostitutes did believe him; and even after you saw this, you had no change of heart to believe him."

Parable of the Vineyard

[33]"Listen to another parable. There was a master of a household who planted a vineyard. He put a hedge around it, dug a winepress in it, and built a tower.[a] Then He leased it to some tenant farmers and went on a journey. [34]Now when fruit season drew near, he sent his servants to the tenants to collect his fruit. [35]But grabbing his servants, the tenants beat up one, killed another, and stoned still another. [36]Again the master sent other servants, even more than the first, and they did the same thing to them. [37]Finally he sent his son to them, saying, 'They will respect my son.'

a 21:33. cf. Isa. 5:1-2.

[38]"But when the tenants saw the son, they said among themselves, 'This is the heir! Come on, let's kill him and get his inheritance!' [39]So grabbing him, they threw him out of the vineyard and killed him. [40]Therefore when the master of the vineyard comes, what will he do to those tenants?"

[41]"He will bring those miserable men to a miserable end," they said to Him, "and will lease the vineyard to other tenants, who will give him his share of the fruits in their seasons." [42]*Yeshua* said to them, "Have you never read in the Scriptures[b]?

'The stone which the builders
rejected,
this has become the chief
cornerstone.
This came from ADONAI,
and it is marvelous in our eyes.'[c]

[43]Therefore I say to you, the kingdom of God will be taken away from you and given to a people producing its fruits. [44]Whoever falls on this stone will be shattered; but the one upon whom it falls, it will crush him."[d]

[45]When the ruling *kohanim* and Pharisees heard *Yeshua's* parables, they realized He was talking about them. [46]Although they were trying to seize Him, they feared the crowds, because they regarded Him as a prophet.

22

Invitation to the Wedding Feast

[1] *Yeshua* answered and spoke to them again in parables, saying, [2]"The kingdom of heaven may be compared to a king who made a wedding feast for his son. [3]He sent out his servants to call those who were invited to the wedding feast,

b 21:42. Lit. *Writings*.

c 21:42. Ps. 118:22-23 (117:22-23 LXX).

d 21:44. cf. Isa. 28:16; Dan. 2:34, 44-45. Some manuscripts omit verse 44.

but they wouldn't come. 4Again he sent
out other servants, saying, 'Tell those
who were invited, "Look, I've prepared
my meal. My oxen and fattened cattle
are killed, and everything is ready. Come
to the wedding feast!"'

5"But paying no attention, they went
away, one to his own farm, another to his
business. 6And the rest grabbed his servants, humiliated them, and killed them.
7Now the king became furious! Sending
his troops, he destroyed those murderers and set fire to their city.

8"Then he said to his servants, 'The
wedding feast is ready, but those who
were invited were not worthy. 9So go
into the highways and byways, and invite
everyone you find to the wedding feast.'
10And those servants went out into the
highways and gathered together all they
found, both bad and good; and the wedding was filled with guests.

11"But when the king came in to look
over the guests, he saw a man there
who wasn't dressed in wedding clothes.
12'Friend,' he said to him, 'how did you
get in here without wedding clothes?'
But the man was silent. 13Then the king
said to his servants, 'Tie him up hand and
foot, and throw him into the outer darkness; in that place will be weeping and
gnashing of teeth.' 14For many are called,
but few are chosen."

A Trap about Paying Taxes

15Then the Pharisees went and plotted
how they might trap Him with a word.
16And they sent to Him some of their disciples, along with the Herodians, saying,
"Teacher, we know that You are honest
and teach the way of God in truth. And
what others think doesn't concern You,
for You do not look at men's appearance.
17Tell us therefore, what do You think? Is
it permitted to pay taxes to Caesar, or
not?"

18But *Yeshua*, knowing their wickedness, said, "Why are you testing Me, you
hypocrites? 19Show Me the tax money."

So they brought Him a denarius.

20And He said to them, "Whose image
is this? And whose inscription?"

21"Caesar's," they said to Him.

Then He said to them, "Give therefore
to Caesar the things that are Caesar's,
and to God the things that are God's."
22And hearing this, they were amazed.
So they left Him and went away.

Religious Leaders Ask a Tricky Question

23On that day, Sadducees (who say
there is no resurrection) came to *Yeshua*
and questioned Him, saying, 24"Teacher,
Moses said, 'If someone dies having no
children, his brother as next of kin shall
marry his widow and father children for
his brother.'[a] 25Now there were seven
brothers among us. The first married
and died; and having no offspring, left
his wife to his brother. 26In the same way
also the second, and the third, down to
the seventh. 27Last of all, the woman
died. 28So in the resurrection, whose
wife of the seven will she be? For they all
had married her."

29But answering, *Yeshua* said to them,
"You've gone astray, because you don't
understand the Scriptures or the power
of God. 30For in the resurrection they neither marry nor are given in marriage, but
are like angels in heaven. 31But concerning the resurrection of the dead, haven't
you read what was spoken to you by God,
saying, 32'I am the God of Abraham, and
the God of Isaac, and the God of Jacob'?
He is not the God of the dead, but of the
living!"[b] 33When the crowds heard this,
they were astounded at His teaching.

The Greatest *Mitzvot*

34But the Pharisees, when they heard
that *Yeshua* had silenced the Sadducees,
gathered together in one place. 35And
testing Him, one of them, a lawyer,

a 22:24. Lit. *raise up seed for his brother*; cf. Dt. 25:5-6; Gen. 38:8.

b 22:32. cf. Exod. 3:6.

asked, 36“Teacher, which is the greatest commandment in the *Torah*?”

37And He said to him, “‘You shall love *ADONAI* your God with all your heart, and with all your soul, and with all your mind.’[a] 38This is the first and greatest commandment. 39And the second is like it, ‘You shall love your neighbor as yourself.’[b] 40The entire *Torah* and the Prophets hang on these two commandments.”

Yeshua Overturns the Arguments

41Now while the Pharisees were gathered together, *Yeshua* asked them a question, 42saying, “What do you think about the Messiah? Whose Son is He?”[c]

“David’s,” they say to Him.

43“Then how is it,” He says to them, “that David by the Spirit calls him ‘Lord’?

> 44For he says, ‘*ADONAI* said to my Lord,
> “Sit at My right hand,
> until I put Your enemies under Your feet.”’[d]

45If David then calls Him ‘Lord,’ how is He his son?” 46No one was able to answer Him a word. Nor did anyone dare from that day on to question Him any longer.

23

Seven Woes

1Then *Yeshua* spoke to the crowds and to His disciples, 2saying, “The *Torah* scholars and Pharisees sit on the seat of Moses. 3So whatever they tell you, do and observe. But don’t do what they do; for what they say, they do not do. 4They tie up heavy loads, hard to carry,[e] and lay them on men’s shoulders; but they themselves aren’t willing to lift a finger to move them. 5All their works they do to be noticed by men. They make their *tefillin* wide and their *tzitziyot* long.[f] 6They love the place of honor at feasts, the best seats in the synagogues, 7greetings in the marketplaces, and to be called rabbi by men.

8“But you are not to be called rabbi; for One is your Teacher, and you are all brothers. 9And call no man on earth your father; for One is your Father, who is in heaven. 10Nor are you to be called teachers; for One is your Teacher, the Messiah. 11But the greatest among you shall be your servant. 12Whoever exalts himself shall be humbled, and whoever humbles himself shall be exalted.

13“But woe to you, *Torah* scholars and Pharisees, hypocrites! For you shut people out of the kingdom of heaven. For you do not enter yourselves, nor do you let those enter who are trying to go in.(14)[g]

15“Woe to you, *Torah* scholars and Pharisees, hypocrites! For you travel over land and sea to make one convert. And when he becomes one, you make him twice as much a son of Gehenna as yourself.

16“Woe to you, blind guides! You say, ‘Whoever swears by the Temple, it is nothing; but whoever swears by the gold of the Temple, he is obligated.’ 17O fools and blind ones! Which is greater, the gold or the Temple that made the gold holy?[h] 18And you say, ‘Whoever swears by the altar, it is nothing; but whoever swears by the offering on it, he is obligated.’ 19O blind ones! Which is greater, the offering or the altar that makes the offering holy?[i] 20Therefore, whoever swears by the altar, swears both by the altar and everything on it. 21And whoever swears by the Temple, swears both by the Temple and by Him who dwells in it. 22And

a 22:37. cf. Deut. 6:5, *v’ahavta*.
b 22:39. Lev. 19:18b, *v’ahavta l’reiacha kamocha*.
c 22:42. cf. Ps. 110:1; Ps. 109:1 (LXX).
d 22:44. Ps. 110:1.
e 23:4. Some mss. omit *hard to carry*.
f 23:5. cf. Exod. 13:9, 16; Deut. 6:8; 11:18; Num. 15:37-41.
g 23:14. Some manuscripts add v. 14: *Woe to you, Torah scholars and Pharisees, hypocrites! For you devour widows’ houses, while praying at length as a show. Therefore you will receive greater condemnation.* cf. Mk. 12:40; Lk. 20:47.
h 23:17ff. cf. Exod. 30:29.
i 23:19. cf. Exod. 29:37.

whoever swears by heaven, swears both
by the throne of God and by Him who sits
on it.

23"Woe to you, *Torah* scholars and Pharisees, hypocrites! You tithe[a] mint and dill
and cumin, yet you have neglected the
weightier matters of *Torah*—justice and
mercy and faithfulness. It is necessary to
do these things without neglecting the
others. 24O blind guides, straining out a
gnat while swallowing a camel!

25"Woe to you, *Torah* scholars and
Pharisees, hypocrites! You clean the outside of the cup and dish, but inside they
are full of greed and uncontrolled desire.
26O blind Pharisee! First clean the inside
of the cup and dish, so that the outside
may become clean as well.

27"Woe to you, *Torah* scholars and
Pharisees, hypocrites! For you are like
whitewashed tombs, which look beautiful on the outside but inside are full
of dead men's bones and everything
unclean. 28In the same way, you appear
righteous to men on the outside, but are
full of hypocrisy and lawlessness.

29"Woe to you, *Torah* scholars and
Pharisees, hypocrites! You build tombs
for the prophets and decorate the monu-
ments of the *tzaddikim*. 30And you say, 'If
we'd been alive in the days of our forefathers, we wouldn't have been partners
with them in shedding the blood of the
prophets.' 31So you testify against yourselves, that you are sons of those who
murdered the prophets. 32Fill up, then,
the measure of your fathers! 33O snakes,
you brood of vipers! How will you escape
the condemnation of Gehenna?

34"Because of this, behold, I'm sending you prophets and wise men and
Torah scholars. Some of them you will
kill and execute at the stake, and some
of them you will scourge in your synagogues and persecute from city to city.
35And so, upon you shall come all the
righteous blood shed on earth, from the
blood of righteous Abel to the blood of
Zechariah son of Berechiah,[b] whom you
murdered between the Temple and the
altar.[c] 36Amen, I tell you, all these things
will come upon this generation."

Holy Temple to Be Destroyed

37"O Jerusalem, Jerusalem who kills
the prophets and stones those sent to
her! How often I longed to gather your
children together, as a hen gathers her
chicks under her wings, but you were not
willing! 38Look, your house is left to you
desolate![d] 39For I tell you, you will never
see Me again until you say, '*Baruch ha-ba
b'shem* ADONAI. Blessed is He who comes
in the name of the LORD!'"[e]

24

1Now when *Yeshua* went out and was
going away from the Temple, His disciples
came up to point out to Him the Temple
buildings. 2"Don't you see all these?" He
responded to them. "Amen, I tell you,
not one stone will be left here on top of
another—every one will be torn down!"

Signs of the End of Time

3As He was sitting on the Mount of
Olives, the disciples came to Him privately, saying, "Tell us, when will these
things happen? What will be the sign of
Your coming and of the end of the age?"

4*Yeshua* answered them, "Be careful
that no one leads you astray! 5For many
will come in My name, saying, 'I am the
Messiah,' and will lead many astray. 6You
will hear of wars and rumors of wars.
See that you are not alarmed, for this
must happen but it is not yet the end.
7For nation will rise up against nation,
and kingdom against kingdom.[f] And
there will be famines and earthquakes in

a 23:23. cf. Lev. 27:30; Deut. 12:6, 17; 14:22-23; Mal. 3:8-10.

b 23:35. Some mss. omit *son of Berechiah*.

c 23:35. cf. Gen. 4:8; Zech. 1:1; 2 Chr. 24:21.

d 23:38. 13:35. cf. Jer. 12:7; 22:5.

e 23:39. Ps. 118:26.

f 24:7. cf. Isa. 19:2; 2 Chr. 15:6.

various places. 8But all these things are only the beginning of birth pains.

9"Then they will hand you over to persecution and will kill you. You will be hated by all the nations because of My name. 10And then many will fall away and will betray one another and hate one other. 11Many false prophets will arise and lead many astray. 12Because lawlessness will multiply, the love of many will grow cold. 13But the one who endures to the end will be saved. 14This Good News of the kingdom shall be proclaimed in the whole world as a testimony to all the nations, and then the end will come.

15"So when you see 'the abomination of desolation,'[a] which was spoken of through Daniel the prophet, standing in the Holy Place (let the reader understand), 16then those in Judea must flee to the mountains. 17The one on the roof must not go down to take what is in his house, 18and the one in the field must not turn back to get his coat. 19Woe to those who are pregnant and to those who are nursing babies in those days! 20Pray that your escape will not happen in winter, or on *Shabbat*. 21For then there will be great trouble,[b] such as has not happened since the beginning of the world until now, nor ever will. 22And unless those days were cut short, no one would be delivered. But for the sake of the chosen, those days will be cut short.

23"Then if anyone says to you, 'Look, here's the Messiah,' or 'There He is,' do not believe it. 24For false messiahs and false prophets will rise up[c] and show great signs and wonders so as to lead astray, if possible, even the chosen. 25See, I have told you beforehand.

26"So if they say to you, 'Look, He is in the wilderness,' do not go out. Or, 'Look, He is in the inner rooms,' do not believe it. 27For just as lightning comes from the east and flashes as far as the west, so also will be the coming of the Son of Man. 28For wherever the carcass is, there the vultures will gather.

29"But immediately after the trouble of those days,

'the sun will be darkened,
and the moon will not give
its light
and the stars will fall from heaven
and the powers of the heavens
will be shaken.'[d]

30Then the sign of the Son of Man will appear in heaven, and then all the tribes of the land will mourn, and they will see 'the Son of Man coming on the clouds of heaven'[e] with power and great glory. 31He will send out His angels with a great *shofar*, and they will gather together His chosen from the four winds, from one end of heaven to the other."[f]

Watching for Messiah's Return

32"Now learn the parable from the fig tree. When its branch becomes tender and puts forth leaves, you know that summer is near. 33So also, when you see all these things, know that it is near, at the door. 34Amen, I tell you, this generation will not pass away until all these things happen. 35Heaven and earth will pass away, but My words will never pass away.[g] 36But of that day and hour no one knows, not even the angels of heaven nor the Son,[h] except the Father alone.

37"For just as the days of Noah were, so will be the coming of the Son of Man. 38For in those days before the flood, they were eating and drinking, marrying and giving in marriage, until the day Noah entered the ark. 39And they did not understand until the flood came and swept them all away.[i] So shall it be at the

a 24:15. Dan. 9:27; 11:31; 12:11.
b 24:21. Dan. 12:1; cf. Jer. 30:7; Joel 2:1-2.
c 24:24. cf. Deut. 13:1ff.; 18:14ff.

d 24:29. cf. Isa. 13:10, 34:4 (LXX); Ezek. 32:7; Joel 2:10; 3:4(2:31); Zeph. 1:15.
e 24:30. Dan. 7:13.
f 24:31. cf. Isa. 11:12; 27:13; Zech. 9:14.
g 24:35. cf. Isa. 40:8; 55:9-11.
h 24:36. Some mss. omit *nor the Son*.
i 24:37-39. cf. Gen. 6:17-24.

coming of the Son of Man. 40Then two men will be in the field, one taken and one left. 41Two women will be grinding at the mill, one taken and one left.[a] 42Therefore stay alert; for you do not know what day your Lord is coming. 43But know this, that if the master of the house had known what time the thief was coming, he would have kept watch and not let his house be broken into. 44So you also must be ready, for the Son of Man is coming at an hour you do not expect."

The Faithful Servant

45"Who then is the faithful and wise servant, whom the master put in charge of his household to give them food at the proper time? 46Blessed is that servant whose master finds him so doing when he comes. 47Amen, I tell you, his master will put him in charge of all his possessions. 48But if that wicked servant says in his heart, 'My master is taking a long time,' 49and he begins to beat his fellow servants, and he eats and drinks with drunkards, 50the master of that servant will come on a day when he does not expect him and at an hour he does not know. 51And he will cut him in two and assign his place with the hypocrites, where there will be weeping and gnashing of teeth."

25

Parable of the Ten Virgins

1"Then the kingdom of heaven will be like ten virgins who took their lamps and went out to meet the bridegroom.[b] 2Five of them were foolish, and five were wise. 3For when the foolish ones took their lamps, they took no oil with them. 4But the wise ones took oil in jars along with their lamps.

5"Now while the bridegroom was taking a long time, they all got drowsy and started falling asleep. 6But in the middle of the night there was a shout, 'Look, the bridegroom! Come out to meet him!' 7Then all those virgins got up and trimmed their lamps. 8Now the foolish ones said to the wise, 'Give us some of your oil, since our lamps are going out.' 9But the wise ones replied, 'No, there won't be enough for us and for you. Instead, go to those who sell, and buy some for yourselves.'

10"But while they were going off to buy, the bridegroom came. And those who were ready went in with him to the wedding feast, and the door was shut. 11Now later, the other virgins came, saying, 'Sir, Sir, open up for us!'

12"But he replied, 'Amen, I tell you, I do not know you.' 13Therefore stay alert, for you know neither the day nor the hour."

Parable of the Talents

14"For it is like a man about to go on a journey. He called his own servants and handed over his possessions to them. 15To one he gave five talents,[c] to another two, and to another one, each according to his own ability. Then he went on his journey.

16"Immediately the one who had received the five talents went and traded with them and gained five more. 17In the same way, the one with two gained two more. 18But the one who received one went off and dug a hole in the ground and hid his master's money.

19"Now after a long time, the master of those servants came and settled accounts with them. 20The one who had received the five talents came up and brought another five talents, saying, 'Master, you handed me five talents. Look, I've gained five more.' 21His master said to him, 'Well done, good and faithful servant! You were faithful with a little, so

a 24:41. cf. Exod. 11:5.
b 25:1. Some mss. add: *and the bride*.
c 25:15. One talent was worth 6000 denarii, or about 16 years' wages.

I'll put you in charge of much. Enter into
your master's joy!'
22"The one who had received the two
talents also came up and said, 'Master,
you handed me two talents. Look, I've
gained two more.' 23His master said to
him, 'Well done, good and faithful servant! You were faithful with a little, so
I'll put you in charge of much. Enter into
your master's joy!'
24"Then the one who had received
the one talent also came up and said,
'Master, I knew that you are a hard man,
reaping where you didn't sow and gathering where you scattered no seed. 25So
I was afraid, and I went off and hid your
talent in the ground. See, you have what
is yours.'
26"But his master responded, 'You
wicked, lazy servant! You knew that I
reap where I didn't sow and gather where
I scattered no seed? 27Then you should
have brought my money to the brokers,
and when I came I would have received it
back with interest. 28Therefore take the
talent away from him, and give it to the
one who has the ten talents. 29For to the
one who has, more shall be given, and he
shall have an abundance. But from the
one who does not have, even what he
does have shall be taken away. 30Throw
the worthless servant out, into the outer
darkness where there will be weeping
and gnashing of teeth.'"

The Righteous Judge

31"Now when the Son of Man comes
in His glory, and all the angels with Him,
then He will sit on His glorious throne.
32All the nations will be gathered before
Him, and He will separate them from
one another, just as the shepherd separates the sheep from the goats.[a] 33And
He will put the sheep on His right, but
the goats on His left. 34Then the King
will say to those on His right, 'Come, you
who are blessed by My Father, inherit
the kingdom prepared for you from the
foundation of the world. 35For I was hungry and you gave Me something to eat; I
was thirsty and you gave Me something
to drink; I was a stranger and you invited
Me in; 36I was naked and you clothed Me;
I was sick and you visited Me; I was in
prison and you came to Me.'[b]
37"Then the righteous will answer
Him, 'Lord, when did we see You hungry
and feed You? Or thirsty and give You
something to drink? 38And when did we
see You a stranger and invite You in? Or
naked and clothe You? 39When did we see
You sick, or in prison, and come to You?'
40"And answering, the King will say to
them, 'Amen, I tell you, whatever you did
to one of the least of these My brethren,
you did it to Me.'[c] 41Then He will also say
to those on the left, 'Go away from Me,
you cursed ones, into the everlasting fire
which has been prepared for the devil
and his angels. 42For I was hungry and
you gave Me nothing to eat; I was thirsty
and you gave Me nothing to drink; 43I
was a stranger and you did not invite Me
in; naked and you did not clothe Me; sick
and in prison and you did not visit Me.'
44"Then they too will answer, saying,
'Lord, when did we see You hungry or
thirsty or a stranger or naked or sick or in
prison, and did not care for You?' 45Then
He will answer them, saying, 'Amen, I tell
you, whatever you did not do for one of
the least of these, you did not do for Me.'
46These shall go off to everlasting punishment, but the righteous into everlasting
life."[d]

26

The Conspiracy Grows

1Now it happened that when *Yeshua*
had finished all these words, He said to
His disciples, 2"You know that Passover
comes in two days, and the Son of Man
will be handed over to be executed."

a 25:32. cf. Ezek. 34:17.

b 25:35-36. cf. Isa. 58:7.

c 25:40. cf. Prov. 19:17.

d 25:46. cf. Dan. 12:2.

3 Then the ruling *kohanim* and elders of the people were gathered together in the court of the *kohen gadol* named Caiaphas. 4 They plotted together in order that they might seize *Yeshua* by stealth and kill Him. 5 "But not during the festival," they were saying, "so there won't be a riot among the people."

A Woman Anoints *Yeshua* for Burial

6 Now while *Yeshua* was in Bethany at the house of Simon *ha-Metzora*, 7 a woman came up to Him with an alabaster jar of very expensive oil. And she poured it on His head as He was reclining at the table. 8 But when the disciples saw this, they were indignant, saying, "Why this waste? 9 It could have been sold for a lot, and the money given to the poor!"

10 But *Yeshua*, knowing this, said to them, "Why do you cause trouble for this woman? She's done Me a *mitzvah*. 11 You always have the poor with you, [a] but you won't always have Me. 12 For when she poured this oil on My body, she did it to prepare Me for burial. 13 Amen, I tell you, wherever this Good News is proclaimed in all the world, what she has done will also be told in memory of her."

Betrayed and Sold for Silver

14 Then one of the Twelve, the one called Judah of Kriot, went to the ruling *kohanim* 15 and said, "What are you willing to give me if I hand Him over to you?" And they weighed out thirty shekels[b] of silver for him. 16 From then on, Judah began looking for a chance to hand Him over.

17 Now on the first day of *matzah*,[c] the disciples came to *Yeshua*, saying, "Where do You want us to prepare for You to eat the Passover?"

18 He said, "Go into the city to a certain man, and tell him, 'The Teacher says, "My time is near; at your house I am to keep the Passover with My disciples."'" 19 The disciples did as *Yeshua* had ordered them, and they prepared the Passover.[d]

20 Now when it was evening, *Yeshua* was reclining at the table with the Twelve. 21 As they were eating, He said, "Amen, I tell you, one of you will betray Me."

22 And being very sorrowful, they began, each one, to say to Him, "I'm not the one, am I, Master?"

23 And He replied, "The one who dipped his hand in the bowl with Me, he's the one who will betray Me.[e] 24 The Son of Man indeed goes, just as it is written about Him; but woe to that man by whom the Son of Man is betrayed![f] It would have been better for that man if he had not been born!"

25 And Judah, the one betraying Him, replied, "I'm not the one, am I, Rabbi?"

Yeshua said to him, "You've said it yourself."

26 Now while they were eating, *Yeshua* took *matzah*;[g] and after He offered the *bracha*, He broke and gave to the disciples and said, "Take, eat; this is My body." 27 And He took a cup; and after giving thanks, He gave to them, saying, "Drink from it, all of you; 28 for this is My blood of the covenant, which is poured out for many for the removal of sins.[h] 29 But I say to you, I will never drink of this fruit of the vine from now on, until that day when I drink it anew with you in My Father's kingdom."

30 After singing the *Hallel*,[i] they went out to the Mount of Olives. 31 Then *Yeshua* said to them, "This night you will all fall away because of Me; for it is written,

a 26:11. cf. Deut. 15:11.
b 26:15. cf. Exod. 21:32; Zech. 11:12.
c 26:17. cf. Exod. 12:15.
d 26:19. cf. Deut. 16:5-8.
e 26:23. cf. Exod. 12:8; Ps. 41:10(9).
f 26:24. cf. Ps. 41:10(9).
g 26:26. Lit. bread (at Passover, unleavened bread).
h 26:28. cf. Exod. 24:8; Jer. 31:31; Heb. 9:22; 10:16-18. Some mss. say: *new covenant*.
i 26:30. Ps. 113-118; Ps. 115-118 was sung after the last cup.

Matthew 26:26

Now while they were eating, Yeshua took matzah; and after He offered the bracha, He broke and gave to the disciples and said, "Take, eat; this is My body."

'I will strike the Shepherd,
and the sheep of the flock will be
scattered.'[a]

32But after I am raised up, I will go
before you to the Galilee."
33But Peter replied to Him, "Though
all fall away because of You, I'll never fall
away."
34*Yeshua* said to him, "Amen, I tell you,
this very night, before a rooster crows,
you will deny Me three times."
35"Even if I must die with You," Peter
says to Him, "I'll never deny You!" And so
said all the disciples.

"Your Will Be Done"

36Then *Yeshua* comes with them to a
place called Gethsemane, and He tells the
disciples, "Sit here, while I go over there
and pray." 37And He took along Peter and
Zebedee's two sons, and He began to be
sorrowful and troubled. 38Then He tells
them, "My soul is deeply grieved, even
to the point of death. Stay here and keep
watch with Me." 39Going a little farther,
He fell face down and prayed, saying,
"My Father, if it is possible, let this cup
pass from Me! Yet not as I will, but as You
will."
40Then He comes to the disciples and
finds them sleeping; and He tells Peter,
"So couldn't you keep watch with Me for
one hour? 41Keep watching and praying,
so that you won't enter into temptation. The spirit is willing, but the flesh
is weak." 42Again for a second time He
went away and prayed, saying, "My
Father, if this cannot pass away unless
I drink it, let Your will be done." 43And
again He came and found them sleeping,
for their eyes were heavy. 44So He left
them again and prayed a third time, saying the same words once more. 45Then
He comes to the disciples and says to
them, "Still sleeping? Taking your rest?
Look, the hour is at hand, and the Son
of Man is being delivered into the hands
of sinners. 46Get up, let's go! Look, My
betrayer is near."

Taken into Custody

47While *Yeshua* was still speaking, here
came Judah, one of the Twelve, and with
him a big crowd with swords and clubs,
from the ruling *kohanim* and elders of
the people. 48Now His betrayer had given
them a sign, saying, 'The One I kiss, He's
the One—seize Him!' 49And immediately
Judah drew near[b] to *Yeshua* and said,
"*Shalom*, Rabbi!" and kissed Him.
50"Friend," *Yeshua* said to him, "do
what you've come to do." Then they
came up and threw their hands on *Yeshua*
and seized Him. 51And suddenly, one of
those with *Yeshua* stretched out his hand
and drew his sword, and he struck the
kohen gadol's servant and cut off his ear.
52Then *Yeshua* said to him, "Put your
sword back in its place! For all who take
up the sword shall perish by the sword.[c]
53Or do you suppose that I cannot call on
My Father, and at once He will place at
My side twelve legions[d] of angels? 54How
then would the Scriptures be fulfilled,
that it must be so?"
55At that hour *Yeshua* said to the
crowds, "Have you come out with
swords and clubs, to capture Me as you
would a revolutionary?[e] Every day I sat
teaching in the Temple, and you didn't
seize Me. 56But all this has happened so
that the writings of the prophets would
be fulfilled." Then all the disciples fled,
abandoning Him.
57Now those who had seized *Yeshua* led
Him away to Caiaphas, the *kohen gadol*,
where the *Torah* scholars and elders had
gathered. 58Peter was following Him
from a distance as far as the courtyard of
the *kohen gadol*. And after going inside,
he was sitting with the guards, to see the
outcome.

a 26:31. Zech. 13:7.

b 26:49. cf. Gen. 44:18.
c 26:52. cf. Gen. 9:6.
d 26:53. 1 legion = 6000 soldiers.
e 26:55. Or robber.

Yeshua's Trial Begins

59Now the ruling *kohanim* and all the
Sanhedrin kept trying to get false testimony against *Yeshua* so they could put
Him to death. 60But they found none,
though many false witnesses came forward. At last two came forward 61and
said, "This fellow said, 'I'm able to
destroy the Temple of God and rebuild it
in three days!'"

62The *kohen gadol* stood up and said
to *Yeshua*, "Have You no answer? What's
this they're testifying against You?" 63But
Yeshua kept silent.

The *kohen gadol* said to Him, "I charge
You under oath by the living God, tell us if
You are *Mashiach Ben-Elohim!*"[a]

64"As you have said," replied *Yeshua*.
"Besides that, I tell you, soon after you
will see the Son of Man sitting at the
right hand of power and coming on the
clouds of heaven."[b]

65Then the *kohen gadol* tore his clothes
and said, "Blasphemy! Why do we need
any more witnesses? Look, you've heard
the blasphemy. 66What's your verdict?"[c]

"Guilty," they answered. "He deserves
death!" 67Then they spat in His face and
pounded Him with their fists.[d] Others
slapped Him and demanded, 68"Prophesy to us, you Messiah! Which one hit
You?"

Peter Denies *Yeshua*

69Meanwhile, Peter was sitting in the
courtyard. A servant girl came over to
him and said, "You also were with *Yeshua*
of the Galilee."

70But he denied it before everyone,
saying, "I don't know what you're talking
about!"

71When he went onto the porch,
another servant girl saw him and said to
those who were there, "This man was
with *Yeshua ha-Natzrati*."

72Again he denied it with an oath: "I
don't know the Man!"

73A little while later, some of the
bystanders approached Peter and said to
him, "Surely you're one of them, too—
your accent gives you away."

74Then he began to curse[e] and to swear
an oath: "I do not know the Man!" Right
then, a rooster crowed. 75Then Peter
reminded himself of the word *Yeshua* had
said: "Before the rooster crows, you will
deny Me three times." And he went away
and wept bitterly.

27

Judah's Remorse

1When daybreak came, the ruling *kohanim* and elders of the people conspired
against *Yeshua* to put Him to death.
2And they tied Him up, led Him away,
and handed Him over to Pilate, the governor. 3Then Judah, His betrayer, saw
that *Yeshua* had been condemned. Feeling remorse, he brought the thirty silver
pieces back to the ruling *kohanim* and
elders, 4saying, "I've sinned, betraying
innocent blood!"

But they said, "What's that to us? You
see to it yourself!" 5After tossing the silver into the Temple sanctuary, he left.
Then he went off and hanged himself.
6But the ruling kohanim took the silver
pieces and said, "It is not permitted to
put these in the treasury, since it is blood
money." 7So after they conferred, they
bought with them the potter's field,
as a cemetery for strangers. 8For this
reason that field has been called the
"Field of Blood" to this day. 9Then was
fulfilled what was spoken by Jeremiah
the prophet, saying, "And they took the
thirty silver pieces, the price of Him on
whom a price had been set by *B'nei-Israel;*
10and they gave them for the potter's
field, just as Adonai arranged for me."[f]

a 26:63. cf. Jn. 20:31.
b 26:64. cf. Dan. 7:13; Ps. 110:1; Isa. 9:6(7).
c 26:66. cf. Lev. 24:16.
d 26:67. cf. Isa. 50:6.
e 26:74. cf. Mk. 14:71.
f 27:7-10. cf. Zech. 11:12-13; Jer. 18:2-6; 32:6-15; 19:1-13.

"Kill the King!"

11Now *Yeshua* stood before the governor. The governor questioned Him, saying, "Are You the King of the Jews?"

"You say so," *Yeshua* said. 12And while He was accused by the ruling *kohanim* and elders, He did not answer.

13Then Pilate said to Him, "Don't You hear how many things they testify against you?" 14*Yeshua* did not answer, not even one word, so the governor was greatly amazed.

15Now during the feast, the governor was accustomed to release to the crowd one prisoner, anyone they wanted. 16At that time they had a notorious prisoner, called *Yeshua Bar-Abba*. 17So when they were gathered together, Pilate said to them, "Which one do you want me to release for you? *Yeshua* who is *Bar-Abba*, or *Yeshua* who is called Messiah?"[a] 18For he knew that they had handed Him over out of envy.

19While Pilate was sitting on the judgment seat, his wife sent him a message, saying, "Don't have anything to do with that righteous Man, for today I've suffered many things in a dream because of Him."

20Now the ruling *kohanim* and elders persuaded the crowds that they should ask for *Bar-Abba* and destroy *Yeshua*. 21But the governor responded, "Which of the two do you want me to release for you?"

And they said, "*Bar-Abba!*"

22Pilate said to them, "What then shall I do with *Yeshua*, who is called Messiah?"

"Execute Him!" all of them say.

23But Pilate said, "Why? What evil has He done?"

But they kept shouting all the more, saying, "Let Him be executed!"

24When Pilate saw he was accomplishing nothing, but instead a riot was starting, he took some water and washed his hands in front of the crowd. "I am innocent of this blood,"[b] he said. "You see to it yourselves!"

25All the people answered and said, "His blood be on us and on our children!"[c]

26Then he released to them *Bar-Abba*. And after he had *Yeshua* scourged, he handed Him over to be crucified.

Nailed to a Stake

27Then the governor's soldiers took *Yeshua* into the Praetorium and gathered the whole cohort around Him. 28They stripped Him and put a scarlet robe around Him. 29And after braiding a crown of thorns, they placed it on His head and put a staff in His right hand. And falling on their knees before Him, they mocked Him, saying, "Hail, King of the Jews!" 30They spat on Him, and they took the staff and beat Him over and over on the head. 31When they finished mocking Him, they stripped the robe off Him and put His own clothes back on Him. And they led Him away to crucify Him.

32As they came out, they found a man from Cyrene, Simon by name. They forced him into service, to carry *Yeshua's* crossbeam.[d] 33And when they came to a place called Golgotha (that is to say, Place of a Skull), 34they offered Him wine mixed with gall to drink;[e] but after tasting, He was unwilling to drink it. 35And when they had crucified Him, they divided His clothing among themselves by casting lots.[f] 36And they sat down and kept guard over Him there. 37Over His head they put the charge against Him, which read: "THIS IS *YESHUA*, THE KING OF THE JEWS."

38Then two outlaws were executed with Him, one on the right and one on the left. 39Those passing by were jeering at Him,[g] shaking their heads 40and

a 27:16-17. Most mss. omit *Yeshua* before *Bar-Abba*. *Bar-Abba* is Aramaic for *Son of the Father*.

b 27:24. Some mss. say *this righteous blood* or *this righteous Man's blood*

c 27:25. cf. Josh. 2:19.

d 27:32. Probably the patibulum, the horizontal piece of the execution stake, weighing about 100 lbs.

e 27:34. cf. Ps. 69:22(21).

f 27:35. Ps. 22:19(18).

g 27:39. cf. Ps. 22:8(7).

saying, "You who are going to destroy the Temple and rebuild it in three days, save Yourself! If you are *Ben-Elohim*, come down from the stake!"

41 Likewise the ruling kohanim, along with the Torah scholars and elders, were also mocking Him. 42 "He saved others," they were saying, "but He can't save Himself? He's the King of Israel! Let Him come down now from the stake, and we'll believe in Him! 43 He trusts in God; let God rescue Him now, if He wants Him.[a] For He said, 'I am Ben-Elohim.'" 44 Even the outlaws who were executed with Him were ridiculing Him in the same way.[b]

Yeshua Lays Down His Life

45 Now from the sixth hour, darkness fell upon all the land until the ninth hour.[c] 46 About the ninth hour *Yeshua* cried out with a loud voice, saying, "*Eli, Eli, lema sabachthani?*"[d] that is, "My God, My God, why have You abandoned Me?"

47 When some of those standing there heard it, they began saying, "This Man is calling for Elijah." 48 Right away one of them ran and took a sponge. He filled it with sour wine and put it on a stick, and was offering it to *Yeshua* to drink.[e] 49 But the rest were saying, "Leave Him alone! Let's see if Elijah comes to save Him." 50 And *Yeshua* cried out again with a loud voice and gave up His spirit.

51 And behold, the curtain[f] of the Temple was split in two, from top to bottom. And the earth quaked and rocks were split apart. 52 And the tombs were opened, and many bodies of the *kedoshim* who were sleeping were raised to life. 53 And coming forth out of the tombs after His resurrection, they went into the holy city and appeared to many.

54 Now the centurion, and those with him keeping guard over *Yeshua*, when they saw the earthquake and what was happening, they became terribly frightened and said, "This really was the Son of God!"

The Tomb Is Sealed

55 Many women were there, watching from a distance. They had followed *Yeshua* from the Galilee, serving Him. 56 Among them were Miriam from Magdala, Miriam the mother of Jacob and Joseph, and the mother of Zebedee's sons.

57 Now when it was evening, there came a rich man from Arimathea, named Joseph, who had also become a disciple of *Yeshua*. 58 This man went to Pilate and asked for *Yeshua's* body. Then Pilate ordered it to be given up. 59 And Joseph took the body and wrapped it in a clean linen cloth. 60 And he laid it in his own new tomb,[g] which he had cut in the rock. Then he rolled a large stone up to the door of the tomb and went away. 61 Now Miriam from Magdala was there, and the other Miriam, sitting opposite the tomb.

Guarding the Tomb

62 Now on the next day, which is after the preparation, the ruling *kohanim* and Pharisees were gathered before Pilate. 63 "Sir," they said, "we remember how that deceiver said while He was still alive, 'After three days I'm to be raised.' 64 Therefore, order the tomb to be made secure until the third day, so His disciples do not come and steal Him away. They will tell the people, 'He is risen from the dead,' and the last deception will be worse than the first!"

65 "You have a guard," Pilate said to them. "Go, make it as secure as you know how." 66 So they went and made the tomb secure, sealing the stone along with the soldiers of the guard.

a 27:43. cf. Ps. 22:8.
b 27:44. cf. Isa. 53:3.
c 27:45. From noon until 3 p.m.; cf. Job 5:14; Ps. 105:28.
d 27:46. Ps. 22:2(1); cf. Deut. 32:20.
e 27:48. cf. Ps. 69:22(21).
f 27:51. Heb. *parokhet, veil or inner curtain*; cf. Exod. 26:33; 2 Chr. 3:14; Heb. 9:3.
g 27:57-60. cf. Isa. 53:9.

28

The Son Is Risen!

[1]Now after *Shabbat*, as it began to dawn on the first day of the week, Miriam of Magdala and the other Miriam came to look at the tomb. [2]And suddenly there was a great earthquake, for an angel of ADONAI descended from heaven and came and rolled back the stone and sat on it. [3]His appearance was like lightning,[a] and his clothing as white as snow. [4]And those keeping watch were shaken for fear of him and became like dead men.

[5]But the angel answered and said to the women, "Do not be afraid, for I know you are looking for *Yeshua* who was crucified. [6]He is not here; for He is risen, just as He said. Come, see the place where He[b] was lying. [7]Go quickly now and tell His disciples that He is risen from the dead. And behold, He's going before you to the Galilee. There you will see Him. See, I have told you!" [8]They quickly left the tomb, with fear yet with great joy, and ran to bring news to His disciples.

The Good News Cannot Be Hidden

[9]And behold, *Yeshua* met them. "*Shalom!*" He said. They drew near, grasped his feet, and worshiped Him. [10]"Don't be afraid," *Yeshua* said to them. "Go tell My brothers to head for the Galilee, and there they will see Me."

[11]Now while they were going, some of the guard came into the city and reported to the ruling *kohanim* all that had happened. [12]And when they had assembled with the elders and consulted together, they gave a large sum of silver to the soldiers, [13]saying, "Tell them, 'His disciples came at night and stole Him away while we were sleeping.' [14]And if this is heard by the governor, we'll appease him and keep you out of trouble." [15]So the soldiers took the money and did as they were instructed. And this story was spread among the Judeans to this day.

Authority to Make Disciples Everywhere

[16]Now the eleven disciples went to the Galilee, to the mountain *Yeshua* had designated. [17]When they saw Him, they worshiped; but some wavered. [18]And *Yeshua* came up to them and spoke to them, saying, "All authority in heaven and on earth has been given to Me.[c] [19]Go therefore and make disciples of all nations, immersing them in the name of the Father and the Son and the *Ruach ha-Kodesh*, [20]teaching them to observe all I have commanded you. And remember! I am with you always, even to the end of the age."

a 28:3. cf. Dan. 10:6.
b 28:6. Some mss. say *the Lord*.
c 28:18. cf. Isa. 9:5-6(6-7); Dan. 7:14.

The Good News According to
Mark

Introduction

Mark, the shortest of the four Gospels, is dated as early as the 40s C.E., though many scholars think it was more likely written in the 50s or 60s. Matthew and Luke may have used Mark's Gospel when constructing their own accounts. John Mark, who traveled with both Barnabas and Paul, authored this account. Though not an eyewitness himself, early tradition tells us that his Gospel was based on the eyewitness testimony of Simon Peter, one of the twelve *shlichim*. Therefore, this writing becomes another apostolic testimony to the message of the Good News.

The Gospel of Mark focuses less on *Yeshua's* teaching than on His deeds, especially His miracles. Events are recounted in an almost breathless fashion. Note the frequent use of "immediately" or equivalent expressions as one event leads into another. Mark's Gospel issues a strong call to discipleship, often placing the suffering of *Yeshua* alongside that call, as in chapters 8-10. As Matthew ends his Gospel with the Great Commission to bring the Good News to all nations, this second Gospel addresses itself to Gentiles, perhaps those living in Rome, the empire's capital.

Mark does not display the fullness of theological reflection on the life of *Yeshua* that the other Gospels do. Nevertheless, Mark's compact directness carries a significant message in itself. The fulcrum is found in Mark 8:29, when *Yeshua* asks, "Who do you say I am?" Peter answers, "You are the Messiah!" Before Peter's confession, the emphasis is on *Yeshua's* miracles. Afterward, it is on His suffering and death. It is as though once we come to recognize that *Yeshua* is the Messiah, we must learn what kind of Messiah He is, something even the disciples could not easily grasp. He is the Messiah who suffers and dies on our behalf—One whose followers must be prepared for costly discipleship as well.

A Look Inside Mark

1

The Kingdom Is Coming Now

[1]The beginning of the Good News of
Yeshua ha-Mashiach, Ben-Elohim. [2]As Isaiah the prophet has written,

"Behold, I send My messenger before
You,
who will prepare Your
way.[a]
[3]The voice of one crying in the
wilderness,
'Prepare the way of
ADONAI,
and make His paths straight.'"[b]

[4]John appeared, immersing in the
wilderness, proclaiming an immersion
involving repentance for the removal
of sins. [5]All the Judean countryside was
going out to him, and all the Jerusalem-
ites. As they confessed their sins, they
were being immersed by him in the Jordan River.

[6]John wore clothes made from camel's hair, with a leather belt around his
waist, and he ate locusts and wild honey.
[7] "After me comes One who is mightier
than I am," he proclaimed. "I'm not worthy to stoop down and untie the strap of
His sandals! [8]I immersed you with water,
but He will immerse you in the *Ruach
ha-Kodesh.*"[c]

The Spirit Rests on *Yeshua*

[9]In those days, *Yeshua* came from
Natzeret in the Galilee and was immersed
by John in the Jordan. [10]Just as He was
coming up out of the water, He saw the
heavens ripping open and the *Spirit* as
a dove coming down upon Him. [11]And
there came a voice from the heavens:
"You are My Son, whom I love; with You I
am well pleased!"[d]

[12]That instant, the *Spirit* drives Him
into the wilderness. [13]He was in the wilderness forty days, being tempted by
satan. And He was with the wild beasts,
and the angels were taking care of Him.

Fishermen Follow Him

[14]Now after John was put in jail, *Yeshua*
came into the Galilee, proclaiming the
Good News of God. [15]"Now is the fullness
of time," He said, "and the kingdom of
God is near! Turn away from your sins,
and believe in the Good News!"

[16]Passing along by the Sea of Galilee, He saw Simon and Simon's brother
Andrew casting a net in the sea, for they
were fishermen. [17]And *Yeshua* said to
them, "Follow Me, and I will make you
become fishers of men." [18]Immediately
they left their nets and followed Him.

[19]Going a little farther, He saw Jacob
the son of Zebedee and John his brother,
who were in their boat mending the nets.
[20]Immediately He called them, and they
left their father Zebedee in the boat with
the hired hands and followed Him.

Demons Flee at His Command

[21]And they went into Capernaum.
Right away, on *Shabbat*, He entered the
synagogue and began to teach. [22]And
they were astounded at His teaching,
for He was teaching them as one having
authority[e] and not as the *Torah* scholars.

[23]Just then there was a man in their
synagogue with an unclean spirit. And
he cried out, [24]"What have we to do with
You, *Yeshua* of *Natzeret*? Have You come
to destroy us? I know who You are! You're
the Holy One of God!"

[25]*Yeshua* rebuked him, saying, "Quiet!
Come out of him!" [26]And the unclean
spirit, after throwing the man into convulsions and crying out with a loud voice,
came out of him.

a 1:2. cf. Ex. 23:20, Mal. 3:1.
b 1:3. Isa. 40:3.
c 1:8. cf. Joel 2:28f; Ezek. 36:26; Zech. 12:10.
d 1:11. cf. Ps. 2:7, 12; Prov. 30:4; Isa. 9:5(6).
e 1:22, 27. cf. Isa. 53:12.

Mark 1:10-11

Just as He was coming up out of the water, He saw the heavens ripping open and the Spirit as a dove coming down upon Him. And there came a voice from the heavens: "You are My Son, whom I love; with You I am well pleased!"

27They were all so amazed that they
asked among themselves, "What is this?
A new teaching with authority! He commands even the unclean spirits, and they
obey Him!" 28And immediately news
about Him spread throughout the region
surrounding Galilee.

The Hurting Become Whole

29As soon as they left the synagogue,
they went with Jacob and John to the
house of Simon and Andrew. 30Now
Simon's mother-in-law was lying sick
with a fever. Right away, they told *Yeshua*
about her. 31He came and raised her up by
taking her hand. The fever left her, and
she began to take care of them.

32When evening came, at sunset, the
people brought to Him all the sick and
those who were afflicted by demons.
33The whole town gathered together at
the door. 34He healed many who were
sick with various diseases and drove out
many demons. And He would not allow
the demons to speak, because they knew
who He was.

35Very early, while it was still night,
Yeshua got up, left, and went away to
a place in the wilderness; and there He
was praying. 36Then Simon and those
with him hunted for *Yeshua*. 37And when
they found Him, they said to Him, "Every-
body's looking for You."

38He said to them, "Let's go somewhere else, to the neighboring towns,
so that I may proclaim the message there
also—this is what I came for." 39And He
went throughout all the Galilee, proclaiming the message in their synagogues and
driving out demons.

40A man with *tzara'at* comes to Him,
begging Him and falling on his knees,
saying, "If You are willing, You can make
me clean."

41Moved with compassion, *Yeshua*
stretched out His hand and touched
him. He said, "I am willing. Be cleansed."
42Immediately, the *tzara'at* left him, and
he was cleansed.

43*Yeshua* sent him away at once,
sternly warning him. 44He said to him,
"See that you say nothing to anyone, but
go show yourself to the *kohen*.[a] Then, for
your cleansing, offer what Moses commanded, as a testimony to them." 45But
he went out and began to proclaim and
spread the word, so much that *Yeshua*
could no longer enter a town openly
but had to stay out in wilderness areas.
Still, they kept on coming to Him from
everywhere.

2

Power to Pardon the Paralyzed

1When He returned to Capernaum
after some days, it was heard that He
was at the house. 2So many were gathered that there was no longer room for
them even outside the door. He kept proclaiming the word to them.

3Some people came bringing to Him
a paralyzed man, carried by four men.
4When they couldn't get near *Yeshua*
because of the crowd, they removed
the roof where He was. After digging
through, they lowered the mat on which
the paralyzed man was lying. 5*Yeshua*,
seeing their faith, said to the paralyzed
man, "Son, your sins are forgiven."

6But some of the *Torah* scholars were
sitting there, questioning in their hearts,
7"Why does this fellow speak like this?
He blasphemes! Who can pardon sins but
God alone?"

8Immediately *Yeshua*, knowing in His
spirit that they were raising questions
this way within themselves, said to them,
"Why are you questioning these things in
your hearts? 9Which is easier, to say to the
paralyzed man, 'Your sins are forgiven,'
or to say, 'Get up, and take your mat and
walk'? 10But so you may know that the
Son of Man has authority to pardon sins
on earth...." He tells the paralyzed man,

a 1:44. cf. Lev. 13:6, 13, 17, 23; 14:39.

11“I tell you, get up, take your mat and go home!”

12At once the man got up, took his mat, and walked before them all. They were all astonished and glorified God, saying, “We've never seen anything like this!”[a]

Fellowship with Sinners

13Again, *Yeshua* went out by the sea. The whole crowd kept coming to Him, and He continued to teach them. 14As He was passing by, He saw Levi the son of Alphaeus sitting at the tax collector's booth. He said to him, “Follow Me.” And he got up and followed Him.

15Now it happens that *Yeshua* was reclining at the table in Levi's house, and many tax collectors and sinners were reclining with *Yeshua* and His disciples. For there were many, and they were following Him. 16When the *Torah* scholars of the Pharisees saw Him eating with sinners and tax collectors, they began to say to His disciples, “With tax collectors and sinners He eats?”

17And when He heard this, *Yeshua* said to them, “Those who are healthy have no need for a doctor, but those who are sick do. I did not come to call the righteous, but the sinful.”

Feasting in His Presence

18Now John's disciples and the Pharisees were fasting. They came and said to Him, “Why do the disciples of John and the disciples of the Pharisees fast, but Your disciples do not fast?”

19And *Yeshua* said to them, “The guests of the bridegroom cannot fast while the bridegroom is with them, can they? As long as they have the bridegroom with them, they cannot fast. 20But the days will come when the bridegroom is taken away from them, and then they will fast in that day.

21“No one sews a patch of unshrunk cloth on an old garment. Otherwise the patch pulls away from the old, and a worse tear happens. 22And no one puts new wine into old wineskins. Otherwise, the wine will burst the skins; and the wine is lost, also the skins. But one puts new wine into fresh wineskins.”

Lord of *Shabbat*

23Now it happened on *Shabbat* that *Yeshua* was going through the grain fields; and His disciples began to make their way, plucking the heads of grain.[b] 24The Pharisees were saying to Him, “Look, why are they doing what is not permitted on *Shabbat*?”[c]

25And He said to them, “Haven't you ever read what David did when he was in need, and he and those with him became hungry?[d] 26How he entered into the house of God when Abiathar was *kohen gadol* and ate the showbread, which is permitted only for the *kohanim* to eat, and gave some even to those who were with him?”

27Then He said to them, “*Shabbat* was made for man, and not man for *Shabbat*. 28So the Son of Man is Lord even of *Shabbat*.”

3

A *Mitzvah* on *Shabbat*

1*Yeshua* entered the synagogue again, and a man with a withered hand was there. 2Now some were carefully watching Him, to see if He would heal him on *Shabbat*, so that they might accuse Him. 3He said to the man with the withered hand, “Stand up here in the center.” 4Then He said to them, “Is it permitted on *Shabbat* to do good or to do evil, to save a life or to kill?”[e] But they kept silent.

5After looking around at them with anger, grieved by their hardness of heart, He says to the man, “Stretch out your hand.” And he stretched it out, and his

a 2:5-12. cf. Isa. 53:12.

b 2:23. cf. Dt. 23:25.

c 2:24. cf. Exod. 20:10; 23:12; Deut. 5:14.

d 2:25 cf. Lev. 24:5-9; 1 Sam. 21:1-6.

e 3:4. cf. Exod. 20:10; Lev. 23:12; Deut. 5:14.

hand was restored. 6The Pharisees went out right away with the Herodians and began plotting against Him, how they might destroy Him.

Crowds Clamor for *Yeshua*

7*Yeshua* withdrew to the sea with His disciples, and a large crowd from the Galilee followed. From Judea, 8and from Jerusalem, and from Idumea, and beyond the Jordan, and around Tyre and Sidon, a great number, hearing all He was doing, came to Him. 9He told His disciples to have a small boat ready for Him because of the crowd, so that they wouldn't mob Him.

10For He had healed many, so that all those afflicted fell down before Him in order to touch Him. 11And the unclean spirits, whenever they saw Him, would fall down before Him and cry out, "You are *Ben-Elohim!*" 12But *Yeshua* strictly ordered them not to make Him known.

Appointing the Twelve

13Now He climbs up on the mountain and calls those He Himself wanted, and they came to Him. 14He appointed twelve (whom He also named *shlichim*), so that they might be with Him and He might send them to proclaim the Good News, 15and to have power to drive out demons. 16And He appointed the Twelve: to Simon He gave the name Peter; 17to Jacob and his brother John, the sons of Zebedee, He gave the name Boanerges, which is Sons of Thunder; 18and Andrew, Philip, Bartholomew, Matthew, Thomas, Jacob the son of Alphaeus, Thaddaeus, Simon the Zealot;[a] 19and Judah from Kriot, who also betrayed Him.

Binding the Strong Man

20Then He comes into a house, and again a crowd gathers so they couldn't even eat. 21When His family heard about this, they went out to take hold of Him; for they were saying, "He's out of His mind!"

22The *Torah* scholars who came down from Jerusalem said, "He's possessed by beelzebul," and, "By the ruler of demons He drives out demons."

23He called them and began speaking to them in parables: "How can satan drive out satan? 24If a kingdom is divided against itself, that kingdom cannot stand. 25And if a house is divided against itself, that house will not be able to stand. 26And if satan has risen up against himself and is divided, he cannot stand but his end has come.

27"But no one can enter a strong man's house to ransack his property, unless he first ties up the strong man. Then he will thoroughly plunder his house. 28Amen, I tell you, all things will be forgiven the sons of men, the sins and whatever blasphemies they utter; 29but whoever slanders[b] the *Ruach ha-Kodesh* never has release, but is guilty of an eternal sin!" 30For they were saying, "He has an unclean spirit."

A Spiritual Family Begins

31Then His mother and brothers come. Standing outside, they sent word to Him, summoning Him. 32A crowd was sitting around Him, and they tell Him, "Look, Your mother and Your brothers are outside looking for You." 33Answering them, He said, "Who are My mother and My brothers?" 34Looking at those sitting in a circle around Him, He said, "Here are My mother and My brothers! 35For whoever does the will of God, he is My brother and sister and mother."

4

Storytelling Opens Hearts

1Again *Yeshua* began to teach by the sea. A large crowd gathered around Him, so He got into a boat on the sea and sat

a 3:18. Lit. *Cananean*, Aramaic for *zealot*, *enthusiast*; perhaps formerly affiliated with the Jewish nationalistic Zealot party.

b 3:29. Lit. *blasphemes*; cf. Mt. 12:31-32.

down. And the crowd was by the sea on the land. [2]He began teaching them many things by parables, and in His teaching, He said to them: [3]"Listen! Behold, a sower went out to spread some seed. [4]It happened that as he sowed, some fell beside the road; and the birds came and ate it up.

[5]"Other seed fell on rocky ground, where it didn't have much soil. It sprang up immediately, because the soil wasn't deep. [6]But when the sun came up, it was scorched; and because it had no root, it withered away.

[7]"Other seed fell among the thorns; and the thorns grew and choked it, and it yielded no crop.

[8]"And others fell into the good soil and were producing fruit, springing up and increasing. They yielded a crop, producing thirty, sixty, and a hundredfold." [9]And He said, "He who has ears to hear, let him hear."

[10]When *Yeshua* was alone, those around Him with the Twelve started asking Him about the parables. [11]And He told them, "To you has been given the secret of the kingdom of God. But for those who are outside, everything is in parables,[a] so that

[12]'Seeing, they may see
and not perceive,
and hearing, they may hear and not
understand,
so they may not turn
back and be forgiven.'"[b]

[13]He said to them, "Don't you grasp this parable? Then how will you understand all the parables? [14]The sower sows the word. [15]These are the ones beside the road where the word is sown. Whenever they hear, satan comes quickly and takes away the word that has been sown in them.

[16]"These are the ones sown on rocky ground. When they hear the word, immediately they receive it with joy. [17]And they have no root in themselves but last only a short while. When trouble or persecution comes because of the word, immediately they fall away.

[18]"And others are the ones sown among the thorns. They have heard the word; [19]but the worries of the world, the seduction of wealth, and the desires for other things enter in and choke the word, and it becomes unfruitful.

[20]"And those are the ones sown on the good soil. They hear the word and accept it and produce fruit, thirty, sixty, and a hundredfold."

Reaping What You Sow

[21]He also was saying to them, "Is a lamp put under a basket or a bed? No, shouldn't it be placed on a lampstand? [22]For there is nothing hidden that will not be revealed, nor anything kept secret except that it would come to light. [23]If anyone has ears to hear, let him hear." [24]Then He continued, "Pay attention to what you hear. With the measure you use, it will be measured to you; and more will be added to you. [25]For whoever has, to him more will be given. And whoever does not have, even what he has will be taken away from him."

What Is the Kingdom of God Like?

[26]And He was saying, "The kingdom of God is like when a man spreads seed on the soil [27]and falls asleep at night and gets up by day, and the seed sprouts and grows. He himself doesn't know how. [28]Automatically, the earth brings forth a crop—first the blade, then the head, then the full grain in the head. [29]But when the grain is ready, at once he sends in the sickle, for the harvest has come."

[30]*Yeshua* also said, "How should we picture the kingdom of God? Or by what story shall we present it? [31]It is like a mustard seed when it's planted in the

a 4:11. cf. Prov. 1:6.
b 4:12. Isa. 6:9-10.

ground. Though the smallest of all seeds in the earth, yet when planted it grows up and becomes the largest of all the herbs. It puts forth big branches, so the birds of the air can nest in its shade."[a]

33With many such parables He used to tell them the word, as much as they were able to hear. 34But apart from a parable, He wasn't speaking to them. Yet when they were alone, to His own disciples He would explain everything.

Power Over Nature

35Now on that same day in the evening, He says to them, "Let's cross over to the other side." 36After leaving the crowd, they take Him along in the boat, just as He was. And other boats were with Him.

37A great windstorm arises, and the waves were rushing into the boat. The boat was beginning to fill up. 38But *Yeshua* was in the back of the boat, sleeping on a pillow. They wake Him up and say to Him, "Teacher, don't you care that we are perishing?"

39So He woke up and rebuked the wind. And He said to the sea, "Quiet! Be still!" Then the wind stopped, and it became totally calm. 40And He said to them, "Why are you afraid? Even now you have no faith?"

41They were struck with awe and said to one another, "Who is this? Even the wind and the sea obey Him!"

5

Power Over Demons

1They came to the other side of the sea, into the country of the Gerasenes. 2As soon as *Yeshua* got out of the boat, a man from the graveyard[b] with an unclean spirit met Him. 3He lived among the tombs, and no one could restrain him anymore, even with a chain. 4For he had often been bound with shackles and chains, but the chains had been ripped apart by him and the shackles broken. No one was strong enough to tame him. 5And through it all, night and day, at the graveyard and in the mountains, he kept screaming and gashing himself with stones.

6When he saw *Yeshua* from a distance, he ran and bowed down before Him. 7Crying out with a loud voice, he said, "What's between You and me, *Yeshua, Ben El Elyon*? I'm warning you, in the name of God, do not torment me!"

8For *Yeshua* had said to him, "Come out of the man, you unclean spirit!" 9Then *Yeshua* began questioning him, "What is your name?"

And he answered, "My name is Legion,[c] for we are many." 10He kept begging Him not to send them out of the country. 11Now a large herd of pigs was feeding on the hillside nearby. 12The unclean spirits urged Him, saying, "Send us to the pigs, so we may enter them." 13So *Yeshua* gave them permission. The unclean spirits came out and entered the pigs. And the herd, about two thousand in number, rushed down the cliff and were drowned in the sea.

14The herdsmen ran away and told the town and countryside, and they came to see what had happened. 15Now they came to *Yeshua* and saw the madman who had had the legion. He was sitting there, dressed in clothes and in his right mind. The people were scared.

16Those who had seen it described in detail what had happened to the man plagued by a demon, and they also told about the pigs. 17And they began to beg *Yeshua* to leave their country. 18As He was getting into the boat, the man who had been infested with demons kept begging to remain with Him. 19*Yeshua* did not let him, but He told him, "Go home to your friends and tell them how much *ADONAI* has done for you, how He showed you mercy."

a 4:30-32. Dan. 2:34-35, 44-45.
b 5:2. Lit. *tombs*.
c 5:9. Latin for *thousands*, a large group of soldiers; cf. Mt. 26:53.

20 So he went away and began to proclaim in the Decapolis[a] how much *Yeshua* had done for him. And all were amazed.

Power in His Touch

21 When *Yeshua* had crossed over in the boat again to the other side, a big crowd gathered around Him; and He was by the sea. 22 Then one of the synagogue leaders, named Jairus, comes. Seeing Him, he falls at His feet. 23 He begs Him a great deal, saying, "My little daughter is near death! Come and lay hands on her so that she may be healed and live!"

24 So *Yeshua* went off with him, and a big crowd was following Him and pressing upon Him. 25 And there was a woman with a blood flow for twelve years,[b] 26 who had suffered much under many doctors. She had spent all that she had without benefit; instead, she grew worse. 27 When she heard about *Yeshua*, she came through the crowd from behind and touched His garment. 28 For she kept saying, "If I touch even His clothes, I shall be healed."

29 Right away the blood flow stopped, and she felt in her body that she was healed from her disease. 30 At once *Yeshua*, knowing in Himself that power had gone out from Him, turned around in the crowd and said, "Who touched My clothes?"

31 His disciples responded, "You see the crowd pressing upon You and you say, 'Who touched Me?'" 32 But He kept looking around to see who had done this.

33 But the woman, scared and shaking, knowing what had happened to her, came and fell down before Him and told Him the whole truth. 34 And He said to her, "Daughter, your faith has made you well. Go in *shalom* and be healed from your disease."

35 While *Yeshua* was still speaking, messengers come from the house of the synagogue leader, saying, "Your daughter is dead. Why do you still trouble the Teacher?"

36 But ignoring what they said, *Yeshua* tells the synagogue leader, "Do not be afraid; only believe." 37 He did not let anyone follow Him except Peter, Jacob, and John, the brother of Jacob.

38 They come to the house of the synagogue leader. He sees a commotion, people weeping and wailing loudly. 39 After entering, He said to them, "Why make such a fuss and weep? The child didn't die, but is sleeping."

40 They start jeering at Him. But after sending all of them out, He takes the child's father and mother, and those with Him, and enters where the child was. 41 Then, taking hold of the child's hand, He tells her, *"Talitha koum,"*[c] which means, "Little girl, I say to you, get up." 42 Immediately, the girl stood up and began to walk around! (She was twelve years old.) And they were overcome with astonishment. 43 But He gave them strict orders that no one should know about this, and He said something to eat should be given to her.

6

Responding to Rejection

1 Now *Yeshua* went out from there, and He comes to His hometown, and His disciples follow Him. 2 When *Shabbat* came, He began to teach in the synagogue. Many listeners were amazed, saying, "Where did this fellow get these things? What's this wisdom given to Him? Such miracles are done by His hands! 3 Isn't this the carpenter, the son of Miriam, and the brother of Jacob and Joseph and Judah and Simon? Aren't His sisters here with us?" And they took offense at Him.

4 Then *Yeshua* began saying to them, "A prophet is not without honor except in his hometown, among his relatives, and

a 5:20. The name means *Ten Cities*.
b 5:25. cf. Lev. 15:25-29.
c 5:41. Greek transliteration for the general Aramaic command to get up; some mss. read *Talitha kumi*, referring directly to the little girl.

in his own house." [5]He was not able to do any miracle, except that He laid hands on a few sick people and healed them. [6]And He was astonished because of their unbelief.[a] And He was going around among the villages teaching.

[7]*Yeshua* summoned the Twelve, and He began to send them out two by two. And He gave them authority over the unclean spirits. [8]He directed them to take nothing for the journey except a walking stick—no bread, no bag, no copper coin in their belt—[9]but to wear sandals and not to put on two shirts.[b]

[10]He was also telling them, "Wherever you enter a house, stay there until you leave that place. [11]And whatever place will not receive you or listen to you, as you leave from there, shake the dust off the bottom of your feet as a witness against them." [12]So they went out and proclaimed that all should repent, [13]and they were driving out many demons and anointing with oil many who were sick and healing them.

[14]King Herod heard, for *Yeshua*'s name had become known. Some were saying, "John the Immerser has risen from the dead! Because of this, these powers are at work in Him!" [15]But others were saying, "It's Elijah!" Still others were saying, "It's a prophet, like one of the prophets of old."[c]

[16]But when Herod heard, he said, "John, the one I beheaded, has been raised!" [17]For Herod himself sent and arrested John and bound him in prison for the sake of Herodias, the wife of his brother Philip, because Herod had married her. [18]For John had been telling Herod, "It is not permitted for you to have your brother's wife."[d] [19]Now Herodias had a grudge against John and wanted to kill him, but she wasn't able. [20]For Herod was in awe of John and kept him safe, knowing him to be a righteous and holy man. When he listened to John he was confused, but he still listened gladly.

[21]An opportunity came—when Herod, on his birthday, gave a banquet for his high officials, military brass, and the leaders of the Galilee. [22]When the daughter of Herodias[e] came in and danced, she pleased Herod and those reclining with him. And the king said to the girl, "Ask me for whatever you want, and I'll give it to you!" [23]He vowed to her, "Whatever you ask of me I'll give you, up to half of my kingdom!"

[24]She left the room and said to her mother, "What should I ask for?"

Her mother said, "The head of John the Immerser!"

[25]Immediately she rushed to the king and requested, "I want you to give me, right now, the head of John the Immerser on a platter!"

[26]The king became very sorrowful; but because of his oaths and those reclining with him, he didn't want to refuse her.

[27]Immediately the king sent an executioner and gave orders to bring John's head. And the executioner went out and beheaded John in the prison, [28]brought his head on a platter, and gave it to the girl; and the girl gave it to her mother. [29]When John's disciples heard, they came and took his body and laid it in a tomb.

Feeding 5000 Families

[30]The twelve *shlichim* gathered together with *Yeshua*, and they reported to Him all they had done and taught. [31] There were many coming and going, and they had no time even to eat. So He said to them, "Come away by yourselves to an isolated place and rest awhile." [32]So they left privately by boat to an isolated place. [33]However, the people saw them leaving, and many recognized them. They ran on foot from all the towns to get there ahead of them. [34]As *Yeshua* came ashore, He saw a large crowd and felt compassion for them, because they were like

a 6:3-6. cf. Isa. 53:1ff.
b 6:9. Lit. *tunic or undershirt*.
c 6:15. cf. Mal. 4:5; Deut. 18:17-19.
d 6:17-18. cf. Exod. 20:8, 17; Lev. 18.
e 6:22. cf. Mt. 14:6. Some mss. say *his daughter Herodias*.

Mark 6:41

And He took the five loaves and the two fish; and looking up to heaven, He offered the bracha. He broke the loaves and kept giving them to the disciples to serve to the people; and He divided the two fish among them all.

sheep without a shepherd.[a] So He taught
them many things.
35When it was already late, His disciples came to Him and said, "This place
is isolated, and the hour is already late.
36Send these people away so they can go
into the nearby countryside and the villages and buy themselves something to
eat."
37But He answered and said to them,
"You give them something to eat!"
And they said to Him, "Should we go
and spend two hundred denarii on bread
to give them something to eat?"
38Then He said to them, "How many
loaves do you have? Go and see."
When they found out, they said, "Five,
and two fish."
39Then *Yeshua* made them all sit down
in groups on the green grass. 40So they
reclined in groups of hundreds and fif-
ties. 41And He took the five loaves and the
two fish; and looking up to heaven, He
offered the *bracha*. He broke the loaves
and kept giving them to the disciples to
serve to the people; and He divided the
two fish among them all. 42They all ate
and were satisfied, 43and the disciples
picked up twelve baskets full of broken
pieces and fish. 44Now there were five
thousand men who ate the loaves.

Walking on Water

45Right away, *Yeshua* made His disciples get into the boat and go ahead of
Him to the other side, to Bethsaida, while
He Himself was sending the crowd away.
46After leaving them, He went up on the
hillside to pray.
47And when evening came, the boat
was in the middle of the sea and He was
alone on the land. 48He saw the disciples
struggling to row, for the wind was
against them. Around the fourth watch
in the night,[b] *Yeshua* comes to them,
walking on the sea; and He wanted to
pass by them. 49But when they saw Him
walking on the sea, they thought He was
a ghost and cried out—50for they all saw
Him and were terrified.
But immediately, He spoke to them.
He said, "Take courage! I am. Do not
be afraid." 51Then He got into the boat
with them, and the wind stopped. They
were utterly dumbfounded, 52for they
still hadn't understood about the loaves.
Instead, their hearts were hardened.

Miracles Multiply

53After they had crossed over, they
came to land at Gennesaret and set
anchor there. 54As they got out of the
boat, immediately people recognized
Yeshua. 55They ran about the region and
began to carry around on their mats all
those who were in bad shape, to wherever they heard He was. 56And wherever
He entered villages, towns, or countryside, people were placing the sick
in the marketplaces and begging Him
to let them touch even the *tzitzit* of His
garment—and all who touched it were
being healed.

7

Hearts Harden

1Now the Pharisees and some of the
Torah scholars who had come from Jerusalem gathered around *Yeshua*. 2And
they saw that some of His disciples
were eating bread with unclean hands,
that is, not washed. 3(For the Pharisees
and all Jewish people do not eat unless
they wash their hands up to the elbow,
keeping the tradition of the elders. 4And
when they come from the marketplace,
they do not eat unless they perform a
ritual washing.[c] There are many other
traditions they have received and hold,
such as the washing of cups, pitchers,
copper vessels.)[d]

a 6:34. cf. Num. 27:17, 2 Chr. 18:16.
b 6:48. Roman time, 3-6 a.m.
c 7:4. Various mss. say *wash* or *immerse*.
d 7:1-4. Some mss. add *and dining couches*; cf. Exod. 30:17-21.

5 The Pharisees and *Torah* scholars questioned *Yeshua*, "Why don't Your disciples walk according to the tradition of the elders? Why do they eat bread with unwashed hands?"

6 And He said to them, "Rightly did Isaiah prophesy about you hypocrites, as it is written,

> 'This people honors Me
> with their lips
> but their heart is far from
> Me.
> 7 And in vain they worship Me,
> teaching as doctrines
> the commandments of men.'[a]

8 Having left behind the commandment of God, you hold on to the tradition of men."

9 He was also telling them, "You set aside the commands of God, in order that you may validate your own tradition. 10 For Moses said, 'Honor your father and your mother,' and, 'He who speaks evil of father or mother must be put to death.'[b] 11 But you say if anyone tells his father or mother, 'Whatever you might have gained from me is *korban* (that is, an offering to God),' 12 then you no longer permit him to do anything for his father or mother, 13 making void the word of God with your tradition that you've handed down. And you do many such things."[c]

14 Then *Yeshua* called the crowd again and began saying to them, "Hear Me, everyone, and understand. 15 There is nothing outside the man that can make him unholy by going into him. Rather, it is what comes out of the man that makes the man unholy."[d] (16)[e]

17 When He had left the crowd and entered the house, His disciples questioned Him about the parable. 18 And He said to them, "Are you then also lacking understanding? Don't you grasp that whatever goes into the man cannot make him unholy? 19 For it does not enter into the heart but into the stomach, and then goes out into the sewer, cleansing all foods."[f]

20 And He continued, "It is what comes out of the man that makes the man unholy. 21 For from within, out of the heart of men, come evil intentions, sexual immorality, theft, murder, 22 adultery, greed, wickedness, deceit, lustfulness, envy, slander, pride, and foolishness. 23 All these evil things come from within and make the man unholy."

Miracles Touch Gentile Lives

24 *Yeshua* got up and left from there to the region of Tyre. When He had entered a house, He didn't want anyone to know; but He couldn't escape notice. 25 A woman whose little daughter had an unclean spirit heard about Him. She came immediately and fell at His feet. 26 The woman was a Greek, from Syrophoenicia. And she kept begging *Yeshua* to drive the demon out of her daughter.

27 He was telling her, "First let the children get their fill, for it's not right to take the children's bread and throw it to the dogs."

28 "Yes, Master," she said to Him, "but even the dogs under the table eat the children's crumbs."

29 Then He said to her, "Because of this word, go your way! The demon has left your daughter." 30 She went home and found the child lying on the bed, and the demon gone.

31 Again He left the region of Tyre and came through Sidon to the Sea of Galilee, within the region of the Decapolis. 32 They bring Him a deaf man who had a speech impediment, and they beg Him to lay His hand on him. 33 *Yeshua* took him aside from the crowd to a private place, and He put His fingers in the man's ears. After spitting, He touched the man's

a 7:7. Isa. 29:13.
b 7:10. Exod. 20:10; Deut. 5:16.
c 7:13ff. cf. Num. 30:1-2. This commandment concerning vows is sometimes abused.
d 7:15. cf. Lev. 10:10.
e 7:16. Some mss. add: *If any man has ears to hear, let him hear.*

f 7:19. cf. Lev. 10:10; Lev. 11; Dt. 14:3ff.

tongue. 34Looking up to heaven, He says to the man, *"Ephphatha,"*[a] which means "Be opened!"

35Immediately the man's ears were opened, his tongue was loosened, and he began to speak plainly. 36*Yeshua* ordered them not to tell anyone. But the more He ordered them, the more they continued proclaiming it. 37People were completely astounded, saying, "He has done all things well. He makes even the deaf hear and the mute speak!"

Do You Still Not Understand?

1In those days, there was another large crowd with nothing to eat, and *Yeshua* called the disciples. He said to them, 2"I have compassion for the crowd, because they've stayed with Me for three days now and have nothing to eat. 3If I send them home hungry they'll pass out on the way, for some of them have come from very far away."

4His disciples answered Him, "How can anyone satisfy these people with bread here in a wasteland?"

5"How many loaves do you have?" *Yeshua* was asking them.

"Seven," they said.

6He directed the crowd to recline on the ground. After taking the seven loaves and giving thanks, He broke them and began giving them to His disciples to serve; and they served them to the crowd. 7They also had a few small fish and, after offering a *bracha* for them, He commanded these to be served as well. 8They ate and were satisfied, and they picked up the broken pieces left over—seven baskets. 9About four thousand[b] were there, and *Yeshua* sent them away.

10Right away, He got into the boat with His disciples and went to the area of Dalmanutha. 11The Pharisees came and began to argue with Him, demanding a sign from heaven, to test Him. 12Sighing deeply in His spirit, *Yeshua* said, "Why does this generation demand a sign? Amen, I tell you, no sign will be given to this generation." 13Leaving them, He got back into the boat and crossed to the other side.

The Un-Seeing Disciples

14Now the disciples had forgotten to take bread, and they had only one loaf in the boat. 15*Yeshua* was warning them, "Watch out! Beware of the leaven of the Pharisees and the leaven of Herod."

16They began to discuss with each other that they had no bread. 17And *Yeshua*, aware of this, said to them, "Why do you discuss that you have no bread? You still don't get it? Don't you understand? Are your hearts hardened? 18Having eyes, don't you see? And having ears, don't you hear? And don't you remember? 19When I broke the five loaves for the five thousand, how many baskets of leftovers did you pick up?"

"Twelve," they say to Him.

20"When I broke the seven loaves for the four thousand, how many baskets of leftovers did you pick up?"

"Seven," they say to Him.

21He said to them, "Do you still not understand?"

Eyes that Need Opening

22They come to Bethsaida. Some people bring a blind man to *Yeshua* and beg Him to touch the man. 23Taking the blind man by the hand, *Yeshua* brought him outside the village. After spitting on the man's eyes and laying His hands on him, *Yeshua* asked the man, "Do you see anything?"

24The man looked up and said, "I see men! They look like trees walking about." 25Then *Yeshua* put His hands on the man's eyes again. The man looked intently, his

a 7:34. Contraction of the Aramaic *etpatach*.
b 8:9. 4000 men or families; cf. Matt. 15:32-39.

Mark 9:2-4

After six days, Yeshua takes with Him Peter and Jacob and John, and brings them up a high mountain by themselves. And He was transfigured before them. His clothes became radiant and brilliantly white, whiter than any launderer on earth could bleach them. Then Elijah appeared to them with Moses, and they were talking with Yeshua.

sight was restored, and he began to see everything clearly.

[26]*Yeshua* sent him straight home, saying, "Don't even enter the village!"

[27]Now *Yeshua* and His disciples went out to the villages around Caesarea Philippi. On the way He asked His disciples, "Who do people say that I am?"

[28]They told Him, "John the Immerser; and others Elijah; but others, one of the prophets."[a]

[29]Then He asked them, "But who do you say that I am?"

Peter answered Him, "You are the Messiah!" [30]And He warned them not to tell anyone about Him.

Revealing the Mission

[31]Then He began to teach them that the Son of Man must suffer many things and be rejected by the elders and ruling *kohanim* and *Torah* scholars, and be killed, and after three days rise again.[b] [32]He was speaking openly about this. And Peter took Him aside and began to rebuke Him. [33]But turning around and looking at His disciples, He rebuked Peter. He said, "Get behind Me, satan! You are not setting your mind on the things of God, but the things of men."

[34]Then He called the crowd, along with His disciples, and said to them, "If anyone wants to follow after Me, he must deny himself, take up his cross, and keep following Me. [35]For whoever wants to save his life will lose it, but whoever loses his life for My sake and the sake of the Good News will save it. [36]For what does it profit a man to gain the whole world, yet forfeit his soul? [37]For what could a man give in exchange for his soul? [38]For whoever is ashamed of Me and My words in this unfaithful and sinful generation, the Son of Man will also be ashamed of him when He comes in the glory of His Father with the holy angels!"

a 8:28. cf. Deut. 18:17-19; Mal. 4:5.
b 8:31. cf. Isa. 53.

9

[1]*Yeshua* was telling them, "Amen, I tell you, there are some standing here who will never taste death until they see the kingdom of God come with power!"

A Glimpse of His Glory

[2]After six days, *Yeshua* takes with Him Peter and Jacob and John, and brings them up a high mountain by themselves. And He was transfigured before them. [3]His clothes became radiant and brilliantly white, whiter than any launderer on earth could bleach them. [4]Then Elijah appeared to them with Moses, and they were talking with *Yeshua*.

[5]Peter responds to *Yeshua*, "Rabbi, it's good for us to be here. Let's make three *sukkot*—one for You, and one for Moses, and one for Elijah." [6](He didn't know what to say, for they were terrified.)

[7]Then a cloud came, overshadowing them;[c] and out of the cloud came a voice, "This is My Son, whom I love. Listen to Him!"[d] [8]Suddenly when they looked around, they no longer saw anyone with them except *Yeshua*.

[9]As they were coming down from the mountain, *Yeshua* ordered them not to tell anyone what they had seen, until the Son of Man rose up from the dead. [10]They kept this word to themselves, discussing among themselves what it is to rise up from the dead. [11]And they questioned Him, saying, "Why do the *Torah* scholars say that Elijah must come first?"

[12]Now He told them, "Indeed Elijah comes first;[e] he restores all things. And how is it written that the Son of Man must suffer much and be treated with contempt?[f] [13]I tell you that Elijah has

c 9:7. cf. Exod. 40:34.
d 9:7. cf. Ps. 2:7; Prov. 30:4; Isa. 9:5(6); Deut. 18:15.
e 9:11. cf. Mal. 4:5.
f 9:12. cf. Isa. 53:1-3; Ps. 118: 22 (117:22 LXX); Ps. 22:6 (21:7 LXX).

come, and they did to him whatever they wanted, just as it is written about him."[a]

The Secret of Prayer

[14]When they came to the disciples, they saw a big crowd around them and the *Torah* scholars arguing with them. [15]Suddenly, when the whole crowd saw *Yeshua*, they were amazed and began running to greet Him. [16]He questioned them, "What are you arguing about with them?"

[17]And a man from the crowd answered Him, "Teacher, I brought You my son, who has a spirit that makes him mute. [18]Whenever it seizes him, it throws him down; he foams at the mouth, grinds his teeth, and becomes stiff. I told Your disciples to drive it out, but they couldn't!"

[19]And answering them, He said, "Oh faithless generation, how long shall I be with you? How long shall I put up with you? Bring him to Me."

[20]They brought the boy to *Yeshua*. When the spirit saw Him, immediately it threw the boy into a convulsion. The boy fell to the ground and began rolling around and foaming at the mouth. [21]*Yeshua* asked the father, "How long has this been happening to him?"

"Since he was a child," the man answered. [22]"It has often thrown him into fire or water to destroy him. But if You can do anything, have compassion and help us!"

[23]"'If You can'?" *Yeshua* said to him. "All things are possible for one who believes!"

[24]Immediately the boy's father cried out, "I believe! Help my unbelief!"

[25]When *Yeshua* saw that a crowd was gathering fast, He rebuked the unclean spirit, telling it, "I command you, deaf and mute spirit, come out of him and do not ever enter him again!"

[26]After howling and shaking the boy wildly, it came out. The boy became so much like a corpse that many were saying, "He's dead!" [27]But *Yeshua* took him by the hand and lifted him, and the boy stood up.

[28]After *Yeshua* came into the house, His disciples began questioning Him in private, "Why couldn't we drive it out?"

[29]And He said to them, "This kind cannot come out except by prayer."[b]

[30]They left from there and passed through the Galilee. *Yeshua* didn't want anyone to know, [31]for He was teaching His disciples and telling them, "The Son of Man is going to be delivered into the hands of men, and they will kill Him. And after He is killed, three days later He will rise up." [32]But the disciples didn't understand this statement, and they were afraid to question Him about it.

The Secret of Childlike Humility

[33]Then they came to Capernaum. And when *Yeshua* was in the house, He began to ask the disciples, "What were you discussing on the way?" [34]But they kept quiet, because on the way they had argued with one another about who was the greatest.

[35]Sitting down, He called the Twelve and said to them, "If any man wants to be first, he shall be least of all and the servant of everyone." [36]Taking a small child, He set him in the midst of them. And taking him in His arms, He said to them, [37]"Whoever welcomes one of these children in My name, welcomes Me; and whoever welcomes Me, welcomes not Me but the One who sent Me."

[38]John said to Him, "Teacher, we saw someone driving out demons in Your name, and we tried to stop him because he wasn't following us."

[39]But *Yeshua* responded, "Don't stop him! No one who does a miracle in My name will be able soon afterward to speak evil about Me. [40]He who is not against us is for us. [41]For whoever gives you a cup of water to drink in My name

a 9:13. cf. 1 Ki. 19:2-3, 10, 14.

b 9:29 Some manuscripts add *and fasting*.

because you belong to Messiah, amen I tell you, he will never lose his reward."

[42]"But whoever causes one of these little ones who trust in Me to stumble, it would be better for him to have a heavy millstone put around his neck and to be thrown into the sea!"

The Secret of Salt

[43]"And if your hand causes you to stumble, cut it off! It is better for you to enter into life crippled than, having two hands, to go to Gehenna,[a] into the unquenchable fire. [(44)b] [45]And if your foot causes you to stumble, cut it off! It's better for you to enter life lame than, having your two feet, to be thrown into Gehenna. [(46)] [47]If your eye causes you to stumble, tear it out! It is better for you to enter the kingdom of God with one eye than, having two eyes, to be thrown into Gehenna, [48]where

'their worm does not die
and the fire is not
quenched.'[c]

[49]"For everyone will be salted with fire. [50]Salt is good; but if the salt becomes unsalty, with what will you flavor it? Have salt in yourselves, and keep *shalom* with one another."

10

Abide in Marriage

[1]Then getting up from there, *Yeshua* goes to the region of Judea beyond the Jordan. Again crowds gather around Him, and, as was His custom, He began to teach them once more.

[2]Pharisees came up, and to test Him they began asking, "Is it permitted for a man to divorce his wife?"

[3]And He replied to them, "What did Moses command you?"

[4]The Pharisees said, "Moses permitted a man to write a bill of divorce and to put her away."[d]

[5]But *Yeshua* said to them, "Because of your hardness of heart he wrote you this commandment! [6]But from the beginning of creation, God 'made them male and female. [7]For this reason a man shall leave his father and mother and be joined to his wife, [8]and the two shall become one flesh.'[e] So they are no longer two, but one flesh. [9]Therefore what God has joined together, let no man separate!"

[10]In the house, the disciples began questioning Him about this again. [11]And He said to them, "Whoever divorces his wife and marries another commits adultery against her. [12]And if she divorces her husband and marries another, she is committing adultery."

Let the Little Ones Come!

[13]Now people were bringing little children to *Yeshua* so He might touch them, but the disciples rebuked those who brought them. [14]But when *Yeshua* saw this, He got angry. He told them, "Let the little children come to Me! Do not hinder them, for the kingdom of God belongs to such as these. [15]Amen, I tell you, whoever does not receive the kingdom of God like a little child will never enter it!" [16]And He took them in His arms and began blessing them, laying His hands on them.

The Cost of Discipleship

[17]As *Yeshua* was setting out on His way, a man ran up to Him, fell on his knees before Him, and asked, "Good Teacher, what shall I do to inherit eternal life?"

[18]"Why do you call Me good?" *Yeshua* said to him. "No one is good except One—that is God. [19]You know the commandments, 'Do not murder, do not commit adultery, do not steal, do not

a 9:43. cf. Isa. 66:24; for more, see Glossary.
b 9:44, 46. Verses omitted; some mss. read: *where their worm does not die, and the fire is not quenched.*
c 9:48. Isa. 66:24.

d 10:4. Deut. 24:1-4.
e 10:6-8a. Gen. 1:27, 5:2, 2:24.

give false testimony,' do not cheat, 'honor your father and mother.'"[a]

[20]The man responded, "Teacher, all these I have kept since my youth!"

[21]Looking at him, *Yeshua* loved him and said, "One thing you lack. Go, sell as much as you have, and give to the poor; and you will have treasure in heaven. Then come, follow Me." [22]But at this statement, the man became sad and went away grieving, for he had much property.

[23]Then looking around, *Yeshua* says to His disciples, "How hard it will be for the rich to enter the kingdom of God!" [24]The disciples were amazed at His words. But *Yeshua* answers again and says to them, "Children, how hard it is to enter the kingdom of God! [25]It is easier for a camel to go through the eye of a needle, than for a rich man to enter the kingdom of God."

[26]The disciples were even more astonished, saying among themselves, "Then who can be saved?"

[27]Looking at them, *Yeshua* said, "With men it is impossible, but not with God. For all things are possible with God!"[b]

[28]Peter began to say to Him, "Look, we've left everything to follow You!"

[29]"Amen, I tell you," *Yeshua* replied, "there is no one who has left house or brothers or sisters or mother or father or children or property, for My sake and for the sake of the Good News, [30]who will not receive a hundred times as much now in this time, houses and brothers and sisters and mothers and children and property, along with persecutions; and in the *olam ha-ba*, eternal life. [31]But many who are first will be last, and the last first."

Death and Resurrection Revealed

[32]They were on the way going up to Jerusalem, and *Yeshua* was going ahead of them. And they were amazed, while those who followed were fearful. Again *Yeshua* took the Twelve aside and began to tell them what was going to happen to Him.

[33]He said, "Look, we are going up to Jerusalem, and the Son of Man will be handed over to the ruling *kohanim* and the *Torah* scholars. They will condemn Him to death and hand Him over to the Gentiles.[c] [34]They will mock Him and spit on Him, scourge Him and kill Him. Yet after three days, He will rise again!"

[35]Then Jacob and John, the sons of Zebedee, come up to Him, saying, "Teacher, we want You to do for us whatever we ask of You."

[36]And He said to them, "What do you want Me to do for you?"

[37]They said to Him, "Let us sit, one on Your right and one on Your left, in Your glory."

[38]But *Yeshua* answered them, "You don't know what you're asking! Are you able to drink the cup I drink, or endure the immersion I must endure?"

[39]They said to Him, "We are able."

And *Yeshua* said to them, "You will drink the cup I drink, and you will endure the immersion I must endure. [40]But to sit on My right or left is not Mine to grant—it is for those for whom it has been prepared."

[41]Now when the ten heard, they started to get angry with Jacob and John. [42]And calling them over, *Yeshua* said to them, "You know those recognized as rulers of the nations lord it over them, and their great ones play the tyrant over them. [43]Yet it is not this way among you. But whoever wants to be great among you shall be your servant, [44]and whoever wants to be first among you shall be slave of all. [45]For even the Son of Man did not come to be served, but to serve, and to give His life as a ransom for many."

Ben-David Heals the Blind

[46]Then they came to Jericho. Now as *Yeshua* was leaving Jericho with His disciples and a large crowd, Bartimaeus the

a 10:19. Exod. 20:12-16; Deut. 5:16-20.
b 10:27. cf. Gen. 18:14.
c 10:33-4. cf. Isa. 42, 49, 50, 53; Dan. 9:26.

son of Timaeus, a blind beggar, was sitting by the roadside. 47When he heard
that it was *Yeshua* of *Natzeret*, he began
to cry out, "*Ben-David*, *Yeshua*! Have
mercy on me!" 48Many were warning him
to be quiet; but he kept crying out all the
more, "*Ben-David*, have mercy on me!"[a]

49*Yeshua* stopped and said, "Call him
over."

So they call the blind man, saying,
"Take heart! Get up, He's calling you!"
50Throwing off his cloak, he jumped up
and came to *Yeshua*.

51And answering him, *Yeshua* said,
"What do you want Me to do for you?"

The blind man said, "*Rabboni*, I want to
see again!"

52*Yeshua* said to him, "Go! Your faith has
made you well." Instantly he regained his
sight and began following *Yeshua* down
the road.

11

Ben-David Enters Jerusalem

1Now as they draw near to Jerusalem,
to Bethphage and Bethany, to the Mount
of Olives, *Yeshua* sends two of His disciples 2and says to them, "Go into the
village ahead of you. Right away as you
enter it, you will find a colt tied up that
no one has ever sat upon.[b] Untie it and
bring it. 3If anyone says to you, 'Why are
you doing this?' say, 'The Master needs
it.' And right away he will send it back
here.'"[c]

4They went and found a colt outside in
the street, tied at a door. And they untied
it. 5Some people standing there began
saying to them, "What are you doing,
untying the colt?"

6They answered just as *Yeshua* had
told them, and the people let them go.
7And they brought the colt to *Yeshua* and
laid their cloaks on it, and He sat on it.
8Many spread their cloaks on the road,
and others spread branches cut from the
fields.[d] 9Those going before and those
following kept shouting,

"*Hoshia-na! Baruch ha-ba b'shem*
Adonai!
Blessed is He who comes in
the name of the Lord!
10Blessed is the coming
kingdom of our father
David!
Hoshia-na in the highest!"[e]

11And He entered Jerusalem and went
into the Temple. After looking around at
everything, He went out to Bethany with
the Twelve, since it was already late.

The Fruit of the Faithful

12The next day, when they had left
Bethany, He became hungry. 13Seeing
from a distance a fig tree in leaf, He went
to see if He would find any fruit on it.
When He came up to it, He found nothing
except leaves, because it wasn't the season for figs. 14And He said to it, "May no
one ever eat fruit from you again!" And
His disciples were listening.

15Then they came to Jerusalem. And
He entered the Temple and started to
drive out those selling and buying in the
Temple. He overturned the tables of the
moneychangers and the seats of those
selling doves, 16and He wouldn't let anyone carry goods through the Temple.
17And He began to teach them, saying,
"Is it not written,

'My house shall be called
a house of prayer for all the
nations'?[f]

But you have made it a 'den of
thieves.'"[g]

18The ruling *kohanim* and *Torah* scholars heard this and began looking for a

a 10:48. cf. Isa. 61:1(LXX); Lk. 4:18.
b 11:2. cf. Zech. 9:9.
c 11:3. cf. Gen. 49:10-11.
d 11:7-8. Lit. *garments, clothing*.
e 11:9-10. cf. Ps. 118:25-26.
f 11:17. Isa. 56:7.
g 11:17. Jer. 7:11.

way to destroy Him; for they were afraid of Him, because the whole crowd was astonished at His teaching. 19Whenever evening came, *Yeshua* and His disciples would leave the city.

20As they were passing by in the morning, they saw the fig tree shriveled from the roots. 21Peter remembered and said to *Yeshua*, "Rabbi, look! The fig tree You cursed has shriveled up!"

22And *Yeshua* answered, saying to them, "Have faith in God! 23Amen, I tell you, if someone says to this mountain, 'Be taken up and thrown into the sea,' and does not doubt in his heart but trusts that what he says is happening, so shall it be for him. 24For this reason I say to you, whatever you pray and ask, believe that you have received it, and it will be yours. 25Whenever you stand praying, if you have anything against anyone, forgive him, so that your Father in heaven may also forgive you your transgressions." (26) [a]

A Question for a Question

27Again they come to Jerusalem. While *Yeshua* was walking in the Temple, the ruling *kohanim*, *Torah* scholars, and elders come up to Him. 28And they start saying to Him, "By what authority are You doing these things? Who gave You this authority to do these things?"

29*Yeshua* said to them, "I will put one question to you. Answer Me, and I will tell you by what authority I do these things. 30The immersion of John—was it from heaven or from men? Answer Me!"

31They began to dialogue among themselves, saying, "If we say, 'From heaven,' He will say, 'Then why didn't you believe him?' 32But if we say, 'From men'...?" They were afraid of the crowd, for all held that John really was a prophet. 33So answering *Yeshua*, they say, "We don't know."

And *Yeshua* tells them, "Neither will I tell you by what authority I do these things."

12

Taking the Kingdom by Force

1*Yeshua* began to speak to them in parables: "A man planted a vineyard. He put a hedge around it, dug a pit for the winepress, and built a tower. He leased it to some tenant farmers and went on a journey. 2And at the season, he sent a servant to collect from the tenants part of the vineyard's fruit. 3But grabbing him, they beat him up and sent him away empty-handed. 4And again the man sent another servant to them, and they wounded his head and treated him shamefully. 5He sent another, and that one they killed; and so on with many others, beating some and killing some. 6He had yet one, a well-loved son. He sent him to them last of all, saying, 'They will respect my son.'

7"But those tenants said to one another, 'This is the heir! Come on, let's kill him and the inheritance will be ours!' 8So grabbing the son, they killed him and threw him out of the vineyard.

9"What then will the master of the vineyard do? He will come and destroy the tenants and give the vineyard to others. 10Haven't you read this Scripture?

'The stone which the builders
  rejected,
this has become the chief
  cornerstone.
11This came from Adonai,
  and it is marvelous in our
  eyes.'"[b]

12They were trying to seize *Yeshua*, because they realized that He spoke the parable against them. But they feared the crowd, so they left Him and went away.

a 11:26. Some mss. add: *But if you don't forgive, neither will your Father in heaven forgive your transgressions.*

b 12:10-11. Ps. 118:22-23(117:22-23 LXX).

A Test of Loyalty

13Then they send some of the Pharisees and Herodians to *Yeshua* in order to trap Him with a word. 14They come and say to Him, "Teacher, we know that You are honest, and what others think doesn't concern You. You don't look at men's appearance, but teach the way of God according to the truth. Is it permitted to pay taxes to Caesar, or not? 15Should we pay, or shouldn't we?"

But *Yeshua* saw through their hypocrisy and said to them, "Why are you testing Me? Bring Me a denarius so I may see it."

16They brought one. And He said to them, "Whose image is this? And whose inscription?"

"Caesar's," they said to Him.

17Then *Yeshua* said to them, "Give to Caesar the things that are Caesar's, and to God the things that are God's." And they were completely amazed at Him.

The Challenge of the Sadducees

18Then Sadducees (who say there is no resurrection) came and began questioning *Yeshua*, saying, 19"Teacher, Moses wrote for us that 'if a man's brother dies and leaves a wife but no children, then his brother should take the widow and father children for his brother.'[a] 20There were seven brothers; and the first took a wife and, when he died, left no offspring. 21And the second took her and died, leaving no offspring, and the third likewise. 22Now the seven left no offspring. Last of all, the woman died, too. 23In the resurrection, when they rise up, whose wife will she be? For all seven had married her."

24*Yeshua* said to them, "Isn't this the reason you've gone astray, because you don't understand the Scriptures or the power of God? 25For when they rise up from the dead, they neither marry nor are given in marriage, but are like angels in heaven. 26But concerning the dead being raised, haven't you read in the book of Moses about the burning bush? How God said to him, 'I am the God of Abraham, and the God of Isaac, and the God of Jacob'?[b] 27He's not the God of the dead, but of the living. You have gone far astray!"

Love Ends the Argument

28One of the *Torah* scholars came and heard them debating. Seeing that *Yeshua* had answered them well, he asked Him, "Which commandment is first of all?"

29*Yeshua* answered, "The first is, '*Shema Yisrael,* ADONAI *Eloheinu,* ADONAI *echad*. Hear, O Israel, the LORD our God, the LORD is One. 30And you shall love ADONAI your God with all your heart, and with all your soul, and with all your mind, and with all your strength.'[c] 31The second is this, 'You shall love your neighbor as yourself.'[d] There is no other commandment greater than these."

32"Well said, Teacher," the *Torah* scholar said to Him. "You have spoken the truth, that He is *echad*, and besides Him there is no other![e] 33And 'to love Him with all the heart, with all the understanding, and with all the strength,'[f] and 'to love the neighbor as oneself,'[g] is much more than all burnt offerings and sacrifices."

34When *Yeshua* saw that he had answered wisely, He said to him, "You are not far from the kingdom of God." And no one dared any longer to question Him.

Who Is King David's Lord?

35While *Yeshua* was teaching in the Temple, He said, "How is it that the *Torah* scholars say that the Messiah is

a 12:19. Lit. *raise up seed for his brother*; cf. Dt. 25:5-6; Gen. 38:8.

b 12:26. Exod. 3:6.

c 12:29-30. Dt. 6:4-5(6:4-5 LXX), *v'ahavta*.

d 12:31. Lev. 19:18b, *v'ahavta l'reiacha kamocha*.

e 12:32. cf. Dt. 4:35 (LXX).

f 12:33. Dt. 6:4-5.

g 12:33. Lev. 19:18b.

Ben-David? 36David himself, through the *Ruach ha-Kodesh*, said,

> 'ADONAI said to My Lord,
> "Sit at My right hand,
> until I put Your enemies
> under Your feet."'[a]

37If David himself calls Him 'Lord,' in what way is He his son?" And the large crowd was listening to Him with delight.

38In His teaching He said, "Watch out for the *Torah* scholars, who like to walk around in long robes. They like greetings in the marketplaces, 39the best seats in the synagogues, and places of honor at feasts. 40They devour widows' houses and make long prayers as a show. These men will receive greater condemnation!"

41He sat down opposite the treasury and began watching how the people were putting money into the offering box. Many rich people were putting in a lot. 42Then a poor widow came and put in two small copper coins, worth less than a penny. 43Calling His disciples over, He said to them, "Amen, I tell you, this poor widow has put in more than all those contributing to the box! 44For they all put in from their surplus; but she, out of her poverty, put in everything she had, her whole living."

13

Signs of the End

1As *Yeshua* was going out of the Temple, one of His disciples said to Him, "Teacher, look! What stones and what buildings!"

2*Yeshua* said to him, "You see these great buildings? Not one stone here will be left upon another. Every one will be torn down!"

3As He was sitting on the Mount of Olives opposite the Temple, Peter, Jacob, John, and Andrew were questioning Him privately, 4"Tell us, when will these things happen? What will be the sign that all these things are about to be accomplished?"

5*Yeshua* began to tell them, "Watch out that no one leads you astray! 6Many will come in My name, saying, 'I am He,' and they will lead many astray. 7When you hear of wars and rumors of wars, do not be alarmed, for this must happen but it is not yet the end. 8For nation will rise up against nation, and kingdom against kingdom. There will be earthquakes in various places, and there will be famines. These things are only the beginning of birth pains.

9"Watch out for yourselves! They will hand you over to the courts, and you will be beaten in the synagogues. You will stand before governors and kings because of Me, as a witness to them. 10The Good News must first be proclaimed to all the nations. 11When they arrest you and hand you over, do not worry beforehand about what to say. Say whatever is given to you in that hour, for it is not you who speaks but the *Ruach ha-Kodesh*. 12Brother will betray brother to death, and a father his child. And children will rise up against parents and have them put to death. 13And you will be hated by all because of My name, but the one who endures to the end will be saved."

Birth Pangs Before Deliverance

14"But when you see 'the abomination of desolation'[b] standing where it should not be (let the reader understand), then those in Judea must flee to the mountains. 15The one on the roof must not go down, nor enter to take anything out of his house. 16And the one in the field must not turn back to get his cloak. 17Woe to those who are pregnant and to those who are nursing babies in those days! 18Pray that it will not happen in winter.

a 12:36. cf. Ps. 110:1; Ps. 109:1 (LXX).

b 13:14. cf. Dan. 9:27; 12:11 (LXX); Mt. 24:15.

19“For in those days there will be trouble such as has never happened,[a] not
since the beginning of the creation which
God created until now, and never will.
20And unless *ADONAI* had cut short those
days, no one would be saved. But for the
sake of the elect, whom He chose, He cut
short the days.

21“And then if anyone says to you,
‘Look, here’s the Messiah!’ or, ‘Look,
there He is!’ do not believe it. 22For false
messiahs and false prophets will rise
up[b] and show signs and wonders to lead
astray, if possible, the chosen. 23So be
careful! See, I have told you everything
beforehand.”

Messianic Victory

24“But in those days, after that
trouble,

> ‘the sun will be darkened,
> and the moon will not give
> its light,
> 25and the stars will be falling from
> heaven,
> and the powers in the heavens will be
> shaken.’[c]

26And then they will see ‘the Son of
Man coming in clouds’[d] with great power
and glory. 27Then He will send out the
angels and will gather together His chosen from the four winds, from the end of
the earth, to the end of heaven.”

Keep Watch

28“Now learn the parable from the fig
tree. When its branch becomes tender
and puts forth leaves, you know that
summer is near. 29So also, when you see
all these things happening, know that it
is near, at the door. 30Amen, I tell you,
this generation will not pass away until
all these things happen. 31Heaven and
earth will pass away, but My words will
never pass away. 32But of that day or
hour no one knows, not even the angels
in heaven nor the Son, except the Father.

33“Keep on the lookout! Stay alert! For
you do not know when the time is. 34It is
like a man away on a journey. After leaving his house and putting his servants in
charge and giving each his task, he also
commanded the doorkeeper to watch.
35Therefore stay alert, for you do not
know when the master of the house is
coming, whether in the evening, at midnight, when the rooster crows, or in the
early morning. 36So watch in case, coming suddenly, he finds you asleep. 37What
I say to you I say to all: ‘Stay alert!’”

14

Anointed for Burial

1Now it was two days before Passover
and the Feast of *Matzah*. The ruling *kohanim* and *Torah* scholars were searching
for a way to grab *Yeshua* by stealth and
kill Him. 2“But not during the festival,”
they were saying, “so there won’t be a
riot among the people.”

3And while *Yeshua* was in Bethany at
the house of Simon *ha-Metzora*, reclining at the table, a woman came with an
alabaster jar of very expensive oil of pure
nard. Breaking open the jar, she poured it
over His head. 4But some got angry and
said among themselves, “Why was this
fragrant oil wasted? 5It could have been
sold for over three hundred denarii, and
the money given to the poor!” And they
kept scolding her.

6But *Yeshua* said, “Leave her alone.
Why do you cause trouble for her? She’s
done Me a *mitzvah*. 7For you always have
the poor with you, and you can do good
for them whenever you want; but you
won’t always have Me. 8She did what she
could—she came beforehand to anoint
My body for burial. 9Amen, I tell you,
wherever the Good News is proclaimed

a 13:19. cf. Dan. 12:1.
b 13:22. cf. Deut. 13:1f; 18:14f.
c 13:24-25. From Isa. 13:10; 34:4 (LXX); Joel 2:10.
d 13:26. Dan. 7:13.

in all the world, what she has done will also be told in memory of her."

10Then Judah from Kriot, one of the Twelve, went out to the ruling *kohanim* to betray *Yeshua* to them. 11They were delighted when they heard this and promised to give him money. And Judah began looking for a chance to hand Him over.

New Covenant at the Last *Seder*

12Now on the first day of *matzah*, when they were slaughtering the Passover lamb, *Yeshua*'s disciples say to Him, "Where do You want us to go and prepare for You to eat the Passover?"

13He sends two of His disciples and tells them, "Go into the city, and a man carrying a jar of water will meet you. Follow him, 14and wherever he enters, tell the homeowner, 'The Teacher says, "Where is My guest room, where I may eat the Passover with My disciples?"' 15He will show you a large upper room, furnished and ready. Make preparations for us there."

16The disciples went out, came to the city, and found just what *Yeshua* had told them. And they prepared the Passover. 17When it was evening, He came with the Twelve. 18As they were reclining and eating, *Yeshua* said, "Amen, I tell you, one of you who is eating with Me will betray Me."

19They began to be sorrowful and to say to Him one by one, "I'm not the one, am I?"

20He said to them, "It's one of the Twelve, one who dips with Me in the bowl.[a] 21For the Son of Man indeed goes, just as it is written about Him; but woe to that man by whom the Son of Man is betrayed! It would have been better for that man if he had not been born!"

22And while they were eating, He took *matzah*;[b] and after He offered the *bracha*, He broke it and gave it to them and said, "Take; this is My body." 23And He took a cup; and after giving thanks, He gave to them and they all drank from it. 24And He said to them, "This is My blood of the covenant, which is poured out for many.[c] 25Amen, I tell you, I will never again drink of the fruit of the vine, until that day when I drink it anew in the kingdom of God."

Denial Predicted

26After singing the *Hallel*,[d] they went out to the Mount of Olives. 27And *Yeshua* said to them, "You will all fall away, for it is written,

'I will strike the Shepherd,
and the sheep will be
scattered.'[e]

28But after I'm raised up, I will go before you to the Galilee."

29Peter said to Him, "Even though all fall away, I won't!"

30And *Yeshua* said to him, "Amen, I tell you, today—this very night—before a rooster crows twice, you will deny Me three times."

31But Peter kept insisting exceedingly, "Even if I must die with You, I'll never deny You!" And they all were saying the same.

A Night of Painful Prayer

32Then they come to a place whose name is Gethsemane; and *Yeshua* says to His disciples, "Sit here while I pray." 33He takes with Him Peter, Jacob, and John; and He began to be deeply distressed and troubled. 34And He tells them, "My soul is deeply grieved, even to the point of death. Stay here and keep watch."

35Going a little farther, He fell to the ground and began praying that if possible this hour might pass Him by. 36And He was saying, "*Abba*, Father, all things are

a 14:20. cf. Exod. 12:8.
b 14:22. Lit. *bread* (at Passover, unleavened bread).
c 14:24. cf. Exod. 24:8; Jer. 31:31; Heb. 9:22; 10:16-18. Some mss. say: *new covenant*.
d 14:26. Ps. 113-118. (After the last cup, Ps. 115-118 is sung.)
e 14:27. Zech. 13:7.

possible for You! Take this cup from Me! Yet not what I will, but what You will."

37 Then He comes and finds them sleeping; and He tells Peter, "Simon, you're asleep? Couldn't you keep watch for one hour? 38 Keep watching and praying, so that you do not enter into temptation. The spirit is willing, but the flesh is weak." 39 Again He went away and prayed, saying the same words. 40 And again He came and found them sleeping, for their eyes were very heavy. They didn't know what to answer Him. 41 And He comes the third time and says to them, "Are you still sleeping and taking your rest? Enough! The hour has come. Look, the Son of Man is being delivered into the hands of sinners. 42 Get up, let's go! Look, My betrayer is near."

Betrayed and Abandoned

43 Right away, while *Yeshua* was still speaking, Judah comes up, one of the Twelve, and with him a crowd with swords and clubs, from the ruling *kohanim*, *Torah* scholars, and elders. 44 Now His betrayer had given them a signal, saying, "The One I kiss, He's the One! Seize Him and lead Him away under guard."

45 As soon as Judah came, he drew near[a] to *Yeshua* and said, "Rabbi!" and kissed Him. 46 Then they threw their hands on *Yeshua* and seized Him. 47 But one of the bystanders, drawing his sword, struck the servant of the *kohen gadol* and cut off his ear.

48 *Yeshua* said to them, "Have you come out with swords and clubs, to capture Me as you would against a revolutionary? 49 Every day I was with you in the Temple teaching, and you didn't seize Me. But this is so that the Scriptures[b] would be fulfilled." 50 And all fled, abandoning Him.[c] 51 A certain young man was following Him, with nothing but a linen cloth around his body, and they grabbed him. 52 But he ran away naked, leaving behind the linen cloth.

a 14:45. cf. Gen. 44:18.

b 14:49. cf. Mt. 26:56, *writings of the prophets*.

c 14:49-50. cf. Zech. 13:7; Mk. 14:27; Mt. 26:31.

Falsely Charged

53 Then they led *Yeshua* away to the *kohen gadol*. And all the ruling *kohanim*, elders, and *Torah* scholars gathered. 54 Peter had followed Him from a distance, right into the courtyard of the *kohen gadol*. He was sitting with the guards, warming himself by the fire.

55 Now the ruling *kohanim* and all the Sanhedrin kept trying to get evidence against *Yeshua* so they could put Him to death, but they weren't finding any. 56 Many were giving false testimony against Him, but their testimony wasn't consistent. 57 Some stood up and began to give false testimony against Him, saying, 58 "We heard Him say, 'I will destroy this Temple made with hands, and in three days I will build another made without hands.'" 59 Yet even then, their testimony didn't agree.

60 The *kohen gadol* stood up in the middle and questioned *Yeshua*, saying, "Do You have no answer? What is this they're testifying against You?"

61 But keeping silent, *Yeshua* did not answer. Again the *kohen gadol* questioned Him, "Are you *Mashiach*, Son of the Blessed One?"[d]

62 "I am," said *Yeshua*, "and you shall see 'the Son of Man sitting at the right hand of the Powerful One,' and 'coming with the clouds of heaven'!"[e]

63 Tearing his clothes, the *kohen gadol* says, "Why do we still need witnesses? 64 You've heard the blasphemy. What seems right to you?"

Then all condemned Him as deserving death. 65 Some began to spit on Him, to blindfold Him, and to beat Him with their fists, saying, "Prophesy!" Also the guards slapped Him around.

The Rooster Crows

66 As Peter was below in the courtyard, one of the servant girls of the *kohen gadol* comes by. 67 Seeing Peter warming

d 14:61. Heb. *Ben-ha-Mvorach*.

e 14:62. cf. Dan. 7:13(LXX); Ps. 110:1(109:1 LXX).

himself, she looked straight at him. "You also were with *Yeshua* of *Natzeret*," she says.

68But he denied it, saying, "I don't know or understand what you're talking about!" Then he went outside to the gateway, and a rooster crowed.

69Seeing him, the servant girl began again to tell the bystanders, "This is one of them."

70But again he denied it. And a little while later, the bystanders were again saying to Peter, "Surely you're one of them, for you're also a Galilean."

71But he began to curse himself and to swear an oath: "I do not know this Man you're talking about!" 72Right then, a rooster crowed a second time. Then Peter called to mind the word *Yeshua* had said to him: "Before a rooster crows twice, you will deny Me three times." And he broke down and began to weep.

15

Handed Over to the Romans

1Right at daybreak, the ruling *kohanim* held a meeting to consult with the elders and *Torah* scholars and the whole Sanhedrin. They tied up *Yeshua*, led Him away, and handed Him over to Pilate. 2Pilate interrogated Him, "Are You the King of the Jews?"

Yeshua answers him, "As you say."

3The ruling *kohanim* began to accuse Him of many things. 4Again, Pilate asked Him, "Aren't you going to answer? Look how many charges they're bringing against You!" 5But *Yeshua* did not answer, so Pilate was amazed.

6Now during the feast, he used to release to them one prisoner, anyone they were asking for. 7Now a man named *Bar-Abba*[a] had been in jail with the rebels who had committed murder during the rebellion. 8The crowd came up and began to request what he was accustomed to do for them. 9But Pilate answered them, saying, "Do you want me to release for you the King of the Jews?" 10For he knew that out of envy the ruling *kohanim* had handed Him over. 11But the ruling *kohanim* stirred up the crowd, so he would release *Bar-Abba* to them instead.

12Then answering again, Pilate said to them, "So what do you want me to do with the One you call the King of the Jews?"

13They shouted back, "Execute Him!"

14Pilate responded, "Why? What evil has He done?"

But they shouted all the more, "Execute Him!"

15Wanting to satisfy the crowd, Pilate released *Bar-Abba* for them. And after he had *Yeshua* scourged, he handed Him over to be crucified.

16The soldiers took Him away, into the palace, the governor's mansion called the Praetorium. And they call together the cohort[b] of soldiers. 17They dress Him up in purple. After braiding a crown of thorns, they put it on Him. 18And they began to salute Him, "Hail, King of the Jews!" 19Over and over, they kept hitting Him on the head with a staff and spitting on Him; and kneeling down, they worshiped Him. 20When they finished mocking Him, they stripped the purple off Him and put His own clothes back on Him. And they led Him out to crucify Him.

Crucified as King of the Jews

21Now Simon of Cyrene, the father of Alexander and Rufus, was coming in from the countryside. The soldiers force this passerby to carry *Yeshua's* cross-beam.[c] 22They bring *Yeshua* to the place called Golgotha (which is translated, Place of a Skull). 23They were offering Him wine mixed with myrrh, but He didn't take it. 24Then they crucify Him and divide up His

a 15:7, 11, 15. Son of Abba or Son of the Father (Aram.).

b 15:16. Lit. *speira*, 600 Roman soldiers.

c 15:21. Probably the patibulum, the horizontal piece of the execution stake, weighing about 100 lbs.

Mark 15:20

When they finished mocking Him, they stripped the purple off Him and put His own clothes back on Him. And they led Him out to crucify Him.

As foretold by Moses: Exodus 12:7 *and* 24:8, Leviticus 17:11, Deuteronomy 18:15
As heralded by Israel's Prophets: Isaiah 53:7-8, Jeremiah 31:31-33, John 1:36

clothing among themselves, casting lots for them[a] to see who should take what.

25 Now it was the third hour[b] when they nailed Him on the stake. 26 And the inscription of the charge against Him was written above: "THE KING OF THE JEWS." 27 And with Him they execute two outlaws, one on His right and one on His left. (28)[c]

29 Those passing by were jeering at Him, shaking their heads and saying, "Ha! You who are going to destroy the Temple and rebuild it in three days, 30 save Yourself by coming down from the stake!"

31 Likewise the ruling *kohanim*, along with the *Torah* scholars, were also mocking Him among themselves. "He saved others," they were saying, "but He can't save Himself? 32 Let the Messiah, the King of Israel, come down now from the stake, so we may see and believe!" Even those executed with Him were ridiculing Him. Death and Burial

33 When the sixth hour had come, darkness fell over the whole land until the ninth hour.[d] 34 At the ninth hour *Yeshua* cried out with a loud voice, "*Eloi, Eloi, lema sabachthani?*"[e] which is translated, "My God, My God, why have You abandoned Me?"[f]

35 When some of the bystanders heard it, they began saying, "Look, He's calling for Elijah." 36 Then someone ran and filled a sponge with sour wine. He put it on a stick and was offering it to *Yeshua* to drink, saying, "Wait, let's see if Elijah comes to take Him down." 37 But letting out a loud cry, *Yeshua* breathed His last.

38 Then the *curtain*[g] of the Temple was split in two, from top to bottom. 39 When the centurion, who was standing in front of Him, saw the way *Yeshua* breathed His last, he said, "This Man really was the Son of God!"

40 There were also women watching from a distance. Among them were Miriam from Magdala, Miriam the mother of Jacob the younger and of Joses,[h] and Salome. 41 They would follow Him and serve Him when He was in the Galilee. Many other women who had gone up together with Him to Jerusalem were there also.

42 Now evening had already come. Since it was the Day of Preparation, that is, the day before *Shabbat*, 43 Joseph of Arimathea, a respected council member who himself was waiting for the kingdom of God, went boldly to Pilate and asked for *Yeshua*'s body.

44 Pilate was surprised that He was already dead. Summoning the centurion, he asked him whether *Yeshua* had been dead for long. 45 When Pilate learned this from the centurion, he granted the body to Joseph. 46 Joseph bought a linen cloth, took Him down, wrapped Him in the linen, and laid Him in a tomb that had been cut out of the rock. Then he rolled a stone against the door of the tomb. 47 Miriam from Magdala and Miriam the mother of Joses were watching where *Yeshua's* body was placed.

16

The Empty Tomb

1 When *Shabbat* was over, Miriam of Magdala, Miriam the mother of Jacob, and Salome bought spices, so that they might come and anoint *Yeshua*'s body. 2 Very early on the first day of the week, when the sun had risen, they come to the tomb. 3 They were saying to each other, "Who will roll away the stone for us from the entrance to the tomb?"

4 Looking up, they see that the stone (it was really huge) had been rolled away.

a 15:24. Ps. 22:19(18)

b 15:25. About nine in the morning.

c 15:28. Later mss. add: *So the Scripture was fulfilled which says, 'He was counted with the sinners.'* See Isa. 53:12.

d 15:33. From noon until 3 p.m.

e 15:34. Eloi, Eloi, l'ma sh'vaktani? See Aramaic Targum Psalm 22:1f; cf. Mt. 27:46.

f 15:34. Ps. 22:2(1); cf. Dt. 32:20.

g 15:38. Heb. *parokhet*, *veil* or *inner curtain*; cf. Exod. 26:33; 2 Chr. 3:14; Heb. 9:3.

h 15:40. A shortened form of the name *Joseph*; cf. Mt. 27:56.

[5]As they entered the tomb, they saw
a young man sitting on the right side,
dressed in a white robe; and they were
startled. [6]But he said to them, "Do not
be alarmed. You are looking for *Yeshua* of
Natzeret, who was crucified. He is risen!
He is not here! See the place where they
put Him. [7]But go, tell His disciples and
Peter, 'He is going before you to the Galilee. There you will see Him, just as He told
you.'"

[8]And going outside, they fled from
the tomb, gripped by trembling and
amazement. They didn't say anything to
anybody, for they were afraid.

He Is Risen[a]

[9]After He had risen early on the first
day of the week, He appeared first to
Miriam of Magdala, from whom He had
driven out seven demons. [10]She went
and brought word to those who had
been with Him, while they were mourning and weeping. [11]When they heard that
He was alive and had been seen by her,
they refused to believe.

[12]After that, He appeared in a different
form to two of them as they were walking on their way to the country. [13]They
went and reported it to the rest, but they
did not believe them either. [14]Later He
appeared to them, the eleven, as they
were reclining at the table. He rebuked
them for their unbelief and hardhearted-
ness, because they did not believe those
who had seen Him after He had been
raised.

Tell the World!

[15]He told them, "Go into all the world
and proclaim the Good News to every
creature. [16]He who believes and is
immersed shall be saved, but he who
does not believe shall be condemned.
[17]These signs will accompany those who
believe: in My name they will drive out
demons; they will speak new languages;
[18]they will handle snakes; and if they
drink anything deadly, it will not harm
them; they will lay hands on the sick, and
they will get well."

19Then the Lord *Yeshua*, after He
had spoken to them, was taken up into
heaven and sat down at the right hand
of God. 20And they went out and proclaimed everywhere, the Lord working
with them and confirming the word by
the signs that follow.

a 16:9-20. The earliest mss. exclude Mark 16:9-20. A shorter version reads: But, they reported briefly to Peter and those with him all they had been told. And after these things, Yeshua Himself, through them, sent out from east to west the sacred, imperishable proclamation of eternal salvation.

The Good News According to Luke

Introduction

The Gospel of Luke was written by a doctor—but possibly not a Jewish one! Luke may have been one of the "God-fearers," a large group of Gentiles who frequented the synagogue and observed some Jewish customs. In any case, Luke was highly knowledgeable about Jewish laws and customs in the land of Israel and the Temple.

Luke was a careful historian who researched others' first-hand accounts before writing his own. He spent time traveling with Paul and also authored the book of Acts, which forms the second volume of what is really a two-part work. The first volume, the Gospel of Luke, is the longest of all the New Covenant books. Luke is unique among the Gospel writers in focusing on the events that took place as *Yeshua* made His way to Jerusalem (9:51-19:27). Some of *Yeshua's* teaching is found only in Luke, such as the well-known parable of the Prodigal Son. We would be much the poorer without this material.

Written about 60-85 C.E., Luke addresses an audience not unlike today's Messianic communities—established by Jewish believers yet with a large Gentile contingent, with great interest and loyalty to the homeland of Biblical faith and hope. In the very first paragraph, Luke tells us his purpose for writing: "so you may know for sure the truth of the words you have been taught" (1:4). Luke stresses God's plan of salvation and the offer of that salvation to both Gentile and Jewish people. Luke resonates with modern Jewish sensibilities, reflecting *Yeshua's* concern for the oppressed and downtrodden as well as for justice—issues of *tikkun olam*, "repairing the world." Luke is also especially inclusive of women, from Elizabeth to Miriam and Martha and the women who are first to meet the resurrected Messiah.

For readers in today's diverse, pluralistic world, Luke gently raises questions about truth and why Yeshua is who He and His followers claim Him to be. He is the fulfillment of Israel's Messianic hope and the One who gives purpose and dignity to all who put their trust in Him.

A Look Inside Luke

Silencing the Opposition (20:20)

Teaching in the Temple (21:1)

The Day before *Pesach* (22:1)
The *Seder* in the Upper Room (22:14)
Yeshua Prays at the Mount
of Olives (22:39)
Betrayed! (22:47)
Denied Three Times (22:55)
Beaten by Roman Soldiers (22:63)
Brought Before the Council (22:66)

Brought Before Pilate (23:1)
Brought Before Herod (23:8)
Pilate's Decree (23:13)
Executed on the Stake (23:26)
Temple Curtain Torn in Two (23:44)
Buried in a Rich Man's Tomb (23:50)
Women Visit the Garden Tomb (24:1)
Eyes Open in Emmaus (24:13)
Good News Spreads to the *Talmidim*
in Jerusalem (24:32)
Yeshua Ascends into Heaven (24:50)

1

A Doctor Charts the Facts

1 Now many have undertaken to organize an account of the events fulfilled among us, 2 just as they were handed down to us from the start by the eyewitnesses and reporters of the word. 3 Therefore it seemed best to me also, because I have carefully investigated everything from the beginning, to write for you an orderly record, most excellent Theophilus, 4 so you may know for sure the truth of the words you have been taught.

Prophecy of Birth to the Barren

5 In the days of Herod, King of Judah, there was a *kohen* named Zechariah from the priestly division of Abijah.[a] Elizabeth, his wife, was from the daughters of Aaron. 6 Together they were righteous before *ADONAI*, walking without fault in all His commandments and instructions. 7 But they were childless, because Elizabeth was barren and both of them were elderly.

8 Now it happened to be Zechariah's time to serve as *kohen* before *ADONAI* in the order of his division. 9 According to the custom of the priestly office, it became his lot to enter the Holy Place of *ADONAI* to burn incense.[b] 10 And the whole crowd of people was praying outside at the hour of incense burning. 11 An angel of *ADONAI* appeared to him, standing at the right side of the altar of incense. 12 Zechariah was in turmoil when he saw the angel, and fear fell upon him. 13 But the angel said, "Do not be afraid, Zechariah, because your prayer has been heard. Your wife, Elizabeth, will give birth to your son, and you will name him John. 14 And you will have joy and gladness, and many will rejoice at his birth. 15 He will be great before *ADONAI*; and he should not drink wine and intoxicating beverage,[c] but he will be filled with the *Ruach ha-Kodesh* just out of his mother's womb. 16 Many of *B'nei-Israel* will turn to *ADONAI* their God. 17 And he will go before Him in the spirit and power of Elijah, to turn the hearts of fathers to the children[d] and the disobedient ones to the wisdom of the righteous, to make ready for *ADONAI* a prepared people.

18 Zechariah said to the angel, "How will I know this for certain? I'm an old man, and my wife is well-advanced in age."

19 And speaking to him, the angel declared, "I am Gabriel, the one standing in God's presence. I was commissioned to tell you and proclaim to you this good news. 20 So look, you will be silent and powerless to speak until the day these things happen, since you did not believe my words which will be fulfilled in their time."

21 The people were waiting for Zechariah and wondering about his long delay in the Holy Place. 22 But when he came out, he couldn't speak to them. Then they realized that he had seen a vision in the Holy Place. He was making signs to them but remained mute. 23 When the days of his priestly *service* had been completed, he went home. 24 After these days, his wife Elizabeth became pregnant and hid herself for five months, saying, 25 "*ADONAI* has done this for me! In these days He looked upon me, to take away my disgrace among the people."[e]

Prophecy of Birth to the Virgin

26 Then in the sixth month, the angel Gabriel was sent by *ADONAI* into a town in the Galilee named *Natzeret* 27 and to a virgin engaged to a man named Joseph, of the house of David. The virgin's name

a 1:5. cf. 1 Chr. 24:10.
b 1:9. cf. Exod. 30:6-8; 1 Chron. 24:10, 19.
c 1:15. cf. Num. 6:3.
d 1:17. cf. Mal. 3:23-24(4:5-6).
e 1:25. cf. Isa. 54:1-10.

was Miriam. 28And coming to her, the angel said, "*Shalom*, favored one! ADONAI is with you.[a]" 29But at the message, she was perplexed and kept wondering what kind of greeting this might be. 30The angel spoke to her, "Do not be afraid, Miriam, for you have found favor with God. 31Behold, you will become pregnant and give birth to a son, and you shall call His name *Yeshua*.[b] 32He will be great and will be called *Ben-Elyon*. ADONAI *Elohim* will give Him the throne of David,[c] His father. 33He shall reign over the house of Jacob for all eternity, and His kingdom will be without end."[d]

34Miriam said to the angel, "How can this be, since I am not intimate with a man?"[e]

35And responding, the angel said to her, "The *Ruach ha-Kodesh* will come upon you, and the power of *Elyon* will overshadow you. Therefore, the Holy One being born will be called *Ben-Elohim*. 36Behold, even your relative Elizabeth has conceived a son in her old age; and the one who was called barren is six months pregnant. 37For nothing will be impossible with God."[f]

38So Miriam said, "Behold, the servant of ADONAI. Let it be done to me according to your word." And the angel left her.

Elizabeth Greets Miriam with Joy

39Now in those days, Miriam got up and quickly traveled into the hill country, to a town in Judah. 40She entered Zechariah's home and happily greeted Elizabeth. 41When Elizabeth heard Miriam's greeting, the unborn child leaped in her womb; and Elizabeth was completely filled with the *Ruach ha-Kodesh*. 42She then cried out with a great shout, saying, "You are blessed among women, and blessed is the fruit of your womb. 43Who am I, that the mother of my Master should come to me? 44For even when I just heard the sound of your greeting in my ear, the unborn child leaped with joy in my womb. 45Blessed is she who trusted that there would be a fulfillment of those things spoken to her by ADONAI."

46Then Miriam said,

"My soul magnifies ADONAI,[g]
47and my spirit greatly rejoices in
God, my Savior.
48For He has looked with care upon
the humble state of His
maidservant.
For behold, from now on all
generations
will call me blessed.
49For the Mighty One has
done a great thing for me,
and holy is His name.
50And His mercy is
from generation to generation
to the ones who fear Him.
51He has displayed power
with His arm
He has scattered the proud
in the thoughts of their hearts.
52He has brought down rulers
from thrones
and exalted humble
ones.
53He has filled the hungry with
good things
and sent away the rich
empty-handed.
54He has helped His servant
Israel,[h]
remembering His mercy,
55just as He spoke to
our fathers,
to Abraham and to his
seed forever."

Zechariah Breaks His Silence

56Miriam stayed with her for three months and then returned to her home. 57Upon Elizabeth's full term to deliver,

a 1:28. Some mss. add *and blessed are you among women*.
b 1:31. cf. Isa. 7:14.
c 1:32. cf. 2 Sam. 7:12-16; Isa. 9:6(7); 11:1; Ps. 132:11-12.
d 1:33. cf. Ps. 45:6; 89:35-37; Dan. 2:44; 7:14.
e 1:34. cf. Isa. 7:14.
f 1:37. cf. Gen. 18:14.
g 1:46-55. cf. 1 Sam. 2:1-10.
h 1:54. cf. Isa. 41:8(41:8 LXX).

Luke 1:43

Who am I, that the mother of my Master should come to me? For even when I just heard the sound of your greeting in my ear, the unborn child leaped with joy in my womb.

she gave birth to a son. 58Her neighbors
and relatives heard how *ADONAI* had
shown her His great mercy, and they
began to rejoice with her.

59Now on the eighth day they came
time to circumcise the child,[a] and they
kept trying to call him by his father's
name, Zechariah. 60But his mother
declared, "No, he will be called John."

61But they said to her, "No one among
your relatives is called by this name." 62So
they began making signs to his father, as
to what he wanted him named.

63Asking for a small tablet, he wrote,
"John is his name." They were all astonished! 64And his mouth was immediately
unlocked as well as his tongue, and he
began to speak, praising God. 65Fear
came on all those who lived around them,
and all these matters were talked about
throughout the hill country of Judah.
66Everyone who heard pondered these
things in their hearts, saying, "What then
will this child become?" For the hand of
ADONAI was on him.

The *Kohen's* Song of Prophecy

67His father Zechariah was filled with
the *Ruach ha-Kodesh* and prophesied,
saying,

68"Blessed be *ADONAI*,
God of Israel,
for He has looked after His people and
brought them redemption.
69He has raised up a horn
of salvation for us
in the house of His servant
David,[b]
70just as He spoke by the mouth of His
holy prophets from ages past,
71salvation from our enemies and from
the hand of all who hate us!
72So He shows mercy to our fathers
and remembers His holy covenant,[c]
73the vow which He swore to Abraham
our father, to grant us—
74rescued fearlessly from the hand of
our enemies[d]—to serve Him,
75in holiness and righteousness before
Him all our days.
76And you, child, will be called a
prophet of *Elyon*.
For you will go before *ADONAI* to prepare His ways,[e]
77to give knowledge of salvation to His
people
through removal of
their sins.[f]
78Through our God's heart
of mercy,
the Sunrise from on high
will come upon us,
79to give light to those
who sit in darkness
and in the shadow of death,[g]
to guide our feet
in the way of *shalom*."

80And the child kept growing and
became strong in spirit; and he lived in
the wilderness until the day of his public
appearance to Israel.

2

Yeshua's Birth in Bethlehem

1Now it happened in those days a
decree went out from Caesar Augustus
to register all the world's inhabitants.
2This was the first census taken when
Quirinius was governor of Syria. 3Every-
one was traveling to be registered in his
own city.

4Now Joseph also went up from the
Galilee, out of the town of *Natzeret* to
Judah, to the city of David, which is called
Bethlehem, because he was from the
house and family of David.[h] 5He went to
register with Miriam, who was engaged
to him and was pregnant.

a 1:59. cf. Gen. 17:12; Lev. 12:3.
b 1.69. cf. 2 Sam. 7; 22:3; Isa. 37:35(37:35 LXX).
c 1:72. cf. Mic. 7:20.
d 1:73-74. cf. Gen. 22:16-17.
e 1:76. cf. Mal. 3:1; Isa. 40:3; Mic. 1:2.
f 1:77. cf. Jer. 31:34(38:34 LXX).
g 1:79. cf. Isa. 9:1(2).
h 2:4. cf. Mic. 5:1(2).

6 But while they were there, the time came for her to give birth— 7 and she gave birth to her firstborn son. She wrapped Him in strips of cloth and set Him down in a manger, since there was no room for them in the inn.

Shepherds Witness Angelic Praises

8 Now there were shepherds in the same region, living out in the fields and guarding their flock at night. 9 Suddenly an angel of *ADONAI* stood before them, and the glory of *ADONAI* shone all around them; and they were absolutely terrified.

10 But the angel said to them, "Do not be afraid! For behold, I proclaim Good News to you, which will be great joy to all the people. 11 A Savior is born to you today in the city of David, who is Messiah the Lord. 12 And the sign to you is this: You will find an infant wrapped in strips of cloth and lying in a manger."

13 And suddenly a multitude of heavenly armies appeared with the angel, praising God and saying,

14 "Glory to God in the highest,
  and on earth *shalom* to men of
  good will."

15 And when the angels departed from them into the heavens, the shepherds were saying to one another, "Let's go to Bethlehem and see this thing that has happened which *ADONAI* has made known to us!" 16 So they hurried off and found Miriam and Joseph, and the Baby lying in the manger. 17 When they had seen this, they made known the word that had been spoken to them concerning this Child. 18 And all those who heard were amazed at the things the shepherds told them. 19 But Miriam treasured all these things, pondering them in her heart. 20 The shepherds returned, glorifying and praising God for all the things they had heard and seen, just as they had been told.

Temple Prophets Rejoice

21 When eight days had passed for His *brit-milah*,[a] He was named *Yeshua*, the name given by the angel before He was conceived in the womb. 22 And when the days of their purification were fulfilled,[b] according to the *Torah* of Moses, they brought Him to Jerusalem to present to *ADONAI*. 23 As it is written in the *Torah* of *ADONAI*, "Every firstborn male that opens the womb shall be called holy to *ADONAI*."[c] 24 So they offered a sacrifice according to what was said in the *Torah* of *ADONAI*: "a pair of turtle doves, or two young pigeons."[d]

25 Now there was a man in Jerusalem whose name was Simeon, and this man was just and pious, waiting for the consolation of Israel.[e] The *Ruach ha-Kodesh* was on him. 26 And it had been revealed to him by the *Ruach ha-Kodesh* that he would not die before he had seen the Anointed One of *ADONAI*. 27 So in the *Spirit*, Simeon came into the Temple; and when the parents brought the Child *Yeshua* to do for Him according to the custom of the *Torah*, 28 Simeon received Him into his arms and offered a *bracha* to God, saying,

29 "Now may You let Your servant go in
  peace, O Sovereign Master,[f]
 according to Your word.
30 For my eyes have seen Your
  salvation,
31 which You have prepared
  in the presence of all peoples:
32 'A light for revelation
  to the nations'[g]
 and the glory of Your people
  Israel."

33 And His father and mother were marveling at the things that were said

a 2:21. cf. Gen. 17:12; Lev. 12:3.
b 2:22. cf. Lev. 12:1-8.
c 2:23. Exod. 13:2, cf. Exod. 13:12, 15.
d 2:24. Lev. 12:8; 5:11 (LXX).
e 2:25. cf. Isa. 40:1; 51:3.
f 2:29. Grk. *Despota*; cf. Heb. *Ha-Adon*, Isa. 3:1; 10:33.
g 2:32. Isa. 42:6; 49:6; cf. 60:1-3.

Luke 2:28-32

Simeon received Him into his arms and offered a bracha to God, saying, "Now may You let Your servant go in peace, O Sovereign Master, according to Your word. For my eyes have seen Your salvation, which You have prepared in the presence of all peoples: 'A light for revelation to the nations' and the glory of Your people Israel."

about Him. 34 And Simeon offered a *bracha* over them and said to Miriam His mother, "Behold, this One is destined to cause the fall and rise of many in Israel, and to be a sign that is opposed, 35 so the thoughts of many hearts may be uncovered. (And even for you, a sword will pierce through your soul.)"

36 Now Anna, a daughter of Phanuel of the tribe of Asher, was a prophetess. She was well advanced in age, having lived with a husband only[a] seven years 37 and then as a widow until age eighty-four. She never left the Temple, serving night and day with fasting and prayers. 38 And coming up at that very instant, she began praising God and speaking about the Child to all those waiting for the redemption of Jerusalem.[b]

39 When Joseph and Miriam had completed everything according to the *Torah* of *ADONAI*, they returned to the Galilee, to their own city of *Natzeret*. 40 The Child kept growing and became strong, filled with wisdom; and the favor of God was upon Him.

The Boy Astonishes Jerusalem Scholars

41 Now His parents were going every year to Jerusalem for the Passover feast.[c] 42 When He became twelve years old, they were going up according to festival custom. 43 As they headed home after completing the days, the boy *Yeshua* remained in Jerusalem, but His parents didn't know. 44 Supposing He was in the caravan, they went a day's journey, then began looking for Him among relatives and friends. 45 When they did not find Him, they returned to Jerusalem to search for Him.

46 After three days they found Him in the Temple, sitting in the center of the teachers, listening to them and asking them questions. 47 And all those hearing Him were astonished at His understanding and His answers. 48 When His parents saw *Yeshua*, they were overwhelmed. And His mother said to Him, "Child, why did you do this to us? Look! Your father and I were searching for You frantically!"

49 He said to them, "Why were you searching for Me? Didn't you know that I must be about the things of My Father?" 50 But they did not grasp the message He was telling them.

51 Then He went down with them to *Natzeret* and was obedient to them. But His mother treasured all these words in her heart. 52 And *Yeshua* kept increasing in wisdom and stature, and in favor with God and men.

3

John the Immerser at the Jordan

1 It was now the fifteenth year of the reign of Tiberius Caesar—when Pontius Pilate was governor of Judea, and Herod was tetrarch of the Galilee, and his brother Philip was tetrarch of the region of Ituraea and Trachonitis, and Lysanias was tetrarch of Abilene. 2 During the high priesthood of Annas and Caiaphas, the word of God came upon John, the son of Zechariah, in the wilderness. 3 And he came into all the surrounding region of the Jordan, proclaiming an immersion of repentance for the removal of sins. 4 As it is written in the scroll of the words of Isaiah the prophet,

> "The voice of one crying in the
>   wilderness,
> 'Prepare the way of
>   *ADONAI*,
> and make His paths
>   straight.
> 5 Every valley shall be filled up
>   and every mountain and hill
>   brought low.

a 2:36. Lit. *from her virginity.*
b 2:38. cf. Isa. 43:1-3; 49:26.
c 2:41. cf. Exod. 23:15; Lev. 23:4-8; Deut. 16:1-8.

Luke 2:46-47

After three days they found Him in the Temple, sitting in the center of the teachers, listening to them and asking them questions. And all those hearing Him were astonished at His understanding and His answers.

The crooked shall be made straight
and the rough ways made smooth,
6and all humanity shall see the
salvation of God.'"[a]

7Therefore John was saying to the crowds that came out to be immersed by him, "You brood of vipers! Who warned you to flee from the coming wrath? 8Therefore produce fruits worthy of repentance; and don't even begin to say among yourselves, 'We have Abraham as our father'! For I tell you that from these stones God can raise up children for Abraham. 9Even now the axe is laid at the root of the trees, so every tree that does not produce good fruit is cut down and thrown into the fire!"

10The crowds were asking him, "What should we do?"

11He answered them, saying, "Whoever has two coats, let him give to the one who has none; and whoever has food, let him do the same."[b]

12Tax collectors also came to him to be immersed. "Teacher," they said to him, "what should we do?"

13He said to them, "Do not take more than you are supposed to."

14Also soldiers asked him, saying, "And what should we do?"

He said to them, "Do not take things from anyone by force, do not falsely accuse anyone, and be content with your wages."[c]

15Now the people were filled with expectation, and all were wondering in their hearts about John, whether he might be the Messiah. 16John answered them all, saying, "As for me, I immerse you with water. But One is coming who is mightier than I am; I am not worthy to untie the strap of His sandals! He will immerse you in the *Ruach ha-Kodesh* and fire. 17His winnowing fork is in His hand to clear His threshing floor and gather the wheat into His barn, but the chaff He will burn up with inextinguishable fire."[d] 18So with many other exhortations, John proclaimed Good News to the people. 19But Herod the tetrarch—after being rebuked by John because of Herodias, his brother's wife, and because of all the evil things Herod had done—20added even this on top of them all: he shut up John in prison.

21Now when all the people were immersed, *Yeshua* also was immersed. And while He was praying, heaven was opened 22and the *Ruach ha-Kodesh* came down upon Him in bodily form like a dove. And from out of heaven came a voice, "You are My Son, whom I love—with You I am well pleased!"[e]

The Lineage of *Yeshua Ben-David Ben-Elohim*

23*Yeshua* was about thirty years old when He began his ministry. He was the son (as was supposed) of Joseph, the son of Heli, 24the son of Matthat, the son of Levi, the son of Melki, the son of Jannai, the son of Joseph, 25the son of Mattathias, the son of Amos, the son of Nahum, the son of Esli, the son of Naggai, 26the son of Maath, the son of Mattathias, the son of Semein, the son of Josech, the son of Joda, 27the son of Joanan, the son of Rhesa, the son of Zerubbabel, the son of Shealtiel, the son of Neri, 28the son of Melki, the son of Addi, the son of Cosam, the son of Elmadam, the son of Er, 29the son of Joshua, the son of Eliezer, the son of Jorim, the son of Matthat, the son of Levi, 30the son of Simeon, the son of Judah, the son of Joseph, the son of Jonam, the son of Eliakim, 31the son of Melea, the son of Menna, the son of Mattatha, the son of Nathan, the son of David,[f] 32the son of Jesse, the son of Obed, the son of Boaz, the son of Salmon, the son of Nahshon, 33the son of Amminadab, the son of Ram, the son of Hezron, the son of Perez, the

a 3:4-6. Isa. 40:3-5.
b 3:11. Isa. 58:7.
c 3:14. cf. Exod. 20:16; 23:1; Lev. 19:11.
d 3:17. cf. Ps. 1:4; Jer. 7:20.
e 3:22. cf. Ps. 2:7; Prov. 30:4; Isa. 9:5(6).
f 3:31. Heb. *Ben-David*.

son of Judah, 34the son of Jacob, the son of Yitzhak, the son of Abraham,[a] the son of Terah, the son of Nahor, 35the son of Serug, the son of Reu, the son of Peleg, the son of Eber, the son of Shelah, 36the son of Cainan, the son of Arphaxad, the son of Shem, the son of Noah, the son of Lamech, 37the son of Methuselah, the son of Enoch, the son of Jared, the son of Mahalalel, the son of Kenan, 38the son of Enosh, the son of Seth, the son of Adam,[b] the son of God.

4

Temptation in the Wilderness

1*Yeshua,* now filled with the *Ruach ha-Kodesh,* returned from the Jordan. He was led by the Spirit in the wilderness 2for forty days, being tested by the devil. Now He ate nothing during those days, and when they had ended, He was hungry.

3The devil said to Him, "If You are *Ben-Elohim*, tell this stone to become bread."

4*Yeshua* answered him, "It is written, 'Man shall not live by bread alone.'"[c]

5And leading Him up, the devil showed Him all the kingdoms of the world in an instant. 6And the devil said to Him, "I'll give to You all this authority along with its glory, because it has been handed over to me and I can give it to anyone I wish. 7Therefore, if you will worship before me, all this shall be Yours."

8But answering, *Yeshua* told him, "It is written, 'You shall worship *Adonai* your God, and Him only shall you serve.'"[d]

9Then he brought *Yeshua* to Jerusalem and placed Him on the highest point of the Temple. He said to Him, "If You are *Ben-Elohim*, throw Yourself down from here. 10For it is written,

'He will command His
angels concerning you,
to guard you,'[e]
11and 'upon their hands
they will lift you up,
so that you may not strike
your foot against a stone.'"[f]

12But answering, *Yeshua* said to him, "It is said, 'You shall not put *Adonai* your God to the test.'"[g] 13And when the devil had completed every test, he departed from Him until another occasion.

Isaiah's Prophecy Fulfilled in *Natzeret*

14*Yeshua* returned in the power of the *Spirit* to the Galilee, and news about Him went out through all the surrounding region. 15He taught in their synagogues, and everyone was praising Him. 16And He came to *Natzeret*, where He had been raised. As was His custom, He went into the synagogue on *Shabbat*, and He got up to read. 17When the scroll of the prophet Isaiah was handed to Him, He unrolled the scroll and found the place where it was written,

18"The Spirit of *Adonai* is on Me,
because He has anointed Me
to proclaim Good News to the poor.
He has sent Me[h] to proclaim
release to the captives
and recovery of sight to the blind,
to set free the oppressed,
19and to proclaim the year of
Adonai's favor."[i]

20He closed the scroll, gave it back to the attendant, and sat down. All eyes in the synagogue were focused on Him. 21Then He began to tell them, "Today this Scripture has been fulfilled in your ears."

a 3:34. Heb. *Ben-Avraham*.
b 3:38. Heb. *Ben-Adam*.
c 4:4. Deut. 8:3.
d 4:8. Deut. 6:13; some mss. begin: *"Get behind Me, satan! It is written..."*
e 4:10. Ps. 91:11.
f 4:11. Ps. 91:12.
g 4:12. Deut. 6:16.
h 4:18. Some mss. add *to heal the brokenhearted.*
i 4:18-19. Isa. 61:1-2a(61:1-2a LXX); 58:6d(58:6d LXX); cf. Lev. 25:10.

22All were speaking well of Him and marveling at the gracious words coming out of His mouth. And they were saying, "Isn't this the son of Joseph?"

23But He said to them, "Doubtless you will say to Me this proverb, 'Doctor, heal yourself!' and 'What we have heard was done at Capernaum, do as much here also in your hometown.'"

24But He said, "Amen, I tell you, 'No prophet is accepted in his own hometown.' 25But with all truthfulness I say to you, that there were many widows in Israel in the days of Elijah, when heaven was closed for three and a half years and there came a great famine over all the land. 26Elijah was not sent to any of them, but only to Zarephath in the land of Sidon, to a widowed woman.[a] 27There were many with *tzara'at* in Israel in the time of Elisha the prophet, and none of them were purified apart from Naaman the Syrian."[b]

28Now all in the synagogue were filled with rage upon hearing these things. 29Rising up, they drove Him out of the town and brought Him as far as the edge of the mountain on which their city had been built, in order to throw Him off the cliff. 30But passing through the middle of them, He went on His way.

Healing and Deliverance in Capernaum and Beyond

31*Yeshua* came down to Capernaum, a town in the Galilee. He was teaching them on *Shabbat*, 32and they were astounded at His teaching because His message had authority. 33In the synagogue was a man who had a unclean demonic spirit, and he cried out with a loud voice, 34"Ah! What have we to do with You, *Yeshua* of *Natzeret*? Have You come to destroy us? I know who You are! You are the Holy One of God!"

35*Yeshua* rebuked him, saying, "Quiet! Come out of him!" And when the demon threw him down in their midst, it came out without hurting him.

36They were all amazed, and they spoke to one another, saying, "What is this message? For with authority and power He commands the unclean spirits, and they come out." 37So His reputation grew, spreading to every place in that region.

38After He left the synagogue, *Yeshua* entered Simon's home. Simon's mother-in-law was suffering from a high fever, and they petitioned Him concerning her. 39Then standing over her, He rebuked the fever and it left her. Immediately she arose to wait on them.

40When the sun was setting, they brought to *Yeshua* all who were sick with various diseases. And He was laying hands on each one and healing them. 41Even demons were coming out from many, shouting out and saying, "You are *Ben-Elohim*!"[c] But He was rebuking them and not permitting them to speak, because they knew Him to be the Messiah.

42Now when it was day, He left and went to a desert place. The crowds were searching for Him, and they came to Him and were trying to keep Him from leaving them. 43But He said to them, "I must proclaim the Good News of the kingdom of God[d] to the other towns also. It was for this purpose I was sent." 44So He kept preaching in the synagogues of Judea.

5

Calling Fishermen at the *Kinneret*

1It happened that the crowds were pressing upon *Yeshua* to hear the word of God as He was standing by the Lake of *Kinneret*, 2when He saw two boats standing beside the lake. Now the fishermen had left them and were washing

a 4:25-26. cf. 1 Kings 17:1, 7-10.
b 4:27. cf. 2 Kings 5:1-14.
c 4:41. cf. Ps.2:7.
d 4:43. cf. Dan. 7:14, 27.

Luke 5:1-2

It happened that the crowds were pressing upon Yeshua to hear the word of God as He was standing by the Lake of Kinneret, when He saw two boats standing beside the lake. Now the fishermen had left them and were washing the nets.

the nets. [3]Getting into one of the boats, Simon's boat, *Yeshua* asked him to push out a ways from the land. Then sitting down, He taught the crowds from the boat.

[4]When He had finished speaking, He said to Simon, "Go out into the deep water, and let down your nets for a catch."

[5]Simon replied, "Master, we've worked hard all night and caught nothing. But at Your word I will let down the nets." [6]When they had done this, they caught so many fish that their nets began to break. [7]So they signaled to their partners in the other boat to come and help them. They came and filled both boats so full that they began to sink. [8]But when Simon Peter saw this, he fell down at *Yeshua's* knees, saying, "Go away from me, Master, for I am a sinful man!" [9]For amazement had gripped him and all who were with him, over the catch of fish they had netted; [10]so also Jacob and John, Zebedee's sons, who were partners with Simon.

But *Yeshua* said to Simon, "Do not be afraid. From now on, you will be catching men." [11]So when they had brought the boats to the landing, they left everything and followed Him.

Yeshua Heals and News Spreads

[12]Now while *Yeshua* was in one of the towns, a man covered with *tzara'at* appeared. And when he saw *Yeshua*, he fell on his face and begged Him, saying, "Master, if You are willing, You can make me clean."

[13]*Yeshua* stretched out His hand and touched him, saying, "I am willing. Be cleansed!" Immediately, the *tzara'at* left him. [14]*Yeshua* ordered him to tell no one, but commanded him, "Go and show yourself to the *kohen*.[a] Then bring an offering for your cleansing, just as Moses commanded, as a testimony to them."

[15]But the news about *Yeshua* was spreading all the more, and many crowds were coming together to hear and to be healed of their diseases. [16]Yet He would often slip away into the wilderness and pray.

Crowds Gather from the Galilee, Judea, and Jerusalem

[17]Now on one of those days, *Yeshua* was teaching. Pharisees and *Torah* scholars were sitting there, who had come from every village of the Galilee and Judea, as well as from Jerusalem. And *ADONAI's* power to heal was in Him. [18]And behold, men were carrying a paralyzed man on a stretcher, trying to bring him in and place him before *Yeshua*. [19]But when they found no way to bring him in because of the crowd, they went up on the roof and let him down with his stretcher through the tiles, right in the middle before *Yeshua*. [20]When He saw their faith, He said, "Man, your sins are forgiven."

[21]Then the *Torah* scholars and the Pharisees began to question, saying, "Who is this fellow speaking blasphemies? Who can pardon sins but God alone?"

[22]*Yeshua*, knowing their thoughts, replied to them, "Why are you raising questions in your hearts? [23]Which is easier, to say, 'Your sins are forgiven you,' or to say, 'Get up and walk'? [24]But so you may know that the Son of Man has authority on earth to pardon sins...." He said to the paralyzed one, "I tell you, get up and take your cot, and go home!"

[25]Immediately he got up before them, picked up what he had been lying on, and went home, glorifying God. 26 Astonishment took hold of them, and they glorified God and all were filled with awe, saying, "We've seen incredible things today!"

The Banquet at Levi's House

[27]After these things, *Yeshua* went out and observed a tax collector named Levi, sitting at the tax booth. He said to him,

a 5:14. cf. Lev. 13:1; 14:2-3.

"Follow Me." [28]And leaving everything, he got up and followed Him.

[29]Levi made a great banquet for *Yeshua* at his house, and there was a large crowd of tax collectors and others who were reclining with them. [30]The Pharisees and their *Torah* scholars began murmuring to His disciples, saying, "Why do you eat and drink with tax collectors and sinners?"

[31]And *Yeshua* answered and said to them, "Those who are healthy have no need for a doctor, but those who are sick do. [32]I did not come to call the righteous, but the sinful to repentance."

[33]But they said to Him, "John's disciples often fast and offer prayers, as do the disciples of the Pharisees. But Your disciples are eating and drinking."

[34]But *Yeshua* said to them, "You cannot make the guests of the bridegroom fast while the bridegroom is with them, can you? [35]But the days will come; and when the bridegroom is taken away from them, then they will fast in those days."

[36]Now he was also telling them a parable. "No one tears a patch from a new garment to use it on an old garment. Otherwise he will rip the new, and the patch from the new will not match the old. [37]And no one puts new wine into old wineskins. Otherwise, the new wine will burst the skins, it will be spilled out, and the skins will be destroyed. [38]But new wine must be put into fresh wineskins. [39]No man who drinks old wine wants new, because he says, 'The old is fine.'"

6

Shabbat in the Grain Fields

[1]Now during *Shabbat*, *Yeshua* was passing through grain fields; and His disciples were picking and eating heads of grain, rubbing them in their hands. [2]But some of the Pharisees said, "Why are you doing what is not permitted on *Shabbat*?"

[3]Then answering them, *Yeshua* said, "Haven't you read what David did when he was hungry, and those with him? [4]How he entered into the house of God, took and ate the showbread which only the *kohanim* are permitted to eat, and even gave it to those with him?"[a] [5]He said to them, "The Son of Man is Lord of *Shabbat*."

Shabbat Controversy at the Synagogue

[6]On a different *Shabbat*, *Yeshua* entered the synagogue and was teaching. A man was there, whose right hand was paralyzed. [7]But closely watching Him were the *Torah* scholars and Pharisees, to see if He heals on *Shabbat*, so that they might find grounds to accuse Him. [8]But He knew their opinions and said to the man with the paralyzed hand, "Get up and stand in our midst." And getting up, the man stood.

[9]*Yeshua* said to them, "I ask you, is it permitted on *Shabbat* to do good or to do evil, to save or to destroy a life?" [10]Then looking around at everyone, He said to the man, "Stretch out your hand." The man did, and his hand was restored. [11]But they were filled with fury and discussed among themselves what they might do to *Yeshua*.

Appointing the Twelve

[12]And it was during these days that *Yeshua* went out to the mountain to pray, and He spent all night in prayer to God. [13]When day came, He called His disciples, choosing from among them twelve whom He also named *shlichim*—[14]Simon, whom He also named Peter, and Andrew his brother; and Jacob and John; and Philip and Bartholomew; [15]and Matthew and Thomas; Jacob the son of Alphaeus; Simon who was called the Zealot; [16]Judah the son of Jacob; and Judah from Kriot, who became a traitor.

a 6:3-4. cf. 1 Sam. 21:2-7(1-6).

The Sermon on the Plain

17Then *Yeshua* came down with them and stood on a level place. A large crowd of His disciples and a multitude of people, from all Judea, Jerusalem, and the coastal region of Tyre and Sidon, 18had come to hear Him and to be healed of their diseases. Even those disturbed by defiling spirits were being healed. 19Everyone in the crowd was trying to touch Him, because power flowed from Him and He was healing them all.

20And looking up at His disciples, He said,

"Blessed are you who are poor,
for yours is the kingdom of God.
21Blessed are you who hunger now,
for you shall be satisfied.
Blessed are you who weep now,
for you shall laugh.
22Blessed are you when people hate you,
and when they exclude you, and revile you,
and spurn your name as evil on account of the Son of Man.

23Rejoice in that day and jump for joy! For behold, your reward is great in heaven! For their fathers used to treat the prophets the same way."[a]

24But woe to you who are rich,
for you are receiving your comfort in full.
25Woe to you who are full,
for you shall be hungry.
Woe to you who are laughing now,
for you shall mourn and weep.
26Woe to you when all men
speak well of you,
for their fathers used to treat the
false prophets the same way."[b]

27"But I say to you who are listening: Love your enemies, do good to those who hate you, 28bless those who curse you, pray for the ones who mistreat you. 29To the one who strikes you on the cheek, offer the other also. And from the one who takes your cloak, do not hold back your shirt. 30Give to every one who asks you; and whoever takes something of yours, make no demands upon him.

31"Do to others as you would have them do to you. 32If you love those who love you, what credit is that to you? For even sinners love those who love them. 33And if you do good to those who are doing good to you, what credit is that to you? Even sinners do this. 34And if you lend to those from whom you expect to take, what credit is that to you? Even sinners lend to sinners in order to receive back the same.

35"But love your enemies, and do good, and lend, expecting nothing in return.[c] Then your reward will be great and you will be sons of *Elyon*, for He is kind to the ungrateful and evil ones. 36Be compassionate, just as your Father is compassionate to you."

37Do not judge, and you will not be judged. Do not condemn, and you will not be condemned. Pardon, and you will be pardoned. 38Give, and it will be given to you—a good measure, pressed down, shaken together, overflowing, will be given into your lap. For whatever measure you measure out will be measured back to you."

39He also spoke this parable to them: "The blind cannot show the way to the blind, can he? Won't they both fall into a pit? 40A disciple is not above his teacher, but everyone who is fully trained will be like his teacher.

41"Why do you look at the speck in your brother's eye, but do not notice the beam in your own eye? 42How can you say to your brother, 'Brother, let me take out the speck in your eye,' when you yourself do not see the beam in your own eye? You hypocrite! First take the beam out

a 6:23. cf. Neh. 9:26.
b 6:26. cf. Jer. 5:11-13.
c 6:35. cf. Prov. 19:17.

of your own eye, and then you will see
clearly the speck in your brother's eye, to
take it out."

43"For there is no good tree that produces rotten fruit, nor again does a
rotten tree produce good fruit. 44Each
tree comes to be known by its own fruit.
For figs are not gleaned out of briars;
neither are bunches of grapes gathered
from thorn bushes.

45"Out of the good treasure of his
heart the good man brings forth good,
and out of evil the evil man brings forth
evil. For from the overflow of the heart
his mouth speaks."

46"Why do you call Me 'Master, Master' and do not do what I say? 47Everyone
who comes to Me and hears My words
and does them, I will show you what he
is like. 48He is like a man building a house,
who dug deep and laid a foundation on
the rock. And when a flood came, the torrent burst against that house but could
not shake it, because it had been well
built.

49"But the one who hears yet does not
do is like a man who built a house upon
land without a foundation. When the
torrent burst against it, immediately it
collapsed—and the destruction of that
house was great!"

7

A Centurion's Faith at Capernaum

1When *Yeshua* finished all His *drash* in
the hearing of the people, He entered
Capernaum. 2Now a certain centurion
had a valued slave, who was ill and about
to die. 3When he heard about *Yeshua*, he
sent Jewish elders to Him, asking Him
to come and save his slave. 4When they
came to *Yeshua*, they begged Him earnestly, saying, "He is worthy for You to
grant this, 5for he loves our people and
even built our synagogue."

6Now *Yeshua* started to go with them;
and when He wasn't far from the house,
the centurion sent friends to say to Him,
"Master, do not trouble Yourself, for I'm
not worthy for You to come under my
roof. 7That is why I didn't consider myself
worthy to come to You. But say the word
and let my servant be healed. 8For I also
am a man under authority, with soldiers
under me. I say to this one, 'Go!' and he
goes; and to another, 'Come!' and he
comes; and to my servant, 'Do this!' and
he does it."

9Now when *Yeshua* heard this, He was
amazed at him. Turning to the crowd
following Him, He said, "I tell you, not
even in Israel have I found such great
faith." 10When those who had been sent
returned to the house, they found the
slave in good health.

An Amazing Report Spreads throughout all Judea

11The next day *Yeshua* traveled to a
town called Nain, and coming along with
Him were His disciples and a large crowd.
12Just as He came near the town gate,
behold, a dead man was being carried
out, the only son of his mother, a widow.
A considerable crowd from the town was
with her.

13When the Lord saw her, He felt
compassion for her and said, "Don't
cry." 14Then He came up and touched
the coffin, and the pallbearers came to
a standstill. He said, "Young man! I tell
you, get up!" 15The dead man sat up and
began speaking, and *Yeshua* gave him to
his mother.[a]

16Fear took hold of them all, and they
glorified God, saying, "A great prophet
has appeared among us, and God has visited His people." 17This report concerning
Him spread throughout all Judea and the
surrounding region.

a 7:15. 1 Kings 17:23.

John Seeks Confirmation from Prison

[18]John's disciples reported to him
about all these things. Calling two of his
disciples, [19]John sent them to the Lord,
saying, "Are you the One who is to come,
or should we look for another?"

[20]When they appeared before Him, the
men said, "John the Immerser sent us to
you, saying, 'Are you the One who is to
come, or shall we look for another?'"

[21]At this very hour He was healing
many of diseases, sicknesses, and evil
spirits; and He granted sight to many who
were blind. [22]And answering, He said to
them, "Go report to John what you saw
and heard: the blind see, the lame walk,
those with *tzara'at* are cleansed, the deaf
hear, the dead are raised, and the poor
have good news proclaimed to them.[a]
[23]Blessed is he who is not led to stumble
because of Me."

[24]And after John's messengers left,
He began to speak about John to the
crowds. "What did you go out to the
wilderness to see? A reed shaken by
the wind? [25]No? So what did you go out
to see? A man dressed in fine garments?
Look, those who wear finery and live in
luxury are in the palaces of kings! [26]Then
what did you go out to see? A prophet?
Yes, I tell you, even more than a prophet.
[27]This is the one about whom it is written,

'Behold, I send My messenger
before You,
who will prepare Your way before
You.'[b]

[28]I say to you, there is no one greater
than John among those born of women;
yet the least in the kingdom of God is
greater than he."

[29]And when all the people heard,
even the tax collectors, they affirmed
God's justice, because they had been
immersed with John's immersion. [30]But
the Pharisees and *Torah* lawyers, not
having been immersed by John, declared
God's purpose invalid for themselves.

[31]"So then, to what shall I compare the
people of this generation? What are they
like? [32]They are like children sitting in the
marketplace and calling to each other,
saying,

'We played the flute for
you,
and you didn't dance.
We sang a dirge,
and you didn't weep.'

[33]"For John the Immerser has come
not eating bread nor drinking wine, and
you say, 'He has a demon.' [34]The Son of
Man has come eating and drinking. and
you say, 'Look, a glutton and a drunkard,
a friend of tax collectors and sinners!'
[35]Yet wisdom is vindicated by all her
children."

An Unwelcome Woman Finds Favor

[36]Now one of the Pharisees was asking *Yeshua* if He would eat with him.
Upon entering the Pharisee's home, He
reclined at the table. [37]And behold, a
woman in the town who was a sinner,
when she discovered that *Yeshua* was
reclining at the Pharisee's home, brought
an alabaster jar of perfume. [38]As she
stood behind Him at His feet, weeping,
she began to drench His feet with tears
and kept wiping them with her head of
hair. Then she was kissing His feet and
anointing them with perfume.

[39]Now when the Pharisee who invited
Him saw this, he said to himself, "If this
were a prophet, He would know what
sort of woman is touching Him—that
she's a sinner."

[40]And answering, *Yeshua* said to him,
"Simon, I have something to say to you."

And he said, "Say it, Teacher!"

a 7:22. Isa. 35:5-6; 61:1-2a.
b 7:27. Mal. 3:1.

41"A moneylender had two debtors. One owed him five hundred denarii,[a] but the other fifty. 42When neither could repay him, he canceled both debts. So which of them will love him more?"

43Simon replied, "I suppose the one who had the bigger debt canceled."

"You have judged correctly," *Yeshua* said. 44Turning toward the woman, He said to Simon, "Do you see this woman? I entered into your house, and you didn't give Me water for My feet. But she has drenched My feet with tears and wiped them with her hair.[b] 45You didn't greet Me with a kiss; but from the time she entered, she has not stopped kissing My feet. 46You didn't anoint My head with oil, but she has anointed My feet with perfume. 47For this reason I tell you, her sins, which are many, have been forgiven—for she loved much. But the one who is forgiven little, loves little. 48He then said to her, "Your sins have been forgiven."

49But those who were reclining at table with Him began to say to one another, "Who is this, who even forgives sins?"

50Then He said to the woman, "Your faith has saved you. Go in *shalom*."

8

Sowing Good News from Town to Town

1Soon afterward, *Yeshua* began traveling throughout towns and villages, preaching and proclaiming the Good News of the Kingdom of God. The twelve were also with Him. 2And certain women who had been healed of evil spirits and infirmities — Miriam, the one called Magdalene, out of whom seven demons had gone; 3Joanna, the wife of Kuza, Herod's finance minister; Susanna; and many others—were supporting them out of their own resources.

4And when a large crowd was gathering and those from various towns were traveling to Him, He spoke by means of a parable. 5"The sower went out to spread his seed. As he sowed, some fell beside the road and was trampled; and the birds of the air ate it up. 6And other seed fell on rock; when it came up, that seed withered away because it had no moisture. 7Other seed fell among the thorns, and the thorns grew up with it and choked it. 8And other seed fell into the good soil; and when it came up, it produced fruit a hundredfold." While saying these things, He would call out, "He who has ears to hear, let him hear."

9Now His disciples were asking Him what this parable meant. 10Then *Yeshua* said to them, "To you has been given to know the secrets of the kingdom of God; but to the others it is given in parables,[c] in order that

'Seeing, they may
  not see,
and hearing, they may
  not understand.'[d]

11"Now the parable is this: the seed is the word of God. 12Those beside the road are the ones who have heard; then the devil comes and takes away the word from their heart, so that they may not believe and be saved. 13But those on the rocky places are the ones who, when they hear, accept the word with joy. But these have no root; they believe for a season, and in a time of testing fall away. 14Now that which fell into the thorns are those who were hearing; but as they go along the way, they are choked by the cares and riches and pleasures of life, and they do not bear mature fruit. 15But the seed in the good soil are those with a praiseworthy and good heart, who have

a 7:41. 1 denarius = 1 day's wage.
b 7:44. cf. Gen. 18:4-8.

c 8:10. cf. Prov. 1:6.
d 8:10. cf. Isa. 6:9; Ezek. 17:2.

heard the word and hold it fast and bear fruit with patient endurance.

16"Now no one after lighting a lamp covers it with some object or places it under a bed. But he puts it on a lampstand so that all those who enter may be able to see the light. 17For nothing is hidden that will not become evident, nor secret that shall not be known and come into open view. 18So pay attention how you listen. For whoever has, to him more will be given. And whoever does not have, even what he supposes he has will be taken away from him."

19*Yeshua*'s mother and brothers came to Him, but were not able to reach Him through the crowd. 20Now it was reported to Him, "Your mother and Your brothers are standing outside, wanting to see You."

21But answering, He said to them, "My mother and My brothers are these who are hearing the word of God and doing it."

Crossing a Stormy Sea

22Now on one of those days *Yeshua* and His disciples got into a boat, and He said to them, "Let's move to the other side of the lake." So they set out. 23Then as they were sailing, He fell asleep. A violent windstorm came down on the lake, and they were swamped with water and in danger.

24They came to *Yeshua* and woke Him, saying, "Master, Master, we're perishing!" He got up and rebuked the wind and the surging wave of water. Then they stopped, and it became calm.[a]

25Then *Yeshua* said to them, "Where is your faith?" But they were afraid and marveled, saying to one another, "Who then is this? He commands even the winds and the water, and they obey Him!"

Not Welcome in the Gerasenes

26They sailed over to the country of the Gerasenes, which is on the opposite side of the Galilee. 27A demon-plagued man from the town met *Yeshua* as He was coming out onto the land. The man hadn't worn any clothing for a long time and was living not in a house but in the tombs.

28Seeing *Yeshua*, he cried out and fell down before *Yeshua*, and with a loud voice said, "What's between You and me, *Yeshua*, *Ben El Elyon*? I'm begging You, do not torment me!" 29For *Yeshua* commanded the defiling spirit to come out of the man. For many times it had seized him so that, even though he was restrained and bound with chains and shackles, he would break the chains and be driven by the demons into the desert.

30*Yeshua* questioned him, "What is your name?"

"Legion," he said, for many demons had entered him. 31They kept begging Him not to command them to depart into the abyss.[b] 32Now a large herd of pigs was feeding on the mountain. The demons urged *Yeshua* to let them enter these pigs, and He gave them permission. 33Then the demons came out of the man and entered into the pigs. The herd rushed down the cliff into the lake and was drowned. 34But when the herdsmen saw what happened, they ran away and reported it in the town and countryside.

35People went out to see what had happened. They came to *Yeshua* and found the man from whom the demons had gone—clothed and in his right mind, sitting at the feet of *Yeshua*. And they were frightened. 36Now those who had seen it reported how the demon-plagued man had been restored. 37And all the people from the region surrounding the Gerasenes asked *Yeshua* to go away from them because they were overcome by great fear. So He got into a boat and returned.

38The man from whom the demons had gone out begged to go with *Yeshua*. But *Yeshua* sent him away, saying, 39"Return to your home, and describe all that God

a 8:24. cf. Ps. 65:8(7).

b 8:31. cf. Rev. 9:1; 20:1-3.

has done for you." So he went away, proclaiming throughout the whole town all that *Yeshua* had done for him.

Interrupted on the Way to a Miracle

40As *Yeshua* returned, the crowd welcomed Him, for they were all expecting Him. 41And here came a man named Jairus, a leader in the synagogue. Falling at *Yeshua*'s feet, he begged Him to come to his house, 42because his only daughter, about twelve years old, was dying. But as He made His way, the masses were crushing in upon Him.

43And there was a woman with a blood flow for twelve years,[a] who could not be healed by anyone. 44She came up from behind and touched the *tzitzit* of *Yeshua's* garment. Immediately, her blood flow stopped. 45*Yeshua* said, "Who touched Me?"

When everyone denied it, Peter said, "Master, the crowds are surrounding You and pressing in!"

46But *Yeshua* said, "Someone touched Me, for I recognized power going out from Me." 47Then seeing that she did not escape notice, the woman came trembling and fell prostrate before Him. In the presence of all the people, she confessed why she had touched Him and how she had been healed immediately. 48He said to her, "Daughter, your faith has made you well. Go in *shalom*."

49While He was still speaking, someone comes from the house of the synagogue leader, saying, "Your daughter has died. Don't bother the Teacher anymore."

50But hearing this, *Yeshua* replied to him, "Do not fear—just keep trusting, and she shall be restored."

51When *Yeshua* came into the house, He didn't let anyone enter with Him except Peter, John, Jacob, and the child's father and mother. 52And everyone was weeping and lamenting her; but He said, "Don't weep, for she didn't die but is sleeping." 53But they were ridiculing Him, knowing she had died.

54But *Yeshua*, took her by the hand and called out, saying, "Child, get up!" 55Her spirit returned, and she arose immediately. *Yeshua* ordered food to be given to her to eat. 56Her parents were utterly astonished, but He ordered them to say nothing of what had happened.

9

Sending Out the Twelve

1Now when *Yeshua* called the twelve together, He gave them power and authority over all the demons and to heal diseases. 2He sent them out to proclaim the kingdom of God and to heal. 3And He said to them, "Take nothing for the journey—no walking stick, no travel bag, no bread, no money, nor even to have two shirts. 4Whatever house you enter, stay there and depart from there. 5And whoever does not receive you, when you leave that town, shake off the dust from your feet as a witness against them." 6So they went out and began traveling throughout the villages, proclaiming the Good News and healing everywhere.

7Now Herod the tetrarch heard all that was happening. He was very confused, because some were saying that John had been raised from the dead, 8but others that Elijah had appeared, and others that some prophet from among the ancients had arisen. 9But Herod said, "I beheaded John, but who is this about whom I hear such things?" And he kept trying to see Him.

A Hungry Crowd in a Desolate Place

10When the *shlichim* returned, they described to *Yeshua* all they had done. Then He took them along and withdrew privately to a city named Bethsaida. 11But

a 8:43. cf. Lev. 15:25; some mss. add *who had spent all her assets on doctors.*

the crowds found out and followed Him. So *Yeshua* welcomed them and began speaking to them about the kingdom of God and curing those in need of healing.

[12]Now the day began to wind down, and the twelve came and said to *Yeshua*, "Send the crowd away, so they might go into the nearby villages and countryside and find food and lodging; for we are in a desolate place here."

[13]But *Yeshua* said to them, "You give them something to eat!"

But they said, "We have no more than five loaves of bread and two fish, unless we go to buy food for all these people."
[14]For there were about five thousand men.

Then *Yeshua* said to His disciples, "Have the people recline in groups of about fifty each."
[15]They did so, and all reclined.
[16]And He took the five loaves and the two fish; and looking up to heaven, He offered the *bracha* and broke them. And He kept giving them to the disciples to set before the crowd.
[17]Then they all ate and were satisfied. And what was left over was picked up, twelve baskets of the fragments.

Secrets Revealed to the Disciples Alone

[18]Once when *Yeshua* was praying alone and His disciples were near, He put a question to them, saying, "Who do the crowds say that I am?"

[19]They replied, "John the Immerser, but others Elijah, and others that some prophet from among the ancients has arisen."

[20]Then He said to them, "But who do you that say I am?"

Then Peter answered and said, "The Messiah of God."

[21]But *Yeshua* warned them, and He ordered them not to tell this to anyone,
[22]saying, "The Son of Man must suffer many things and be rejected by the elders and ruling *kohanim* and *Torah* scholars, and be killed, and on the third day be raised."

[23]Then *Yeshua* was saying to everyone, "If anyone wants to follow Me, he must deny himself, take up his cross every day, and follow Me.
[24]For whoever wants to save his life will lose it, but whoever loses his life for My sake will save it.

[25]"For what does it profit a man if he gains the whole world but loses or forfeits himself?
[26]For whoever is ashamed of Me and My words, the Son of Man will be ashamed of him when He comes in His glory and the glory of the Father and the holy angels.[a]
[27]But I tell you truthfully, there are some standing here who will never taste death until they see the kingdom of God."

Glorified on a Mountain

[28]About eight days after these teachings, *Yeshua* took Peter, John, and Jacob with Him and went up the mountain to pray.
[29]While He was praying, the appearance of His face changed, and His clothing flashed like white lightning.
[30]And behold, two men were talking with Him, Moses and Elijah.
[31]Appearing in glory, they were speaking of *Yeshua*'s departure, which was about to take place in Jerusalem.

[32]Now Peter and those with him were overcome with sleep. But when they awakened, they saw *Yeshua's* glory and the two men standing with Him.
[33]And as they were leaving *Yeshua*, Peter said to Him, "Master, it's good for us to be here. Let's make three *sukkot*: one for You, and one for Moses, and one for Elijah"—not knowing what he was saying.

[34]While he was yet saying these things, a cloud came and overshadowed them; and they were afraid as they entered the cloud.
[35]Then a voice came out of the cloud, saying, "This is My Son, the One I have chosen. Listen to Him!"[b]
[36]And after the voice happened, *Yeshua* was found alone. They kept quiet and told no

a 9:26. cf. Dan. 7:10.
b 9:35. cf. Ps. 2:7; Prov. 30:4; Isa. 9:5(6); Deut. 18:15.

one in those days any of the things they had seen.

Coming Down from the Mountaintop

37On the next day as they came down from the mountain, a large crowd met *Yeshua*. 38Suddenly a man from the crowd shouted out loudly, saying, "Teacher, I'm begging You to look at my son, for he's my only child! 39You see, a spirit takes hold of him, and he immediately screams. It throws him into convulsions with frothing. It hardly ever leaves him—it's crushing him! 40I begged Your disciples to drive it out, but they couldn't."

41Then answering, *Yeshua* said, "O faithless and twisted generation,[a] how long shall I be with you and put up with you? Bring your son here." 42And while the boy was still approaching *Yeshua*, the demon knocked him down to the ground and threw him into convulsions. But *Yeshua* rebuked the unclean spirit, healed the boy, and restored him to his father. 43And all were amazed at the mighty power of God. But as everyone was marveling at all He was doing, He said to His disciples, 44"Put these words into your ears: the Son of Man is about to be delivered into the hands of men." 45But they did not understand this statement; it was yet concealed from them so they could not grasp it. And they were afraid to ask Him about this statement.

46Now a dispute began between the disciples as to who might be the greatest among them. 47But *Yeshua*, knowing the reasoning of their heart, took a child and set him by His side. 48He said to them, "Whoever welcomes this child in My name, welcomes Me. And whoever welcomes Me, welcomes the One who sent Me. The one who is the least among all of you is the one who is great."

49John replied, "Master, we saw someone driving out demons in Your name, and we tried to stop him because he doesn't follow along with us."

50*Yeshua* said to him, "Do not stop him, for he who is not against you is for you."

Samaria Turns *Yeshua* Away

51When the days were approaching for Him to be taken up, *Yeshua* was determined to go up to Jerusalem. 52He sent messengers before Him, and they went and entered a Samaritan village to make His arrangements. 53But they did not receive Him, because He was focused on going up to Jerusalem. 54When His disciples Jacob and John saw this, they said, "Master, do You want us to command fire to come down from heaven and consume them[b]?" 55But *Yeshua* turned and rebuked them.[c]

56Then they moved on to another village. 57As they were traveling on the road, someone said to Him, "I will follow You wherever You go."

58But *Yeshua* said to him, "Foxes have dens and birds of the air have nests, but the Son of Man has nowhere to lay His head." 59He said to another, "Follow Me."

But that one said, "First let me go and bury my father."

60But *Yeshua* said to him, "Let the dead bury their own dead. But you, go and proclaim the kingdom of God."

61Then another also said, "I will follow You, Master, but first let me say goodbye to those in my home."

62But *Yeshua* said to him, "No one who has put his hand to the plow and looked back is fit for the kingdom of God."

10

Yeshua Sends Out the Seventy

1Now after these things, the Lord assigned seventy[d] others and sent them

a 9:41. cf. Deut. 32:5.

b 9:54. Some mss. add *just as Elijah did.*

c 9:55b, 56a. Some mss. add *and said, "You do not know what kind of spirit you have—for the Son of Man did not come to destroy men's lives, but to save."*

d 10:1, 17. Some mss. say *seventy-two.*

out by twos before Him into every town and place where He Himself was about to go. [2]And He was telling them, "The harvest is plentiful, but the workers are few. Therefore, beg the Lord of the harvest to send out workers into His harvest.

[3]"Go forth! Look, I am sending you as lambs in the midst of wolves. [4]Do not be burdened with a money belt, travel bag, or shoes; and do not greet anyone along the way. [5]Whatever home you enter, first say, "*Shalom* be on this home." [6]If a son of *shalom* is there, your *shalom* will rest on him; but if not, it will return to you. [7]And remain in this same home, eating and drinking the things they offer, for the worker is deserving of his wage. Do not keep moving from house to house.

[8]"Whatever town you enter and they welcome you, eat what they set before you. [9]Then heal the sick in that town, and say to them, 'The kingdom of God has come near to you.' [10]But if you enter a town and they do not welcome you, then go out into its streets and say, [11]'Even the dust of your town sticking to our feet, we wipe off as a witness to you. But know this! The kingdom of God has come near.' [12]I tell you, it will be more tolerable for Sodom[a] on that day than for that town.

[13]"Woe to you, Chorazin! Woe to you, Bethsaida! For if the miracles done in you had been done in Tyre and Sidon, they would have turned long ago, sitting in sackcloth and ashes. [14]Yet it will be more bearable for Tyre and Sidon at the Judgment than for you![b] [15]And you, Capernaum? You won't be lifted up to heaven, will you? No, you will go down as far as *Sheol*. [16]The one who listens to you hears Me, and the one who rejects you rejects Me, and the one who rejects Me rejects the One who sent Me."

Returning with a Good Report

[17]Then the seventy returned with joy, saying, "Master, even the demons submit to us in Your name!"

a 10:12. cf. Gen. 19:24-28..
b 10:13-14. cf. Ezek. 26-28.

[18]And *Yeshua* said to them, "I was watching satan fall like lightning from heaven. [19]Behold, I have given you authority to trample upon serpents and scorpions, and over all the power of the enemy; nothing will harm you. [20]Nevertheless, do not rejoice that the spirits submit to you, but rejoice that your names have been written in the heavens."[c]

[21]In that very hour, He was overjoyed in the *Ruach ha-Kodesh* and said, "I praise You, Father, Master of the universe, that You have hidden these things from the wise and discerning and revealed them to infants. Yes, Father, for this way was pleasing to You. [22]All things have been handed over to Me by My Father. No one knows who the Son is except the Father, and who the Father is except the Son and anyone to whom the Son chooses to reveal Him."

[23]Then turning to the disciples, He said privately, "Blessed are the eyes that see what you see! [24]For I tell you, many prophets and kings desired to see what you are seeing yet did not see, and to hear what you are hearing yet did not hear."

Who Is My Neighbor?

[25]Now a certain *Torah* lawyer stood up to entrap *Yeshua*, saying, "Teacher, what should I do to gain eternal life?"

[26]Then *Yeshua* said to him, "What has been written in the *Torah*? How do you read it?"

[27]And he replied, "You shall love *ADONAI* your God with all your heart, and with all your soul, and with all your strength, and with all your mind; and your neighbor as yourself."[d]

[28]*Yeshua* said to him, "You have answered correctly. Do this and you will live."

c 10:20. cf. Exod. 32:32; Dan. 12:1.
d 10:27. cf. Deut. 6:5(6:5 LXX), *v'ahavta et ADONAI*; Lev. 19:18b, *v'ahavta l'reiacha*.

29But wanting to vindicate himself, he said to *Yeshua*, "Then who is my neighbor?"

30*Yeshua* replied, "A certain man was going down from Jerusalem to Jericho. He was attacked by robbers, who stripped him and beat him. Then they left, abandoning him as half dead. 31And by chance, a *kohen* was going down that road; but when he saw the man, he passed by on the opposite side. 32Likewise a Levite also, when he came to the place and saw him, passed by on the opposite side. 33But a Samaritan who was traveling came upon him; and when he noticed the man, he felt compassion. 34He went up to him and bandaged his wounds, pouring on olive oil and wine. Then setting him on his own animal, he brought him to a lodge for travelers and took care of him. 35The next day he took out two denarii[a] and gave them to the innkeeper, saying, 'Take care of him. And whatever else you spend, upon my return I will repay you myself.' 36Which of these three seems to you a neighbor to the one attacked by robbers?"

37And he said, "The one who showed mercy to him."

Then *Yeshua* said to him, "Go, and you do the same."

At Home with Miriam and Martha

38Now while they were traveling, *Yeshua* entered a certain village; and a woman named Martha welcomed Him into her house. 39She had a sister called Miriam, who was seated at the Master's feet, listening to His teaching. 40But Martha was distracted with much serving; so she approached *Yeshua* and said, "Master, doesn't it concern you that my sister has left me to serve alone? Then tell her to help me!"

41But answering her, the Lord said, "Martha, Martha, you are anxious and bothered about many things; 42but only one thing is necessary. For Miriam has chosen the good part, which will not be taken away from her."[b]

11

Praying Along the Way

1Now *Yeshua* was praying in a certain place. When He finished, one of His disciples said to Him, "Master, teach us to pray, just as John taught his disciples."

2Then *Yeshua* said to them, "When you pray, say,

'Father,
sanctified be Your Name,
Your kingdom come.[c]
3Give us each day our daily
bread.
4And forgive us our sins,
for we also forgive
everyone indebted to us.
And lead us not into
temptation."

5Then *Yeshua* said to them, "Which of you has a friend and will go to him in the middle of the night and say to him, 'Friend, lend me three loaves of bread, 6because a friend of mine has come to me on his journey and I have nothing to set before him.' 7Then from within he may answer, saying, 'Don't bother me. The door is already locked, and my children and I are in bed. I can't get up to give you anything.' 8I tell you, even if the friend will not get up and give him anything out of friendship, yet because of the man's persistence he will get up and give him as much as he needs.

9"So I say to you, 'Ask, and it shall be given to you. Seek, and you shall find. Knock, and it shall be opened to you. 10For everyone who asks receives, and the one who seeks finds, and to the one who knocks it will be opened.' 11What

a 10:35. 1 denarius = 1 day's wages

b 10:42. cf. Ps. 27:4.

c 11:2. cf. Matt. 6:9-13.

father, if his son asks for a fish, will give him a snake instead? [12]And if he asks for an egg, will he give him a scorpion? [13]If you then, being evil, know how to give good gifts to your children, how much more will your heavenly Father give the *Ruach ha-Kodesh*[a] to those who ask Him!"

Crowds Demand a Sign from Heaven

[14]Now *Yeshua* was driving out a demon, and it was mute. When the demon had gone out, the mute one spoke and the crowds were amazed. [15]But some among them said, "By beelzebul, the ruler of demons, He drives out demons." [16]Others, testing Him, were demanding from Him a sign from heaven.

[17]But *Yeshua*, knowing their thoughts, said to them, "Every kingdom divided against itself is destroyed, and a house against a house falls. [18]Now if satan is divided against himself, how will his kingdom stand? For you say by beelzebul I drive out the demons. [19]But if by beelzebul I drive out demons, by whom do your sons drive them out? For this reason, they will be your judges. [20]But if by the finger of God[b] I drive out demons, then the kingdom of God has come to you.

[21]"When a strong one, fully-armed, protects his own estate, his possessions are safe. [22]But as soon as someone stronger than he attacks and overpowers him, then he takes away the armor that he had trusted in and divides up his plunder. [23]He who is not with Me is against Me, and he who does not gather with Me scatters.

[24]"When an unclean spirit goes out of a man, it passes through waterless places looking for rest. Not finding any, it says, 'I will return to my house where I came from.' [25]And when it comes, it finds the house swept and put in order. [26]Then it goes and takes along seven other spirits more evil than itself, and they go in and settle there. And that man's last condition becomes worse than the first."

[27]Then as *Yeshua* was saying these things, a certain woman in the crowd, raising her voice, said to Him, "Blessed is the womb that carried You and the breasts that nursed You!"

[28]But He said, "Rather, blessed are those who hear the word of God and obey it."

[29]With the crowds increasing, *Yeshua* began to say, "This generation is a wicked generation. It demands a sign, yet no sign will be given to it except the sign of Jonah. [30]For just as Jonah became a sign to the Ninevites,[c] so also the Son of Man will be to this generation. [31]The Queen of the South will rise up at the Judgment with the men of this generation and condemn them, for she came from the ends of the earth to hear the wisdom of Solomon.[d] And behold, something greater than Solomon is here. [32]The men of Nineveh will rise at the judgment with this generation and will condemn it, because they repented at Jonah's proclamation. And indeed, one greater than Jonah is here.

[33]"No one lighting a lamp puts it in a cellar or under a basket, but on the lampstand so that those entering may see the light. [34]Your eye is the lamp of your body. When your eye is healthy, your whole body is full of light. But when it is sick, your body is full of darkness. [35]Therefore, watch out that the light in you is not darkness. [36]If then your body is full of light, with no part of it dark, it will be as full of light as when a lamp gives you light with its gleam."

Dinner with a Pharisee

[37]As He spoke, a Pharisee asked *Yeshua* to eat with him, so He entered and sat down. [38]But the Pharisee was surprised when he saw that *Yeshua* did not do the ritual handwashing before the meal. [39]But the Lord said to him,

a 11:13. cf. Joel 3:1-5(2:28-32); Zech. 12:10.
b 11:20. cf. Exod. 8:15(19).
c 11:30. cf. Jon. 3:4-5.
d 11:31. cf. 1 Kings 10:1-10.

"You Pharisees clean the outside of the cup and plate, but inside you are full of greed and wickedness. 40Fools! Didn't He who created the outside also create the inside? 41But give as *tzedakah* those things that are within, and indeed everything is pure to you.

42"But woe to you Pharisees, for you tithe the mint, rue, and every garden herb,[a] yet bypass justice and the love of God. It is necessary to do these things without neglecting the others. 43Woe to you Pharisees, for you love the best seats in the synagogues and the greetings in the marketplaces. 44Woe to you, for you are like unmarked tombs, and people walk over them without knowing."

45But answering, one of the *Torah* lawyers says to Him, "Teacher, when You say these things, You insult us too."

46Then *Yeshua* said, "Woe to you *Torah* lawyers as well, for you weigh the people down with burdens hard to carry, yet you yourselves will not touch the burdens with even a finger.

47"Woe to you, for you build the tombs of the prophets whom your own fathers killed! 48So you are witnesses and approve the deeds of your fathers, for indeed they killed them and you are building their tombs.

49"For this reason also the wisdom of God said, 'I will send them prophets and *shlichim*, and some of them they will kill and persecute, 50so that the blood of the prophets shed since the foundation of the world might be required from this generation— 51from the blood of Abel to the blood of Zechariah, the one who perished between the altar and the house of God.[b] Yes, I tell you, it will be required from this generation.'

52"Woe to you, *Torah* lawyers, for you have taken away the key of knowledge. You yourselves did not enter, and you stood in the way of those entering."

53When *Yeshua* left there, the *Torah* scholars and the Pharisees began to be very hostile and to interrogate Him on many issues, 54plotting against Him to catch Him in His words.

12

An Aside with the Disciples

1Meanwhile, when thousands of people had gathered, so many that they were trampling one another, *Yeshua* began speaking first to His disciples, "Be on guard yourselves against the *hametz* of the Pharisees, which is hypocrisy. 2There is nothing covered up that will not be revealed, and nothing hidden that will not be made known. 3Therefore, whatever you have said in the dark will be heard in the light, and what you have spoken in private rooms will be proclaimed from the housetops.

4"I say to you, My friends, "You should not be afraid of those who kill the body, since after this they have nothing more they can do. 5But I will show you whom you should fear. Fear the One who, after the killing, has authority to cast into Gehenna. Yes, I tell you, fear this One!

6"Aren't five sparrows being sold for two pennies?[c] Yet not one of them is forgotten before God. 7Indeed, even the hairs of your head are all numbered. So do not fear; you are more valuable than many sparrows. 8Now I tell you, whoever acknowledges Me before men, the Son of Man also will acknowledge him before the angels of God. 9But the one who denies Me before men will be denied before the angels of God. 10And everyone who speaks a word against the Son of Man will be forgiven, but the one who slanders[d] the *Ruach ha-Kodesh* will not be forgiven. 11And when they bring you to the synagogues, rulers, and authorities, do not worry about how you should defend yourself or what you should say,

a 11:42. cf. Lev. 27:30.

b 11:51. cf. Gen. 4:8; 2 Chr. 24:20-21.

c 12:6. Lit. *assarion*, a small, nearly worthless Roman copper coin.

d 12:10. Lit. *blasphemes*.

12because the *Ruach ha-Kodesh* will teach you at that time what is necessary to say."

A Request from the Crowd

13Then someone from the crowd said to him, "Teacher, tell my brother to divide the inheritance with me."

14But *Yeshua* said to him, "Man, who made Me a judge or arbitrator over you?" 15Then He said to them, "Watch out! Be on guard against all kinds of greed, because one's life does not consist in the abundance of the material goods he possesses."[a] 16And *Yeshua* told them a parable, saying, "The land of a certain rich man produced good crops. 17And he began thinking to himself, saying, 'What shall I do? I don't have a place to store my harvest!' 18And he said, 'Here's what I'll do! I'll tear down my barns and build larger ones, and there I'll store all my grain and my goods. 19And I'll say to myself, "O my soul, you have plenty of goods saved up for many years! So take it easy! Eat, drink, and be merry."' 20But God said to him, 'You fool! Tonight your soul is being demanded back from you! And what you have prepared, whose will that be?'[b] 21So it is with the one who stores up treasure for himself and is not rich in God."

Instructions for the Disciples

22Then *Yeshua* said to His disciples, "So I say to you, do not worry about life, what you will eat; nor about the body, what you will wear. 23For life is more than food and the body more than clothing. 24Consider the ravens. They do not sow or reap, they have no storeroom or barn, yet God feeds them. How much more valuable you are than birds!

25"And which of you by worrying can add a single hour to his life?[c] 26So if you cannot do even something very little, why do you worry about other things? 27Consider the lilies, how they grow. They neither toil nor spin. Yet I tell you that not even Solomon in all his glory was clothed like one of these.[d] 28But if God so clothes the grass in the field—which is here today and thrown into the furnace tomorrow—then how much more will He clothe you, O you of little faith?

29"So do not seek what you will eat and what you will drink, and do not keep worrying. 30For all the nations of the world strive after these things. But your Father knows that you need these things. 31Instead, seek His kingdom, and these things shall be added to you. 32Do not be afraid, little flock, for your Father chose to give you the kingdom.

33"Sell your possessions and do *tzedakah*. Make money pouches for yourselves that do not get old—a treasure in the heavens that never runs out, where no thief approaches and no moth destroys. 34For where your treasure is, there will your heart be also.

35"Have your belt strapped on and lamps burning. 36Be like people waiting for their master to return from a wedding feast, so that when he comes and knocks, they may open to him immediately.

37"Happy are those slaves whose master finds them alert when he comes. Amen, I tell you, he will prepare himself and have them recline at table, and will come and serve them.

38And if he comes in the second or even the third watch[e] and finds them so, they will be happy. 39But understand this, that if the master of the house had known at what hour the thief was coming, he would not have allowed his house to be broken into. 40You also must be ready, for the Son of Man is coming at an hour you don't expect."

41Then Peter said, "Master, are You telling this parable for us, or for everyone?"

42And the Lord said, "Who then is the faithful and wise manager, whom the

a 12:15. cf. Exod. 20:14(17).

b 12:20. cf. Ps. 39:6(5); Job 27:8; Jer. 17:11.

c 12:25. Or *a cubit to his height*; 1 cubit = 1.5 feet.

d 12:27. cf. 1 Ki. 10:4-7.

e 12:38. 2nd watch: 9 pm – 12am; 3rd watch: 12 am – 3 am.

master will put in charge of his servants, to give them their food portion at the proper time? 43Blessed is that servant whose master finds him so doing when he comes. 44Truly I tell you, his master will put him in charge of all his possessions.

45"But if that servant says in his heart, 'My master is taking a long time to come,' and he begins to beat the young slave boys and girls and to eat and drink and get drunk, 46the master of that servant will come on a day when he does not expect him and at an hour he does not know. And he will cut him in two and assign him a place with the unfaithful.

47"That slave who knew his master's will but did not prepare or act according to his desire will be harshly whipped. 48But the one who did not know and did things worthy of a beating will be whipped lightly. From everyone given much, much will be required; and from the one for whom more is provided, all the more they will ask of him.

49"I came to pour out fire on the earth, and how I wish it were already ablaze! 50But I have an immersion to endure,[a] and how distressed I am until it is finished!

51"Do you suppose that I have come to bring *shalom* on earth? No, I tell you, but rather division. 52From now on there will be five in one house in opposition, three against two and two against three. 53They will be divided,

father against son and son against father,
mother against daughter and daughter against mother,
mother-in-law against daughter-in-law and daughter-in-law against mother-in-law."[b]

Lessons for the Crowds

54Then He also was saying to the crowds, "When you see a cloud rising in the west, instantly you say, 'A rainstorm is coming'—and so it is. 55And when a south wind is blowing, you say, 'It will be a scorcher'—and so it is. 56Hypocrites! The surface of the earth and sky you know how to interpret yet you don't know how to interpret this present time? 57Why can't you judge for yourselves what is right? 58For while you are going with your accuser to the authorities, make an effort to come to a settlement with him—so he doesn't drag you before the judge, and the judge hand you over to the officer of the court, and the officer of the court throw you into prison. 59I tell you, you will never get out of there until you have paid back the last little bit."[c]

13

1Now there were some present at the same time who told *Yeshua* about the Galileans whose blood Pilate had mixed with their sacrifices. 2He answered and said to them, "Do you suppose that these Galileans are worse sinners than the rest of the Galileans because they have suffered these things? 3No, I tell you! But unless you repent, you all will perish the same way.

4"Or those eighteen upon whom the tower in Siloam fell and were killed, do you suppose that they are worse sinners than all the people living in Jerusalem? 5No, I tell you! But unless you repent, you all will perish the same way.

6Then *Yeshua* began telling this parable: "A man had a fig tree he had planted in his vineyard, and he came looking for fruit on it and found none. 7So he said to the gardener, 'Indeed, for three years I've come searching for fruit on this fig tree and found none. Remove it! Why does it use up the ground?'

8"But answering, the gardener said to him, 'Master, leave it alone for this year also, until I dig around it and apply fertilizer. 9And if it bears fruit, good. But if not, cut it down.'"

a 12:50. cf. Mk. 10:38.
b 12:53. cf. Mic. 7:6-7(LXX).
c 12:59. Lit. *the last lepton*, a small copper coin of little value.

Teaching by Example at the Synagogue

10 Now *Yeshua* was teaching in one of the synagogues on *Shabbat*. 11 And behold, there was a woman with a disabling spirit for eighteen years, bent over and completely unable to stand up straight. 12 When *Yeshua* saw her, He called out to her and said, "Woman, you are set free from your disability." 13 Then He laid hands on her, and instantly she stood up straight and began praising God.

14 But the synagogue leader, indignant that *Yeshua* had healed on *Shabbat*, started telling the crowd, "There are six days in which work should be done[a]—so come to be healed on those days and not on *Yom Shabbat*!"

15 But the Lord answered him and said, "Hypocrites! On *Shabbat* doesn't each of you untie his ox or donkey from the stall and lead it away to give it drink? 16 So this one, a daughter of Abraham incapacitated by satan for eighteen years, shouldn't she be set free from this imprisonment on *Yom Shabbat*?" 17 When *Yeshua* said these things, all His opponents were put to shame; but the whole crowd was rejoicing at all the glorious things done by Him.[b]

Teaching throughout the Towns and Villages

18 So *Yeshua* was saying, "What is the kingdom of God like? To what shall I compare it? 19 It is like a mustard seed, which a man took and dropped into his own garden. It grew and became a tree, and the birds of the air nested in its branches."[c] 20 Again He said, "To what shall I compare the kingdom of God? 21 It is like *hametz*, which a woman took and hid in three measures of flour, until it was all leavened.

a 13:14. cf. Exod. 20:9; Deut. 5:13.
b 13:17. cf. Ps. 132:18; Isa. 12:5.
c 13:19. cf. Ezek. 17:23.

22 And He continued on His journey through the towns and villages, teaching and making His way to Jerusalem. 23 And someone said to Him, "Master, are only a few being saved?"

Then *Yeshua* said to them, 24 "Make every effort to enter through the narrow door; for many, I tell you, will try to enter and will not be able. 25 Once the Master of the household gets up and shuts the door, and you're standing outside and begin knocking on the door, saying, 'Master, open up for us,' then He will say to you, 'I don't know where you come from.' 26 Then you will start to say, 'We ate and drank in Your company, and You taught in our streets.' 27 But He will say, 'I tell you, I don't know where you come from. Get away from Me, all of you evildoers!'"[d]

28 "There will be weeping and the gnashing of teeth when you see Abraham and Isaac and Jacob and all the prophets in the kingdom of God, but you yourselves thrown out. 29 And they will come from the east and west and from the north and south, and they will recline at table in the kingdom of God. 30 And indeed, some are last who shall be first, and some are first who shall be last."

A Warning to Move On

31 In that hour, some Pharisees came up and said to *Yeshua*, "Get out and leave from here, because Herod wants to kill You!"

32 But *Yeshua* said to them, "Go and tell that fox, 'Indeed, I'm driving out demons and performing healings today and tomorrow, and on the third day I will reach My goal.' 33 But I must keep going today and tomorrow, because it just can't be that a prophet would perish outside Jerusalem.

34 "O Jerusalem, Jerusalem who kills the prophets and stones those sent to her! How often I longed to gather your

d 13:27. cf. Ps. 6:9(8).

children together, as a hen gathers her chicks under her wings, but you were not willing. 35Look, your house is left to you desolate![a] For I tell you, you will never see Me until you say, '*Baruch ha-ba b'shem* ADONAI. Blessed is He who comes in the name of the LORD!'[b]"

14

A Dinner Conversation on *Shabbat*

1Now when *Yeshua* went into the home of one of the leaders of the Pharisees to eat a meal on *Shabbat*, they were watching Him closely. 2And there before Him was a man swollen with fluid. 3So *Yeshua* said to the *Torah* lawyers and the Pharisees, "Is it permitted to heal on *Shabbat*, or not?"

4But they kept silent. So *Yeshua* took hold of him and healed him, and He sent him away. 5Then He said to them, "Which of you, with a son or an ox falling into a well on *Yom Shabbat*, will not immediately pull him out?"[c] 6And they could not reply to these things.

7*Yeshua* began telling a parable to those who had been invited, when He noticed how they were choosing the seats of honor. He said to them, 8"When you are invited by someone to a wedding, don't take the seat of honor, for someone more highly esteemed than you may have been invited by him. 9Then the one who invited both of you will come to you and say, 'Give up this seat.' And with shame, you would proceed to take the lowest seat. 10But when you are invited, go and recline in the lowest seat so that when the one who invited you comes, he may say to you, 'Friend, move up higher.' Then you shall be honored in the presence of all those who are dining with you. 11For everyone who exalts himself will be humbled, and the one who humbles himself will be exalted."[d]

12Then *Yeshua* was also saying to the one who invited Him, "When you host a luncheon or dinner, don't invite your friends or your brothers or your relatives or rich neighbors. Otherwise they might invite you in return as your payback. 13But when you host a banquet, invite the poor, the crippled, the lame, and the blind; 14and you will be blessed, since they cannot repay you. You will be repaid at the resurrection of the righteous."

15Now hearing this, one of those dining with *Yeshua* said to Him, "Blessed is he who eats bread in the kingdom of God."

16But *Yeshua* said to him, "A certain man was hosting a large banquet, and he invited many. 17At the time for the banquet, he sent his slave to tell those who had been invited, 'Come, everything is already prepared.'

18"But every one of them began to beg off. The first said to him, 'I bought a farm, and I'm obligated to go out to see it. I'm asking you to have me excused.' 19Then another one said, 'I've purchased five teams of oxen, and I'm going to check them out. I'm asking you to have me excused.' 20Still another said, 'I've married a wife, so I cannot come.'[e]

21"The slave came and reported these things to his master. Then the master of the house got angry and said to his slave, 'Quickly go out into the squares and alleys of the city and bring here the poor, the maimed, the blind, and the lame.'

22"And the slave said, 'Master, I have done as you instructed, and still there is room.'

23"So the master said to the slave, 'Go out into the thoroughfares and fenced areas, and press them to come in so my home may be filled. 24For I tell you, none

a 13:35. Lit. *your house is left to you*—; cf. Jer. 12:7; 22:5.
b 13:35. Ps. 118:26a.
c 14:5. cf. Exod. 21:33; Deut. 22:4.
d 14:11. cf. Prov. 29:23.
e 14:18-20. cf. Deut. 20:5-7; 24:5.

of those men who were invited will taste my banquet.'"

Telling Parables Along the Road

25Now great crowds were traveling with *Yeshua*; and He turned and said to them, 26"If anyone comes to Me and does not hate his own father, mother, wife, children, brothers, and sisters—and yes, even his own life—he cannot be My disciple. 27Whoever does not carry his own cross and follow Me cannot be My disciple.

28"For which of you, wanting to build a tower, doesn't first sit down and figure out the cost, to see if he has enough to finish it? 29Otherwise, when he has laid a foundation and isn't able to finish everything, all who see it begin to mock him, saying, 'This man began to build and wasn't able to finish!'

31"Or what king, going to make war against another king, won't first sit down to consider whether he is able with ten thousand to confront the one coming against him with twenty thousand?[a] 32If not, while the other is still far away, he sends an ambassador and asks for peace. 33So in the same way, whoever does not renounce all that he has, cannot be My disciple.

34"Therefore, salt is good; but if the salt should lose its flavor, how shall it be made salty again? 35It is not suitable for the soil or for a manure heap—it is thrown out. The one who has ears to hear, let him hear."

15

1Now all the tax collectors and sinners were drawing near to hear *Yeshua*. 2The Pharisees and the *Torah* scholars began to complain, saying, "This man welcomes sinners and eats with them."

a 14:31. cf. Prov. 20:18.

3So He told this parable to them, saying, 4"Which man among you, if he has a hundred sheep and loses one of them, will not leave the ninety-nine in the wilderness and go after the lost one until he finds it? 5When he has found it, he puts it on his shoulders, rejoicing. 6And when he comes home, he calls together his friends and neighbors and says, 'Rejoice with me, for I've found my sheep that was lost!' 7I tell you, in the same way there will be more joy in heaven over one repenting sinner than over the ninety-nine righteous people who have no need of repentance."

8"Or which woman, if she has ten silver coins and loses one coin,[b] does not light a lamp, sweep the house, and search thoroughly until she finds it? 9When she has found it, she calls together her friends and neighbors, saying, 'Rejoice with me, for I've found the coin I had lost!' 10In the same way, I tell you, there is joy in the presence of the angels of God over one sinner who repents."

11Then *Yeshua* said, "A certain man had two sons, 12and the younger of them said to the father, 'Father, give me the share of the property that comes to me.' So he divided his wealth between them.

13"Not many days later, the younger son gathered everything and traveled to a far country, and there he squandered his inheritance on wild living. 14Now when he had spent everything, a severe famine came against that country, and he began to be in need. 15So he went and joined himself to one of the citizens of that country, who sent him into his fields to feed pigs. 16And he was longing to fill up on the carob pods the pigs were eating, but no one was giving him any.

17"But when he came to his senses, he said, 'How many of my father's hired workers have food overflowing, but here I am dying of hunger! 18I'll get up and go to my father, and I'll say to him, 'Father, I

b 15:8-10. Lit. *drachma*, a Greek coin. 1 drachma = 1 denarius = 1 day's wage.

have sinned against heaven and in your
presence. 19I am no longer worthy to be
called your son. Make me like one of your
hired workers.
20"And he got up and went to his own
father. But while he was still far away, his
father saw him and felt compassion. He
ran and fell on his neck and kissed him.
21Then the son said to him, 'Father, I have
sinned against heaven and in your presence. I am no longer worthy to be called
your son.'
22"But the father said to his slaves,
'Quick! Bring out the best robe and put it
on him! Put a ring on his hand and sandals
on his feet. 23Bring the fattened calf and
kill it! Let's celebrate with a feast! 24For
this son of mine was dead and has come
back to life—he was lost and is found!'
Then they began to celebrate.
25"Now his older son was out in the
field. And as he came near the house, he
heard music and dancing. 26And he called
out to one of the servants and began to
ask what these things could be.
27"The servant said to him, 'Your
brother has come, and your father has
killed the fattened calf because he got
him back safe and sound.'
28"But the older son was angry and
didn't want to go in. So his father came
outside and pleaded with him. 29But he
answered and said to his father, 'Look,
so many years I've slaved away for you—
not once did I ignore your order. Yet
you've never given me a young goat so
I could celebrate with my friends. 30But
when this son of yours came—the one
who has squandered your wealth with
prostitutes—for him you killed the fattened calf!"
31"Then the father said to him, 'Son,
you are always with me, and everything
that is mine is yours. 32But it was right
to celebrate and rejoice, because this
brother of yours was dead but has come
back to life! He was lost, but is found.'"

16

A Lesson for the Disciples

1Now *Yeshua* was also saying to the
disciples, "There was a rich man who had
a household manager, and this manager
was accused of squandering his belong-
ings. 2So he called the manager and said
to him, 'What's this I hear about you?
Give an accounting of your management,
because you cannot be manager any
longer.'
3"Then the manager said to himself,
'What shall I do, since my master is taking the management away from me? I'm
not strong enough to dig; I'm ashamed
to beg. 4I know what I'll do, so that when
I'm put out of management others will
welcome me into their homes.' 5So he
called in each one of his master's debtors, and he said to the first, 'How much
do you owe my master?'
6"He said, 'One hundred units of olive
oil.'
"The manager said to him, 'Take your
bill, sit down quickly, and write fifty.'
7Then he said to another, 'Now how
much do you owe?'
"He said, 'A hundred units of wheat.'
"The manager said to him, 'Take your
bill and write eighty.'
8"Now the master praised the crooked
manager because he had acted shrewdly,
for the sons of this age are smarter when
dealing with their own generation than
the sons of light. 9I say to you, make
friends for yourselves from the wealth of
the world, so when it runs out, they will
welcome you into the eternal shelters.
10"One who is faithful in the smallest
matters is also faithful in much, and the
one unjust in the smallest matters will
likewise be unjust in much. 11So then, if
you cannot be trusted with unjust wealth,
who will trust you with true wealth?
12Now if you have not been trustworthy

with what belongs to another, who will give you anything of your own? 13No servant can serve two masters; for either he will hate the one and love the other, or he will stick by one and look down on the other. You cannot serve God and money."[a]

The Pharisees Listen In

14Now the Pharisees, who were lovers of money, were listening to all these things and sneering at *Yeshua*. 15But He said to them, "You are the ones who justify yourselves before the people, but God knows your hearts.[b] For what is prized among men is detestable in God's sight."

16"The *Torah* and the Prophets were proclaimed until John. Since then, the Good News of the kingdom of God is being proclaimed, and everyone tries forcing his way in. 17But it is easier for heaven and earth to pass away than for a single serif[c] of the *Torah* to fail. 18Everyone who divorces his wife and marries another commits adultery. And he who marries one who is divorced from a husband commits adultery.

19"Now there was a rich man dressed in purple and fine linen, living it up in luxury every day. 20But a poor man named Lazarus had been laid at his gate, covered with sores 21and longing to be fed with what fell from the rich man's table. Besides, even the dogs were coming to lick his sores.

22"It happened that the poor man died and was carried by the angels to Abraham's side. Then the rich man also died and was buried. 23And from *Sheol*, as he was in torment, he raised his eyes. And he sees Abraham far off, and Lazarus at his side.[d] 24So he cried out and said, 'Father Abraham, have mercy on me! And send Lazarus so he may dip the tip of his finger in water and cool off my tongue, because I am suffering torment in this flame.'[e]

25"But Abraham said, 'Son, remember that in your life you received your good things, even as Lazarus received the bad things. But now he is comforted here, and you are tormented. 26Besides all this, between us and you a great chasm is firmly set, so that those who want to cross over to you cannot, nor can those from there cross over to us.

27"Then the rich man said, 'I beg you then, Father Abraham, send Lazarus to my father's house! 28For I have five brothers to warn, so that they will not also come to this place of torment.'

29"But Abraham says, 'They have Moses and the Prophets. Let them listen to them.'

30"But he said, 'No, Father Abraham, but if someone from the dead goes to them, they will repent.'

31"But Abraham said, 'If they do not listen to Moses and the Prophets, neither will they be convinced even if someone rises from the dead!'"

17

Back to Teaching His Own

1Then *Yeshua* said to His disciples, "Stumbling blocks are bound to come, but woe to the one by whom they come! 2It would be better for him to have a millstone put around his neck and to be hurled into the sea, than for him to cause one of these little ones to stumble.

3"Keep yourselves alert! If your brother sins, rebuke him; and if he repents, forgive him. 4Even if he sins against you seven times a day, and seven times returns to you, saying, 'I repent,' you shall forgive him."

5Then the *shlichim* said to the Lord, "Increase our faith!"

6Then the Lord said, "If you have faith like a mustard seed, you could say to this

a 16:13. Lit. *mammon*, Aramaic for *wealth, property*; sometimes personified as Mammon.

b 16:15. cf. 1 Sam. 16:7; Prov. 21:2.

c 16:17. Lit. one horn/projection/hook; in Hebrew, one crown/ornament/stroke.

d 16:22-23. Lit. bosom, chest. Note: Gen. 15:15; 47:30

e 16:24. cf. Isa. 66:24.

mulberry tree, 'Be uprooted and planted in the sea,' and it would obey you. 7But if you have a slave who is plowing or tending sheep, who among you will say to him when he comes in from the field, 'Come right in, and recline at table'? 8But won't he instead say to him, 'Prepare something for me to eat! Dress yourself and wait on me while I eat and drink; and afterward, you may eat and drink'? 9He doesn't thank the slave because he did what he was commanded, does he? 10So you too, when you've done everything you are commanded, say, 'We are unworthy slaves. We have done only what we were supposed to do.'"

On the Move through Samaria

11Now while going up to Jerusalem, *Yeshua* was passing between Samaria and the Galilee. 12As He entered a certain village, ten men with *tzara'at* came toward Him. They stood some distance away[a] 13and raised their voices, saying, "*Yeshua*, Master, have mercy on us!"

14When He saw them, He said to them, "Go and show yourselves to the *kohanim*."[b] And as they went, they were cleansed. 15Now one of them, when he saw that he was healed, came back, glorifying God with a loud voice. 16And he fell at *Yeshua*'s feet, facedown, giving Him thanks. And he was a Samaritan.

17Then *Yeshua* answered and said, "Weren't ten cleansed? But where are the nine? 18Weren't any found who came back to give glory to God except this foreigner?" 19Then *Yeshua* said to the man, "Stand up and go! Your faith has made you well."

20Now when *Yeshua* was asked by the Pharisees when the kingdom of God would come, He answered them and said, "The kingdom of God does not come with signs to be seen. 21Nor will they say, 'Look, here!' or 'There!' For behold, the kingdom of God is in your midst."

a 17:12. cf. Lev. 13:45-46.
b 17:14. cf. Lev. 14:1-3ff.

22Then *Yeshua* said to the disciples, "The days will come when you will long to see one of the days of the Son of Man, and you will not see it. 23They will say to you, 'Look, there!' or 'Look, here!' Do not go and chase after them. 24For just as the lightning flashes from one part of the sky and lights up another part, so will the Son of Man be in His day. 25But first He must suffer much and be rejected by this generation. 26As it was in the days of Noah,[c] so will it also be in the days of the Son of Man. 27They were eating, drinking, marrying, and being given in marriage, until the day Noah entered the ark. Then the flood came and destroyed them all.

28"It was just the same in the days of Lot.[d] They were eating, drinking, buying, selling, planting, building. 29But on the day Lot left Sodom, it rained fire and sulfur from heaven and destroyed them all. 30Things will be the same on the day when the Son of Man is made fully known. 31In that day, the one who is on the roof, and his possessions in the house, must not go down to take them away. In the same way, the one who is in the field must not turn back. 32Remember Lot's wife![e] 33Whoever tries to keep his life will lose it; but whoever loses his life will preserve it.

34"I tell you, on that night there will be two in one bed. One will be taken along and the other left. 35There will be two women grinding at the same place. One will be taken and the other left."(36)[f]

37"Where, Lord?" they replied.

And He said to them, "Where there is a corpse, there also will the vultures be gathered."[g]

18

1Then *Yeshua* told them a parable to show that they should always pray and

c 17:26. cf. Gen. 6:11-13.
d 17:28. cf. Gen. 19:24-25.
e 17:32. cf. Gen. 19:26.
f 17:36. Some mss. add: There will be two in the field. One will be taken along, and the other left.
g 17:37. cf. Rev. 19:17-19.

not be discouraged, 2He said, "There
was a judge in a certain city who neither
feared God nor respected people. 3And
there was a widow in that city who kept
coming to him, saying, 'Give me justice
against my opponent.'

4"He was unwilling at the time. But
afterward he said to himself, 'Although
I don't fear God or respect people, 5yet
because this widow keeps bothering me,
I will give her justice so she won't wear
me out by her incessant coming.'"

6Then the Lord said, "Hear what the
unjust judge is saying. 7Won't God do
justice for His chosen ones, who cry out
to Him day and night? Will He be slow to
help them? 8I tell you, He will quickly give
them justice. But when the Son of Man
comes, will He find faith on the earth?"

9Then *Yeshua* spoke this parable to
some who trusted in themselves that
they were righteous, while holding others in contempt. 10"Two men went up to
the Temple to pray, one a Pharisee and
the other a tax collector. 11The Pharisee
stood and was praying this to himself: 'O
God, I thank You that I am not like other
people—thieving, unjust, adulterers, or
even like this tax collector. 12I fast twice a
week and tithe on all that I get.'

13"But the tax collector, standing some
distance away, wouldn't even lift his eyes
toward heaven, but beat his chest, saying, 'God, be merciful to me, the sinner!'[a]
14I tell you, this man, rather than the
other, went down to his home declared
righteous. For everyone who exalts himself will be humbled, but the one who
humbles himself will be exalted."

15Now they were bringing even their
babies to *Yeshua*, so He might touch
them. But when the disciples saw this,
they began rebuking them. 16But *Yeshua*
called for them, saying, "Let the little
children come to Me and do not hinder
them, for the kingdom of God belongs to
such as these. 17Amen, I tell you, whoever
does not receive the kingdom of God like
a little child will never enter it.

18And a religious leader inquired of
Yeshua, saying, "Good Teacher, what
shall I do to inherit eternal life?"

19"Why are you calling Me good?"
Yeshua said to him. "No one is good
except One—that is God. 20You know the
commandments: 'Do not commit adultery, do not murder, do not steal, do not
give false testimony, honor your father
and mother.'[b]"

21The man said, "All these I have kept
since my youth."

22When *Yeshua* heard this, He said to
him, "One thing you still lack. Sell all,
as much as you have, and distribute to
the poor, and you will have treasure in
heaven. Then come, follow Me." 23But
upon hearing these things, he became
deeply distressed, for he was very rich.

24Gazing at him, *Yeshua* said, "How
hard it is for the rich to enter into the
kingdom of God! 25It is easier for a camel
to go through the eye of a needle than
for a rich man to enter the kingdom of
God."

26Then those who heard said, "Then
who can be saved?"

27But *Yeshua* said, "What is impossible
with men is possible with God."[c]

28Then Peter said, "Look, we've left
everything of our own to follow You."

29And *Yeshua* said to them, "Amen,
I tell you, there is no one who has left
house or wife or brothers or parents or
children, for the sake of the kingdom of
God, 30who will not receive many times
as much in this age; and in the *olam ha-ba*,
eternal life."

31Then *Yeshua* took the twelve aside
and said to them, "Look, we're going up
to Jerusalem, and everything written by
the prophets about the Son of Man will
be carried out. 32He will be handed over
to the Gentiles, and He will be mocked
and insulted and spat upon. 33After they
have scourged Him, they will kill Him. Yet
on the third day, He will rise again." 34But
they understood none of these things;

a 18:13. cf. Ezra 9:6.

b 18:20. Exod. 20:12-13(12-16); Deut. 5:16-17(16-20).

c 18:27. cf. Jer. 32:17.

this message was hidden from them, and they did not understand what He was saying.

Approaching Jericho

35Now as *Yeshua* was approaching Jericho, a certain blind man was sitting by the road, begging. 36But when he heard the crowd going by, he asked what was happening. 37They told him that *Yeshua ha-Natzrati* was passing by. 38And he cried out, saying, "*Yeshua, Ben-David*, have mercy on me!"

39And those leading the way were scolding him, so he would be quiet. But he kept shouting all the more, "*Ben-David*, have mercy on me!"

40So *Yeshua* stopped and ordered the blind man to be brought to Him. And when he came near, *Yeshua* asked him, 41"What do you want Me to do for you?"

And he said, "Master, I want to see again!"

42*Yeshua* said to him, "Receive your sight. Your faith has made you well." 43Immediately the man received his sight and began following *Yeshua*, glorifying God. And when all the people saw it, they also gave praise to God.

19

Visiting Zacchaeus in Jericho

1Now *Yeshua* entered Jericho and was passing through. 2And here was a man by the name of Zacchaeus; he was a chief tax collector, and he was rich. 3Zacchaeus was trying to see who *Yeshua* was, but he couldn't because of the crowd, for he was short in height. 4So he ran ahead and climbed up into a sycamore tree to see *Yeshua*, for He was about to pass through that way.

5When *Yeshua* came to the place, He looked up and said to him, "Zacchaeus, hurry and come down, for I must stay at your house today."

6Zacchaeus hurried and came down and welcomed Him joyfully.

7But when everyone saw it, they began to grumble, saying, "*Yeshua* has gone to be the guest of a sinner!"

8But Zacchaeus stood there and said to the Lord. "Look, Master, half of my possessions I give to the poor, and if I have somehow cheated anyone, I repay four times as much!"[a]

9Then *Yeshua* said to him, "Today salvation has come to this home, because he also is a son of Abraham. 10For the Son of Man came to seek and to save the lost."

11As they were listening to this, *Yeshua* went on to tell a parable, because He was near Jerusalem and they supposed that the kingdom of God was about to appear at once. 12Therefore He said, "A certain nobleman went to a faraway land to receive for himself a kingdom and then return. 13And calling ten of his own slaves, he gave them ten minas[b] and said to them, 'Do business until I come back.' 14But his citizens detested him and they sent a delegation after him, saying, 'We don't want this fellow to reign over us!' 15When he returned after receiving the kingdom, he called for those slaves to whom he had given the money. He wanted to know how much business they had done. 16Now the first appeared, saying, 'Master, your one mina has made ten.' 17The master said to him, 'Well done, good slave! Because you were faithful with so little, take charge over ten cities.' 18Also, the second slave came, saying, 'Your mina, Master, made five.' 19Then he also said to this one, 'You are likewise over five cities.' 20But another came, saying, 'Master, here is your mina. I was keeping it safe in a handkerchief, 21for I was afraid of you because you are a strict man. You take what you did not make and reap what you did not sow.' 22He said to him, 'By the words of your own mouth I will judge you, you wicked

a 19:8. cf. Exod. 22:1-3(2-4); 2 Sam. 12:6.

b 19:13, 18, 20, 24, 25. 1 mina = 100 denarii = about four months' wages for an average worker.

slave! You knew that I am strict, taking what I did not make and reaping what I did not sow? 23Then why didn't you put my money in the bank, so that when I came back I could have collected it with interest?' 24Then to the bystanders he said, 'Take the mina from him, and give it to the one who has ten minas.' 25But they said to him, 'Sir, he has ten minas!' 26'I tell you, to everyone who has, more shall be given. But from the one who doesn't have, even what he does have shall be taken away. 27But those hostile to me, who didn't want me to reign over them, bring them here and execute them before me.'"

Riding into Jerusalem

28After saying these things, *Yeshua* was going on ahead, up to Jerusalem. 29When He got near Bethphage and Bethany, at the Mount of Olives,[a] He sent two of the disciples, 30saying, "Go into the village ahead. As you enter, you will find a colt tied up, that no one has ever sat upon. Untie it and bring it. 31And if anyone asks you, 'Why are you untying it?' you shall say, 'The Master needs it.'"

32Those who were headed out found things just as He told them. 33Then as they were untying the colt, his owners said to them, "Why are you untying the colt?"

34They said, "The Master needs it." 35Then they brought it to *Yeshua*, threw their cloaks[b] on the colt, and set *Yeshua* on it.[c] 36And as He went along, the people were spreading their cloaks on the road.[d] 37When *Yeshua* came near the slope of the Mount of Olives, the whole crowd of disciples began to rejoice. They praised God with a loud voice for all the miracles they had seen, 38saying,

"Blessed is the King who
comes in the
name of *ADONAI*![e]
Shalom in heaven and glory in the
highest!"

39Some of the Pharisees from the crowd said to Him, "Teacher, rebuke Your disciples!"

40But answering, *Yeshua* said, "I tell you that if these keep silent, the stones will shout out!"[f]

41As He drew near and saw Jerusalem, He wept over her, 42saying, "If only you had recognized this day the things that lead to *shalom*! But now they are hidden from your eyes. 43For the days will come upon you when your enemies will surround you with barricades and hem you in on all sides.[g] 44And they will smash you to the ground—you and your children within you. And they won't leave within you one stone upon another, because you did not recognize the time of your visitation."

Confrontation at the Temple

45Then *Yeshua* entered the Temple and began to drive out the merchants, 46saying to them, "It is written,

'My house shall be a house of prayer,'[h]
but you have made it a 'den of thieves.'"[i]

47And He was teaching every day in the Temple. The ruling *kohanim* and the *Torah* scholars, even the leaders of the people, were trying to destroy Him; 48but they could not find any way to do it, because all the people were hanging on His words.

20

1On one of the days while *Yeshua* was teaching the people in the Temple and proclaiming the Good News, the

a 19:29. Lit. *the mountain called "of Olives."*
b 19:35. Lit. *garments, clothing.*
c 19:35. cf. Zech. 9:9.
d 19:36. cf. 2 Kings 9:13.
e 19:38. cf. Ps. 118:26a.
f 19:40. cf. Hab. 2:11.
g 19:43. cf. Isa. 29:3.
h 19:46. Isa. 56:7.
i 19:46. Jer. 7:11.

ruling *kohanim* and the *Torah* scholars, together with the elders, confronted Him. 2And they spoke, saying to Him, "Tell us by what authority are You doing these things? Or who is the one who gave You this authority?"

3But answering, *Yeshua* said to them, "I also will ask you a question, and you tell Me: 4the immersion of John—was it from heaven or from men?"

5They reasoned among themselves, saying, "If we say, 'From heaven,' He will say, 'Why didn't you believe him?' 6But if we say, 'From men,' then all the people will stone us, because they are convinced that John is a prophet." 7So they answered that they didn't know where it came from.

8And *Yeshua* said to them, "Neither will I tell you by what authority I do these things."

9Then He began to tell the people this parable: "A man planted a vineyard,[a] leased it to tenant farmers, and went on a journey for a long time. 10And at the season, he sent a servant to the tenants so that they would give him part of the vineyard's fruit. But the tenants beat him up and sent him away empty-handed. 11So he proceeded to send another servant. They beat him too and treated him shamefully, and they sent him away empty-handed. 12And he proceeded to send a third one. They wounded this one too, and they threw him out.

13"Now the master of the vineyard said, 'What shall I do? I will send my son, whom I love. Probably they will show him respect.' 14But when the tenants saw him, they discussed the matter among themselves, saying, 'This is the heir! Let's kill him so the inheritance will be ours.' 15So they threw him out of the vineyard and killed him. What then will the master of the vineyard do to them? 16He will come and destroy those tenants and give the vineyard to others."

But when they heard this, they said, "May it never happen!"

a 20:9. cf. Isa. 5:1-7.

17Then *Yeshua* looked right at them and said, "Then what is this that has been written,

'The stone which the builders
rejected,
this has become the chief
cornerstone'?[b]

18Everyone who falls on that stone will be shattered; but the one upon whom it falls, it will crush him."[c]

19The *Torah* scholars and the ruling *kohanim* tried to grab Him that very hour, because they realized that He spoke this parable against them—but they feared the people.

Silencing the Opposition

20Now they watched Him and sent spies who pretended to be righteous, in order to trap Him in His words so they could hand Him over to the power and authority of the governor. 21And they asked Him, saying, "Teacher, we know that You tell it straight and You teach it straight. You show no partiality, but teach the way of God according to the truth. 22Is it permitted for us to pay taxes to Caesar, or not?"

23But carefully considering their treachery, *Yeshua* said to them, 24"Show me a denarius.[d] Whose image and inscription does it have?"

And they said, "Caesar's."

25Then He said to them, "Well then, give to Caesar the things that are Caesar's, and to God the things that are God's." 26And they could not trap Him in His words in the presence of the people. Astonished by His answer, they kept silent.

27Then some of the Sadducees (who deny there is a resurrection) came and questioned *Yeshua*. 28"Teacher," they said, "Moses wrote for us that 'if a man's brother dies' having a wife 'but

b 20:17. Ps. 118:22 (117:22 LXX).
c 20:18. cf. Isa. 8:14-15; 28:16; Dan. 2:34, 44-45.
d 20:24. A Roman coin.

no children, then his brother should
take the widow and father children for
his brother.'[a] 29Now there were seven
brothers, and the first took a wife and
died childless; 30and the second 31and the
third took her, but in this same way, each
of the seven brothers died and left no
children. 32Finally the woman died too.
33So in the resurrection, whose wife is
she? For all seven had married her."

34*Yeshua* said to them, "The sons of
this age marry and are given in marriage.
35But those considered worthy to reach
the *olam ha-ba* and the resurrection of
the dead neither marry nor are given in
marriage. 36For they can no longer die,
because they are like angels and are sons
of God, being sons of the resurrection.
37But at the burning bush even Moses
revealed that the dead are raised, when
he calls *ADONAI* 'the God of Abraham, and
the God of Isaac, and the God of Jacob.'[b]
38Now He is God not of the dead but of
the living, for to Him they all are living."

39Some of the *Torah* scholars replied,
"Teacher, You have said it well." 40For
they no longer dared to question Him
about anything.

41Then *Yeshua* said to them, "How can
they say that the Messiah is *Ben-David*?
42For David himself says in the Book of
Psalms,

'*ADONAI* said to my Lord,
"Sit at My right hand,
43until I make Your enemies a footstool
for Your feet."'[c]

44David then calls Him 'Lord'; so how is
He his son?"

45Then with all the people listening,
Yeshua said to the disciples, 46"Beware
of the *Torah* scholars, who like to walk
around in long robes. They love greetings in the marketplaces, the best seats
in the synagogues, and places of honor
at feasts. 47They devour widows' houses
and make long prayers as a show. These
men will receive greater condemnation!"

21

Teaching in the Temple

1Then *Yeshua* looked up and saw the
rich dropping their gifts into the treasury
box. 2He also saw a poor widow dropping in two small copper coins.[d] 3And He
said, "Truly I say to you, this poor widow
has put in more than all the rest. 4For all
these put in their gifts from their surplus.
But she, out of her poverty, put in all she
had to live on."

5And while some were talking about
the Temple, how it was decorated with
beautiful stones and offerings, *Yeshua*
said, 6"As for these things you are looking at, the days will come when not one
stone will be left upon another. Every
one will be torn down!"

7And they questioned Him, saying,
"Teacher, so when will these things happen? What will be the sign that these
things are about to take place?"

8And He said, "Watch out that you are
not led astray! For many will come in My
name, saying, 'I am He' and 'The time is
near!' Do not follow them. 9And when
you hear of wars and chaos, do not be
terrorized. For these things need to happen first, but the end will not come at
once."

10Then He continued telling them,
"Nation will rise up against nation, and
kingdom against kingdom. 11There will
be great earthquakes along with famines and epidemics in various places, and
there will be terrors along with great
signs from heaven. 12But before all these
things, they will grab you and persecute
you, handing you over to the synagogues
and prisons, and leading you away to
kings and governors on account of My
name. 13This will lead you to be a witness.

a 20:28. Deut. 25:5.
b 20:37. cf. Exod. 3:4-6.
c 20:42b-43. Ps. 110:1(109:1 LXX).

d 21:2. Lit. *lepta*, the smallest coins, almost worthless in value.

14So make up your minds not to prepare ahead of time to defend yourselves—15for I Myself will give you speech and wisdom that none of your opponents will be able to resist or refute. 16But you will be handed over even by parents, brothers, relatives, and friends—and they will put some of you to death. 17And you will be hated by all because of My name. 18Yet not a hair of your head will be lost. 19By your endurance, you will gain your souls.

20"But when you see Jerusalem surrounded by armies, then recognize that her desolation is near. 21Then those in Judea must flee to the mountains, and those inside the city must get out, and those in the countryside must not enter her. 22For these are the days of punishment, to fulfill all that has been written.[a]

23"Woe to those who are pregnant and to those who are nursing babies in those days! For there will be great distress in the land and wrath on this people. 24They will fall by the edge of the sword and be led away captive into all the nations. Jerusalem will be trampled by the Gentiles until the times of the Gentiles are fulfilled.[b]

25"There will be signs in the sun and moon and stars. And upon the earth nations will be confused by the roaring of the sea and its waves.[c] 26People will lose heart from fear and anticipation of what is overtaking the earth, for the powers of the heavens will be shaken.[d] 27And then they will see the Son of Man coming in a cloud with power and great glory.[e] 28Now when these things begin to happen, stand straight and lift up your heads, because your salvation is near!"

29Then *Yeshua* told them a parable: "Look at the fig tree and all the trees. 30As soon as they sprout their leaves, you see it and you know at once that summer is near. 31So also, when you see these all these things happening, know that the kingdom of God is near. 32Amen, I tell you, this generation will not pass away until all these things happen. 33Heaven and earth will pass away, but My words will never pass away.[f]

34"But watch out so your hearts are not weighed down by carousing, strong drink, and the worries of life. Do not let that day come upon you suddenly like a trap. 35For it will come rushing upon all who live on the face of the whole earth. 36But stay alert at all times, praying that you may have the strength to escape all these things about to happen, and to stand before the Son of Man."

37So during the days *Yeshua* was teaching in the Temple, but in the nights He went out and stayed on the Mount of Olives.[g] 38And all the people would come early in the morning to hear Him in the Temple.

22

The Day before *Pesach*

1Now the Feast of *Matzah*, which is called Passover, was approaching. 2The ruling *kohanim* and *Torah* scholars were searching for a way to do away with *Yeshua*, for they were afraid of the people.

3Then satan entered into Judah, the one from Kriot, one of the twelve. 4And he went away and talked with the ruling *kohanim* and officers of the Temple guard about how he might deliver *Yeshua* over to them. 5They were delighted and agreed to give him money. 6So he agreed and began looking for a chance to hand *Yeshua* over to them without a crowd.

7Then came the day of *matzah* when the Passover lamb had to be sacrificed. 8Now *Yeshua* sent Peter and John, saying, "Go and prepare the Passover for us, so we may eat."

a 21:22. cf. Hos. 9:7; Dan. 9:24-27.
b 21:24. cf. Dan. 8:13-14; Rom. 11:25.
c 21:25. cf. Joel 3:3-4(2:30-31); Isa. 17:12.
d 21:26. cf. Isa. 34:4 (LXX); Hag. 2:6.
e 21:27. cf. Dan. 7:13-14.

f 21:33. cf. Isa. 40:8; 55:9-11.
g 21:37. cf. Lit. *the mountain called "of Olives."*

[9]Then they said to Him, "Where do You
want us to prepare?"
[10]And He said to them, "Behold, when
you have entered the city, a man carrying
a jar of water will meet you. Follow him
into the house that he enters. [11]And say
to the owner of the house, 'The Teacher
says to you, "Where is the guest room
where I may eat the Passover with My
disciples?"' [12]And with that, he will show
you a large upper room, fully furnished.
Make preparations there." [13]So they left
and found just what *Yeshua* had told
them, and they prepared the Passover.

The *Seder* in the Upper Room

[14]When the hour came, *Yeshua* reclined
at table, and the *shlichim* with Him. [15]And
He said to them, "I have eagerly desired
to eat this Passover with you before I suffer. [16]For I tell you, I will never it eat again
until it is fulfilled in the kingdom of God."
[17]And when He had taken a cup and
offered the *bracha*, He said, "Take this
and share it among yourselves. [18]For I tell
you that I will never drink of the fruit of
the vine from now on, until the kingdom
of God comes."
[19]And when He had taken *matzah*[a] and
offered the *bracha*, He broke it and gave
it to them, saying, "This is My body, given
for you. Do this in memory of Me." [20]In
the same way, He took the cup after the
meal, saying, "This cup is the new covenant in My blood, which is poured out
for you.[b] [21]But look, the hand of the one
betraying Me is with Mine on the table.[c]
[22]For indeed, the Son of Man is going as
has been predetermined; but woe to that
man by whom He is betrayed!"
[23]So they began to discuss among
themselves which of them it might be
who would do this thing. [24]But there was
also a quarrel among them about which
of them is considered the greatest. [25]And
Yeshua said to them, "The kings of the
nations have mastery over them, and
those exercising authority over them
are called 'benefactors.' [26]But with you,
it is not so. Rather, let the one who is
greatest among you become like the
youngest, and the one who leads like the
one who serves. [27]For who is greater, the
one who reclines or the one who serves?
Is it not the one who reclines? But I am
among you as one who serves.
[28]"You are the ones who have
remained with Me in My times of testing.
[29]And just as My Father has granted Me a
kingdom, so I grant to you [30]that you may
eat and drink at My table in My kingdom,
and you shall sit upon thrones judging
the twelve tribes of Israel.
[31]"Simon, Simon! Indeed, satan has
demanded to sift you all like wheat. [32]But
I have prayed for you, Simon, that your
faith will not fail. And when you have
turned back, strengthen your brothers."
[33]But Simon said to Him, "Master, I am
ready to go with You even to prison and
to death!"
[34]But *Yeshua* said, "I tell you, Peter, a
rooster will not crow today until you have
denied three times that you know Me."
[35]And He said to them, "When I sent
you out without a money pouch and
travel bag and sandals, you didn't lack
anything, did you?"

They said, "No, nothing."

[36]Then He said to them, "But now,
whoever has a money pouch must carry it
as well as a travel bag. And whoever does
not own a sword must sell his cloak and
buy one. [37]For I tell you that this which is
written must be fulfilled in Me: 'And he
was counted with the lawless.'[d] For what
is written about Me is being fulfilled."
[38]But they said, "Master, look here!
Two swords!"

And He said to them, "It is enough."

Yeshua Prays at the Mount of Olives

[39]And *Yeshua* came out and went
as usual to the Mount of Olives, and

a 22:19. Lit. *bread* (at Passover, unleavened bread).
b 22:20. cf. Exod. 24:8; Jer. 31:31-34.
c 22:21. cf. Ps. 41:10(9).
d 22:37. Isa. 53:12.

the disciples followed Him. [40]When he reached the place, He said to them, "Pray that you will not enter into temptation." [41]And He pulled back about a stone's throw from them, got on His knees, and began to pray, [42]saying, "Father, if You are willing, take this cup from Me; yet not My will, but Yours be done."

[43]Now an angel from heaven appeared to Him and strengthened Him. [44]And in His anguish, He was praying fervently; and His sweat was like drops of blood falling down on the ground. [45]When He rose up from prayer, He came to the disciples and found them asleep, exhausted from grief. [46]And He said to them, "Why are you sleeping? Get up and pray, so that you won't enter into temptation."

Betrayed!

[47]While *Yeshua* was speaking, suddenly a crowd came, and the one called Judah, one of the Twelve, approached *Yeshua* to kiss Him. [48]But *Yeshua* said to him, "Judah, with a kiss you betray the Son of Man?"[a]

[49]When those around Him saw what was going to happen, they said to Him, "Master, shall we strike with the sword?" [50]And one of them struck the servant of the *kohen gadol* and cut off his right ear.

[51]But *Yeshua* answered and said, "Stop this now!" And He touched the man's ear and healed him.

[52]Then *Yeshua* said to the ruling *kohanim*, officers of the Temple guard, and the elders who had come against Him,, "Have you come out with swords and clubs as you would against a revolutionary? [53]Every day I was with you in the Temple, yet you did not lay a finger on Me. But this is yours—the hour and the power of darkness." [54]Then they seized *Yeshua* and led Him away and brought Him into the house of the *kohen gadol*. But Peter was following from a distance.

a 22:47. cf. Ps. 55:12-13, 20.

Denied Three Times

[55]Now they had lit a fire in the center of the courtyard and sat down together, and Peter was sitting among them. [56]Then a servant girl saw him sitting at the fire. She looked straight at him and said, "This one was with Him too!"

[57]But he denied it, saying, "Woman, I don't know Him!"

[58]A little later, another saw him and said, "You too are one of them."

But Peter said, "Man, I am not!"

[59]And about an hour later, another began to insist, saying, "Certainly this fellow was with Him, for he too is a Galilean!"

[60]But Peter said, "Man, I don't know what you're talking about!" And immediately, while he was still speaking, a rooster crowed. [61]And the Lord turned and looked straight at Peter. Then Peter remembered the word of the Lord, how He had told him, 'Before the rooster crows today, you will deny Me three times.'

[62]And Peter went out and wept bitterly.

Beaten by Roman Soldiers

[63]Now the men who were guarding *Yeshua* began mocking and beating Him. [64]They blindfolded Him and kept asking Him, saying, "Prophesy! Who is the one who hit You?" [65]And reviling Him, they were saying many other things against Him.

Brought Before the Council

[66]As it become day, the elders of the people gathered together, both ruling *kohanim* and *Torah* scholars, and they led Him away to their council, saying, [67]"If You are *Mashiach*, tell us."

But *Yeshua* said to them, "If I tell you, you will never believe; [68]and if I ask you, you will never answer. [69]But from now on, the Son of Man is seated at the right hand of the power of God."[a]

70Then they all said, "Are You then *Ben-Elohim*?"

And to them He said, "You say that I am."

71Then they said, "What further need do we have for testimony? For we have heard it ourselves from His own mouth!"

23

Brought Before Pilate

1Then the entire assembly got up and brought *Yeshua* to Pilate. 2And they began to accuse Him, saying, "We found this fellow subverting our nation, forbidding payment of taxes to Caesar and saying that He Himself is Messiah—a king."

3So Pilate questioned Him, saying, "Are You the King of the Jews?"

"As you say," *Yeshua* replied.

4Then Pilate said to the ruling *kohanim* and the crowds, "I find no case against this Man."

5But they kept insisting, saying, "He stirs up the people, teaching throughout all Judea, starting from the Galilee to as far as here."

6But when Pilate heard this, he asked whether the Man was a Galilean. 7And when he learned that *Yeshua* was from Herod's jurisdiction, he sent Him to Herod, who was also in Jerusalem at that time.

Brought Before Herod

8Now Herod was overjoyed when he saw *Yeshua*, for he had wanted to see Him for a long time, because he had heard about Him and was hoping to see some miracle done by Him. 9He was questioning *Yeshua* on many issues, but *Yeshua* did not answer at all.[b] 10And the ruling *kohanim* and the *Torah* scholars stood their ground, strongly accusing Him.

11Now Herod together with his soldiers were treating Him with contempt and mocking Him.[c] They put splendid clothing on Him and sent Him back to Pilate. 12And Herod and Pilate became friends with one another from that very day, for previously they had been enemies with one another.

Pilate's Decree

13Now Pilate called together the ruling *kohanim*, the leaders, and the people. 14And he said to them, "You brought this Man to me as one who incites the people to revolt. But having examined Him in your presence, I have found no case against this Man regarding what you accuse Him of doing. 15Nor did Herod, for he sent Him back to us. Indeed, He has done nothing that is worthy of death. 16Therefore I will scourge Him and release Him."(17)[d]

18But they shouted out all together, saying, "Take this fellow away! Release to us *Bar-Abba*!"[e] 19(He was someone who had been thrown into prison for a rebellion in the city and murder.)

20Again Pilate addressed them, wanting to release *Yeshua*; 21but they kept shouting out, saying, "Execute, execute Him!"

22And a third time he spoke to them, "Why? What evil has this One done? I have found in Him no fault deserving of death. Therefore, I will scourge and release Him."

23But they were insistent, demanding with loud shouts that He be executed. And their voices prevailed. 24So Pilate decreed that their demand be put into effect. 25And He released the one they were asking for, the one thrown in jail for insurrection and murder. But he handed over *Yeshua* to their will.

a 22:69. cf. Dan. 7:13(LXX); Ps. 110:1(109:1 LXX).
b 23:9. cf. Isa. 53:7.
c 23:11. cf. Isa. 53:3.
d 23:17. Some mss. add: *Now Pilate needed to release one prisoner to them at the feast.*
e 23:18. Also Barabbas, *Son of the Father* (Aram.).

Executed on the Stake

26 As they led Him away, they grabbed
a man, Simon of Cyrene, coming in from
the countryside. They placed on him the
cross-beam,[a] to carry behind *Yeshua*.
27 Now a great multitude of people was
following Him, including women who
were mourning and singing dirges for
Him. 28 But *Yeshua*, turning to them, said,
"Daughters of Jerusalem, do not weep
for Me, but for yourselves and your children. 29 For indeed, the days are coming
when they will say, 'Blessed are barren,
and the wombs that never gave birth,
and the breasts that did not feed.'

30 Then they will begin to say to the
mountains, 'Fall on us!'
and to the hills, 'Cover us!'[b]

31 For if they do these things when the
wood is green, what will happen when it
is dry?"
32 Others, two evildoers, were also
led away to be put to death with Him.
33 When they came to the place called the
Skull, there they crucified Him and the
evildoers, one on His right and the other
on His left.
34 But *Yeshua* was saying, "Father, forgive them, for they do not know what
they are doing." Then they cast lots,
dividing up His clothing.[c]
35 The people stood there watching.
And even the leaders were sneering at
Him, saying, "He saved others; let Him
save Himself if He is the Messiah of God,
the Chosen One!"[d]
36 The soldiers likewise mocked Him,
coming up and bringing Him sour wine,[e]
37 and saying, "If You are the King of the
Jews, save Yourself."
38 Now there was also an inscription
over Him:[f] THIS IS THE KING OF THE
JEWS. 39 One of the evildoers hanging
there was jeering at Him, saying, "Aren't
You the Messiah? Save Yourself—and
us!"
40 But the other one, rebuking him,
replied, "Don't you fear God, since you
are under the same sentence? 41 We're
getting what we deserve for our actions,
and rightly so—but this One has done
nothing wrong." 42 And he said, "*Yeshua*,
remember me when You come into Your
kingdom."
43 *Yeshua* said to him, "Amen, I tell you,
today you shall be with Me in Paradise."

Temple Curtain Torn in Two

44 It was now about the sixth hour, and
darkness fell over the whole land until
the ninth hour,[g] 45 for the sun died out.
And the curtain[h] of the Temple was torn
in two.
46 And *Yeshua*, crying out with a loud
voice, said, "Father, 'into Your hands I
entrust My spirit.'"[i] When He had said
this, He breathed His last.
47 Now when the centurion saw what
had happened, he began glorifying God,
saying, "Truly this was a righteous Man."
48 And all the crowds assembled for this
spectacle, when they saw what had happened, began to turn back, beating their
breasts. 49 But all *Yeshua's* acquaintances,
and the women who were following Him
from the Galilee, were standing at a distance, watching these things.

Buried in a Rich Man's Tomb

50 Now there was a man named Joseph,
a council member, a good and righteous
man. 51 (He had not been in agreement
with the council and their action.), He
was from the Judean town of Arimathea,
and he was waiting for the kingdom of
God. 52 This man went to Pilate and asked
for *Yeshua's* body. 53 And he took it down,
wrapped it in a linen cloth, and laid Him

a 23:26. Probably the patibulum, the horizontal piece of the execution stake, weighing about 100 lbs.
b 23:30. cf. Hos. 10:8.
c 23:34. cf. Ps. 22:19(18).
d 23:35. cf. Ps. 22:7-9(6-8).
e 23:36. cf. Ps. 69:22(21).
f 23:38. Some mss. add *in letters of Greek and Latin and Hebrew*.
g 23:44. From noon until 3 p.m.
h 23:45. Heb. *parokhet, veil or inner curtain*; cf. Exod. 26:33; 2 Chr. 3:14; Heb. 9:3.
i 23:46. Ps. 31:6(5), cf. Ps. 30:5 (LXX).

in a tomb[a] cut out of the rock, where no one had ever yet been laid.

[54]Now it was the Day of Preparation, and *Shabbat* was approaching. [55]The women who had come with Him from the Galilee followed, and they saw the tomb and how His body was laid. [56]Then they returned and prepared spices and perfumes. But on *Shabbat* they rested according to the commandment.

24

Women Visit the Garden Tomb

[1]Now on the first day of the week, at daybreak, the women came to the tomb, carrying the spices they had prepared. [2]They found the stone had been rolled away from the tomb; [3]but when they entered, they did not find the body of the Lord *Yeshua*.

[4]And while they were perplexed about this, suddenly two men in dazzling clothes stood beside them. [5]The women were terrified and bowed their faces to the ground, but the men said to them, "Why do you search for the living among the dead? [6]He is not here, but He is risen! Remember what He told you when He was still in the Galilee, [7]saying that the Son of Man must be delivered into the hands of sinful men, and be executed, and on the third day rise up."

[8]And they were reminded of His words. [9]And when they returned from the tomb, they told all these things to the eleven and to everyone else. [10]Now it was Miriam from Magdala, Joanna, the Miriam of Jacob and others together with them who were telling these things to the *shlichim*. [11]But these words appeared to them as nonsense, and they would not believe them. [12]But Peter got up and ran to the tomb. Leaning in, he sees only the linen cloths. And he went away to his home, marveling at what had happened.

a 23:53. cf. Isa. 53:9b.

Eyes Open in Emmaus

[13]Now behold, two of them on that very day were traveling to a village named Emmaus, a distance of about seven miles[b] from Jerusalem. [14]They were speaking with one another about all the things that had been happening. [15]While they were talking and discussing, *Yeshua* Himself approached and began traveling with them. [16]But their eyes were kept from recognizing Him.

[17]Then He said to them, "What are these things you are discussing with one another as you are walking along?"

They stood still, looking gloomy. [18]Then the one named Cleopas answered and said to Him, "Are You the only one visiting Jerusalem who doesn't know the things that happened there in these days?"

[19]*Yeshua* said to them, "What kind of things?"

And they said to Him, "The things about *Yeshua* from *Natzeret*, who was a Prophet, powerful in deed and word before God and all the people—[20]how the ruling *kohanim* and our leaders handed Him over to be sentenced to death, and they executed Him. [21]But we were hoping that He was the One about to redeem Israel. Besides all this, today is the third day since these things happened.

[22]"But also some women among us amazed us. Early in the morning they were at the tomb. [23]When they didn't find His body, they came saying that they had also seen a vision of angels, who said He is alive! [24]Some of those with us went to the tomb and found it just as the women said, but they did not see Him."

[25]*Yeshua* said to them, "Oh foolish ones, so slow of heart to put your trust in all that the prophets spoke! [26]Was it not necessary for Messiah to suffer these things and to enter into His glory?" [27]Then beginning with Moses and all the Prophets, He explained to them the

b 24:13. Lit. 60 stadia; 1 stadion is about 607 feet or 187 meters.

things written about Himself in all the Scriptures.

28They approached the village where they were going, and He acted as though He were going farther on. 29But they urged Him, saying, "Stay with us, for it is nearly evening and the day is already gone." So He went in to stay with them.

30And it happened that when He was reclining at the table with them, He took the *matzah*,[a] offered a *bracha* and, breaking it, gave it to them. 31Then their eyes were opened and they recognized Him, and He disappeared from them.

Good News for the *Talmidim* in Jerusalem

32They said to one another, "Didn't our heart burn within us while He was speaking with us on the road, while He was explaining the Scriptures to us?" 33And they got up that very hour and returned to Jerusalem. They found the eleven and others with them gathered together, 34saying, "The Lord is risen indeed! He has appeared to Simon!" 35Then they began telling about the events on the road and how He became recognized by them in the breaking of the *matzah*.

36While they were speaking of these things, *Yeshua* Himself stood in the midst of them and said, "*Shalom Aleichem*!" 37But they were startled and terrified, thinking they were seeing a ghost.

38Then He said to them, "Why are you so shaken? And why do doubts arise in your heart? 39Look at My hands and My feet—it is I Myself! Touch Me and see! For a spirit doesn't have flesh and bones, as you see I have." 40And when He had said this, He showed them His hands and His feet.

41But while they were still in disbelief due to joy and wonder, He said to them, "Do you have anything to eat here?"

42They gave Him a piece of broiled fish, 43and He took it and ate it in their presence. 44Then He said to them, "These are My words which I spoke to you while I was still with you—everything written concerning Me in the *Torah* of Moses and the Prophets and the Psalms must be fulfilled.

45Then He opened their minds to understand the Scriptures, 46and He said to them, "So it is written, that the Messiah is to suffer and to rise from the dead on the third day, 47and that repentance for the removal of sins[b] is to be proclaimed in His name to all nations, beginning from Jerusalem.[c] 48You are witnesses of these things. 49And behold, I am sending the promise of My Father upon you; but you are to stay in the city until you are clothed with power from on high."

Yeshua Ascends into Heaven

50Then *Yeshua* led them out as far as Bethany, and He lifted up His hands[d] and blessed them. 51And while blessing them, He departed from them from them and was taken up into heaven. 52After worshiping Him, they returned to Jerusalem with great joy. 53And they were continually in the Temple, praising God.

a 24:30, 35. Lit. *bread* (at Passover, unleavened bread).

b 24:47. cf. Heb. 9:22; 10:18.

c 24:47. cf. Mal. 1:11.

d 24:50. cf. Num. 6:22-27.

The Good News According to John

Introduction

John, one of the twelve original *shlichim*, wrote this fourth Gospel or *Besorah*. He was one of the sons of Zebedee, along with Jacob. Written in a style completely different than the other three, it probably dates from the end of the first century (about 90–95 C.E.). Writing many years after *Yeshua's* resurrection, John includes in his account the kinds of deep insights one would expect of a young student who was present with *Yeshua* and has now grown into a mature and wise sage.

At one time, John was believed to be the least Jewish of the Gospels. Now that scholars have learned more about first-century Judaism (including the discovery and study of the Dead Sea Scrolls), John is recognized to be very Jewish indeed. Other Jewish writers of this period also attribute divinity to the Word (Logos in Greek, *Memra* in Aramaic). Some of the speeches of *Yeshua* in John resemble a rabbinic commentary or *midrash*, and a wealth of references point to the Jewish traditions and institutions dating from the time of the *Tanakh*: Jacob's Ladder, *Shabbat*, *Sukkot*, *Hanukkah*, *Pesach*, the serpent in the wilderness, and *manna* all make their appearance here.

John was written at a time when intra-Jewish conflicts over *Yeshua* and the claims of his followers were running high. In some instances, Jewish believers in *Yeshua* were no longer welcome in the synagogues. In this context, some believe that John wrote to Jewish nonbelievers to answer the question, "Who is the Messiah?" John's answer, of course, is *Yeshua*, seen as both human and divine in nature, the Son of God or *Ben-Elohim*. Others think it was written primarily to encourage Jewish believers to pursue a deeper, persevering level of faith in light of the opposition. Either way, the audience appears to be largely Jewish. John works both to encourage those who believe in *Yeshua* and to lead to faith those who do not yet put their trust in Him. *Yeshua's* words and deeds reveal who He is: the Word of God who tabernacled among us, the Lamb of God who takes away the sin of the world, the Light of the World, and much more.

A Look Inside John

The Word Becomes Flesh (1:1)
John's Witness to Israel's Leaders (1:19)
Behold, the Lamb of God (1:29)
Yeshua's First *Talmidim* (1:35)
Talmidim Offer Witness (1:43)

Water to Wine (2:1)
Yeshua Purges the Temple (2:12)

A Pharisee Comes Seeking Truth (3:1)
The Father's Love Revealed (3:9)

The Living Word, Source of Life (3:22)
Yeshua Offers Living Water (4:1)
Ready for Harvest (4:27)
Life for a Dying Son (4:43)

Healing on *Shabbat* (5:1)
Sent by the Father (5:16)
The Father Testifies about the Son (5:31)

New *Manna* in the Wilderness (6:1)
The Savior on the Sea (6:16)
The Bread from Heaven (6:25)
Fallout from a Hard Teaching (6:60)

Anticipating Hostility at *Sukkot* (7:1)
Teaching at the Temple (7:14)
Satisfying Spiritual Thirst (7:37)
Religious Adversaries (7:45)

Mercy for a Sinful Woman (8:1)
The Light of the World (8:12)

Bringing Light to the Blind (9:1)
Is Seeing Believing? (9:35)

The Faithful Hear *the Shepherd's* Voice (10:1)
Some Despise the Light and Harden (10:22)

Lazarus Is Dead (11:1)
Comforting the Mourners (11:17)
Yeshua's Word Raises the Dead (11:38)
Better that One Man Die (11:45)

Miriam Anoints the Messiah (12:1)
Israel's King Has Come (12:12)
Fallen Seed Produces a Harvest (12:20)
Choose Either the Light or the Darkness (12:35)

Modeling Servanthood (13:1)
Yeshua Reveals His Betrayer (13:18)
Leaving A Legacy of Love (13:31)

The Way to the Father's House (14:1)
The Believer's Helper (14:15)

Abiding in the Vine (15:1)
The World Hates God's Own (15:18)

The *Spirit* Reveals Truth (16:5)
Death and Resurrection Foretold (16:16)

The Son Glorifies the Father (17:1)
Yeshua Prays for His *Talmidim* (17:6)
Interceding for All Believers (17:20)

Betrayed and Arrested (18:1)
Interrogated and Tried (18:12)

Bound and Sentenced (19:1)
The Lamb of God Is Sacrificed (19:17)
Buried in a Rich Man's Tomb (19:38)

The Tomb Is Empty (20:1)
Yeshua Appears to Miriam (20:11)
Yeshua Appears to the Disciples (20:19)
The Reason for Signs and Wonders (20:30)

Fish for Breakfast with the Risen One (21:1)
Love Restores Peter (21:15)
John's Witness (21:24)

John 1:14a

And the Word became flesh and tabernacled among us.

1

The Word Becomes Flesh

1 In the beginning was the Word.[a] The Word was with God, and the Word was God. 2 He was with God in the beginning. 3 All things were made through Him, and apart from Him nothing was made that has come into being. 4 In Him was life, and the life was the light of men. 5 The light shines in the darkness, and the darkness has not overpowered it.

6 There came a man sent from God, whose name was John. 7 He came as a witness to testify about the light, so that through him everyone might believe. 8 He was not the light, but he came to bear witness concerning the light. 9 The true light, coming into the world, gives light to every man.

10 He was in the world, and the world was made through Him; but the world did not know Him. 11 He came to His own, but His own did not receive Him. 12 But whoever did receive Him, those trusting in His name, to these He gave the right to become children of God. 13 They were born not of a bloodline, nor of human desire, nor of man's will, but of God. 14 And the Word became flesh and tabernacled among us. We looked upon His glory,[b] the glory of the one and only[c] from the Father, full of grace and truth.

15 John testifies about Him. He cried out, saying, "This is He of whom I said, 'The One who comes after me is above me, because He existed before me.'" 16 Out of His fullness, we have all received grace on top of grace. 17 *Torah* was given through Moses; grace and truth came through *Yeshua* the Messiah. 18 No one has ever seen God; but the one and only God,[d] in the Father's embrace, has made Him known.

John's Witness to Israel's Leaders

19 This is John's testimony, when the Judean leaders sent *kohanim* and Levites from Jerusalem to ask him, "Who are you?"

20 He openly admitted and did not deny; he admitted, "I am not the Messiah."

21 "What then? Are you Elijah?" they asked him.

"I am not," said John.

"Are you the Prophet?"

"No," he answered.

22 So they said to him, "Who are you? Give us an answer for those who sent us. What do you say about yourself?"

23 He said, "I am 'the voice of one crying in the wilderness, "Make straight the way of ADONAI,"'[e] as the prophet Isaiah said."

24 Now those sent were from the Pharisees. 25 They asked him, "If you're not the Messiah, Elijah, or the Prophet, why then are you immersing?"

26 "I immerse in water," John answered. "Among you stands One you do not know, 27 coming after me, whose sandals I'm not worthy to untie." 28 These things happened in Bethany beyond the Jordan, where John was immersing.

Behold, the Lamb of God

29 The next day, John sees *Yeshua* coming to him and says, "Behold, the Lamb[f] of God who takes away the sin of the world! 30 This is the One about whom I told you, 'He who comes after me is above me, because He was before me.' 31 I didn't know Him, but I came immersing with water so that He might be revealed to Israel."

32 Then John testified, "I have seen the Spirit coming down like a dove out of

a 1:1. cf. Gen. 1:1; Prov. 8:23.
b 1:14. cf. Exod. 40:34.
c 1:14, 18; 3:16, 18. Lit. *unique*, sometimes translated *only begotten*.
d 1:18. Some mss. say *the only Son*.
e 1:23. Is. 40:3.
f 1:29. cf. Exod. 12:21; Num. 28:8; Isa. 53:5-7.

heaven, and it remained on Him. 33 I did not know Him; but the One who sent me to immerse in water said to me, 'The One on whom you see the *Spirit* coming down and remaining, this is the One who immerses in the *Ruach ha-Kodesh*.' 34 And I have seen and testified that this is *Ben-Elohim*."[a]

Yeshua's First *Talmidim*

35 Again the next day, John was standing with two of his disciples 36 and watched *Yeshua* walking by. He said, "Behold, the Lamb of God!" 37 The two disciples heard him say this, and they followed *Yeshua*.

38 *Yeshua* turned around and saw them following. He said to them, "What are you looking for?"

They said to Him, "Rabbi" (which is translated Teacher), "where are you staying?"

39 "Come and see," *Yeshua* tells them. So they came and saw where He was staying, and they spent that day with Him. It was about the tenth hour.[b]

40 Andrew, the brother of Simon Peter, was one of the two who heard John speak and followed *Yeshua*. 41 First he finds his own brother Simon and tells him, "We've found the Messiah!" (which is translated Anointed One).

42 Andrew brought Simon to *Yeshua*. *Yeshua* looked at him and said, "You are Simon, son of John. You shall be called Kefa (which is translated Peter)."

Talmidim Offer Witness

43 The next day, *Yeshua* decided to go to the Galilee. He finds Philip and says to him, "Follow Me!" 44 Now Philip was from Bethsaida, the same town as Andrew and Peter.

45 Philip finds Nathanael and tells him, "We've found the One that Moses in the *Torah*, and also the prophets, wrote about—*Yeshua* of *Natzeret*, the son of Joseph!"

46 "*Natzeret*!" Nathanael answered. "Can anything good come from there?"

Philip said to him, "Come and see."

47 *Yeshua* saw Nathanael coming toward Him. He said, "Look, a true Israelite! There's nothing false in him."

48 Nathanael said to Him, "How do you know me?"

Yeshua answered, "Before Philip called you, when you were under the fig tree, I saw you."

49 "Rabbi," Nathanael answered, "You are *Ben-Elohim*! You are the King of Israel!"[c]

50 "Because I told you that I saw you under the fig tree, you believe?" *Yeshua* replied to him. "You will see greater things than that!" 51 And He said, "Amen, amen I tell you, you will see heaven opened and the angels of God going up and coming down on the Son of Man!"[d]

2

Water to Wine

1 On the third day, there was a wedding at Cana in the Galilee. *Yeshua's* mother was there, 2 and *Yeshua* and His disciples were also invited to the wedding. 3 When the wine ran out, *Yeshua's* mother said to Him, "They don't have any wine!"

4 *Yeshua* said to her, "Woman, what does this have to do with you and Me? My hour hasn't come yet."

5 His mother said to the servants, "Do whatever He tells you."

6 Now there were six stone jars, used for the Jewish ritual of purification, each holding two to three measures.[e] 7 *Yeshua* said to them, "Fill the jars with water!" So they filled them up to the top. 8 Then He said to them, "Take some water out, and give it to the headwaiter." And they brought it.

a 1:34. cf. Ps. 2:7; Prov. 30:4.
b 1:39. 4 p.m.
c 1:49. cf. Ps. 2:6-7.
d 1:51. cf. Gen. 28:12-13; Dan. 7:13.
e 2:6. About 20-25 gallons; 1 measure is about 9 gallons.

9Now the headwaiter did not know where it had come from, but the servants who had drawn the water knew. As the headwaiter tasted the water that had become wine, he calls the bridegroom 10and says to him, "Everyone brings out the good wine first, and whenever they are drunk, then the worse. But you've reserved the good wine until now!" 11*Yeshua* did this, the first of the signs, in Cana of the Galilee—He revealed His glory, and His disciples believed in Him.

Yeshua Purges the Temple

12After this *Yeshua* went down to Capernaum with His mother, brothers,[a] and disciples, and they stayed there a few days. 13The Jewish feast of Passover was near, so *Yeshua* went up to Jerusalem. 14In the Temple, He found the merchants selling oxen, sheep, and doves; also the moneychangers sitting there. 15Then He made a whip of cords and drove them all out of the Temple, both the sheep and oxen. He dumped out the coins of the moneychangers and overturned their tables. 16To those selling doves, He said, "Get these things out of here! Stop making My Father's house a marketplace!" 17His disciples remembered that it is written, "Zeal for your House will consume Me!"[b]

18The Judean leaders responded, "What sign do You show us, since You are doing these things?"

19"Destroy this Temple," *Yeshua* answered them, "and in three days I will raise it up."

20The Judean leaders then said to Him, "Forty-six years this Temple was being built, and You will raise it up in three days?" 21But He was talking about the temple of His body. 22So after He was raised from the dead, His disciples remembered that He was talking about this. Then they believed the Scripture and the word that *Yeshua* had spoken.

23Now when He was in Jerusalem for the Passover, during the feast, many believed in His name, seeing the signs He was doing. 24But *Yeshua* did not entrust Himself to them, because He knew all men. 25He did not need anyone to testify about man, for He knew what was in man.

3

A Pharisee Comes Seeking Truth

1Now there was a man, a Pharisee named Nicodemus, a ruler of the Jewish people. 2He came to *Yeshua* at night and said, "Rabbi, we know that You, a teacher, have come from God. For no one can perform these signs which You do unless God is with Him!"

3*Yeshua* answered him, "Amen, amen I tell you, unless one is born from above,[c] he cannot see the kingdom of God."

4"How can a man be born when he is old?" Nicodemus said to Him. "He cannot enter his mother's womb a second time and be born, can he?"

5*Yeshua* answered, "Amen, amen I tell you, unless one is born of water and spirit,[d] he cannot enter the kingdom of God. 6What is born of the flesh is flesh, and what is born of the Spirit is spirit. 7Do not be surprised that I said to you, 'You all must be born from above.' 8The wind blows where it wishes and you hear its sound, but you do not know where it comes from or where it goes. So it is with everyone born of the Spirit."

The Father's Love Revealed

9"How can these things happen?" Nicodemus said.

10*Yeshua* answered him, "You're a teacher of Israel and you do not understand these things? 11Amen, amen I tell

a 2:12. Some mss. say *brothers and sisters*.
b 2:17. Ps. 69:10(9).
c 3:3, 7. Or born *again*.
d 3:5. cf. Ezek. 36:24-27.

you, We speak about what We know and testify about what We have seen. Yet you all do not receive Our testimony! [12]If you do not believe the earthly things I told you, how will you believe when I tell you about heavenly things? [13]No one has gone up into heaven except the One who came down from heaven—the Son of Man. [14]Just as Moses lifted up the serpent in the desert,[a] so the Son of Man must be lifted up, [15]so that whoever believes in Him may have eternal life!

[16]"For God so loved the world that He gave His one and only Son, that whoever believes in Him shall not perish but have eternal life. [17]God did not send the Son into the world to condemn the world, but in order that the world might be saved through Him. [18]The one who believes in Him is not condemned; but whoever does not believe has been condemned already, because he has not put his trust in the name of the one and only *Ben-Elohim.*

[19]"Now this is the judgment, that the light has come into the world and men loved the darkness instead of the light,[b] because their deeds were evil. [20]For everyone who does evil hates the light and does not come to the light, so that their deeds will not be exposed. [21]But whoever practices the truth comes to the light, so that it may be made known that his deeds have been accomplished in God."

The Living Word, Source of Life

[22]Afterwards, *Yeshua* and His disciples came to the land of Judea. There He was staying with them and immersing. [23]Now John also was immersing at Aenon near Salim, because much water was there and many were coming and being immersed; [24]for John had not yet been thrown into prison.

[25]Now an argument came up between John's disciples and a Judean concerning purification. [26]They came to John and said, "Rabbi, the One who was with you beyond the Jordan, the One you testified about—look, He is immersing, and all are coming to Him!"

[27]John answered, "A man can receive nothing unless it has been given to him from heaven. [28]You yourselves testify that I said, 'I am not the Messiah,' but rather, 'I am sent before Him.' [29]The one who has the bride is the bridegroom, but the best man rejoices when he stands and hears the bridegroom's voice. So now my joy is complete! [30]He must increase, while I must decrease."

[31]The One who comes from above is above all. The one who is from the earth is of the earth, and of the earth he speaks. The One who comes from heaven is above all. [32]And what He has seen and heard, He testifies to that; yet no one receives His testimony. [33]Whoever receives His testimony has certified that God is true.

[34]The One whom God has sent speaks the words of God, for God gives the Spirit without limit. [35]The Father loves the Son and has given everything into His hand. [36]He who trusts in the Son has eternal life. He who does not obey the Son will not see life, but the wrath of God remains on him.

4

Yeshua Offers Living Water

[1]Now *Yeshua* knew that the Pharisees heard that He was making and immersing more disciples than John. [2](Although *Yeshua* Himself was not immersing, His disciples were.) [3]So He left Judea and went back again to the Galilee.

[4]But He needed to pass through Samaria. [5]So He comes to a Samaritan town called Shechem, near the plot of

a 3:14. cf. Num. 21:8.
b 3:19. cf. Is. 5:20.

land that Jacob gave to his son Joseph.[a] 6 Now Jacob's well was there. So *Yeshua*, exhausted from the journey, was sitting by the well. It was midday.[b]

7 A Samaritan woman comes to draw water. "Give me a drink," *Yeshua* tells her, 8 for His disciples had gone away to the town to buy food.

9 Then the Samaritan woman tells Him, "How is it that You, a Jew, ask me, a Samaritan woman, for a drink?" (For Jewish people don't deal with Samaritans.)

10 *Yeshua* replied to her, "If you knew the gift of God, and who it is who is saying to you, 'Give Me a drink,' you would have asked Him, and He would have given you living water."

11 "Sir," the woman tells Him, "You don't have a bucket, and the well is deep. Then from where do You get this living water? 12 You're not greater than our father Jacob, are You? He gave us this well. He drank out of it himself, with his sons and his cattle."

13 *Yeshua* replied to her, "Everyone who drinks from this water will get thirsty again. 14 But whoever drinks of the water that I will give him shall never be thirsty. The water that I give him will become a fountain of water within him, springing up to eternal life!"

15 "Sir," the woman tells Him, "give me this water, so I won't get thirsty or have to come all the way here to draw water!"

16 He tells her, "Go call your husband, and then come back here."

17 "I don't have a husband," the woman replied.

Yeshua tells her, "You've said it right, 'I have no husband.' 18 For you've had five husbands, and the man you have now isn't your husband. This you've spoken truthfully!"

19 "Sir," the woman tells Him, "I see that You are a prophet! 20 Our fathers worshiped on this mountain, but you all say that the place where we must worship is in Jerusalem."

21 *Yeshua* tells her, "Woman, believe Me, an hour is coming when you will worship the Father neither on this mountain nor in Jerusalem. 22 You worship what you do not know; we worship what we know, for salvation is from the Jews. 23 But an hour is coming—it is here now—when the true worshipers will worship the Father in Spirit and truth, for the Father is seeking such people as His worshipers. 24 God is Spirit, and those who worship Him must worship in spirit and truth."

25 The woman tells Him, "I know that Messiah is coming (He who is called the Anointed One.)[c] When He comes, He will explain everything to us."

26 *Yeshua* tells her, "I—the One speaking to you—I am."

Ready for Harvest

27 At this moment, His disciples came back. They were amazed that He was speaking with a woman. Yet no one said, "What do You want?" or "Why are You speaking with her?"

28 So the woman left her water jar and went back to the town. She tells the people, 29 "Come see a man who told me everything I ever did! He couldn't be the Messiah, could He?" 30 The people left the town and began coming to Him.

31 Meanwhile, the disciples were pressing Him, "Rabbi, eat!"

32 But He said to them, "I have food to eat that you know nothing about."

33 So the disciples were saying to each other, "No one brought Him food to eat, did they?"

34 *Yeshua* tells them, "My food is to do the will of the One who sent Me and to accomplish His work. 35 Don't you say, 'Four more months, and then comes the harvest'? Look, I tell you, lift up your eyes and look at the fields! They are white and ready for harvest.

a 4:5. Most mss. say *Sychar*; cf. Gen. 33:18-19; 48:22(48:22 LXX); Josh. 24:32.

b 4:6. Lit. *about the sixth hour*.

c 4:25. *Christ* (Gk.) and *Messiah* (Heb.) both mean *Anointed One*.

36“The reaper receives a reward and gathers fruit for eternal life, so that the sower and reaper may rejoice together. 37For the saying is true, ‘One sows and another reaps.’ 38I sent you to reap what you haven’t worked for. Others have worked hard, and you have joined in their work.”

39Many of the Samaritans from that town put their trust in Him because of the word of the woman testifying, “He told me everything I ever did!” 40So when the Samaritans came to Him, they kept asking Him to stay with them. He stayed there two days, 41and many more believed because of His word. 42They kept telling the woman, “It’s no longer because of your words that we believe. We’ve heard for ourselves! Now we know that this really is the Savior of the world!”

Life for a Dying Son

43After the two days, He went on from there into the Galilee. 44Now *Yeshua* Himself had testified that a prophet has no honor in his own country. 45But when He came into the Galilee, they welcomed Him. For they had seen all He had done at the feast in Jerusalem, since they also had gone up to celebrate.

46So He went again to Cana of the Galilee, where He had turned the water into wine. Now there was a nobleman whose son was sick in Capernaum. 47When he heard that *Yeshua* had come from Judea to the Galilee, he went to Him and begged Him to come down and heal his son; for he was about to die.

48Then *Yeshua* said to him, “Unless you all see signs and wonders, you’ll never believe!”

49The nobleman said to Him, “Sir, come down before my child dies!”

50*Yeshua* tells him, “Go! Your son lives!”

The man believed the word that *Yeshua* said to him and started off. 51While on his way down, his servants met him, saying that his son was living. 52So he asked them the hour when the boy began to get better. They said, “The fever left him yesterday at about the seventh hour.”[a]

53Then the father realized that it was the same hour *Yeshua* said to him, “Your son lives!” Now he himself believed, along with his whole household. 54*Yeshua* did this as the second sign, after He had come again from Judea into the Galilee.

5

Healing on *Shabbat*

1After this there was a Jewish feast, and *Yeshua* went up to Jerusalem. 2Now in Jerusalem there is a pool by the sheep gate, called Bethzatha in Aramaic,[b] which has five porches. 3In these a crowd of invalids was lying around—blind, lame, disabled.(4)[c]

5Now a certain man had been an invalid there for thirty-eight years. 6Seeing him lying there and knowing he had been that way a long time, *Yeshua* said to him, “Do you want to get well?”

7The invalid answered Him, “Sir, I have nobody to put me into the pool when the water is stirred up. While I’m trying to get in, somebody else steps down before me!”

8*Yeshua* tells him, “Get up! Pick up your mat and walk!”

9Immediately, the man was healed! He took up his mat and started walking around. Now that day was *Shabbat*, 10so Judean leaders were saying to the man who was healed, “It’s *Shabbat*! It’s not permitted for you to carry your mat.”

11But he answered them, “The man who made me well told me, ‘Pick up your mat and walk.’”

12They asked him, “Who is the man who told you, ‘Pick up your mat and walk’?”

a 4:52. One o’clock.

b 5:2. Lit. *in Hebrew*. *Bethesda* (Heb.) means *House of Mercy*. *Bethzatha* (Aram.) means *the place of poured out water*.

c 5:3. ASV adds: *They waited for the water to be moved.* Other mss. also add verse 4: *because an angel of the Lord sometimes went to the pool and moved the water. Then, whoever went into the water first was healed from whatever disease he had.*

13But the man who had been healed didn't know who it was, for *Yeshua* had slipped away into the crowd in that place.

14Afterwards, *Yeshua* finds him in the Temple. He said to him, "Look, you've been healed! Stop sinning, so nothing worse happens to you." 15The man left and told the Judean leaders that it was *Yeshua* who had made him well.

Sent by the Father

16Because *Yeshua* was doing these things on *Shabbat*, the Judean leaders started persecuting Him. 17But *Yeshua* said to them, "My Father is still working, and I also am working." 18So for this reason the Judean leaders kept trying even harder to kill Him—because He was not only breaking *Shabbat*,[a] but also calling God His own Father, making Himself equal with God.

19Therefore *Yeshua* answered them, "Amen, amen I tell you, the Son cannot do anything by Himself. He can do only what He sees the Father doing. Whatever the Father does, the Son does likewise. 20For the Father loves the Son and shows Him everything He does. He will show Him even greater works than these, so that you will be amazed. 21For just as the Father raises the dead and gives them life, so also the Son gives life to whomever He wants. 22The Father does not judge anyone, but has handed over all judgment to the Son 23so that all should honor the Son, just as they honor the Father. Whoever does not honor the Son does not honor the Father who sent Him.

24"Amen, amen I tell you, whoever hears My word and trusts the One who sent Me has eternal life. He does not come into judgment, but has passed over from death into life. 25Amen, amen I tell you, an hour is coming and is now here, when the dead will hear the voice of *Ben-Elohim*. Those who hear will live! 26For just as the Father has life in Himself, so also He has granted the Son to have life in Himself. 27Also He has given the Son authority to judge, because He is the Son of Man.

28"Do not be amazed at this, for an hour is coming when all who are in their graves will hear His voice 29and come out![b] Those who have done good will come to a resurrection of life, and those who have done evil will come to a resurrection of judgment. 30I can do nothing on My own. Just as I hear, I judge; and My judgment is just, for I do not seek My own will, but the will of the One who sent Me."

The Father Testifies about the Son

31"If I testify about Myself, My witness is not valid. 32There is another who testifies about Me, and I know that the testimony He gives is true. 33You have sent to John, and he has testified to the truth. 34I do not receive the testimony of man, but I say these things so that you may be saved. 35He was the lamp that was burning and shining, and you wanted to rejoice for a while in his light.

36"But the testimony I have is greater than that from John. The works the Father has given Me to finish—the very works I am doing—testify about Me, that the Father has sent Me. 37And the Father who sent Me has testified concerning Me. You have never heard His voice nor seen His form. 38Nor do you have His Word living in you, because you do not trust the One He sent. 39You search the Scriptures because you suppose that in them you have eternal life. It is these that testify about Me. 40Yet you are unwilling to come to Me so that you may have life!

41"I do not accept glory from men. 42But I know you, that you do not have the love of God in yourselves. 43I have come in My Father's name, and you do not receive Me. But if another comes in his own name, you will receive him. 44How can you believe, when you receive

a 5:18. cf. Mk. 2:27; Lk. 13:16.

b 5:28-29. cf. Ezek. 37:12; Ps. 16:10; Dan. 12:2.

glory from one another and you do not seek the glory that comes from God alone?

[45]"Do not think that I will accuse you before the Father. The one who accuses you is Moses, in whom you have put your hope. [46]For if you were believing Moses, you would believe Me—because he wrote about Me. [47]But since you do not believe his writings, how will you believe My words?"[a]

6

New *Manna* in the Wilderness

[1]Afterwards, *Yeshua* went away to the other side of the Sea of Galilee, also known as the Sea of Tiberias. [2]A large crowd kept following Him, because they were watching the signs He was performing on the sick. [3]Then *Yeshua* went up the mountainside and sat down there with His disciples. [4]Passover, the Jewish feast, was near.

[5]Lifting up His eyes and seeing a large crowd coming to Him, *Yeshua* said to Philip, "Where will we buy bread so these may eat?" [6]Now *Yeshua* was saying this to test him, for He knew what He was about to do.

[7]Philip answered Him, "Two hundred denarii[b] isn't enough to buy bread for each to get a little bit!"

[8]One of His disciples, Andrew, Simon Peter's brother, said to Him, [9]"There's a boy here who has five barley loaves and two fish—but what's that for so many?"

[10]*Yeshua* said, "Make the people recline." There was much grass in the area. So the men reclined, about five thousand in number. [11]Then *Yeshua* picked up the loaves. And having given thanks, He distributed bread to everyone who was reclining. He did the same with the fish, as much as they wanted.

a 5:46-47. cf. Deut. 18:15-19.
b 6:7. One denarius was the daily wage for a laborer.

[12]When the people were full, *Yeshua* said to His disciples, "Gather up the leftovers, so nothing is wasted." [13]So they gathered them and filled twelve baskets with broken pieces from the five barley loaves, which were left over by those who had finished eating.

[14]When the people saw the sign that *Yeshua* performed, they began to say, "This is most certainly the Prophet who is to come into the world!"[c] [15]Realizing that they were about to come and seize Him by force to make Him king, *Yeshua* withdrew again to the mountain, Himself alone.

The Savior on the Sea

[16]Now when evening came, *Yeshua's* disciples went down to the sea. [17]Getting into a boat, they set out to cross the sea toward Capernaum. By now it had become dark, and still *Yeshua* had not come to them. [18]A great wind began to blow, stirring up the sea.

[19]After they had rowed about twenty-five or thirty stadia,[d] they catch sight of *Yeshua* walking on the sea, approaching the boat. They were terrified! [20]But *Yeshua* says to them, "I am. Don't be afraid."[e] [21]Then they wanted to take Him into the boat, and right away the boat reached the shore where they were headed.

The Bread from Heaven

[22]The next day, the crowd remaining on the other side of the sea realized that no other boat had been there except the one, and that *Yeshua* hadn't gone into the boat with His disciples, but that His disciples had gone away alone. [23]Some other boats from Tiberias came close to the place where they had eaten the bread after the Master had given thanks. [24]So when the crowd realized that neither *Yeshua* nor His disciples were there, they

c 6:14. cf. Dt. 18:15.
d 6:19. About three or four miles, halfway across the sea.
e 6:20. Lit. *I am. Don't be afraid*; cf. Jn. 8:24, 18:6.

got into the boats and set off for Capernaum to find Him. 25 When they found
Him on the other side of the sea, they
said, "Rabbi, when did You get here?"
26 *Yeshua* responded to them, "Amen,
amen I tell you, you seek Me not because
you saw signs, but because you ate all
the bread and were filled. 27 Don't work
for food that spoils, but for the food that
endures to eternal life, which the Son of
Man will give to you. For on Him, God the
Father has put the seal of approval."
28 Then they said to Him, "What shall
we do to perform the works of God?"
29 *Yeshua* answered them, "This is the
work of God, to trust in the One He sent."
30 So they said to Him, "Then what sign
do You perform, so that we may see and
believe You? What work do You do? 31 Our
fathers ate the manna in the wilderness;
as it is written, 'Out of heaven He gave
them bread to eat.'"[a]
32 *Yeshua* answered them, "Amen,
amen I tell you, it isn't Moses who has
given you bread from heaven, but My
Father gives you the true bread from
heaven. 33 For the bread of God is the One
coming down from heaven and giving life
to the world."
34 So they said to Him, "Sir, give us this
bread from now on!"
35 *Yeshua* said to them, "I am the bread
of life. Whoever comes to Me will never
be hungry, and whoever believes in Me
will never be thirsty. 36 But I told you that
you have seen Me, yet you do not believe.
37 Everyone the Father gives Me will come
to Me, and anyone coming to Me I will
never reject. 38 For I have come down
from heaven not to do My own will but
the will of the One who sent Me.
39 "Now this is the will of the One who
sent Me, that I lose not one of all He has
given Me, but raise each one on the last
day. 40 For this is the will of My Father,
that everyone who sees the Son and
trusts in Him may have eternal life; and I
will raise him up on the last day."

a 6:31. Ps. 78:24; cf. Exod. 16:4-36; Neh. 9:15.

41 Some of the Judeans[b] started to
grumble about Him, because He said,
"I am the bread that came down from
heaven." 42 They were saying, "Isn't this
Yeshua the son of Joseph, whose father
and mother we know? How can He now
say, 'I have come down from heaven'?"
43 *Yeshua* answered, "Stop grumbling
among yourselves! 44 No one can come to
Me unless My Father who sent Me draws
him—and I will raise him up on the last
day. 45 It is written in the Prophets, 'They
will all be taught by God.'[c] Everyone who
has listened and learned from the Father
comes to Me. 46 Not that anyone has seen
the Father except the One who is from
God—He has seen the Father.
47 "Amen, amen I tell you, he who
believes has eternal life. 48 I am the bread
of life. 49 Your fathers ate the manna in
the desert, yet they died. 50 This is the
bread that comes down from heaven,
so that one may eat and not die. 51 I am
the living bread, which came down from
heaven. If anyone eats this bread, he will
live forever. This bread is My flesh, which
I will give for the life of the world."
52 Then the Jews began arguing with
one another, "How can this man give us
His flesh to eat?"
53 So *Yeshua* said to them, "Amen, amen
I tell you, unless you eat the flesh of the
Son of Man and drink His blood, you have
no life in yourselves. 54 He who eats My
flesh and drinks My blood has eternal
life, and I will raise him up on the last day.
55 "For My flesh is real food and My
blood is real drink. 56 He who eats My
flesh and drinks My blood abides in Me,
and I in him. 57 Just as the living Father
sent Me and I live because of the Father,
so the one who eats of Me will also live
because of Me. 58 This is the bread that
came down from heaven—not like the
bread your fathers ate and then died. He
who eats this bread will live forever."
59 He said these things while teaching
at the synagogue in Capernaum.

b 6:41. Perhaps *Galileans*.
c 6:45. cf. Isa 54:13.

Fallout from a Hard Teaching

[60]So when many of His disciples heard this, they said, "This is a hard teaching. Who can listen to it?"

[61]But *Yeshua* knew His disciples were murmuring, so He said to them, "Does this offend you? [62]Then what if you see the Son of Man going back up to the place where He was before? [63]It is the Spirit who gives life; the flesh is of no benefit. The words I have spoken to you are Spirit and are life! [64]Yet some of you do not trust." *Yeshua* knew from the beginning who were the ones who did not trust, as well as which one would betray Him.

[65]Then He told them, "For this reason I've told you that no one can come to Me unless it has been granted to him by the Father."

[66]From this time, many of His disciples left and quit walking with Him. [67]So *Yeshua* said to the Twelve, "You don't want to leave also, do you?"

[68]Simon Peter answered Him, "Lord, to whom shall we go? You have the words of eternal life! [69]We have trusted and have come to know that you are the Holy One of God."

[70]*Yeshua* answered them, "Didn't I choose you, the Twelve? Yet one of you is the adversary!" [71]Now He was speaking of Judah, the son of Simon of Kriot—for he, one of the Twelve, was about to betray Him.

7

Anticipating Hostility at *Sukkot*

[1]After these events, *Yeshua* was walking about in the Galilee. He did not want to walk in Judea, because the Judean leaders wanted to kill Him. [2]Now the Jewish Feast of Tabernacles[a] was near. [3]Therefore His brothers said to Him, "Leave here and go to Judea, so Your disciples also may see the works You are doing. [4]No one who wants to be well known does everything in secret. If You are doing these things, show Yourself to the world!" [5]For not even His brothers were trusting in Him.

[6]Therefore *Yeshua* said to them, "My time has not yet come, but your time is always at hand. [7]The world cannot hate you, but it hates Me because I testify that its works are evil. [8]You go on up to the Feast. I'm not going to this Feast, because My time hasn't yet fully come." [9]After saying these things, He stayed in the Galilee.

[10]But after His brothers went to the Feast, He also went, not openly but secretly. [11]Then the Judean leaders were searching for Him at the Feast and kept asking, "Where is that fellow?" [12]There was a lot of murmuring about Him in the crowds. Some were saying, "He is good." But others were saying, "Not so! He leads the people astray." [13]Yet no one spoke openly about Him for fear of the Judean leaders.

Teaching at the Temple

[14]About halfway through the Feast, *Yeshua* went up to the Temple and began teaching. [15]Then the Judean leaders were amazed, saying, "How does this man know so much, having never been taught?"[b]

[16]*Yeshua* answered, "My teaching is not from Me, but from Him who sent Me. [17]If anyone wants to do His will, he will know whether My teaching comes from God or it is Myself speaking. [18]Whoever speaks from himself seeks his own glory; but He who seeks the glory of the One who sent Him, He is true and there is no unrighteousness in Him. [19]Hasn't Moses given you the *Torah*? Yet none of you keeps it. Why are you trying to kill Me?"

[20]The crowd answered, "You have a demon! Who's trying to kill you?"

a 7:2. cf. Deut. 16:16.

b 7:15. Lit. *knows letters, not having learned.*

21*Yeshua* answered, "I did one good work, and all of you are amazed. 22Because Moses has given you circumcision (though it is not from Moses, but from the patriarchs), you circumcise a man on *Shabbat*. 23If a man receives circumcision on *Shabbat* so that the *Torah* of Moses may not be broken, why are you angry that I healed a man's whole body on *Shabbat*? 24Do not judge by appearance, but judge righteously."

25Then some of the people from Jerusalem were saying, "Isn't this the person they're trying to kill? 26Look, He speaks openly and they're saying nothing to Him. Can it be that the leaders know He is the Messiah? 27But we know where this person is from. But the Messiah, whenever He may come, no one knows where He is from."

28Then, while teaching in the Temple courts, *Yeshua* cried out, "You know both who I am and where I am from! I have not come on My own, but the One who sent Me is true. You do not know Him, 29but I know Him because I am from Him and He sent Me."

30Then they were trying to seize Him; but no one laid a hand on Him, because His hour had not yet come. 31Yet many from the crowd believed in Him and were saying, "When the Messiah comes, He won't perform more signs than this person has, will He?" 32The Pharisees heard people in the crowd murmuring these things about Him, and the ruling *kohanim* and Pharisees sent guards to arrest Him.

33*Yeshua* said, "I am with you only a little while longer, and then I am going to the One who sent Me. 34You will look for Me but will not find Me. Where I am, you cannot come."

35The Judean leaders then said among themselves, "Where is this person about to go that we shall not find Him? He's not going to the Diaspora to teach the Greeks, is He? 36What did He mean by saying, 'You will look for Me but will not find Me. Where I am, you cannot come'?"

Satisfying Spiritual Thirst

37On the last and greatest day of the Feast, *Yeshua* stood up and cried out loudly, "If anyone is thirsty, let him come to Me and drink. 38Whoever believes in Me, as the Scripture says, 'out of his innermost being will flow rivers of living water.'"[a] 39Now He said this about the *Spirit*, whom those who trusted in Him were going to receive; for the *Spirit*[b] was not yet given, since *Yeshua* was not yet glorified.

40When they heard these words, some of the crowd said, "This man really is the Prophet." 41Others were saying, "This is the Messiah." Still others were saying, "*The Messiah* doesn't come from the Galilee, does He? 42Didn't the Scripture say that the Messiah comes from the seed of David and from Bethlehem, David's town?"[c] 43So a division arose in the crowd because of *Yeshua*. 44Some wanted to capture Him, but no one laid hands on Him.

Religious Adversaries

45Then the guards returned to the ruling *kohanim* and Pharisees, who asked them, "Why didn't you bring Him?"

46"Never has anyone spoken like this man," the guards answered.

47The Pharisees responded, "You haven't been led astray also, have you? 48Have any of the rulers or Pharisees believed in Him? 49No, but this mob that doesn't know the *Torah*—they are cursed!"

50Nicodemus, the one who had come to *Yeshua* before and was one of them, said to them, 51"Our *Torah* doesn't judge a man unless it first hears from him and knows what he's doing, does it?"

52They answered him, "You aren't from the Galilee too, are you? Search,

a 7:38. cf. Isa. 44:3, 55:1, 58:11; Ezek. 47; Zech. 14:8.

b 7:39. Some mss. read *Holy Spirit* (Heb. *Ruach ha-Kodesh*).

c 7:42. cf. Mic. 5:1(2).

and see that no prophet comes out of the Galilee!"[a]

53Then everyone went to his own house.

8

Mercy for a Sinful Woman

1But *Yeshua* went to the Mount of Olives. 2At dawn, He came again into the Temple. All the people were coming to Him, and He sat down and began to teach them.

3The *Torah* scholars and Pharisees bring in a woman who had been caught in adultery. After putting her in the middle, 4they say to *Yeshua*, "Teacher, this woman has been caught in the act of committing adultery. 5In the *Torah*, Moses commanded us to stone such women. So what do You say?" 6Now they were saying this to trap Him, so that they would have grounds to accuse Him.

But *Yeshua* knelt down and started writing in the dirt with His finger. 7When they kept asking Him, He stood up and said, "The sinless one among you, let him be the first to throw a stone at her." 8Then He knelt down again and continued writing on the ground.

9Now when they heard, they began to leave, one by one, the oldest ones first, until *Yeshua* was left alone with the woman in the middle. 10Straightening up, *Yeshua* said to her, "Woman, where are they? Did no one condemn you?"

11"No one, Sir," she said.

"Then neither do I condemn you," *Yeshua* said. "Go, and sin no more."

The Light of the World

12*Yeshua* spoke to them again, saying, "I am the light of the world. The one who follows Me will no longer walk in darkness, but will have the light of life."

a 7:52. The earliest manuscripts do not include John 7:53-8:11. Others locate the passage after 7:36 or after 21:25.

13Then the Pharisees said to Him, "You are testifying about Yourself, so Your testimony is not valid."

14*Yeshua* answered them, "Even if I testify about Myself, My testimony is valid. For I know where I came from and where I am going. But you don't know where I come from or where I am going. 15You judge according to the flesh, but I do not judge anyone. 16Yet even if I do judge, My judgment is true, because it is not I alone but I with the Father who sent Me. 17Even in your *Torah* it is written that the testimony of two men is true.[b] 18I am one witness for Myself, and the Father who sent Me bears witness for Me."

19Then they said to Him, "Where is your Father?"

Yeshua answered, "You know neither Me nor My Father. If you knew Me, you would also know My Father." 20He spoke these words in the treasury while teaching in the Temple, but no one arrested Him because His hour had not yet come.

21Then again *Yeshua* spoke to them, "I am going away. You will look for Me and die in your sin. Where I am going, you cannot come."

22"He won't kill Himself, will He?" the Judeans asked. "Is that why He says, 'Where I am going, you cannot come'?"

23*Yeshua* said, "You are from below; I am from above. You are of this world; I am not of this world. 24Therefore I told you that you will die in your sins. If you don't believe that I am, you will die in your sins."

25So they asked Him, "Who are you?"

Yeshua replied, "What have I been telling you from the beginning? 26I have much to say and judge about you. But the One who sent Me is true, and I tell the world what I heard from Him." 27They didn't understand that He was talking to them about the Father.

28So *Yeshua* said, "When you have lifted up the Son of Man, then you will know who I am. I do nothing by Myself, but speak just what the Father has taught

b 8:17. cf. Dt. 17:6; 19:15.

Me. [29]The One who sent Me is with Me. He has not left Me alone, because I always do what is pleasing to Him."

[30]As He was speaking these things, many people put their trust in Him.

[31]Then *Yeshua* said to the Judeans who had trusted Him, "If you abide in My word, then you are truly My disciples. [32]You will know the truth, and the truth will set you free!"

[33]They answered Him, "We are Abraham's children and have never been slaves to anyone! How can you say, 'You will become free'?"

[34]*Yeshua* answered them, "Amen, amen I tell you, everyone who sins is a slave to sin. [35]Now the slave does not remain in the household forever; the son abides forever. [36]So if the Son sets you free, you will be free indeed! [37]I know you are Abraham's children; yet you are trying to kill Me, because My word has no place in you. [38]I tell of what I have seen with the Father; so also you do what you heard from the father."[a]

[39]"Abraham is our father," they replied to Him.

Yeshua said to them, "If you are Abraham's children, do the deeds of Abraham. [40]But now you are seeking to kill Me—a Man who has told you the truth, which I heard from God. This Abraham did not do! [41]You are doing the deeds of your father."

They said to Him, "We were not born as illegitimate children—we have one Father, God Himself!"

[42]*Yeshua* said to them, "If God were your Father, you would love Me, for from God I came and now I am here. For I have not come on My own, but He sent Me. [43]Why don't you understand My speech? Because you're not able to hear My word! [44]You are of your father the devil, and you want to do the desires of your father. He was a murderer from the beginning and does not stand in the truth, because there is no truth in him. Whenever he speaks lies he is just being himself—for he is a liar and the father of lies.

[45]"But because I speak the truth, you do not believe Me. [46]Which one of you convicts Me of sinning? If I am telling the truth, why don't you believe Me? [47]He who belongs to God hears the words of God. The reason you don't hear[b] is because you do not belong to God."

[48]The Judean leaders responded, "Aren't we right to say you are a Samaritan and have a demon?"

[49]*Yeshua* answered, "I do not have a demon! I honor My Father, yet you dishonor Me. [50]But I do not seek My own glory; there is One who is seeking and judging. [51]Amen, amen I tell you, if anyone keeps My word, he will never see death."

[52]"Now we know You have a demon!" the Judean leaders said to Him. "Abraham and the prophets died. Yet You say, 'If anyone keeps My word, he will never taste death.' [53]You are not greater than our father Abraham who died, are You? The prophets also died! Who do You make Yourself out to be?"

[54]*Yeshua* answered, "If I glorify Myself, My glory is nothing. It is My Father who gives Me glory—the One of whom you say, 'He is our God.'[c] [55]Yet you do not know Him, but I know Him. If I say I do not know Him, I will be a liar like you. Yet I do know Him and keep His Word. [56]Your father Abraham rejoiced to see My day; he saw it and was thrilled."

[57]Then the Judeans said to Him, "You're not even fifty years old and you've seen Abraham?"[d]

[58]*Yeshua* answered, "Amen, amen I tell you, before Abraham was, I am!"

[59]Then they picked up stones to throw at Him, but *Yeshua* hid Himself and went out from the Temple.[e]

a 8:38. Some mss. say *My Father... your father.*

b 8:47. Dt. 6:4; Ex. 24:7.

c 8:54. Some mss. *say your God.*

d 8:57. Some mss. *say has Abraham seen You?*

e 8:59. Some mss. *add passing through their midst, he went away in this manner.*

9

Bringing Light to the Blind

1As *Yeshua* was passing by, He saw a
man who had been blind since birth. 2His
disciples asked Him, "Rabbi, who sinned,
this man or his parents, that he should be
born blind?"

3*Yeshua* answered, "Neither this man
nor his parents sinned. This happened so
that the works of God might be brought
to light in him. 4We must do the work of
the One who sent Me, so long as it is day!
Night is coming when no one can work.
5While I am in the world, I am the light of
the world."

6Having said these things, He spat on
the ground, made mud with the saliva,
and spread the mud on the blind man's
eyes. 7He told him, "Go, wash in the Pool
of Siloam" (which is translated Sent). So
he went away, washed, and came back
seeing.

8Therefore his neighbors and those
who had seen him as a beggar kept saying, "Isn't this the one who used to sit
and beg?"

9"This is the one!" some said.

"No, but it looks like him," said others.

But the man himself kept saying, "I
am!"

10So they asked him, "Then how were
your eyes opened?"

11He answered, "The Man who is called
Yeshua made mud, rubbed it on my eyes,
and said to me, 'Go to Siloam and wash.'
So I went away and washed, and then I
received my sight!"

12"Where is He?" they asked him.

"I don't know," he said.

13They bring to the Pharisees the man
who once was blind. 14Now the day was
Shabbat when *Yeshua* made the mud
and opened the man's eyes. 15So again
the Pharisees were asking him how he
received his sight. He responded, "He
put mud on my eyes, and I washed, and
I see!"

16So some of the Pharisees began saying, "This man isn't from God, because
He doesn't keep *Shabbat*!" But others
were saying, "How can a sinner perform
such signs?" So there was a split among
them.

17Again they say to the blind man,
"What do you say about Him, since He
opened your eyes?"

And he said, "He's a prophet."

18So the Judean leaders didn't believe
that he had been blind and received his
sight until they called his parents. 19They
questioned them, "Is this your son,
whom you say was born blind? Then how
does he see now?"

20Then his parents answered, "We
know that this is our son and that he
was born blind. 21We don't know how he
now sees, nor do we know who opened
his eyes. Ask him—he's old enough. He
will speak for himself." 22His parents
said this because they were afraid of
the Judean leaders. For the Judean leaders had already agreed that anyone who
professed *Yeshua* to be Messiah would
be thrown out of the synagogue. 23That's
why his parents said, "He's old enough—
ask him."

24So a second time they called the
man who had been blind and said, "Give
glory to God! We know that this man is a
sinner!"

25The man replied, "I don't know
whether He's a sinner. One thing I do
know is that I was blind, but now I see!"

26So they asked him, "What did He do
to you? How did He open your eyes?"

27"I told you already and you didn't listen!" the man responded. "What, do you
want to hear it again? You don't want to
become His disciples too, do you?"

28They railed at him and said, "You're
a disciple of that One, but we're disciples
of Moses! 29We know that God has spoken to Moses; but as for this fellow, we
don't know where He is from."

30The man replied to them, "That's amazing! You don't know where He is from, yet He opened my eyes! 31We know that God doesn't listen to sinners; but if anyone fears Him and does His will, He hears this one. 32Since the beginning of the world, no one has ever heard that anyone has opened the eyes of a man born blind. 33If this man were not from God, He couldn't do anything."

34They replied to him, "You were born completely in sin, and you're teaching us?" And they threw him out.

Is Seeing Believing?

35*Yeshua* heard that they had thrown him out. Finding him, He said, "Do you believe in the Son of Man?"[a]

36The man answered, "Who is He, Sir? Tell me, so that I may believe in Him!"

37*Yeshua* said, "You have seen Him—He is the One speaking with you."

38He said, "Lord, I believe!" And he worshiped Him.

39*Yeshua* said, "For judgment I came into this world, so that those who don't see may see, and the ones who do see may become blind."

40Some of the Pharisees who were with Him heard Him say this and asked, "We're not blind too, are we?"

41*Yeshua* said to them, "If you were blind, you would have no sin. But now you say, 'We see.' So your sin remains."

10

The Faithful Hear *the Shepherd's* Voice

1"Amen, amen I tell you, he who does not enter the sheepfold by the door, but climbs in some other way, is a thief and a robber. 2But he who enters through the door is the shepherd of the sheep. 3To him the doorkeeper opens, and the sheep hear his voice. The shepherd calls his own sheep by name and leads them out.

4"When he has brought out all his own, he goes ahead of them; and the sheep follow him because they know his voice. 5They will never follow a stranger, but will run away from him, for they do not know the voice of strangers." 6*Yeshua* told them this parable, but they did not understand what He was telling them.

7So *Yeshua* said again, "Amen, amen I tell you, I am the gate for the sheep. 8All those who came before Me are thieves and robbers, but the sheep did not listen to them. 9I am the gate![b] If anyone comes in through Me, he will be saved. He will come and go and find pasture. 10The thief comes only to steal, slaughter, and destroy. I have come that they might have life, and have it abundantly!

11"I am the Good Shepherd.[c] The Good Shepherd lays down His life for the sheep. 12The hired worker is not the shepherd, and the sheep are not his own. He sees the wolf coming and abandons the sheep and flees. Then the wolf snatches and scatters the sheep. 13The man is only a hired hand and does not care about the sheep.

14"I am the Good Shepherd. I know My own and My own know Me, 15just as the Father knows Me and I know the Father. And I lay down My life for the sheep. 16I have other sheep that are not from this fold; those also I must lead, and they will listen to My voice. So there shall be one flock, one Shepherd.

17"For this reason the Father loves Me, because I lay down My life, so that I may take it up again. 18No one takes it away from Me, but I lay it down on My own. I have the authority to lay it down, and I have the authority to take it up again. This command I received from My Father."

19Again a division arose among the Judeans because of these words. 20Many of them were saying, "He has a demon.

a 9:35. Some mss. say *the Son of God* (Ben-Elohim).

b 10:7, 9. Or *door*.

c 10:11. cf. Gen. 48:15; Ps. 23; Ezek. 37:24.

He's insane! Why listen to Him?" [21]Others said, "These are not the sayings of someone who is plagued by a demon. A demon cannot open the eyes of the blind, can it?"

Some Despise the Light and Harden

[22]Then came *Hanukkah;*[a] it was winter in Jerusalem. [23]*Yeshua* was walking in the Temple around Solomon's Colonnade. [24]Then the Judean leaders surrounded Him, saying, "How long will You hold us in suspense? If You are the Messiah, tell us outright!"

[25]*Yeshua* answered them, "I told you, but you don't believe! The works I do in My Father's name testify concerning Me. [26]But you don't believe, because you are not My sheep. [27]My sheep hear My voice. I know them, and they follow Me. [28]I give them eternal life! They will never perish, and no one will snatch them out of My hand. [29]My Father, who has given them to Me, is greater than all. And no one is able to snatch them out of the Father's hand. [30]I and the Father are one."

[31]Again the Judean leaders picked up stones to stone Him. [32]*Yeshua* answered them, "I've shown you many good works from the Father. For which of these are you going to stone Me?"

[33]The Judean leaders answered, "We aren't stoning you for a good work, but for blasphemy. Though You are a man, You make Yourself God!"

[34]*Yeshua* answered them, "Isn't it written in your Writings,[b] 'I have said you are gods'? [35]If he called them 'gods,' to whom the Word of God came (and the Scripture cannot be broken), [36]do you say of Him, the One the Father set apart and sent into the world, 'You speak blasphemy,' because I said, 'I am *Ben-Elohim*'?

[37]"If I don't do the works of My Father, don't believe Me! [38]But if I do, even if you don't trust Me, trust the deeds. Then you may come to know and continue to understand that the Father is in Me, and I am in the Father." [39]Therefore they tried to capture Him again, but He escaped from their hand.

[40]Again He went back across the Jordan to the place where John first started immersing, and He stayed there. [41]Many people came to Him and were saying, "John performed no sign, but all John said about this man was true." [42]And many trusted in Him there.

11

Lazarus Is Dead

[1]Now a man named Lazarus was sick. He was from Bethany, the village of Miriam and her sister Martha. [2]This was the same Miriam who anointed the Master with perfume and wiped His feet with her hair. It was her brother Lazarus who was sick. [3]So the sisters sent a word to *Yeshua*, saying, "Master, the one you love is sick!"

[4]When *Yeshua* heard this, He said, "This sickness will not end in death. It is for God's glory, so that *Ben-Elohim* may be glorified through it." [5]Now *Yeshua* loved Martha and her sister and Lazarus. [6]However, when He heard that Lazarus was sick, He stayed where He was for two more days.

[7]Then after this, He said to His disciples, "Let's go up to Judea again."

[8]"Rabbi," the disciples say to Him, "just now the Judean leaders were trying to stone You! And You're going back there again?"

[9]*Yeshua* answered, "Aren't there twelve hours in the day? If a man walks in the day, he doesn't stumble, because he sees the light of the world. [10]But if a man should walk around at night, he stumbles, because the light is not in him."

[11]After He said this, He tells them, "Our friend Lazarus has fallen asleep, but I'm going there to wake him up."

a 10:22. Lit. Rededication.
b 10:34. Lit. *Law*, here applied to the *Torah*, Prophets, and Writings; quote is from Ps. 82:6.

[12]So the disciples said to Him, "Master,
if he has fallen asleep, he will get better." [13]Now *Yeshua* had spoken about his
death, but they thought He was talking
about ordinary sleep.

[14]Then *Yeshua* told them clearly, "Lazarus is dead! [15]I'm glad for your sake I
wasn't there, so that you may believe.
Anyway, let's go to him!"

[16]Then Thomas called the Twin[a] said to
the other disciples, "Let's go too, so that
we may die with Him!"

Comforting the Mourners

[17]So when *Yeshua* arrived, He discovered that Lazarus had been in the tomb
already for four days. [18]Bethany was less
than two miles[b] from Jerusalem, [19]and
many of the Judeans had come to Martha and Miriam to console them about
their brother.

[20]When Martha heard that *Yeshua* was
coming, she went out to meet Him; but
Miriam sat in the house. [21]Martha said to
Yeshua, "Master, if You had been here,
my brother wouldn't have died! [22]But I
know, even now, that whatever You may
ask of God, He will give You."

[23]*Yeshua* said to her, "Your brother will
rise again."

[24]Martha said to Him, "I know, he will
rise again in the resurrection on the last
day."

[25]*Yeshua* said to her, "I am the resurrection and the life! Whoever believes in Me,
even if he dies, shall live. [26]And whoever
lives and believes in Me shall never die.
Do you believe this?"

[27]She says to Him, "Yes, Lord, I believe
that you are the Messiah, *Ben-Elohim*
who has come into the world." [28]After
she said this, she left and secretly told
her sister Miriam, "The Teacher is here,
and He's calling for you." [29]As soon as
Miriam heard, she quickly got up and
was coming to Him. [30]Now *Yeshua* had
not yet come into the village, but was still
in the place where Martha had met Him.
[31]The Judeans, who were with Miriam in
the house and comforting her, seeing
how quickly she got up and went out, followed her. They thought she was going
to the tomb to weep there.

[32]So when Miriam came to where
Yeshua was, she saw Him and fell at His
feet, saying to Him, "Master, if You had
been here, my brother would not have
died!"

[33]When *Yeshua* saw her weeping, and
the Judeans who came with her weeping, He was deeply troubled in spirit and
Himself agitated. [34]"Where have you laid
him?" He asked.

"Come and see, Master," they tell Him.
[35]*Yeshua* wept. [36]So the Judeans said,
"See how He loved him!"

[37]But some of them said, "Couldn't
this One, who opened the eyes of the
blind man, have also kept this man from
dying?"

Yeshua's Word Raises the Dead

[38]So *Yeshua*, again deeply troubled
within Himself, comes to the tomb. It was
a cave, and a stone was lying against it.
[39]*Yeshua* says, "Roll away the stone!"

Martha, the dead man's sister, said to
Him, "Master, by this time he stinks! He's
been dead for four days!"

[40]*Yeshua* says to her, "Didn't I tell you
that if you believed, you would see the
glory of God?"

[41]So they rolled away the stone. *Yeshua*
lifted up His eyes and said, "Father, I
thank you that you have heard Me. [42]I
knew that You always hear Me; but
because of this crowd standing around I
said it, so that they may believe that You
sent Me."

[43]And when He had said this, He cried
out with a loud voice, "Lazarus, come
out!" [44]He who had been dead came out,
wrapped in burial clothes binding his
hands and feet, with a cloth over his face.

a 11:16; 20:24; 21:2. Grk. *Didymus*.

b 11:18. Lit. 15 *stadia*; 1 stadion is about 607 feet or 187 meters.

And *Yeshua* tells them, "Cut him loose, and let him go!"

Better that One Man Die

45Therefore many of the Judeans, who had come to Miriam and had seen what *Yeshua* had done, put their trust in Him. 46But some of them went to the Pharisees and told them what *Yeshua* had done.

47So the ruling *kohanim* and Pharisees called a meeting of the Sanhedrin. "What are we doing?" they asked. "This Man is performing many signs! 48If we let Him go on like this, everyone will believe in Him, and the Romans will come and take away both our holy place and our nation."

49But one of them, Caiaphas, who was *kohen gadol* that year, said to them, "You know nothing! 50You don't take into account that it is better for you that one man die for the people rather than for the whole nation to be destroyed."

51Now he did not say this by himself; but as the *kohen gadol* that year, he prophesied that *Yeshua* would die for the nation.[a] 52And not for the nation only, but also so that He might gather together into one the scattered children of God.[b]

53So from that day on, they plotted to kill Him. 54Therefore *Yeshua* no longer walked openly among the Judeans, but went from there to the country near the wilderness, to a city called Ephraim. He stayed there with His disciples.

55Now the Jewish Passover was near; and many people went up out of the regions to Jerusalem before Passover, to purify themselves. 56So they were searching for *Yeshua*, saying to one another as they stood in the Temple, "What do you think? Won't He come to the feast at all?" 57Now the ruling *kohanim* and Pharisees had given orders that if anyone knew where He was, he should report it so that they might arrest Him.

a 11:51. cf. Is. 53:8.
b 11:52. cf. Is. 11:10-11; 56:6-7; Jer. 3:17; Mic. 2:12-13.

12

Miriam Anoints the Messiah

1Six days before Passover, *Yeshua* came to Bethany, where Lazarus was, whom *Yeshua* had raised from the dead. 2So they prepared a dinner there for *Yeshua*. Martha was serving, and Lazarus was one of those reclining at the table with Him. 3Then Miriam took a pound[c] of very expensive oil of pure nard and anointed *Yeshua's* feet, and she wiped His feet dry with her hair. Now the house was filled with the fragrance of the oil.

4But Judah from Kriot, one of His disciples, the one who was about to betray Him, said, 5"Why wasn't this oil sold for three hundred denarii[d] and the money given to the poor?" 6Now he said this not because he cared about the poor, but because he was a thief. Since he had the moneybox, he used to steal from what was put in it.

7Therefore *Yeshua* said, "Leave her alone! She set it aside for the day of My burial. 8You will always have the poor among you, but you will not always have Me."

9Now a large crowd of Judeans knew He was there and came, not only for *Yeshua* but also to see Lazarus, whom He had raised from the dead. 10So the ruling *kohanim* made plans to kill Lazarus also, 11because on account of him many of the Jewish people were going and putting their trust in *Yeshua*.

Israel's King Has Come

12The next day, the huge crowd that had come up for the feast heard that *Yeshua* was coming to Jerusalem. 13So they took palm branches and went out to meet Him, shouting,

c 12:3. a Roman pound, about 12 ounces.
d 12:5. One denarius was the daily wage for a laborer.

John 12:3

Then Miriam took a pound of very expensive oil of pure nard and anointed Yeshua's feet, and she wiped His feet dry with her hair. Now the house was filled with the fragrance of the oil.

"'*Hoshia-na!*
Baruch ha-ba b'shem ADONAI!
Blessed is He who comes
in the name of the LORD!'[a]
The King of Israel!"

14 Finding a young donkey, *Yeshua* sat
on it, as it is written,

15"Fear not,
Daughter of Zion!
Look! Your King is coming,
sitting on a donkey's colt."[b]

16His disciples did not understand
these things at first. But when *Yeshua*
was glorified, then they remembered
that these things were written about
Him and that the crowd had done these
things for Him.
17So the crowd, which had been with
Yeshua when He called Lazarus out of the
tomb and raised him from the dead, kept
on telling everyone about it. 18It was also
for this reason that the crowd came out
to meet Him, because they heard that He
had performed this sign. 19So the Pharisees said to each other, "You see that you
can't do anything. Look, the whole world
has taken off after Him!"

Fallen Seed Produces a Harvest

20Now there were some Greeks among
those who were going up to worship at
the feast. 21These came to Philip, who
was from Bethsaida in the Galilee. "Sir,"
they said, "we want to see *Yeshua*."
22Philip comes and tells Andrew; Andrew
and Philip come and tell *Yeshua*.
23*Yeshua* answers them, saying, "The
hour has come for the Son of Man to be
glorified! 24Amen, amen I tell you, unless
a grain of wheat falls to the earth and
dies, it remains alone. But if it dies, it produces much fruit. 25He who loves his life
will lose it, and the one who hates his life
in this world will keep it forever. 26If any
man serves Me, he must follow Me; and
where I am, there also will My servant
be. If anyone serves Me, the Father will
honor him.
27"Now My soul is troubled. And what
shall I say? 'Father, save Me from this
hour'? But it was for this reason I came to
this hour. 28Father, glorify Your name!"
Then a voice came out of heaven, "I
have glorified it, and again I will glorify
it!"
29Therefore the crowd that was standing there and heard it was saying that it
had thundered. Others were saying, "An
angel has spoken to Him."
30*Yeshua* responded, "This voice hasn't
come for My sake, but for yours. 31Now
is the judgment of this world! Now the
prince of this world will be driven out!
32And as I am lifted up from the earth, I
will draw all to Myself." 33He said this to
show the kind of death He was about to
die.
34The crowd answered Him, "We've
heard from *Scripture*[c] that the Messiah
remains forever. How can You say, 'The
Son of Man must be lifted up'? Who is
this Son of Man?"

Choose Either the Light or the Darkness

35Therefore *Yeshua* said to them, "The
light is with you for a little longer. Walk
while you have the light, so that the
darkness will not overtake you. The one
who walks in darkness doesn't know
where he is going. 36While you have the
light, believe in the light so that you may
become sons of light." *Yeshua* spoke
these things, then left and hid Himself
from them.
37But even though He had performed
so many signs before them, they weren't
trusting in Him. 38This was to fulfill the
word of Isaiah the prophet, who said,

a 12:13. Ps. 118:25a, 26a.
b 12:15. Zech. 9:9.

c 12:34. Lit. *Law*, here applied to the *Torah*, Prophets, and Writings; cf. Isa. 9:6(7); Dan. 7:14.

"ADONAI, who has believed
our report?
To whom has the arm
of ADONAI been revealed?"[a]

39For this reason they could not
believe, for Isaiah also said,

40"He has blinded their eyes
and hardened their hearts,
so they might not see
with their eyes
nor understand
with their hearts
and turn back,
and I would heal them."[b]

41Isaiah said these things because he
saw His glory and spoke of Him.
42Nevertheless many, even among
the leaders, put their trust in Him. But
because of the Pharisees, they were not
confessing *Yeshua*,[c] so they would not be
thrown out of the synagogue;[d] 43for they
loved the glory of men more than the
glory of God.
44*Yeshua* cried out, "Whoever puts
trust in Me believes not in Me but in
the One who sent Me! 45And whoever
beholds Me beholds the One who sent
Me. 46As light I have come into the world,
so that everyone who trusts in Me should
not remain in darkness.
47"If anyone hears My words but
doesn't keep them, I do not judge him;
for I came to save the world, not to judge
the world. 48The one who rejects Me and
doesn't receive My words has a judge;
the word I spoke will judge him on the
last day. 49For I did not speak on My own,
but the Father Himself who sent Me has
commanded Me what to say and speak.
50And I know that His commandment is
life everlasting. Therefore what I say, I
say just as the Father has told Me."

a 12:38. Is. 53:1(LXX).
b 12:40. cf. Is. 6:10.
c 12:42. cf. Jn. 9:22.
d 12:42. Lit. *from the synagogue*, i.e. excommunicated, cut off from all community, banned; cf. Mt. 18:17.

13

Modeling Servanthood

1Now it was just before the feast of
Passover. *Yeshua* knew that His hour had
come to depart from this world to the
Father. Having loved His own who were
in the world, He loved them until the
end.[e]
2While the *seder* meal was happening,
the devil had already put in the heart of
Judah from Kriot that he should hand
over *Yeshua*. 3*Yeshua* knew that the
Father had given all things into His hands,
and that He had come from God and was
returning to God. 4So He gets up from
the meal and lays aside His outer garment; and taking a towel, He wrapped it
around His waist. 5Then He pours water
into a basin. He began to wash the disciples' feet, drying them with the towel
wrapped around Him.
6Then He comes to Simon Peter, who
says to Him, "Master, are You going to
wash my feet?"
7*Yeshua* responded, "You don't know
what I am doing now, but you will understand after these things."
8Peter said to Him, "You shall never
wash my feet!"
Yeshua answered him, "If I don't wash
you, you have no part with Me."
9Simon Peter said to Him, "Master,
then not only my feet, but also my hands
and my head!"
10*Yeshua* said to him, "He who has
bathed has no need to wash, except the
feet; he is completely clean. And you
all are clean, though not every one."
11He knew who was betraying Him; for
this reason, He said, "Not all of you are
clean."
12So after He had washed their feet
and put His robe back on and reclined
again, He said to them, "Do you understand what I have done for you? 13You call

e 13:1. cf. John 19:30.

Me 'Teacher' and 'Master'—and rightly you say, for I am. 14So if I, your Master and Teacher, have washed your feet, you also ought to wash each other's feet. 15I have given you an example—you should do for each other what I have done for you.

16"Amen, amen I tell you, a servant isn't greater than his master, and the one who is sent isn't greater than the one who sent him. 17If you know these things, you are blessed if you do them!"

Yeshua Reveals His Betrayer

18"I am not speaking to all of you—I know whom I have chosen. But so the Scripture may be fulfilled, 'He who eats My bread has lifted up his heel against Me.'[a] 19From now on I am telling you, before it happens, so that when it happens you may believe that I am. 20Amen, amen I tell you, he who receives the one I send, receives Me; and he who receives Me, receives the One who sent Me."

21After He said these things, *Yeshua* was agitated in spirit and testified, "Amen, amen I tell you, one of you will betray Me!"

22The disciples began looking at each other, perplexed—who was He talking about? 23One of His disciples, whom *Yeshua* loved, was reclining at His side. 24Simon Peter nods to him and says, "Ask Him—who is He talking about?"

25Then he who leaned on *Yeshua*'s chest says to Him, "Master, who is it?"

26*Yeshua* answers, "It's the one I will give this bit of *matzah* to, after I dip it." After dipping the *matzah*,[b] He takes it and gives it to Judah from Kriot, the son of Simon. 27And with that bit, satan entered into him. Then *Yeshua* tells him, "What you're about to do, do quickly!"

28But no one reclining at the table knew why *Yeshua* said this to him. 29Since Judah had the moneybox, some thought *Yeshua* was telling him, "Buy what we need for the feast," or that he should give something to the poor. 30So after Judah received the bit of *matzah*, he left immediately. Now it was night.

Leaving a Legacy of Love

31Then when Judah had gone out, *Yeshua* said, "Now the Son of Man is glorified, and God is glorified in Him! 32If God is glorified in Him,[c] God will glorify Him in Himself, and will glorify Him at once. 33Little children, I am with you only a little longer. You will search for Me; and just as I told the Judean leaders, so I say to you now, 'Where I am going, you cannot come.'

34"I give you a new commandment, that you love one another. Just as I have loved you, so also you must love one another. 35By this all will know that you are My disciples, if you have love for one another."

36"Master, where are You going?" Simon Peter said to Him.

Yeshua answered, "Where I am going, you cannot follow Me now; but you will follow Me later."

37Peter said to Him, "Master, why can't I follow You now? I'll lay down my life for You!"

38*Yeshua* answers, "Will you lay down your life for Me? Amen, amen I tell you, before the rooster crows, you will deny Me three times!"

14

The Way to the Father's House

1"Do not let your heart be troubled. Trust in God; trust also in Me. 2In My Father's house there are many dwelling places. If it were not so, would I have told you that I am going to prepare a place for you? 3If I go and prepare a place for you, I will come again and take you to Myself, so that where I am you may also be. 4And you know the way to where I am going."[d]

a 13:18. cf. Ps. 41:10(9).

b 13:26. Lit. *bit, small piece*; cf. Exod. 12:8.

c 13:32. Early mss. missing this first part.

d 14:4. Some mss. say *Where I am going you know, and the way you know.*

5Thomas said to Him, "Master, we don't know where You are going. How can we know the way?"

6*Yeshua* said to him, "I am the way, the truth, and the life! No one comes to the Father except through Me. 7If you have come to know Me, you will know My Father also. From now on, you do know Him and have seen Him."

8Philip said to Him, "Master, show us the Father, and it is enough for us."

9*Yeshua* said to him, "Have I been with you for so long a time, and you haven't come to know Me, Philip? He who has seen Me has seen the Father. How can you say, 'Show us the Father'? 10Don't you believe that I am in the Father and the Father is in Me? The words I say to you, I do not speak on My own; but the Father dwelling in Me does His works. 11Believe Me that I am in the Father and the Father is in Me—or at least believe because of the works themselves.

12"Amen, amen I tell you, he who puts his trust in Me, the works that I do he will do; and greater than these he will do, because I am going to the Father. 13And whatever you ask in My name, that I will do, so that the Father may be glorified in the Son. 14If you ask Me[a] anything in My name, I will do it."

The Believer's Helper

15"If you love Me, you will keep My commandments. 16I will ask the Father, and He will give you another Helper[b] so He may be with you forever—17the Spirit of truth, whom the world cannot receive, because it does not behold Him or know Him. You know Him, because He abides with you and will be in you. 18I will not abandon you as orphans;[c] I will come to you. 19In a little while, the world will no longer behold Me, but you will behold Me. Because I live, you also will live! 20"In that day, you will know that I am in My Father, you are in Me, and I am in you. 21He who has My commandments and keeps them is the one who loves Me. He who loves Me will be loved by My Father, and I will love him and reveal Myself to him."

22Judah (not the one from Kriot) said to Him, "Master, what has happened, that You are about to reveal Yourself to us and not the world?"

23*Yeshua* answered and said to him, "If anyone loves Me, he will keep My word. My Father will love him, and We will come to him and make Our dwelling with him. 24He who does not love Me does not keep My words. And the word you hear is not Mine, but the Father's who sent Me. 25These things I have spoken to you while dwelling with you. 26But the Helper, the *Ruach ha-Kodesh* whom the Father will send in My name, will teach you everything and remind you of everything that I said to you.

27"*Shalom* I leave you, My *shalom* I give to you; but not as the world gives! Do not let your heart be troubled or afraid. 28You've heard Me say, 'I am going away and I am coming back to you.' If you loved Me, you would rejoice that I am going to the Father, because the Father is greater than I. 29I have told you now before it happens, so that when it happens you may believe!

30"I will not talk with you much longer, for the ruler of this world is coming. He has nothing on Me. 31But in order that the world may know that I love the Father, I do exactly as the Father commanded Me.

"Get up, let's go from here!"

15

Abiding in the Vine

1"I am the true vine, and My Father is the gardener. 2Every branch in Me that does not bear fruit, He takes away; and

a 14:14. Some mss. omit Me.

b 14:16. *Intercessor, Advocate, Comforter,* or *Counselor;* lit. *Paraclete*. Alsow in 14:26; 15:26; 16:7.

c 14:18. cf. Exod. 22:21-23(22-24); Jer. 49:11.

every branch that bears fruit, He trims so that it may bear more fruit. 3You are already clean because of the word I have spoken to you. 4Abide in Me, and I will abide in you. The branch cannot itself produce fruit, unless it abides on the vine. Likewise, you cannot produce fruit unless you abide in Me.

5"I am the vine; you are the branches. The one who abides in Me, and I in him, bears much fruit; for apart from Me, you can do nothing. 6If anyone does not abide in Me, he is thrown away like a branch and is dried up. Such branches are picked up and thrown into the fire and burned.

7"If you abide in Me and My words abide in you, ask whatever you wish, and it shall be done for you. 8In this My Father is glorified, that you bear much fruit and so prove to be My disciples."

9"Just as the Father has loved Me, I also have loved you. Abide in My love! 10If you keep My commandments, you will abide in My love, just as I have kept My Father's commandments and abide in His love. 11These things I have spoken to you so that My joy may be in you, and your joy may be full.

12"This is My commandment, that you love one another just as I have loved you.[a] 13No one has greater love than this: that he lay down his life for his friends. 14You are My friends if you do what I command you.

15"I am no longer calling you servants, for the servant does not know what his master is doing. Now I have called you friends, because everything I have heard from My Father I have made known to you.

16"You did not choose Me, but I chose you. I selected you so that you would go and produce fruit, and your fruit would remain. Then the Father will give you whatever you ask in My name.

17"These things I command you, so that you may love one another."

a 15:12. cf. Lev. 19:18.

The World Hates God's Own

18"If the world hates you, know that it has hated Me before you. 19If you were of the world, the world would love you as its own. But you are not of the world, since I have chosen you out of the world; therefore the world hates you.

20"Remember the word I spoke to you: 'A servant is not greater than his master.'[b] If they persecuted Me, they will persecute you also. If they kept My word, they will keep yours also.

21"But all these things they will do to you for the sake of My name, because they do not know the One who sent Me. 22If I had not come and spoken to them, they would have no sin. But now they have no excuse for their sin.

23"He who hates Me also hates My Father. 24If I had not done works among them that no one else did, they would have no sin. But now they have seen and have hated both Me and My Father. 25So is fulfilled the word written in their Scripture,[c] 'They hated Me for no reason.'[d]

26"When the Helper comes—whom I will send to you from the Father, the Spirit of truth who goes out from the Father—He will testify about Me. 27And you also testify, because you have been with Me from the beginning."

16

1"I have spoken these things to you so that you may be kept from stumbling. 2They will throw you out of the synagogues. Yes, an hour is coming when whoever kills you will think he is offering service to God. 3They will do these things because they have never known the Father or Me. 4But I have spoken these things to you so that when their hour comes, you may remember that I told you of them. I did not tell you these

b 15:20. Jn. 13:16.

c 15:25a. Lit. *Torah or the Law*; cf. Lk. 24:44-45.

d 15:25b. cf. Ps. 35:19; 69:5(4); (Heb. *sinat chinam*).

things from the beginning, because I was with you."

The *Spirit* Reveals Truth

5"But now I am going to the One who sent Me, and not one of you is asking Me, 'Where are you going?' 6Because I have spoken these things to you, grief has filled your heart. 7But I tell you the truth, it is to your advantage that I go away! For if I do not go away, the Helper will not come to you; but if I go, I will send Him to you.

8"When He comes, He will convict the world about sin, righteousness, and judgment: 9concerning sin, because they do not believe in Me; 10concerning righteousness, because I am going to the Father and you will no longer see Me; 11and concerning judgment, because the ruler of this world has been judged.

12"I still have much more to tell you, but you cannot handle it just now. 13But when the Spirit of truth comes, He will guide you into all the truth. He will not speak on His own; but whatever He hears, He will tell you. And He will declare to you the things that are to come. 14He will glorify Me, because He will take from what is Mine and declare it to you. 15Everything that the Father has is Mine. For this reason I said the *Spirit* will take from what is Mine and declare it to you."

Death and Resurrection Foretold

16"A little while, and you will no longer see Me; and again in a little while, you will see Me."

17Then some of His disciples said to one other, "What does He mean by telling us, 'A little while, and you will no longer see Me; and again in a little while, you will see Me'? And, 'Because I am going to the Father'?"

18They kept on saying, "What's this He's saying, 'A little while'? We don't know what He's talking about!"

19*Yeshua* knew that they wanted to question Him, so He said to them, "Are you asking each other about this, that I said, 'A little while, and you will no longer see Me; and again in a little while, you will see Me'? 20Amen, amen I tell you, you will weep and mourn, but the world will celebrate. You will be filled with sorrow, but your sorrow will turn to joy!

21"When a woman is in labor, she has pain because her hour has come.[a] But when she gives birth to the child, she no longer remembers the anguish, because of the joy that a human being has been born into the world. 22So also you have sorrow now; but I will see you again, and your heart will rejoice, and no one will take your joy away from you!

23"In that day, you will ask Me nothing. Amen, amen I tell you, whatever you ask the Father in My name, He will give you. 24Up to now, you have not asked for anything in My name. Ask and you will receive, so that your joy may be full.

25"These things I have spoken to you in metaphors. An hour is coming when I will no longer speak to you in metaphors, but will tell you plainly about the Father. 26In that day, you will ask in My name—and I'm not telling you that I will ask the Father on your behalf. 27For the Father Himself loves you, because you have loved Me and have believed that I came forth from God. 28I came forth from the Father and have come into the world. Again I am leaving the world and going to the Father."

29His disciples say, "See, now You're speaking plainly and not in metaphors. 30Now we know that You know everything and have no need to be asked anything. By this we believe that You came forth from God."

31*Yeshua* answered them, "Do you now believe? 32Look, the hour is coming—indeed has come—when you will be scattered, each to his own, and you will abandon Me. Yet I am not alone, because

a 16:21. cf. Isa. 26:17; Mic. 4:9-10.

the Father is with Me. [33]These things I have spoken to you, so that in Me you may have *shalom*. In the world you will have trouble, but take heart! I have overcome the world!"

17

The Son Glorifies the Father

[1]*Yeshua* spoke these things; then, lifting up His eyes to heaven, He said, "Father, the hour has come. Glorify Your Son, so the Son may glorify You. [2]Even as You gave Him authority over all flesh, so may He give eternal life to all those You have given Him. [3]And this is eternal life, that they may know You, the only true God, and *Yeshua* the Messiah, the One You sent. [4]I glorified You on earth by finishing the work that You have given Me to do. [5]Now, Father, glorify Me together with Yourself, with the glory which I had with You before the world came to be."

Yeshua Prays for His *Talmidim*

[6]"I have made Your name known to the men of this world that You gave Me. They were Yours; You gave them to Me, and they have kept Your word. [7]Now they have come to know that everything You have given Me is from You. [8]The words, which You gave Me, I have given to them. They received them and truly understood that I came from You, and they believed that You sent Me. [9]I ask on their behalf. Not on behalf of the world do I ask, but on behalf of those You have given Me, for they are Yours. [10]All Mine are Yours, and Yours are Mine; and I have been glorified in them. [11]I am no longer in the world; but they are in the world, and I am coming to You. Holy Father, keep them in Your name that You have given Me, so that they may be one just as We are. [12]While I was with them, I was keeping them in Your name that You have given Me. I guarded them, and not one of them was lost except the son of destruction,[a] so that the Scripture would be fulfilled.

[13]"But now I am coming to You. I say these words while I am still in the world, so that they may have My joy made full in themselves. [14]I have given them Your word; and the world hated them, because they are not of the world just as I am not of the world. [15] I am not asking that You take them out of the world, but that You keep them from the evil one. [16]They are not of the world, just as I am not of the world.

[17]"Make them holy in the truth. Your word is truth. [18]Just as You sent Me into the world, so I have sent them into the world. [19]And for their sakes I make Myself holy, so that they also may be made holy in truth."

Interceding for All Believers

[20]"I pray not on behalf of these only, but also for those who believe in Me through their message, [21]that they all may be one. Just as You, Father, are in Me and I am in You, so also may they be one in Us, so the world may believe that You sent Me. [22]The glory that You have given to Me I have given to them, that they may be one just as We are one—[23]I in them and You in Me—that they may be perfected in unity, so that the world may know that You sent Me and loved them as You loved Me.

[24]"Father, I also want those You have given Me to be with Me where I am, so that they may see My glory—the glory You gave Me, for You loved Me before the foundation of the world. [25]Righteous Father, the world did not know You, but I knew You; and these knew that You sent Me. [26]I made your Name known to them, and will continue to make it known, so that the love with which You loved Me may be in them, and I in them."

a 17:12. cf. Ps. 41:10(9).

18

Betrayed and Arrested

[1]When *Yeshua* had said these things, He went out with His disciples across the Kidron Valley,[a] where there was a garden, which He and His disciples entered. [2]Now Judah, who was betraying Him, also knew the place, because *Yeshua* had often met there with His disciples. [3]So Judah, having taken a band of soldiers and some officers from the ruling *kohanim* and Pharisees, comes there with lanterns, torches, and weapons. [4]Then *Yeshua*, knowing all the things coming upon Him, went forward. He said to them, "Who are you looking for?"

[5]"*Yeshua ha-Natzrati*," they answered Him.

Yeshua tells them, "I am." Now Judah, the one betraying Him, was also standing with them. [6]So when *Yeshua* said to them, "I am," they drew back and fell to the ground.

[7]So again He asked them, "Who are you looking for?"

And they said, "*Yeshua ha-Natzrati*."

[8]*Yeshua* answered, "I told you, I am! If you're looking for Me, let these men go their way." [9]This was so the word would be fulfilled that He spoke: "I did not lose one of those You have given Me."[b]

[10]Then Simon Peter, who had a sword, drew it and struck the servant of the *kohen gadol*, and cut off his right ear. Now the servant's name was Malchus. [11]So *Yeshua* said to Peter, "Put the sword into the sheath! The cup the Father has given Me—shall I never drink it?"

Interrogated and Tried

[12]Then the band of soldiers, with the captain and the officers of the Judeans, seized *Yeshua* and tied Him up. [13]They led Him first to Annas, for he was the father-in-law of Caiaphas, the *kohen gadol* that year. [14]Now Caiaphas was the one who had advised the Judean leaders that it was better for one man to die on behalf of the people.

[15]Simon Peter was following *Yeshua* with another disciple. Now that disciple was known to the *kohen gadol*, so he went with *Yeshua* into the court of the *kohen gadol*. [16]But Peter was left standing outside by the door. So the other disciple, who was known to the *kohen gadol*, went out and spoke to the doorkeeper and brought Peter in.

[17]The maidservant at the door says to Peter, "Aren't you one of this Man's disciples too?"

He says, "No, I'm not." [18]The servants and officers were standing around a fire they had made, because it was cold and they were warming themselves. And Peter was also with them, standing and warming himself.

[19]The *kohen gadol* then questioned *Yeshua* about His disciples and His teaching. [20]"I have spoken openly to the world," *Yeshua* answered him. "I always taught in the synagogues and the Temple, where all the Jewish people come together. I spoke nothing in secret. [21]Why question Me? Ask those who have heard what I spoke to them. Look, they know what I said."

[22]When He had said this, one of the officers standing nearby gave *Yeshua* a slap, saying, "Is that the way you answer the *kohen gadol*?"

[23]*Yeshua* answered him, "If I have spoken wrongly, give evidence of the wrong; but if rightly, why hit Me?" [24]Then Annas sent Him, still tied up, to Caiaphas, the *kohen gadol*.

[25]Now Simon Peter was standing outside and warming himself. So they said to him, "Aren't you one of His disciples too?"

He denied it and said, "No, I'm not!"

[26]One of the servants of the *kohen gadol*, a relative of the man whose ear

a 18:1. cf. 2 Sam. 15:23.
b 18:9. Similar to Jn. 6:39, 17:12.

Peter had cut off, said, "Didn't I see you in the garden with Him?"

27 Again Peter denied it, and immediately a rooster crowed.

28 Then they led *Yeshua* from Caiaphas to the Praetorium.[a] It was early. They themselves did not enter the Praetorium, so they would not become unclean but might eat the Passover. 29 Therefore Pilate came out to them and said, "What charge do you bring against this man?"

30 They answered, "If He weren't an evildoer, we wouldn't have handed Him over to you."

31 Then Pilate said to them, "Take Him yourselves, and judge Him by your *Torah*!"

The Judean leaders responded, "We are not authorized to put anyone to death." 32 This happened so that the word *Yeshua* spoke would be fulfilled, signifying what kind of death He was about to die.

33 So Pilate went back into the Praetorium, called for *Yeshua*, and asked Him, "Are you the King of the Jews?"

34 "Are you saying this on your own," *Yeshua* answered, "or did others tell you about Me?"

35 Pilate answered, "I'm not a Jew, am I? Your own nation and ruling *kohanim* handed You over to me! What have You done?"

36 *Yeshua* answered, "My kingdom is not of this world. If My kingdom were of this world, then My servants would be fighting so that I wouldn't be handed over to the Judean leaders. But as it is, My kingdom is not from here."

37 So Pilate said to Him, "Are you a king, then?"

Yeshua answered, "You say that I am a king. For this reason I was born, and for this reason I came into the world, so that I might testify to the truth. Everyone who is of the truth hears My voice."

38 Pilate said to Him, "What is truth?" After he said this, he went out again to the Judean leaders. He said to them, "I find no case against Him. 39 But it's your custom that I release someone for you at Passover. So do you want me to release to you the King of the Jews?"

40 They shouted back, "Not this One, but *Bar-Abba*!" Now *Bar-Abba*[b] was a revolutionary.

a 18:28, 33; 19:9. The Roman governor's Jerusalem residence.

19

Bound and Sentenced

1 Then Pilate took *Yeshua* and had Him scourged. 2 The soldiers twisted together a crown of thorns and put it on His head, and dressed Him in a purple robe. 3 They kept coming up to Him, saying, "Hail, King of the Jews!" and slapping Him over and over.

4 Pilate came out again. He said to them, "Look, I'm bringing Him out to you, to let you know that I find no case against Him." 5 So *Yeshua* came out, wearing the crown of thorns and the purple robe. "Behold, the Man!" Pilate said to them.

6 When the ruling *kohanim* and officers saw Him, they yelled out, "Execute Him! Execute Him!"[c]

Pilate said to them, "Take Him yourselves and execute Him! For I don't find a case against Him."

7 The Judean leaders answered him, "We have a law,[d] and according to the *Torah* He must die, because He claimed to be *Ben-Elohim*!"

8 When Pilate heard this word, he became even more fearful. 9 He went into the Praetorium again and said to *Yeshua*, "Where are You from?" But *Yeshua* gave him no answer. 10 So Pilate said to Him, "You aren't speaking to me? Don't You know that I have the authority to release You, and I have the authority to crucify You?"

b 18:40. Also Barabbas, *Son of the Father* (Aram.).

c 19:6. Lit. *crucify* or *crucified* in 19:6, 10, 15, 16, 18, 20, 23, 32, 41; a Roman method of execution.

d 19:7. cf. Lev. 24:16

11 *Yeshua* answered, "You would have no authority over Me if it hadn't been given to you from above. For this reason, the one who handed Me over to you has the greater sin."

12 Pilate tried to let Him go after this; but the Judean leaders cried out, saying, "If you release this Man, you are no friend of Caesar. Everyone who makes himself a king opposes Caesar!"

13 So when Pilate heard these words, he brought *Yeshua* out and sat down on the judge's seat at a place called the Stone Pavement (but in Aramaic,[a] Gabbatha). 14 It was the Day of Preparation for Passover, about the sixth hour.[b] And Pilate said to the Judean leaders, "Behold, your king!"

15 They shouted back, "Take Him away! Take Him away! Execute Him!"

Pilate said to them, "Should I execute your king?"

The ruling *kohanim* answered, "We have no king but Caesar!"

16 Finally, Pilate handed *Yeshua* over to be crucified.

The Lamb of God Is Sacrificed

17 Then they took *Yeshua*. He went out, carrying His own crossbar, to the Place of a Skull, which in Aramaic[c] is called Golgotha. 18 There they crucified Him, and with Him two others, one on each side and *Yeshua* in between.

19 Pilate also wrote a sign and put it on the execution stake. It was written, "YESHUA HA-NATZRATI, THE KING OF THE JEWS." 20 Many Judeans read this sign, because the place where *Yeshua* was executed was near the city; it was written in Hebrew, Latin, and Greek.

21 The ruling *kohanim* of the Judeans were saying to Pilate, "Don't write, 'The King of the Jews,' but that He said, 'I am King of the Jews.'"

22 "What I have written, I have written," Pilate answered.

23 So the soldiers, when they executed *Yeshua*, took His outer garments and made four parts, a part for each soldier. They took His tunic also, but it was seamless, woven top to bottom in one piece. 24 So they said to one another, "Let's not tear it, but cast lots for it to see whose it will be." This was so the Scripture would be fulfilled,

> "They divided My garments among
> them,
> and for My clothing they cast lots."[d]

So the soldiers did these things.

25 Standing near the execution stake of *Yeshua* were His mother, His mother's sister, Miriam the wife of Clopas, and Miriam from Magdala. 26 *Yeshua* saw His mother and the disciple whom He loved standing nearby. He tells His mother, "Woman, behold, your son!" 27 Then He tells the disciple, "Behold, your mother!" From that very hour, the disciple took her into his own home.

28 After this, when *Yeshua* knew that all things were now completed, to fulfill the Scripture *He* said, "I am thirsty."[e] 29 A jar full of sour wine was sitting there, so they put a sponge soaked with the sour wine on a hyssop branch and brought it to His mouth. 30 When *Yeshua* tasted the sour wine, He said, "It is finished!" And He bowed His head and gave up His spirit.

31 It was the Day of Preparation, and the next day was a festival *Shabbat*. So that the bodies should not remain on the execution stake during *Shabbat*, the Judean leaders asked Pilate to have the legs broken and to have the bodies taken away.

32 So the soldiers came and broke the legs of the first and then the other who had been executed with *Yeshua*. 33 Now when they came to *Yeshua* and saw that He was already dead, they did not break His legs. 34 But one of the soldiers pierced His side with a spear, and immediately

a 19:13. Lit. *in Hebrew*.
b 19:14. i.e. noon.
c 19:17. Lit. *in Hebrew*.
d 19:24. Ps. 22:19(18).
e 19:28. cf. Ps. 69:21.

blood and water came out. 35He who has seen it has testified, and his testimony is true. He knows that he is telling the truth, so that you also may believe. 36These things happened so that the Scripture would be fulfilled, "Not a bone of His shall be broken."[a] 37And again another Scripture says, "They shall look on Him whom they have pierced."[b]

Buried in a Rich Man's Tomb

38After these things, Joseph of Arimathea asked Pilate if he could take *Yeshua's* body away. Joseph was a disciple of *Yeshua*, but secretly for fear of the Judean leaders. Pilate gave permission, so Joseph came and took the body away. 39Nicodemus, who had first visited *Yeshua* at night, also came bringing a mixture of myrrh and aloes, about a hundred pounds.[c] 40Then they took the body of *Yeshua* and wrapped it in linen with the spices, as is the Jewish burial custom.

41Now in the place where He was executed, there was a garden. In the garden was a new tomb[d] where no one had yet been buried. 42Because it was the Jewish Day of Preparation and the tomb was nearby, they laid *Yeshua* there.

20

The Tomb Is Empty

1Early in the morning on the first day of the week, while it is still dark, Miriam from Magdala comes to the tomb. She sees that the stone had been rolled away from the tomb. 2So she comes running to Simon Peter and the other disciple, the one *Yeshua* loved. She tells them, "They've taken the Master out of the tomb, and we don't know where they've put Him!"

3Then Peter and the other disciple set out, going to the tomb. 4The two were running together, but the other disciple outran Peter and arrived at the tomb first. 5Leaning in, he sees the linen strips lying there. But he didn't go in.

6Then Simon Peter comes following him, and he entered the tomb. He looks upon the linen strips lying there, 7and the face cloth that had been on His head. It was not lying with the linen strips, but was rolled up in a place by itself. 8So then the other disciple, who had reached the tomb first, also entered. He saw and believed. 9For they did not yet understand from Scripture that *Yeshua* must rise from the dead.[e] 10So the disciples went back to their own homes.

Yeshua Appears to Miriam

11But Miriam stood outside the tomb weeping. As she was weeping, she bent down to look into the tomb. 12She sees two angels in white sitting, one at the head and one at the feet, where *Yeshua's* body had been lying.

13"Woman, why are you crying?" they say to her.

She says to them, "Because they took away my Master, and I don't know where they've put Him." 14After she said these things, she turned around. And she sees *Yeshua* standing there. Yet she didn't know that it was *Yeshua*.

15*Yeshua* says to her, "Woman, why are you weeping? Who are you looking for?"

Thinking He's the gardener, she says to Him, "Sir, if You've carried Him away, tell me where You've put Him, and I will take Him away."

16*Yeshua* says to her, "Miriam!"

Turning around, she says to Him in Aramaic,[f] "*Rabboni!*" (which means Teacher).

17*Yeshua* says to her, "Stop clinging to Me, for I have not yet gone up to the Father. Go to My brothers and tell them, 'I am going up to My Father and your Father, to My God and your God.'"

a 19:36. cf. Ex. 12:46; Num. 9:12; Ps. 34:21(20).
b 19:37. Zech. 12:10.
c 19:39. Roman pound=12 oz; 100 Roman pounds=75 pounds.
d 19:41. cf. Is. 53:9.
e 20:9. cf. Ps. 16:10.
f 20:16. Lit. *in Hebrew*.

John 20:2b

"They've taken the Master out of the tomb, and we don't know where they've put Him!"

[18]Miriam from Magdala comes, announcing to the disciples, "I've seen the Lord," and what He had said to her.

Yeshua Appears to the Disciples

[19]It was evening on that day, the first of the week. When the doors were locked where the disciples were, for fear of the Judean leaders, *Yeshua* came and stood in their midst! And He said to them, "*Shalom aleichem!*" [20]After He said this, He showed them His hands and His side. Then the disciples rejoiced when they saw the Lord. [21]*Yeshua* said to them again, "*Shalom aleichem!* As the Father has sent Me, I also send you."

[22]And after He said this, He breathed on them. And He said to them, "Receive the *Ruach ha-Kodesh!* [23]If you forgive anyone's sins, they are forgiven; but if you hold back, they are held back."

[24]One of the Twelve, Thomas called the Twin, was not with them when *Yeshua* came. [25]The other disciples were saying to him, "We've seen the Lord!"

But he replied to them, "Unless I see the nail prints in His hands, and put my finger into the mark of the nails, and put my hand in His side, I will never believe!"

[26]Eight days later the disciples were again inside, and Thomas was with them. *Yeshua* comes, despite the locked doors. He stood in their midst and said, "*Shalom aleichem!*" [27]Then He said to Thomas, "Put your finger here, and look at My hands. Reach out your hand and put it into My side. Stop doubting and believe!"

[28]Thomas answered and said to Him, "My Lord and my God!"

[29]*Yeshua* said to Him, "Because you have seen Me, you have believed? Blessed are the ones who have not seen and yet have believed!"

The Reason for Signs and Wonders

[30]*Yeshua* performed many other signs in the presence of the disciples, which are not written in this book. [31]But these things have been written so that you may believe that *Yeshua* is *Mashiach Ben-Elohim*, and that by believing you may have life in His name.

21

Fish for Breakfast with the Risen One

[1]After these things, *Yeshua* revealed Himself again to the disciples at the Sea of Tiberias. Now here is how He appeared. [2]Simon Peter, Thomas called the Twin, Nathanael of Cana in the Galilee, the sons of Zebedee, and two of the other disciples were together.

[3]Simon Peter said to them, "I'm going fishing."

"We're coming with you too," they said. They went out and got into the boat, and that night they caught nothing.

[4]At dawn, *Yeshua* stood on the beach; but the disciples didn't know that it was *Yeshua*. [5]So *Yeshua* said to them, "Boys, you don't happen to have any fish, do you?"

"No," they answered Him.

[6]He said to them, "Throw the net off the right side of the boat, and you'll find some." So they threw the net, and they were not able to haul it in because of the great number of fish.

[7]Therefore the disciple whom *Yeshua* loved said to Peter, "It's the Lord!" When Simon Peter heard that it was the Lord, he tied his outer garment around himself—for he was stripped down for work—and threw himself into the sea. [8]But the other disciples came in the boat from about two hundred cubits[a] offshore, dragging the net full of fish.

[9]So when they got out onto the land, they saw a charcoal fire with fish placed on it, and bread. [10]*Yeshua* said to them, "Bring some of the fish you've just caught." [11]Simon Peter went aboard and hauled the net to shore. There were 153

a 21:8. One cubit is about eighteen inches.

John 21:7b

When Simon Peter heard that it was the Lord, he tied his outer garment around himself—for he was stripped down for work—and threw himself into the sea.

fish, many of them big; but the net was
not broken. 12*Yeshua* said to them, "Come,
have breakfast." None of the disciples
dared ask Him, "Who are You?"—knowing it was the Lord.13*Yeshua* comes and
takes the bread and gives it to them, and
likewise the fish. 14This was now the third
time that *Yeshua* was revealed to the disciples after He was raised from the dead.

Love Restores Peter

15When they had finished breakfast,
Yeshua said to Simon Peter, "Simon,
son of John, do you love Me more than
these?"

"Yes, Lord," he said to Him, "You know that I love you."

He said to him, "Feed My lambs!"

16He said to him again a second time,
"Simon, son of John, do you love Me?"

"Yes, Lord," he said, "You know that I love You."

He said to him, "Take care of My sheep!"

17He said to him a third time, "Simon,
son of John, do you love Me?"

Peter was grieved because He said to him for a third time, "Do you love Me?" And he said to Him, "Lord, You know everything! You know that I love You!"

Yeshua said to him, "Feed My sheep!"[a]

18"Amen, amen I tell you, when you
were younger, you used to dress yourself and walk wherever you wanted; but
when you grow old, you will stretch out
your hands, and someone else will dress
you and carry you where you do not want
to go." 19Now this He said to indicate by
what kind of death Peter was going to
glorify God. And after this, *Yeshua* said to
him, "Follow Me!"

20Peter, turning around, sees the disciple following. This was the one whom
Yeshua loved, who also had reclined
against *Yeshua's* chest at the *seder* meal
and said, "Master, who is the one who is
betraying You?" 21Seeing him, Peter said
to *Yeshua*, "Lord, what about him?"

22*Yeshua* said to him, "If I want him to
remain until I come, what is that to you?
You follow Me!" 23Therefore this saying
went out among the brothers, that this
disciple would not die. Yet *Yeshua* did not
say to him that he would not die, but, "If
I want him to remain until I come, what is
that to you?"

John's Witness

24This is the disciple who is an eyewitness of these things and wrote these
things. We know that his testimony is
true. 25There are also many other things
that *Yeshua* did. If all of them were to be
written one by one, I suppose that not
even the world itself will have room for
the books being written!

a 21:15-17. Some mss. say *Simon, son of Jonah*.

The Acts of the *Shlichim*

Introduction

Acts is the second volume of Luke's historical account that began with his gospel. It falls into two parts: chapters 1–12 focus on Peter in Jewish and Samaritan geographic regions, while chapters 13–28 are concerned with Paul in largely Gentile areas. Rather abruptly, Acts ends with Paul's house arrest in Rome, around 62 c.e.—and with no mention of the destruction of the Temple in 70 c.e., this book was likely written between those two events.

Acts is above all about God's work through the *Ruach ha-Kodesh*, filling and empowering the *shlichim* and other Jews to spread the Good News. It has been observed that Acts pauses to summarize the growth and spread of God's Word five times (6:7, 9:31, 12:24, 16:5, and 19:20). Thus, Acts shows that *Yeshua's* statement in Acts 1:8 is being fulfilled—a fulfillment whose promise stretches back to Genesis 12:1-3.

Along the way, we see that the inclusion of Gentiles in God's plan—one of Luke's key themes—occurs amidst dissension, debate (including the issue of the place of the Torah for Gentiles), and compromise. Yet through the riots and imprisonments, arguments and personality conflicts, Luke shows that the *Ruach ha-Kodesh* is at work. In fact, the *Ruach ha-Kodesh* is another key theme of Luke, as are the ideas that we are living in the "last days" and that salvation comes through forgiveness and what follows—the removal of sins.

In writing Acts, Luke may have wanted to help Jewish and Gentile believers reconcile. He may also be spreading the Good News to Romans (much of Acts consists of Paul's trials and defenses), as well as to Jews (to show that Paul was not opposed to Jewish compliance with the written *Torah*). Luke is also concerned about helping both Gentile and Jewish believers work out the question of their identity in a pluralistic world and vis-à-vis the opposing claims of the Jewish leadership. All this makes Acts relevant for believers today. Luke's message to us is that despite competing religious voices and official opposition to *Yeshua* from Jewish leadership, God will continue to fulfill His promised plan of salvation.

A Look Inside Acts

When Will *Yeshua* Restore
the Kingdom? (1:1)
Appointing a New *Shaliach* (1:12)

The *Ruach* Fills the *Talmidim* (2:1)
Peter Speaks to the *Shavuot* Crowd (2:14)
Teshuvah—Thousands Immersed (2:37)
New Covenant Community Begins (2:42)

A Lame Beggar Walks (3:1)
Peter Speaks at the Temple (3:11)

Standing before the Sanhedrin (4:1)
Prayer for Courage (4:23)
Spirit-Filled Community Life (4:32)

Ananias and Sapphira Lie
to the *Ruach* (5:1)
Signs and Wonders, Angelic Jailbreak,
and Bold Witness (5:12)

Appointed for Service (6:1)
Stephen's Testimony
and Martyrdom (6:8)

Saul Persecutes Messiah's
Community (8:1)
The Good News Spreads to Samaria (8:4)
An Ethiopian Asks about Isaiah 53 (8:26)

Saul Turns from Murder to Messiah (9:1)
Signs and Wonders Follow Peter (9:32)

The Centurion's Vision (10:1)
Peter's Vision (10:9)
Peter Goes to Cornelius (10:24)
The *Ruach* Falls on the Gentiles (10:44)

Peter Reports to Jerusalem (11:1)
Discipling in Diaspora (11:19)

Persecution and Deliverance (12:1)
Herod Gets His Due (12:20)

Sent Out from Antioch (13:1)
Paul's Message in
Diaspora Synagogues (13:13)

Mixed Crowds Believe
Amidst Persecution (14:1)

Jerusalem Council Rules
on Circumcision (15:1)
Letter to Diaspora Communities (15:22)
New Teams Strengthen
Communities (15:36)

Going West to Macedonia (16:6)
Salvation for a Jailer's Household (16:25)

Synagogue Responses Vary (17:1)
An Unknown God in Athens (17:16)

Many Respond in Corinth (18:1)
Sailing East to Revisit
Communities (18:18)
Discipling New Leaders (18:24)

God's Power Displayed in Ephesus (19:8)
Idol-Makers Start a Riot (19:21)

Escaping Death (20:1)
Prophetic Warnings (20:13)

Going to Jerusalem
Despite Warnings (21:1)
Advice from Jacob and the Elders (21:17)
Trouble at the Temple (21:27)

Paul's Testimony on
the Temple Stairs (22:1)
The Romans Intervene (22:23)
Delivered to the Council (22:30)

Conspiracy to Kill Paul (23:12)
Escorted to Caesarea (23:23)

Defense Before Governor Felix (24:1)
In Prison for Two Years (24:22)

Appeal to Caesar (25:1)
Festus Seeks Agrippa's Counsel (25:13)

Defense Before King Agrippa (26:1)

1

When Will *Yeshua* Restore the Kingdom?

1 I wrote the first volume, Theophilus, about all that *Yeshua* began to do and teach— 2 up to the day He was taken up, after He had given orders by the *Ruach ha-Kodesh* to the *shlichim* He had chosen. 3 To them He showed Himself to be alive after His suffering through many convincing proofs, appearing to them for forty days and speaking about the kingdom of God.

4 Now while staying with them, He commanded them not to leave Jerusalem, but to wait for what the Father promised—which, He said, "you heard from Me. 5 For John immersed with water, but you will be immersed in the *Ruach ha-Kodesh* not many days from now."

6 So when they gathered together, they asked Him, "Lord, are You restoring the kingdom to Israel at this time?"

7 He said to them, "It is not your place to know the times or seasons which the Father has placed under His own control. 8 But you will receive power when the *Ruach ha-Kodesh* has come upon you; and you will be My witnesses in Jerusalem, and through all Judah, and Samaria, and to the end of the earth."

9 After saying all this—while they were watching—He was taken up, and a cloud received Him out of their sight. 10 While they were staring into heaven as He went up, suddenly two men stood with them in white clothing. 11 They said, "Men of Galilee, why do you keep standing here staring into heaven? This *Yeshua*, who was taken up from you into heaven, will come in the same way as you saw Him go into heaven."

Appointing a New *Shaliach*

12 Then they returned to Jerusalem from the Mount of Olives[a] (which is near Jerusalem, a *Shabbat* day's journey[b]). 13 When they had entered, they went up to the upper room where they were staying—Peter and John and Jacob and Andrew; Philip and Thomas, Bartholomew and Matthew; Jacob son of Alphaeus and Simon the Zealot and Judah son of Jacob. 14 All these with one mind were continuing together in prayer—along with the women and Miriam, *Yeshua*'s mother, and His brothers.

15 In those days, Peter stood up among the brothers and sisters (the number of names all together was about a hundred and twenty) and said, 16 "Brothers,[c] the Scripture had to be fulfilled, which the *Ruach ha-Kodesh* foretold by the mouth of David, concerning Judah—who became a guide to those who seized *Yeshua*. 17 For he was counted among us and received his share of this office." 18 (Now this man Judah bought a field with the reward of his wickedness. Falling headfirst, he burst open in the middle and his intestines splattered out. 19 And it became known to all those living in Jerusalem, so in their own language that field was called Akeldama[d]—that is, 'Field of Blood.') 20 For it is written in the Book of Psalms,

> 'Let his dwelling place become desolate,
> and let there be no one living in it'[e]
> and 'Let another take his position.'[f]

21 Therefore one of the men who have accompanied us all the time that the Lord *Yeshua* went in and out among us— 22 beginning with His immersion by John until the day He was taken up from us—must become a witness with us of His resurrection."

23 So they nominated two—Joseph, called Barsabbas (also called Justus), and

a 1:12. Lit. *the hill called Olivet*, meaning *olive grove*.

b 1:12. About one-half mile.

c 1:16; 2:29; 7:2; 13:15, 26, 38; 15:7, 13; 23:1, 6; 28:17. Lit. *men brothers*, addressing in particular the males in this mixed group of believers.

d 1:19. Grk. *Hakeldamach*; Aram. *Chakel-d'ma*.

e 1:20. cf. Ps. 69:26(25).

f 1:20. cf. Ps. 109:8(108:8 LXX).

Matthias. [24]And they prayed and said, "You, O Lord, who knows the hearts of all men, show us which of these two You have chosen [25]to take the position in this office as *shaliach*, from which Judah turned aside to go to his own place." [26]Then they cast lots for them, and the lot fell upon Matthias; and he was added to the eleven *shlichim*.

2

The *Ruach* Fills the *Talmidim*

[1]When the day of *Shavuot*[a] had come, they were all together in one place. [2]Suddenly there came from heaven a sound like a mighty rushing wind, and it filled the whole house where they were sitting. [3]And tongues like fire spreading out appeared to them and settled on each one of them. [4]They were all filled with the *Ruach ha-Kodesh* and began to speak in other tongues as the Spirit enabled them to speak out.

[5]Now Jewish people were staying in Jerusalem, devout men from every nation under heaven. [6]And when this sound came, the crowd gathered. They were bewildered, because each was hearing them speaking in his own language. [7]And they were amazed and astonished, saying, "All these who are speaking—aren't they Galileans? [8]How is it that we each hear our own birth language? [9]Parthians and Medes and Elamites and those living in Mesopotamia, Judea and Cappadocia, Pontus and Asia,[b] [10]Phrygia and Pamphylia, Egypt and parts of Libya toward Cyrene, and visitors from Rome [11](both Jewish people and proselytes), Cretans and Arabs—we hear them declaring in our own tongues the mighty deeds of God!" [12]And they were all amazed and perplexed, saying to each other, "What does this mean?"

[13]Others, poking fun, were saying, "They are full of sweet new wine!"

Peter Speaks to the *Shavuot* Crowd

[14]But Peter, standing with the Eleven, raised his voice and addressed them: "Fellow Judeans and all who are staying in Jerusalem, let this be known to you, and pay attention to my words. [15]These men are not drunk, as you suppose—for it's only the third hour of the day![c] [16]But this is what was spoken about through the prophet Joel:

[17]'And it shall be in the last days,' says God,
'that I will pour out My Spirit on all flesh.
Your sons and your daughters shall prophesy,
your young men shall see visions,
and your old men shall dream dreams.
[18]Even on My slaves, male and female,
I will pour out My Spirit in those days,
and they shall prophesy.
[19] And I will give wonders in the sky above
and signs on the earth beneath—
blood, and fire, and smoky vapor.
[20]The sun shall be turned to darkness
and the moon to blood
before the great and glorious Day of *ADONAI* comes.
[21]And it shall be that everyone who calls on the name of *ADONAI*
shall be saved.'[d]

[22]"Men of Israel, hear these words! *Yeshua ha-Natzrati*—a Man authenticated to you by God with mighty deeds and wonders and signs God performed through Him in your midst, as you yourselves know—[23]this *Yeshua*, given over by God's predetermined plan and

a 2:1. Grk. *Pentecost*; Heb. *Shavuot*; *Feast of Weeks*.
b 2:9; 6:9; 16:6; 19:10, 22, 26, 27, 31; 20:4, 16, 18; 21:27; 24:19; 27:2. The Roman province of Asia, in the western part of Asia Minor (now part of Turkey).
c 2:15. 9 a.m.
d 2:17-21. cf. Joel 2:28-32.

foreknowledge, nailed to the cross by the hand of lawless men, you killed. 24But God raised Him up, releasing Him from the pains of death, since it was impossible for Him to be held by it. 25For David says about Him,

'I saw *ADONAI* always before me,
for He is at my right hand
so that I might not be shaken.
26Therefore my heart was glad and my tongue rejoiced;
moreover, my body also will live in hope,
27because You will not abandon my soul to *Sheol*
or let Your Holy One see decay.
28You have made known to me the paths of life;
You will fill me with joy in Your presence.'[a]

29"Brothers, I can confidently tell you that the patriarch David died and was buried—his tomb is with us to this day. 30So because he was a prophet and knew God had sworn with an oath to him to seat one of his descendants on his throne,[b] 31David saw beforehand and spoke of Messiah's resurrection—that He was not abandoned to *Sheol*, and His body did not see decay.[c]

32"This *Yeshua* God raised up—we all are witnesses! 33Therefore, being exalted to the right hand of God and receiving from the Father the promise of the *Ruach ha-Kodesh*, He poured out this—what you now see and hear. 34For David did not ascend into the heavens; yet he himself says,

'*ADONAI* said to my Lord,
"Sit at my right hand,
35until I make Your enemies a footstool for Your feet."'[d]

a 2:29. cf. Ps. 16:8-11.
b 2:30. cf. Ps. 132:11; 2 Sam. 7:12ff; Ps. 89:3ff.
c 2:31. cf. Ps. 16:10.
d 2:34-35. Ps. 110:1(109:1 LXX).

36"Therefore let the whole house of Israel know for certain that God has made Him—this *Yeshua* whom you had crucified—both Lord and Messiah!"

Teshuvah—Thousands Immersed

37Now when they heard this, they were cut to the heart and said to Peter and the rest of the *shlichim*, "Fellow brothers, what shall we do?"

38Peter said to them, "Repent, and let each of you be immersed in the name of Messiah *Yeshua* for the removal of your sins, and you will receive the gift of the *Ruach ha-Kodesh*. 39For the promise is for you and your children, and for all who are far away—as many as *ADONAI* our God calls to Himself."

40With many other words he warned them and kept urging them, saying, "Save yourselves from this twisted generation!"[e] 41So those who received his message were immersed, and that day about three thousand souls were added.

New CovenantCommunity Begins

42They were devoting themselves to the teaching of the *shlichim* and to fellowship, to breaking bread and to prayers. 43Fear lay upon every soul, and many wonders and signs were happening through the *shlichim*. 44And all who believed were together, having everything in common. 45They began selling their property and possessions and sharing them with all, as any had need. 46Day by day they continued with one mind, spending time at the Temple and breaking bread from house to house. They were sharing meals with gladness and sincerity of heart, 47praising God and having favor with all the people. And

e 2:40. cf. Deut. 32:5.

Acts 2:38

Peter said to them, "Repent, and let each of you be immersed in the name of Messiah Yeshua for the removal of your sins, and you will receive the gift of the Ruach ha-Kodesh.

every day the Lord was adding to their number[a] those being saved.

3

A Lame Beggar Walks

1 Now Peter and John were going up to the Temple at the ninth hour,[b] the time of prayer. 2 A man lame from birth was being carried—every day they used to put him at the Temple gate called Beautiful, so he could beg for *tzedakah* from those entering the Temple. 3 When he saw Peter and John about to go into the Temple, he began asking to receive *tzedakah*.

4 But Peter, along with John, looked straight at him and said, "Look at us!" 5 So he gave them his attention, expecting to receive something from them. 6 But Peter said, "Silver and gold I do not have, but what I do have I give to you—in the name of *Yeshua ha-Mashiach ha-Natzrati*, get up and walk!" 7 Then grabbing him by the right hand, he raised him up; and immediately the man's feet and ankles were made strong. 8 Jumping up, he stood and began walking; and he went with them into the Temple, walking and leaping and praising God!

9 Now all the people saw him walking and praising God. 10 They began to realize he was the one who used to sit begging for *tzedakah* at the Beautiful Gate of the Temple, and they were filled with wonder and astonishment over what had happened to him.

Peter Speaks at the Temple

11 While he was clinging to Peter and John, all the people together came running toward them in the place called Solomon's Portico. 12 But when Peter saw, he responded to the people, "Men of Israel, why are you amazed at this? Why do you stare at us—as if by our own power or godliness we had made this man walk? 13 The God of Abraham and Isaac and Jacob, the God of our fathers, has glorified His Servant[c] *Yeshua*—the One you handed over and disowned before Pilate, though he had decided to release Him. 14 But you rejected the Holy and Righteous One and asked for a murderer to be granted to you. 15 You killed the Author of life—the One God raised from the dead! We are witnesses of it. 16 Now through faith in the name of *Yeshua*, His name has strengthened this man whom you see and know. Indeed, the faith through *Yeshua* has given this man perfect health in front of you all.

17 "Now brothers, I know that you acted in ignorance, just as your leaders did. 18 But what God foretold through the mouth of all His prophets—that His Messiah was to suffer—so He has fulfilled. 19 Repent, therefore, and return—so your sins might be blotted out, 20 so times of relief might come from the presence of *Adonai* and He might send *Yeshua*, the Messiah appointed for you. 21 Heaven must receive Him, until the time of the restoration of all the things that God spoke about long ago through the mouth of His holy prophets. 22 Moses said, '*Adonai* your God will raise up for you a Prophet like me from among your brothers. Hear and obey Him in all that He shall say to you. 23 And it shall be that every soul that will not listen to that Prophet shall be completely cut off from the people.'[d] 24 Indeed, all the prophets who have spoken from Samuel on have announced these days. 25 You are the sons of the prophets and also of the covenant that God cut with your fathers,[e] saying to Abraham, 'In your seed shall all the families of the earth be blessed.'[f] 26 God raised up His Servant and sent Him first to you, to bless you all by turning each of you from your wicked ways."

a 2:47. Some mss. read *to the community* (Grk. *ekklesia*).
b 3:1. 3 p.m., the time of the daily offering, *minchah*.
c 3:13. cf. Isa. 52:13-53:12.
d 3:23. cf. Deut. 18:15-19(LXX); Lev. 23:29(LXX).
e 3:25. cf. Exod. 24:8; Heb. 10:16.
f 3:25. cf. Gen. 12:3; 22:18.

4

Standing Before the Sanhedrin

[1]As Peter and John were speaking to
the people, the *kohanim* and the captain of the Temple and the Sadducees
came up to them. [2]They were indignant
because Peter and John were teaching
the people and announcing in *Yeshua*
the resurrection of the dead. [3]So they
grabbed them and put them in jail until
the next day, for it was already evening.
[4]But many who heard the message
believed, and the number of the men
came to about five thousand.

[5]On the next day, the rulers and
elders and *Torah* scholars were gathered
together in Jerusalem. [6]Annas the *kohen
gadol* was there, and Caiaphas and John
and Alexander, and all those who were
of high-priestly descent. [7]When they had
placed Peter and John in their midst, they
began to inquire, "By what power or in
what name did you do this?"

[8]Then Peter, filled with the *Ruach ha-
Kodesh*, said to them, "Rulers and elders
of the people! [9]If we are on trial today
for a *mitzvah* done for a sick man, as to
how this fellow was healed, [10]let it be
known to all of you and to all the people
of Israel, that by the name of *Yeshua ha-
Mashiach ha-Natzrati*—whom you had
crucified, whom God raised from the
dead—this one stands before you whole.
[11]This *Yeshua* is 'the stone—rejected by
you, the builders—that has become the
chief cornerstone.'[a] [12]There is salvation
in no one else, for there is no other name
under heaven given to mankind by which
we must be saved!"

[13]Now when they saw the boldness
of Peter and John and figured out they
were laymen without training, they were
amazed. They began to realize that these
men had been with *Yeshua*. [14]But seeing
the healed man standing with them, they
had nothing to say in response. [15]When
they had ordered Peter and John to go
out of the council chamber, they began
to confer with one another, [16]saying,
"What shall we do with these men? For
indeed, it's obvious to everyone living in
Jerusalem that a remarkable miracle has
happened through them, and we cannot
deny it. [17]But so it won't spread any further among the people, let's warn them
not to speak anymore to anyone in this
name."

[18]So they called them in and ordered
them not to speak or teach at all in the
name of *Yeshua*. [19]But Peter and John
replied, "Whether it is right in the sight
of God to listen to you rather than to
God, you decide. [20]For we cannot stop
speaking about what we have seen and
heard."

[21]After threatening them again, they
let them go—finding no way they could
punish them on account of the people,
because they all were glorifying God for
what had happened. [22]For the man in
whom this miracle of healing had happened was more than forty years old.

Prayer for Courage

[23]As soon as they were released, Peter
and John went to their own people and
reported all that the ruling *kohanim* and
elders had said to them. [24]When they
heard it, they lifted their voices together
to God and said, "O Sovereign Master,
'You made heaven and earth and the sea,
and everything in them.'[b] [25]You said by
the *Ruach ha-Kodesh*, through the mouth
of our father David Your servant,

'Why did the nations rage
and the peoples plot foolish things?
[26]The kings of the earth took their
stand
and the rulers were gathered
together
against ADONAI and against His
Anointed One.'[c]

a 4:21. Ps. 118:22.

b 4:24. cf. Exod. 20:11; Ps. 146:6; Neh. 9:6.

c 4:25-26. Ps. 2:1-2(LXX).

27"For truly both Herod and Pontius Pilate, along with the Gentiles and
the peoples of Israel, were gathered
together in this city against Your holy
Servant *Yeshua*, whom You anointed.
28They did whatever Your hand and Your
purpose predetermined to happen.
29And now, Lord, look at their threats,
and grant Your servants to speak Your
word with utmost courage— 30while You
stretch out Your hand to heal, and signs
and wonders take place through the
name of Your holy Servant *Yeshua*."
31When they had prayed, the place
where they were gathered was shaken.
And they were all filled with the *Ruach
ha-Kodesh* and began to speak the word
of God with boldness.

Spirit-Filled Community Life

32Now the whole group of those who
believed was one in heart and mind. No
one would say anything he owned was
his own, but they had everything in common. 33With great power the *shlichim*
were giving witness to the resurrection
of the Lord *Yeshua*, and abundant favor
was upon them all. 34No one among
them was needy, for all who were owners of lands or houses would sell them
and bring the proceeds 35and set them
at the feet of the *shlichim*. And the proceeds were distributed according to the
need each one had.
36Now Joseph, also called Barnabas
by the *shlichim* (which is translated Son
of Encouragement), was a Levite and
native of Cyprus. 37He sold a field that he
owned and brought the money and laid it
at the feet of the *shlichim*.

5

Ananias and Sapphira Lie to the *Ruach*

1On the other hand, a man named Ananias together with his wife, Sapphira,
sold a property. 2He kept back some of
the proceeds, with his wife's full knowledge, and brought part of it and set it at
the feet of the *shlichim*.
3But Peter said, "Ananias, why has
satan filled your heart to lie to the *Ruach
ha-Kodesh* and keep back part of the proceeds of the land? 4While it remained
unsold, it was your own, wasn't it? And
after it was sold, wasn't it at your dis-
posal? How did this deed get into your
heart? You haven't lied to men but to
God."
5As soon as he heard these words,
Ananias fell down and died. Great fear
came upon all who heard about it. 6The
young men got up and wrapped him in a
shroud, then carried him out and buried
him.
7After an interval of about three hours,
his wife came in, not knowing what had
happened. 8Peter responded to her, "Tell
me if you sold the land for this much."
She said, "Yes, for that much."
9Then Peter said to her, "How did you
agree to test the Spirit of the Lord? Look,
the feet of those who buried your husband are at the door—they will carry you
out, too!"
10Immediately she fell down at his feet
and died. When the young men came
back in, they found her dead and carried her out and buried her beside her
husband. 11And great fear came over
the whole community and all who heard
these things.

Signs and Wonders, Angelic Jailbreak, and Bold Witness

12Meanwhile, through the hands of the
shlichim many signs and wonders were
happening among the people. And they
were all together in Solomon's Portico.
13But no one else dared to join them,
though the people continued to think
highly of them. 14Yet more than ever
those trusting in the Lord were added—
large numbers of men and women. 15They

even carried the sick into the streets and laid them on stretchers and cots, so that when Peter passed by at least his shadow might fall on some of them. [16]Crowds were also gathering from the towns around Jerusalem, bringing those who were sick or tormented by unclean spirits, and they were all being healed.

[17]But the *kohen gadol* rose up, and all those with him (that is, the sect of the Sadducees), and they were filled with jealousy. [18]They grabbed the *shlichim* and put them in a public jail. [19]But during the night an angel of ADONAI opened the prison doors, and leading them out he said, [20]"Go, stand in the Temple and speak to the people the whole message about this Life." [21]Now when they heard that, they entered the Temple at daybreak and began teaching.

When the *kohen gadol* and those with him arrived, they called together the Sanhedrin, even the council of elders of *B'nei-Israel*, and sent to the prison to have the prisoners brought in. [22]But when the officers came, they did not find them in the prison. So they returned and reported, [23]saying, "We found the prison locked with maximum security and the guards standing at the doors; but when we opened up, we found no one inside."

[24]When the captain of the Temple and the ruling *kohanim* heard these words, they were perplexed about them, wondering where this would lead. [25]But someone came and reported to them, "The men you put in prison are standing in the Temple and teaching the people!" [26]Then the captain went off with the officers and brought the *shlichim*—but not with force, because they feared they might be stoned by the people.

[27]When they had brought them, they placed them before the Sanhedrin. The *kohen gadol* questioned them, [28]saying, "We gave you strict orders not to teach in this name—and look, you have filled Jerusalem with your teaching, and you intend to bring on us the blood of this Man!"

[29]Peter and the *shlichim* replied, "We must obey God rather than men. [30]The God of our fathers raised up *Yeshua*, whom you seized and had crucified.[a] [31]This One God exalted at His right hand as Leader and Savior,[b] to give repentance to Israel and removal of sins. [32]And we are witnesses of these events—as is the *Ruach ha-Kodesh*, whom God has given to those who obey Him."

[33]Now when they heard this, they became enraged and wanted to kill them. [34]But a certain Pharisee named Gamaliel, a teacher of the *Torah* respected by all the people, stood up in the Sanhedrin and gave orders to put the men outside for a little while. [35]Then he said to them, "Men of Israel, be careful what you are about to do with these men. [36]For some time ago Theudas rose up, claiming to be somebody; and a number of men, maybe four hundred, joined up with him. He was killed, and all who followed him were scattered and came to nothing. [37]After this fellow, Judah the Galilean rose up in the days of the census and got people to follow him. He also perished, and all who followed him were scattered. [38]So now I tell you, stay away from these men and leave them alone. For if this plan or undertaking is of men, it will come to an end; [39]but if it is of God, you will not be able to stop them. You might even be found fighting against God." They took his advice, [40]called in the *shlichim*, flogged them, ordered them not to continue speaking in the name of *Yeshua*, and let them go.

[41]So they left the presence of the Sanhedrin, rejoicing that they were considered worthy to be dishonored on account of His name.[c] [42]And every day, in the Temple and from house to house, they never stopped teaching and proclaiming *Yeshua* as the Messiah.

a 5:30. Lit. *killed by hanging Him on a tree.*
b 5:31, 13:23. cf. Ps. 27:1(26:1 LXX).
c 5:41. Lit. *the name*; cf. Phil. 2:9; 3 Jn. 7.

6

Appointed for Service

[1]Now in those days, when the disciples were multiplying, grumbling arose[a] among the Hellenists against the Hebrews, because their widows were being overlooked in the daily support. [2]So the Twelve called together the whole group of the disciples and said, "It is not right for us to neglect the word of God in order to serve tables. [3]So, brothers, select from among you seven reputable men, full of the Spirit and wisdom, whom we may put in charge of this duty. [4]But we will devote ourselves to prayer and to the service of the Word."

[5]The statement pleased the whole group; and they chose Stephen, a man full of faith and the *Ruach ha-Kodesh*, and Philip, Prochorus, Nicanor, Timon, Parmenas, and Nicolas, a proselyte from Antioch. [6]They placed these men before the *shlichim*; and after praying, they laid hands on them.[b]

[7]The word of God kept on spreading, and the number of disciples in Jerusalem greatly multiplied; even a great number of the *kohanim* were becoming obedient to the faith.

Stephen's Testimony and Martyrdom

[8]Now Stephen, full of grace and power, was doing great wonders and signs among the people. [9]But some men from what was called the Synagogue of the Freedmen—both Cyrenians and Alexandrians, as well as some from Cilicia and Asia[c]—stood up and began arguing with Stephen. [10]But they could not withstand the wisdom and the Spirit by whom he was speaking.

[11]Then they secretly instigated men into saying, "We have heard him speaking blasphemous words against Moses and against God!" [12]They also incited the people, the elders, and the *Torah* scholars; and they rushed at Stephen, seized him, and led him away to the Sanhedrin. [13]They set up false witnesses who said, "This man never stops speaking words against this holy place and the *Torah*. [14]For we have heard him saying that this *Yeshua ha-Natzrati* will destroy this place and change the customs that Moses handed down to us." [15]Watching him intently, everyone who was sitting in the Sanhedrin saw that his face was like the face of an angel.

7

[1]Then the *kohen gadol* said, "Are these things so?"

[2]Stephen declared, "Brothers and fathers, listen. The God of glory appeared to our father Abraham when he was in Mesopotamia, before he lived in Haran. [3]He said to him, 'Leave your country and your relatives, and come here to the land that I will show you.' [4]Then he left the land of the Chaldeans and settled in Haran. From there, after his father died, God moved him to this land where you now live. [5]He gave him no inheritance in it—not even a foothold—yet He promised 'to give it to him as a possession to him and to his descendants after him,' even though he had no child.

[6]"But God spoke in this way, that his 'descendants would be foreigners in a land belonging to others, and they would enslave and mistreat them for four hundred years. [7]But I will judge the nation they serve as slaves,' God said, 'and afterward they shall come out and serve Me in this place.'[d]

[8]"Then God gave Abraham the covenant of circumcision.[e] So he became

a 6:1. cf. Exod. 16:7-8.
b 6:6. cf. Num. 8:10; 27:18; Deut. 34:9.
c 6:9. The Roman province of Asia, in the western part of Asia Minor (now part of Turkey).
d 7:6-7. Gen. 15:13-14.
e 7:8. Heb. *brit milah*.

the father of Isaac and circumcised him on the eighth day, and so Isaac with Jacob, and Jacob with the twelve patriarchs. 9The patriarchs became jealous of Joseph and sold him into Egypt. Yet God was with him. 10He rescued him out of all his troubles and granted him favor and wisdom before Pharaoh, king of Egypt, who made him governor over Egypt and all his household.

11"Famine and great suffering came over all Egypt and Canaan, and our fathers could find no food. 12But when Jacob heard that there was grain in Egypt, he sent our fathers there the first time. 13On the second visit, Joseph made himself known to his brothers, and his family became known to Pharaoh. 14So Joseph sent and called for Jacob and all his relatives—seventy-five persons. 15Jacob went down to Egypt and died, he and our fathers. 16They were carried to Shechem and laid in the tomb that Abraham had bought for a sum of money from the sons of Hamor in Shechem.

17"But as the time drew near for the promise God had sworn to Abraham, the people increased and multiplied in Egypt—18until 'there arose another king over Egypt who knew nothing about Joseph.'[a] 19Dealing with our people with cruel cunning, this king mistreated our fathers and forced them to abandon their infants so they would not survive.

20"At this time Moses was born—extraordinary before God. For three months he was nurtured in his father's house. 21And when he was set outside, Pharaoh's daughter took him and raised him as her own son. 22Moses was educated in all the wisdom of the Egyptians, and he was powerful in his words and deeds.

23"When he was approaching forty years of age, it came into his heart to visit his brothers, *B'nei-Israel*. 24When he saw one of them being treated unjustly, he went to the defense of the oppressed man and avenged him by striking down the Egyptian. 25He was assuming that his brothers understood that by his hand God was delivering them, but they did not understand. 26So on the next day he appeared to them as they were fighting. He tried to reconcile them in *shalom*, saying, 'Men, you are brothers. Why do you wrong one another?'

27"But the one doing wrong to his neighbor pushed him away, saying, 'Who appointed you ruler and judge over us? 28You don't want to kill me as you killed the Egyptian yesterday, do you?'[b] 29At this remark, Moses fled and became an exile in the land of Midian, where he became the father of two sons.

30"When forty years had passed, an angel appeared to him in the wilderness of Mount Sinai in the flame of a burning bush. 31When Moses saw it, he was amazed at the sight. But when he came up to look, there came the voice of ADONAI: 32'I am the God of your fathers, the God of Abraham and Isaac and Jacob.'[c]

"Moses trembled in fear and did not dare to look. 33But *ADONAI* said to him, 'Take the sandals off your feet, for the place where you are standing is holy ground. 34I have surely seen the oppression of my people in Egypt and have heard their groaning, and I have come down to deliver them. Now come—let Me send you to Egypt.'

35"This Moses—whom they rejected, saying, 'Who appointed you as ruler and judge?'—is the one whom God sent as both ruler and redeemer, by the hand of the angel who appeared to him in the bush. 36This man led them out, performing wonders and signs in the land of Egypt, and at the Red Sea, and in the wilderness for forty years. 37This is the Moses who said to *B'nei-Israel*, 'God will raise up for you a prophet like me from among your brothers.'[d]

38"This is the one who was in the community in the wilderness, with the

a 7:18. Exod. 1:8.

b 7:28. Exod. 2:14.

c 7:32. Exod. 3:6.

d 7:37. Exod. 12:41; 33:1.

angel who spoke to him on Mount Sinai,
and with our fathers. He received living
words to pass on to us. 39Our fathers
did not want to be obedient to him, but
shoved him aside. And in their hearts
they turned back to Egypt, 40 saying to
Aaron, 'Make gods for us who will go
before us. For this Moses who led us out
of the land of Egypt—we have no idea
what has happened to him.'[a]

41"And they made a calf in those days,
offered a sacrifice to the idol, and were
rejoicing in the works of their hands.
42But God turned and gave them over to
serve the host of heaven, just as it is written in the book of the Prophets:

'It was not to Me that you brought
sacrifices and offerings
for forty years in the wilderness,
was it, O House of Israel?
43You also took up the tent of Moloch
and the star of your god Rephan,
the images you made to worship.
And I will deport you beyond
Babylon.'[b]

44"Our fathers had the Tent of Witness in the wilderness—just as the One
speaking to Moses had directed him to
make it according to the design he had
seen. 45Our fathers received it in turn and
brought it in with Joshua when they took
possession of the land of the nations that
God drove out before our fathers. So it
remained until the days of David, 46who
found favor in God's sight. He asked
to find a dwelling place for the God[c] of
Jacob. 47But Solomon built a house for
Him. 48However, *Elyon* does not dwell in
man-made houses. As the prophet says,

49'Heaven is My throne,
and the earth is the footstool of My
feet.
What kind of house will you build for
Me, says *ADONAI*,
or what is the place of My rest?
50Did not My Hand make all these
things?'[d]

51"O you stiff-necked people! You uncircumcised of heart and ears! You always
resist the *Ruach ha-Kodesh*; just as your
fathers did, you do as well. 52Which of
the prophets did your fathers not persecute? They killed the ones who foretold
the coming of the Righteous One. Now
you have become His betrayers and murderers—53you who received the *Torah* by
direction of angels and did not keep it!"

54When they heard these things, they
became enraged and began gnashing
their teeth at him. 55But Stephen, full of
the *Ruach ha-Kodesh*, gazed into heaven
and saw the glory of God—and *Yeshua*
standing at the right hand of God. 56And
he said, "Look, I see the heavens opened
and the Son of Man standing at the right
hand of God!"

57But they covered their ears; and crying out with a loud voice, they rushed
at him with one impulse. 58Driving him
out of the city, they began stoning him,
and the witnesses laid down their cloaks
at the feet of a young man named Saul.
59They went on stoning Stephen as he
was calling out, "Lord *Yeshua*, receive my
spirit!" 60Then he fell on his knees and
cried out with a loud voice, "Lord, do not
hold this sin against them!" After he said
this, he died.[e]

8

Saul Persecutes Messiah's Community

1Now Saul was in agreement with Stephen's execution. On that day a great
persecution arose against Messiah's
community in Jerusalem, and they were

a 7:40. Exod. 32:1, 23.
b 7:42-43. Amos 5:25-27.
c 7:46. Lit. *house*; cf. Ps. 132:3-5(LXX).
d 7:50. Isa. 66:2.
e 7:60. Lit. *he fell asleep.*

all scattered throughout the region of
Judea and Samaria, except the *shlichim*.
[2]Some devout men buried Stephen and
mourned deeply for him.

[3]But Saul was destroying Messiah's
community, entering house after house;
and dragging off men and women, he
was throwing them into prison.

The Good News Spreads to Samaria

[4]Now those who had been scattered
went around proclaiming the Word.
[5]Philip went down to the main city of
Samaria and proclaimed the Messiah to
them. [6]The crowds were paying close
attention to what Philip was saying—as
they both heard and saw the signs that
he was doing. [7]For unclean spirits were
coming out of many who were plagued,
shrieking with a loud voice. Many paralyzed and crippled were healed also. [8]So
there was great joy in that city.

[9]Now a man named Simon had been
practicing magic in the city and astonish-
ing the people of Samaria, saying he was
someone great. [10]They all were paying
special attention to him, saying, "This
man is the power of God that is called
'Great.'" [11]And they kept paying attention
to him, because for a long time he had
astonished them with his magical arts.
[12]But when they believed Philip proclaiming the Good News about the kingdom
of God and the name of Messiah *Yeshua*,
both men and women were immersed.
[13]Even Simon himself believed; and after
being immersed, he continued with
Philip. And when he saw signs and great
miracles happening, he was continually
amazed.

[14]Now when the *shlichim* in Jerusalem
heard that Samaria had accepted the
message of God, they sent Peter and
John to them. [15]They came down and
prayed for them to receive the *Ruach ha-Kodesh*. [16]For He had not yet come upon
them; they had only been immersed in
the name of the Lord *Yeshua*. [17]Then they
began laying their hands on them, and
they were receiving the *Ruach ha-Kodesh*.

[18]Now when Simon saw that the *Ruach
ha-Kodesh* was given through the laying
on of hands by the *shlichim*, he offered
them money, [19]saying, "Give this power
to me, too—so that anyone on whom I lay
hands may receive the *Ruach ha-Kodesh*."

[20]Peter said to him, "May your silver
go to ruin, and you with it—because you
thought you could buy God's gift with
money![a] [21]You have no part or share in
this matter, because your heart is not
right before God. [22]Therefore repent of
this wickedness of yours, and pray to the
Lord that, if possible, the intent of your
heart may be pardoned. [23]For I see in you
the poison of bitterness and the bondage of unrighteousness!"

[24]Simon replied, "Pray for me, so that
none of what you have said may come
upon me."

[25]So when they had testified and spoken the word of the Lord, they returned
to Jerusalem, proclaiming the Good
News to many Samaritan villages.

An Ethiopian Asks about Isaiah 53

[26]Now an angel of the Lord spoke to
Philip, saying, "Get up, and go south on
the road going down from Jerusalem to
Gaza." (This is a desert road.) [27]So he got
up and went. And behold, an Ethiopian
eunuch—an official who was responsible
for all the treasure of Candace, queen of
the Ethiopians—had traveled to Jerusalem to worship [28]and was now returning.
Sitting in his chariot, he was reading the
prophet Isaiah.

[29]The Spirit said to Philip, "Go, catch up
with this chariot."

[30]Philip ran up and heard him reading the prophet Isaiah and said, "Do you
understand what you are reading?"

[31]"How can I," he said, "unless someone guides me?" So he invited Philip to
come up and sit with him. [32]Now the

a 8:21. cf. 2 Kings 5:20–27.

passage of Scripture that he was reading
was this:

"He was led as a sheep to slaughter;
and as a lamb before its shearer is
silent,
so He opens not His Mouth.
33 In His humiliation justice was denied
Him.
Who shall recount His generation?
For His life is taken away from the
earth."[a]

34 The eunuch replied to Philip, "Please
tell me, who is the prophet talking
about—himself or someone else?"
35 Then Philip opened his mouth, and
beginning with this Scripture he proclaimed the Good News about *Yeshua*.
36 Now as they were going down the
road, they came to some water. The
eunuch said, "Look, water! What's to
prevent me from being immersed?"
37[b] 38 He ordered the chariot to stop.
They both got down into the water, Philip
and the eunuch, and Philip immersed
him. 39 When they came up out of the
water, the Spirit of the Lord snatched
Philip away.[c] The eunuch saw no more of
him, for he went on his way, rejoicing.
40 But Philip found himself at Azotus.
And as he passed through, he kept proclaiming the Good News to all the towns
until he came to Caesarea.

9

Saul Turns from Murder to Messiah

1 Now Saul, still breathing out threats
and murder against the Lord's disciples,
went to the *kohen gadol*. 2 He requested
letters of introduction from him to the
synagogues in Damascus, so that if he
found any men or women belonging to
the Way, he might bring them as prisoners to Jerusalem.
3 As he was traveling, approaching
Damascus, suddenly a light from heaven
flashed around him. 4 Falling to the
ground, he heard a voice saying to him,
"Saul, Saul, why are you persecuting
Me?"
5 "Who are You, Lord?" Saul said.
"I am *Yeshua*—whom you are persecuting.[d] 6 But get up and go into the city,
and you will be told what you must do."[e]
7 The men travelling with him stood
speechless, hearing the voice but seeing
no one.[f] 8 Saul got up from the ground—
but opening his eyes, he could see
nothing. They led him by the hand and
brought him into Damascus. 9 For three
days he could not see, and he did not eat
or drink.
10 Now there was a disciple named Ananias in Damascus. The Lord said to him,
"Ananias."
He said, "Here I am, Lord."
11 The Lord said to him, "Get up and go
to the street named Straight, and ask in
the house of Judah for someone from
Tarsus named Saul. For look, he is praying; 12 and in a vision he has seen a man
named Ananias coming in and laying his
hands on him, so that he might regain his
sight."
13 But Ananias answered, "Lord, I have
heard from many about this man—how
much harm he has done to your *kedoshim*
in Jerusalem. 14 And here he has authority
from the ruling *kohanim* to tie up all who
call on Your name."
15 But the Lord said to him, "Go, for he
is a choice instrument to carry My name
before nations and kings and *B'nei-Israel*.
16 For I will show him how much he must
suffer for My name's sake."

a 8:32-33. Isa. 53:7-8.
b 8:37. Some mss. include: *And he said, "If you believe with all your heart, you may." He replied, I believe that Yeshua the Messiah is the Son of God!"*
c 8:40. cf. 1 Kings 18:12.
d 9:5. Some mss. add: *It is hard for you to kick against the goads.*
e 9:6. Some mss. begin: *So he, trembling and astonished, said, "Lord, what do You want me to do?" Then the Lord said to him, "But get up..."*
f 9:7. cf. Dan 10:7.

Acts 9:3-4

As he was traveling, approaching Damascus, suddenly a light from heaven flashed around him. Falling to the ground, he heard a voice saying to him, "Saul, Saul, why are you persecuting Me?"

17So Ananias left and entered into the
house. Laying hands on Saul, he said,
"Brother Saul, the Lord—*Yeshua*, the
One who appeared to you on the road by
which you were coming—has sent me,
so that you might regain your sight and
be filled with the *Ruach ha-Kodesh*."
18Immediately, something like scales
fell from Saul's eyes, and he regained his
sight. Then he got up and was immersed;
19and when he had taken food, he was
strengthened. Now for several days,
he was with the disciples in Damascus.
20Immediately he began proclaiming
Yeshua in the synagogues, saying, "He is
Ben-Elohim."
21All those hearing him were amazed.
They were saying, "Isn't this the one
who made havoc in Jerusalem for all
those who call on this name? And hasn't
he come here to bring them as prisoners before the ruling *kohanim*?" 22But
Saul kept growing stronger, and he was
confounding the Jewish people living in
Damascus by proving that *Yeshua* is the
Messiah. 23When many days had passed,
these Jewish people plotted to kill him—
24but their plot became known to Saul.
They were watching the gates day and
night, to kill him. 25But the disciples took
Saul by night and let him down over the
wall, lowering him in a basket.
26When Saul arrived in Jerusalem, he
made attempts to join up with the disciples—but they were all afraid of him,
not believing that he was a disciple. 27But
Barnabas took him in and brought him to
the *shlichim*. He described to them how
Saul had seen the Lord on the road and
the Lord had spoken to him, and how he
had spoken boldly in the name of *Yeshua*.
28So Saul was with them, going in and
out in Jerusalem, speaking boldly in the
name of the Lord. 29He was speaking
and arguing with the Hellenists, but they
were trying to kill him. 30When the brothers found out, they brought him down to
Caesarea and sent him off to Tarsus.

31So Messiah's community throughout
all Judea and Galilee and Samaria had
shalom and was built up. Walking in the
fear of the Lord and in the comfort of the
Ruach ha-Kodesh, it kept multiplying.

Signs and Wonders Follow Peter

32Peter went here and there among
them all. He came down as well to the
kedoshim living in Lydda. 33There he
found a man named Aeneas, who had
been bedridden for eight years—he was
paralyzed. 34Peter said to him, "Aeneas,
Messiah *Yeshua* heals you. Get up and
pack up your bed." Immediately, he got
up! 35All who lived in Lydda and the Plain
of Sharon saw him, and they turned to
the Lord.
36In Joppa, there was a disciple named
Tabitha (which translates as Dorcas). She
was full of *mitzvot* and *tzedakah*, which
she continually did. 37In those days, she
became ill and died. When they had
washed her for burial, they placed her
in an upstairs room. 38Since Lydda was
near Joppa, the disciples—hearing that
Peter was there—sent two men to him,
begging him, "Please come to us without
delay!"
39So Peter got up and went with them.
When he arrived, they took him to the
upstairs room. All the widows were crying, showing all the tunics and other
clothing Dorcas had made while she was
with them. 40But Peter sent them all outside, and he got down on his knees and
prayed. Then, turning to the body, he
said "Tabitha, get up!" She opened her
eyes, and when she saw Peter, she sat up.
41He gave her his hand and raised her up.
Then he called the *kedoshim* and widows
and presented her alive.[a]
42It became known throughout Joppa,
and many came to believe in the Lord.
43So it happened that Peter stayed on
in Joppa for several days with Simon, a
tanner.[b]

a 9:37-41. cf. Elijah raising a child in 1 Kings 17:18-23.

b 9:43; 10:6, 32. Either a profession (e.g. *Simon, a leatherworker*) or a surname (e.g. *Simon Burseus; Simon Tanner*).

10

The Centurion's Vision

1Now in Caesarea there was a man named Cornelius, a centurion of what was called the Italian Cohort. 2He was a devout man, revering God with all his household. He gave *tzedakah* generously to the people and prayed to God continually. 3About the ninth hour of the day,[a] he saw clearly in a vision an angel of God coming and saying to him, "Cornelius!"

4He stared at him in terror and said, "What is it, Lord?"

The angel said to him, "Your prayers and *tzedakah* have gone up as a memorial offering before God. 5Now send men to Joppa and call for Simon, also named Peter. 6He is being entertained as a guest by Simon the tanner, whose house is beside the sea."

7When the angel speaking to him had left, he called two of his servants and a soldier from among those attached to his command. 8After he explained everything to them, he sent them to Joppa.

Peter's Vision

9The next day, as the soldiers were traveling and approaching the city, Peter went up to the rooftop to pray, at about the sixth hour.[b] 10Now he became very hungry and wanted to eat; but while they were preparing something, he fell into a trance. 11He saw the heavens opened, and something[c] like a great sheet coming down, lowered by its four corners to the earth. 12In it were all sorts of four-footed animals and reptiles and birds of the air.

13A voice came to him, "Get up, Peter. Kill and eat."

14But Peter said, "Certainly not, Lord! For never have I eaten anything unholy or unclean."[d]

15 Again a voice came to him, a second time: "What God has made clean, you must not consider unholy." 1This happened three times, and the sheet was immediately taken up to heaven.

17Now while Peter was puzzling about what the vision he had seen might mean, behold, the men sent by Cornelius found Simon's house and appeared before the gate. 18They called out and began to ask whether Simon, also called Peter, was staying in this place as a guest.

19Now while Peter was mulling over the vision, the Spirit said to him, "Look here, three men are looking for you. 20But get up, go downstairs, and go with them without hesitating, because I Myself have sent them."

21Going down to the men, Peter said, "Here, I'm the one you're looking for. What is the reason for your coming?"

22And they said, "Cornelius, a centurion, a righteous and God-fearing man well-spoken of by all the Jewish people, was directed by a holy angel to summon you to his house and to hear a message from you."

23So Peter invited them in to be his guests. The next day he got up and went with them, and some of the brothers from Joppa accompanied him.

Peter Goes to Cornelius

24The following day he entered Caesarea. Cornelius was waiting for them and had called together his relatives and close friends. 25As Peter entered, Cornelius met him and fell down at his feet and worshiped him.

26But Peter pulled him up, saying, "Stand up! I too am just a man."

27Talking with him, Peter went inside and found many people gathered. 28He said to them, "You yourselves know that it is not permitted for a Jewish man to

a 10:3. 3 p.m., *minchah*, time of the daily offering at the Temple.

b 10:9. Noon.

c 10:11, 16; 11:5. Lit. *thing, object, vessel.*

d 10:14. cf. Lev. 10:10; 11:7-45; Deut. 14:4-20; Ezek. 4:14; Dan. 1:8.

associate with a non-Jew or to visit him. Yet God has shown me that I should call no one unholy or unclean. 29So I came without objection when I was sent for. I ask, then, what is the reason why you sent for me?"

30Cornelius declared, "Four days ago at this hour, I was praying *minchah*[a] in my house. Suddenly, a man stood in front of me in shining clothes. 31He says, 'Cornelius, your prayer has been heard and your *tzedakah* remembered before God. 32Therefore send to Joppa and ask for Simon, who is also called Peter. He is staying in the house of Simon the tanner, by the sea.' 33So I sent for you immediately, and you have been kind enough to come. Now then, we are all here before God to hear all that you have been commanded by the Lord."

34Then Peter opened his mouth and said, "I truly understand that God is not one to show favoritism,[b] 35but in every nation the one who fears Him and does what is right is acceptable to Him. 36You know the message He sent to *B'nei-Israel*, proclaiming *shalom* through Messiah *Yeshua*—He is Lord of all. 37You know the message that has spread throughout all Judea, beginning from Galilee after the immersion that John proclaimed. 38You know how God anointed *Yeshua* of *Natzeret* with the *Ruach ha-Kodesh* and power—how He went about doing good and healing all who were oppressed by the devil, because God was with Him. 39We are witnesses to all He did, both in the Judean countryside and in Jerusalem. They put Him to death by hanging Him on a tree, 40but God raised Him up on the third day and caused Him to be visible— 41not to all the people, but to us, witnesses who were chosen beforehand by God. We ate and drank with Him after He rose from the dead. 42And He commanded us to proclaim to the people and to testify that He is the One ordained by God as Judge of the living and the dead. 43All the prophets testify about Him—that everyone who puts his trust in Him receives forgiveness of sins through His name."

The *Ruach* Falls on the Gentiles

44While Peter was still speaking these words, the *Ruach ha-Kodesh* fell on all those hearing the message. 45All the circumcised believers who came with Peter were astonished, because the gift of the *Ruach ha-Kodesh* had been poured out even on the Gentiles. 46For they were hearing them speaking in tongues and magnifying God.

Then Peter answered, 47 "Can anyone refuse water for these to be immersed, who have received the *Ruach ha-Kodesh* just as we did?" 48So he commanded them to be immersed in the name of Messiah *Yeshua*. Then they asked him to stay for a few days.

11

Peter's Report to Jerusalem

1Now the *shlichim* and brothers throughout Judea heard that the Gentiles also had received the word of God. 2But when Peter went up to Jerusalem, those of the circumcision took issue with him, 3saying, "You went to uncircumcised men and ate with them!"

4So Peter began explaining to them point by point, saying, 5"I was in the city of Joppa praying, and in a trance I saw a vision—something like a great sheet coming down, being lowered from heaven by its four corners, and it came right to me. 6I looked inside, considering it carefully, and saw four-footed creatures of the earth, wild animals, reptiles, and birds of the air. 7I also heard a voice saying, 'Get up, Peter. Kill and eat.'

8"But I said, 'Certainly not, Lord! For never has anything unholy or unclean

a 10:30. Lit. *the ninth hour*, 3 p.m., time of afternoon prayer.

b 10:34. cf. Deut. 10:17; 2 Chr. 19:7

entered my mouth.' 9But a voice from
heaven answered a second time, 'What
God has made clean, you must not consider unholy.' 10This happened three
times, and then everything was pulled
up to heaven.

11"At that very moment, three men
arrived at the house where we were,
sent to me from Caesarea. 12The Spirit
told me to go with them without hesitating. These six brothers also went with
me, and we entered the man's house.
13He reported to us how he had seen an
angel standing in his house and saying,
'Send to Joppa and bring Simon called
Peter. 14He will speak words to you by
which you will be saved—you and all
your household.'

15"As I began to speak, the *Ruach ha-
Kodesh* fell on them, just as on us at the
beginning. 16And I remembered the
word of the Lord, how He used to say,
'John immersed with water, but you will
be immersed in the *Ruach ha-Kodesh*.'
17Therefore if God gave them the same
gift as also to us after we put our trust
in the Lord Messiah *Yeshua*, who was I to
stand in God's way?"

18When they heard this they became
quiet, and they glorified God, saying,
"Then even to the Gentiles God has
granted repentance leading to life!"

Discipling in Diaspora

19Now those scattered because of the
persecution that happened in connection
with Stephen traveled as far as Phoenicia
and Cyprus and Antioch, telling the message only to Judeans. 20However, there
were some of them, men of Cyprus and
Cyrene, who came to Antioch and began
speaking to the Hellenists also, proclaiming the Lord *Yeshua*. 21 The hand of the
Lord was with them, and a great number
who believed turned to the Lord.

22News about these things reached
the ears of the community in Jerusalem, and they sent Barnabas to Antioch.
23When he arrived and saw the grace
of God, he was thrilled. He encouraged
them all to remain true to the Lord with
heartfelt devotion. 24For Barnabas was
a good man, full of the *Ruach ha-Kodesh*
and faith. And a large number was added
to the Lord.

25Then Barnabas left for Tarsus to look
for Saul, 26and when he had found him,
he brought him to Antioch. For a whole
year they met together with Messiah's
community and taught a large number.
Now it was in Antioch that the disciples
were first called "Christianoi."[a]

27Now in these days prophets came
down from Jerusalem to Antioch. 28One
of them, named Agabus, stood up and
predicted through the Spirit that there
was going to be a great famine over all
the world. (This took place during the
reign of Claudius.) 29So the disciples
decided to send relief to those brothers
and sisters living in Judea, each according to his ability. 30This they did, sending
it to the elders by the hand of Barnabas
and Saul.

12

Persecution and Deliverance

1Now at that time Herod the king
seized some from Messiah's community
to do them harm. 2He had Jacob, John's
brother, put to death with the sword.
3Seeing it pleased the Judean leaders,
he proceeded to capture Peter as well.
This was during the Days of *Matzah*.
4After seizing him, he put him in prison,
handing him over to four squads with
four soldiers each to guard him. He was
intending to bring him before the people after Passover. 5So Peter was kept
in prison, but prayer for him was being
offered fervently to God by Messiah's
community.

6Now that very night when Herod
was about to bring him out, Peter was

a 11:26. Grk. *Christianoi* (Christians); Heb. *M'shichim* (Messianics); Eng. *anointed ones*; cf. Acts 26:28; 1 Pet. 4:16.

sleeping—bound with two chains between two soldiers, while guards before the gate were keeping watch over the prison. 7Suddenly an angel of the Lord appeared, and a light shone in the cell. He poked Peter on the side and woke him up, saying, "Get up! Quick!" And the chains fell off his hands. 8Then the angel said to him, "Get dressed and put on your sandals," and he did so. Then he tells him, "Put on your cloak and follow me." 9Peter went out and kept following him—he didn't know that what was happening with the angel was real, but thought he was seeing a vision. 10After they passed a first guard and a second, they came to the iron gate leading into the city. It opened for them by itself. They went out and walked along a narrow street. Suddenly the angel left him.

11When Peter came to himself, he said, "Now I know for real that the Lord has sent His angel[a] and delivered me from the hand of Herod and from all that the Judean people were expecting." 12When he realized this, he went to the house of Miriam, the mother of John (also called Mark), where many were assembled together and praying. 13When he knocked on the door of the entrance gate, a maid named Rhoda came to answer. 14Although she recognized Peter's voice, out of joy she did not open the gate but ran in and announced that Peter was standing in front of the gate. 15They said to her, "You're crazy!" But she kept insisting it was so. But they were saying, "It is his angel."

16But Peter kept on knocking. When they opened the gate, they saw him and were amazed! 17But he motioned with his hand for them to be silent, and he explained to them how the Lord had brought him out of the prison. He said, "Go tell these things to Jacob and the brothers." Then he left and went to another place.

18When day came, there was no small commotion among the soldiers as to what had become of Peter. 19After Herod made a search for him and did not find him, he interrogated the guards and commanded that they be led away to execution. Then he went down from Judea and stayed in Caesarea.

Herod Gets His Due

20Now it happened that Herod was furious with the people of Tyre and Sidon. So they came to him, united. Having won over Blastus, the king's personal aide, they began asking for peace—because their country was supplied with food from the king's country.

21On an appointed day, Herod donned his royal robes and, taking his seat upon the throne, began to make a speech to them. 22The people were shouting, "The voice of a god and not a human!" 23Immediately, an angel of the Lord struck him down—because he did not give God the glory. And he was eaten by worms and died.

24But the word of God kept on growing and multiplying. 25And Barnabas and Saul returned to Jerusalem when they had fulfilled their service, taking along John (who was also called Mark).

13

Sent Out from Antioch

1Now in the Antioch community, there were prophets and teachers: Barnabas, Simeon called Niger, Lucius the Cyrenian, Manaen (brought up since childhood with Herod the Tetrarch), and Saul. 2While they were serving the Lord and fasting, the *Ruach ha-Kodesh* said, "Set apart for me Barnabas and Saul for the work to which I have called them." 3Then after fasting, praying, and laying hands on them, they sent them off.

4So, sent out by the *Ruach ha-Kodesh*, they went down to Seleucia, and from there they sailed to Cyprus. 5When they

a 12:11. cf. Ps. 34:7; Dan. 3:28; 6:22.

arrived at Salamis, they began to proclaim the word of God in the Jewish synagogues. They also had John[a] as a helper.

6When they had gone throughout the whole island as far as Paphos, they found a man who was a magician—a Jewish false prophet, whose name was Bar-Yeshua. 7He was with the proconsul, Sergius Paulus, an intelligent man. This man summoned Barnabas and Saul and sought to hear the word of God. 8But Elymas the magician (for so his name is translated) was opposing them, seeking to turn the proconsul away from the faith. 9But Saul, who is also Paul, filled with the *Ruach ha-Kodesh*, fixed his gaze on him 10and said, "O you, full of all deceit and trickery, son of the devil, enemy of all righteousness—will you not stop making crooked the straight paths of the Lord?[b] 11Now, behold, the hand of the Lord is upon you,[c] and you shall be blind and not see the sun for awhile." Immediately, cloudiness and darkness fell upon him, and he went about seeking people to lead him by the hand. 12When he saw what had happened, the proconsul believed, because he was astonished at the teaching about the Lord.

Paul's Message in Diaspora Synagogues

13Setting sail from Paphos, Paul's company came to Perga in Pamphylia. John left them and returned to Jerusalem. 14But they passed on from Perga and came to Antioch of Pisidia. Entering the synagogue on the *Shabbat*, they sat down. 15After the reading of the *Torah* and the Prophets, the synagogue leaders sent to them, saying, "Brothers, if you have any word of encouragement for the people, speak."

16So Paul, standing up and motioning with his hand, said, "Men of Israel and God-fearers, listen. 17The God of this people Israel chose our fathers and made the people great during their stay in the land of Egypt,[d] and with an outstretched arm He led them out of there. 18For about forty years He put up with them in the wilderness.[e] 19And when He had destroyed seven nations in the land of Canaan, He gave their land as an inheritance[f]—20all of this took about 450 years. After that, he gave them judges until Samuel the prophet. 21Then they asked for a king, and God gave them Saul, son of Kish, of the tribe of Benjamin, for forty years. 22After removing him, He raised up David to be their king. He also testified about him and said, 'I have found David, the son of Jesse, a man after My heart, who will do My will.'[g]

23"From this man's seed, in keeping with His promise, God brought to Israel a Savior[h]—*Yeshua*. 24Before His coming, John had proclaimed an immersion of repentance to all the people of Israel. 25As John was completing his service, he said, 'What do you suppose me to be? I am not He. But behold, One is coming after me, whose sandal I'm not worthy to untie.'

26"Brothers, sons of the family of Abraham and those among you who are God-fearers, it is to us the message of this salvation has been sent. 27For those who live in Jerusalem and their rulers—not recognizing Him or the sayings of the Prophets that are read every *Shabbat*—fulfilled these words by condemning Him. 28Though they found no charge worthy of a death sentence, they asked Pilate to have Him executed. 29When they had carried out all that had been written about Him, they took Him down from the tree and laid Him in a tomb. 30But God raised Him from the dead! 31For many days He appeared to those who had come up from the Galilee to Jerusalem, who are now His witnesses to the people.

a 13:5. cf. Acts 12:25.
b 13:10. cf. Deut. 32:4-6; Prov. 10:9; 11:20.
c 13:11. cf. 1 Sam. 5:6-7; Job 19:21.
d 13:17. cf. Exod. 6:1, 6; 13:14, 16; Deut. 7:6-8.
e 13:18. cf. Num. 14:34.
f 13:19. cf. Deut. 7:1; Josh. 19:51.
g 13:22. cf. Ps. 89:20; 1 Sam 13:14.
h 13:23. cf. 1 Sam 13:14; Ps. 27:1(26:1 LXX).

32And we proclaim to you Good News—the promise to the fathers has arrived! 33For God has fulfilled this promise to the children—to us—by raising up *Yeshua*, as it is also written in the second psalm:

'You are My Son.
Today I have become Your Father.'[a]

34"But since He raised Him up from the dead, never to return to decay, He has spoken in this way, 'I will give you the holy and sure mercies of David.'[b] 35Therefore He also says in another psalm, 'You will not permit Your Holy One to see decay.'[c] 36For after David had served God's purpose in his own generation, he went to sleep and was laid with his fathers and saw decay. 37But the One whom God raised up did not see decay.

38"Therefore, let it be known to you, brothers, that through this One is proclaimed to you the removal of sins, including all those from which you could not be set right by the *Torah* of Moses. 39Through this One everyone who keeps trusting is made righteous.

40"Be careful, then, so that what is said in the Prophets may not come upon you:

41'Look, you scoffers,
be amazed and vanish away.
For I am doing a work in your days—
a work you will never believe,
even if someone tells it to you in detail.'[d]"

42As Paul and Barnabas were going out, the people kept begging them to speak these things to them the next *Shabbat*. 43When the synagogue meeting broke up, many of the Jewish people and God-fearing inquirers followed Paul and Barnabas, who were speaking with them and trying to persuade them to continue in the grace of God.

a 13:33. Ps. 2:7; cf. 2 Sam. 7:14.
b 13:34. Isa. 55:3.
c 13:35. Ps. 16:10.
d 13:41. Hab. 1:5.

44The following *Shabbat*, almost the entire city came together to hear the word of the Lord. 45When the Jewish leaders saw the crowds, they were filled with jealousy and tried to contradict what Paul was saying by reviling him. 46Both Paul and Barnabas spoke out boldly and said, "It was necessary for the word of God to be spoken to you first. Since you reject it and judge yourselves unfit for eternal life—behold, we turn to the Gentiles. 47For so the Lord has commanded us,

'I have placed you as a light to the nations,
so that you may bring salvation to the end of the earth.'[e]"

48When the Gentiles heard this, they were thrilled and glorified the word of the Lord; and as many as had been inscribed for eternal life believed.[f]

49Now the word of the Lord spread throughout the whole region. 50But the Jewish leaders incited the God-fearing women of high standing and the leading men of the city. They stirred up persecution against Paul and Barnabas, and they drove them out of their district. 51But Paul and Barnabas shook the dust off their feet against them,[g] and they went on to Iconium. 52And the disciples were filled with joy and the *Ruach ha-Kodesh*.

14

Mixed Crowds Believe Amidst Persecution

1Now in Iconium, the same thing happened—they entered as usual into the Jewish synagogue and spoke in such a way that a large number of Jewish and Greek people believed. 2But the Jewish people who would not believe stirred up

e 13:47. Isa. 49:6.
f 13:48. cf. Exod. 32:33; Ps. 69:28; Dan. 12:1.
g 13:51. cf. Matt. 10:14; Mk. 6:11; Lk. 9:5.

the Gentiles and poisoned their minds against the brothers.

[3]So they stayed there a considerable time, speaking boldly in the Lord—who was testifying to the message of His grace, granting signs and wonders to come about by their hands. [4]But the population of the city split; some were with the Jewish leaders and some were with the *shlichim*. [5]Now it happened that an attempt was made by both the Gentiles and Jewish people, along with their rulers, to abuse and stone them. [6]But they found out about it and fled to the Lycaonian cities of Lystra and Derbe and the surrounding countryside. [7]There they proclaimed the Good News.

[8]Now a man was sitting in Lystra without strength in his feet, lame from birth, who had never walked. [9]This man heard Paul speaking. When Paul looked intently at him and saw that he had faith to be healed, [10]he said with a loud voice, "Stand right up! On your feet!" And the man leaped up and began to walk around!

[11]Now the crowd, seeing what Paul had done, lifted up their voices, saying in Lycaonian, "The gods have become like men and come down to us!" [12]And they began calling Barnabas "Zeus" and Paul "Hermes" (because he was the main speaker).

[13]The priest of Zeus, whose temple was before the front gate of the city, brought bulls and garlands; he wanted to offer a sacrifice with the people. [14]But when the *shlichim* Barnabas and Paul heard of it, they tore their clothes and rushed out among the crowd, crying out [15] and saying, "Men, why are you doing these things? We too are human, just like you! We proclaim the Good News to you, telling you to turn from these worthless things to the living God, who made the heaven and the earth and the sea and all that is in them.[a] [16]In past generations He allowed all the nations to go their own ways.[b] [17]Yet He did not leave Himself without a witness—He did good by giving you rain from heaven and fruitful seasons, filling your hearts with joy and gladness."[c] [18]Even saying these things, they barely restrained the crowd from sacrificing to them.

[19]But Jewish people came from Antioch and Iconium; and after they won the crowd over and stoned Paul, they were dragging him out of the city, supposing him to be dead. [20]But while the disciples surrounded him, he got up and went back into the city. On the next day he left with Barnabas for Derbe. [21]After proclaiming the Good News to that city and making many disciples, they returned to Lystra and to Iconium and to Antioch. [22]They were strengthening the souls of the disciples, encouraging them to persevere in faith, and saying, "It is through many persecutions that we must enter the kingdom of God." [23]When they had handpicked elders for them in every community, and prayed with fasting, they placed them in the care of the Lord—in whom they had put their trust.

[24]Then they passed through Pisidia and came to Pamphyllia. [25]After speaking the message in Perga, they went down to Attalia. [26]From there they sailed back to Antioch (where they had been entrusted to the gracious care of God for the work now completed). [27]When they arrived and gathered together Messiah's community, they began to report all that God had done in helping them and that He had opened a door of faith to the Gentiles. [28]And they stayed quite awhile with the disciples.

15

Jerusalem Council Rules on Circumcision

[1]Now some men coming down from Judea were teaching the brothers, "Unless you are circumcised according to the custom of Moses, you cannot be saved." [2]When Paul and Barnabas had a

a 14:15. cf. Ex. 20:11; Ps. 146:6.
b 14:16. cf. Ps. 81:12; Mic. 4:5.
c 14:17. cf. Deut. 11:14; Ps. 65:10; Ezek. 34:26; Joel 2:23.

big argument and debate with them, the
brothers appointed Paul and Barnabas
with some others from among them to
go up to Jerusalem to the *shlichim* and
elders about this issue.

3So they were sent on their way by the
Antioch community. They were passing
through both Phoenicia and Samaria,
describing in detail the conversion of the
Gentiles, and they were bringing great
joy to all the brothers and sisters. 4When
they arrived in Jerusalem, they were
welcomed by the community and the
shlichim and the elders. They reported all
that God had done in helping them.

5But some belonging to the party of
the Pharisees who had believed stood
up, saying, "It is necessary to circumcise
them and to command them to keep the
Torah of Moses."

6The *shlichim* and elders were gathered
together to examine this issue. 7After
much debate, Peter stood up and said to
them, "Brothers, you know that in the
early days God chose from among you,
that by my mouth the Gentiles should
hear the message of the Good News and
believe. 8And God, who knows the heart,
testified to them by giving them the
Ruach ha-Kodesh—just as He also did for
us. 9He made no distinction between us
and them, purifying their hearts through
faith. 10Why then do you put God to the
test by putting a yoke on the neck of the
disciples—which neither our fathers nor
we have been able to bear? 11But instead,
we believe that we are saved through
the grace of the Lord *Yeshua*, in the same
way as they are."

12Then the whole group became silent
and were listening to Barnabas and Paul
as they were describing in detail all the
signs and wonders God had done through
them among the Gentiles. 13After they
finished speaking, Jacob answered,
"Brothers, listen to me. 14Simon has
described how God first showed His concern by taking from the Gentiles a people
for His Name. 15The words of the Prophets agree, as it is written:

16'After this I will return
and rebuild the fallen tabernacle of David.
I will rebuild its ruins
and I will restore it,
17so that the rest of humanity may seek the Lord—
namely all the Gentiles who are called by My name—
says *Adonai*, who makes these things[a]
18known from of old.'[b]

19Therefore, I judge not to trouble
those from among the Gentiles who are
turning to God— 20but to write to them
to abstain from the contamination of
idols, and from sexual immorality, and
from what is strangled, and from blood.[c]
21For Moses from ancient generations
has had in every city those who proclaim
him, since he is read in all the synagogues
every *Shabbat*."

Letter to Diaspora Communities

22Then it seemed good to the *shlichim*
and elders, with the whole community, to
choose men from among themselves to
send to Antioch with Paul and Barnabas.
They sent Judah (also called Barsabbas)
and Silas, leading men among the brothers, 23and this letter along with them:

"The *shlichim* and the elders, your brothers,
To the Gentile brothers and sisters of Antioch, Syria, and Cilicia:
Greetings!
24Since we have heard that some from
among us have troubled you with
words disturbing to your souls,[d]

a 15:16-17. Amos 9:11-12(LXX); cf. Zech. 8:20-23; Dan. 9:19.

b 15:18. cf. Isa. 45:21(LXX).

c 15:20. cf. Exod. 34:15-17; Lev. 18:6-26; Exod. 22:31; Lev. 3:17.

d 15:24. Some mss. add saying, *"You must be circumcised and keep the law,"*

> although we gave them no such authorization, [25]it seemed good to us, having come to one accord, to select men to send to you with our beloved Barnabas and Paul— [26]men who have risked their lives for the name of our Lord *Yeshua* the Messiah. [27]We therefore have sent to you Judah and Silas, who themselves will report to you the same things by word of mouth. [28]It seemed good to the *Ruach ha-Kodesh* and to us not to place on you any greater burden than these essentials: [29]that you abstain from things offered to idols, from blood, from things strangled, and from sexual immorality. By keeping away from these things, you will do well.
>
> *Shalom!*"

[30]So when they were sent off, they went down to Antioch; and when they had gathered the whole group together, they delivered the letter. [31] he people read it and rejoiced over its encouragement. [32]Judah and Silas, prophets themselves, encouraged the brothers and sisters with a long message and strengthened them.

[33]After spending some time there, they were sent off with *shalom* by the brothers and sisters to those who had sent them. [34a] [35]But Paul and Barnabas remained in Antioch, teaching and proclaiming the word of the Lord with many others.

New Teams Strengthen Communities

[36]After some days Paul said to Barnabas, "Let's return and visit the brothers and sisters in every city where we have proclaimed the word of the Lord, to see how they are." [37]Barnabas was planning to take along John, called Mark. [38]But Paul was insisting that they shouldn't take him along—the one who had deserted them in Pamphylia, not accompanying them in the work. [39]A sharp disagreement took place, so that they split off from one another. Barnabas took Mark with him and sailed away to Cyprus. [40]But Paul selected Silas and went out, being entrusted by the brothers and sisters to the gracious care of the Lord. [41]He went through Syria and Cilicia, strengthening the communities.

16

[1]Now Paul came to Derbe and Lystra. There was a disciple there named Timothy, son of a woman who was a Jewish believer and a Greek father, [2]who was well-spoken of by the brothers at Lystra and Iconium. [3]Paul wanted this man to accompany him, and he took him and circumcised him for the sake of the Jewish people in those places—for they all knew that his father was Greek.

[4]As they were traveling through the cities, they were handing down the rulings that had been decided upon by the *shlichim* and elders in Jerusalem, for them to keep. [5]So Messiah's communities were strengthened in the faith and kept increasing daily in number.

Going West to Macedonia

[6]They went through the region of Phrygia and Galatia, having been forbidden by the *Ruach ha-Kodesh* to speak the word in Asia.[b] [7]When they came to Mysia, they were trying to proceed into Bithynia, but the Spirit of *Yeshua* would not allow them. [8]So they passed by Mysia and went down to Troas.

[9]Now a vision appeared to Paul in the night. A man from Macedonia was standing and pleading with him, saying, "Come over to Macedonia and help us!" [10]As soon as he had seen the vision, immediately we tried to go to Macedonia,

a 15:34. Some mss. add verse 34: *But it seemed good to Silas to remain there.*

b 16:6. The Roman province of Asia, in the western part of Asia Minor (now part of Turkey).

concluding that God had called us to proclaim the Good News to them.

[11]So we put out to sea from Troas and made a straight course for Samothrace, the next day on to Neapolis, [12]and from there to Philippi—which is a leading city of the district of Macedonia as well as a Roman colony. We stayed in this city for several days.

[13]On *Yom Shabbat*, we went outside the gate to the river, where we expected a place of prayer to be. We sat down and began speaking with the women who had gathered. [14]A woman named Lydia—a seller of purple cloth from the city of Thyatira, a God-fearer—was listening. The Lord opened her heart to respond to what Paul was saying.

[15]When she was immersed, along with her household, she urged us, saying, "If you have judged me to be faithful to the Lord, come and stay at my house." And she insisted.[a]

[16]It so happened that as we were going to prayer, we met a slave girl who had a spirit of divination, who was bringing her masters much profit from her fortune-telling.[b] [17]Following after Paul and us, she kept shouting, saying, "These men are servants of *El Elyon*, who are proclaiming to you the way of salvation." [18]She kept doing this for many days. But Paul was irritated and turned and said to the spirit, "I command you in the name of Messiah *Yeshua* to come out of her!" And it came out of her that very moment.

[19]But when her masters saw that the hope of profit was gone, they grabbed Paul and Silas and dragged them into the marketplace before the authorities. [20]And when they brought them to the chief authorities, they said, "These men are throwing our city into an uproar! Being Jewish, [21]they advocate customs which are not permitted for us to accept or practice,[c] being Romans."

[22]Then the crowd joined in the attack on them. So the chief authorities ripped their clothes off them and commanded them to be beaten with rods. [23] After inflicting many blows on them, they threw them into prison, ordering the jailer to guard them securely. [24]Having received this charge, he threw them into the inner prison and fastened their feet in the stocks.[d]

Salvation for a Jailer's Household

[25]But about midnight, Paul and Silas were praying and singing hymns to God, and the prisoners were listening to them. [26]Suddenly there was such a great earthquake that the foundations of the prison were shaken. Immediately all the doors were unlocked, and everyone's chains came loose.

[27]When the jailer woke up and saw the prison doors opened, he drew his sword and was about to kill himself, supposing the prisoners had escaped. [28]But Paul cried out with a loud voice, saying, "Don't harm yourself! We're all here!"

[29]The jailer called for lights and rushed in; and trembling with fear, he fell down before Paul and Silas. [30]After he brought them out, he said, "Sirs, what must I do to be saved?"

[31]They said, "Put your trust in the Lord *Yeshua*[e] and you will be saved—you and your household!"

[32]Then they spoke the word of the Lord to him, along with everyone in his household. [33]He took them that very hour and washed their wounds, and at once he was immersed—he and all his household. [34]The jailer brought them to his house and set food before them, and he was overjoyed that he with his entire household had put their trust in God.

[35]When day came, the chief authorities sent their police officers, saying, "Release those men."

a 16:15. cf. 2 Kings 4:8-10.
b 16:16. cf. Lev. 19:26; Deut. 18:9-10; Jer. 27:9-10.
c 16:21. cf. Esth. 3:8.
d 16:24. cf. Jer. 20:2-3.
e 16:31. Some mss. add *the Messiah*.

Acts 16:25-26

But about midnight, Paul and Silas were praying and singing hymns to God, and the prisoners were listening to them. Suddenly there was such a great earthquake that the foundations of the prison were shaken. Immediately all the doors were unlocked, and everyone's chains came loose.

36 But the jailer reported these words
to Paul, saying, "The chief authorities
have sent orders to release you. So come
out now, and go in *shalom*."
37 But Paul said to the officers, "They
have beaten us publicly without a trial—
men who are Roman citizens—and have
thrown us into prison. And now they are
sending us away secretly? No! Let them
come themselves and lead us out!"
38 The police officers reported these
words to the chief authorities. They
became afraid when they heard they
were Romans, 39 so they came and apolo-
gized to them. After they escorted them
out, they kept begging them to leave the
city. 40 When Paul and Silas went out of
the prison, they visited Lydia's house.
And when they saw the brothers, they
encouraged them and then departed.

17

Synagogue Responses Vary

1 After passing through Amphipolis and
Apollonia, they came to Thessalonica,
where there was a Jewish synagogue.
2 As was his custom, Paul went to the
Jewish people; and for three *Shabbats*,
he debated the Scriptures with them.
3 He opened them and gave evidence
that Messiah had to suffer and rise from
the dead, saying, "This *Yeshua*, whom I
declare to you, is the Messiah." 4 Some
of them were convinced and became
attached to Paul and Silas, as were a large
number of the God-fearing Greeks and
no small number of the leading women.
5 But some of the Jewish people
became jealous. Taking some wicked
fellows of the marketplace and gathering a crowd, they stirred the city into
an uproar. They attacked Jason's house,
trying to bring Paul and Silas out to the
mob. 6 When they did not find them, they
instead began dragging Jason and some
of the brothers before the city officials,
shouting, "These men who have upset
the world have come here too, 7 and
Jason has welcomed them! They are all
acting against the decrees of Caesar,
saying there is another king, *Yeshua*."
8 Hearing these things, the crowd and the
city officials were confused. 9 But after
receiving bail from Jason and the rest,
they released them.
10 As soon as it was night, the brothers sent Paul and Silas to Berea. Upon
arrival, they made their way to the Jewish synagogue. 11 Now these were more
noble-minded than those in Thessalonica,
because they received the message with
goodwill, searching the Scriptures each
day to see whether these things were
true. 12 Therefore many of them believed,
as well as quite a few prominent Greek
women and men.
13 But when the Jewish people of Thessalonica learned that the word of God
had been proclaimed by Paul in Berea,
they came there too, agitating and
inciting the people. 14 Then the brothers
immediately sent Paul away to the sea,
but Silas and Timothy remained there.
15 Those escorting Paul brought him as far
as Athens. After receiving an order for
Silas and Timothy to come to him as soon
as possible, they left.

An Unknown God in Athens

16 Now while Paul was waiting for them
in Athens, his spirit was aroused within
him when he saw that the city was full of
idols. 17 So he was debating in the synagogue with the Jewish people and the
God-fearers, as well as in the marketplace every day with all who happened
to be there. 18 Also some of the Epicurean
and Stoic philosophers were conversing
with him. Some were saying, "What's
this babbler trying to say?" while others, "He seems to be a proclaimer of
foreign deities"—because he was proclaiming the Good News of *Yeshua* and
the resurrection. 19 So they took Paul to
the Aereopagus, saying, "May we know
what this new teaching is that you are

talking about? 20For you are bringing some strange things to our ears, so we want to know what these things mean." 21Now all the Athenians and foreigners visiting there used to pass their time doing nothing but telling or hearing something new.

22So Paul stood in the middle of the Aereopagus and said, "Men of Athens, I see that in all ways you are very religious. 23For while I was passing through and observing the objects of your worship, I even found an altar with this inscription: 'To an Unknown God.' Therefore what you worship without knowing, this I proclaim to you. 24The God who made the world and all things in it, since He is Lord of heaven and earth,[a] does not live in temples made by hands.[b] 25Nor is He served by human hands, as if He needed anything,[c] since He Himself gives to everyone life and breath and all things.[d] 26From one He made every nation of men to live on the face of the earth, having set appointed times and the boundaries of their territory.[e] 27They were to search for Him, and perhaps grope around for Him and find Him. Yet He is not far from each one of us,[f] 28for

'In Him we live and move and have our being.'

As some of your own poets have said,
'For we also are His offspring.'[g]

29Since we are His offspring, we ought not to suppose the Deity is like gold or silver or stone, an engraved image of human art and imagination.[h] 30Although God overlooked the periods of ignorance, now He commands everyone everywhere to repent. 31For He has set a day on which He will judge the world in righteousness, through a Man whom He has appointed.[i] He has brought forth evidence of this to all men, by raising Him from the dead."

32Now when they heard about the resurrection of the dead, some began scoffing. But others said, "We will hear from you again about this."

33So Paul left from their midst. 34But some men joined with him and believed—among them Dionysius (a member of the council of the Areopagus), a woman named Damaris, and others with them.

18

Many Respond in Corinth

1After these things, Paul left Athens and went to Corinth. 2There he found a Jewish man named Aquila—a native of Pontus having recently come from Italy with his wife Priscilla, because Claudius had commanded all Jewish people to leave Rome. Paul went to see them; 3and because he was of the same trade, he stayed with them and began working, for by trade they were tent-makers. 4And he was debating every *Shabbat* in the synagogue, trying to persuade both Jewish and Greek people.

5Now when Silas and Timothy arrived from Macedonia, Paul became occupied with the message, urgently testifying to the Jewish people that *Yeshua* is the Messiah. 6But when they resisted and reviled him, he shook out his garments[j] and said, "Your blood be upon your own heads—I am clean![k] From now on, I will go to the Gentiles."

7After leaving there, Paul went into the house of a man named Titius Justus, a God-fearer whose house was next door to the synagogue. 8Crispus, the synagogue leader, put his faith in the Lord, along with his whole household. And many of the Corinthians, upon hearing, were believing and being immersed.

a 17:24a. cf. Isa. 42:5; Deut. 10:14; Ps. 115:16.
b 17:24b. cf. 1 Kings 8:27.
c 17:25a. cf. Job 22:2; Ps. 50:10-12.
d 17:25b. cf. Gen. 2:7; Job 27:3.
e 17:26. cf. Deut. 32:8; Job 12:23.
f 17:27. cf. Deut. 4:7; Jer. 23:23.
g 17:28. Quotes from Epimenides and Aratus.
h 17:29. cf. Isa. 40:18-19.
i 17:31. cf. Ps. 2; 9:8; 96:13; 98:9.

j 18:6a. cf. Neh. 5:13.
k 18:6b. cf. 2 Sam. 1:16; 1 Kings 2:33; Ezek. 18:13.

9Now the Lord said to Paul through a vision in the night, "Do not be afraid, but speak and do not be silent! 10For I am with you and no one shall attack you to harm you—many people in this city are for Me." 11So he stayed a year and six months, teaching the word of God among them.

12But while Gallio was proconsul of Achaia, the Jewish leaders made a united attack against Paul and brought him before the judgment seat, 13saying, "This man persuades men to worship God contrary to the *Torah*."

14But when Paul was about to open his mouth, Gallio said to the Jewish people, "If it were a matter of wrongdoing or a vicious crime, there would be a reason to put up with you, O Jews. 15But since it is issues about words, names, and your own law, see to it yourselves. I do not wish to be a judge of these." 16And he drove them from the judgment seat. 17Then they all grabbed Sosthenes, the synagogue leader, and began beating him in front of the judgment seat. But Gallio paid no attention to these things.

Sailing East to Revisit Communities

18Paul, having stayed many more days, said farewell to the brothers and set sail to Syria, and with him were Priscilla and Aquila. At Cenchrea Paul had his hair cut off, for he was keeping a vow. 19When they arrived at Ephesus, Paul left Priscilla and Aquila there. But he himself went into the synagogue and debated with the Jewish people. 20When they asked him to stay longer, he declined, 21instead taking leave of them while saying, "God willing, I'll return to you again."

He set sail from Ephesus. 22After landing at Caesarea, he went up and greeted Messiah's community; then he went down to Antioch. 23After spending some time there, he departed and went one place after another throughout the region of Galatia and Phrygia, strengthening all the disciples.

Discipling New Leaders

24Now a Jewish man named Apollos, a native of Alexandria, came to Ephesus. He was a learned man, well versed in the Scriptures. 25He had been instructed in the way of the Lord. With a fervent spirit, he was speaking and teaching accurately the facts about *Yeshua*—while only being acquainted with the immersion of John. 26This man began speaking out boldly in the synagogue. But when Priscilla and Aquila heard him, they took him aside and explained the way of God more accurately.

27When Apollos wanted to cross over to Achaia, the brothers encouraged him and wrote to the disciples to welcome him. Upon arrival, he greatly helped those who by grace had believed. 28For he powerfully refuted the Jewish people in public, demonstrating through the Scriptures that the Messiah was *Yeshua*.

19

1While Apollos was at Corinth, Paul traveled through the upper region and came to Ephesus. He found some disciples 2and said to them, "Did you receive the *Ruach ha-Kodesh* when you believed?"

They replied to him, "No, we've never even heard that there is a *Ruach ha-Kodesh*.

3He said, "Into what were you immersed?"

They said, "Into John's immersion."

4Paul said, "John immersed with an immersion of repentance, telling the people that they should believe in the One coming after him—that is, in *Yeshua*."

5When they heard this, they were immersed in the name of the Lord *Yeshua*. 6And when Paul laid hands upon them, the *Ruach ha-Kodesh* came upon them, and they began speaking in tongues and prophesying. 7In all, there were about twelve men.

God's Power Displayed in Ephesus

8Paul went into the synagogue and for three months spoke boldly, debating and persuading them about the kingdom of God. 9But when they were hardening and refusing to believe, speaking evil of the Way before the whole group, he withdrew from them, taking the disciples with him, debating daily in the hall of Tyrannus. 10This continued for two years, so that all the residents of Asia[a] heard the word of the Lord—Jewish as well as Greek people.

11God was doing extraordinary miracles by Paul's hands, 12so that even handkerchiefs and aprons that touched his skin were brought to the sick, and the diseases left them and the evil spirits went out of them.

13But some traveling Jewish exorcists also tried to invoke the name of the Lord *Yeshua*, saying, "I charge you by the *Yeshua* whom Paul preaches." 14Seven sons of a Jewish ruling *kohen* named Sceva were doing this. 15But the evil spirit answered them, "I know *Yeshua* and I know about Paul, but who are you?"

16Then the man with the evil spirit sprang at them, subduing and overpowering all of them, so that they fled out of that house naked and wounded. 17This became known to all who lived in Ephesus, both Jewish and Greek people. Fear fell upon them all, and the name of the Lord *Yeshua* was being magnified.

18Many also of those who had believed came confessing and announcing their practices. 19And many of those who practiced magic arts brought their books together in a heap, burning them before everyone. They totaled the value of the books and found it to be about fifty thousand pieces of silver. 20So the word of the Lord was growing in power and prevailing.

Idol-Makers Start a Riot

21Now after these things were accomplished, Paul resolved in the Spirit to go to Jerusalem after passing through Macedonia and Achaia, saying, "After I have been there, I must also see Rome." 22So after sending two who were assisting him, Timothy and Erastus, he himself stayed in Asia for a while.

23Around that time, there arose no small uproar concerning the Way. 24For a man named Demetrius—a silversmith, a maker of silver shrines of Artemis—was providing no small amount of business to the craftsmen. 25He gathered these together, along with those of related occupations, and he said, "Men, you know that our wealth is from this business. 26You see and hear that not only in Ephesus but also throughout all Asia, Paul has persuaded and perverted a considerable crowd, saying that handmade gods are not gods at all.[b] 27Not only is there a danger that this trade of ours might come into disrepute, but also that the temple of the great goddess Artemis might be considered as nothing. She whom all Asia and the world worships might even be thrown down from her majesty."

28When they heard, they were filled with fury and began shouting, "Great is Artemis of the Ephesians!" 29The city was filled with confusion. They rushed into the theater, dragging with them Gaius and Aristarchus, Macedonians who were travel companions of Paul. 30Paul was wishing to enter among the crowd, but the disciples would not let him. 31Some of the chiefs of Asia,[c] being his friends, sent to him and begged him not to surrender himself in the theater.

a 19:10, 22, 26, 27, 31. The Roman province of Asia, in the western part of Asia Minor (now part of Turkey).

b 19:26. cf. Deut. 4:28; Isa. 44:10-20; Jer. 10:3-5.

c 19:31. Lit. *Asiarchs*, high-ranking government officials of Asia.

[32]Now some cried out one thing, some another, for the assembly was in confusion. Most did not know why they had come together. [33]Some of the crowd solicited Alexander, whom the Jewish people put forward. Alexander motioned with his hand. He wished to offer a defense to the crowd. [34]But recognizing that he was Jewish, for about two hours they all with one voice cried out, "Great is Artemis of the Ephesians!"

[35]After the town clerk quieted the crowd, he said, "Men of Ephesus, what man is there who doesn't know that the city of the Ephesians is temple keeper of the great Artemis and of her image fallen from heaven? [36]Since these things are undeniable, you must be calm and do nothing reckless. [37]For you have brought these men here who are neither sacrilegious nor revilers of our goddess. [38]If Demetrius and the craftsmen with him have a complaint against anyone, the courts are open and there are proconsuls. Let them accuse them. [39]But if you seek anything further, it will be settled in the lawful assembly. [40]For we are in danger of being charged with rioting today, there being no reason which we are able to give to justify this mob." Upon saying this, he dismissed the assembly.

20

Escaping Death

[1]After the uproar ended, Paul sent for the disciples; and when he had encouraged them and said farewell, he departed to go to Macedonia. [2]When he had passed through these parts and given them a great word of encouragement, he came to Greece, [3]where he spent three months. When a plot was formed against him by the Jewish leaders as he was about to sail to Syria, he decided to return via Macedonia. [4]Sopater of Berea, son of Pyrrhus, accompanied him; as well as Aristarchus and Secundus of Thessalonica; Gaius of Derbe, and Timothy; Tychicus and Trophimus of Asia.[a] [5]These went on ahead and were waiting for us at Troas. [6]But we sailed from Philippi after the Days of *Matzah*. In five days we came to them in Troas, where we stayed for seven days.

[7]Now on the first day of the week, we gathered to break bread. Paul was talking with them, intending to leave the next day, so he prolonged his speech till midnight. [8]There were many lamps in the upper chamber where we were meeting. [9]Now a young man named Eutychus was sitting in a windowsill, sinking into a deep sleep as Paul kept on talking. Overcome by sleep, he fell from the third story and was picked up—dead.

[10]But Paul went down, fell on him and threw his arms around him. He said, "Don't be upset, for his life is within him."[b]

[11]After he went back up and broke the bread and ate, he talked with them a long while until daybreak and then left. [12]So they took the boy away alive, greatly relieved.

Prophetic Warnings

[13]But we went on ahead to the ship and set sail for Assos, intending to take Paul aboard there—for so he had arranged, intending himself to travel there by land. [14]When he met us at Assos, we took him on board and went to Mitylene. [15]Sailing from there, we arrived the next day opposite Chios; the next day we crossed over to Samos, and the day after that we came to Miletus. [16]For Paul had decided to sail past Ephesus so that he might not spend much time in Asia, because he was hurrying to be in Jerusalem, if possible, by the day of *Shavuot*.

[17]From Miletus, dispatching someone to Ephesus, he called for the elders of the community. [18]When they came to him, he said to them, "You yourselves know how

a 20:4, 16, 18. The Roman province of Asia, in the western part of Asia Minor (now part of Turkey).

b 20:10. cf. 1 Kings 17:21; 2 Kings 4:34.

I behaved among you all the time from the first day I set foot in Asia, [19]serving the Lord with all humility and tears and trials which fell upon me through the plots of the Jewish leaders. [20]I did not shrink back from proclaiming to you anything that was profitable, teaching you publicly as well as from house to house, [21]testifying to both Jewish and Greek people repentance to God and trust in our Lord *Yeshua*.

[22]"And now, look, bound by the Spirit, I am going to Jerusalem—not knowing what will happen to me there, [23]except that the *Ruach ha-Kodesh* bears witness to me from city to city, saying that bondage and afflictions await me. [24]However, I don't consider my life of any value, except that I might finish my course and the office I received from the Lord *Yeshua*, to declare the Good News of the grace of God.

[25]"Now, look! I know that none of you, among whom I have gone proclaiming the kingdom, will ever see my face again. [26]Therefore, I testify to you this day that I am innocent of the blood of all. [27]For I did not shrink back from declaring to you the whole purpose of God.

[28]"Take care of yourselves and all the flock of which the *Ruach ha-Kodesh* has made you overseers, to shepherd the community of God—which He obtained with the blood of His own.[a] [29]I know that after my departure, savage wolves will come in among you, not sparing the flock.[b] [30]Even from among yourselves will arise men speaking perversions, to draw the disciples away after themselves. [31]Therefore be alert, remembering that night and day for three years I did not stop warning you with tears.

[32]"Now I commit you to God and the word of His grace, which is strong to build you up and to give you the inheritance among all who have been made holy. [33]I coveted no one's silver or gold or clothing. [34]You yourselves know that these hands of mine have provided for my own needs as well as for those with me. [35]In all things I have shown you an object lesson—that by hard work one must help the weak, remembering the words of the Lord *Yeshua*, that He Himself said, 'It is more blessed to give than to receive.'"[c]

[36]When he had said these things, he knelt down and prayed with them all. [37]They all began weeping and falling upon Paul's neck and kissing him, [38]grieving most of all over the statement he made that they would never see his face again. Then they accompanied him to the ship.

21

Going to Jerusalem Despite Warnings

[1]After tearing ourselves away from them and setting sail, we set a straight course to Cos, the next day to Rhodes, and from there to Patara. [2] Finding a ship crossing to Phoenicia, we went aboard and set sail. [3]When we came in sight of Cyprus, passing it by on the left, we kept sailing to Syria and landed at Tyre—for there the ship was to unload the cargo. [4]We looked up the disciples and stayed there seven days. They kept telling Paul through the Spirit not to set foot in Jerusalem.

[5]When our days there were over, we departed and went on our journey. They all, with wives and children, accompanied us until we were outside the city. After kneeling down on the shore and praying, [6]we said farewell to one another. Then we boarded the ship, and they returned home.

[7]When we had finished the trip from Tyre, we arrived at Ptolemais. We greeted the brothers and sisters and stayed with them for one day. [8]On the next day, we departed and came to Caesarea. We

a 20:28. cf. Gen. 22:2, 8; Lk. 22:20; Heb. 9:12; Rev. 5:9-10.
b 20:29. cf. Ezek. 22:27.
c 20:35. cf. Matt. 10:8.

entered the home of Philip, the proclaimer of Good News, who was one of the seven, and we stayed with him. 9Now this man had four virgin daughters who prophesied.

10While we stayed there for a number of days, a prophet named Agabus came down from Judea. 11He came to us, took Paul's belt, tied his own hands and feet, and said, "The *Ruach ha-Kodesh* says this: 'In this way shall the Jewish people in Jerusalem bind the man who owns this belt and deliver him into the hands of the Gentiles.'"

12When we heard these things, both we and the local people urged Paul not to go up to Jerusalem. 13Then Paul responded, "What are you doing, weeping and breaking my heart? For I am ready not only to be bound but to die for the name of the Lord *Yeshua*!"

14Since he would not be persuaded, we fell silent, saying only, "May the Lord's will be done."

15After these days, we packed and started going up to Jerusalem. 16Some of the disciples from Caesarea also went with us, bringing us to Mnason of Cyprus—one of the early disciples by whom we might be hosted.

Advice from Jacob and the Elders

17When we arrived in Jerusalem, the brothers welcomed us gladly. 18On the next day, Paul went in with us to Jacob; all the elders were present. 19After greeting them, he reported to them in detail what God had done among the Gentiles through his service. 20And when they heard, they began glorifying God.

They said, "You see, brother, how many myriads there are among the Jewish people who have believed—and they are all zealous for the *Torah*. 21They have been told about you—that you teach all the Jewish people among the Gentiles to forsake Moses, telling them not to circumcise their children or to walk according to the customs. 22What's to be done then? No doubt they will hear that you have come.

23"So do what we tell you. We have four men who have a vow on themselves.[a] 24Take them, and purify yourself[b] along with them and pay their expenses, so that they may shave their heads. That way, all will realize there is nothing to the things they have been told about you, but that you yourself walk in an orderly manner, keeping the *Torah*.

25"As for Gentiles who have believed, however, we have written by letter what we decided—for them to abstain from what is offered to idols, and from blood, and from what is strangled, and from immorality."

26The next day Paul took the men, purifying himself along with them. He went into the Temple, announcing when the days of purification would be completed and the sacrifice would be offered for each one of them.

Trouble at the Temple

27When the seven days were about to be completed, the Jewish leaders from Asia[c] saw Paul in the Temple and began stirring up the whole crowd. They grabbed him, 28shouting, "Men of Israel, help! This is the man who is teaching all men everywhere against our people and the *Torah* and this place. Besides, he has even brought Greeks into the Temple and defiled[d] this holy place!"

29For they had previously seen Trophimus the Ephesian in the city with him, and they assumed that Paul had brought him into the Temple. 30The whole city was stirred up, and the people rushed together. They grabbed Paul and dragged him out of the Temple, and the gates were shut at once.

31As they were trying to kill him, news came to the commander of the cohort

a 21:23. cf. Num. 6:13-21.

b 21:24. cf. Num. 19:17-22; Acts 24:18.

c 21:27; 24:19; 27:2. The Roman province of Asia, in the western part of Asia Minor (now part of Turkey).

d 21:29. Lit. *made common or unholy*; cf. Lev. 10:10.

that all Jerusalem was in chaos. [32]Immediately he took soldiers and centurions and rushed down to them. Upon seeing the commander and the soldiers, they stopped beating Paul. [33]Then the commander came up, arrested Paul, ordered him to be bound with two chains, and began investigating what he had done. [34]Some in the crowd shouted one thing, and some another. As he could not determine the facts because of the uproar, he ordered him to be brought into headquarters.

[35]When he came to the steps, he had to be carried by the soldiers because of the violence of the crowd. [36]For the multitude of people that followed kept shouting, "Away with him!"

[37]As Paul was about to be brought into the headquarters, he said to the commander, "Can I say something to you?"

The commander said, "You know Greek? [38]Then you're not the Egyptian who stirred up a rebellion some time ago—and led four thousand men of the Assassins out into the desert?"

[39]Paul said, "I am a Jewish man from Tarsus in Cilicia, a citizen of no insignificant city. I beg you, let me speak to the people."

[40]When the commander had given him permission, Paul stood on the steps and motioned to the people with his hand. When there was a great hush, he spoke to them in Aramaic,[a] saying:

22

Paul's Testimony on the Temple Stairs

[1]"Brothers and fathers, listen to my defense which I now present to you." [2]When they heard that Paul was addressing them in Aramaic, they became even more quiet. Then he said, [3]"I am a Jewish man, born in Tarsus of Cilicia but brought up in this city at the feet of Gamaliel, trained strictly according to the *Torah* of our fathers, being zealous for God just as all of you are today. [4]I persecuted this Way to the death, arresting both men and women and throwing them in prisons— [5]as the *kohen gadol* and all the council of elders can testify about me. I also received letters from them to the brothers, and I went to Damascus to bring back to Jerusalem even those who were there in chains—to be punished.

[6]"But it happened that as I was traveling and drawing near to Damascus, about noon a great light from heaven suddenly flashed all around me. [7]I fell to the ground and heard a voice saying to me, 'Saul, Saul, why do you persecute Me?'

[8]"I answered, 'Who are you, Lord?'

"He said to me, 'I am *Yeshua ha-Natzrati*, whom you are persecuting.'

[9]"Now those who were with me saw the light, but did not understand the voice of the One who was speaking to me. [10]So I said, 'What shall I do, Lord?'

"And the Lord said to me, 'Get up, and go to Damascus. There you will be told all that you have been appointed to do.'

[11]"But since I could not see because of the brilliance of that light, I was led by the hand by those who were with me and came into Damascus. [12]Then a certain Ananias—a devout man according to the *Torah*, well spoken of by all the Jewish people living there— [13]came to me. Standing before me, he said to me, 'Brother Saul, look up!' In that very moment, I looked and saw him!

[14]"And he said, 'The God of our fathers handpicked you to know His will—to see the Righteous One and to hear an utterance from His mouth. [15]For you will be a witness for Him to all people of what you have seen and heard. [16]Now why are you waiting? Get up and be immersed, and wash away your sins, calling on His Name.'

a 21:40; 22:2; 26:14. Lit. *the Hebrew dialect.*

[17]"It happened that when I returned to
Jerusalem and was praying in the Temple, I fell into a trance; [18]and I saw Him
saying to me, 'Hurry! Get out of Jerusalem quickly, because they will not accept your witness about Me.'

[19]"And I said, 'Lord, they themselves know that in one synagogue after another, I was imprisoning and beating those trusting in You. [20]Even when
the blood of Your witness Stephen was spilled, I too was standing by and approving, and guarding the clothing of those who were killing him.'

[21]"And he said to me, 'Go! For I will send you far away to the Gentiles.'"

[22]Up to this statement they listened to him. Then they raised their voices, saying, "Away from the earth with this fellow! For he's not fit to live!"

The Romans Intervene

[23]As they were crying out and flinging off their cloaks and throwing dust into
the air,[a] [24]the commander ordered Paul
to be brought into headquarters. He said Paul should be examined by lashing, so that he might find out why they were
shouting against him so. [25]But when they
stretched him out with straps, Paul said to the centurion standing there, "Is it legal for you to scourge a man who is a Roman citizen without due process?"

[26]Now when the centurion heard this, he went to the commander and reported it, saying, "What are you going to do? For this man is Roman."

[27]The commander came and said to him, "Tell me, are you Roman?"

And he said, "Yes."

[28]The commander answered, "I bought this citizenship for a large sum."

Paul said, "But I was born so."

[29]Therefore, those who were about to interrogate him instantly drew back from him. And the commander also was afraid when he found out that Paul was a Roman and that he had bound him.

a 22:23. cf. 2 Sam. 16:13.

Delivered to the Council

[30]But on the next day, desiring to know exactly why Paul had been accused by the Judeans, he released him and commanded the ruling *kohanim* and all the Sanhedrin to meet together. And he brought Paul and set him before them.

23

[1]Paul, looking intently at the Sanhedrin, said, "Brothers, I have lived my life in all good conscience for God up to
this day." [2]But the *kohen gadol* Ananias
ordered those standing by him to strike him on the mouth.

[3]Then Paul said to him, "God is going to strike you on the mouth, you whitewashed wall! Do you sit judging me according to the *Torah*, and yet in violation of the *Torah* you order me to be struck?"[b]

[4]Those standing nearby said, "Do you insult God's *kohen gadol*?"

[5]Paul said, "I didn't know, brothers, that he is the *kohen gadol*. For it has been written, 'You shall not speak evil of a ruler of your people.'"[c]

[6]But recognizing that one group was Sadducees and the other Pharisees, Paul began crying out in the Sanhedrin, "Brothers, I am a Pharisee, a son of Pharisees! I am on trial because of the hope of the resurrection of the dead!"

[7]When he said this, a dispute broke out between the Pharisees and Sadducees, and the assembly was divided. [8]For
the Sadducees say there is no resurrection or angel or spirit, but the Pharisees
affirm them all. [9]Then there was a great
uproar. Some of the *Torah* scholars of the Pharisees' party stood up and protested sharply, "We find nothing wrong with this man! What if a spirit or angel has spoken to him?"

b 23:3. cf. Lev. 19:15; Deut. 25:2.
c 23:5. Exod. 22:28.

10As a big dispute was developing, the commander was afraid that Paul would be torn to pieces by them. So he ordered the soldiers to go down and take him by force from among them and to bring him into headquarters.

11The following night the Lord stood beside Paul and said, "Take courage! For just as you have testified about Me in Jerusalem, so you must also testify in Rome!"

Conspiracy to Kill Paul

12When it was day, the Judean leaders formed a conspiracy. They bound themselves by an oath not to eat or drink until they had killed Paul. 13There were more than forty who formed this plot. 14They went to the ruling *kohanim* and elders and said, "We have bound ourselves with a solemn oath to taste nothing until we have killed Paul. 15So now you and the Sanhedrin serve notice to the commander to bring him down to you—like you are about to investigate his case more thoroughly. But we are ready to kill him before he comes near."

16But the son of Paul's sister heard of their ambush. He went into the headquarters and told Paul. 17Paul called one of the centurions and said, "Take this young man to the commander, for he has a message for him."

18So the centurion took him and led him to the commander and said, "The prisoner Paul called me and asked me to bring this young man to you, as he has something to say to you."

19The commander took him by the hand, stepped aside, and began asking him privately, "What is it that you have to report to me?"

20And he said, "The Judean leaders have agreed to ask you to bring Paul down to the Sanhedrin tomorrow—as if they are about to investigate more thoroughly about him. 21But do not give in to them, for more than forty of them have bound themselves by an oath not to eat or drink until they have killed him. Even now, they are ready and waiting for your consent."

22So the commander dismissed the young man, charging him, "Tell no one that you have informed me about these things."

Escorted to Caesarea

23Calling two of his centurions, he said, "At the third hour of the night,[a] prepare two hundred soldiers, along with seventy horsemen and two hundred spearmen, to proceed as far as Caesarea. 24Also provide mounts for Paul to ride, so that he might be brought safely to Felix the governor."

25He wrote a letter to this effect:

26"Claudius Lysias,
To the Most Excellent Governor Felix:

Greetings!

27This man was seized by the Judean leaders and was about to be killed by them, when I came on the scene with the soldiers and rescued him, having learned that he is a Roman citizen. 28Desiring to know the charge of which they were accusing him, I brought him down to their Sanhedrin. 29I found that he was accused concerning issues of their law, but charged with nothing worthy of death or imprisonment. 30When I was informed that there was a plot against the man, I sent him to you immediately, also ordering his accusers to state before you what they have against him."

31So the soldiers, in keeping with their orders, took Paul and brought him by night to Antipatris. 32On the next day, they returned to headquarters, leaving the horsemen to go on with him. 33When they came to Caesarea and delivered the letter to the governor, they also presented Paul before him. 34Upon reading

a 23:23. 9 p.m.

the letter, the governor asked what province he was from. When he learned that Paul was from Cilicia, [35]he said, "I will give you a hearing when your accusers have arrived also." Then he gave orders for Paul to be guarded in Herod's Praetorium.

24

Defense Before Governor Felix

[1]After five days, the *kohen gadol* Ananias came down with some of the elders and an attorney named Tertullus. They brought formal charges against Paul before the governor. [2]When Paul was called in, Tertullus began to accuse him, saying, "We are enjoying much peace through you, and reforms are introduced for this nation because of your foresight. [3]We acknowledge this, most excellent Felix, in every way and every place with all gratitude.

[4]"But in order that I may not weary you any longer, I beg you in your kindness to hear us briefly. [5]For we have found this man to be a pest, stirring up riots among all the Jewish people throughout the world, and a ringleader of the sect of the *Natzratim*. [6]He even tried to defile the Temple, but we seized him.[a] [8]By examining him yourself, you will be able to learn from him all these things about which we accuse him."

[9]The Judean leaders also joined in the attack, affirming that these things were true. [10]When the governor nodded for him to speak, Paul responded: "Knowing that you have been judge over this nation for many years, I gladly make my own defense. [11]As you can verify, it is no more than twelve days since I went up to Jerusalem to worship. [12]They did not find me arguing with anyone or inciting a riot—not in the Temple or in the synagogues or anywhere else in the city. [13]Nor can they prove to you the charges they now bring against me.

[14]"But this I confess to you, that according to the Way (which they call a sect), I worship the God of our fathers,[b] believing everything written in the *Torah* and the Prophets. [15]In God I have a hope—which these men also wait for—that there will surely be a resurrection of both the righteous and the unrighteous.[c]

[16]"Therefore I do my best always to have a clear conscience before both God and men. [17]Now after several years, I came to bring *tzedakah* to my country for the poor and to present offerings. [18]As I was doing this, they found me in the Temple, having been purified—without any crowd or uproar. [19]But there were some Jewish people from Asia, who ought to be here before you to press charges if they have anything against me. [20]Or let these men themselves tell what wrongdoing they found when I stood before the Sanhedrin— [21]except for this one cry I shouted out while standing among them: 'It is about the resurrection of the dead that today I am on trial before you.'"

In Prison for Two Years

[22]But Felix, having a rather extensive knowledge of the Way, put them off, saying, "When Lysias the commander comes down, I will rule on your case." [23]Then he gave the centurion orders for Paul to be kept in custody and yet have some freedom, and not to prevent any of his friends from attending to his needs.

[24]Now some days later Felix came with his wife Drusilla, who was Jewish. He sent for Paul and listened to him speak about faith in Messiah *Yeshua*. [25]But as he was arguing about righteousness, self-control, and the coming judgment, Felix became afraid and said, "Go away for now! When I find time, I will summon you."

a Some mss. add 24:6b-8a: *We wanted to judge him according to our own Torah. But the commander Lysias came along, and with much violence took him out of our hands, ordering his accusers to come before you.*

b 24:14. cf. Exod. 3:15.

c 24:15. cf. Dan. 12:2; Isa. 26:19; Ezek. 37:12-14.

26At the same time too, he was hoping that money would be given to him
by Paul; so he sent for him frequently
and would talk with him. 27But after two
years had passed, Felix was succeeded
by Porcius Festus; and wishing to do the
Judean leaders a favor, Felix left Paul in
prison.

25

Appeal to Caesar

1Three days after Festus arrived in
the province, he went up to Jerusalem
from Caesarea. 2There the ruling *kohanim* and the leading Judeans brought
charges against Paul. They were urging
him, 3asking a favor—to have Paul sent
to Jerusalem, planning an ambush to kill
him on the road.

4Festus then answered that Paul was
being guarded at Caesarea, and that he
himself was about to go there shortly.
5"So then," he said, "let the prominent
men among you go down with me; and
if there is any wrong in the man, let them
accuse him."

6After spending not more than eight
to ten days with them, he went down
to Caesarea. The next day, he sat on
the judgment seat and ordered Paul to
be brought in. 7When he arrived, the
Judeans who had come down from
Jerusalem stood around him, bringing
against him many serious charges which
they could not prove.

8Paul said in his defense, "I have committed no offense against the *Torah* of
the Jewish people, or against the Temple, or against Caesar."

9But Festus, wanting to do the Jewish leaders a favor, said to Paul, "Are you
willing to go up to Jerusalem to be tried
before me?"

10But Paul said, "I am standing before
Caesar's judgment seat, where I ought
to be tried. I have done no wrong to the
Judeans, as you very well know. 11If then
I am in the wrong and have committed
anything worthy of death, I do not seek
to escape death. But if there is nothing to
their charges, no one can turn me over to
them. I appeal to Caesar!"

12Then when Festus had consulted
with the council, he responded, "You
have appealed to Caesar—to Caesar you
shall go!"

Festus Seeks Agrippa's Counsel

13Now after several days had passed,
King Agrippa and Bernice arrived at Caesarea to pay their respects to Festus.
14While they were staying there several
days, Festus laid Paul's case before the
king, saying, "There is a man left behind
as a prisoner by Felix. 15When I was in
Jerusalem, the ruling *kohanim* and elders
of the Judeans brought charges against
him, asking for a judgment against him.
16I answered them that it is not Roman
practice to turn over anyone before
the accused meets his accusers face to
face and has an opportunity to make his
defense concerning the charges. 17So
when they came together here, I did not
delay, but on the next day sat on the judgment seat and ordered the man to be
brought in. 18When the accusers stood
up, they were not bringing a charge of
what crimes I suspected. 19Instead, they
had certain issues with him about their
own religion and about a certain *Yeshua*,
who had died, whom Paul claimed to be
alive.

20"Since I was at a loss as to how
to investigate these matters, I asked
whether he was willing to go to Jerusalem to be tried there in regard to them.
21But when Paul appealed to be held in
custody for the decision of His Majesty
the Emperor, I ordered him to be held
until I could send him to Caesar."

22Then Agrippa said to Festus, "I would
like to hear the man myself."

"Tomorrow," he said, "you shall hear
him."

23So on the next day, Agrippa and Bernice came with great pageantry. They entered the audience hall with the commanders and the most prominent men of the city. Then at the order of Festus, Paul was brought in.

24Festus said, "King Agrippa and all present with us, you see this man about whom the whole Judean population petitioned me, both in Jerusalem and here, shouting out that he ought not live any longer. 25But I found that he had done nothing deserving of death; and when he himself appealed to His Majesty the Emperor, I decided to send him. 26Yet I have nothing specific to write to my lord about him. Therefore I have brought him before you—and especially before you, King Agrippa—so that after the investigation has taken place, I might have something to write. 27For it seems illogical to me when sending a prisoner, not to report also the charges against him."

26

Defense Before King Agrippa

1Agrippa said to Paul, "It is permitted for you to speak for yourself."

Then Paul stretched out his hand and began his defense. 2"Concerning all I am accused of by the Judean leaders, I consider myself fortunate, King Agrippa, that it is before you that I am about to make my defense today— 3since you are especially knowledgeable about all Jewish customs and issues. Therefore I beg you to listen patiently to me.

4"Now all the Jewish people have known my manner of life ever since my youth, starting from the beginning in my own nation and also in Jerusalem. 5They have known about me for a long time—if they were willing to testify—that according to the strictest sect of our religion, I lived as a Pharisee.

6"Yet now I stand here being judged for the hope in the promise made by God to our fathers. 7It is the promise that our twelve tribes hope to attain, as they earnestly worship night and day. And for this hope I am accused by Jewish people, O King! 8Why is it judged incredible by any of you that God raises the dead?

9"In fact, I myself thought it was necessary do many things in opposition to the name of *Yeshua ha-Natzrati.* 10And that is what I did in Jerusalem. Not only did I lock up many of the *kedoshim* in prisons by the authority I received from the ruling *kohanim*, but I cast my vote against them when they were being condemned to death. 11I tried to cause them to blaspheme by punishing them often in the synagogues. In furious rage against them, I persecuted them even in foreign cities.

12"While journeying to Damascus with the authority and commission of the ruling *kohanim*, 13at midday, O King, I saw on the road a light from heaven, brighter than the sun, shining around me and those traveling with me. 14When we had all fallen to the ground, I heard a voice saying to me in Aramaic, 'Saul, Saul, why are you persecuting Me? It is hard for you to kick against goads!'

15"Then I said, 'Who are you, Lord?'

"And the Lord said, 'I am *Yeshua*—whom you are persecuting. 16But get up, and stand on your feet.[a] For I have appeared to you for this purpose—to appoint you as a servant and witness to the things you have seen as well as to the things I will yet reveal to you. 17I will rescue you[b] from your own people, and from the Gentiles to whom I am sending you, 18to open their eyes—so they may turn from darkness to light[c] and from the power of satan to God, that they may receive release from sins as well as a place among those who are made holy through trusting in Me.'

19"Therefore, O King Agrippa, I was not disobedient to the heavenly vision.

a 26:16a. cf. Ezek. 2:1; Dan. 10:11.
b 26:17. cf. Jer. 1:8, 19.
c 26:18. cf. Isa. 35:5; 42:7, 16.

[20]Rather, I kept declaring—first to those
in Damascus, and then Jerusalem and
throughout all the region of Judea, and
also the Gentiles—that they should
repent and turn to God, performing
deeds consistent with that repentance.
[21]"For this reason some Judeans seized
me in the Temple and tried to put me to
death. [22]Since I have had God's help, to
this day I have stood here testifying to
both small and great. I am saying nothing but what the Prophets and Moses
said was going to happen— [23]that the
Messiah was to suffer and that, being
first to rise from the dead, He would proclaim light both to our people and to the
nations.[a]"
[24]As Paul was thus making his defense,
Festus says with a loud voice, "You're
crazy, Paul! Your great learning is driving
you insane!"
[25]But Paul declares, "I am not insane,
most noble Festus! Rather I am speaking the sober truth. [26]For the king knows
about these things, and I speak freely to
him, since I am convinced that none of
these things escape his notice—for this
was not done in a corner. [27]King Agrippa,
do you believe the Prophets? I know that
you do believe!"
[28]Agrippa said to Paul, "In a short
time you are trying to persuade me to be
Messianic!"[b]
[29]And Paul said, "Whether short or
long, I would pray to God that not only
you, but also all who hear me today
would be such as I am—except for these
chains!"
[30]Then the king stood up, as well as the
governor, Bernice, and those sitting with
them. [31]When they had gone away, they
began talking among themselves, saying,
"This man is doing nothing deserving of
death or chains."
[32]Then Agrippa said to Festus, "This
man could have been set free, if he had
not appealed to Caesar."

a 26:23. cf. Isa. 42:6; 49:6.
b 26:28. Grk. *Christianos*; Heb. *M'shichim*; cf. Acts 11:26; 1 Pet. 4:16.

27

Sailing for Rome

[1]When it was decided that we should
sail for Italy, they handed Paul and some
other prisoners over to a centurion
named Julius, of the Augustan Cohort.
[2]So we boarded a ship from Adramyttium, which was about to sail to the ports
along the coast of Asia, and we set out
to sea—accompanied by Aristarchus, a
Macedonian from Thessalonica.
[3]The next day, we set down at Sidon.
Julius, treating Paul kindly, let him go to
his friends to receive care. [4]Setting out
to sea from there, we sailed under the
shelter of Cyprus, because the winds
were against us. [5]When we had sailed
across the open sea along the coast of
Cilicia and Pamphylia, we came down to
Myra in Lysia. [6]There the centurion found
a ship from Alexandria sailing for Italy
and put us on board.
[7]Sailing slowly for a number of days,
with difficulty we made it to Cnidus. As
the wind did not allow us to go further,
we sailed under the shelter of Crete, off
Salmone. [8]Coasting along it with difficulty, we came to a place called Fair
Havens, near the city of Lasea.
[9]Since considerable time had passed
and the voyage was already dangerous
because the Fast[c] had already gone by,
Paul kept warning them, [10]telling them,
"Men, I can see that the voyage is about
to end in disaster and great loss—not
only of the cargo and the ship, but also
of our lives!"
[11]But the centurion was persuaded
more by the pilot and the captain of the
ship than by what was said by Paul. [12]And
because the harbor was unsuitable for
wintering, the majority reached a decision to set out to sea from there—if
somehow they might reach Phoenix, a

c 27:9. After *Yom Kippur*, when autumn winds were increasing.

harbor of Crete facing northeast and southeast, and spend the winter there.

Storm and Shipwreck

13 When the south wind blew gently,
supposing they had obtained their purpose, they raised the anchor and started
coasting along the shore by Crete. 14 But
before long, a hurricane-force wind
called "the Northeaster" swept down
from the island. 15 When the ship was
caught and could not face into the wind,
we gave way to it and were driven along.
16 As we ran under the shelter of a small
island called Cauda, we were barely able
to get control of the dinghy. 17 When the
crew had hoisted it up, they made use of
ropes to undergird the ship. Then fearing
they might run aground on the Syrtis,[a]
they let down the anchor and so were
driven along. 18 But as we were violently
battered by the storm, the next day they
began throwing cargo overboard. 19 On
the third day, they threw out the ship's
gear with their own hands. 20 With neither sun nor stars appearing for many
days, and no small storm pressing on us,
all hope of our survival was vanishing.

21 As they had long been without food,
Paul stood up in their midst and said,
"Men, you should have listened to me
and not sailed from Crete, to avoid this
disaster and loss. 22 Yet now I urge you
to take heart, for there will be no loss
of life among you—but only of the ship.
23 For this very night, there came to me an
angel of the God to whom I belong and
whom I serve. 24 He said, 'Do not fear,
Paul. You must stand before Caesar; and
indeed, God has granted you all who are
sailing with you.' 25 So take heart, men,
for I trust God that it will be exactly as
I have been told. 26 But we must run
aground on some island."

27 Now when the fourteenth night had
come, as we were drifting across the
Adriatic Sea, about midnight the sailors
began to sense that they were nearing
some land. 28 So they took soundings
and found the water was twenty fathoms deep.[b] A bit farther along, they
took another sounding and found it was
fifteen fathoms deep. 29 Fearing that we
might run aground on the rocks, they
threw out four anchors from the stern.
They were longing for day to come.

30 Now the sailors were trying to
escape from the ship and had lowered
the dinghy into the sea, pretending they
were going to put out anchors from the
bow. 31 Paul said to the centurion and the
soldiers, "Unless these men remain on
the ship, you cannot be saved!"

32 Then the soldiers cut away the ropes
of the dinghy and let it drift away. 33 As
day was about to dawn, Paul urged them
all to take some food, saying, "Today is
the fourteenth day that you have kept
waiting and going without food, having
taken nothing. 34 Therefore, I urge you to
take some food—for this is for your survival, since not one of you will lose a hair
from his head."

35 And when he had said these things,
he took bread, gave thanks to God
before them all, broke it, and began to
eat. 36 Then all were encouraged and took
some food themselves. 37 (In all we were
276 persons on the ship.)

38 When they had eaten enough, they
began to lighten the ship, throwing the
wheat into the sea. 39 Then when daylight
came, they did not recognize the land; but
they noticed a bay with a beach, where
they planned to run the ship aground if
they could. 40 So they cut off the anchors
and left them in the sea, while loosen-
ing the ropes of the rudders at the same
time. Then, hoisting the forward sail to
the wind, they made for the beach. 41 But
they struck a sandbar between the seas
and ran the ship aground. The bow stuck
fast and remained immovable, and the
stern began to break up by the pounding
of the waves.

42 The plan of the soldiers was to kill
the prisoners, so that none of them

a 27:17. An area known for shallow water and shifting sandbars.

b 27:28. 20 fathoms=120 feet; 15 fathoms=90 feet.

would escape by swimming away. [43]But the centurion, wanting to save Paul, kept them from carrying out their plan. He ordered those able to swim to throw themselves overboard first and get to land— [44]and the rest to get there on boards and pieces of the ship. And in this way all were brought safely to land.

28

From Malta to Rome

[1]Once safely ashore, we learned that the island was called Malta. [2]The natives showed us unusual kindness. Because it had started raining and it was cold, they kindled a fire and welcomed us all.

[3]But when Paul had gathered a bundle of brushwood and placed it on the fire, a viper came out because of the heat and fastened on his hand. [4]When the natives saw the snake hanging from his hand, they began saying to one another, "No doubt this man is a murderer! Though he has been saved from the sea, Justice[a] has not allowed him to live."

[5]However, Paul shook the snake off into the fire and suffered no harm. [6]They were expecting him to swell up or suddenly fall down dead—but after they waited a long time and saw no harm come to him, they changed their minds and began to say he was a god.

[7]Now in the vicinity around that place were lands belonging to the most prominent man of the island, named Publius. He welcomed us and hosted us warmly for three days. [8]It so happened that the father of Publius was lying in bed sick with a fever and dysentery. Paul visited him and, when he had prayed and laid hands on him, he healed him. [9]After this happened, the rest of the sick on the island started coming and getting healed. [10]They also heaped honors on us; and when we sailed, they put on board all the supplies we needed.

a 28:4. Grk. *Dike*, the goddess of justice.

[11]After three months, we set sail in a ship from Alexandria that had wintered at the island, with the Twin Brothers[b] as its figurehead. [12]Setting down at Syracuse, we stayed there three days. [13]From there we got underway[c] and reached Rhegium; and a day later a south wind came up, and on the second day we came to Puteoli. [14]There we found some brothers and sisters, and we were invited to stay with them for seven days. And in this way we came to Rome.

[15]Now the brothers there, when they heard about us, came as far as the Forum of Appius and the Three Taverns to meet us. When Paul saw them, he gave thanks to God and took courage. [16]When we entered Rome, Paul was permitted to remain in his own quarters, with a soldier guarding him.

Paul Keeps Spreading the Good News

[17]It happened that after three days, Paul called together those who were the prominent Jewish leaders. When they had gathered he said to them, "Brothers, although I had done nothing against our people or the customs of our fathers, I was delivered as a prisoner from Jerusalem into the hands of the Romans. [18]When they examined me, they wanted to release me because there was no basis for the death penalty. [19]But when the Judean leaders protested, I was forced to appeal to Caesar—not that I had any charge to bring against my own nation. [20]For this reason, therefore, I have requested to see you and to speak with you—since it is for the hope of Israel that I am bearing this chain."

[21]They said to him, "We have received no letters from Judea about you, and none of the brothers coming here has reported or spoken any evil about you. [22]But we think it appropriate to hear from

b 28:11. Grk. *Dioscuri, Sons of Zeus*; the twin brothers Castor and Pollux, the gods of navigation, were the ship's patron deities.

c 28:13. Lit. *took away* [the anchor]; cf. Acts 27:40.

you about what you think. For indeed, it
is known to us that regarding this sect, it
is spoken against everywhere."
[23]They set a day to meet Paul and came
to him at his quarters in large numbers.
From morning until evening he was
explaining everything to them, testifying about the kingdom of God and trying
to persuade them about *Yeshua* from
both the *Torah* of Moses and the Prophets. [24]Some were convinced by what he
said, while others refused to believe.
[25]So when they disagreed among themselves, they began leaving after Paul had
said one last statement: "The *Ruach ha-*
Kodesh rightly spoke through Isaiah the
prophet to your fathers, [26]saying,

'Go to this people and say,
"You will keep on hearing but will
never understand;
you will keep looking, but will never
see.
[27]For the heart of this people has
become dull,
their ears can barely hear,
and they have shut their eyes.
Otherwise they might see with their
eyes,
hear with their ears,
and understand with their hearts.
Then they would turn back,
and I would heal them."'[a]

[28]Therefore let it be known to you that
this salvation of God has been sent to the
Gentiles, and they will listen!" [29][b]
[30]Paul remained two whole
years in his own rented quarters and
continued to welcome all who came to
him— [31]proclaiming the kingdom of God
and teaching about the Lord *Yeshua* the
Messiah with all boldness and without
hindrance.

a 28:26-27. Isa. 6:9-10; Matt. 13:15.

b 28:29. Some mss. insert: *When he had said these words, the Jewish people left, having a great dispute among themselves.*

Paul's Letter to the Romans

Introduction

Romans is considered in many ways to be Paul's greatest letter. In it, Paul outlines his theology in broad, majestic terms while also giving attention to practical matters. We can date Romans with some confidence to the winter of 56-57 C.E., written at the end of Paul's third journey, possibly from Corinth (see 1 Cor. 16:6).

Uniquely among New Covenant communities, the Roman community seems to have begun independently of the *shlichim*, perhaps by Jewish people from Rome who had visited Jerusalem during the *Shavuot* of Acts 2 and come to faith there. The Roman historian Suetonius and Acts 18:2 both tell us that there were disturbances in Rome over the proclamation of *Yeshua*, and in 49 C.E. the emperor Claudius expelled the Jewish leaders, making little distinction between *Yeshua's* followers and others—thus Priscilla and Aquila came from Rome to Corinth, where they met Paul. By the time Jewish leaders could return about a decade later, two things would have happened: first, the Gentile component of the Messianic communities would have grown considerably; and second, the broader Jewish community would have resented the believers whose *Yeshua* "caused" the expulsion. By the time Paul writes, we are dealing with a community with growing tensions: between Gentile and Jewish believers, between Messianic communities and the larger Jewish community, and between believers and the secular society. Paul's audience then is a mixed group of Jewish and Gentile believers, with the latter probably in the majority.

From chapter 15, we learn that Paul will soon be heading to Jerusalem to bring an offering from the Gentile believers. Then it will be on to Spain via Rome in order to continue spreading the Good News there with the support of the community in Rome. Each travel plan underscores an important emphasis in Paul's letter to the Romans. First is the nature of the Good News and its proclamation (1:16-17), which develops into a full discussion of sin, the way to salvation through faith in *Yeshua*, the place of the *Torah* in Messiah's community, and life in the Spirit. Second is the relationship of Jewish and Gentile people living in community and issues regarding those with strong and weak convictions. In matters both theological and practical, the letter provides important instruction for unity within this mixed community. Relating to God and to community—these are two timeless emphases of Paul in all his writings!

A Look Inside Romans

Introducing Paul and His Message (1:1)
Eager to Visit (1:8)
The Righteous Shall Live by Faith (1:16)
Yet All Are Guilty (1:18)

God's Judgment on Unrighteousness (2:1)
Jewish People Fall Short Too (2:17)

No One Is Acceptable (3:1)
How God Accepts Us (3:21)

Abraham Set Right by Faith (4:1)
Trusting in the Promise (4:13)

Shalom with God through Messiah (5:1)
Yet Sin Reigns through Death (5:12)

Who Is Your Master? (6:1)

Two Laws at War (7:1)

Life in the *Ruach* (8:1)
The Coming Glory (8:18)

The Role of Israel (9:1)

Misdirected Zeal (10:1)

Israel Not Rejected (11:1)
The Mystery Revealed! (11:25)

Be Dead to Self (12:1)

Respecting Authority (13:1)

Unity in Community (14:1)

Salvation for the Gentiles (15:7)
Going to the Ends of the Earth (15:22)

Welcome the Apostolic Team (16:1)
Closing Blessing (16:25)

1

Introducing Paul and His Message

[1]Paul, a slave of Messiah *Yeshua*, called to be a *shaliach* and set apart for the Good News of God, [2]which He announced beforehand through His prophets in the Holy Scriptures. [3]Concerning His Son, He came into being from the seed of David according to the flesh. [4]He was appointed *Ben-Elohim* in power according to the Spirit of holiness, by the resurrection from the dead. He is Messiah *Yeshua* our Lord.

[5]Through Him we have received grace and the office of *shaliach*, to bring about obedience of faith among all the nations on behalf of His name. [6]And you also are called to *Yeshua* the Messiah.

[7]To all those in Rome, loved by God, called to be *kedoshim*:

Grace to you and *shalom* from God our Father and the Lord *Yeshua* the Messiah!

Eager to Visit

[8]First, I thank my God through Messiah *Yeshua* for all of you, because your faithfulness is made known throughout the whole world. [9]For God is my witness, whom I serve with my spirit in the Good News of His Son. How unceasingly I make mention of you, [10]always pleading in my prayers, if somehow by God's will now at last I will be granted a good journey to come to you. [11]For I long to see you, so I may share with you some spiritual gift to strengthen you. [12]That is to say, we would be encouraged together by one another's faithfulness—both yours and mine.

[13]I do not want you to be unaware, brothers and sisters,[a] that many times I planned to come to you (though I was prevented until now)—so I might have some fruit among you also, just as I have among the rest of the nations. [14]I have an obligation to both Greeks and barbarians, to both the wise and the foolish. [15]So I am eager to proclaim the Good News also to you who are in Rome.

The Righteous Shall Live by Faith

[16]For I am not ashamed of the Good News, for it is the power of God for salvation to everyone who trusts—to the Jew first and also to the Greek. [17]In it the righteousness of God is revealed, from trust to trust.[b] As it is written, "But the righteous shall live by *emunah*."[c]

Yet All Are Guilty

[18]For the wrath of God is revealed from heaven against all ungodliness and unrighteousness of men. In unrighteousness they suppress the truth, [19]because what can be known about God is plain to them—for God has shown it to them. [20]His invisible attributes—His eternal power and His divine nature—have been clearly seen ever since the creation of the world, being understood through the things that have been made.[d] So people are without excuse— [21]for even though they knew God, they did not glorify Him as God or give Him thanks. Instead, their thinking became futile, and their senseless hearts were made dark.[e] [22]Claiming to be wise, they became fools. [23]They exchanged the glory of the immortal God for an image in the form of mortal man and birds and four-footed beasts and creeping things.[f]

[24]Therefore God gave them over in the evil desires of their hearts to impurity, to dishonor their bodies with one another. [25]They traded the truth of God for a lie and worshiped and served the creation rather than the Creator, who is blessed

a 1:13; 7:1, 4; 8:29; 10:1; 11:25; 12:1; 15:14, 30; 16:14, 16. Lit. *brothers* (in Messiah's community).

b 1:17. Or *from trusting-faith to trusting-faith.*

c 1:17. Grk. *pistis*; cf. Hab. 2:4(2:4 LXX).

d 1:20. cf. Ps. 19:1-6; Jer. 5:21-22.

e 1:21. cf. 2 Kin. 17:15; Isa. 59:1-15; Jer. 2:5; Ps. 14:1-3.

f 1:23. cf. Deut. 4:16-18.

forever. Amen. 26For this reason God gave them up to shameful passions. Even their women exchanged natural relations for what is against nature. 27Likewise the men abandoned natural relations with women and were burning with passion toward one another—men committing shameful acts with other men[a] and receiving in themselves the due penalty for their error.

28And just as they did not see fit to recognize God, God gave them over to a depraved mind, to do what is not fitting. 29They became filled with all unrighteousness, wickedness, greed, evil. They are full of envy, murder, strife, deceit, malice. They are gossips, 30slanderers, God-haters, insolent, haughty, boastful, inventors of evil, disobedient to parents. 31They are foolish, faithless, heartless, ruthless. 32Though they know God's righteous decree—that those who practice such things deserve death—they not only do them but also approve of others who practice the same.

2

God's Judgment on Unrighteousness

1Therefore you are without excuse, O man—every one of you who is judging. For by whatever you judge another, you condemn yourself. For you who judge practice the same things.[b] 2We know that God's judgment on those who practice such things is based on truth. 3But you, O man—judging those practicing such things yet doing the same—do you suppose that you will escape the judgment of God? 4Or do you belittle the riches of His kindness and tolerance and patience—not realizing that God's kindness leads you to repentance?

5But by your hard and unrepentant heart, you are storing up wrath for yourself on the day of wrath, when God's righteous judgment is revealed.[c] 6He will pay back each person according to his deeds.[d] 7To those who by perseverance in doing good are seeking glory, honor, and immortality—eternal life. 8But to those who are self-seeking and do not obey the truth, but obey unrighteousness—wrath and fury. 9There will be trouble and hardship for every human soul that does evil—to the Jew first and also to the Greek. 10But there will be glory, honor, and *shalom* to everyone who does good—to the Jew first and also to the Greek. 11For there is no partiality with God.[e]

12For all who have sinned outside of *Torah* will also perish outside of *Torah*, and all who have sinned according to *Torah* will be judged by *Torah*. 13For it is not the hearers of *Torah* who are righteous before God; rather, it is the doers of *Torah* who will be justified. 14For when Gentiles, who do not have the *Torah*, do by nature the things of the *Torah*, they are a law to themselves even though they do not have the *Torah*. 15They show that the work of the *Torah* is written in their hearts, their conscience bearing witness and their thoughts switching between accusing or defending them 16on the day when God judges the secrets of men according to my Good News through Messiah *Yeshua*.

Jewish People Fall Short Too

17But if you call yourself Jewish and rely upon the *Torah* and boast in God 18and know His will and determine what matters because you are instructed from the *Torah*— 19and you are sure that you are a guide to the blind, a light to those who are in darkness, 20a corrector of the foolish, a teacher of the immature, having in the *Torah* the embodiment of knowledge and the truth—

a 1:27. cf. Lev. 18:22; 20:13.
b 2:1. cf. 2 Sam. 12:5-7; Matt. 7:1-2.
c 2:5. cf. Deut. 32:34-35.
d 2:6. cf. Ps. 62:12, Prov. 24:12, Matt. 16:27, 2 Cor. 5:10, Col. 3:25, 2 Tim. 4:14, 1 Pet. 1:17, Rev. 2:23.
e 2:11. cf. Deut. 10:17.

21you then who teach another, do you
not teach yourself?
You who preach not to steal, do you
steal?
22You who say not to commit adultery,
do you commit adultery?
You who detest idols, do you rob
temples?
23You who take pride in the *Torah*,
through your violation of the *Torah*, do
you dishonor God?
24For as it is written, "the name of God
is slandered among the nations because
of you."[a]
25Circumcision is indeed worthwhile
if you keep the *Torah*; but if you break
the *Torah*, your circumcision has become
uncircumcision.[b] 26Therefore, if the uncircumcised keeps the righteous decrees of
the *Torah*, will not his uncircumcision be
counted as circumcision?[c] 27 Indeed, the
one not circumcised physically who fulfills the *Torah* will judge you[d] who—even
with the written code[e] and circumcision—break the *Torah*. 28For one is not
a Jew who is one outwardly, nor is circumcision something visible in the flesh.
29Rather, the Jew is one inwardly, and
circumcision is of the heart—in Spirit not
in letter. His praise is not from men, but
from God.[f]

3

No One Is Acceptable

1Then what is the advantage of being
Jewish? Or what is the benefit of circumcision? 2Much in every way. First of all,
they were entrusted with the sayings of
God. 3So what if some did not trust? Will
their lack of faith nullify God's faithfulness? 4May it never be! Let God be true
even if every man is a liar, as it is written,

"that You may be righteous in Your
words
and prevail when You are judged."[g]

5But if our unrighteousness demonstrates the righteousness of God, what
shall we say? God is not unrighteous
to inflict wrath, is He? (I am speaking in
human terms.) 6May it never be! For otherwise, how will God judge the world?
7But if by my lie the truth of God abounds
to His glory, why am I still judged as a sinner? 8And why not say, "Let us do evil, so
that good may come" — just as we are
being slandered and as some claim that
we say. Their condemnation is deserved!
9What then? Are we better than they?
No, not at all.[h] For we have already made
the case that all—both Jewish and Greek
people—are under sin. 10As it is written,

"There is no one righteous—no, not
one.
11There is no one who understands,
no one who seeks after God.
12All have turned aside; together they
have become worthless.
There is no one who does good—
no, not even one!
13Their throat is an open grave;
with their tongues they keep
deceiving.
The poison of vipers is under their
lips.
14Their mouth is full of cursing and bitterness.
15Their feet are swift to shed blood.
16Ruin and misery are in their paths,
17and the way of *shalom* they have
not known.
18There is no fear of God before their
eyes."[i]

a 2:24. Isa. 52:5b(LXX).
b 2:25. cf. Jer. 9:24-26.
c 2:26. cf. Deut. 10:16; 30:6; Jer. 4:4.
d 2:27a. cf. Matt. 12:41-42; 19:28; Lk. 11:31; 22:30.
e 2:27b. Lit. *letter*.
f 2:29. cf. Gen. 29:35, 49:8.
g 3:4. Ps. 51:4b(50:6b LXX).
h 3:9. Or possibly, *What then do we hold before ourselves as a defense?*
i 3:18. Ecc. 7:20; Ps. 13:2-3; Ps. 5:10; Ps. 139:4; Ps. 9:28; Isa. 59:7-8; Ps. 35:2.

19Now we know that whatever the *Torah* says, it says to those within the *Torah*, so that every mouth may be shut and the whole world may become accountable to God. 20For no human, on the basis of *Torah* observance, will be set right in His sight[a]—for through the *Torah* comes awareness of sin.

How God Accepts Us

21But now God's righteousness apart from the *Torah* has been revealed, to which the *Torah* and the Prophets bear witness—22namely, the righteousness of God through putting trust in Messiah *Yeshua*,[b] to all who keep on trusting. For there is no distinction, 23for all have sinned and fall short of the glory of God. 24They are set right as a gift of His grace, through the redemption that is in Messiah *Yeshua*.[c] 25God set forth *Yeshua* as an atonement,[d] through faith in His blood, to show His righteousness in passing over sins already committed. 26Through God's forbearance, He demonstrates His righteousness at the present time—that He Himself is just and also the justifier of the one who puts his trust in *Yeshua*.[e]

27Where, then, is boasting? It is excluded. By what principle? Of works? No, but by the principle of faith.[f] 28For we consider a person to be set right apart from *Torah* observance. 29Is God the God of the Jewish people only? Is He not also the God of the Gentiles? Yes, of the Gentiles also. 30 Since God is One, He will set right the circumcised by faith and the uncircumcised through faith. 31Do we then nullify the *Torah* through faithfulness? May it never be! On the contrary, we uphold the *Torah*.

a 3:20. cf. Ps. 143:2.
b 3:22. Or *the faithfulness of Messiah Yeshua*; cf. Ps. 143:1-2.
c 3:24. cf. Isa. 53:10-12.
d 3:25. Lit. *a mercy seat*, the place of atonement (Heb. *kaporet*); cf. Rom. 5:10; 2 Cor. 5:19, 21.
e 3:26. Or *the one who lives on the basis of Yeshua's faithfulness*.
f 3:27. cf. Eph. 2:8-9.

4

Abraham Set Right by Faith

1What then shall we say that Abraham, our forefather according to the flesh, has found? 2For if Abraham was set right by works, he has something to boast about—but not before God. 3For what does the Scripture say? "Abraham believed God, and it was credited to him as righteousness."[g] 4Now to the one who works, the pay is not credited as a gift, but as what is due. 5But to the one who does not work, but trusts in Him who justifies the ungodly, his trust is credited as righteousness— 6just as David also speaks of the blessing on the man to whom God credits righteousness apart from works:

7"Blessed are those whose lawless
  deeds are forgiven
  and whose sins are covered.
8Blessed is the man whose sin ADONAI
  will never count against him."[h]

9Is this blessing then only on the circumcised, or also on the uncircumcised? For we say, "trust was credited to Abraham as righteousness."[i]

10In what state then was it credited? While circumcised, or uncircumcised? Not while circumcised, but while uncircumcised! 11And he received the sign of circumcision as a seal of the righteousness of the trust he had while he was uncircumcised, so he might be the father of all who are trusting while uncircumcised—that righteousness might be credited to them as well. 12Also he is the father of the circumcised, to those not only circumcised but also walking in the footsteps of the trust of our father Abraham before his circumcision.[j]

g 4:3. Gen. 15:6; cf. Gal. 3:6; Jacob 2:23.
h 4:8. Ps. 31:1-2(LXX); cf. Ps. 32:1-2.
i 4:9. Gen. 15:6.
j 4:12. cf. Gen. 17:1ff.

Trusting in the Promise

[13]For the promise to Abraham or to his seed—to become heir of the world—was not through law, but through the righteousness based on trust. [14]For if those who are of the *Torah* are heirs, trust has become empty and the promise is made ineffective. [15]For the *Torah* brings about wrath; but where there is no law, neither is there a violation.

[16]For this reason it depends on trust, so that the promise according to grace might be guaranteed to all the offspring—not only to those of the *Torah* but also to those of the faith of Abraham. He is the father of us all [17](as it is written, "I have made you a father of many nations"[a]). He is our father in the sight of God in whom he trusted, who gives life to the dead and calls into existence that which does not exist. [18]In hope beyond hope, he trusted that he would become the father of many nations according to what was spoken—"So shall your descendants be."[b] [19]And without becoming weak in faith, he considered his own body—as good as dead, since he was already a hundred years old—and the deadness of Sarah's womb. [20]Yet he did not waver in unbelief concerning the promise of God. Rather, he was strengthened in faith, giving glory to God. [21]He was fully convinced that what God has promised, He also is able to do.[c] [22]That is why "it was credited to him as righteousness."[d]

[23]Now not only for his sake was it written that it was credited to him, [24]but for our sake as well. It is credited to us as those who trust in Him who raised *Yeshua* our Lord from the dead. [25]He was handed over for our transgressions and raised up for the sake of setting us right.[e]

a 4:17. Gen. 17:5.
b 4:18. Gen. 15:5.
c 4:21. cf. Gen. 18:14.
d 4:22. cf. Gen. 15:6; 17:17, 21-27; 18:14; 21:2.
e 4:25. cf. Isa. 53:4, 11.

5

Shalom with God through Messiah

[1]Therefore, having been made righteous by trusting, we have *shalom* with God through our Lord *Yeshua* the Messiah.[f] [2]Through Him we also have gained access by faith into this grace in which we stand and boast in the hope of God's glory. [3]And not only that, but we also boast in suffering—knowing that suffering produces perseverance; [4]and perseverance, character; and character, hope. [5]And hope does not disappoint, because God's love has been poured into our hearts through the *Ruach ha-Kodesh* who was given to us.

[6]For while we were still helpless, at the right time Messiah died for the ungodly. [7]For rarely will anyone die for a righteous man—though perhaps for a good man someone might even dare to die. [8]But God demonstrates His own love toward us, in that while we were yet sinners, Messiah died for us. [9]How much more then, having now been set right by His blood, shall we be saved from God's wrath through Him. [10]For if, while we were yet enemies, we were reconciled to God through the death of His Son, how much more, having been reconciled, shall we be saved by His life. [11]And not only that, but we also boast in God through our Lord *Yeshua* the Messiah, through whom we have now received reconciliation.

Yet Sin Reigns through Death

[12]So then, just as sin came into the world through one man and death through sin, in the same way death spread to all men because all sinned. [13]For up until the *Torah*, sin was in the world; but sin does not count as sin when there

f 5:1. cf. Isa. 54:17.

is no law. 14Nevertheless death reigned from Adam until Moses, even over those who had not sinned in a manner similar to the violation of Adam, who is a pattern of the One to come.

15But the gracious gift is not like the transgression. For if many died because of the transgression of one man, how much more did the grace of God overflow to many through the gift of one Man—*Yeshua* the Messiah. 16Moreover, the gift is not like what happened through the one who sinned. For on the one hand, the judgment from one violation resulted in condemnation; but on the other hand, the gracious gift following many transgressions resulted in justification.[a] 17For if by the one man's transgression, death reigned through the one,[b] how much more shall those who receive the overflow of grace and the gift of righteousness reign in life through the One, Messiah *Yeshua*.

18So then, through the transgression of one, condemnation came to all men; likewise, through the righteousness of one came righteousness of life to all men. 19For just as through the disobedience of one man, many were made sinners, so also through the obedience of one man, many will be set right forever.[c]

20Now the *Torah* came in so that transgression might increase. But where sin increased, grace overflowed even more— 21so that just as sin reigned in death, so also grace might reign through righteousness, to eternal life through Messiah *Yeshua* our Lord.

6

Who Is Your Master?

1What shall we say then? Are we to continue in sin so that grace may abound? 2May it never be! How can we who died to sin still live in it? 3Or do you not know that all of us who were immersed into Messiah *Yeshua* were immersed into His death? 4Therefore we were buried together with Him through immersion into death—in order that just as Messiah was raised from the dead by the glory of the Father, so we too might walk in newness of life.

5For if we have become joined together in the likeness of His death, certainly we also will be joined together in His resurrection— 6knowing our old man was crucified with Him so that the sinful body might be done away with, so we no longer serve sin. 7For he who has died is set free from sin.

8Now if we have died with Messiah, we believe that we shall also live with Him. 9We know that Messiah, having been raised from the dead, no longer dies; death no longer is master over Him. 10For the death He died, He died to sin once for all; but the life He lives, He lives to God. 11So also continually count yourselves both dead to sin and alive to God in Messiah *Yeshua*.

12Therefore do not let sin rule in your mortal body so that you obey its desires. 13And do not keep yielding your body parts to sin as tools of wickedness; but yield yourselves to God as those alive from the dead, and your body parts as tools of righteousness to God. 14For sin shall not be master over you, for you are not under law but under grace.

15What then? Shall we sin because we are not under law but under grace? May it never be! 16Do you not know that to whatever you yield yourselves as slaves for obedience, you are slaves to what you obey—whether to sin resulting in death, or to obedience resulting in righteousness? 17But thanks be to God that though you were slaves of sin, you wholeheartedly obeyed the form of teaching under which you were placed; 18and after you were set free from sin, you became enslaved to righteousness.

a 5:16. Lit. *judgment from one to condemnation ... gift from many trespasses to acquittal.*
b 5:17. cf. Gen. 2:17; 3:6, 19.
c 5:19. Lit. *made righteous*, cf. Rom. 1:17.

19I speak in human terms because of the weakness of your flesh. For just as you yielded your body parts as slaves to uncleanness and lawlessness, leading to more lawlessness, so now yield your body parts as slaves to righteousness, resulting in holiness. 20For when you were slaves of sin, you were free with regard to righteousness. 21So then, what outcome did you have that you are now ashamed of? For the end of those things is death. 22But now, having been set free from sin and having become enslaved to God, you have your fruit resulting in holiness. And the outcome is eternal life. 23For sin's payment[a] is death, but God's gracious gift is eternal life in Messiah *Yeshua* our Lord.

7

Two Laws at War

1Or do you not know, brothers and sisters (for I speak to those who know law), that the law is master over a person as long as he lives? 2For the married woman is bound by law to her husband while he lives; but if the husband dies, she is released from the law concerning the husband. 3So then, if she is joined to another man while her husband is living, she will be called an adulteress. But if her husband dies, she is free from the law—so she is not an adulteress, though she is joined to another man.

4Therefore, my brothers and sisters, you also were made dead to the *Torah* through the body of Messiah, so that you might be joined to another—the One who was raised from the dead—in order that we might bear fruit for God. 5For when we were in the flesh, the sinful passions that came through the *Torah* were working in our body parts to bear fruit for death. 6But now we have been released from the law, having died to what confined us, so that we serve in the new way of the Spirit and not in the old way of the letter.

7What shall we say then? Is the *Torah* sin? May it never be! On the contrary, I would not have known sin except through the *Torah*. For I would not have known about coveting if the *Torah* had not said, "You shall not covet."[b] 8But sin, taking an opportunity, worked in me through the commandment all kinds of coveting. For apart from the *Torah*, sin is dead.

9Once I was alive apart from the *Torah*; but when the commandment came, sin came to life 10and I died. The commandment meant for life was found to cause death.[c] 11Sin, taking an opportunity through the commandment, deceived me and through it killed me.[d] 12So then, the *Torah* is holy, and the commandment is holy and righteous and good.

13Therefore did that which is good become death to me? May it never be! Rather it was sin working death in me—through that which is good—so that sin might be shown to be sin, and that through the commandment sin might become utterly sinful. 14For we know that the *Torah* is spiritual; but I am of the flesh, sold to sin. 15For I do not understand what I am doing—for what I do not want, this I practice; but what I hate, this I do. 16But if I do what I do not want to do, then I agree with the *Torah*—that it is good.

17So now it is no longer I doing it, but sin dwelling in me. 18For I know that nothing good dwells in me—that is, in my flesh. For to will is present in me, but to do the good is not. 19For the good that I want, I do not do; but the evil that I do not want, this I practice. 20But if I do what I do not want, it is no longer I doing it, but sin that dwells in me.

21So I find the principle—that evil is present in me, the one who wants to do good. 22For I delight in the *Torah* of God

a 6:23. Or *the wages of sin.*

b 7:7. Exod. 20:17; Deut. 5:21.

c 7:10. cf. Lev. 18:5; Deut. 30:19.

d 7:11. cf. Gen. 3:13.

with respect to the inner man, 23but I see a different law in my body parts, battling against the law of my mind and bringing me into bondage under the law of sin which is in my body parts. 24Miserable man that I am! Who will rescue me from this body of death? 25Thanks be to God—it is through Messiah *Yeshua* our Lord![a] So then, with my mind I myself serve the *Torah* of God; but with my flesh, I serve the law of sin.

8

Life in the *Ruach*

1Therefore, there is now no condemnation for those who are in Messiah *Yeshua*. 2For the law of the Spirit of life in Messiah *Yeshua* has set you free from the law of sin and death. 3For what was impossible for the *Torah*—since it was weakened on account of the flesh—God has done. Sending His own Son in the likeness of sinful flesh and as a sin offering, He condemned sin in the flesh— 4so that the requirement of the *Torah* might be fulfilled in us, who do not walk according to the flesh but according to the Spirit.

5For those who live according to the flesh set their minds on the things of the flesh, but those who live according to the Spirit set their minds on the things of the Spirit. 6For the mindset of the flesh is death, but the mindset of the Spirit is life and *shalom*. 7For the mindset of the flesh is hostile toward God, for it does not submit itself to the law of God—for it cannot. 8So those who are in the flesh cannot please God.

9However, you are not in the flesh but in the Spirit—if indeed the Spirit of God dwells in you. Now if anyone does not have the Spirit of Messiah, he does not belong to Him. 10But if Messiah is in you, though the body is dead because of sin, yet the Spirit is alive because of righteousness. 11 And if the Spirit of the One who raised *Yeshua* from the dead dwells in you, the One who raised Messiah *Yeshua* from the dead will also give life to your mortal bodies through His Spirit who dwells in you.

12So then, brothers, we do not owe anything to the flesh, to live according to the flesh. 13For if you live according to the flesh, you must die; but if by the Spirit you put to death the deeds of the body, you shall live. 14For all who are led by the Spirit of God, these are sons of God. 15For you did not receive the spirit of slavery to fall again into fear; rather, you received the Spirit of adoption, by whom we cry, "*Abba*! Father!" 16The Spirit Himself bears witness with our spirit that we are children of God.[b] 17And if children, also heirs—heirs of God and joint-heirs with Messiah—if indeed we suffer with Him so that we may also be glorified with Him.

The Coming Glory

18For I consider the sufferings of this present time not worthy to be compared with the coming glory to be revealed to us. 19For the creation eagerly awaits the revelation of the sons of God. 20For the creation was subjected to futility[c]—not willingly but because of the One who subjected it[d]—in hope 21 that the creation itself also will be set free from bondage to decay into the glorious freedom of the children of God. 22For we know that the whole creation groans together and suffers birth pains until now— 23and not only creation, but even ourselves. We ourselves, who have the firstfruits[e] of the Spirit, groan inwardly as we eagerly wait for adoption—the redemption of our body.

24For in hope we were saved. But hope that is seen is not hope. For who hopes for what he sees? 25But if we hope for what

a 7:25. Lit. *Grace be to God through Messiah Yeshua our Lord*; cf. Jn. 14:6.

b 8:16. cf. Hos. 1:10.
c 8:19a. cf. Ps. 39:5-6; Eccl. 1:2.
d 8:19b. cf. Gen. 3:17; 5:29.
e 8:23. cf. Exod. 34:22; Lev. 23:10, 20; Num. 18:12.

Romans 7:24-25a

Miserable man that I am! Who will rescue me from this body of death? Thanks be to God—it is through Messiah Yeshua our Lord!

we do not see, then we eagerly wait for it with perseverance. 26In the same way, the Spirit helps in our weakness. For we do not know how to pray as we should, but the Spirit Himself intercedes for us with groans too deep for words. 27And He who searches the hearts[a] knows the mind of the Spirit, because He intercedes for the *kedoshim* according to the will of God.

28Now we know that all things work together for good for those who love God, who are called according to His purpose. 29For those whom He foreknew He also predestined to be conformed to the image of His Son, so that He might be the firstborn among many brothers and sisters. 30And those whom He predestined, He also called; and those whom He called, He also justified; and those whom He justified, He also glorified.

31What then shall we say in view of these things? If God is for us, who can be against us?[b] 32He who did not spare His own Son but gave Him up for us all, how shall He not also with Him freely give us all things? 33Who shall bring a charge against God's elect? It is God who justifies.[c] 34Who is the one who condemns? It is Messiah,[d] who died, and moreover was raised,[e] and is now at the right hand of God and interceding for us. 35Who shall separate us from the love of Messiah? Shall tribulation, or distress, or persecution, or famine, or nakedness, or danger, or sword? 36As it is written,

> "For Your sake we are being put to
> death all day long;
> we are counted as sheep for the
> slaughter."[f]

37But in all these things we are more than conquerors through Him who loved us. 38For I am convinced that neither death nor life, nor angels nor principalities, nor things present nor things to come, nor powers, 39nor height nor depth, nor any other created thing will be able to separate us from the love of God that is in Messiah *Yeshua* our Lord.

9

The Role of Israel

1I tell the truth in Messiah—I do not lie, my conscience assuring me in the *Ruach ha-Kodesh*— 2that my sorrow is great and the anguish in my heart unending. 3For I would pray that I myself were cursed, banished from Messiah for the sake of my people—my own flesh and blood,[g] 4who are Israelites. To them belong the adoption[h] and the glory[i] and the covenants and the giving of the *Torah*[j] and the Temple service[k] and the promises. 5To them belong the patriarchs—and from them, according to the flesh, the Messiah, who is over all, God, blessed forever. Amen.

6But it is not as though the word of God has failed. For not all those who are descended from Israel are Israel, 7nor are they all children because they are Abraham's seed; rather, "Your seed shall be called through Isaac."[l] 8That is, it is not the children of the flesh who are children of God; rather, the children of the promise are counted as seed. 9For the word of promise is this: "At this time I will come, and Sarah shall have a son."[m] 10And not only this, but also Rebecca having twins, from one act with our father Isaac. 11Yet before the sons were even born and had not done anything good or bad—so that God's purpose and choice might stand not because of works but because of Him who calls— 12it was said to her, "The

a 8:27. cf. Ps. 139:1-5.
b 8:31. cf. Ps. 118:6.
c 8:33. cf. Isa. 50:8-9.
d 8:34. Some mss. read *Messiah Yeshua*.
e 8:34. Some mss. add *from the dead*.
f 8:36. Ps. 44:23(22)(43:23 LXX); cf. Zech. 11:4, 7.

g 9:3. Lit. *my brothers, my kinsmen according to the flesh*.
h 9:4a. cf. Exod. 4:22; Hos 11:1.
i 9:4b. cf. Exod. 40:34; 1 Kin. 8:11; Ezek. 1:28.
j 9:4c. cf. Deut. 4:13-14.
k 9:4d. Heb. *avodah*; cf. Deut. 7:6; Josh. 22:27; 1 Chr. 28:13.
l 9:7. Gen. 21:12(LXX).
m 9:9. Gen. 18:10, 14.

older shall serve the younger."[a] 13As
it is written, "Jacob I loved, but Esau I
hated."[b]

14What shall we say then? There is no
injustice with God, is there? May it never
be! 15For to Moses He says,

"I will have mercy on whom I have
mercy,
and I will have compassion on
whom I have compassion."[c]

16So then it does not depend on the
one who wills or the one who strives,
but on God who shows mercy. 17For the
Scripture says to Pharaoh, "For this very
purpose I raised you up—to demonstrate
My power in you, so My name might be
proclaimed in all the earth."[d] 18So then
He has mercy on whom He wills, and He
hardens whom He wills.

19You will say to me then, "Why does
He still find fault? For who has resisted
His will?" 20But who in the world are you,
O man, who talks back to God? Will what
is formed say to the one who formed it,
"Why did you make me like this?"[e] 21Does
the potter have no right over the clay,
to make from the same lump one vessel
for honor and another for common use?
22Now what if God, willing to demonstrate His wrath and to make His power
known, endured with much patience
vessels of wrath designed for destruction? 23And what if He did so to make
known the riches of His glory on vessels
of mercy, which He prepared beforehand
for glory?

24Even us He called—not only from the
Jewish people, but also from the Gentiles— 25as He says also in Hosea,

"I will call those who were not My
people, 'My people,'
and her who was not loved,
'Beloved.'

26And it shall be that in the place where
it was said to them,
'You are not My people,'
there they shall be called sons of
the living God."[f]

27Isaiah cries out concerning Israel,
"Though the number of *B'nei-Israel* be
as the sand of the sea,
only the remnant shall be saved.
28For *ADONAI* will carry out His word
upon the earth,
bringing it to an end and finishing
quickly."[g]
29And just as Isaiah foretold,
"Unless *ADONAI-Tzva'ot* had left us
seed,
we would have become like Sodom
and resembled Gomorrah."[h]

30What shall we say then? That Gentiles, who did not pursue righteousness,
attained righteousness—that is, a righteousness of faith. 31But Israel, who
pursued a *Torah* of righteousness, did
not reach the *Torah*. 32Why? Because they
pursued it not by faith, but as if it were
from works. They stumbled over the
stone of stumbling, 33just as it is written,

"Behold, I lay in Zion
a stone of stumbling
and a rock of offense,
and whoever believes in Him
shall not be put to shame."[i]

10

Misdirected Zeal

1Brothers and sisters, my heart's desire
and my prayer to God for Israel is for their
salvation. 2For I testify about them that
they have zeal for God—but not based
on knowledge. 3For being ignorant of
God's righteousness and seeking to
establish their own, they did not submit

a 9:12. Gen. 25:23.
b 9:13. Mal. 1:2-3.
c 9:15. Exod. 33:19.
d 9:17. Exod. 9:16.
e 9:20. Isa. 29:16(LXX); 45:9.
f 9:26. Hos. 2:23; 1:10(2:1 LXX).
g 9:27-28. cf. Isa. 10:22-23.
h 9:29. Isa. 1:9.
i 9:33. Isa. 28:16.

themselves to the righteousness of God.
[4]For Messiah is the goal[a] of the *Torah* as
a means to righteousness for everyone
who keeps trusting.
[5]For Moses writes about the righteousness that is based on *Torah*, "The
man who does these things shall live by
them."[b] [6]But the righteousness based on
faith speaks in this way:

"Do not say in your heart,[c] 'Who will
go up into heaven?'[d]
(that is, to bring Messiah down),
[7]or, 'Who will go down into the abyss?'[e]
(that is, to bring Messiah up from
the dead)."
[8]But what does it say?
"The word is near you,
in your mouth and in your heart"[f]
—that is, the word of faith that we
are proclaiming.
[9]For if you confess with your mouth
that *Yeshua* is Lord,
and believe in your heart that God
raised Him from the dead,
you will be saved.
[10]For with the heart it is believed for
righteousness,
and with the mouth it is confessed for
salvation.

[11]For the Scripture says, "Whoever
trusts in Him will not be put to shame."[g]
[12]For there is no distinction between Jew
and Greek, for the same Lord is Lord of
all—richly generous to all who call on
Him. [13]For "Everyone who calls upon the
name of *ADONAI* shall be saved." [h]
[14]How then shall they call on the One
in whom they have not trusted? And how
shall they trust in the One they have not
heard of? And how shall they hear without someone proclaiming? [15]And how
shall they proclaim unless they are sent?
As it is written, "How beautiful are the
feet of those who proclaim good news
of good things!"[i] [16]But not all heeded
the Good News. For Isaiah says, "*ADONAI*,
who has believed our report?"[j] [17]So faith
comes from hearing, and hearing by the
word of Messiah.
[18]But I say, have they never heard?
Indeed they have, for

"Their voice has gone out into all the
earth,
and their words to the ends of the
world."[k]

[19]But I say, did Israel not understand?
First Moses says,

"I will provoke you to jealousy by
those who are not a nation,
with a nation empty of understanding I will vex you."[l]
[20]And Isaiah is so bold as to say,
"I was found by those who did not
seek Me;
I became visible to those who did
not ask for Me."[m]

[21]But about Israel He says,

"All day long I stretched forth my
hands
to a disobedient and contrary
people."[n]

11

Israel Not Rejected

[1]I say then, God has not rejected His
people, has He?[o] May it never be! For I
too am an Israelite, of the seed of Abraham, of the tribe of Benjamin. [2]God has

a 10:4. Or *end-goal*.
b 10:5. Lev. 18:5.
c 10:6. Deut. 9:4.
d 10:6. Deut. 30:12.
e 10:7. Deut. 30:13; cf. Ps. 71:20.
f 10:8. Deut. 30:14.
g 10:11. Isa. 28:16.
h 10:13. Joel 2:32(LXX); cf. Joel 3:5.
i 10:15. Isa. 52:7; Nah. 1:15.
j 10:16. Isa. 53:1.
k 10:18. Ps. 19:4; Ps. 18:5(LXX).
l 10:19. Deut. 32:21.
m 10:20. Isa. 65:1.
n 10:21. Isa. 65:2.
o 11:1. cf. Jer. 31:37; 33:24-26.

not rejected His people whom He knew beforehand.[a] Or do you not know what the Scripture says about Elijah, how he pleads with God against Israel? 3"ADONAI, they have killed your prophets, they have destroyed your altars; I alone am left, and they are seeking my life."[b] 4But what is the divine response to him? "I have kept for Myself seven thousand men who have not bowed the knee to Baal."[c] 5So in the same way also at this present time there has come to be a remnant[d] according to God's gracious choice. 6But if it is by grace, it is no longer by works; otherwise grace would no longer be grace.

7What then? What Israel is seeking, it has not obtained; but the elect obtained it, and the rest were hardened— 8just as it is written,

"God gave them a spirit of stupor,
eyes not to see and ears not to hear,
until this very day."[e]

9And David says,

"Let their table become a snare and a trap,
a stumbling block and a retribution for them.
10Let their eyes be darkened so they do not see,
and bend their back continually."[f]

11I say then, they did not stumble so as to fall, did they?[g] May it never be! But by their false step salvation has come to the Gentiles, to provoke Israel to jealousy.[h] 12Now if their transgression leads to riches for the world, and their loss riches for the Gentiles, then how much more their fullness! 13But I am speaking to you who are Gentiles. Insofar as I am a *shaliach* to the Gentiles, I spotlight my ministry 14if somehow I might provoke to jealousy my own flesh and blood[i] and save some of them. 15For if their rejection leads to the reconciliation of the world, what will their acceptance be but life from the dead?

16If the firstfruit is holy, so is the whole batch of dough;[j] and if the root is holy, so are the branches. 17But if some of the branches were broken off and you—being a wild olive—were grafted in among them and became a partaker of the root of the olive tree with its richness,[k] 18do not boast against the branches. But if you do boast, it is not you who support the root but the root supports you. 19You will say then, "Branches were broken off so that I might be grafted in." 20True enough. They were broken off because of unbelief, and you stand by faith. Do not be arrogant, but fear— 21for if God did not spare the natural branches, neither will He spare you. 22Notice then the kindness and severity of God: severity toward those who fell; but God's kindness toward you, if you continue in His kindness; otherwise you too will be cut off! 23And they also, if they do not continue in their unbelief, will be grafted in;
for God is able to graft them in again.
24For if you were cut out of that which by nature is a wild olive tree, and grafted contrary to nature into a cultivated olive tree, how much more will these natural branches be grafted into their own olive tree?

The Mystery Revealed!

25For I do not want you, brothers and sisters, to be ignorant of this mystery—lest you be wise in your own eyes[l]—that a partial hardening has come upon Israel until the fullness of the Gentiles has come in[m]; 26and in this way[n] all Israel will be saved, as it is written,

a 11:2. cf. 1 Sam. 12:22; Ps. 94:14.
b 11:3. 1 Ki. 19:4a, 10, 14.
c 11:4. 1 Ki. 19:18.
d 11:5. cf. 2 Kings 19:4; Ezra 9:8; Isa. 10:20-22; 11:11, 16; 37:31-32; Jer. 23:3; 31:7; Ezek. 6:8; Mic. 2:12; 5:7-8; 7:18; Zeph. 2:7; Zech. 8:11-12.
e 11:8. Deut. 29:4; Isa. 29:10.
f 11:10. Ps. 69:22-23.
g 11:11. cf. Hos. 14:1-2, 6-10(13:16-14:1, 5-9).
h 11:11. cf. Deut. 32:21.
i 11:14. Lit. *my flesh*; my fellow countrymen.
j 11:16. cf. Num. 15:21; Neh. 10:37; Ezek. 44:30.
k 11:17. cf. Jer. 11:16.
l 11:25a. cf. Prov. 3:7; Rom. 12:16.
m 11:25b. cf. Dan. 8:13-14; Lk. 21:24
n 11:26. Or *and so*.

Romans 11:24

For if you were cut out of that which by nature is a wild olive tree and grafted contrary to nature into a cultivated olive tree, how much more will these natural branches be grafted into their own olive tree?

"The Deliverer shall come out of Zion.
He shall turn away ungodliness
from Jacob.
27And this is My covenant with them,[a]
when I take away their sins."[b]

28Concerning the Good News, they are hostile for your sake; but concerning chosenness, they are loved on account of the fathers[c]— 29for the gifts and the calling of God are irrevocable.[d] 30For just as you once were disobedient to God but now have been shown mercy because of their disobedience, 31in like manner these also have now been disobedient with the result that, because of the mercy shown to you, they also may receive mercy. 32For God has shut up all in disobedience, so that He might show mercy to all.

33O the depth of the riches,
both of the wisdom and knowledge
of God!
How unsearchable are His judgments
and how incomprehensible His
ways!
34For "who has known the mind of
ADONAI,
or who has been His counselor?"[e]
35Or "who has first given to Him,
that it shall be repaid to him?"[f]

36For from Him and through Him and to Him are all things. To Him be the glory forever! Amen.

12

Be Dead to Self

1I urge you therefore, brothers and sisters, by the mercies of God, to present your bodies as a living sacrifice—holy, acceptable to God—which is your spiritual service. 2Do not be conformed to this world but be transformed by the renewing of your mind, so that you may discern what is the will of God—what is good and acceptable and perfect.

3For through the grace given me, I say to everyone among you not to think more highly of yourself than you ought to think—but to use sound judgment, as God has assigned to each person a measure of faith. 4For just as we have many parts in one body—and all the parts do not have the same function— 5so we, who are many, are one body in Messiah and everyone parts of one another. 6We have gifts that differ according to the grace that was given to us—if prophecy, in proportion to our faith; 7if service, in our serving; or the one who teaches, in his teaching; 8or the one who exhorts, in his exhortation; the one who gives, in generosity; the one who leads, with diligence; the one who shows mercy, with cheerfulness.

9Let love be without hypocrisy—detesting what is evil, holding fast to the good. 10Be tenderly devoted to one another in brotherly love; outdo one another in giving honor. 11Do not be lagging in zeal; be fervent in spirit. Keep serving the Lord, 12rejoicing in hope, enduring in distress, persisting in prayer, 13contributing to the needs of the *kedoshim*, extending hospitality.

14Bless those who persecute you—bless and do not curse. 15Rejoice with those who rejoice; weep with those who weep.[g] 16Live in harmony with one another; do not be proud, but associate with the lowly. Do not be wise in your own eyes.[h] 17Repay no one evil for evil;[i] give thought to what is good in the eyes of all people. 18If possible, so far as it depends on you, live in *shalom* with all people. 19Never take your own revenge, loved ones, but give room for God's

a 11:27. Isa. 59:20-21(LXX).
b 11:27. Isa. 27:9; cf. Jer. 31:31-34.
c 11:28. cf. Deut. 7:8; 10:15.
d 11:29. cf. 2 Cor. 7:10.
e 11:34. Isa. 40:13.
f 11:35. Job 41:3(11); cf. Job 41:3(LXX).
g 12:14. cf. Job 30:25.
h 12:16. cf. Prov. 3:7.
i 12:17. cf. Prov. 20:22; 24:29.

wrath—for it is written, "Vengeance is Mine; I will repay,"[a] says ADONAI. [20]Rather,

> "If your enemy is hungry, feed him;
> if he is thirsty, give him a drink.
> For by doing so you will heap coals of
> fire upon his head."[b]

[21]Do not be overcome by evil, but overcome evil with good.

13

Respecting Authority

[1]Let every person submit himself to the governing authorities. For there is no authority except from God, and those that exist are put in place by God.[c] [2]So whoever opposes the authority has resisted God's direction, and those who have resisted will bring judgment on themselves. [3]For leaders cause no fear for good behavior, but for bad. Now if you do not want to fear the authority, do what is good and you will get his approval— [4]for he is God's servant to you for your good. But if you do evil, be afraid—for he does not carry the sword for no reason; for he is God's servant, an avenger who inflicts punishment on the evildoer. [5]Therefore it is necessary to be in submission—not only because of punishment but also because of conscience. [6]For this reason you also pay taxes, for the authorities are God's servants, attending diligently to this very thing. [7]Pay to everyone what is due them—tribute to whom tribute is due; tax to whom tax is due; respect to whom respect is due; honor to whom honor is due.

[8]Owe no one anything except to love one another, for the one who loves another has fulfilled the *Torah*. [9]For the commandments—"You shall not commit adultery, you shall not murder, you shall not steal, you shall not covet,"[d] and any other commandment—are summed up in this word: "You shall love your neighbor as yourself."[e] [10]Love does no harm to a neighbor; therefore love is the fullness of the *Torah*.

[11]Besides this, you know the time—that it is already the hour for you to awaken from sleep; for now our salvation is nearer than when we first came to trust. [12]The night is almost gone and the day is near, so let us put off the works of darkness and put on the armor of light. [13]Let us walk properly as in the day—not in carousing and drunkenness, not in sexual promiscuity and sensuality, not in strife and envy. [14]Instead, put on the Lord Messiah *Yeshua*, and stop making provision for the flesh—for its cravings.

14

Unity in Community

[1]Now accept the one who is weak in faith, but not for the purpose of disputes about opinions. [2]One person has faith to eat anything, but the weak eats only vegetables. [3]Don't let the one who eats disparage the one who does not eat, and don't let the one who does not eat judge the one who eats, for God has accepted him. [4]Who are you to judge another's servant? Before his own master he stands or falls. Yes, he shall stand, for the Lord is able to make him stand.

[5]One person esteems one day over another while another judges every day alike. Let each be fully convinced in his own mind. [6]The one who observes that day does so to the Lord. The one who eats, eats to the Lord, for he gives thanks to God; and the one who abstains, abstains to the Lord, and he gives thanks to God. [7]For none of us lives for himself, and none dies for himself. [8]For if we live, we live for the Lord; and if we die, we die

a 12:19. Deut. 32:35.
b 12:20. Prov. 25:21-22(LXX).
c 13:1. cf. Dan. 2:21; 4:17.
d 13:9. Exod. 20:13-15, 17; Deut. 5:17-19, 21.
e 13:9. Lev. 19:18.

for the Lord. So whether we live or die,
we belong to the Lord. 9For this reason
Messiah died and lived again, so that He
might be Lord of both the dead and the
living.
10But you, why do you judge your
brother or sister?[a] Or you too, why do
you look down on your brother or sister?
For we all will stand before the judgment
seat of God.[b] 11For it is written,

"As I live, says *ADONAI*, every knee
shall bow to Me,
and every tongue shall give praise
to God."[c]

12So then each one of us shall give
account of himself to God.
13Therefore let us not judge one
another from now on, but rather decide
this—not to put a stumbling block or
a trap in the way of a brother or sister.
14I know, and am persuaded in the Lord
Yeshua, that nothing is unholy in itself;
but it is unholy for the one who consid-
ers it unholy.[d] 15For if your brother or
sister is grieved on account of food, you
are no longer walking according to love.
Do not destroy by your food the one for
whom Messiah died. 16Therefore do not
let what is good for you be spoken of as
evil— 17for the kingdom of God is not
about eating and drinking, but righteousness and *shalom* and joy in the *Ruach
ha-Kodesh*. 18For the one who serves
Messiah in this manner is pleasing to God
and approved by men.
19So then let us pursue what makes
for *shalom* and for the building up of one
another.[e] 20Stop tearing down the work
of God for the sake of food. Indeed all
things are clean, but wrong for the man
who by eating causes stumbling. 21It is
good not to eat meat or drink wine or do
anything by which your brother or sister
stumbles. 22The faith you have, keep it
to yourself before God. How fortunate
is the one who does not condemn himself for what he approves. 23But the one
who has doubts is condemned if he eats,
because it is not of faith. And whatever is
not of faith is sin.

a 14:10a, b; 13:13; 14:15, 21. Lit. *brother*.
b 14:10b. Other mss. read of *Messiah*.
c 13:11. Isa. 49:18; 45:23, cf. Gen. 29:35.
d 14:14. cf. Lev. 10:10.
e 14:19. cf. Ps. 34:14.

15

1Now we who are strong ought to
bear the weaknesses of the powerless
and not just please ourselves. 2Let each
of us please his neighbor for his good,
for building him up. 3For even Messiah
did not please Himself, but as it is written, "The insults of those who insulted
You have fallen on Me."[f] 4For whatever
was written before was written for our
instruction, so that through patience and
the encouragement of the Scriptures we
might have hope.[g] 5Now may the God of
patience and encouragement grant you
to be like-minded with one another in
the manner of Messiah *Yeshua*, 6so that
together with one voice you may glorify
the God and Father of our Lord *Yeshua*
the Messiah.

Yet All Are Guilty

7Therefore accept one another just as
Messiah also accepted you, to the glory
of God. 8For I declare that Messiah has
become a servant to the circumcised for
the sake of God's truth, in order to con-
firm the promises given to the patriarchs
9and for the Gentiles to glorify God for
His mercy. As it is written,

"For this reason I will give You praise
among the Gentiles,
and I will sing to Your name."[h]

10And again it says, "Rejoice, O Gentiles, with His people."[i] 11And again,

f 15:3. Ps. 69:9(68:10 LXX).
g 15:4. cf. Ps. 119:9, 11, 105; 2 Tim. 3:16-17.
h 15:9. 2 Sam. 22:50; Ps. 18:49(17:50 LXX).
i 15:10. Deut. 32:43(LXX).

> "Praise *ADONAI* all you Gentiles,
> and let all the peoples praise Him."[a]

12And again, Isaiah says,

> "There shall be a shoot of Jesse;
> and the One who arises to rule the Gentiles,
> in Him shall the Gentiles hope."[b]

13Now may the God of hope fill you with all joy and *shalom* in trusting, so you may overflow with hope in the power of the *Ruach ha-Kodesh.*

14Now I myself am convinced about you, my brothers and sisters, that you also are full of goodness, filled with all knowledge and also able to counsel one another. 15But I have written rather boldly to you on some points as a reminder—because of the grace given to me by God 16to be a servant of Messiah *Yeshua* to the Gentiles, in priestly service to the Good News of God—so that the offering up of the Gentiles might be pleasing,[c] made holy by the *Ruach ha-Kodesh.*

17So in Messiah *Yeshua*, I have reason to boast before God. 18For I will not dare to speak of anything except what Messiah accomplished through me, to bring about the obedience of the Gentiles by word and deed, 19in the power of signs and wonders, in the power of the Spirit of God. So from Jerusalem and around even to Illyricum, I have fully proclaimed the Good News of Messiah. 20In this way I make it my aim to proclaim the Good News not where Messiah was already named, lest I build on another person's foundation, 21but as it is written,

> "Those who have never been told shall see,
> and those who have not heard shall understand."[d]

Going to the Ends of the Earth

22For this reason I was often hindered from coming to you. 23But now with no place in these regions, and since I have had a desire for many years to come to you, 24I hope to see you while traveling through when I go to Spain—and to be helped on my journey there by you, if first I may enjoy your company for a bit.

25But now I am going to Jerusalem, bringing aid to the *kedoshim.* 26For Macedonia and Achaia were pleased to make some contribution for the poor among the believers in Jerusalem. 27Yes, they were pleased to do so, and they are under obligation to them. For if the Gentiles have shared in their spiritual blessings, they also ought to serve them in material blessings. 28So when I have finished delivering the collection safely to them, I will head for Spain by way of you. 29Now I know that when I come to you, I will come in the fullness of the blessing of Messiah.

30Now I urge you, brothers and sisters, through our Lord *Yeshua* the Messiah and through the love of the Spirit, to press on together with me—with prayers to God on my behalf. 31Pray that I might be rescued from the unbelieving Judeans, and that my service for Jerusalem might be acceptable to the *kedoshim.* 32Then, God willing, I may come to you in joy, and together with you find rest.

33Now may the God of *shalom* be with you all. Amen.

16

Welcome the Apostolic Team

1Now I recommend to you our sister Phoebe—who is a *shammash* of Messiah's community at Cenchrea— 2so you may receive her in the Lord, in a way worthy of *kedoshim*, and help her in whatever matter she may need from you. For she

a 15:11. Ps. 117:1(116:1 LXX).
b 15:12. Isa. 11:10.
c 15:16. cf. Mal. 3:4; Isa. 66:20.
d 15:21. Isa. 52:15(LXX).

herself has become a patroness of many, including me as well.

3Greet Prisca[a] and Aquila, my fellow workers in Messiah *Yeshua*, 4who risked their own necks for my life. Not only I give them thanks, but also all of Messiah's communities among the Gentiles. 5Greet also the community that meets in their house. Greet Epaenetus whom I dearly love, who is the first fruit in Asia[b] for Messiah.

6Greet Miriam, who has worked hard for you.

7Greet Andronicus and Junia, my kin and fellow prisoners who are well known[c] among the *shlichim*. They were in Messiah before me.

8Greet Ampliatus, whom I dearly love in the Lord.

9Greet Urbanus, our fellow worker in Messiah, and Stachys whom I dearly love.

10Greet Apelles, who is approved in Messiah. Greet those from the household of Aristobulus.

11Greet Herodion, my kinsman. Greet those from the household of Narcissus, who are in the Lord.

12Greet Tryphaena and Tryphosa, workers in the Lord. Greet Persis whom I dearly love, who has worked hard in the Lord.

13Greet Rufus, chosen in the Lord, and his mother—who was also a mother to me.

14Greet Asyncritus, Phlegon, Hermes, Patrobas, Hermas, and the brothers and sisters with them.

15Greet Philologus and Julia, Nereus and his sister, also Olympas and all the *kedoshim* with them.

16Greet one another with a holy kiss. All of Messiah's communities greet you. 17Now I urge you, brothers and sisters, to keep your eye on those who are causing divisions and stumbling blocks, contrary to the teaching that you learned. Turn away from them. 18For such people do not serve our Lord the Messiah, but only their own belly. By their smooth talk and flattery they deceive the hearts of the unsuspecting. 19Your obedience has become known to all, so I rejoice over you—but I want you to be wise about what is good and innocent about what is evil. 20Now the God of *shalom* will soon crush satan under your feet. May the grace of our Lord *Yeshua* be with you.

21Timothy, my fellow worker, greets you; so do Lucius and Jason and Sosipater, my kin.

22I, Tertius, who wrote this letter, greet you in the Lord.

23Gaius, host to me and the whole community, greets you. Erastus, the city treasurer, greets you, and so does brother Quartus.[d]

Closing Blessing

25Now to the One who is able to strengthen you according to my Good News and the proclamation of *Yeshua* the Messiah, according to the revelation of the mystery which has been kept secret for long ages 26but now is revealed and through the Writings of the Prophets has been made known to all the nations, according to the commandment of the eternal God to bring about obedience of faith—27to the only wise God, through *Yeshua* the Messiah, to Him be the glory forever. Amen.

a 16:3. Also *Priscilla*; cf. Acts 18:2, 18, 26; 1 Cor. 16:19; 2 Tim. 4:19.

b 16:5. The Roman province of Asia, in the western part of Asia Minor (now part of Turkey).

c 16.7. Lit. *bearing a mark*.

d 16:24. Some mss. add: *The grace of our Lord Yeshua the Messiah be with you all. Amen.*

Paul's First Letter to the Corinthians

Introduction

Corinth, considered the number three city in the Roman empire after Rome and Alexandria, also sported a major Jewish community. It was listed by Philo as one of the cities of Jewish Diaspora, and it is evident that Paul was conscious of this presence, even if Gentiles were a majority of the community at Corinth (Acts 10:32).

The Corinthian community began when Paul visited fellow Jewish believers Priscilla and Aquila. Eventually, Paul's witness led to a local synagogue leader, Crispus, along with his household, coming to faith. As a result, many in the Corinthian community were immersed (Acts 18:1-8, 1 Cor. 1:4).

Though the community was majority Gentile, it was likely knowledgeable about Jewish customs and concerns and trying to figure out how Jews and Gentiles could live together in unity and good order. Many Corinthians had come to faith out of a pagan background that still exercised far too much influence on their ethics and social behavior.

1 Corinthians is an intensely personal and practical letter, written about 55 C.E. from Ephesus and addressed to the wider believing community in Corinth. The letter often seems to jump from one subject to another, as Paul responds to a "laundry list" of issues in the life of Messiah's community:

• Divisions and factionalism (1:10-13). In the culture of that day, sophisticated speakers were put on pedestals. Rather than submitting to one another and to Paul in humility, the Corinthians ran after their favorite pop-stars. Spiritual unity was a hard commodity to come by.

• Ethical issues. The Corinthians were deeply divided over matters such as extramarital sex, incest, lawsuits against fellow believers, and eating food sacrificed to idols. They were not mature enough to effectively resolve them, or to discern at what points their culture was shaping their faith rather than vice-versa.

• Conduct at public meetings of believers. Paul addresses the roles of men and women, the issue of head coverings, the Lord's supper, and spiritual gifts. Notably, the Corinthians valued spiritual gifts and status over love and unity.

• Doctrinal issues. In particular, the resurrection was badly misunderstood. The Corinthians mistakenly thought of themselves as having "arrived" spiritually, thus sanctioning widespread immorality.

Above all, Paul shows us how the Good News challenges us to be shaped by *Yeshua*, not by our culture—whether that culture is 1st century Greek paganism, or 21st century Jewish American lifestyle.

A Look inside 1 Corinthians

Greetings (1:1)
Thanksgiving (1:4)
Concern about Disunity (1:10)
Whose Wisdom Is Foolish? (1:18)

Wisdom that Rests on God's Power (2:1)

Building Together on
God's Foundation (3:1)

Learning to Imitate
Messiah's *Shaliach* (4:1)

Removing the "*Hametz*"
from Your House (5:1)

Settle Disputes Within
the Community (6:1)
Morality in the Temple of God (6:9)

Counsel About Marriage (7:1)
Remain As You Were Called (7:17)

Concerning Idol Sacrifices (8:1)

Servant Leadership Wins Over All (9:1)

Warnings from History (10:1)
Feast with the Lord—
Not with Idols (10:16)

Headship and Coverings (11:2)
Unity at the Lord's Table (11:17)

Spiritual Gifts for the Body (12:1)

The Superior Way of Love (13:1)

Orderly Governing of the Gifts (14:1)

The Victory of the Resurrection (15:1)

Collection for Jerusalem
and Final Greetings (16:1)

1

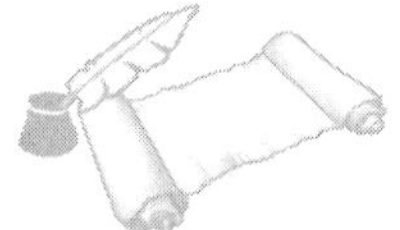

Greetings

1Paul, called as a *shaliach* of Messiah *Yeshua* by the will of God, and Sosthenes our brother,

2To God's community in Corinth—having been made holy in Messiah *Yeshua*, called as *kedoshim*—with all who everywhere call on the name of our Lord *Yeshua* the Messiah, both theirs and ours:

3Grace to you and *shalom* from God our Father, and the Lord *Yeshua* the Messiah!

Thanksgiving

4I always thank my God for you because of God's grace that was given to you in Messiah *Yeshua*. 5For in Him you were made rich in every way—in all speaking and all knowledge— 6just as the evidence of Messiah was confirmed among you. 7So you are not lacking in any spiritual gift, as you eagerly wait for the revealing of our Lord *Yeshua* the Messiah. 8He will also strengthen you until the end—blameless in the Day of our Lord *Yeshua* the Messiah. 9God is faithful,[a] through whom you were called into the fellowship of His Son, *Yeshua* the Messiah our Lord.

Concern about Disunity

10Now I urge you, brothers and sisters, through the name of our Lord *Yeshua* the Messiah, that you all speak the same thing and that there be no divisions among you, but that you be united in the same mind and in the same purpose. 11For it has been reported to me concerning you, my brothers and sisters, by those who are from Chloe's household, that there are rivalries among you. 12I say this because you are each saying, "I follow Paul," or "I follow Apollos," or "I follow Kefa," or "I follow Messiah." 13Has Messiah been divided? Paul wasn't crucified for you, was he? Or were you immersed into the name of Paul? 14I thank God that I immersed none of you, except Crispus and Gaius, 15so that no one should say that I had immersed you into my own name. 16(I also immersed the household of Stephanas; besides them, I don't recall if I immersed anyone else.) 17For Messiah sent me not to immerse, but to proclaim the Good News—not with cleverness of speech, so that the cross of Messiah would not be made of no effect.

Whose Wisdom Is Foolish?

18For the message of the cross is foolishness to those who are perishing, but to us who are being saved it is the power of God. 19For it is written,

"I will destroy the wisdom of the wise
and bring to nothing the understanding of the intelligent."[b]

20Where is the wise one? Where is the *Torah* scholar? Where is the debater of this age? Hasn't God made foolish the wisdom of the world?[c] 21For seeing that—in God's wisdom—the world through its wisdom did not know God, God was pleased—through the foolishness of the message proclaimed—to save those who believe. 22For Jewish people ask for signs and Greek people seek after wisdom, 23but we proclaim Messiah crucified—a stumbling block to Jewish people and foolishness to Gentile people, 24but to those who are called (both Jewish and Greek people), Messiah, the power of God and the wisdom of God. 25For the foolishness of God is wiser than men, and the weakness of God is stronger than men.

26For you see your calling, brothers and sisters, that not many are wise according to human standards,[d] not many are powerful, and not many are born well. 27Yet God chose the foolish things of the world

a 1:9. cf. Deut. 7:9.

b 1:19. Isaiah 29:14.

c 1:20. cf. Job 12:17; Is. 19:11-12.

d 1:26. Lit. *the flesh*.

so He might put to shame the wise; and God chose the weak things of the world so He might put to shame the strong;
[28]and God chose the lowly and despised things of the world, the things that are as nothing, so He might bring to nothing
the things that are— [29]so that no human
might boast before God. [30]But because of Him you are in Messiah *Yeshua*, who became to us wisdom from God and righteousness and holiness and redemption—[31]so that, just as it is written, "Let him who boasts, boast in ADONAI."[a]

2

Wisdom that Rests on God's Power

[1]When I came to you, brothers and sisters, I did not come with excellence of speech or wisdom, proclaiming to you
the mystery[b] of God. [2]For I decided not to know about anything among you except *Yeshua* the Messiah—and Him crucified.
[3]I was with you in weakness and in fear
and in much trembling. [4]My speech and my preaching were not with persuasive words of wisdom, but in demonstration
of the Spirit and of power—[5]so that your faith would not be in the wisdom of men but in the power of God.

[6]We do speak wisdom, however, among those who are mature—but not a wisdom of this age or of the rulers of this
age, who are coming to nothing. [7]Rather, we speak God's wisdom in a mystery—a wisdom that has been hidden, which God destined for our glory before the ages.
[8]None of the rulers of this age understood it—for if they had, they would not
have crucified the Lord of glory. [9]But as it is written,

"Things no eye has seen
and no ear has heard,
that have not entered the heart of mankind—
these things God has prepared for those who love Him."[c]

[10]But God revealed these things to us through the Spirit.[d] For the Spirit searches all things—even the depths
of God. [11]For who among men knows the things of a man, except the man's spirit within him? In the same way, no one knows the things of God except the
Spirit of God. [12]Now we have received not the spirit of the world, but the Spirit who is from God—so we might come to know the things freely given to us by
God. [13]These things we also speak—not in words taught by human wisdom but in words taught by the Spirit, explaining the spiritual to the spiritual.

[14]Now a natural man does not accept the things of the Spirit of God, for they are foolishness to him; and he cannot understand them, because they are spiritually discerned. [15]But the one who is spiritual discerns all things, and he himself is discerned by no one. For

[16]"who has known the mind of ADONAI,
that he will instruct Him?"[e]

But we have the mind of Messiah.

3

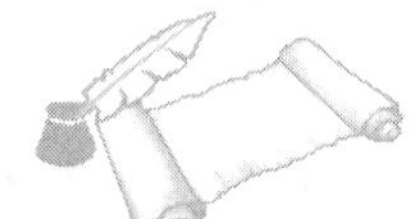

Building Together on God's Foundation

[1]And I, brothers and sisters, could not speak to you as spirit-filled but as
worldly[f]—as infants in Messiah. [2]I gave you milk, not solid food, for you were not yet ready. Indeed, even now you are not
yet ready, [3]for you are still worldly. For since there is jealousy and strife among

a 1:31. Jeremiah 9:23(24).
b 2:1. Some mss. say *testimony*.
c 2:19. Isa. 64:3(4).
d 2:10-15. Both the Heb. *Ruach* and Eng. *spirit* or *Spirit* are expressions of the Grk. *pneuma*.
e 2:16. Isa. 40:13.
f 3:1, 3. Lit. *fleshly*.

you, aren't you worldly and walking in a human way? 4For when one says, "I follow Paul," and another, "I follow Apollos," are you not mere humans[a]?

5What then is Apollos? And what is Paul? Servants through whom you came to trust—and to each as the Lord gave. 6I planted, Apollos watered, but God gave the increase. 7So neither the one who plants nor the one who waters is anything, but only God who makes things grow. 8Now he who plants and he who waters work as one, but each will receive his own reward according to his own labor. 9For we are God's co-workers; you are God's field, God's building.

10According to the grace of God which was given to me, like a skilled master builder I laid a foundation, and another builds on it. But let each consider carefully how he builds on it. 11For no one can lay any other foundation than what is already laid[b]—which is *Yeshua* the Messiah. 12Now if anyone builds on the foundation with gold, silver, precious stones, wood, hay, straw, 13each one's work will become clear. For the Day will show it, because it is to be revealed by fire; and the fire itself will test each one's work—what sort it is. 14If anyone's work built on the foundation survives, he will receive a reward. 15If anyone's work is burned up, he will suffer loss—he himself will be saved, but as through fire.

16Don't you know that you are God's temple and that God's Spirit dwells among you? 17If anyone destroys God's temple, God will destroy him; for God's temple is holy, and you are that temple.

18Let no one deceive himself. If anyone thinks he is wise in this age, let him become a fool so he may become wise.[c] 19For the wisdom of this world is foolishness in the sight of God. For it is written, "He catches the clever in their craftiness."[d] 20And again, "The Lord knows the thoughts of the wise, that they are useless."[e] 21So let no one boast about men. For all things are yours—22whether Paul or Apollos or Kefa, or the world or life or death, or things present or things to come. All are yours, 23and you are Messiah's, and Messiah is God's.

a 3:4. Some mss. say *fleshly*.
b 3:11. cf. Isa. 28:16.
c 3:18. cf. Isa. 5:21; Jer. 8:8–9.
d 3:19. Job 5:13.

4

Learning to Imitate Messiah's *Shaliach*

1So let each one think of us in this way—as Messiah's helpers and stewards of the mysteries of God. 2In this case, moreover, what is required of stewards is to be found trustworthy. 3But to me it matters very little to be judged by you or by any human court. In fact, I do not even judge myself. 4For I know of nothing against myself, yet I am not justified by this. It is the Lord who judges me. 5Therefore do not judge anything before the time—wait until the Lord comes. He will bring to light the things hidden in darkness and also make clear the motives of the hearts. Then the praise for each one will come from God.

6Now I have applied these things to myself and Apollos for your benefit, brothers and sisters, so you might learn from us not to go beyond what is written. Then none of you will be puffed up in favor of one against the other. 7For who makes you different? And what do you have that you did not receive? But if you did receive it, why do you boast as if you had not received it?

8Already you are full! Already you have become rich! Without us you have become kings! Indeed, I wish you were kings, so we also might be kings with you! 9For it seems to me that God has put us, the *shlichim*, on display last of all—like men sentenced to death. For we have become a spectacle to the world, both to angels and to people. 10We are fools for Messiah's sake, but you are

e 3:20. cf. Ps. 94:11(Ps. 93:11 LXX).

wise in Messiah! We are weak, but you are strong! You are honored, but we are dishonored! 11To this very hour we are both hungry and thirsty, dressed in rags and mistreated and homeless. 12We toil, working with our own hands. When we are cursed, we bless. When we are persecuted, we endure. 13When we are slandered, we speak kindly. We have become the scum of the earth, the dregs of all things—even to this moment.

14I do not write these things to make you ashamed, but to warn you as my dearly loved children. 15For though you may have ten thousand guardians in Messiah, yet you do not have many fathers. For in Messiah *Yeshua*, I became your father through the Good News. 16I urge you therefore—be imitators of me. 17For this reason I have sent you Timothy, my dearly loved and faithful child in the Lord. He will remind you of my ways in Messiah, just as I teach everywhere in every community.

18Now some are puffed up, as though I were not coming to you. 19But I will come to you soon, if the Lord is willing; and I will find out not the talk of those who are puffed up, but their power. 20For the kingdom of God does not consist of talk but of power. 21What do you want? Shall I come to you with a rod, or in love and a spirit of gentleness?

5

Removing the "*Hametz*" from Your House

1It is actually reported that among you there is sexual immorality, and such immorality as is not even among the pagans—that someone has his father's wife. 2And you are puffed up! Shouldn't you have mourned instead, so that the one who did this deed might be removed from among you? 5:3 For even though I am absent in body, I am present in spirit—I have already passed judgment on the one who has done this thing, as though I were present. 4When you are gathered together in the name of our Lord *Yeshua*, I am with you in spirit. With the power of our Lord *Yeshua*, 5you are to turn such a fellow over to satan for the destruction of his fleshly nature,[a] so that his spirit may be saved in the day of the Lord *Yeshua*.

6Your boasting is no good. Don't you know that a little *hametz* leavens the whole batch of dough? 7Get rid of the old *hametz*,[b] so you may be a new batch, just as you are unleavened—for Messiah, our Passover Lamb, has been sacrificed. 8Therefore let us celebrate the feast not with old *hametz*,[c] the *hametz* of malice and wickedness, but with unleavened bread—the *matzah* of sincerity and truth.

9I wrote to you in my letter not to mix together[d] with sexually immoral people—10not at all meaning the sexually immoral people of this world or the greedy or swindlers or idolaters, for then you would have to exit the world. 11But now I am writing to you not to mix together with anyone who is being called a brother if he is sexually immoral or greedy or an idolater or a slanderer or a drunkard or a swindler—not even to eat with such a fellow. 12For what business do I have judging outsiders? Don't you judge those who are inside? 13But those who are outside, God judges. Put away the wicked fellow from among yourselves.[e]

6

Settle Disputes Within the Community

1Does any one of you, when he has a matter against his neighbor, dare to go

a 5:5. cf. Prov. 23:14.
b 5:7. cf. Exod. 12:19.
c 5:8. cf. Exod. 13:7; Deut. 16:3.
d 5:9. cf. 2 Thes. 3:14.
e 5:13. cf. Deut. 13:6(5); 17:7, 12; 19:19; 21:21; 22:21, 24; 24:7.

to court before the unrighteous and not before the *kedoshim*? [2]Don't you know that the *kedoshim* will judge the world? And if the world is to be judged by you, are you incompetent to judge trivial matters? [3]Don't you know that we will judge angels? How much more the matters of this life! [4]So if you have courts for matters of this life, why do you appoint as judges those who have no standing in the community? [5]I say this to put you to shame! Isn't there even one wise man among you who will be able to settle disputes between his brothers? [6]Instead, a brother goes to court against a brother—and before unbelievers at that!

[7]Therefore, it is already an utter failure for you that you have lawsuits among yourselves. Why not rather be wronged? Why not rather be cheated? [8]But you yourselves do wrong and cheat—and against your brothers and sisters at that!

Morality in the Temple of God

[9]Or don't you know that the unrighteous will not inherit the kingdom of God? Don't be deceived! The sexually immoral, idolaters, adulterers, those who practice homosexuality, [10]thieves, the greedy, drunkards, slanderers, swindlers—none of these will inherit the kingdom of God. [6:11] That is what some of you were—but you were washed, you were made holy, you were set right in the name of the Lord *Yeshua* the Messiah and by the Spirit of our God.

[12]"Everything is permitted for me"—but not everything is helpful. "Everything is permitted for me"—but I will not be controlled by anything. [13]"Food is for the stomach, and the stomach is for food"—but God will do away with both of them. Yet the body is not for sexual immorality but for the Lord, and the Lord is for the body. [14]Now God raised up the Lord and will also raise us up by His power. [15]Don't you know that your bodies are members of Messiah? Shall I then take the members of Messiah and make them members of a prostitute? May it never be! [16]Or don't you know that the one who joins himself to a prostitute is one body with her? For it is said, "The two shall become one flesh."[a] [17]But the one who joins himself to the Lord is one spirit with Him.

[18]Flee from sexual immorality! Every other sin that a man commits is outside the body—but the one committing sexual immorality sins against his own body. [19]Or don't you know that your body is a temple of the *Ruach ha-Kodesh* who is in you, whom you have from God, and that you are not your own? [20]For you were bought with a price. Therefore glorify God in your body.[b]

7

Counsel About Marriage

[1]Now concerning the things about which you wrote to me, it is good for a man not to touch a woman. [2]But because of much immorality, let each man have his own wife, and let each woman have her own husband. [3]Let the husband fulfill his obligation to his wife, and likewise also the wife to her husband. [4]The wife does not have the rights to her own body, but the husband. Likewise also the husband does not have the rights to his own body, but the wife. [5]Do not deprive one another—except by mutual consent for a time, so that you may devote yourselves to prayer.[c] Then come together again, so that satan doesn't tempt you because of your lack of self-control. [6]But this I say as a concession, not as a command.[7]Yet I wish that all men were like me. However, each man has his own gift from God, one in this way and another that.

[8]But I say to the unmarried and to widows that it is good for them to remain as I am. [9]But if they do not have self-control, let them marry. For it is better to marry than to burn with desire.

a 6:16. Gen. 2:24.

b 6:20. Some mss. add *and in your spirit, which are God's*.

c 7:5. cf. Exod. 19:15; some mss. say *fasting and prayer*.

[10]But to the married I command—not I, but the Lord[a]—a wife is not to be separated from her husband [11](but if she gets separated, let her remain unmarried or else be reconciled to her husband), and the husband is not to divorce his wife.

[12]But to the rest I say—I, not the Lord—if any brother has a wife who is not a believer, and she agrees to live with him, he must not divorce her. [13]And if any woman has a husband who is not a believer, and he agrees to live with her, she must not divorce him. [14]For the unbelieving husband is made holy through the wife, and the unbelieving wife is made holy through her husband.[b] Otherwise your children would be unclean, but now they are holy. [15]But if the unbeliever separates, let him be separated. The brother or the sister is not bound in such cases, but God has called you to *shalom*. [16]For how do you know, wife, whether you will save your husband? Or how do you know, husband, whether you will save your wife?

Remain As You Were Called

[17]Only, as the Lord has assigned to each one, as God has called each, let him walk in this way. I give this rule in all of Messiah's communities. [18]Was anyone called when he already had been circumcised? Let him not make himself uncircumcised. Has anyone been called while uncircumcised? Let him not allow himself to be circumcised. [19]Circumcision is nothing and uncircumcision is nothing[c]—but keeping God's commandments matters. [20]Let each one remain in the calling in which he was called. [21]Were you called as a slave? Don't let that bother you—but if indeed you can become free, make the most of the opportunity. [22]For the one who was called in the Lord as a slave is the Lord's freedman. Likewise the one who was called while free is Messiah's slave. [23]You were bought with a price; do not become slaves of men. [24]Brothers and sisters, let each one—in whatever way he was called—remain that way with God.

[25]Now concerning virgins I have no command from the Lord, but I give an opinion as one who by the Lord's mercy is trustworthy. [26]I think then, because of the present distress, that it is good for a man to remain as he is. [27]Are you bound to a wife? Don't seek a divorce. Are you free from a wife? Don't seek a wife. [28]But if you marry, you have not sinned; and if a virgin marries, she has not sinned. Yet such people will have trouble in this fleshly life, and I am trying to spare you. [29]But this I say, brothers and sisters—the time is short. From now on those who have wives should be as though they had none; [30]and those who weep, as though not weeping; and those who rejoice, as though not rejoicing; and those who buy, as though not possessing; [31]and those who use the world, as though not using it to the fullest. For the present form of this world is passing away.

[32]But I want you to be free from cares. An unmarried man cares about the things of the Lord—how he may please the Lord; [33]but the married man cares about the things of the world—how he may please his wife— [34]and he is divided. The unmarried woman, as well as the virgin, cares about the things of the Lord, so that she may be holy both in body and in spirit. But the married woman cares about the things of the world—how she may please her husband. [35]Now I say this for your own benefit—not to put a restraint on you, but to promote proper and constant service to the Lord without distraction.

[36]But if any man thinks that he is behaving inappropriately toward his virgin, if the time is ripe and it is meant to be, let him do what he decides. He does not sin. Let them marry. [37]But he who stands firm in his heart—who has no pressure, but has power over his own will

a 7:10-11. cf. Matt. 5:32; 19:9.
b 7:14. Lit. *the brother.*
c 7:19. cf. Gal. 5:6; 6:15.

and has so determined in his own heart
to keep her a virgin—he will do well. [38]So
then both he who marries the virgin does
well, and he who doesn't marry her does
better.

[39]A wife is bound to her husband as
long as he lives; but if her husband dies,
she is free to be married to anyone she
wishes—only in the Lord.[a] [40]But in my
judgment she is happier if she stays as
she is—and I also think that I have God's
Spirit.

8

Concerning Idol Sacrifices

[1]Now concerning idol sacrifices,
we know that we all have knowledge.
Knowledge puffs up, but love builds up.
[2]If anyone thinks he knows anything, he
doesn't yet know as he ought to know.
[3]But if anyone loves God, he is known by
Him.

[4]Therefore concerning the
eating of idol sacrifices, we know that
an idol is nothing in the world, and that
there is no God but one.[b] [5]For even if
there are so-called "gods," whether in
heaven or on earth (as indeed there are
many "gods" and many "lords"),

[6]yet for us there is one God, the
Father,[c]
from whom are all things, and we
exist for Him;
and one Lord, *Yeshua* the Messiah,
through whom are all things, and
we exist through Him.

[7]But that knowledge is not in everyone—some, so accustomed to idols up
until now, eat food as an idol sacrifice;
and their conscience, being weak, is
defiled. [8]But food will not bring us before
God. We are no worse off if we do not eat
and no better off if we do eat. [9]But watch
out that this freedom of yours does not
somehow become a stumbling block to
the weak.[d] [10]For suppose someone sees
you—who have this knowledge—dining in an idol's temple. If his conscience
is weak, won't he be emboldened to eat
idol sacrifices? [11]For the one who is weak
is destroyed by your knowledge—the
brother for whom Messiah died. [12]In this
way, when you sin against the brothers
and sisters and wound their conscience
when it is weak, you sin against Messiah. [13]For this reason, if food causes my
brother to stumble, I will never eat meat
again, so that I do not cause my brother
to stumble.

9

Servant Leadership Wins Over All

[1]Am I not free? Am I not a *shaliach*?
Have I not seen *Yeshua* our Lord? Are
you not my work in the Lord? [2]If to others I am not a *shaliach*, at least I am to
you—for you are the seal of my office of
shaliach in the Lord.

[3]My defense to those who examine
me is this. [4]Don't we have the right to
food and drink? [5]Don't we have the right
to take along a believing wife, as do the
other *shlichim* and the Lord's brothers
and Kefa? [6]Or is it only Barnabas and I
who have no right to not work? [7]What
soldier ever serves at his own expense?
Who plants a vineyard and does not eat
its fruit? Or who tends a flock and does
not drink its milk?

[8]I don't say these things merely as a
man, do I? Doesn't *Torah* also say these
things? [9]For it is written in the *Torah* of
Moses, "You shall not muzzle an ox while
it is threshing."[e] Is it the oxen that concern God, [10]or is He speaking entirely for

a 7:39. cf. 2 Cor. 6:14.
b 8:4. cf. Deut. 4:35, 39; 6:4; some mss. say *there is no other God but one*.
c 8:6. cf. Deut 6:4, Isa. 46:9; Jer. 10:6, 7; 1 Cor. 8:4, Mal. 2:10.
d 8:9. cf. Exod. 23:33.
e 9:9. Deut. 25:4.

our sake? Yes, it was written for our sake, because the one plowing ought to plow in hope and the one threshing in hope of a share in the crop. [11]If we sowed spiritual things into you, is it too much if we reap material things from you? [12]If others have a share in this claim over you, shouldn't we even more?

Nevertheless we did not use this right, but we put up with all things so that we cause no hindrance to the Good News of Messiah. [13]Don't you know that those who perform the holy services eat from the Temple, and those who wait on the altar receive a share at the altar?[a] [14]So also the Lord ordered those who proclaim the Good News to get their living from the Good News.

[15]But I have used none of these things, and I am not writing these things so it will happen this way in my case—for I would rather die than let anyone deprive me of my reason to boast. [16]For if I proclaim the Good News, I have no reason to boast—for pressure is put on me and woe to me if I don't proclaim the Good News! [17]For if I do this of my own will, I have a reward. But if not of my own will, I have been entrusted with a commission. [18]What then is my reward? That when I preach, I may present the Good News free of charge, not making use of my right[b] in the Good News.

[19]For though I am free from all men, I have made myself a slave to all, so that I might win over more of them. [20]To the Jewish people I identified[c] as a Jew, so that I might win over the Jewish people. To those under *Torah* I became like one under *Torah* (though not myself being under *Torah*), so that I might win over those under *Torah*; [21]to those outside *Torah*, like one outside *Torah* (though not being outside God's *Torah* but in Messiah's *Torah*), so that I might win over those outside *Torah*. [22]To the weak I became weak, so that I might win over the weak. I have become all things to all men, so that by all means possible I might save some. [23]I do it all for the sake of the Good News, so that I might be a fellow partaker of it.

[24]Don't you know that in a stadium the runners all run, but one receives the prize? Run in such a way that you may win! [25]Every competitor exercises self-control in all respects. They do it to receive a perishable crown, but we do it to receive an imperishable one. [26]So I run in this way—not aimlessly. So I box in this way—not beating the air. [27]Rather, I punish my body and bring it into submission, so that after I have preached to others, I myself will not be disqualified.

a 9:13. cf. Lev. 6:16, 26; 7:6, 31-32; Num. 5:9-10; 18:8-20, 31; Deut. 18:1.
b 9:18. cf. 1 Cor. 9:12b, 14.
c 9:20. Or *became*.

10

Warnings from History

[1]For I do not want you to be ignorant, brothers and sisters, that our fathers were all under the cloud and all passed through the sea.[d] [2]They all were immersed into Moses in the cloud and in the sea. [3]And all ate the same spiritual food, [4]and all drank the same spiritual drink—for they were drinking from a spiritual rock that followed them, and the Rock was Messiah.[e] [5]Nevertheless, God was not pleased with most of them, for they were struck down in the desert.[f]

[6]Now these things happened as examples for us, so we wouldn't crave evil things, just as they did.[g] [7]Do not be idolaters, as some of them were. As it is written, "The people sat down to eat and drink, and rose up to play."[h] [8]And let's not commit sexual immorality, as some of them did—and in one day 23,000 fell.[i] [9]And let's not test the Lord, as some of them did—and were destroyed by serpents.[j] [10]And let's not grumble, as some

d 10:1. cf. Exod. 13:21; Exod. 14:22, 29; Ps. 105:39; Neh. 9:11.
e 10:4. cf. Exod. 17:6; Num. 20:7-13.
f 10:5. cf. Num. 14:29-35.
g 10:6. cf. Num. 11:4, 34; Ps. 106:14.
h 10:7. Exod. 32:6.
i 10:8. cf. Num. 25:1-9.
j 10:9. cf. Num. 21:5-6.

of them did—and were destroyed by the destroying angel.[a] 11Now these things happened to them as an example, and it was written down as a warning to us—on whom the ends of the ages have come. 12Therefore let the one who thinks that he stands watch out that he doesn't fall. 13No temptation has taken hold of you except what is common to mankind. But God is faithful—He will not allow you to be tempted beyond what you can handle. But with the temptation He will also provide a way of escape, so you will be able to endure it.

Feast with the Lord—Not with Idols

14Therefore, my dearly loved ones, flee from idolatry. 15I speak as to sensible people—judge for yourselves what I say. 16The cup of blessing that we bless—isn't it a sharing of Messiah's blood? The bread which we break—isn't it a sharing of Messiah's body? 17Since there is one bread, we who are many are one body—for we all partake of the one bread. 18Consider physical Israel. Those who eat the sacrifices—aren't they partners in the altar?[b]

19What am I saying then—that an idol sacrifice is anything, or that an idol is anything? 20No, I'm saying that what the pagans sacrifice is to demons and not to God, and I don't want you to become partners with demons.[c] 21You cannot drink the cup of the Lord and the cup of demons. You cannot partake of the table of the Lord and the table of demons. 22Or do we provoke the Lord to jealousy?[d] We are not stronger than He, are we?

23"Everything is permitted"—but not everything is helpful. "Everything is permitted"—but not everything builds up. 24Let no one seek his own good, but the good of his neighbor. 25Eat whatever is sold in the meat market, without raising questions of conscience. 26For "the earth is the Lord's, and its fullness."[e] 27If an unbeliever invites you over and you want to go, eat whatever is set before you, without raising questions of conscience. 28But if anyone says to you, "This is from an idol sacrifice," do not eat it, for the sake of the one who informed you, and for the sake of conscience— 29not your own conscience, I mean, but the other person's. For why is my freedom judged by another's conscience? 30If I partake with thankfulness, why am I denounced because of something I give thanks for?

31Therefore, whether you eat or drink or whatever you do, do all to the glory of God. 32Give no offense either to Jewish or Greek people or to God's community— 33just as I also try to please everyone in everything, not seeking my own benefit but the benefit of many, so that they may be saved.

11

1Be imitators of me, just as I also am of Messiah.

Headship and Coverings

2Now I praise you because you remember me in everything and hold firm the traditions just as I passed them on to you. 3But I want you to know that the head of every man is Messiah, and the head of the woman is the man, and the head of Messiah is God. 4Every man praying or prophesying with his head covered dishonors his head. 5But every woman praying or prophesying with her head uncovered dishonors her head. For it is one and the same as having been shaved. 6For if a woman does not cover her head, let her cut off her hair. But if it is shameful for a woman to have her hair cut off or to be shaved, let her cover her head.

7For surely a man ought not to cover his head, since he is the image and glory

a 10:10. cf. Num. 16:41-50.
b 10:18. cf. Lev. 7:6, Deut. 12:17-19.
c 10:20. cf. Deut. 32:17,
d 10:22. cf. Deut. 32:21.
e 10:26. Ps. 24:1.

of God.[a] But the woman is the glory of man. [8]For man is not from woman, but woman from man. [9]Neither was man created for the woman's sake, but woman for the man's sake.[b] [10]For this reason the woman ought to have a symbol of authority on her head, because of the angels. [11]In any case—in the Lord—woman is not independent of man and man is not independent of woman. [12]For just as the woman came from the man, so also the man comes through the woman—but all things are from God.

[13]Judge for yourselves—is it proper for a woman to pray to God with her head uncovered? [14]Doesn't the natural order of things[c] teach you—if a man has long hair, it is a disgrace for him; [15]but if a woman has long hair, it is her glory, for her hair was given to her as a covering. [16]But if anyone intends to be contentious, we have no such custom—nor do God's communities.

Unity at the Lord's Table

[17]But in giving you this instruction I do not praise you, for when you meet together it does more harm than good. [18]For first of all, when you come together as Messiah's community, I hear that there are divisions among you; and to some extent I believe it— [19]for there must be factions among you, so that those among you who are tried and true may be evident. [20]Therefore, when you meet together in the same place, it is not to eat the Lord's Supper—[21]for each one takes his own supper beforehand, and one goes hungry while another gets drunk. [22]What! It is certainly not that you do not have houses, is it? Don't you have houses to eat and drink in? Or do you despise God's community and try to humiliate those who have nothing? What shall I say to you? Shall I praise you? I don't praise you for this!

[23]For I received from the Lord what I also passed on to you—that the Lord *Yeshua,* on the night He was betrayed, took *matzah;*[d] [24]and when He had given thanks, He broke it and said,[e] "This is My body, which is for you. Do this in memory of Me." [25]In the same way, He also took the cup, after supper, saying, "This cup is the new covenant[f] in My blood. Do this, as often as you drink it, in memory of Me." [26]For as often as you eat this bread and drink this cup, you proclaim the Lord's death until He comes.

[27]Therefore whoever eats the bread or drinks the Lord's cup in an unworthy manner will be guilty of the body and the blood of the Lord. [28]But a man must examine himself, and then let him eat of the bread and drink from the cup. [29]For the one who eats and drinks without recognizing the body, eats and drinks judgment on himself. [30]For this reason many among you are weak and sick, and quite a few have died.[g] [31]For if we were judging ourselves thoroughly, we wouldn't be coming under judgment. [32]But when we are judged, we are being disciplined by the Lord so that we might not be condemned along with the world.

[33]So then, my brothers and sisters, when you come together to eat, wait for one another. [34]If anyone is hungry let him eat at home, so that when you meet it doesn't lead to judgment. And the rest I will put in order when I come.

12

Spiritual Gifts for the Body

[1]Now concerning spiritual gifts, brothers and sisters, I do not want you to be ignorant. [2]You know that when you were

a 11:7. cf. Gen. 1:26-27.
b 11:8-9. cf. Gen. 2:21-23.
c 11:14. Lit. *nature itself.*

d 11:23. Lit. *bread* (at Passover, unleavened bread).
e 11:24. Some mss. begin *"Take, eat; this is My body..."*; cf. Matt. 26:26.
f 11:25. Heb. *Brit Hadashah*; cf. Exod. 24:8, Jer. 31:31.
g 11:30. Lit. *have fallen asleep.*

pagans, you were enticed by idols that
cannot speak, and you got led astray.[a]
[3]Therefore I make known to you that
no one speaking by God's Spirit says,
"*Yeshua* be cursed," and no one can say,
"*Yeshua* is Lord," except by the *Ruach*
ha-Kodesh.

[4]Now there are various kinds of gifts,
but the same Spirit. [5]There are various
kinds of service, but the same Lord.
[6]There are various kinds of working, but
the same God who works all things in all
people. [7]But to each person is given the
manifestation of the Spirit for the benefit of all. [8]For to one is given through
the Spirit a word of wisdom, to another
a word of knowledge according to the
same Spirit, [9]to another faith by the
same Spirit, to another gifts of healings
by the one Spirit, [10]to another workings
of miracles, to another prophecy, to
another discerning of spirits, to another
different kinds of tongues, to another
the interpretation of tongues. [11]But one
and the same Spirit activates all these
things, distributing to each person individually as He wills.

[12]For just as the body is one and has
many parts, and all the parts of the
body—though many—are one body, so
also is Messiah. [13]For in one Spirit we were
all immersed into one body—whether
Jewish or Greek, slave or free—and all
were made to drink of one Spirit.

[14]For the body is not one part, but
many. [15]If the foot says, "Since I'm not
a hand, I'm not part of the body," is it
therefore not part of the body? [16]And if
the ear says, "Since I'm not an eye, I'm
not part of the body," is it for this reason
any less part of the body? [17]If the whole
body were an eye, where would the hearing be? If the whole were hearing, where
would the sense of smell be? [18]But now
God has placed the parts—each one of
them—in the body just as He desired.
[19]If they were all one part, where would
the body be? [20]But now there are many
parts, yet one body.

a 12:2. cf. Ps. 115-4-5; Jer. 10:5; Hab. 2:18-19.

[21]The eye cannot tell the hand, "I don't
need you!" or in turn the head to the
feet, "I don't need you!" [22]On the contrary, those parts of the body that seem
to be less important are indispensable.
[23]Those parts of the body that we think
to be less honorable, we clothe with
greater honor; and our unpresentable
parts are treated with greater modesty;
[24]but our presentable parts have no such
need. Rather God assembled the body,
giving more honor to those who are lacking, [25]so that there may be no division in
the body, but so that the parts may have
the same care for one another. [26]If one
part suffers, all the parts suffer together.
If one part is honored, all the parts
rejoice together.

[27]Now you are the body of Messiah,
and members individually. [28]God has put
into His community first *shlichim*, second
prophets, third teachers, then miracles,
then healings, helps, leadership, various
kinds of tongues. [29]All are not *shlichim*,
are they? All are not prophets, are they?
All are not teachers, are they? All do not
work miracles, do they? [30]All do not have
gifts of healing, do they? All do not speak
in tongues, do they? All do not interpret, do they? [31]But earnestly desire the
greater gifts. And still I show you a far
better way:

13

The Superior Way of Love

[1]If I speak with the tongues of men and
of angels
but have not love,
I have become a noisy gong
or a clanging cymbal.

[2]If I have the gift of prophecy
and know all mysteries and all
knowledge,
and if I have all faith so as to remove
mountains
but have not love,

I am nothing.

[3]If I give away all that I own
and if I hand over my body so I might boast[a]
but have not love,
I gain nothing.

[4]Love is patient,
love is kind,
it does not envy,
it does not brag,
it is not puffed up,
[5]it does not behave inappropriately,
it does not seek its own way,
it is not provoked,
it keeps no account of wrong,
[6]it does not rejoice over injustice
but rejoices in the truth;
[7]it bears all things,
it believes all things,
it hopes all things,
it endures all things.

[8]Love never fails—
but where there are prophecies,
they will pass away;
where there are tongues,
they will cease;
where there is knowledge,
it will pass away.

[9]For we know in part and we prophesy in part;
[10]but when that which is perfect has come,
then that which is partial will pass away.

[11]When I was a child,
I spoke like a child,
I thought like a child,
I reasoned like a child.
When I became a man,
I put away childish things.

[12]For now we see in a mirror dimly,
but then face to face.
Now I know in part,
but then I will know fully,
even as I have been fully known.

[13]But now these three remain—
faith, hope, and love.
And the greatest of these is love.

a 13:3. Other mss. say *be burned*.

14

Orderly Governing of the Gifts

[1]Pursue love and eagerly desire spiritual gifts, but especially that you may
prophesy. [2]For one who speaks in a
tongue speaks not to people but to
God—for no one understands, but in
the Spirit he speaks mysteries. [3]But one
who prophesies speaks to people for
building up, urging on, and uplifting.
[4]One who speaks in a tongue builds up
himself, but one who prophesies builds
up the community. [5]Now I want you all
to speak in tongues, but even more that
you would prophesy.[b] One who prophesies is greater than one who speaks in
tongues—unless he interprets, so that
the community may be built up.

[6]But now, brothers and sisters, if I
come to you speaking in tongues, how
will I benefit you—unless I speak to you
by way of revelation or knowledge or
prophecy or teaching? [7]It is the same for
lifeless things that make a sound—like
a flute or a harp. If they make no distinction in the tones, how will what is
played be recognized? [8]For if the trumpet[c] makes an unclear sound, who will
prepare himself for battle? [9]So also with
you with your tongue—unless you utter
speech that is intelligible, how will what
is spoken be understood? For you will
be talking to the wind! [10]It may be that
there are many kinds of languages in the
world—and none without meaning. [11]If
then I do not understand the meaning
of the language, I will be a foreigner[d] to
the speaker, and the speaker will be a foreigner to me. [12]Likewise with you—since
you are zealous for spiritual gifts, keep

b 14:5. cf. Num. 11:29.

c 14:8. Grk. *salpigx* (*trumpet*), Heb. *chatzotzrah* (*trumpet*); cf. Num. 10:2, 9, *chatzotzrot kesef* (*silver trumpets*).

d 14:11. Lit. *barbarian*.

trying to excel for the building up of the community.

13 Therefore let one who speaks in a tongue pray that he may interpret. 14 For if I pray in a tongue, my spirit prays, but my mind is unfruitful. 15 What is it then? I will pray in my spirit, but I will also pray with my mind. I will sing praises with my spirit, and I will also sing praises with my mind. 16 Otherwise if you give thanks and praise in the spirit, how will one filling the place of the ungifted say the "Amen" to your thanksgiving, since he has no idea what you're saying? 17 For you certainly give thanks well, but the other person is not built up. 18 I thank God that I speak in tongues more than all of you. 19 However, in Messiah's community I would rather speak five words with my mind, so I may also instruct others, than ten thousand words in a tongue.

20 Brothers and sisters, stop being children in your thinking—rather, be infants in evil, but in your thinking be mature. 21 In the Prophets[a] it is written,

"By those with strange tongues and by the lips of strangers
I will speak to this people.
And not even then will they listen to me," says ADONAI.

22 Therefore tongues are a sign not for believers but for unbelievers—but prophecy is a sign not for unbelievers but for believers. 23 So if Messiah's whole community comes together and everyone speaks in tongues, and uninstructed or unbelieving people come in, won't they say that you are crazy? 24 But if all are prophesying and some unbelieving or ungifted person comes in, he is convicted by all, he is called to account by all. 25 The secrets of his heart become known, and so he will fall down on his face and worship God, declaring, "God really is among you!"[b]

26 What is it then, brothers and sisters? Whenever you come together, each one has a psalm, a teaching, a revelation, a tongue, an interpretation. Let all things be done for edification. 27 If someone speaks in a tongue, let it be by two or at most three, and each in turn; and let one interpret. 28 But if there is no interpreter, let him keep silent in the community but speak to himself and to God. 29 Let two or three prophets speak, and let the others evaluate. 30 But if something is revealed to another sitting nearby, let the first one become silent. 31 For you can all prophesy one by one, so all may learn and be encouraged. 32 The spirits of the prophets are subject to the prophets, 33 for God is not a God of confusion, but *shalom*.

As in all the communities of the *kedoshim*, 34 let women keep silent in the communities, for it is not permitted for them to speak out. Rather let them be in order, as the *Torah* also says.[c] 35 If they want to learn something, let them ask their own husbands at home—for it is disgraceful for a woman to speak out in the community. 36 Did the word of God originate with you? Or did it reach you alone?

37 If anyone thinks he is a prophet or spiritual, let him recognize that what I write to you is the Lord's command. 38 But if someone does not recognize it, he is not recognized. 39 Therefore, brothers and sisters, be eager to prophesy, and do not forbid speaking in tongues. 40 But let everything be done decently and in order.

15

The Victory of the Resurrection

1 Now I make known to you, brothers and sisters, the Good News which I proclaimed to you. You also received it, and you took your stand on it, 2 and by it you are being saved if you hold firm to the word I proclaimed

a 14:21. Lit. *Law*, here applied to *Torah*, Prophets, and Writings; the quote is from Isa. 28:11-12.

b 14:26. cf. Isa. 45:14; Dan. 2:47; Zech. 8:23.

c 14:34. cf. Gen. 3:16.

to you—unless you believed without proper consideration. 3For I also passed on to you first of all what I also received—

that Messiah died for our sins according to the Scriptures,[a]

4that He was buried,

that He was raised on the third day according to the Scriptures,

5and that He appeared to Kefa, then to the Twelve.

6Then He appeared to over five hundred brothers and sisters at one time—

most of them are still alive, though some have died.[b]

7Then He appeared to Jacob, then to all the *shlichim*,

8and last of all, as to one untimely born, He also appeared to me.

9For I am the least of the *shlichim*, unworthy to be called a *shaliach* because I persecuted God's community. 10But by the grace of God I am what I am. His grace toward me was not in vain. No, I worked harder than them all—yet not I, but the grace of God that was with me. 11Whether then it is I or they, so we proclaim, and so you believed.

12Now if Messiah is proclaimed—that He has been raised from the dead—how can some among you say that there is no resurrection of the dead? 13But if there is no resurrection of the dead, not even Messiah has been raised! 14And if Messiah has not been raised, then our proclaiming is meaningless and your faith also is meaningless. 15Moreover, we are found to be false witnesses of God, because we testified about God that He raised up Messiah—whom He did not raise up, if in fact the dead are not raised. 16For if the dead are not raised, not even Messiah has been raised. 17And if Messiah has not been raised, your faith is futile—you are still in your sins. 18Then those also who have fallen asleep in Messiah have perished. 19If we have hoped in Messiah in this life alone, we are to be pitied more than all people.

20But now Messiah has been raised from the dead, the firstfruits of those who have fallen asleep. 21For since death came through a man, the resurrection of the dead also has come through a Man.[c] 22For as in Adam all die, so also in Messiah will all be made alive.

23But each in its own order: Messiah the firstfruits; then, at His coming, those who belong to Messiah; 24then the end, when He hands over the kingdom to God the Father after He has destroyed all rule and all authority and power.[d] 25For He must reign until He has put all His enemies under His feet.[e] 26The last enemy to be destroyed is death. 27For God has "put all things in subjection underneath His feet."[f] But when the psalmist says that "all" has been put in subjection, it is clear that this does not include God Himself, who put all things under Messiah. 28Now when all things become subject to Him, then the Son Himself will also become subject to the One who put all things under Him, so that God may be all in all.

29Otherwise, what will they do who are immersed for the dead? If the dead are not raised at all, then why are they immersed for them? 30And why are we in danger every hour? 31I die every day—yes, as surely as the boast in you, brothers and sisters, which I have in Messiah *Yeshua* our Lord. 32If, for human reasons, I fought with "wild animals" at Ephesus, what good is that to me? If the dead are not raised, "let us eat and drink, for tomorrow we die!"[g] 33Do not be deceived!

"Bad company corrupts good morals."

34Come to your senses as you ought, and stop sinning! For some have no knowledge of God—I say this to your shame.

a 15:3-4. cf. Isa. 53:8-10; Ps. 16:10-11; 22:15-16; Hos. 6:2; Dan. 9:24.

b 15:6. Lit. *most of whom remain until now, but some have fallen asleep.*

c 15:21-22. cf. Rom. 5:12, 21.

d 15:24. cf. Dan. 2:44; 7:14, 27.

e 15:25. cf. Ps. 110:1.

f 15:27. Ps. 8:6b(LXX); cf. Ps. 8:7b(6b); cf. Heb. 2:6-10.

g 15:32. cf. Isa. 22:13; 56:12.

35But someone will say, "How
are the dead raised?"[a] and, "With what
kind of body do they come?" 36Fool! What
you sow does not come to life unless it
dies. 37As for what you sow—you are
not sowing the body that will be, but a
bare seed, maybe of wheat or something
else. 38But God gives it a body just as He
planned, and to each of the seeds a body
of its own. 39All flesh is not the same
flesh, but there is one flesh of humans,
another flesh of animals, another of
birds, and another of fish. 40There are
also heavenly bodies and earthly bodies, but the glory of the heavenly is one
thing while the earthly is another. 41There
is one glory of the sun, another glory of
the moon, and another glory of the stars;
for one star differs from another star in
glory.

42So also is the resurrection of the
dead:

Sown in corruption, raised in
incorruption!
43Sown in dishonor, raised in glory!
Sown in weakness, raised in power!
44Sown a natural body, raised a spiritual body!

If there is a natural body, there is also
a spiritual body. 45So also it is written,
"The first man, Adam, became a living
soul."[b] The last Adam became a life-giving spirit. 46However, the spiritual is not
first, but the natural; then the spiritual.
47The first man is of the earth, made of
dust; the second man is from heaven.

48Like the one made of dust,
so also are those made of dust[c];
and like the heavenly,
so also are those who are heavenly.
49And just as we have borne the image
of the one made from dust,
so also shall we bear[d] the image of
the One from heaven.

50Now I say this, brothers and sisters,
that flesh and blood cannot inherit the
kingdom of God, and what decays cannot
inherit what does not decay. 51Behold, I
tell you a mystery:

We shall not all sleep,
but we shall all be changed—
52in a moment, in the twinkling of an
eye,
at the last *shofar*.[e]
For the *shofar* will sound,
and the dead will be raised
incorruptible,
and we will be changed.
53For this corruptible must put on
incorruptibility ,
and this mortal must put on
immortality.
54But when this corruptible will have
put on incorruptibility
and this mortal will have put on
immortality,
then shall come to pass the saying that
is written:

"Death is swallowed up in victory."[f]
55"Where, O Death, is your victory?
Where, O Death, is your sting?"[g]

56Now the sting of death is sin, and the
power of sin is the *Torah*. 57But thanks be
to God, who keeps giving us the victory
through our Lord *Yeshua* the Messiah!
58Therefore, my dearly loved brothers
and sisters, be steadfast, immovable,
always excelling in the work of the
Lord—because you know that your labor
in the Lord is not in vain.

16

Collection for Jerusalem and Final Greetings

1Now concerning the collection for the
kedoshim, as I directed Messiah's communities in Galatia, you do likewise. 2On
the first day of the week, let each of you

a 15:35. cf. Ezek. 37:3.
b 15:45. cf. Gen. 2:7.
c 15:48. cf. Gen. 3:19.
d 15:49. Many mss. say *let us bear*.
e 15:52. Grk. *salpigx (trumpet)*, Heb. *shofar (ram's horn)*; cf. Exod. 19:16(19:16LXX); Isa. 27:13.
f 15:54. Isa. 25:8.
g 15:55. cf. Hos. 13:14 (LXX); some mss. say *O death, where is your sting? O grave, where is your victory?*

set something aside, saving up whatever is gained, so no collections take place when I come. 3Then whenever I arrive, I will send whomever you approve with letters of introduction to carry your gift to Jerusalem. 4If it is advisable for me to go also, they will go with me.

5But I will come to you after I have passed through Macedonia—for I am passing through Macedonia. 6Perhaps I will stay with you, or even spend the winter, so that you can help me on my journey—wherever I go. 7For I do not wish to see you now just in passing—for I hope to stay on with you for a while, if the Lord permits. 8But I will stay on at Ephesus until *Shavuot*, 9for a great door has opened wide for me, though many are in opposition.

10Now if Timothy comes, see that he has nothing to fear among you—for he is doing the Lord's work, just as I am. 11No one, then, should treat him with disrespect. But set him on his way in *shalom*, so that he might come to me; for I am expecting him, along with the brothers.

12Now about our brother Apollos, I strongly urged him to come to you with the brothers, and he was quite unwilling to come now—but he will come when he has an opportunity.

13Be on the alert! Stand firm in the faith! Be men of courage! Be strong![a] 14Let all that you do be done in love.

15Now I urge you, brothers and sisters (you know the household of Stephanas, that it is the firstfruits of Achaia, and that they have devoted themselves in service to the *kedoshim*), 16also to submit to people such as these, and to everyone working together and laboring. 17I rejoice at the coming of Stephanas and Fortunatus and Achaicus, for they made up for your absence. 18For they refreshed my spirit and yours. Therefore acknowledge such men.

a 16:13. cf. Ps. 30:24(LXX); 31:25(24).

19Messiah's communities in Asia[b] greet you. Aquila and Prisca[c] greet you warmly in the Lord, with the community that meets in their house. 20All the brothers and sisters greet you. Greet one another with a holy kiss.

21This greeting is in my own hand—Paul's. 22If anyone does not love the Lord, let him be cursed. *Marana, tha!* Our Lord, come![d]

23The grace of the Lord *Yeshua* be with you. 24My love be with you all in Messiah *Yeshua*.

b 16:19a. The Roman province of Asia, in the western part of Asia Minor (now part of Turkey).

c 16:19b. Also *Priscilla*; cf. Acts 18:2, 18, 26; 1 Cor. 16:19; 2 Tim. 4:19.

d 16:22. Some mss. say *Maran atha! Our Lord has come!* or *Our Lord is coming!* (Aram.)

Paul's Second Letter to the Corinthians

Introduction

2 Corinthians, like 1 Corinthians, is intensely personal. It was written from Macedonia a year or so after the first letter (so around 56-57), addressed once again to the troubled believers of Corinth.

This time around, the problems are not so much the Corinthians' own behavior and their own questions, but the presence of troublemakers who put themselves forward as authorities in place of the Paul. In chapters 1–7 it seems that a single person was causing trouble in the community; in chapters 10–13 it is a whole group of "false *shlichim*." The false *shlichim* were proclaiming a message that was not the Good News. On top of that, they claimed that a "real *shaliach*" would have charisma, a "take-charge" attitude. He would be a man who saw visions and performed miracles.

The application is not hard to see for believers today. Not only do we have to understand the content of the Good News in order to proclaim it (in contrast to the teaching of the false *shlichim*), but we also need to be the kind of people God wants to use to proclaim that message—not eloquent, good-looking, flashy superstars, but devoted people who have real problems and real weaknesses.

For this reason Paul speaks of believers as having a treasure in fragile jars of clay, to show that this all-surpassing power is from God and not from us (4:7). In fact, Paul says that "if I must boast, I will boast of my weakness" (11:30), because God's power is shown through human weakness. After all, it was the same with *Yeshua* Himself: "For though He was crucified in weakness, yet He lives through the power of God." (13:4).

The Jewish people should be no strangers to this idea. Every year at Passover, we celebrate how God's power was used to deliver His weak, downtrodden people. We see that Yeshua became weak even to the point of death, but through that weakness God showed His power in the resurrection. Today that power enables His people to live transformed lives and even transform the world around them.

A Look Inside 2 Corinthians

1

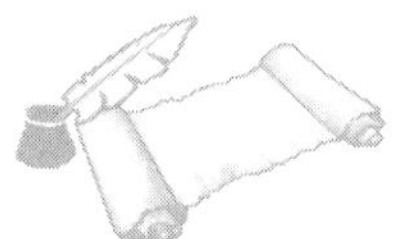

Greetings

[1]Paul, a *shaliach* of Messiah *Yeshua* through the will of God, and Timothy our brother, To God's community at Corinth, with all the *kedoshim* who are throughout Achaia:

[2]Grace to you and *shalom* from God our Father and the Lord *Yeshua* the Messiah.

Encouragement Through Hardships

[3]Blessed be the God and Father of our Lord *Yeshua* the Messiah, the Father of compassion and God of all encouragement. [4]He encourages us in every trouble, so that we may be able to encourage those who are in any trouble, through the very encouragement with which we ourselves are encouraged by God. [5]For just as the sufferings of Messiah overflow into us, so also through Messiah our encouragement overflows. [6]If we are suffering hardship, it is for your encouragement and salvation. Or if we are encouraged, it is for your encouragement, which produces in you the patient endurance of the same sufferings that we also suffer. [7]Our hope for you is firm, since we know that as you are partners in our sufferings, so also in our encouragement.

[8]For we do not want you to be unaware, brothers and sisters, of our trouble that happened in Asia.[a] We were under great pressure—so far beyond our strength that we despaired even of living. [9]In fact, we had within ourselves the death sentence—so that we might not rely on ourselves, but on God who raises the dead. [10]He who rescued us from so great a danger of death will continue to rescue us—we have set our hope on Him that He will rescue us again. [11]You also are helping by your prayer for us, so that from many people thanks may be given on our behalf for the gracious gift given us through the help of many.

[12]For our reason for boasting is this: the testimony of our conscience, that we behaved in the world, and most especially toward you, with simplicity and godly sincerity—not by human wisdom but by the grace of God. [13]For we write nothing to you other than what you can read and understand—and I hope you will understand in full[14]just as you understood us in part, so that we are your reason for boasting just as you also are ours in the Day of our Lord *Yeshua*.

Paul's Change of Plans

[15]Because of this confidence, I was planning to come to you first, so that you might have a second benefit— [16]to pass by you on my way to Macedonia and again from Macedonia to come back to you, and to be helped by you on my journey to Judea. [17]So when I was planning to do this, I didn't do so lightly, did I? Or the things I plan, do I plan according to the flesh—so it might be with me "Yes, yes" and "No, no" at the same time? [18]But as God is faithful, our message to you is not both "Yes" and "No."[b] [19]For *Ben-Elohim*—*Yeshua* the Messiah, who was proclaimed among you by us, by myself and Silvanus[c] and Timothy—was not "Yes" and "No." Rather, in Him it has always been "Yes." [20]For in Him all the promises of God are "Yes." Therefore also through Him is the "Amen" by us, to the glory of God.[d] [21]Now it is God who establishes us with you in Messiah. He anointed us, [22]set His seal on us, and gave us the Spirit in our hearts as a pledge.

[23]But I call God as my witness[e]—to spare you, I didn't come to Corinth again. [24]Not that we lord it over you in matters

a 1:8. The Roman province of Asia, in the western part of Asia Minor (now part of Turkey).

b 1:18. cf. Num. 23:19.

c 1:19. Or *Silas*; cf. Acts 15:22ff.

d 1:20. cf. Ps. 72:19.

e 1:23. Lit. *as witness against my soul.*

of faith, but we are fellow workers for your joy—for in the faith you are standing firm.

2

Forgive the Repentant Sinner

1So I made up my mind that I would not come to you again causing sorrow. 2For if I cause you sorrow, then who is there cheering me on but the one I have made sorrowful? 3And I wrote this very thing to you, so that when I came I wouldn't have sorrow from those who ought to make me rejoice—having confidence in you all that my joy is yours. 4For out of much distress and anguish of heart I wrote to you with many tears—not to make you sorrowful, but to let you know the love that I have especially for you.

5But if anyone has caused sorrow, he has caused sorrow not to me, but to some extent—not to exaggerate—to all of you. 6For such a person, this punishment by the majority is enough. 7So instead you should forgive him and encourage him. Otherwise such a person might be swallowed up by excessive sorrow. 8Therefore I urge you to reaffirm your love for him. 9For to this end I also wrote, that I might know your character, whether you are obedient in all things. 10Now anyone you forgive, I also forgive. For indeed, what I have forgiven (if I have forgiven anything), I did it for you in the presence of Messiah, 11so that we might not be outwitted by satan—for we are not ignorant of his schemes.

Revealing Messiah's Fragrance

12Now when I arrived in Troas for the Good News of Messiah, and a door was opened to me by the Lord, 13I had no rest in my spirit, because I didn't find Titus my brother. So I said farewell to them, and I set out for Macedonia. 14But thanks be to God, who in Messiah always leads us in triumphal procession, and through us reveals everywhere the aroma[a] of the knowledge of Himself. 15For we are the aroma of Messiah to God, among those who are being saved and those who are perishing—16to the one an aroma from death to death, to the other an aroma from life to life. Who is competent for these things? 17For we are not like many, peddling the word of God. Rather, in Messiah we speak in the sight of God with sincerity, as persons sent from God.

3

A New Covenant on Hearts of Flesh

1Are we beginning to commend ourselves again? Or do we need, as some do, letters of recommendation to you or from you? 2You are our letter, written on our hearts, known and read by everyone. 3It is clear that you are a letter from Messiah delivered by us—written not with ink but with the Spirit of the living God, not on tablets of stone but on tablets of human hearts.[b]

4Such is the confidence we have through Messiah toward God—5not that we are competent in ourselves to consider anything as coming from ourselves, but our competence is from God. 6He also made us competent as servants of a new covenant[c]—not of the letter, but of the Spirit. For the letter kills, but the Spirit gives life.

7Now if the ministry of death, carved in letters on stone, came with such glory that *B'nei-Israel* could not look intently upon Moses' face because of its glory-[d]although it was passing away—8how will the ministry of the Spirit not be even

a 2:14. cf. Song 1:3; Ezek. 20:41.
b 3:3. cf. Exod. 24:12; 31:18; 32:15-16; Prov. 3:3; 7:3; Jer. 31:33; Ezek. 11:19; 36:26.
c 3:6. cf. Jer. 31:31.
d 3:7. Lit. *the glory of his face*; cf. Exod. 33:18-19; 34:5-6, 29-35.

more glorious? 9For if there is glory in the ministry of condemnation,[a] the ministry of righteousness overflows even more in glory. 10For even what was glorious is not glorious in comparison to the glory that surpasses it. 11For if what is passing away is glorious, much more what remains is glorious.

12Therefore, having such a hope, we act with great boldness. 13We are not like Moses, who used to put a veil over his face in order for *B'nei-Israel* not to look intently upon the end of what was passing away. 14But their minds were hardened. For up to this very day the same veil remains unlifted at the reading of the ancient covenant, since in Messiah it is passing away. 15But to this day, whenever Moses is read, a veil lies over their heart. 16But whenever someone turns to the Lord, the veil is taken away.[b] 17Now the Lord is the Spirit and where the Spirit of the Lord is, there is freedom.[c] 18But we all, with unveiled face beholding as in a mirror the glory of the Lord, are being transformed into the same image from glory to glory—just as from the Lord, who is the Spirit.

4

Treasures in Jars of Clay

1For this reason, since we have this ministry, just as we received mercy, we do not lose heart. 2Instead, we renounced the hidden shameful ways—not walking in deception or distorting the word of God, but commending ourselves before God to everyone's conscience by the open proclamation of the truth. 3And even if our Good News is veiled, it is veiled to those who are perishing. 4In their case, the god of this world has blinded the minds of the unbelieving, so they might not see the light of the Good News of the glory of Messiah, who is the image of God. 5For we do not proclaim ourselves, but Messiah *Yeshua* as Lord—and ourselves as your slaves for *Yeshua*'s sake. 6For God, who said, "Let light shine out of darkness,"[d] is the One who has shone in our hearts, to give the light of the knowledge of the glory of God in the face of Messiah.[e]

7But we have this treasure in jars of clay,[f] so that the surpassing greatness of the power may be from God and not from ourselves. 8We are hard pressed in every way, yet not crushed; perplexed, yet not in despair; 9persecuted, yet not forsaken; struck down, yet not destroyed; 10always carrying in the body the death of *Yeshua*, so that the life of *Yeshua* may also be revealed in our mortal body. 11For we who live are always being handed over to death for *Yeshua*'s sake, so that the life of *Yeshua* may be revealed in our mortal body. 12So death is at work in us, but life is at work in you. 13But we have the same spirit of faith, according to what is written, "I believed, and therefore I spoke."[g] So we also believe, and therefore we also speak, 14knowing that the One who raised the Lord *Yeshua* will raise us also with *Yeshua*, and will bring us with you into His presence. 15For all things are for your sakes, so that the grace that is spreading through more and more people may cause thanksgiving to overflow—to the glory of God.

16Therefore we do not lose heart. Though our outward man is decaying, yet our inward man is renewed day by day.[h] 17For our trouble, light and momentary, is producing for us an eternal weight of glory far beyond all comparison, 18as we look not at what can be seen but at what cannot be seen. For what can be seen is temporary, but what cannot be seen is eternal.

a 3:9. cf. Deut. 27:26.
b 3:16. cf. Exod. 34:34.
c 3:17. cf. Isa. 61:1.
d 4:6. Gen. 1:3.
e 4:6. Some mss. say *in the face of Messiah Yeshua*.
f 4:7. cf. Job 33:6; Lam. 4:2.
g 4:13. Ps. 116:10(LXX).
h 4:16. cf. Isa. 40:29, 31.

5

Earthly Tents, Eternal Dwellings

1For we know that if the tent, our earthly home, is torn down, we have a building from God—a home not made with human hands, eternal in the heavens. 2For in this we groan, longing to be clothed with our heavenly dwelling—3if indeed, after we have put it on, we will not be found naked. 4For we groan while we are in this tent—burdened because we don't want to be unclothed but to be clothed, so that what is mortal may be swallowed up by life. 5Now the One who prepared us for this very purpose is God, who gave us the Spirit as a pledge. 6Therefore we are always confident and know that while we are at home in the body, we are absent from the Lord. 7For we walk by faith, not by sight. 8We are confident, I say, and prefer rather to be absent from the body and at home with the Lord. 9So whether at home or absent, we make it our aim to be pleasing to Him. 10For we must all appear before the judgment seat of Messiah, so that each one may receive what is due for the things he did while in the body—whether good or bad.

Ambassadors for Messiah

11Therefore, knowing the fear of the Lord,[a] we are trying to persuade people, but what we are is known to God—and I hope it is known to your consciences as well. 12For we are not commending ourselves to you again, but giving you an opportunity for boasting about us, so that you may have something to answer those who boast in outward appearance and not in the heart.[b] 13For if we are out of our minds, it is for God; if we are in our right mind, it is for you. 14For the love of Messiah compels us, since we have concluded that One died for all; as a result all died. 15And He died for all so that those who live might no longer live for themselves, but for the One who died for them and was raised.

16So from now on we recognize no one according to the flesh. Even though we have known Messiah according to the flesh, yet now we no longer know Him this way. 17Therefore if anyone is in Messiah, he is a new creation. The old things have passed away; behold, all things have become new.[c] 18Now all these things are from God, who reconciled us to Himself through Messiah and gave us the ministry of reconciliation. 19That is, in Messiah God was reconciling the world to Himself, not counting their trespasses against them; and He has entrusted the message of reconciliation to us. 20We are therefore ambassadors for Messiah, as though God were making His appeal through us. We beg you on behalf of Messiah, be reconciled to God. 21He made the One who knew no sin to become a sin offering on our behalf,[d] so that in Him we might become the righteousness of God.

6

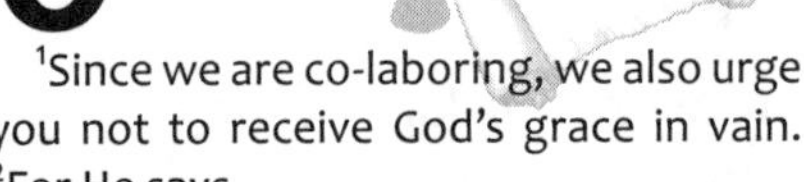

1Since we are co-laboring, we also urge you not to receive God's grace in vain. 2For He says,

> "At a favorable time I listened to you,
> in a day of salvation I helped you."[e]

Behold, now is the favorable time. Behold, now is the day of salvation. 3We give no cause for offense in anything, so that our ministry may not be blamed. 4But as God's servants, we are commending ourselves in every way—in great endurance, in afflictions, in hardships, in distresses, 5in beatings, in

a 5:11. cf. Prov. 1:7, 29; 2:9; 8:13; 10:27; 14:26-27; 19:23; Isa. 11:2-3; etc.

b 5:12. cf. 1 Sam. 16:7(LXX).

c 5:17. cf. Isa. 43:18–19; 65:17.

d 5:21. cf. Lev. 16:15; Isa. 53:4-6, 10.

e 6:2. Isa. 49:8; cf. Isa. 55:6.

imprisonments, in riots, in troubles, in
sleeplessness, in hunger; 6in purity, in
knowledge, in patience, in kindness, in
the *Ruach ha-Kodesh*, in genuine love,
7in truthful speech, in the power of God;
with the weapons of righteousness in
the right hand and in the left; 8through
honor and dishonor, through evil report
and good report. We are regarded as
deceivers and yet true; 9as unknown and
yet well-known; as dying, yet behold, we
live; as disciplined yet not put to death;[a]
10as grieving yet always rejoicing; as poor
yet enriching many; as having nothing
yet possessing everything.

11We have spoken openly to you, O
Corinthians; our heart is open wide!
12You are not restricted by us, yet you are
restricted in your own feelings. 13Now in
return—I speak as to my children—open
wide to us also.

Preserving Sanctity in God's Living Temple

14Do not be unequally yoked with
unbelievers.[b] For what partnership is
there between righteousness and lawlessness? Or what fellowship does light
have with darkness? 15What harmony
does Messiah have with Beliar[c]? Or what
part does a believer have in common
with an unbeliever? 16What agreement
does God's Temple have with idols?[d] For
we are the temple of the living God—just
as God said,

"I will dwell in them and walk among
them;
and I will be their God,
and they shall be My people.[e]
17Therefore, come out from among
them,
and be separate, says ADONAI.
Touch no unclean thing.[f]
Then I will take you in.[g]
18I will be a father to you,
and you shall be My sons and
daughters,
says ADONAI-*Tzva'ot*."[h]

7

1Therefore, since we have these promises, loved ones, let us cleanse ourselves
from all defilement of body and spirit,
perfecting holiness in the fear of God.

Godly Sorrow and Joy

2Make room for us in your hearts. We
wronged no one, ruined no one, took
advantage of no one. 3I do not say this to
condemn you, for I have said before that
you are in our hearts—to die together
and to live together with you. 4Great
is my boldness of speech toward you.
Great is my boasting on your behalf. I
have been filled with encouragement. I
overflow with joy in all our troubles.

5For even when we came into Macedonia, our body had no rest. But we were
hard pressed on every side—conflicts
outside, fears within. 6But God, who
encourages the downcast, encouraged
us with the arrival of Titus; 7and not only
by his coming, but also by the encouragement with which he was encouraged by
you, as he told us of your longing, your
mourning, and your deep concern for
me—so that I rejoiced still more.

8For even if I grieved you with my
letter, I do not regret it—though I did
regret it, for I see that my letter grieved
you, but just for a while. 9Now I rejoice,
not that you were grieved, but that you
were grieved to the point of repentance.
For you were grieved according to God's
will, so that you might in no way suffer
loss from us. 10For the grief that God

a 6:9. cf. Ps. 118:18.
b 6:14. cf. Deut. 22:9-11.
c 6:14-15. A spelling variant of Grk. *belial, the devil*; Heb. *b'liya'al, worthlessness*, possibly a wordplay on Heb. *b'li 'ol, without a yoke*.
d 6:16a. cf. Ezek. 8:3, 10.
e 6:16. cf. Exod. 29:45; Lev. 26:11-12; Jer. 32:38; Ezek. 37:27.

f 6:17a. cf. Isa. 52:11.
g 6:17b. cf. Ezek. 20:34, 41.
h 6:18. Grk. *Kurios Pantokrator* (*Lord Almighty*); cf. 2 Sam. 7:8, 14(2 Ki. 7:8, 14 LXX); 1 Chr. 17:13; Isa. 43:6; Hos. 12:6(5).

wills brings a repentance that leads to salvation, leaving no regret. But the world's grief brings death. 11For see what this very thing—this grieving that God wills—has brought you! What diligence, what defense, what indignation, what fear, what longing, what zeal, what rendering of justice! In everything you have proved yourselves to be innocent in this matter. 12So although I wrote to you, I wrote not for the sake of the wrongdoer or for the sake of the one who was wronged, but to make known to you your diligence for us in the sight of God. 13For this reason we have been encouraged.

Besides our own encouragement, we rejoiced even more at the joy of Titus, because his spirit has been refreshed by all of you. 14For if I have boasted some to him about you, I was not put to shame. But as we spoke all things truthfully to you, so also our boasting to Titus has proved to be the truth. 15His feelings toward you overflow when he remembers everyone's obedience—how you received him with fear and trembling. 16I rejoice that in everything I have confidence in you.

Eagerness to Give

1Now we make known to you, brothers and sisters, the grace God has given to Messiah's communities in Macedonia— 2that in much testing by affliction, the abundance of their joy and their extreme poverty overflowed in a wealth of generosity on their part. 3For I testify that according to their ability, and even beyond their ability, they gave of their own free will—4begging us with much urging for the favor of sharing in the relief of the *kedoshim*. 5Moreover, it was not just as we had hoped, but they gave of themselves first to the Lord and then to us in keeping with God's will. 6So we urged Titus that, just as he had made a start before, so he should also complete this gracious service for you. 7But as you excel in everything—in faith and speech and knowledge and all diligence, and in your love for us—also excel in this grace. 8I am saying this not as a command, but I am trying to prove by the diligence of others the genuineness of your love as well. 9For you know the grace of our Lord *Yeshua* the Messiah—that even though He was rich, yet for your sakes He became poor, so that through His poverty you might become rich. 10Now I give my opinion in this matter, that it is a credit to you that a year ago you were the first to start—not only to do but even to be willing. 11But now finish doing it, so that just as there was eagerness to be willing, so also to finish it, out of what you have. 12For if the eagerness is present, the gift is acceptable according to what a person has, not according to what he doesn't have. 13For it is not relief for others and hardship for you, but as a matter of equality. 14Your abundance at this present time meets their need, so that their abundance may also meet your need—so that there may be equality. 15As it is written, "He who gathered much did not have too much, and he who gathered little did not have too little."[a]

An Offering by Special Delivery

16But thanks be to God, who put into the heart of Titus the same devotion for you. 17For indeed he not only accepted our appeal, but went to you with eagerness and on his own initiative. 18We are sending along with him the brother whose fame in connection with the Good News has spread throughout all of Messiah's communities. 19Not only that, but he has also been appointed by the communities as our travel companion with this gracious gift, which is administered by us for the glory of the Lord Himself and to show our eagerness to help. 20We are

a 8:15. Exod. 16:18.

taking this precaution, so that no one will blame us in regard to the way we administer this generous gift. 21 We have regard for what is honorable—not only before the Lord, but also before people. 22 Also with them we are sending our brother whom we have tested many times and found to be diligent in many things, but now even more diligent because of his great confidence in you. 23 As for Titus, he is my partner and fellow worker among you; as for our brothers, they are the *shlichim* of the communities, a glory to Messiah. 24 Therefore, before Messiah's communities show them the proof of your love and of our boasting about you.

9

1 Now about this service to the *kedoshim*, it is indeed unnecessary for me to write to you— 2 for I know your eagerness. I boast about it to the Macedonians, that Achaia has been preparing for a year already; and your zeal has stirred up most of them. 3 But I am sending the brothers in order that our boasting about you may not be in vain in this case, so that you may be prepared, just as I kept saying. 4 Otherwise, if any Macedonians were to come and find you unprepared, we—not to mention you—would be put to shame in this undertaking. 5 So I thought it necessary to urge the brothers to go on to you and arrange ahead of time your generous gift that had been promised beforehand, so that it would be ready as a gift and not as an extortion.

Sowing and Reaping Generosity

6 The point is this: whoever sows sparingly shall also reap sparingly, and whoever sows bountifully shall also reap bountifully.[a] 7 Let each one give as he has decided in his heart, not grudgingly or under compulsion—for God loves a cheerful giver.[b] 8 And God is able to make all grace overflow to you, so that by always having enough of everything, you may overflow in every good work. 9 As it is written,

> "He scattered widely, He gave to the poor;
> His righteousness endures forever."[c]

10 Now the One who supplies seed to the sower and bread for food will supply and multiply your seed and increase the harvest of your righteousness.[d] 11 You will be enriched in everything for all generosity, which through us brings about thanksgiving to God. 12 For this service of giving is not only supplying the needs of the *kedoshim*, but is also overflowing with many thanksgivings to God. 13 Because of the evidence of this service, they praise God for the obedience of your affirmation of the Good News of Messiah and for the generosity of your contribution to them and to everyone. 14 And in their prayer for you, they long for you because of the surpassing grace of God upon you. 15 Thanks be to God for His indescribable gift!

10

Tearing Down Strongholds

1 Now I, Paul, appeal myself to you by the meekness and gentleness of Messiah—I who am humble when face to face with you, but bold toward you when far away. : 2 I beg of you that when I am present I won't need to be bold with the courage I consider showing against some who judge us as walking in the flesh. 3 For though we walk in the flesh, we do not wage war according to the flesh. 4 For the weapons of our warfare are not fleshly but powerful through God for the

a 9:6. cf. Prov. 11:24-25; 22:9.

b 9:7. cf. Exod. 25:2; 1 Chr. 29:17.

c 9:9. Ps. 112:9.

d 9:10. cf. Isa. 55:10; Hos. 10:12.

tearing down of strongholds.[a] We are tearing down false arguments 5and every high-minded thing that exalts itself[b] against the knowledge of God. We are taking every thought captive to the obedience of Messiah—6ready to punish all disobedience, whenever your obedience is complete.

7Look at what is before your eyes.[c] If anyone is confident in himself that he belongs to Messiah, let him reconsider that just as he belongs to Messiah, so also do we. 8For even if I boast a little more about our authority—which the Lord gave for building you up and not for tearing you down—I will not be put to shame. 9Not that I would try to terrify you by my letters—10for they say, "His letters are weighty and strong, but his presence in person is weak and his speech of no account." 11Let such a person consider this, that what we are in word through letters when we are absent, we also are in action when we are present.

12For we do not dare to classify or compare ourselves with some of those who commend themselves. But when they measure themselves by themselves and compare themselves with themselves, they have no understanding. 13But we will not boast beyond limits, but within the limits of the area that God has assigned to us—to reach even as far as you. 14We are not extending ourselves too far, as if we did not reach you—for we did come even as far as to you with the Good News of Messiah. 15Neither are we boasting beyond limits based on the labors of others, but we have hope while your faith is growing for our area among you to be greatly enlarged—16so that we may proclaim the Good News even to regions beyond you, not boasting about what has been accomplished in another's area. 17But "let him who boasts boast in the Lord."[d] 18For it Is not the one who commends himself who is approved, but the one whom the Lord commends.

a 10:4. cf. Isa. 25:11; Jer. 51:53.
b 10:5. cf. Isa. 2:11–12, 17.
c 10:7. Some mss. say *Do you look at things according to outward appearance?*
d 10:17. Jer. 9:23(24).

11

True and False Apostles

1I wish that you would put up with a little foolishness from me, but indeed you are putting up with me. 2For I am jealous over you with a godly jealousy. For I betrothed you to one husband, to present you to Messiah as a pure virgin.[e] 3But I am afraid that somehow, as the serpent deceived Eve by his cunning, your minds might be led astray from a sincere and pure devotion and purity to the Messiah. 4For if someone comes and proclaims another *Yeshua* whom we did not proclaim, or if you receive a different spirit that you did not receive, or a different "good news" that you did not accept, you put up with that well enough!

5For I consider myself in no way inferior to the "super special" *shlichim*. 6Even if I am unskilled in speech, yet I am not so in knowledge. No, in every way we have made this clear to you in all things. 7Or did I commit a sin in humbling myself so that you might be exalted, because I proclaimed to you God's Good News free of charge? 8I robbed other communities by taking wages from them for service to you. 9When I was present with you and I was in need, I did not burden anyone; for the brothers who came from Macedonia supplied my need. In everything I kept myself from being a burden to you, and I will continue to do so. 10As the truth of Messiah is in me, this boasting of mine will not be silenced in the regions of Achaia. 11Why? Because I do not love you? God knows I do!

12But what I am doing I will continue to do, so that I may cut off the opportunity from those who want an opportunity in what they boast about to also be regarded just as we are. 13For such men

e 11:2. cf. Hos. 2:21-22 (19-20).

are false *shlichim*, deceitful workers masquerading as Messiah's *shlichim*. 14 And no wonder, for even satan masquerades as an angel of light. 15 It is no great thing therefore if his servants also masquerade as servants of righteousness, Their end will be according to their deeds.

Paul Boasts in the Lord

16 I say again, let no one consider me to be a fool. But if you do, accept me as a fool, so that I also may boast a little. 17 What I am saying, I am saying not according to the Lord, but as in foolishness, in this self-confident boasting. 18 Since many boast according to the flesh, I too will boast. 19 For you, being so wise, put up with fools gladly. 20 For you put up with it if someone enslaves you, if someone devours you, if someone takes advantage of you, if someone puts on airs, if someone slaps you on the face. 21 To my shame I must say that we have been weak.

Yet whatever anyone else dares to boast about—I speak in foolishness—I dare, too. 22 Are they Hebrews? So am I. Are they Israelites? So am I. Are they the descendants of Abraham? So am I. 23 Are they servants of Messiah? I am more so—I speak like I'm out of my mind—in labors much more, in prisons much more, in beatings more brutal, near death often. 24 Five times from the Jewish leaders I received forty lashes minus one.[a] 25 Three times I was beaten with rods. Once I was stoned. Three times I suffered shipwreck. A night and a day I spent in the open sea. 26 In my many journeys I have been in dangers from rivers, dangers from robbers, dangers from my countrymen, dangers from the Gentiles, dangers in the city, dangers in the desert, dangers in the sea, dangers among false brothers, 27 in labor and hardship, through many sleepless nights, in hunger and thirst, often without food, in cold and exposure. 28 Besides these other things, there is daily pressure on me of concern for all of Messiah's communities. 29 Who is weak, and I am not weak? Who is led into sin, and I do not burn with indignation? 30 If I must boast, I will boast of my weakness. 31 The God and Father of the Lord *Yeshua*, who is blessed forever, knows that I am not lying. 32 In Damascus the governor under King Aretas was guarding the city of the Damascenes in order to seize me, 33 and I was lowered in a basket through a window in the wall and escaped his hands.[b]

12

Boasting in Visions and Weakness

1 I must go on boasting—though it does no good, I will go on to visions and revelations of the Lord. 2 I know a man in Messiah (whether in the body I don't know, or whether out of the body I don't know—God knows)—fourteen years ago, he was caught up to the third heaven.[c] 3 I know such a man (whether in the body or outside of the body I don't know—God knows)— 4 he was caught up into Paradise and heard words too sacred to tell, which a human is not permitted to utter. 5 On behalf of such a man I will boast—but about myself I will not boast, except in regard to my weaknesses. 6 For if I should want to boast, I would not be foolish—for I will speak the truth. But I refrain, so that no one may think more of me than what he sees in me or hears from me— 7 even in the extraordinary quality of the revelations. So that I would not exalt myself, a thorn in the flesh was given to me—a a messenger of satan to torment me,[d] so I would not exalt myself. 8 I pleaded with the Lord three times about this, that it might leave me. 9 But He said to me, "My grace is

a 11:24. cf. Deut. 25:3.

b 11:32-33. cf. Acts 9:23-25.

c 12:2. cf. Ezek. 8:3.

d 12:7. Cf. Num. 33:55; Job 2:6.

sufficient for you, for power is made perfect in weakness." Therefore I will boast all the more gladly in my weaknesses, so that the power of Messiah may dwell in me. 10For Messiah's sake, then, I delight in weaknesses, in insults, in distresses, in persecutions, in calamities. For when I am weak, then I am strong.

11I have become a fool—you drove me to it, for I ought to have been commended by you. For I am in no way inferior to the super-special *shlichim*—though I am nothing. 12Truly the signs of a *shaliach* were worked out among you, with patient endurance, by signs and wonders and mighty miracles. 13For in what respect were you treated worse than the rest of Messiah's communities—except that I myself did not burden you? Pardon me this injustice!

14Look, I am ready to come to you this third time, and I will not burden you—for I seek not your possessions, but you! For the children are not obliged to save up for the parents, but the parents for the children. 15I will most gladly spend and be spent for your souls. If I love you more, am I to be loved less? 16But be that as it may, I did not burden you myself. Nevertheless, crafty fellow that I am, I caught you with trickery! 17I haven't taken advantage of you through any of those I sent to you, have I? 18I did urge Titus to visit you, and I sent the brother with him. Titus didn't take any advantage of you, did he? Didn't we walk in the same spirit, in the same footsteps?

19All along you've been thinking that we are defending ourselves to you.[a] It is before God that we've been speaking in Messiah—and all for building you up, loved ones. 20For I am afraid that perhaps when I come, I may find you not as I wish, or I may be found by you not as you wish—that there may be strife, envy, outbursts of anger, self-seeking disputes, *lashon ha-ra*, gossip, arrogance, unruly commotions. 21I am afraid that when I come again my God may humiliate me before you, and I will mourn for many of those who have sinned before and not repented of the impurity and sexual immorality and indecency which they committed.

13

Final Warnings

1This is the third time I am coming to you. "By the testimony[b] of two or three witnesses shall every word be established."[c] 2I spoke a warning, when I was with you the second time. Though now I am away, I am again speaking a warning to those who have sinned before, as well as to all the rest, that if I come again, I will not spare anyone—3since you are demanding proof that Messiah is speaking through me. He is not weak toward you, but powerful among you. 4For He was crucified in weakness, yet He lives through the power of God. For we also are weak in Him, yet we shall live with Him by God's power toward you.

5Test yourselves, to see whether you are in the faith. Examine yourselves! Or don't you know yourselves—that Messiah Yeshua is in you? Unless of course you failed the test. 6But I hope that you will realize that we haven't failed the test. 7Now we pray to God that you do no wrong—not so that we may appear to have passed the test, but in order that you may do what is right even if we may seem to have failed. 8For we can do nothing against the truth, but only for the truth. 9For we rejoice when we are weak and you are strong. We also pray for this—your perfecting. 10For this reason I write these things while I am absent, so that when I am present I need not proceed harshly, according to the authority which the Lord gave me—for building up and not for tearing down.

a 12:19. Some mss. say *Do you think all along that we are defending ourselves to you?*

b 13:1. Lit. *mouth.*

c 13:1. Deut. 19:15; cf. Matt. 18:16; 1 Tim. 5:19.

Final Greetings

[11]Finally, brothers and sisters, rejoice!
Aim for restoration, encourage one
another, be of the same mind, live in *shalom*—and the God of love and *shalom* will
be with you.

[12]Greet one another with a holy kiss.

All the *kedoshim* greet you.[a]

[13]The grace of the Lord *Yeshua* the
Messiah and the love of God and the fellowship of the *Ruach ha-Kodesh* be with
you all. Amen.

a 13:12-13. Some versions have three verses: 12 *Greet...* 13 *All...* 14 *The grace...*

Paul's Letter to the Galatians

Introduction

Together with Romans, Paul's letter to the Galatians speaks directly to the pressing issue of Jewish-Gentile relations in the body of Messiah. Written early in Paul's career, some time in the late 40s, Paul here speaks sharply against those, maybe some variety of *Yeshua*-believing Jews, who were teaching Torah-observance for Gentiles as a way of justification. In no uncertain terms, he declares that justification comes by faith, not by *Torah* observance (compare Acts 15). Along the way he draws on illustrations from the Hebrew Bible—Abraham, Sarah, and Hagar—to make his point.

Justification by faith in *Yeshua* is a reality for Jews and Gentiles alike. The well-known verse in Galatians 3:28 does not seek to abolish all distinctions between Jews and Gentiles (any more than it abolishes all distinctions between men and women!), but rather tells us that all people have equal access to God and that all come to him in the same way. As a result, there is a unity in the body of Messiah that transcends the Jewish-Gentile distinction. Moreover, our justification by faith is no license for unethical living, but rather through the *Ruach ha-Kodesh* we bear the fruit of a righteous and ethical life (chapters 5–6).

Paul's opponents were attempting to alienate the Galatians from Paul. In 1 Corinthians 1:11-15, the division came from following various *Yeshua*-believing leaders. Here in Galatians the division may come either from outside the body of Messiah or from certain Jewish believers, but the result was a compromise of the Good News for the non-Jewish Galatians.

In Galatians, Paul points us beyond divisions to the unity that we all share in Messiah—a unity of equal opportunity to come into relationship with God (3:28—the same access); a unity of the same way of salvation (2:16—through faith in God's Messiah); and a practical unity that manifests itself in behavior (5:14—love and self-sacrifice).

A Look Inside Galatians

1

Greetings from Paul

[1]Paul, a *shaliach* (sent not from men or by man, but by *Yeshua* the Messiah and God the Father, who raised Him from the dead), [2]and all the brothers with me.

To Messiah's communities of Galatia:

[3]Grace to you and *shalom* from God our Father and our Lord *Yeshua* the Messiah— [4]who gave Himself for our sins to rescue us from this present evil age, according to the will of our God and Father— [5]to Him be the glory forever and ever! Amen.

No Other Gospel

[6]I am amazed that you are so quickly turning away from the One who called you by the grace of Messiah, to a different "good news"— [7]not that there is another, but only some who are confusing you and want to distort the Good News of Messiah. [8]But even if we (or an angel from heaven) should announce any "good news" to you other than what we have proclaimed to you, let that person be cursed! [9]As we have said before, so I now repeat: if anyone proclaims to you "good news" other than what you received, let that person be under a curse! [10]Am I now trying to win people's approval, or God's? Or am I trying to please people? If I were still trying to please people, I would not be a servant of Messiah.

How Paul Was Sent Out

[11]Now I want you to know, brothers and sisters, that the Good News proclaimed by me is not man-made. [12]I did not receive it from any human, nor was I taught it, but it came through a revelation of *Yeshua* the Messiah.

[13]For you have heard of my earlier behavior in Judaism—how I persecuted God's community beyond measure and tried to destroy it. [14]I was even advancing within Judaism beyond many my own age among my people, being a more extreme observer of my fathers' traditions. [15]But when God—who set me apart from birth and called me through His grace[a]—was pleased [16]to reveal His Son to me so I would proclaim Him among the Gentiles, I did not immediately consult with any human. [17]I did not go up to Jerusalem to those who were *shlichim* before me, either. Instead I went away to Arabia and returned again to Damascus.

[18]Then three years later I went to Jerusalem to visit with Peter, and I stayed with him fifteen days. [19]But I saw no other *shlichim* except Jacob, the Lord's brother. [20](In what I'm writing you, before God, I do not lie.)

[21]Then I went to the regions of Syria and Cilicia. [22]But I was personally unknown to Messiah's communities of Judea; [23]they only kept hearing, "The one who once persecuted us now proclaims the Good News he once tried to destroy!" [24]So they were praising God because of me.

2

Accepted in Jerusalem

[1]Then after fourteen years I went up again to Jerusalem with Barnabas, taking Titus with me. [2]Because of a revelation, I went up and presented to them the Good News that I proclaim among the Gentiles. But I did so privately to those who seemed to be influential, to make sure I would not run—or had not run—in vain.[b] [3]Yet not even Titus who was with me, a Greek, was forced to be circumcised. [4]Now this issue came up because of false brothers secretly brought in (who slipped in to spy out our freedom in

a 1:15. cf. Isa. 49:1, 5; Jer. 1:5.
b 2:2. cf. Isa. 49:4.

Messiah, in order to bring us into bondage). [5]But we did not give in to them even for a moment, so that the truth of the Good News might be preserved for you. [6]But from those who seemed to be influential (whatever they were makes no difference to me; God shows no partiality)—well, those influential ones added nothing to my message. [7]On the contrary, they saw that I had been entrusted with the Good News for the uncircumcised just as Peter was for the circumcised. [8](For the same God who was at work in Peter as a *shaliach* to the Jews, also was at work in me as a *shaliach* to the Gentiles.) [9]Realizing the favor that had been given to me, Jacob and Peter[a] and John—who are the recognized pillars—shook hands in partnership with Barnabas and me,[b] so that we would go to the Gentiles and they to the Jews. [10]They asked only that we remember the poor—something I also was eager to do.

Confronting Hypocrisy

[11]But when Peter came to Antioch, I opposed him to his face, because he was clearly in the wrong—[12]for before certain people came from Jacob, he regularly ate with the Gentiles; but when they came, he began to withdraw and separate himself, fearing those from the circumcision. [13]And the rest of the Jews joined him in hypocrisy, so that even Barnabas was carried away with their hypocrisy. [14]But when I saw that they were not walking in line with the truth of the Good News, I said to Peter in front of everyone, "If you—being a Jew—live like the Gentiles and not like the Jews, how can you force the Gentiles to live like Jews?"

[15]We are Jews by birth and not sinners from among the Gentiles. [16]Yet we know that a person is set right not by deeds based on *Torah*, but rather through putting trust in Messiah *Yeshua*.[c] So even we have put our trust in Messiah *Yeshua*, in order that we might be set right based on trust in Messiah and not by deeds based on *Torah*—because no human will be justified[d] by deeds based on *Torah*. [17]But if, while seeking to be justified in Messiah, we ourselves also were found to be sinners, is Messiah then an agent of sin? May it never be! [18]For if I rebuild the very things I tore down, I prove myself to be a law-breaker. [19]For through law I died to law, so that I might live for God. I have been crucified with Messiah; [20]and it is no longer I who live, but Messiah lives in me. And the life I now live in the body, I live by trusting in *Ben-Elohim*[e]—who loved me and gave Himself up for me. [21]I do not nullify the grace of God—for if righteousness comes through *Torah*, then Messiah died for no reason!

3

By Deeds or by Faith?

[1]O foolish Galatians, who cast a spell on you? Before your eyes *Yeshua* the Messiah was clearly portrayed as crucified. [2]I want to find out just one thing from you: did you receive the Spirit by deeds based on *Torah*, or by hearing based on trust? [3]Are you so foolish? After beginning with the Spirit, will you now reach the goal in the flesh? [4]Did you endure so much for nothing—if it really was for nothing? [5]So then, the One who gives you the Spirit and works miracles among you—does He do it because of your deeds based on *Torah* or your hearing based on trust and faithfulness?

[6]Just as Abraham "believed God, and it was credited to him as righteousness,"[f] [7]know then that those who have faith are children of Abraham. [8] The Scriptures, foreseeing that God would justify the Gentiles by faith, proclaimed the Good News to Abraham in advance, saying,

a 2:9, 11, 14. Lit. *Cephas*, or *Kefa* (Aram.).
b 2:9. Lit. *gave right hands of fellowship (Grk. koinonia)*; cf. 2 Kings 10:15.
c 2:16a. Or *the faithfulness of Messiah Yeshua*.
d 2:16b. cf. Ps. 14:3; 53:3; 143:2; Eccl. 7:20.
e 2:20. Of *the faithfulness of Ben-Elohim*.
f 3:6. Gen. 15:6; cf. Rom. 4:3; Jacob 2:23.

"All the nations shall be blessed through you."[a] 9So then, the faithful are blessed along with Abraham, the faithful one.

10For all who rely on the deeds of *Torah* are under a curse—for the Scriptures say, "Cursed is everyone who does not keep doing everything written in the scroll of the *Torah*."[b] 11It is clear that no one is set right before God by *Torah*, for "the righteous shall live by *emunah*."[c] 12However, *Torah* is not based on trust and faithfulness; on the contrary, "the one who does these things shall live by them."[d] 13Messiah liberated us from *Torah*'s curse, having become a curse for us (for it is written, "Cursed is everyone who hangs on a tree"[e])— 14in order that through Messiah *Yeshua* the blessing of Abraham might come to the Gentiles, so we might receive the promise of the Spirit through trusting faith.

Slaves or Sons?

15Brothers and sisters, I speak in human terms: even with a man's covenant, once it has been confirmed, no one cancels it or adds to it. 16Now the promises were spoken to Abraham and to his seed. It doesn't say, "and to seeds," as of many, but as of one, "and to your seed," who is the Messiah. 17What I am saying is this: *Torah*, which came 430 years later, does not cancel the covenant previously confirmed by God, so as to make the promise ineffective. 18For if the inheritance is based on law, it is no longer based on a promise. But God has graciously given it to Abraham by means of a promise.

19Then why the *Torah*? It was added because of wrongdoings until the Seed would come—to whom the promise had been made. It was arranged through angels by the hand of an intermediary. 20Now an intermediary is not for one party alone—but God is one. 21Then is the *Torah* against the promises of God? May it never be! For if a law had been given that could impart life, certainly righteousness would have been based on law. 22But the Scripture has locked up the whole world under sin, so that the promise based on trust in Messiah *Yeshua*[f] might be given to those who trust.

23Now before faith came, we were being guarded under *Torah*—bound together until the coming faith would be revealed. 24Therefore the *Torah* became our guardian to lead us to Messiah, so that we might be made right based on trusting. 25But now that faith has come, we are no longer under a guardian. 26For you are all sons of God through trusting in Messiah *Yeshua*. 27For all of you who were immersed in Messiah have clothed yourselves with Messiah. 28There is neither Jew nor Greek, there is neither slave nor free, there is neither male nor female—for you are all one in Messiah *Yeshua*. 29And if you belong to Messiah, then you are Abraham's seed—heirs according to the promise.

4

Living as Heirs

1Now I am saying, so long as the heir is underage, he is no different from a slave, even though he is the owner of everything. 2Instead, he is under guardians and managers until the date set by the father. 3So also, when we were underage, we were subservient to the basic principles of the world. 4But when the fullness of time came, God sent out His Son, born of a woman and born under law— 5to free those under law, so we might receive adoption as sons. 6Now because you are sons, God sent the Spirit of His Son into our hearts, who cries out, "*Abba!* Father!" 7So you are no longer a slave but a son—and if a son, also an heir through God.[g] 8But at that time, when you did

a 3:8. cf. Gen. 12:3; 18:18.
b 3:10. cf. Deut. 27:26(27:26 LXX).
c 3:11. Hab. 2:4.
d 3:12. Lev. 18:5.
e 3:13. Deut. 21:23.

f 3:22. Or *the faithfulness of Messiah Yeshua.*
g 4:7. Some mss. read *heir of God through Messiah.*

not know God, you served those who by nature are not gods at all. [9]But now you have come to know God—or rather you have come to be known by God. So how can you turn back again to those weak and worthless principles? Do you want to be enslaved to them all over again? [10]You observe days and months and seasons and years. [11]I fear for you, that perhaps I have labored over you in vain!

[12]I plead with you, brothers and sisters, become like me, for I became like you. You have done me no wrong— [13]you know it was because of a physical ailment that I proclaimed the Good News to you the first time; [14]and though my physical condition was a trial to you, you did not hate or reject me. No, you welcomed me as a messenger of God—or even as Messiah *Yeshua*. [15]So where is your sense of joy? For I testify that you would have torn out your eyes and given them to me, if possible. [16]So have I become your enemy by telling you the truth?! [17]Others zealously court you—not in a good way, but they wish to shut you out so that you will court them. [18]To be courted is good, but let it always be in a good way—and not just when I am there with you. [19]My dear children! Again I suffer labor pains until Messiah is formed in you. [20]I wish I could be with you now and change my tone, for I don't know what to make of you.

Midrash on Abraham's Two Sons

[21]Tell me, you who want to be under law, don't you understand[a] the *Torah*? [22]For it is written that Abraham had two sons, one by the slave woman and one by the free woman.[b] [23]But one—the son by the slave woman—was born naturally;[c] while the other—the son by the free woman—was through the promise. [24]Now these things are being treated allegorically, for these are two covenants. One is from Mount Sinai, giving birth to slavery—this is Hagar. [25]But this Hagar is Mount Sinai in Arabia and corresponds to the present Jerusalem, for she is in slavery along with her children. [26]But the Jerusalem above is free—she is our mother. [27]For it is written:

> "Rejoice, O barren woman
> who bears no children.
> Break forth and shout,
> you who suffer no labor pains.
> For more are the children of the desolate
> than of the one who has a husband."[d]

[28]Now you, brothers and sisters—like Isaac, you are children of promise. [29]But just as at that time the one born according to the flesh persecuted the one born according to the Spirit, so it is now. [30]But what does the Scripture say? "Drive out the slave woman and her son, for the son of the slave woman shall not inherit with the son"[e] of the free woman. [31]So then, brothers and sisters, we are not children of the slave woman but of the free woman.

5

Freedom Based on Favor

[1]For freedom, Messiah set us free—so stand firm, and do not be burdened by a yoke of slavery again. [2]Listen—I, Paul, tell you that if you let yourselves be circumcised, Messiah will be of no benefit to you. [3]Again I testify to every man who lets himself be circumcised, that he is obligated to keep the whole *Torah*. [4]You who are trying to be justified by law[f] have been cut off from Messiah; you have fallen away from grace. [5]For through the Spirit, by faith, we eagerly wait for the hope of righteousness. [6]For in Messiah

a 4:21. Or *hear, listen to the law*; cf. Deut. 6:4; 18:15; Exod. 24:7.
b 4:22. cf. Gen. 16:15; Gen. 21:2.
c 4:23. Lit. *according to the flesh*.
d 4:27. Isa. 54:1.
e 4:30. Gen. 21:10(LXX).
f 5:4. Or *made right by Torah*.

Yeshua, neither circumcision nor uncircumcision has any meaning—but only trust and faithfulness expressing itself through love.

[7]You were running a great race! Who blocked you from following the truth? [8]This detour doesn't come from the One who calls you. [9]A little *hametz* works its way through the whole batch of dough! [10]I am confident in the Lord that you will not think otherwise. But the one who is confusing you will pay the penalty, whoever he is. [11]As for me, brothers and sisters, if I still proclaim circumcision, why am I still being persecuted? In that case, the stumbling block of the cross has been eliminated. [12]I only wish those who are agitating you would castrate themselves![a]

Walking by the Spirit

[13]Brothers and sisters, you were called to freedom—only do not let your freedom become an opportunity for the flesh, but through love serve one another. [14]For the whole *Torah* can be summed up in a single saying: "Love your neighbor as yourself."[b] [15]But if you bite and devour one another, watch out that you are not destroyed by one another.

[16]But I say, walk by the Spirit, and you will not carry out the desires of the flesh. [17]For the flesh sets its desire against the Spirit, but the Spirit sets its desire against the flesh—for these are in opposition to one another, so that you cannot do what you want. [18]But if you are led by the Spirit, you are not under law. [19]Now the deeds of the flesh are clear: sexual immorality, impurity, indecency, [20]idolatry, witchcraft, hostility, strife, jealousy, rage, selfish ambition, dissension, factions, [21]envy, drunkenness, carousing, and things like these. I am warning you, just as I warned you before, that those who do such things will not inherit God's kingdom. [22]But the fruit of the Spirit is love, joy, peace, patience, kindness, goodness, faithfulness, [23]gentleness, and self-control—against such things there is no law. [24]Now those who belong to Messiah[c] have crucified the flesh with its passions and desires.

[25]If we live by the Spirit, let us also walk by the Spirit. [26]Let us not become conceited—provoking one another, envying one another.

Bearing Burdens

[1]Brothers and sisters, if someone is caught doing something wrong, you who are directed by the Spirit, restore such a person in a spirit of gentleness—looking closely at yourself so you are not tempted also. [2]Bear one another's burdens, and in this way you fulfill the *Torah* of Messiah. [3]For if anyone thinks he is something when he is nothing, he is fooling himself. [4]Rather let each one examine his own work. Then he will have pride in himself alone and not in comparison to anyone else. [5]For each one will carry his own load.

[6]Now let the one who is taught the word share all good things with his teacher. [7]Do not be deceived—God is not mocked. For whatever a man sows, that he also shall reap. [8]For the one who sows in the flesh will reap corruption from the flesh.[d] But the one who sows in the Spirit will reap from the Spirit eternal life. [9]So let us not lose heart in doing good, for in due time we will reap if we don't give up. [10]Therefore, whenever we have an opportunity, let us do good toward all[e]—especially those who belong to the household of faith.

Living under God's Favor

[11]Notice the large letters—I am writing to you with my own hand. [12]Those

a 5:12. cf. Phil. 3:2.
b 5:14. Lev. 19:18.
c 5:24. Some mss. add *Yeshua*.
d 6:8. cf. Job 4:8.
e 6:10. cf. Prov. 3:27.

wanting to look good outwardly[a] are
trying to force you to be circumcised—
only so they will not be persecuted for
the cross of Messiah. 13For not even the
circumcised keep *Torah* themselves. Yet
they want to have you circumcised so
that they may boast about your flesh.
14But may I never boast—except in the
cross of our Lord *Yeshua* the Messiah.
Through Him the world has been crucified to me, and I to the world. 15For
neither circumcision nor uncircumcision means[b] anything—but only a new
creation. 16Now as many as live by this
rule[c]—*shalom* and mercy on them and
on the Israel of God.

17From now on let no one make trouble
for me, for I bear on my body the scars[d]
of *Yeshua*.

18The grace of our Lord *Yeshua* the
Messiah be with your spirit, brothers and
sisters. Amen.

---

a 6:12. Lit. *in flesh*.
b 6:15. Most mss. read *is*.
c 6:16. Or *standard, straight rod*; Grk. *kanon*.
d 6:17. Lit. *marks, branding marks*; Grk. *stigma* (pl. *stigmata*).

Paul's Letter to the
Ephesians

Introduction

Ephesians is a wide-ranging and encouraging letter, which is remarkable since Paul wrote it from prison, as said at 3:1, 4:1, and 6:20. This may well be when he was imprisoned in Rome in the early 60s. But Paul apparently looked on his jail time as "for the Lord" (4:1) and for others—"for the sake of you Gentiles " (3:1).

Unlike many of Paul's other letters, Ephesians is not addressed to a specific situation in the Ephesian community. There is no heresy he speaks against, no ethical lapse to correct, no tension between Jewish believers and the Gentile believers who made up the majority. That is not to say that the Ephesians had no problems! But this particular letter is a positive exposition of teaching and encouragement, applicable to all of Messiah's communities regardless of their particular situations.

It is almost impossible to give a summary of the rich teachings of Ephesians. One focus is the *ekklesia*—the community of those who put their trust in *Yeshua*. There is more in Ephesians about the *ekklesia* than in any other of Paul's letters. The existence of this body is a direct result of God's gracious actions in choosing us as His people. His grace is especially seen in *Yeshua*, the great reconciler between Jews and Gentiles and the One who will in fact bring redemption to the entire universe. It is Messiah *Yeshua* who is the head of this body and the cornerstone of God's Temple.

Along with the emphasis on what God has done come exhortations to grow in the knowledge of God and in His love, which includes living according to His will and striving for unity among believers. *Yeshua's* followers must live in imitation of Him—particularly in household relationships (husbands/wives; parents/children; masters/slaves) that mirror the various ways we as believers relate to God.

Of special interest to Messianic believers are Paul's remarks in 2:11-22. Here Paul tells his Gentile readers that they have joined the commonwealth of Israel as fellow citizens through the reconciling work of *Yeshua*. Likewise, in 3:6 he tells us that the Gentiles who have come to faith inherit the promises with Israel as "joint heirs," belong to the same people as "fellow members," and benefit equally as "co-sharers of the promise." In contrast with supersessionism, which teaches that the church *replaces* Israel, Paul says that the Gentiles have *joined* Israel, receiving blessings and promises from which they were once excluded. Messiah's community is not a replacement for Israel, but rather the Body that unites Jews and Gentiles together in Messiah *Yeshua*. No wonder Paul breaks into a deep and lengthy prayer for the Ephesians at the end of the third chapter!

A Look Inside Ephesians

Greetings (1:1)
God's Glorious Grace (1:3)
God's Glorious Power Working in Us (1:15)

Destined for Wrath, Saved by Grace (2:1)
Jew and Gentile, One in Messiah (2:11)

The Mystery of the Gentiles Revealed (3:1)
Prayer for Power and Understanding (3:14)

Unity of the Body and of God (4:1)
Put Off The Old, Put On The New (4:17)

Walk in the Light (5:1)
Orderly Relationships: Marriage (5:21)

Orderly Relationships: Parents (6:1)
Orderly Relationships: Workplace (6:5)
Put on the Armor of God (6:10)

1

Greetings

1 Paul, a *shaliach* of Messiah *Yeshua* by God's will,

To the *kedoshim* in Ephesus[a]—those trusting in Messiah *Yeshua:*

2 Grace and *shalom* to you, from God our Father and the Lord *Yeshua* the Messiah!

God's Glorious Grace

3 Blessed be the God and Father of our Lord *Yeshua* the Messiah, who has blessed us with every spiritual blessing in the heavenly places in Messiah. 4 He chose us in the Messiah before the foundation of the world, to be holy and blameless before Him in love. 5 He predestined us for adoption as sons through Messiah *Yeshua,* in keeping with the good pleasure of His will— 6 to the glorious praise of His grace, with which He favored us through the One He loves!

7 In Him we have redemption through His blood—the removal of trespasses—in keeping with the richness of His grace 8 that He lavished on us. In all wisdom and insight, 9 He made known to us the mystery of His will, in keeping with His good pleasure that He planned in Messiah. 10 The plan of the fullness of times is to bring all things together in the Messiah—both things in heaven and things on earth, all in Him. 11 In Him we also were chosen,[b] predestined according to His plan. He keeps working out all things according to the purpose of His will— 12 so that we, who were first to put our hope in Messiah, might be for His glorious praise.

13 After you heard the message of truth—the Good News of your salvation—and when you put your trust in Him, you were sealed with the promised *Ruach ha-Kodesh.* 14 He is the guarantee of our inheritance, until the redemption of His possession—to His glorious praise!

God's Glorious Power Working in Us

15 Therefore, ever since I heard of your trust in the Lord *Yeshua* and of your love for all the *kedoshim,* 16 I never stop giving thanks for you as I mention you in my prayers— 17 that the God of our Lord *Yeshua* the Messiah, our glorious Father, may give you spiritual wisdom and revelation in knowing Him. 18 I pray that the eyes of your heart may be enlightened, so that you may know what is the hope of His calling, what is the richness of His glorious inheritance in the *kedoshim,* 19 and what is His exceedingly great power toward us who keep trusting Him—in keeping with the working of His mighty strength.

20 This power He exercised in Messiah when He raised Him from the dead and seated Him at His right hand in heaven.[c] 21 He is far above any ruler, authority, power, leader, and every name that is named—not only in the *olam ha-zeh* but also in the *olam ha-ba.* 22 God placed all things under Messiah's feet[d] and appointed Him as head over all things for His community— 23 which is His body, the fullness of Him who fills all in all.

2

Destined for Wrath, Saved by Grace

1 You were dead in your trespasses and sins. 2 At that time, you walked in the way of this world, in conformity to the ruler of the domain of the air—the ruler of the spirit who is now operating in the sons of disobedience. 3 We too all lived among them in the cravings of our flesh,

a 1:1. Some mss. omit *in Ephesus.*
b 1:11. cf. Deut. 9:29; 32:8-9.
c 1:20. cf. Ps. 110:1.
d 1:22. cf. Ps. 8:6.

indulging the desires of the flesh and the mind. By nature we were children of wrath, just like the others. 4But God was rich in mercy,[a] because of His great love with which He loved us. 5Even when we were dead in our trespasses, He made us alive together with Messiah. (By grace you have been saved!) 6And He raised us up with Him and seated us with Him in the heavenly places in Messiah *Yeshua*— 7to show in the *olam ha-ba* the measureless richness of His grace in kindness toward us in Messiah *Yeshua*.

8For by grace you have been saved through faith. And this is not from yourselves—it is the gift of God. 9It is not based on deeds, so that no one may boast. 10For we are His workmanship—created in Messiah *Yeshua* for good deeds, which God prepared beforehand so we might walk in them.

Jew and Gentile, One in Messiah

11Therefore, keep in mind that once you—Gentiles in the flesh—were called "uncircumcision" by those called "circumcision" (which is performed on flesh by hand). 12At that time you were separate from Messiah, excluded from the commonwealth of Israel and strangers to the covenants of promise, having no hope and without God in the world. 13But now in Messiah *Yeshua*, you who once were far off have been brought near by the blood of the Messiah. 14For He is our *shalom*, the One who made the two into one and broke down the middle wall of separation. Within His flesh He made powerless the hostility— 15the law code of *mitzvot* contained in regulations. He did this in order to create within Himself one new man from the two groups, making *shalom*, 16and to reconcile both to God in one body through the cross—by which He put the hostility to death. 17And He came and proclaimed *shalom* to you who were far away and *shalom* to those who were near[b]— 18for through Him we both have access to the Father by the same Spirit. 19So then you are no longer strangers and foreigners, but you are fellow citizens with God's people and members of God's household. 20You have been built on the foundation made up of the *shlichim* and prophets, with Messiah *Yeshua* Himself being the cornerstone.[c] 21In Him the whole building, being fitted together, is growing into a holy temple for the Lord. 22In Him, you also are being built together into God's dwelling place[d] in the Spirit.

3

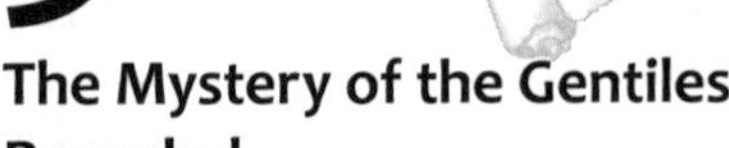

The Mystery of the Gentiles Revealed

1For this reason I, Paul, am a prisoner of Messiah *Yeshua* for the sake of you Gentiles. 2Surely you have heard about the plan of God's grace given to me for you— 3that the mystery was made known to me by revelation, as I wrote before briefly. 4When you read this, you can understand my insight into the mystery of Messiah— 5which was not made known to the sons of men in other generations, as it has now been revealed by the Spirit to His holy *shlichim* and prophets. 6This mystery is that the Gentiles are joint heirs and fellow members of the same body and co-sharers of the promise in Messiah *Yeshua* through the Good News. 7I became a servant of this Good News by the gift of God's favor given to me through the exercise of His power.

8This favor was given to me, the very least of His *kedoshim*, to proclaim to the Gentiles the endless riches of the Messiah 9and to bring to light the plan of the mystery—which for ages was hidden in God, who created all things. 10The purpose is that through Messiah's

a 2:4. cf. Exod. 34:6; Ps. 145:8.

b 2:17. cf. Isa. 57:19.

c 2:20. cf. Ps. 118:22-23; Isa. 28:16.

d 2:22. cf. 1 Ki. 8:13, 39, 43, 39.

Ephesians 2:13-14a

But now in Messiah Yeshua, you who once were far off have been brought near by the blood of the Messiah. For He is our shalom, the One who made the two into one and broke down the middle wall of separation.

community the multi-faceted wisdom of God might be made known to the rulers and authorities in the heavenly places, [11]which is in keeping with the eternal purpose that He carried out in Messiah *Yeshua* our Lord. [12]In Him we have boldness and access with confidence through trusting in Him.[a] [13]So I ask you not to be discouraged by my troubles on your behalf—they are your glory.

Prayer for Power and Understanding

[14]For this reason I bow my knees before the Father[b]— [15]from Him every family in heaven and on earth receives its name. [16]I pray that from His glorious riches He would grant you to be strengthened in your inner being with power through His Spirit, [17]so that Messiah may dwell in your hearts through faith. I pray that you, being rooted and grounded in love, [18]may have strength to grasp with all the *kedoshim* what is the width and length and height and depth, [19]and to know the love of Messiah which surpasses knowledge, so you may be filled up with all the fullness of God.

[20]Now to Him who is able to do far beyond all that we ask or imagine, by means of His power that works in us, [21]to Him be the glory in the community of believers and in Messiah *Yeshua* throughout all generations[c] forever and ever! Amen.

4

Unity of the Body and of God

[1]Therefore I, a prisoner for the Lord, urge you to walk in a manner worthy of the calling to which you were called— [2]with complete humility and gentleness, with patience, putting up with one another in love, [3]making every effort to keep the unity of the Spirit in the bond of *shalom*.

[4]There is one body and one Spirit,
just as you also were called in one hope of your calling;
[5]one Lord, one faith, one immersion;
[6]one God and Father of all,[d]
who is over all and through all and in all.

[7]But to each one of us grace was given in keeping with the measure of Messiah's gift. [8]Therefore it says,

"When He went up on high,
He led captive a troop of captives
and gave gifts to his people."[e]

[9]Now what does "He went up" mean, except that He first went down to the lower regions of the earth?[f] [10]The One who came down is the same One who went up far above all the heavens, in order to fill all things.

[11]He Himself gave some to be *shlichim*, some as prophets, some as proclaimers of the Good News, and some as shepherds and teachers— [12]to equip the *kedoshim* for the work of service, for building up the body of Messiah. [13]This will continue until we all come to the unity of the faith and of the knowledge of *Ben-Elohim*—to mature adulthood, to the measure of the stature of Messiah's fullness. [14]As a result, we are no longer to be like children, tossed around by the waves and blown all over by every wind of teaching, by the trickery of men with cunning in deceitful scheming. [15]Instead, speaking the truth in love, we are to grow up in all ways into Messiah, who is the Head. [16]From Him the whole body is fitted and held together by every supporting ligament. The proper working of each individual part produces the body's growth, for building itself up in love.

a 3:12. Or *through His faithfulness.*
b 3:14. Some mss. add *of our Lord Yeshua the Messiah.*
c 3:21. cf. Ps. 145:4; 13.
d 4:6. cf. Deut. 6:4.
e 4:8. cf. Ps. 68:19(18)(68:18LXX).
f 4:9. cf. Isa. 44:23.

Put Off The Old, Put On The New

17So I tell you this, indeed I insist on it in the Lord—walk no longer as the pagans do, stumbling around in the futility of their thinking. 18They are darkened in their understanding, alienated from the life of God because of the ignorance in them due to the hardness of their heart. 19Since they are past feeling, they have turned themselves over to indecency for the practice of every kind of immorality, with greed for more.

20However, you did not learn Messiah in this way— 21if indeed you have heard Him and were taught in Him, as the truth is in *Yeshua*. 22With respect to your former lifestyle, you are to lay aside the old self corrupted by its deceitful desires, 23be renewed in the spirit of your mind, 24and put on the new self—created to be like God in true righteousness and holiness.

25So lay aside lying and "each one of you speak truth with his neighbor,"[a] for we are members of one another. 26"Be angry, yet do not sin."[b] Do not let the sun go down on your anger,[c] 27nor give the devil a foothold. 28The one who steals must steal no longer—instead he must work, doing something useful with his own hands, so he may have something to share with the one who has need. 29Let no harmful word come out of your mouth, but only what is beneficial for building others up according to the need, so that it gives grace to those who hear it. 30Do not grieve the *Ruach ha-Kodesh* of God,[d] by whom you were sealed for the day of redemption. 31Get rid of all bitterness and rage and anger and quarreling and slander, along with all malice. 32Instead, be kind to one another, compassionate, forgiving each other just as God in Messiah also forgave you.

a 4:25. Zech. 8:16.
b 4:26. Ps. 4:5(4)(4:5LXX).
c 4:26. cf. Ps. 37:8; Matt. 5:22.
d 4:30. cf. Isa. 63:10.

5

Walk in the Light

1Therefore be imitators of God, as dearly loved children; 2and walk in love, just as Messiah also loved us[e] and gave Himself up for us as an offering and sacrifice to God for a fragrant aroma. 3But sexual immorality and any impurity or greed—don't even let these be mentioned among you, as is proper for *kedoshim*. 4Obscene, coarse, and stupid talk are also out of place, but instead let there be thanksgiving. 5Know for certain that no immoral, indecent, or greedy person—who is really an idol worshipper at heart—has any inheritance in the kingdom of Messiah and God.

6Let no one deceive you with empty words, for because of such things God's judgment comes on the children of disobedience. 7Therefore do not be partners with them. 8For once you were darkness, but now in union with the Lord you are light. Walk as children of light 9(for the fruit of light is in all goodness and righteousness and truth), 10trying to learn what is pleasing to the Lord. 11Take no part in the fruitless deeds of darkness, but rather expose them— 12for it is disgraceful even to mention the things that are done by them in secret. 13Yet everything exposed by the light is being made visible, 14for everything made visible is light. This is why it says,

"Wake up, O sleeper!
 Rise from the dead,
 and Messiah will shine on you."[f]

15So pay close attention to how you walk—not as unwise people but as wise. 16Make the most of your time because the days are evil. 17For this reason do not be foolish, but understand what the

e 5:2. Some mss. read you.
f 5:14. cf. Isa. 26:19; 52:1; 60:1.

Lord's will is. [18]And do not get drunk on
wine, for that is recklessness.[a] Instead,
be filled with the Spirit, [19]speaking to
one another in psalms, hymns, and spiritual songs, singing and making music in
your heart to the Lord— [20]always giving thanks for everything to God the
Father, in the name of the Lord *Yeshua*
the Messiah.

Orderly Relationships: Marriage

[21]Also submit yourselves to one
another out of reverence for Messiah—
[22]wives to your own husbands as to the
Lord. [23]For the husband is head of the
wife, as Messiah also is head of His community—Himself the Savior of the body.
[24]But as Messiah's community is submitted to Messiah, so also the wives to their
husbands in everything.

[25]Husbands, love your wives just as
Messiah also loved His community and
gave Himself up for her [26]to make her
holy, having cleansed her by immersion[b]
in the word. [27]Messiah did this so that
He might present to Himself His glorious
community—not having stain or wrinkle
or any such thing, but in order that she
might be holy and blameless. [28]In the
same way, husbands ought to love their
own wives as their own bodies. He who
loves his wife loves himself.

[29]For no one ever hated his own flesh,
but nourishes and cherishes it—just
as Messiah also does His community,
[30]because we are members of His body.
[31]"For this reason a man shall leave his
father and mother and be joined to his
wife, and the two shall become one
flesh."[c] [32]This mystery is great—but I am
talking about Messiah and His community. [33]In any case, let each of you love
his own wife as himself, and let the wife
respect her husband.

a 5:18. cf. Prov. 20:1; 23:31ff.

b 5:26. Lit. *the washing of the water; mikveh.*

c 5:31. Gen. 2:24.

6

Orderly Relationships: Parents

[1]Children, obey your parents in the
Lord, for this is right.[d] [2]"Honor your
father and mother" (which is the first
commandment with a promise), [3]"so
that it may be well with you, and you may
live long on the earth."[e] [4]Fathers, do not
provoke your children to anger, but bring
them up in the discipline and instruction
of the Lord.[f]

Orderly Relationships: Workplace

[5]Slaves, obey your human masters, with respect and reverence, with
sincerity of heart, as you would the Messiah— [6]not just under your master's
eye as people-pleasers, but as slaves of
Messiah doing God's will from the soul.
[7]Serve with a positive attitude, as to the
Lord and not to men—[8]knowing that
whatever good each one does, this he
will receive back from the Lord, whether
slave or free. [9]And masters, treat your
slaves in the same way. Stop using
threats, knowing that the Master—of
them and of you, too—is in heaven,[g] and
there is no favoritism with Him.

Put on the Armor of God

[10]Finally, be strong in the Lord and in
His mighty power. [11]Put on the full armor
of God, so that you are able to stand
against the schemes of the devil. [12]For
our struggle is not against flesh and
blood, but against the rulers, against the
powers, against the worldly forces of this
darkness, and against the spiritual forces
of wickedness in the heavenly places.
[13]Therefore, take up the full armor of

d 6:1. Cf. Prov. 1:8; 6:20; 23:22.

e 6:2-3. Deut. 5:16; cf. Exod. 20:12.

f 6:4. Cf. Deut. 6:7; 11:19; Ps. 78:4; Prov. 22:6.

g 6:9. cf. Job 31:13-15.

God, so that you may be able to resist
when the times are evil, and after you
have done everything, to stand firm.
[14]Stand firm then! Buckle the belt of
truth around your waist, and put on the
breastplate of righteousness.[a] [15]Strap
up your feet in readiness with the Good
News of *shalom*.[b] [16]Above all, take up
the shield of faith with which you will be
able to extinguish all the flaming arrows
of the evil one.[c] [17]And take the helmet
of salvation[d] and the sword of the Spirit,
which is the word of God.[e] [18]Pray in the
Spirit on every occasion, with all kinds of
prayers and requests. With this in mind,
keep alert with perseverance and sup-
plication for all the *kedoshim*. [19]And pray
for me when I open my mouth to make
known with boldness the mystery of the
Good News, [20]for which I am an ambassador in chains. Pray that I may speak
boldly, the way I should.

[21]Now Tychicus, my dearly loved
brother and faithful servant in the Lord,
will give you all the news about me so
you may know how I'm doing. [22]I have
sent him to you for this very reason, so
you may know how we are and he may
encourage your hearts.

[23]*Shalom* to the brothers and sisters,
and trusting love from God the Father
and the Lord *Yeshua* the Messiah. [24]Grace
be with all those who love our Lord
Yeshua the Messiah with undying love.

---

a 6:14. Isa. 11:5.
b 6:15. Isa. 52:7; Ps. 9:17.
c 6:16. Ps 28:7; 76:3; 91;4-5.
d 6:17. Isa. 59:17.
e 6:18. Isa. 49:2.

Paul's Letter to the Philippians

Introduction

Philippians is one of Paul's "prison letters," written during one of his confinements in jail—in Rome, Caesarea, or Ephesus—in the late 50s or early 60s. Unlike some other communities, the Philippians seem to have gotten on quite well in their faith. Nevertheless, they are still exhorted to be on guard against false teachers whose lifestyle does not match their message (3:18-19). Even if we are growing in our faith, we need to be alert to influences that will try to disengage us from God.

Many consider Philippians 4:4 to be the key verse of the letter: "Rejoice in the Lord always—again I will say, rejoice!" Paul rejoices that the Messiah is proclaimed even if from wrong motives (1:18). He rejoices even though he is in prison, and he encourages the Philippians to do the same (2:17-18). He exhorts them to rejoice in the Lord Himself (3:1 and 4:4). He prays with joy (1:4). There is joy in faith (1:25) and specifically in *Yeshua* (1:26). The unity of believers increases his joy (2:2), and the Philippians are Paul's special joy (4:1) as he sees God's work in them.

Finally, Philippians 2:5-11 contains one of the most magnificent pieces of poetry in the New Covenant scriptures—possibly a hymn that had made the rounds among the first believers, which Paul now puts into this letter. *Yeshua* was God by nature, yet became a humble and lowly servant, dying in obedience to the Father in order to bring us salvation. Now He has been exalted to the highest place and with the highest name, and someday all humanity will bow to Him.

With *Yeshua* as our example and also our Savior, we can rejoice even in the midst of suffering. Moreover, we find the motivation to live as God wants us to live—a life which in a mysterious way (2:12-13) is both God's work and yet our responsibility to cultivate (for example, through obedience, prayer, and Scripture reading). There is ample cause to rejoice as we see in Philippians the reality of who *Yeshua* is and what He has done for us!

A Look inside Philippians

Greetings (1:1)
Thanksgiving and Prayers of Joy (1:3)
Even in Chains, Proclaiming Messiah (1:12)
To Live Is Messiah (1:19)

Messiah's Example of Humility (2:1)
Work Out Your Salvation (2:12)
Sending and Receiving Encouragement (2:19)

Where Do You Put Your Confidence? (3:1)
Pursuing the Goal (3:12)

Rejoice in the Lord Always (4:2)
The Secret of Contentment (4:10)
Final Greetings and Blessings (4:21)

1

Greetings

[1]Paul and Timothy, slaves of Messiah
Yeshua,
To all the *kedoshim* in Messiah *Yeshua*
who are in Philippi with the overseers
and *shammashim:*
[2]Grace to you and *shalom* from God our
Father and the Lord *Yeshua* the Messiah.

Thanksgiving and Prayers of Joy

[3]I thank my God at every memory of
you, [4]always praying with joy in every
prayer of mine for you all, [5]because of
your sharing in the Good News from the
first day until now. [6]I am sure of this very
thing—that He who began a good work
in you will carry it on to completion until
the Day of Messiah *Yeshua*. [7]It is right
for me to feel this way about you all,
because I have you in my heart—for you
all are partakers of grace with me, both
in my imprisonment and in the defense
and confirmation of the Good News. [8]For
God is my witness, how I long for all of
you with the affection of Messiah *Yeshua*.
[9]Now this I pray, that your love might
overflow still more and more in knowledge and depth of discernment, [10]in
order to approve what is excellent—so
that in the Day of Messiah you may be sincere and blameless, [11]filled with the fruit
of righteousness that comes through
Yeshua the Messiah, to the glory and
praise of God.

Even in Chains, Proclaiming Messiah

[12]Now I want you to know, brothers
and sisters, that what has happened to
me has actually resulted in the advance-
ment of the Good News. [13]And so my
imprisonment in the cause of Messiah
has become well known throughout the
whole Praetorian Guard and to everyone
else. [14]Because of my imprisonment,
most of the brothers and sisters have
become confident in the Lord to dare
more than ever to speak the message
fearlessly. [15]Some are proclaiming the
Messiah out of envy and strife, but others out of good will. [16]The latter do so out
of love, knowing that I am appointed for
the defense of the Good News. [17]The former proclaim Messiah not sincerely, but
out of selfishness—expecting to stir up
trouble for me in my imprisonment. [18]But
what does it matter? Only that in every
way, whether in dishonesty or in truth,
Messiah is being proclaimed—and in this
I rejoice!

To Live Is Messiah

Yes, and I will keep rejoicing, [19]for I
know that this will turn out for my deliverance, through your intercession and
the help of the Spirit of Messiah *Yeshua*.
[20]My eager expectation and hope is that
in no way will I be put to shame, but that
with complete boldness Messiah will
even now, as always, be exalted in my
body—whether through life or through
death. [21]For to me, to live is Messiah and
to die is gain. [22]But if to live on in the
body means fruit from my work, what
shall I choose? I do not know. [23]I am torn
between the two—having a desire to
leave and be with Messiah, which is far
better; [24]yet for your sake, to remain in
the body is more necessary. [25]Convinced
of this, I know that I will remain and continue with you all, for the sake of your
progress and joy in the faith— [26]so that
your confidence in Messiah *Yeshua* might
overflow because of me through my
coming to you again.
[27]Only live your lives in a manner worthy of the Good News of the Messiah.
Then, whether I come and see you or I
am absent, I may hear of you that you are
standing firm in one spirit—striving side
by side with one mind for the faith of the

Good News 28and not being frightened in any way by your opponents. For them this is a sign of destruction, but for you salvation—and that from God. 29For to you was granted for Messiah's sake not only to trust in Him, but also to suffer for His sake— 30experiencing the same struggle you saw in me and now you are hearing in me.

2

Messiah's Example of Humility

1Therefore if there is any encouragement in Messiah, if there is any comfort of love, if there is any fellowship of the Spirit, if there is any mercy and compassion, 2then make my joy complete by being of the same mind, having the same love, united in spirit, with one purpose. 3Do nothing out of selfishness or conceit, but with humility consider others as more important than yourselves, 4looking out not only for your own interests but also for the interests of others. 5Have this attitude in yourselves, which also was in Messiah *Yeshua*,

6Who, though existing in the form of God,
did not consider being equal to God
a thing to be grasped.
7But He emptied Himself—
taking on the form of a slave,
becoming the likeness of men
and being found in appearance as a man.
8He humbled Himself—
becoming obedient to the point of death,
even death on a cross.
9For this reason God highly exalted Him
and gave Him the name
that is above every name,
10that at the name of *Yeshua*
every knee should bow,[a]
in heaven and on the earth and
under the earth,
11and every tongue profess
that *Yeshua* the Messiah is Lord—
to the glory of God the Father.

Work Out Your Salvation

12Therefore, my loved ones, just as you have always obeyed—not only in my presence, but now even more in my absence—work out your salvation with fear and trembling. 13For the One working in you is God—both to will and to work for His good pleasure.

14Do everything without grumbling or arguing, 15so that you might be blameless and innocent, children of God in the midst of a crooked and twisted generation.[b] Among them you shine as lights in the world, 16holding fast to the word of life, so that I may boast in the day of Messiah that I did not run or labor in vain. 17But even if I am being poured out as a drink offering upon the sacrifice and the service of your faith, I rejoice and share my joy with you all. 18The same way, you also—rejoice and share your joy with me!

Sending and Receiving Encouragement

19But I hope in the Lord *Yeshua* to send Timothy to you soon, so that I too might be encouraged when I know the news about you. 20I have no one else like him who will genuinely care about you— 21for all seek after their own interests, not those of Messiah *Yeshua*. 22But you know Timothy's proven character, that he served with me in spreading the Good News like a son with his father. 23Therefore I hope to send him immediately, as soon as I see how things go with me. 24And I trust in the Lord that soon I too will come myself.

25But I thought it necessary to send to you Epaphroditus—my brother and co-worker and fellow soldier, as well as

a 2:10-11. cf. Isa. 45:23.

b 2:15. cf. Deut. 32:5.

your messenger and aide to my need. 26For he was longing for you all and troubled because you heard that he was sick. 27He certainly was sick, close to death. But God had mercy on him—and not only on him but also on me, so that I would not have sorrow upon sorrow. 28Therefore I have sent him with special urgency, so that when you see him again you might rejoice and I might be less worried about you. 29So welcome him in the Lord with all joy, and hold men like him in high regard, 30because he came close to death for the work of Messiah, risking his life to make up for what was lacking in your service to me.

3

Where Do You Put Your Confidence?

3:1 Finally, my brothers and sisters, rejoice in the Lord! To keep writing the same things to you is not troublesome for me—but for you it is a safeguard.

2Beware of the dogs,[a] beware of the evil workers, beware of the mutilation.[b] 3For it is we who are the circumcision, who worship by the Spirit of God and glory in Messiah *Yeshua* and have not depended on the flesh— 4though I myself might have confidence in the flesh also. If anyone else thinks he might depend on the flesh, I far more— 5circumcised the eighth day; of the nation of Israel; from the tribe of Benjamin; a Hebrew of Hebrews; in regard to the *Torah*, a Pharisee; 6as for zeal, persecuting Messiah's community; as for Torah righteousness, found blameless.

7But whatever things were gain to me, these I have considered as loss for the sake of the Messiah. 8More than that, I consider all things to be loss in comparison to the surpassing value of the knowledge of Messiah *Yeshua* my Lord. Because of Him I have suffered the loss of all things; and I consider them garbage[c] in order that I might gain Messiah 9and be found in Him not having my righteousness derived from *Torah*, but one that is through trusting in Messiah—the righteousness from God based on trust.[d] 10My aim is to know Him and the power of His resurrection and the sharing of His sufferings, becoming like Him in His death— 11if somehow I might arrive at the resurrection from among the dead.

Pursuing the Goal

12Not that I have already obtained this or been perfected, but I press on if only I might take hold of that for which Messiah *Yeshua* took hold of me.[e] 13Brothers and sisters, I do not consider myself as having taken hold of this. But this one thing I do: forgetting what is behind and straining toward what is ahead, 14I press on toward the goal for the reward of the upward calling of God in Messiah *Yeshua*.[f] 15Therefore let all who are mature have this attitude; and if you have a different attitude in anything, this also God will reveal to you. 16Nevertheless, let us live up to the same standard we have attained.

17Brothers and sisters, join in following my example and notice those who walk according to the pattern you have in us. (18For many walk who are enemies of the cross of Messiah—I have often told you about them, and now I am even weeping as I tell you. 19Their end is destruction—their god is their belly and their glory is in their shame. They set their minds on earthly things.)

20For our citizenship is in heaven,
and from there we eagerly wait for the Savior,
the Lord *Yeshua* the Messiah.

a 3:1. cf. Ps. 22:16, 20.
b 3:2. cf. Gal. 5:12.

c 3:8. Lit. *excrement*.
d 3:9. Or *one that is through Messiah's faithfulness—the righteousness from God based on faithfulness*.
e 3:12. Lit. *I was taken hold of by Messiah Yeshua*.
f 3:14. cf. 1 Cor. 9:24; Heb. 12:2.

21 He will transform this humble body
of ours
into the likeness of His glorious
body,
through the power that enables
Him
even to put all things in subjection
to Himself.

4

1 Therefore, my brothers and sisters whom I love and long for, my joy and crown—stand firm in the Lord in this way, my loved ones.

Rejoice in the Lord Always

2 I urge Euodia and Syntyche to be in harmony in the Lord. 3 Yes, and I ask you, true companion,[a] to help these women—they labored side by side with me in spreading the Good News, together with Clement also and the rest of my fellow workers, whose names are in the Book of Life.

4 Rejoice in the Lord always—again I will say, rejoice! 5 Let your gentleness be known to all people. The Lord is near. 6 Do not be anxious about anything—but in everything, by prayer and petition with thanksgiving, let your requests be made known to God. 7 And the *shalom* of God, which surpasses all understanding, will guard your hearts and your minds in Messiah *Yeshua*.[b]

8 Finally, brothers and sisters, whatever is true, whatever is honorable, whatever is just, whatever is pure, whatever is lovely, whatever is commendable—if there is any virtue and if there is anything worthy of praise—dwell on these things. 9 What you have learned and received and heard and seen in me—put these things into practice, and the God of *shalom* will be with you.

The Secret of Contentment

10 I rejoiced in the Lord greatly, that now at last you have revived your concern for me (though you were concerned before but lacked opportunity to show it). 11 I am not saying this because I am in need—for whatever circumstance I am in, I have learned to be content. 12 I know what it is to live with humble means, and I know what it is to live in prosperity. In any and every circumstance I have learned the secret of contentment—both to be filled and to go hungry, to have abundance and to suffer need. 13 I can do all things through Messiah[c] who strengthens me.

14 Nevertheless, you have done well to share in my trouble. 15 Now you Philippians also know that in the beginning of the Good News, when I left Macedonia, not a single community partnered with me in giving and receiving—except you alone. 16 For even in Thessalonica you sent something for my need more than once. 17 Not that I am looking for a gift, but for fruit that overflows to your credit. 18 But I have received everything and have more than enough. I am amply supplied, having received from Epaphroditus what you sent—a fragrant aroma, an acceptable sacrifice, pleasing to God.[d] 19 My God will fulfill every need of yours according to the riches of His glory in Messiah *Yeshua*. 20 To our God and Father be the glory forever and ever! Amen.

Final Greetings and Blessings

21 Greet all the *kedoshim* in Messiah *Yeshua*. The brothers who are with me greet you. 22 All the *kedoshim* greet you, especially those of Caesar's household.

23 The grace of the Lord *Yeshua* the Messiah be with your spirit.

a 4:3. Possibly a proper name.
b 4:7. cf. Isa. 26:3.
c 4:13. Lit. *Him*; cf. 1 Tim. 1:12.
d 4:18. cf. Exod. 29:18.

Paul's Letter to the Colossians

Introduction

Written in the late 50s or early 60s from prison, Paul's letter to the Colossians was intended to help Messiah's community in Colossae fight the false teaching that had entered their midst.

The false teaching seems to have been a combination of Greek and Jewish ideas, perhaps not unlike today when some in the Jewish community attempt to overlay New Age ideas onto Jewish ways of thinking. An assortment of spiritual "options" was characteristic of the ancient world, where various spiritualities downplay who *Yeshua* really is. Therefore Paul upholds Him as the fully supreme One who reconciled Jews and Gentiles through his atoning death. There is no need for anyone or anything to bring us to God—no special leader, ritual, technique, or spirituality.

Paul speaks of principalities, powers, and basic principles of the world that to some degree held sway over the Colossians (2:15, 20). Modern secular people may think that our genes or our upbringing charts the course for our lives. But *Yeshua* is victorious over all things that try to stand between us and God.

Finally, Paul emphasizes the unity of Messiah's body—how *Yeshua* has reconciled Jews and Gentiles. Yet he also recognizes diversity in the unity, as he speaks to wives, to husbands, to children, to parents, to slaves, to masters. Nevertheless, *Yeshua* is the head of the body, His community. Let us do all we can to preserve our unity with all believers. And let us exalt *Yeshua*, our Head, both individually and in our communities.

Supreme over all, victorious over all, reconciler of all—this is our Messiah!

A Look Inside Colossians

Greetings (1:1)
Thanksgiving and Prayer (1:3)
Ben-Elohim Is Supreme (1:15)
The Mystery Revealed (1:24)
Living Out the Mystery (2:6)
The Danger of False Wisdom (2:16)
Put Off the Old, Put on the New (3:1)
Orderly, Mutual Relationships (3:18)
Devote Yourselves to Prayer (4:2)
Further Instructions and Greetings (4:7)

1

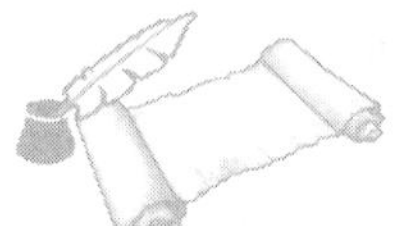

Greetings

[1]Paul, a *shaliach* of Messiah *Yeshua* by God's will, and Timothy our brother,

[2]To the *kedoshim*, the faithful brothers and sisters in Messiah, who are at Colossae:

Grace and *shalom* to you from God our Father![a]

Thanksgiving and Prayer

[3]We always thank God, the Father of our Lord *Yeshua* the Messiah, whenever we pray for you. [4]For we heard of your trust in Messiah *Yeshua* and the love you have for all the *kedoshim* [5]because of the hope stored up for you in heaven. You heard before about this hope in the true message of the Good News [6]that has come to you. In all the world this Good News is bearing fruit and growing,[b] just as it has in you since you first heard it and came to truly know God's grace. [7]You learned it from Epaphras—our dearly loved fellow slave, who is a faithful servant of Messiah on our behalf. [8]He also made clear to us your love in the Spirit.

[9]For this reason also, ever since we heard about you, we have not stopped praying for you. We keep asking God that you might be filled with the knowledge of His will in all wisdom and spiritual understanding— [10]to walk in a manner worthy of the Lord, to please Him in all respects, bearing fruit in every good work and growing in the knowledge of God. [11]We pray that you may be strengthened with all the power that comes from His glorious might, for you to have all kinds of patience and steadfastness. With joy [12]we give thanks to the Father, who qualified you to share in the inheritance of the *kedoshim* in the light. [13]He rescued us from the domain of darkness and brought us into the kingdom of the Son whom He loves. [14]In Him we have redemption—the release of sins.

Ben-Elohim Is Supreme

[15]He is the image of the invisible God,
the firstborn of all creation.
[16]For by Him all things were created—
in heaven and on earth,
the seen and the unseen,
whether thrones or angelic powers
or rulers or authorities.
All was created through Him and for
Him.
[17]He exists before everything,
and in Him all holds together.
[18]He is the head of the body, His
community.
He is the beginning, the firstborn
from the dead—
so that He might come to have first
place in all things.
[19]For God was pleased to have all His
fullness dwell in Him[c]
[20]and through Him to reconcile all
things to Himself,
making peace through the blood of
His cross—
whether things on earth or things
in heaven!

[21]Once you were alienated from God and hostile in your attitude by wicked deeds. [22]But now He has reconciled you in Messiah's physical body through death, in order to present you holy, spotless and blameless in His eyes— [23]if indeed you continue in the faith, established and firm, not budging from the hope of the Good News that you have heard. This Good News has been proclaimed throughout all creation under heaven, and I, Paul, have become its servant.

The Mystery Revealed

[24]Now I rejoice in my sufferings for you, and in my physical body—for the sake of His body, Messiah's community—I fill up

a 1:2. Some mss. add: *and the Lord Yeshua the Messiah.*
b 1:6. cf. Gen 1:28; 9:1, 7; 17:2; 22:17; 28:3; 35:11.
c 1:19. cf. Isa. 6:3; Ezek. 43:5; 44:4.

what is lacking in the afflictions of Messiah. [25]I became its servant according to God's commission, given to me for you, in order to declare His message in full— [26]the mystery that was hidden for ages and generations, but now has been revealed to His *kedoshim*. [27]God chose to make known to them this glorious mystery regarding the Gentiles—which is Messiah in you, the hope of glory! [28]We proclaim Him, warning and teaching everyone in all wisdom, so that we may present every person complete[a] in Messiah. [29]To this end I labor, striving with all His strength which is powerfully at work in me.

2

[1]I want you to know how great a struggle I have for you and for those in Laodicea, as well as for those who have still not seen me face to face. [2]My purpose is that their hearts, joined together in love, may be encouraged. May they have all the riches of the full assurance of understanding, leading to a true knowledge of the mystery of God—that is, Messiah. [3]In Him all the treasures of wisdom and knowledge are hidden.[b] [4]I am telling you this so that no one will deceive you with persuasive-sounding arguments. [5]For even though I am absent in body, yet I am with you in spirit—rejoicing to see your good order and the steadfastness of your trust in Messiah.

Living Out the Mystery

[6]Therefore as you received Messiah Yeshua as Lord, so continue to walk in Him— [7]rooted and built up in Him and established in your faith just as you were taught, overflowing with thankfulness. [8]See that no one takes you captive through philosophy and empty deception, according to the tradition of men and the basic principles of the world rather than Messiah. [9]For all the fullness of Deity lives bodily in Him, [10]and in Him you have been filled to fullness. He is the head over every ruler and authority.

[11]In Him you were also circumcised with a circumcision done not by hand, in the stripping away of the body of the flesh through the circumcision of Messiah. [12]You were buried along with Him in immersion, through which you also were raised with Him by trusting in the working of God, who raised Him from the dead. [13]When you were dead in your sins and the uncircumcision of your flesh, God made you alive together with Him when He pardoned us all our transgressions. [14]He wiped out the handwritten record of debts with the decrees against us, which was hostile to us. He took it away by nailing it to the cross. [15]After disarming the principalities and powers, He made a public spectacle of them, triumphing over them in the cross.[c]

The Danger of False Wisdom

[16]Therefore, do not let anyone pass judgment on you in matters of food or drink, or in respect to a festival or new moon or *Shabbat*.[d] [17]These are a foreshadowing of things to come, but the reality is Messiah.[e] [18]Let no one disqualify you by insisting on false humility and worship of angels—going into detail about what he has seen, puffed up without cause by his fleshly mind. [19]He is not holding fast to the Head. It is from Him that the whole body, nourished and held together by its joints and tendons, grows with a godly increase. [20]If you died with Messiah to the basic principles of the world, why—as though living in the world—do you subject yourselves to their rules? [21]"Don't handle! Don't taste! Don't touch!" [22]These all lead to decay with use, based as they are on man-made

a 1:28. cf. 1 Ki. 8:61; 11:4.
b 2:3. cf. Prov. 3:19; Isa. 11:2; 45:3.
c 2:15. Lit. *in it* or *in Him.*
d 2:16. cf. Lev 23:2-4, 2 Chr. 23:31; 2 Chr. 31:3; Neh. 10:33; Ps. 81:3; Isa. 66:23; Ezek. 46:1, etc.
e 2:17. Lit. *the body is of Messiah.*

commands and teachings.[a] 23Indeed, these are matters that have an appearance of wisdom in self-made religion and humility and self-denial of the body—yet none are of any value for stopping indulgence of the flesh.

3

Put Off the Old, Put On the New

1Therefore, if you have been raised up with Messiah, keep seeking the things above—where Messiah is, sitting at the right hand of God.[b] 2Focus your mind on things above, not on things on the earth.[c] 3For you have died, and your life is hidden with Messiah in God. 4When Messiah, who is your[d] life, is revealed, then you also will be revealed with Him, in glory!

5Therefore, put to death what is earthly in you—sexual immorality, impurity, lust, evil desire, and greed—for that is idolatry. 6Because of such things God's wrath is coming upon the sons of disobedience. 7At one time you also walked in these ways, when you used to live in these ways. 8But now, set them all aside—anger, rage, malice, slander, and foul language out of your mouth. 9Do not lie to one another.[e] After all, you have taken off the old self with its practices 10and have put on the new self that is being renewed in knowledge, according to the image of the One who created him.[f] 11Here there is no longer Greek and Jew, circumcised and uncircumcised, barbarian, savage,[g] slave and free; but Messiah is all, and in all.

12Therefore, as God's chosen people, holy and dearly loved, clothe yourselves in tender compassion, kindness, humility, gentleness, and patience— 13bearing with one another and forgiving each other, if anyone has a grievance against another. Just as the Lord pardoned you, so also you must pardon others. 14But above all these things put on love, which is the bond of perfect harmony. 15Let the *shalom* of Messiah rule in your hearts—to this *shalom* you were surely called in one body. Also be thankful. 16Let the word of Messiah dwell in you richly, teaching and admonishing one another with all wisdom in psalms and hymns and spiritual songs, singing with gratitude in your hearts to God. 17And whatever you do in word or deed, do all in the name of the Lord *Yeshua*, giving thanks to God the Father through Him.

Orderly, Mutual Relationships

18Wives, submit yourselves to your husbands, as is fitting in the Lord. 19Husbands, love your wives and do not become harsh toward them.

20Children, obey your parents in every respect, for this is pleasing to the Lord. 21Fathers, do not provoke your children, so they will not become discouraged.

22Slaves, obey your human masters in every respect—not just within your master's sight as people-pleasers, but with sincerity of heart, fearing the Lord. 23Whatever you do, work at it from the soul, as for the Lord and not for people. 24For you know that from the Lord you will receive the inheritance as a reward. It is to the Lord Messiah you are giving service. 25For the one doing wrong will be paid back for what he did wrong, and there is no favoritism.[h]

4

1Masters, give your slaves what is just and fair, knowing that you also have a Master in heaven.

a 2:22. cf. Isa. 29:13.
b 3:1. cf. Ps. 80:15, 17; 89:13; 110:1; 118:15-16, etc.
c 3:2. cf. Ps. 57:5, 7; 103:11; 115:16; Isa. 40:22; 55:9.
d 3:4. Other mss. read *our*.
e 3:9. cf. Lev. 19:11; Ps. 24:4.
f 3:10. cf. Gen. 1:26-27.
g 3:11. Lit. *Scythian*.
h 3:25. cf. Deut. 10:17.

Devote Yourselves to Prayer

[2]Devote yourselves to prayer, keeping alert in it with thanksgiving. [3]At the
same time, keep praying for us as well,
that God may open up to us a door for
the message, to proclaim the mystery
of Messiah—for which I am in prison.
[4]Pray that I may make the mystery clear,
as I ought to speak. [5]Conduct yourselves
with wisdom toward outsiders, making
the most of the opportunity. [6]Let your
speech always be with grace, seasoned
with salt, to know how you ought to
answer everyone.

Further Instructions and Greetings

[7]Tychicus—a dearly loved brother and
trustworthy servant and fellow slave to
the Lord—will tell you all the news about
me. [8]I sent him to you for this very purpose, so you may know about us and he
may encourage your hearts. [9]With him
I sent Onesimus—a faithful and dear
brother, who is one of your own. They
will tell you about everything here.

[10]My fellow prisoner Aristarchus
sends you his greetings, as does Mark,
the cousin of Barnabas. (You received
instructions about him—if he comes
your way, welcome him.) [11]*Yeshua* who
is called Justus also sends his greetings.
These are the only fellow workers for the
kingdom of God that are from among the
circumcision—they have been a comfort
to me.

[12]Epaphras, who is one of your own,
a slave of Messiah *Yeshua*, greets you.
He is always laboring in prayer on your
behalf, so you may stand complete and
fully assured about everything that is
God's will. [13]For I testify that he has gone
to much trouble for you and for those
in Laodicea and Hierapolis. [14]Luke, the
dearly loved physician, sends you greetings, and so does Demas.

[15]Greet the brothers and sisters in
Laodicea, as well as Nympha and the
community that meets in her house.
[16]When this letter has been read among
you, make sure that it is also read in Messiah's community of Laodicea. In turn,
you should read my letter coming from
Laodicea.

[17]Tell Archippus, "See to it that you
complete the service you have received
in the Lord, that you may fulfill it."

[18]This greeting is in my own hand—
Paul's. Remember my chains!

Grace be with you.

Paul's First Letter to the Thessalonians

Introduction

One of Paul's earliest letters, 1 Thessalonians was written around the year 50 from the city of Corinth. His readers were largely non-Jewish, as we gather from his remark in 1:9 that they had "turned from idols" to the true God.

The letter is a mix of personal, ethical, and pastoral material. Paul speaks well of the Thessalonians and their faith, especially commending how they initially "welcomed" the message of the Good News (1:4). Several times Paul speaks of "imitating" himself (1:5), God (1:5 also), and other believers (2:14), and says that the Thessalonians have become a "model" of faith to others (1:7). Paul then describes his own behavior while in Thessalonica — sincere, seeking to please God, sharing his own life with them. The theme of imitation and modeling is a key to the life of the believer. Though we primarily seek to imitate *Yeshua*, we also learn how to imitate him by modeling the lives of mature and godly believers. Paul then moves on to specific ways to imitate God, by showing what ethical, godly living means in the first part of chapter four.

A word about 2:14-16. This passage has sometimes been taken as an example of anti-Semitism in the New Covenant. The same Greek word can be translated as "Jewish" or "Judean," but the use of "Judeans" rather than "Jews" in verse 14 highlights Paul's parallel. The Thessalonians were persecuted by non-believing Thessalonians just like Messiah's communities in Judea were persecuted by non-believing Judeans. The persecution took the form of preventing the preaching of the Good News to Gentiles. In speaking of "heaping up sins to the limit" and "the wrath of God has come upon them at last," Paul is not speaking of the Jewish people, but of opponents of the Good News, Jewish or Gentile, actually employing ideas taken from the *Tanakh*.

The last part of the letter is devoted to helping the Thessalonians work through their thoughts on fellow believers who have recently died. It seems as though they thought that those who had already passed on would "miss out" on the return of the Lord in some way. Paul comforts them with a word of "hope" (4:13), then reminds them further to live godly lives in light of *Yeshua's* return. The beautiful benediction of 5:23, coming near the end of the letter, is an encouragement to all believers.

A Look Inside 1 Thessalonians

Greetings (1:1)
Good News with Power (1:2)

Cherishing Spiritual Children (2:1)
Longing to Visit and Reassure (2:17)

Thanks, Joy, and Love Before God (3:11)

Walking in Sanctification (4:1)
The *Shofar* Call of
Messiah's Return (4:13)

Keep Watch for the Day of the Lord (5:1)
Instructions for Community Life (5:12)
Closing Greetings (5:25)

1

Greetings

1Paul, Silvanus,[a] and Timothy,

To the community of the Thessalonians in God the Father and the Lord *Yeshua* the Messiah:

Grace to you and *shalom*.

Good News with Power

2We always give thanks to God for all of you, mentioning you in our prayers—continually 3remembering before our God and Father your work of faith and labor of love and steadiness of hope in our Lord *Yeshua* the Messiah. 4We know, brothers and sisters loved by God, that you are chosen, 5because our Good News did not come to you in word only, but also in power and in the *Ruach ha-Kodesh* and with complete certainty—just as you know what kind of men we proved to be while among you for your sake. 6You also became imitators of us and of the Lord, having accepted the message in much tribulation, with the joy of the *Ruach ha-Kodesh*. 7So you became an example to all the believers in Macedonia and Achaia. 8For the word of the Lord rang out from you—not just in Macedonia and Achaia, but also in every place your faithfulness toward God has gone out, so that we have no need to say anything. 9For they themselves bring news about what kind of welcome we had among you, and how you turned to God from idols, to serve the living and true God, 10and to wait for His Son from heaven, whom He raised from the dead—*Yeshua*, the One delivering us from the coming wrath.

2

Cherishing Spiritual Children

1For you yourselves know, brothers and sisters, that our visit to you was not in vain. 2On the contrary, after we had first suffered and been mistreated in Philippi, as you know,[b] we had boldness in our God to tell you the Good News of God—even in the midst of much opposition. 3For our urging is not out of deceit or impure motives or trickery. 4But just as we have been approved by God to be entrusted with the Good News, so we declare it—not pleasing men but rather God, who examines our hearts.[c]

5For as you know and God is witness, we never came with a word of flattery or a motive of greed— 6or seeking glory from people, whether from you or from others, 7even though we could have thrown our weight around as *shlichim* of Messiah. Rather, we proved to be infants[d] among you. Like a nursing mother[e] cherishes her children, 8in this way we were yearning for you. We were delighted to share with you not only the Good News of God but also our very souls, because you had become dear to us.

9For you recall, brothers, our labor and hardship—working night and day, so as not to burden any of you while we proclaimed to you the Good News of God. 10You are witnesses, along with God, of how devoutly and righteously and blamelessly we behaved toward you who believe. 11For you know how, as a father with his own children, 12we exhorted and encouraged and urged each one of you to walk in a manner worthy of God, who calls you into His own kingdom and glory.

13For this reason, we also thank God constantly that when you received the word of God which you heard from us, you accepted it not as the word of men, but as it truly is—the word of God, which does its work in you who believe. 14For you, brothers and sisters, became imitators of God's communities in Messiah *Yeshua* that are in Judea—for you suffered the same things at the hands of your own countrymen as they did from

a 1:1. Or *Silas*; cf. Acts 15:22ff.

b 2.2 cf. Ac. 16:19-40

c 2:4. cf. Ps. 17:3; Prov. 21:2.

d 2:7. Some mss. read *gentle*.

e 2:7. cf. Deut. 22:6.

the Judean leaders, 15who killed both the
Lord *Yeshua* and the prophets and drove
us out.[a] They are not pleasing to God and
hostile to all people, 16hindering us from
speaking to the Gentiles so that they
might be saved. As a result, they constantly fill up the measure of their sins.
But wrath has come upon them at last.

Longing to Visit and Reassure

17But brothers and sisters, after we
were orphaned by separation from you
for a short time (in person, not in heart),
we were all the more eager in our great
longing to see you face to face. 18For we
wanted to come to you—I, Paul, more
than once—but satan thwarted us.
19For who is our hope or joy or crown of
boasting[b] before our Lord *Yeshua* at His
coming? Is it not you? 20For you are our
glory and joy!

3

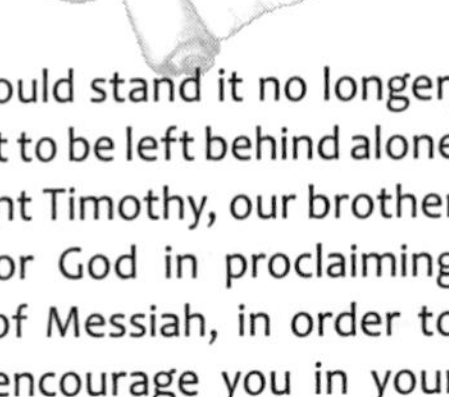

1So when we could stand it no longer,
we thought it best to be left behind alone
in Athens. 2We sent Timothy, our brother
and co-worker for God in proclaiming
the Good News of Messiah, in order to
strengthen and encourage you in your
faith, 3so that no one would be shaken
by these afflictions. For you yourselves
know we are destined for this. 4For even
when we were with you, we kept telling
you in advance that we were going to suffer persecution— just as has happened,
as you know. 5For this reason, when I
could stand it no longer, I sent to find out
about your faithfulness, for fear that the
tempter had tempted you and that our
labor might be in vain.

6But now that Timothy has come to
us from you and brought us the good
news of your faithfulness and love, and
that you always have good memories of
us, longing to see us just as we long to
see you— 7because of this, brothers and
sisters, in all our distress and trouble,
we were comforted about you by your
faithfulness. 8For now we live, since you
are standing firm in the Lord. 9For what
thanks would be enough to offer to God,
in return for all the joy we feel before our
God because of you? 10Night time and
day time we keep praying more than ever
to see you face to face,[c] and mend any
shortcomings in your faith.

Thanks, Joy, and Love Before God

11Now may our God and Father Himself and *Yeshua* our Lord direct our way
to you. 12May the Lord also cause you
to increase and overflow in love for one
another and for all people, just as we also
do for you, 13in order to strengthen your
hearts as blameless in holiness before
our God and Father at the coming of our
Lord *Yeshua* with all His *kedoshim*. Amen.

4

Walking in Sanctification

1Finally then, brothers and sisters, we
ask you and appeal in the Lord *Yeshua*—
just as you received from us the way you
ought to walk and please God (as in fact
you are walking)—that you keep progressing more and more.[d] 2For you know
what instructions we gave you through
the Lord *Yeshua*. 3For this is the will of
God—your sanctification:[e]

to abstain from sexual immorality;

4to know, each of you, how to gain
control over his own body[f] in holiness
and honor— 5not in the passion of lust
like the pagans who do not know God;

6and not to overstep his brother and
take advantage of him in this matter—

a 2:15. cf. Acts 17:5-10.
b 2:19. cf. Jer. 9:23-24; Rom. 5:1-2; 15:17.
c 3:10. Lit. *to see your face.*
d 4:1. cf. Jn. 15:8.
e 4:3. cf. Lev. 19:2.
f 4:4. Lit. *possess his own vessel.*

because the Lord is the avenger in all these things, as we told you before and solemnly warned you. 7For God did not call us to impurity, but in holiness. 8Consequently, the one who rejects this is not rejecting man, but God, who gives His *Ruach ha-Kodesh* to you. 9Now concerning brotherly love, you have no need for anyone to write you—for you yourselves are taught by God[a] to love one another. 10In fact, you even practice it toward all your brothers and sisters throughout Macedonia. But we urge you, brothers and sisters, to keep progressing more and more 11and aspire to lead a quiet life, to mind your own affairs, and to work with your hands, just as we directed you— 12so you may behave properly toward outsiders and not have need of anything.

The *Shofar* Call of Messiah's Return

13Now we do not want you to be uninformed, brothers and sisters, about those who are asleep, so that you may not grieve like the rest who have no hope. 14For if we believe that *Yeshua* died and rose again, so with Him God will also bring those who have fallen asleep in *Yeshua*.[b] 15For this we tell you, by the word of the Lord, that we who are alive and remain until the coming of the Lord shall in no way precede those who are asleep. 16For the Lord Himself shall come down from heaven with a commanding shout, with the voice of the archangel and with the blast of God's *shofar*,[c] and the dead in Messiah shall rise first. 17Then we who are alive, who are left behind, will be caught up together with them in the clouds, to meet the Lord in the air—and so we shall always be with the Lord. 18Therefore encourage one another with these words.

a 4:9. cf. Isa. 54:13.
b 4:14. cf. 1 Cor. 15:20.
c 4:16. cf. Exod 19:16(19:16 LXX).

5

Keep Watch for the Day of the Lord

1Now concerning the times and seasons,[d] brothers and sisters, you have no need for anything to be written to you. 2For you yourselves know very well that the Day of the Lord[e] comes like a thief in the night. 3When they are saying, "*Shalom* and safety,"[f] sudden destruction comes upon them like a woman having birth pains in the womb—there is no way they will escape. 4But you, brothers and sisters, are not in the dark, so that the Day might overtake you like a thief.[g] 5For you all are sons of light and sons of day. We are not of night or of darkness— 6so then, let us not sleep as the others do, but let us remain on the alert and sober-minded. 7For those who sleep, sleep at night; and those who get drunk, get drunk at night. 8But since we are of the day, let us be sober-minded—putting on the breastplate of faithfulness and love, and the hope of salvation as a helmet.[h] 9For God did not destine us for wrath but for obtaining salvation through our Lord *Yeshua* the Messiah. 10He died for us so that, whether we may be awake or asleep,[i] we may live together with Him. 11Therefore encourage one another and build each other up—just as you in fact are doing.

Instructions for Community Life

12Now we ask you, brothers and sisters, to recognize those who work hard among you and are over you in the Lord

d 5:1. cf. Dan. 2:21; Acts 1:7.
e 5:2. cf. Isa. 13:6, 9; Ezek 30:3; Joel 1:15, 2:1, 11, Obad. 15, Zeph. 1:14, Mal. 3:23(4:5).
f 5:3. cf. Jer. 6:14; 8:11; Ezek. 13:10.
g 5:4. cf. Job 24:13-17.
h 5:8. cf. Isa 59:17.
i 5:10. Or *whether we may be alive or dead.*

and correct[a] you, [13]and to esteem them
beyond all measure in love because of their
work. Keep *shalom* among yourselves.
[14]We urge you, brothers and sisters,
correct the unruly, comfort the faint-
hearted, help the weak, be patient with
everyone. [15]See that no one repays evil
for evil to anyone, but always pursue
what is good for one another and for all.

[16]Rejoice always,

[17]pray constantly,

[18]in everything give thanks; for this is
God's will for you in Messiah *Yeshua*.

[19]Do not quench the Spirit,

[20]do not despise prophetic messages,

[21]but test all things, hold fast to what
is good,

[22]keep away from every kind of evil.

[23]Now may the God of *shalom* Himself
make you completely holy; and may your
whole spirit and soul and body be kept
complete, blameless at the coming of
our Lord *Yeshua* the Messiah. [24]Faithful is
the One who calls you—and He will make
it happen!

Closing Greetings

[25]Brothers and sisters, pray for us.

[26]Greet all the brothers and sisters
with a holy kiss. [27]I charge you under
oath, by the Lord, that this letter be read
to all the brothers and sisters.

[28]The grace of our Lord *Yeshua* the
Messiah be with you.[b]

---

a 5:12. cf. 1 Cor. 4:14.

b 5:28. Some mss. add *Amen.*

Paul's Second Letter to the Thessalonians

Introduction

Paul's second letter to the Thessalonians was written not long after the first one, about the year 50 or 51. The focus this time is on suffering and persecution (1:5), put into perspective by the thought of *Yeshua's* return and judgment on evil. This gives believers a second way to think about the return of the Lord. In First Thessalonians, His return was an encouragement to live a godly life; here, it is an encouragement that in the end God will right all wrongs.

A second focus of the letter concerns some matters that may be connected to the persecution the Thessalonians were experiencing. First, some believed the Day of the Lord—the time of God's final judgment—had already come (2:2), possibly because that Day would be accompanied by great turmoil (such as their persecution) in the world. Paul reminds them that certain things must take place first; this is not yet the end. Second, there were some in the community who had quit their jobs, probably also because they thought the end of the world was happening now. Paul exhorts them all to work, and as in the first letter, holds himself up as a model of behavior (3:7).

Though the Thessalonians were healthy in their faith and even an example for others, that did not mean they were a perfect community. Wrong teaching (concerning the Day of the Lord) and wrong behavior (failing to work for a living) had made inroads. The problem was that some of the Thessalonians had misinterpreted what their sufferings meant. It did not mean the end of the world was upon them. Rather, it meant that they were following *Yeshua* and suffering for the kingdom of God (1:5). But on the whole most of the Thessalonians continued to do well, so that Paul could say that "among God's communities we boast about your perseverance and faith in all the persecutions and trials you are enduring" (1:4). What a wonderful commendation!

A Look Inside 2 Thessalonians

Greetings (1:1)
Troubles From an Eternal
Perspective (1:3)

The Man of Lawlessness (2:1)
Firstfruits of Salvation (2:13)

No Time To Be Lazy (3:6)
Final Words (3:16)

1

Greetings

1Paul, Silvanus,[a] and Timothy,

To the community of the Thessalonians in God our Father and the Lord *Yeshua* the Messiah:

2Grace to you and *shalom* from God our Father and the Lord *Yeshua* the Messiah!

Troubles From an Eternal Perspective

3We ought to always thank God for you, brothers and sisters, as is appropriate, because your faithfulness grows wonderfully, and the love of each one of you for one another continually increases. 4Therefore, we ourselves boast of you among the communities of God—about your perseverance and faithfulness through all the persecutions and troubles that you endure. 5This is evidence of the righteous judgment of God, so that you may be considered worthy of the kingdom of God, for which indeed you are suffering.

(6For after all, it is right in the sight of God to pay back trouble to those who trouble you, 7and relief to you who suffer trouble along with us. At the revelation of the Lord *Yeshua* from heaven with His mighty angels 8in flaming fire,[b] He will command judgment on those who do not know God and do not heed the Good News of our Lord *Yeshua*.[c] 9They will pay the price of eternal ruin, away from the presence of the Lord and the glory of His power[d]— 10on that Day when He comes to be glorified among His *kedoshim* and marveled at by all who have believed,[e] because our testimony to you was believed.)

11With this in mind, we pray for you constantly, that our God may consider you worthy of the calling and fulfill with power every good desire and work of faith, 12so the name of our Lord *Yeshua* may be glorified in you, and you in Him, in keeping with the grace of our God and the Lord *Yeshua* the Messiah.

2

The Man of Lawlessness

1Now we ask you, brothers and sisters, concerning the coming of our Lord *Yeshua* the Messiah and our gathering together to Him, 2not to get shaken out of your mind or disturbed—either by a spirit or a word or a letter as if through us—as though the Day of the Lord[f] has come. 3Let no one deceive you in any way, for the Day will not come unless the rebellion comes first and the man of lawlessness is revealed, the one destined to be destroyed.[g] 4He opposes and exalts himself above every so-called god or object of worship, so that he sits in the Temple of God, proclaiming himself that he is God.[h]

5Don't you remember that when I was still with you I was telling you these things? 6And you know what now holds back, for him to be revealed in his own time. 7For the mystery of lawlessness is already operating; only there is one who holds back just now, until he is taken out of the way. 8Then the lawless one will be revealed. The Lord *Yeshua* will slay him with the breath of His mouth and wipe him out with the appearance of His coming.[i] 9The coming of the lawless one is connected to the activity of satan, with all power and signs and false wonders, 10and with every kind of wicked deception toward those who are perishing. They perish because they did

a 1:1. Or *Silas*; cf. Acts 15:22ff.
b 1:8. cf. Exod. 3:2; 19:18; Isa. 66:15; Ezek. 1:13; Dan. 7:9.
c 1:8. cf. Ps. 79:6; Isa. 66:15; Jer. 10:25.
d 1:9. cf. Isa. 2:10, 19, 21(LXX).
e 1:10. cf. Isa. 24:15; 49:3; 66:5; Mal. 1:11.

f 2:2. cf. Joel 1:15; 2:1,11.
g 2:3. Lit. *son of destruction*; cf. Dan. 7:25; 8:25; 11:36.
h 2:4. cf. Isa. 14:14; Ezek. 28:2.
i 2:8. cf. Isa. 11:4; 30:28, Job 4:9.

not accept the love of the truth so as
to be saved. 11For this reason God sends
them a delusional force, to lead them to
believe what is false,[a] 12so that they may
be judged—all those who did not believe
the truth but delighted in wickedness.[b]

Firstfruits of Salvation

13But we should always give thanks to
God for you, brothers and sisters loved
by the Lord, because God chose you as
firstfruits for salvation[c] through sanctification by the Spirit and belief in the truth.
14He called you to this salvation through
our proclaiming the Good News, for you
to gain the glory of our Lord *Yeshua* the
Messiah. 15So then, brothers and sisters,
stand firm and hold on to the traditions
which you were taught, whether by word
of mouth or by our letter.

16Now may our Lord *Yeshua* the Messiah Himself and God our Father, who
loved us and by grace gave us eternal
comfort and good hope, 17comfort and
strengthen your hearts in every good
deed and word.

3

1Finally, brothers and sisters, pray for
us that the word of the Lord may spread
quickly and be glorified—just as it is with
you. 2Also pray that we may be rescued
from perverse and evil people, for not all
are trustworthy. 3But the Lord is trustworthy—and He will strengthen and
protect you from the evil one. 4We have
confidence in the Lord concerning you,
that you are doing and will keep doing
what we command. 5May the Lord direct
your hearts into the love of God and into
the patience of Messiah.

No Time to Be Lazy

6Now we command you, brothers and
sisters, in the name of our Lord *Yeshua*
the Messiah, to keep away from every
brother who behaves irresponsibly
and not according to the tradition they
received from us. 7For you yourselves
know how you ought to imitate us, for we
did not behave inappropriately among
you. 8And we did not eat anyone's bread
without paying for it, but worked night
and day with labor and hardship, so as
not to burden any of you. 9It wasn't that
we had no right, but rather to offer ourselves as an example for you to imitate.
10For even when we were with you, we
would give you this order: if anyone will
not work, neither shall he eat. 11For we
hear that some among you are behaving
irresponsibly—not busy, but busybodies. 12Now such people we command and
urge in the Lord Messiah *Yeshua* to work
in a quiet demeanor, so they may eat
their own bread. 13But as for you, brothers and sisters, do not grow weary of
doing good.

14If anyone does not obey our message
in this letter, take special note of him and
do not associate with him, so that he
may be put to shame. 15Yet do not consider him as an enemy, but warn him as
a brother.

Final Words

16Now may the Lord of *shalom* Himself
give you *shalom* at all times and in every
way. The Lord be with you all!

17The greeting is in my own hand—
Paul's. It is a sign in every letter—in this
way I write.[d]

18The grace of our Lord *Yeshua* the
Messiah be with you all.[e]

a 2:11. cf. 1 Kings 22:22-23.
b 2:12. cf. Exod. 10:1-2; Rom. 9:22.
c 2:13. cf. 1 Cor. 15:20-23.
d 3:17. cf. 1 Cor. 16:21; Col. 4:18; Gal. 6:11; Phlm. 19.
e 3:18. Some mss. add *Amen*.

Paul's First Letter to Timothy

Introduction

Timothy was a young leader (4:12), who it seemed, had a timid or introverted side. Paul often entrusted him with a mission (see 1 Thessalonians 3:2, Philippians 2:20), trusted him completely as a fellow worker (see 1 Thessalonians 3:2), saw him as a spiritual son (1 Timothy 1:18), and in many letters brings greetings to Messiah's community from Timothy as well as from himself.

In this letter, Paul addresses Timothy personally in order to encourage him. First Timothy is one of Paul's final letters written in the 60s not long before he died. At this point Timothy is in Ephesus (1:3) overseeing the community there. The letter therefore gives us insight into the life of a community in which we might see our own reflection. There are some who are teaching falsehoods or arguing over unessential matters (1:3), and Timothy is to tell them to cease. On the positive side, Timothy is to encourage prayer (2:10). Paul also sets out the qualification for community leaders (chapter 3), and the implication is that Timothy is to utilize these criteria in overseeing the selection of those leaders (5:22). Treatment of older people, widows, and elders is included, and since it was a personal letter, Paul also addresses Timothy's diet! (5:23).

The letter contains some well-known exhortations and "trustworthy sayings" (1:15), such as: "Messiah *Yeshua* came into the world to save sinners" (1:15), "fight the good fight" (1:18; again at 6:12), and the famous "The love of money is the root of all kinds of evil" (6:10—note, not money in itself, as it is often misquoted). A poem appears in 3:16 summarizing the amazing nature of the Good News. Above all, Timothy is to "guard" his commission (6:20). Paul over and over encourages Timothy to be the man of God he has been called to be, overcoming his natural timidity by God's gifts, a timidity which perhaps allowed him to be too easily influenced by others (6:20 again).

The enduring value of the letter is first, to encourage both men and women, especially those young and a bit uncertain, to live up to their calling, to exercise their gifts, and to live a godly life in the sight of the Lord, "who alone is immortal and who lives in unapproachable light" (6:16). And second, 1 Timothy paints a picture of what a healthy community looks like in its leadership, its treatment of members, and its focus on *Yeshua* and godliness (6:6).

A Look Inside 1 Timothy

Greeting (1:1)
Beware of False Teachers (1:3)
Mercy to the Worst of Sinners (1:12)
Fight the Good Fight (1:18)

Godliness in Prayer and Worship (2:1)

Qualifications for Oversight
and Service (3:1)

Advice to a Young Leader (4:1)

Giving Honor in the Community (5:1)

Finding True Riches (6:3)

1

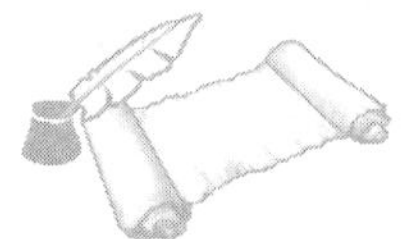

Greeting

[1]Paul, a *shaliach* of Messiah *Yeshua* by the command of God our Savior and Messiah *Yeshua*, our hope.

[2]To Timothy, a true child in faith:

Grace, mercy, *shalom* from God the Father and Messiah *Yeshua*, our Lord!

Beware of False Teachers

[3]As I urged you, when I was leaving for Macedonia, stay in Ephesus to direct certain people not to pass on different instruction, [4]or to pay attention to myths and endless genealogies. These give rise to useless speculations rather than God's training which is in faithfulness. [5]Now the goal of this command is love from of a pure heart and a clear conscience and a genuine faith. [6]Some, having missed the mark, have turned away to fruitless discussion— [7]wanting to be teachers of *Torah*, even though they do not understand what they keep saying or what they so dogmatically assert.

[8]But we know that the *Torah* is good if one uses it legitimately, [9]knowing that the *Torah* is not given for a *tzaddik* but for the lawless and rebellious, for the ungodly and sinful, for the unholy and worldly, for those who kill their fathers or mothers, for murderers, [10]the sexually immoral, homosexuals, slave-traders, liars, perjurers, and for anything else that opposes sound teaching— [11]in keeping with what was entrusted to me, the glorious Good News of the blessed God.

Mercy to the Worst of Sinners

[12]I thank Messiah *Yeshua* our Lord, who has strengthened me, because He considered me faithful, appointing me to service— [13]even though I was formerly a blasphemer, a persecutor, and a violent man. Yet I was shown mercy because I had acted ignorantly in unbelief, [14]and the grace of our Lord overflowed with the faith and love that are in Messiah *Yeshua*. [15]Trustworthy is the saying and deserving of complete acceptance: "Messiah *Yeshua* came into the world to save sinners"—of whom I am foremost. [16]Yet for this reason I was shown mercy—so that in me as the foremost, Messiah *Yeshua* might demonstrate His complete patience, as an example for those about to put their trust in Him for eternal life. [17]Now to the King eternal, immortal, invisible, the only God,[a] be honor and glory forever and ever. Amen.

Fight the Good Fight

[18]This charge I entrust to you, Timothy my son, in keeping with the prophecies once spoken about you, so that by them you fight the good fight, [19]holding onto faith and a good conscience. By rejecting these, some have suffered shipwreck regarding their faith. [20]Among these are Hymenaeus and Alexander—whom I have handed over to satan to be disciplined not to blaspheme.

2

Godliness in Prayer and Worship

[1]Therefore, first of all I urge that requests, prayers, intercessions, and thanksgiving be made on behalf of all people— [2]for kings and all who are in authority[b]—so we may live a peaceful and quiet life in all godliness and respectfulness. [3]This is good and pleasing in the sight of God our Savior. [4]He desires all men to be saved and come into the knowledge of the truth.[c] [5]For

there is one God[d]

and there is one Mediator between God and men[e]—

a 1:17. Some mss. read *the only wise God*.
b 2:2. cf. Ezra 6:10.
c 2:4. cf. Ezek. 18:23, 32.
d 2:5. cf. Deut. 6:4.
e 2:5. cf. Isa. 41:14, 49:7.

a human, Messiah *Yeshua*,
6who gave Himself as a ransom for all[a]—
the testimony at the proper time.
7For this I was appointed a herald and a *shaliach* (I am telling the truth; I am not lying), a teacher of the Gentiles in faithfulness and truth.

8So I desire all men to pray everywhere, lifting up holy hands,[b] without anger and argument. 9Likewise, women
are to adorn themselves in appropriate clothing with modesty and sound judgment—not in seductive hairstyles[c] and gold or pearls or costly clothing, 10but
what is suitable for women claiming godliness, through good deeds. 11Let a woman
receive training in a quiet demeanor with complete respect for order. 12But I do
not allow a woman to train or dictate to a man, but to be in a quiet demeanor.
13For Adam was formed first, then Eve.[d]
14Also Adam was not deceived but the woman—being deceived, she fell into transgression.[e] 15Nevertheless, she will
be sustained through childbearing[f]—if they continue in faithfulness and love and holiness, with sound judgment.

3

Qualifications for Oversight and Service

1Trustworthy is the saying: "If any man aspires to the office of overseer,[g] he desires a good work." 2An overseer,
then, must be beyond criticism—the husband of one wife, clear-minded, self-controlled, respectable, hospitable, able to teach, 3not addicted to wine, not violent but gentle, peaceable, free from the love of money, 4managing his own
household well, keeping his children under control with all respectfulness.
5(But if someone does not know how to manage his own household, how will he care for God's community?) 6He must not
be a new believer,[h] or he may become puffed up and fall into the same judgment as the devil. 7Furthermore, he must
have a good reputation with those outside, so that he will not fall into disgrace and the devil's trap.

8*Shammashim* likewise must be dignified, not double-speaking, not addicted to much wine, not greedy for dishonest
gain. 9They must keep hold of the mystery of the faith with a clear conscience.
10Also let them first be tested—then let those who are blameless serve as
shammashim. 11Women likewise must be dignified, not backbiting; clear-minded,
trustworthy in every respect. 12Let
shammashim be husbands of one wife, managing their children and their own
households well. 13For those who have served well as *shammashim* gain for themselves a good standing and great confidence in the faith that is in Messiah *Yeshua*.

14These things I write to you, hoping
to come to you shortly. 15But if I delay, I write so you may know how one ought to conduct himself in the household of God—which is the community of the living God, a pillar and foundation of truth.
16Now beyond question, great is the mystery of godliness:

He was revealed in the flesh,
Vindicated in the Spirit,
Seen by angels,
Proclaimed among the nations,
Trusted throughout the world,
Taken up in glory.

4

Advice to a Young Leader

1Now the Spirit clearly says that in later times some will fall away from the faith,

a 2:6. cf. Mk. 10:45.
b 2:8. cf. Ps. 63:4.
c 2:9. Lit. *braided hair.*
d 2:13. cf. Gen. 2:7, 22.
e 2:14. cf. Gen. 3:6.
f 2:15. cf. Gen. 3:16.
g 3:1. cf. Num. 4:16(LXX); 31:14(LXX).
h 3:6. Lit. *newly planted* (Grk. neofutos).

following deceitful spirits and teachings of demons [2]through the hypocrisy of false speakers—whose own conscience has been seared. [3]They forbid people to marry; they command people to abstain from foods that God created for the faithful to share with thanksgiving, having come to know the truth. [4]For everything created by God is good, and nothing is to be rejected if it is received with thanksgiving; [5]for it is sanctified through the word of God and prayer.

[6]In pointing out these things to the brothers and sisters, you will be a good servant of Messiah *Yeshua*, nourished in the words of the faith and the sound teaching that you have been following. [7]But avoid godless myths and old wives' tales; instead, train yourself in godliness. [8]For physical exercise has some benefit; but godliness is beneficial for all things, holding promise for both the present life and the one to come. [9]Trustworthy is the saying and deserving of complete acceptance [10](for to this end we work hard and strive): "We have set our hope on the living God, who is the Savior of all people, especially those who trust." [11]Insist on these things and teach them.

[12]Let no one look down on your youthfulness, but become an example of the faithful—in speech, in conduct, in love, in faithfulness, and in purity. [13]Until I come, devote yourself to the public reading of Scripture, to encouragement, and to teaching. [14]Do not neglect the spiritual gift[a] within you, which was given to you through prophecy with the laying on of hands of the elders. [15]Practice these things—be absorbed in them, so that your progress may be clear to all. [16]Give attention to yourself and your teaching. Persevere in these things, for in doing so you will save yourself[b] and those who hear you.

a 5:14. Grk. *charisma*.
b 4:16. cf. 2 Tim. 4:18.

5

Giving Honor in the Community

[1]Never speak harshly to an older man[c] but appeal to him as a father; to younger men as brothers; [2]older women as mothers; and younger women as sisters—with complete purity.

[3]Honor widows who are really widows— [4]but if any widow has children or grandchildren, they must first learn to show devotion to their own home and give back to their parents, for this is pleasing before God. [5]Now she who is really a widow and has been left alone, has put her hope in God and continues in petitions and prayers night and day. [6]But she who is self-indulgent is dead even while she lives. [7]Insist on these things, so that they might be beyond criticism. [8]But if anyone does not provide for his own, especially those in his own house, he has denied the faith and is worse than an unbeliever.

[9]Let a widow be listed only if she is at least sixty, was the wife of one husband, [10]well known for good deeds, if she raised children, if she showed hospitality, if she washed the feet of the *kedoshim*, if she helped those in trouble, and if she devoted herself to every good work.

[11]But refuse younger widows; for when their sensual desires draw them away from the Messiah, they want to get married— [12]facing judgment because they have set aside their previous pledge. [13]And at the same time, they also learn to be idle, going around from house to house—and not just idle, but also gossipers and busybodies, saying things they should not. [14]Therefore, I want the younger widows to get married, have children, manage a household, and give

c 5:1. cf. Lev. 19:32.

no opportunity to the enemy for slander. 15For some have already gone astray after satan. 16If any woman of faith has widows in need, let her help them and not let the community be burdened, so it may help the real widows.

17The elders who lead well are worthy of honor and honorarium[a]—especially those who work hard in the word and teaching. 18For the Scripture says, "You shall not muzzle the ox while he is threshing,"[b] and, "The worker is worthy of his wage."[c] 19Do not accept an accusation against an elder except on the evidence of two or three witnesses.[d] 20Correct those who continue sinning in the presence of everyone, so that the rest also may fear.[e]

21I solemnly charge you—before God and Messiah *Yeshua* and the chosen angels—to observe these things without taking sides, doing nothing out of favoritism. 22Do not lay hands on anyone hastily or take part in the sins of others—keep yourself pure. 23(No longer drink only water, but use a little wine for your stomach and for your frequent ailments.)

24The sins of some people are obvious, going before them into judgment; but for others, their sins follow. 25Likewise, good deeds are obvious, and the others cannot stay hidden.

6

1Let all who are under the yoke as slaves consider their own masters worthy of full respect, so that God's name and our teaching may not be slandered. 2And let those who have believing masters not disrespect them because they are brothers, but serve them even more, since those who share in the benefit are believers and loved. Teach and encourage these things.

Finding True Riches

3If anyone passes on a different teaching and does not agree with sound words, those of our Lord *Yeshua* the Messiah, and with the instruction in keeping with godliness, 4he is prideful, understanding nothing. Instead he is obsessed with arguments and disputes about words—out of which come envy, strife, slander, evil suspicions, 5and constant friction between people corrupted in mind and deprived of the truth, who suppose that godliness is a means of gain.

6Now godliness with contentment is
great gain.[f]
7For we brought nothing into this
world,
So we cannot take anything out of
it.[g]
8But having food and clothing,
with these things we shall be
content.[h]

9But those who want to be rich fall into temptation and a trap and many foolish and harmful desires that plunge men into ruin and destruction.[i] 10For the love of money is the root of all kinds of evil—some, longing for it, have gone astray from the faith and pierced themselves through with many sorrows.

11But you, O man of God, flee from these things and pursue righteousness, godliness, faithfulness, love, perseverance, and gentleness. 12Fight the good fight of faith! Take hold of the eternal life—you were called to it, and you made the good confession for it in the presence of many witnesses. 13I charge you before God who gives life to all things and Messiah *Yeshua* who testified the good confession before Pontius Pilate, 14to keep this command without spot or blame until the appearing of our Lord *Yeshua* the Messiah. 15This He will reveal

a 5:17. Lit. *double honor*.
b 5:18a. Deut. 25:4.
c 5:18b. Lev. 19:13; Deut. 24:15; cf. Lk. 10:7.
d 5:19. cf. Deut. 17:6; 19:15; Matt. 18:16.
e 5:20. cf. Matt. 18:17.

f 1:6. cf. Ps. 37:16; Prov, 15:16; 16:8.
g 1:7. cf. Job 1:21; Ps. 49:17; Eccles. 5:15.
h 1:8. cf. Prov. 30:8.
i 1:9. cf. Prov. 15:27; 23:4; 28:20.

in His own time—the blessed and only
Ruler, the King of kings and the Lord
of lords,[a] 16who alone has immortality,
dwelling in unapproachable light, whom
no man has seen or is able to see.[b] To Him
be honor and eternal dominion! Amen.

17Direct those who are rich in this present age not to be proud or to fix their
hope on the uncertainty of riches,[c] but
rather on God—who richly provides us
with everything to enjoy. 18Direct them
to do good, to be rich in good deeds, to
be generous, sharing, 19storing up for
themselves a good foundation for the
future, so they might take hold of the
true life.

20O Timothy, guard what has been
entrusted to you, turning away from
pointless chatter and the contradictions
of so-called knowledge—21by professing
it, some have missed the mark concerning the faith.

Grace be with you.

a 1:15. cf. Deut. 10:17; Ps 136:2-3,
b 1:16. cf. Ex. 33:20.
c 1:17. cf. Ps. 62:10.

Paul's Second Letter to
Timothy

Introduction

Paul wrote 2 Timothy in the 60s, a short time after 1 Timothy, and in the knowledge that he would soon be executed by Rome (4:6). As in other letters, Paul's own attitude is a model for anyone undergoing persecution or even martyrdom—a situation not common in the West but well known to believers in many other countries.

From this letter we learn that Timothy is a third-generation Jewish believer on his mother's side (1:5; compare Acts 16:1, 3). As in the first letter to Timothy, Paul encourages him to use the gifting God has given him, not giving in to his natural timidity but being bold in the Lord (1:6-8).

In the end, Paul focuses not on Timothy's own gifts and personality, but on what God has done in the Messiah. "I know in whom I have trusted," Paul says (1:12), Timothy is to guard the the good entrusted to him (1:14) so that it can be passed along to others in a kind of chain of proclamation (2:2). Paul describes the life of a believer with powerful images: we are like soldiers who need to endure hardship and obey our superior (2:3-4); we are like athletes in a spiritual contest who need to follow the rules; we are like farmers who work hard to see a harvest of crops. In other words, the believing life takes work and endurance; it takes obedience to the Lord; it takes following the "rules"—by which Paul means not a list of things to do but the basic unshakeable reality of the Good News which alone can bring us to the "finish line" of life.

Some of Paul's admonitions repeat what he said in the first letter: avoid needless controversies (2:14, 23), false teaching (2:17) and ungodly behavior (2:22). But here in 2 Timothy is also found the well-known verses (3:16-17) concerning the Scriptures: "All Scripture is inspired by God and useful for teaching, for reproof, for restoration, and for training in righteousness, so that the person belonging to God may be capable, fully equipped for every good deed." The believer's life is one of fighting for what is right (4:7), enduring hardships (4:5) and suffering (1:8) in the face of continued ungodliness, but above all in looking to God and "the salvation that is in Messiah *Yeshua* with eternal glory" (2:10).

A Look Inside 2 Timothy

1

Greeting

[1]Paul, a *shaliach* of Messiah *Yeshua* through the will of God, according to the promise of life in Messiah *Yeshua.*

[2]To Timothy my beloved child:

Grace, mercy, and *shalom* from God the Father and Messiah *Yeshua* our Lord!

Stir up God's Charisma in You

[3]I thank God, whom I serve with a clear conscience as my forefathers did, when I continually remember you in my prayers night and day. [4]I remember your tears, and I long to see you so that I may be filled with joy. [5]I recall the genuine faithfulness within you, which first lived in your grandmother Lois and your mother Eunice, and I am sure it is within you as well. [6]For this reason I remind you to fan into flame the gift[a] of God, which is in you through the laying on of my hands. [7]For God has not given us a spirit of timidity but of power and love and self-discipline.

Suffer with Me—for the Good News!

[8]Therefore do not be ashamed of the testimony of our Lord or of me His prisoner, but share in suffering for the Good News according to the power of God.

[9]He has saved us
and called us with a holy calling—
not because of our deeds
but because of His own purpose
and grace.
This grace was given to us
in Messiah *Yeshua*
before time began,
[10]but now has been revealed
through the appearing of our Savior
Messiah *Yeshua*.
Indeed, He nullified the power of
death

and brought life and immortality to light through the Good News.

[11]For this Good News I was appointed a herald and a *shaliach* and a teacher. [12]For this reason I also am suffering these things—but I am not ashamed, for I know in whom I have trusted and I am convinced He is able to safeguard what I have entrusted to Him until that Day.

[13]Keep the standard of sound words you have heard from me, in the faithfulness and love that are in Messiah *Yeshua*. [14]Guard the good that has been entrusted to you, through the *Ruach ha-Kodesh* who dwells in us.

[15]You are aware that everyone in Asia has turned away from me—including Phygelus and Hermogenes. [16]May the Lord grant mercy to the household of Onesiphorus, because he often refreshed me and was not ashamed of my imprisonment. [17]On the contrary, when he was in Rome he zealously searched for me and found me. [18]May the Lord grant him to find mercy from the Lord in that day! You know very well how much he served in Ephesus.

2

Disciples from Generation to Generation

[1]Therefore, my child, be strengthened in the grace that is in Messiah *Yeshua.* [2]And what you have heard from me among many witnesses, entrust to faithful people who will be capable to teach others also. [3]Suffer hardship with me, as a good soldier of Messiah *Yeshua*. [4]No one serving as a soldier entangles himself in the activities of everyday life, so that he might please the one who enlisted him. [5]Also, if anyone competes as an athlete, he is not crowned victorious unless he

a 1:6. Grk. *charisma.*

competes according to the rules. 6The
hard-working farmer ought to receive
the first share of the crops. 7Consider
what I am saying, for the Lord will give
you understanding in everything.

8Remember *Yeshua* the Messiah, raised
from the dead, from the seed of David—
according to my Good News. 9For this I
suffer hardship as a criminal, even to the
point of chains—though the word of
God is not chained. 10Therefore I endure
everything for the sake of the chosen, so
they might obtain the salvation that is in
Messiah *Yeshua* with eternal glory.

11Trustworthy is the saying:

If we died with Him,
  we will also live with Him;
12if we endure,
  we will also reign with Him;
if we deny Him,
  He will also deny us;
13if we are faithless,
  He remains faithful,
  for He cannot deny Himself.

A Workman with the Word

14Remind them of these things and
solemnly charge them before God not to
quarrel about words, which is useless—
to the ruin of those who are listening.
15Make every effort to present yourself before God as tried and true, as an
unashamed worker cutting a straight
path with the word of truth.[a] 16But
avoid godless chatter, for it will lead to
further ungodliness 17and their words
will spread like cancer. Among them are
Hymeneaus and Philetus— 18men who
have missed the mark concerning the
truth, saying that the resurrection has
already taken place. They are overturn-
ing the faith of some. 19Nevertheless,
the firm foundation of God stands, having this seal: "The Lord knows those
who are His,"[b] and, "Let everyone who
names the name of the Lord keep away
from unrighteousness."[c] 20Now in a
great house there are not only vessels
of gold and silver, but also of wood and
clay—some for honor and some for common use. 21Therefore, if anyone cleanses
himself from these, he will be a vessel for
honor—sanctified, useful to the Master,
prepared for every good work.

22Now flee from youthful desires;
instead, pursue righteousness, faithfulness, love, and *shalom*, with those who
call on the Lord from a pure heart. 23But
avoid foolish and ignorant disputes,
knowing that they produce quarrels.
24The Lord's slave must not be quarrelsome, but be kind to all, able to teach,
tolerant. 25Let him give guidance with
humility to those who are in opposition—perhaps God may grant them a
change of mind, leading to the knowledge of truth. 26Then they may regain
their senses and escape the devil's snare,
in which they had been held captive by
him to do his will.

3

Opposition in the Last Days

1But understand this, that in the last
days[d] hard times will come— 2for people
will be lovers of self, lovers of money,
boastful, arrogant, blasphemers, disobedient to parents, ungrateful, unholy,
3hardhearted, unforgiving, backbiting,
without self-control, brutal, hating what
is good, 4treacherous, reckless, conceited, lovers of pleasure rather than
lovers of God, 5holding to an outward
form of godliness but denying its power.
Avoid these people! 6For among these
are those who slip into households and
deceive weak women weighed down
with sins, led away by various desires,
7always learning yet never able to come
to the knowledge of truth. 8Just as
Jannes and Jambres opposed Moses,[e] so

a 2:15. cf. Isa. 40:3, 9.
b 2:19a. cf. Num. 16:5.
c 2:19b. cf. Num 16:26.
d 3:1. Heb. *acharit ha-yamim*.
e 3:7. cf. Exod. 7:11-12 (Aram., *Targum Jonathan*).

do these people oppose the truth, men corrupted in mind and worthless concerning the faith. [9]But these people will not make any more progress—for their folly, like that of Jannes and Jambres, will be obvious to everyone.

[10]You, however, closely followed my teaching, manner of life, purpose, faithfulness, patience, love, perseverance— [11]as well as persecutions and sufferings that happened to me in Antioch, Iconium, and Lystra. What persecutions I endured! And the Lord rescued me from them all! [12]Indeed, all who desire to live a godly life in Messiah *Yeshua* will be persecuted. [13]But evil men and imposters will go from bad to worse, deceiving and being deceived.

All Scripture Equips God's People

[14]You, however, continue in what you have learned and what you have become convinced of. For you know from whom you have learned, [15]and that from childhood you have known the sacred writings that are able to make you wise, leading to salvation through trusting in Messiah *Yeshua*. [16]All Scripture is inspired by God[a] and useful for teaching, for reproof, for restoration, and for training in righteousness, [17]so that the person belonging to God may be capable, fully equipped for every good deed.

4

[1]I solemnly charge you—in the presence of God and Messiah *Yeshua*, who is about to judge the living and the dead at His appearing and His Kingdom— [2]proclaim the Word! Be ready when it is convenient or inconvenient.[b] Confront, rebuke, encourage—with complete patience and instruction. [3]For the time will come when they will not put up with sound instruction, but they will pile up for themselves teachers in keeping with their own desires, to have their ears tickled. [4]And they will turn away from hearing the truth and wander off to myths. [5]You, however, keep a clear mind in all things, withstand hardship, do the work of proclaiming the Good News, and fulfill your service.

Finishing the Fight, Receiving the Crown

[6]For I am already being poured out like a drink offering, and the time of my departure has come. [7]I have fought the good fight, I have finished the course, I have kept the faith. [8]In the future there is reserved for me a crown of righteousness, which the Lord, the righteous Judge, will award to me on that day—and not to me only, but also to everyone who has longed for His appearing.

[9]Do all you can to come to me quickly— [10]for Demas, having loved this world, has deserted me and gone to Thessolonica; Crescens has gone to Galatia, and Titus to Dalmatia. [11]Luke is the only one with me. Get Mark and bring him with you, for he is useful to me for service. [12]I have sent Tychius to Ephesus. [13]When you come, bring the cloak which I left with Carpus in Troas, along with the scrolls, and especially the parchments. [14]Alexander the coppersmith did me much harm—the Lord will repay him according to his deeds. [15]Be on guard against him too, for he vehemently opposed our message.

[16]At my first defense, no one stood by me; instead, they all deserted me—may it not be counted against them! [17]But the Lord stood by me and strengthened me, so that through me the message might be proclaimed in full measure, and all the nations might hear—and I was rescued from the lion's mouth![c] [18]The Lord will rescue me from every evil deed and will deliver me safely into His heavenly

a 3:16. Or *God-breathed*.
b 4:2. Lit. *in season, out of season*.
c 4:17. cf. Ps. 7:3(2); Dan. 6:21(20), 28(27).

Kingdom. To Him be the glory forever
and ever. Amen.

Final Greetings

[19]Greet Prisca and Aquila, and the
household of Onesiphorus. [20]Erastus
stayed in Corinth, and I left Trophimus
sick in Miletus. [21]Do all you can to come
before winter. Eubulus sends you greetings, as do Pudens, Linus, Claudia, and all
the brothers and sisters. [22]The Lord be
with your spirit. Grace be with you.

Paul's Letter to
Titus

Introduction

Titus is another personal letter of Paul, again probably from the mid-60s, this time written to Titus, who was a Gentile (see Galatians 2:3) and a longtime co-worker of Paul (see Galatians 2:1, 2 Corinthians 8:23). Paul had left Titus on the island of Crete to "straighten out what was left unfinished" as well as to "appoint elders in every city" (1:5). Presumably Paul's unfinished business included putting leadership in place in the various communities, a task now entrusted to Titus.

Much of the letter repeats what we have seen in 1 and 2 Timothy: the criteria for being an elder, the problem of ungodly people insisting on false teaching and useless debates, relationships between young and old. One contrast with Timothy's situation is that the communities in Crete were recently formed, with leadership not even in place. And the description of the inhabitants of Crete as "always liars, evil beasts, lazy gluttons," while sounding harsh to us in the 21st century, reminds us that the Good News can radically transform anyone no matter what their background.

And once again, we find false teachers, this time belonging to the "circumcision group" (1:10-11). Perhaps there were some who still insisted that Gentiles needed to become Jews to be saved—but Titus was a case in point that they did not need to.

One of the most well-known biblical phrases to be found in this letter is in 2:13: the "blessed hope," described as the appearing of *Yeshua*, who is here called both God and Savior. Until that wonderful day, we are to live according to God's will, both leaders (the elders Titus is to appoint) and the average, everyday person (some of whom were liars and gluttons!). Whether leader or follower, it is only God's grace that saves us and sustains us (2:11; 3:7).

A Look inside Titus

Greetings (1:1)
Setting the Community in Order (1:5)

Advice for Behavior in Community (2:1)

Be Ready for Good Deeds (3:1)
Final Words (3:12)

1

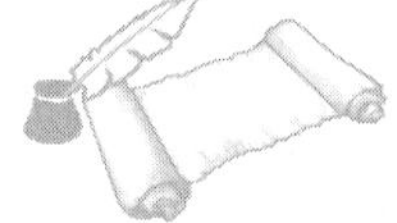

Greetings

[1]Paul, a slave of God and a *shaliach* of Messiah *Yeshua*, for the faith of God's chosen and the knowledge of truth that is in keeping with godliness, [2]based on the hope of eternal life. God—who cannot lie[a]—promised this before the beginning of time. [3]But in His own time He made His message known, through a proclamation with which I was entrusted, by the command of God our Savior.

[4]To Titus, a true child of our common faith:

Grace and shalom from God the Father and Messiah Yeshua, our Savior!

Setting the Community in Order

[5]The reason I left you in Crete was so that you would set in order the things that remain and appoint elders in every city as I directed you— [6]if anyone is blameless, the husband of one wife, having children of faith with no charge of wild living or rebellion. [7]For the overseer must be blameless as God's administrator—not arrogant, not quick-tempered, not addicted to wine, not violent, not greedy for dishonest gain. [8]Rather he must be hospitable, loving what is good, self-controlled, upright, devout, disciplined. [9]He must hold firmly to the trustworthy message in keeping with the teaching, so he can both encourage by instruction that is sound and convict those who speak against it.

[10]For there are many who are rebellious, vain talkers and deceivers, especially those from the circumcision. [11]They must be silenced—those who upset entire households by teaching what they should not, for the sake of dishonest gain. [12]One of them, one of their own prophets, said, "Cretans are always liars, evil beasts, lazy gluttons." [13]This testimony is true. For this reason rebuke them sharply, so they might be sound in the faith, [14]not paying attention to Judaic myths and commands of men who turn away from the truth. [15]To the pure all things are pure; but to those who are defiled and unbelieving, nothing is pure. Both their mind and conscience are defiled. [16]They claim to know God but their deeds deny Him. They are despicable and disobedient and worthless for any good deed.

a 1:2. cf. Num. 23:19.

2

Advice for Behavior in Community

[1]But as for you, speak things that are fitting for sound instruction. [2]Older men are to be clear-minded, dignified, self-controlled, sound in faith, in love, in patience. [3]Likewise, older women are to be sanctified in demeanor—not backbiting or enslaved to much wine. Let them be teachers of what is good, [4]so that they may train the young women to love their husbands, to love their children, [5]to be self-controlled, pure, managing their household, kind, submitted to their own husbands, so that God's word may not be dishonored.

[6]Likewise urge the younger men to be self-controlled, [7]in all things showing yourself to be an example of good deeds—integrity in instruction, dignity, [8]sound speech beyond criticism—so that an opponent may be put to shame, having nothing bad to say about us.

[9]Urge slaves to submit themselves to their own masters in all things, well-pleasing and not back-talking, [10]not stealing but showing all good faithfulness, so that they may do credit to the teaching about God our Savior in everything.

11For the grace of God has appeared,
bringing salvation to all men, 12training
us to deny ungodliness and worldly
desires and to live in a manner that is self-
controlled and righteous and godly in the
present age. 13We wait for the blessed
hope and appearance of the glory of our
great God and Savior, Messiah *Yeshua*.
14He gave Himself for us so that He might
redeem us from every lawless deed and
so that He might purify for Himself a chosen people, zealous for good deeds.[a] 15So
communicate these things, and encourage and correct with complete authority.
Let no one look down on you.

3

Be Ready for Good Deeds

1Remind the people to be submitted
to rulers and authorities, to be obedient, to be ready for every good deed, 2to
slander no one, without fighting, gentle,
showing every courtesy to all people.
3For we also once were foolish, disobedient, deluded, enslaved to various desires
and pleasures, spending our lives in
malice and envy, hateful and hating one
another.

4But when the kindness of God our Savior
and His love for mankind appeared—
5not by deeds of righteousness
which we had done ourselves,
but because of His mercy—
He saved us through the *mikveh* of rebirth
and renewing of the *Ruach ha-Kodesh*,
6whom He abundantly poured out on us
through Messiah *Yeshua* our Savior,
7so that being set right by His grace,
we might become heirs
with the confident hope of eternal life!

8Trustworthy is the saying, and I want
you to insist on these things, so that
those who have put their trust in God
may be careful to devote themselves to
good deeds. These things are good and
beneficial for people.
9But avoid foolish controversies and
genealogies and strife and disputes
about *Torah*, for they are unprofitable
and useless. 10Dismiss a quarrelsome
person after a first and second warning,
11knowing that such a person is twisted
and is sinning—he is self- condemned.

Final Words

12When I send Artemas or Tychicus to
you, hurry to come to me in Nicopolis,
for I have decided to winter there. 13Send
Zenas the lawyer and Apollos on their
journey with great care, so that nothing
is lacking for them. 14And let our people
learn to devote themselves to doing
mitzvot to meet urgent needs, so they
will not be unfruitful.
15All who are with me greet you. Greet
those who love us in the faith. Grace be
with you all.

a 2:14, cf. Ex 19:5–6; Deut. 26:18.

Philemon

Introduction

Philemon is a very personal letter, yet one that has application to all believers. In Paul's time, slavery was common, though quite different than the racially-based slavery of modern times, and it had even less in common with the "human trafficking" of slaves in many countries today. Household slaves—there were other kinds—could work for their freedom and even do well for themselves after freedom.

Onesimus, a runaway slave of Philemon has come to faith in *Yeshua* through Paul's ministry. Paul is now returning Onesimus to Philemon. In his letter, Paul asks Philemon, a believer, to receive Onesimus as a brother in the faith, and suggests that he might even free Onesimus to serve in ministry with Paul. At the time of this letter Paul was in prison, most likely in Rome in the early 60s of the first century.

In Philemon, Paul sets an example of godly behavior for all believers. Paul appeals to Philemon to receive back Onesimus—not with a heavy hand but as brother to brother. Paul's hope is that Philemon will act towards Onesimus out of the love of God, not simply out of obedience to authority. All three men must make a personal sacrifice: Paul in giving up Onesimus as a useful partner in ministry; Philemon in giving up his pride and rights as a master and receiving Onesimus back, and perhaps even releasing him from slavery; and Onesimus in risking returning to his master with whatever consequences that would entail.

Then there is the question of slavery. Even if it was different than the slavery of modern America, it was not always humane. How then could Paul not call for its abolition? Some think that it was such a part of life that it could not have been abolished at that time, and so Paul does not speak against it. He is more concerned with the personal relationship between Philemon and Onesimus than with an institution he could not do anything about. It is also possible that a *humane* situation in which a master treated his slaves well and his slaves obeyed without rebelling could be a picture of what our own relationship of serving God should be like.

Philemon certainly stimulates discussion on this subject, while at the same time stressing that love and self-sacrifice should characterize all our relationships in life.

A Look Inside Philemon

Greetings to a House Group

1Paul, a prisoner of Messiah *Yeshua*,
and Timothy our brother, to Philemon
our beloved and fellow worker.
2To Apphia our sister, to Archippus our
fellow soldier, and to the community that
meets in your house:
3Grace to you and *shalom* from God
our Father and the Lord Messiah *Yeshua*!

Thanks for Love and Comfort

4I thank my God always when mentioning you in my prayers, 5hearing of your
love and the trust you have toward the
Lord *Yeshua* and all the *kedoshim*. 6May
the fellowship of your faith become
effective, with the recognition of all the
good that is ours in Messiah. 7For I've
received much joy and comfort in your
love, brother, because the hearts of the
kedoshim have been refreshed through
you.

Request for Philemon's Runaway

8Therefore, though I have plenty of
boldness in Messiah to order you to do
what's right, 9yet for love's sake I appeal
to you instead. I, Paul, am an old man
and now also a prisoner belonging to
Messiah *Yeshua*. 10I beg you for my child
Onesimus—for whom I became a spiritual father while in chains. 11He once was
useless to you, but now is useful both to
you and me. 12I sent him back to you—he
is my very heart. 13I really wanted to keep
him with me, so that on your behalf he
might serve me while I am in chains for
the Good News. 14But I didn't want to do
anything without your consent, so that
your goodness wouldn't be by force but
by free will.
15For perhaps he was separated from
you for a while in order that you might
have him back forever, 16no longer as
a slave but more than a slave—as a
beloved brother, especially to me but
even more so to you, both in the flesh
and in the Lord.
17So if you consider me a partner, welcome him as you would welcome me.
18But if he has done you any wrong or
owes you anything, charge that to my
account. 19I, Paul, am writing this with
my own hand: I will repay. (Not to mention that you owe me your very self.)
20Yes, brother, let me have some benefit
from you in the Lord. Refresh my heart
in Messiah.

Added Request and Farewell

21Having confidence in your obedience,
I write to you, knowing that you will do
even more than what I say. 22At the same
time also, prepare a guest room for me—
for I hope that through your prayers I will
be given back to you. 23Epaphras, my fellow prisoner in Messiah *Yeshua*, greets
you. 24So do Mark, Aristarchus, Demas,
and Luke, my fellow workers. 25May the
grace of our Lord Messiah *Yeshua* be with
your spirit. Amen.

The Letter to the Hebrews

Introduction

The Letter to the Hebrews—though the title is not original to the book—is written to Jewish believers in *Yeshua* of the first century, as we can tell from the content. At one time the author, who is not named, was thought to be Paul; but scholars today agree that the author is unknown. Whoever he is, he is thoroughly skilled in his handling of the Greek language, the Septuagint, and Jewish thought—particularly with reference to the Temple service. The date, though not firmly known, appears to be before 70 C.E. We can conclude this from remarks that the old covenant is "close to vanishing" (8:13) and the question "Would they not have ceased to be offered?" (10:2), which suggest that the Temple sacrificial system was still operative.

More important than the author or date is the situation of the Jewish believers being addressed. Despite their maturity and sophistication, some were on the road to abandoning their faith altogether and returning to a Judaism minus *Yeshua*. They were being treated as outsiders or even traitors to the Jewish people (13:13) and undergoing trials and persecution (12:3, 7)—though apparently no one had yet become a martyr (12:4). Others were following strange teachings (13:9) and had even stopped meeting with other believers for worship (10:25). But returning to traditional Judaism would also mean laying aside the faith that *Yeshua* had opened a way into the heavenly sanctuary, allowing for direct access to God and face-to-face prayer (10:19-22).

The author of Hebrews is quite concerned for the faith of these Jewish followers of *Yeshua*. Much of the letter is given to showing that *Yeshua*, the incarnate God of Israel Himself, is greater than anyone else—greater than the angels, greater than Moses, the bringer of a greater covenant with a greater priesthood than before and a greater sacrifice that fully atones for our sins. Since this is true, abandoning *Yeshua* is equivalent to turning away from the God of Israel. Along with the emphasis on *Yeshua* come several passages, illustrated from the *Tanakh*, warning that turning from trust in *Yeshua* will bring consequences. But the author wants to encourage, not scold. He points in chapter 11 to a "hall of fame" of Jewish heroes who followed God in spite of obstacles and even persecution, setting an example for us today. To those who persevere, a Sabbath-rest with the Lord is promised (4:8). And how does perseverance come? By "focusing on *Yeshua*, the initiator and perfecter of faith" (12:2). Amen!

A Look Inside Hebrews

1

Superiority of the Son

[1]At many times and in many ways, God
spoke long ago to the fathers through
the prophets. [2]In these last days He has
spoken to us through a Son,[a] whom He
appointed heir of all things and through
whom He created the universe. [3]This
Son is the radiance of His glory and the
imprint of His being, upholding all things
by His powerful word.[b] When He had
made purification for our sins, He sat
down at the right hand of the Majesty
on high.[c] [4]Thus He became as far above
the angels as the name He has inherited
is more excellent than theirs.

[5]For to which of the angels did God
ever say,

"You are My Son.
Today I have become Your Father"?[d]

And again,

"I will be to Him a Father,
and He will be to Me a Son"?[e]

[6]And again, when He brings the firstborn into the world, He says,

"Let all the angels of God worship
Him."[f]

[7]And regarding the angels He says,

"He makes His angels winds,
and His servants a flame of fire."[g]

[8]But regarding the Son He says,

"Your throne, O God, is forever and
ever,
and a scepter of uprightness is the
scepter of Your Kingdom.
[9]You have loved righteousness and
hated lawlessness;
therefore God, Your God, has
anointed You with the oil of gladness
above Your companions."[h]

[10]And,

"In the beginning, *ADONAI*, You laid the
foundation of the earth,
and the heavens are the works of
Your hands.
[11]They shall pass away, but You remain.
And they will all wear out like
clothing.[i]
[12]And like a robe You will roll them up,
and like clothing they will be
changed;
but You are the same,
and Your years shall never end."[j]

[13]But to which of the angels has He
ever said,

"Sit at My right hand,
until I make Your enemies a footstool[k] for Your feet"?[l]

[14]Are they not all ministering
spirits, sent out for service to those
about to inherit salvation?

2

Warning Not to Drift Away

[1]For this reason it is necessary for us to
pay especially close attention to what we
have heard, so that we do not drift away.
[2]For if the word spoken through angels

a 1:2. cf. Matt. 21:37.
b 1:3. Lit. *the word of His power.*
c 1:3. cf. Ps. 110:1(109:1 LXX).
d 1:5. Ps. 2:7.
e 1:5b 2 Sam. 7:14; 1 Chr. 17:13.
f 1:6. Deut. 32:43(LXX); cf. Ps. 96:7(LXX).
g 1:7. Lit. *He who makes …*; cf. Ps. 104:4(103:4 LXX).
h 1:8-9. Ps. 45:6-7(6-7)(44:7-8 LXX).
i 1:11. cf. Isa. 50:9; 51:6.
j 1:10-12. Ps. 102:26-28(25-27); 101:26-28(LXX).
k 1:13. cf. Isa. 66:1; Mt. 5:35.
l 1:13. cf. Ps. 110:1(109:1 LXX).

proved to be firm, and every violation and disobedience received a just payback, [3]how shall we escape if we neglect so great a salvation? It was first spoken through the Lord and confirmed to us by those who heard. [4]At the same time, God was testifying by signs and wonders and various miracles and gifts of the *Ruach ha-Kodesh*, according to His will.

Yeshua Greater than Angels

[5]For it is not to angels that God has subjected the *olam ha-ba*—about which we speak. [6]But somewhere someone has testified, saying,

"What is man, that You are mindful
of him,
or the son of man, that You care for
him?
[7]For a little while, You made him lower
than the angels.
You crowned him with glory and
honor.
[8]You put all things in subjection underneath his feet."[a]

For when He put all things in subjection to him, He left nothing outside his control. But for now we do not yet see all things subjected to him. [9]But we see One who was made for a little while lower than the angels—namely, *Yeshua*. He is now crowned with glory and honor, because of the death He suffered so that, by the grace of God, He might taste death for everyone.

[10]For it was fitting for God—for whom and through whom all things exist—in leading many sons to glory, to perfect through sufferings the initiator of their salvation. [11]For both He who sanctifies and those being sanctified are all from one—so He is not ashamed to call them brothers and sisters,[b] [12]saying,

"I will proclaim Your name to My
brothers and sisters.
In the midst of the congregation I
will sing praise to You."[c]

[13]And again,

"I will put My trust in Him."[d]

And again,

"Here am I and the children God has
given Me."[e]

[14]Therefore, since the children share in flesh and blood, He Himself likewise shared the same humanity—so that through death He might break the power of the one who had the power of death (that is, the devil) [15]and free those who by fear of death were in bondage all their lives. [16]For surely He is not concerned about angels, but about the seed of Abraham. [17]Therefore He had to be made like His brothers in all things, so He might become a merciful and faithful *Kohen Gadol* in matters relating to God, to make atonement for the sins of the people.[f] [18]Because He Himself suffered when put to the test, He is able to help those being tested.

3

Yeshua Greater than Moses

[1]Therefore, holy brothers and sisters, partners in a heavenly calling, take notice of *Yeshua*—the *Shaliach* and *Kohen Gadol* we affirm. [2]He was faithful to the One who appointed Him in His house—as was Moses also.[g] [3]For He has been considered worthy of more glory than Moses, even as the builder of the house has more honor than the house. [4]For

a 2:5-8. Ps. 8:4-6 (5-7 LXX); cf. Gen. 1:26-30.
b 2:11, 12; 3:1, 12; 10:19; 13:22. Lit. *brothers* (in Messiah's community).
c 2:12. Ps. 22:23(22) (21:23 LXX); cf. Mk. 8:38; Lk. 9:26; Heb. 11:16.
d 2:13. Isa. 8:17; 12:2(LXX).
e 2:13. Isa. 8:18(LXX).
f 2:17. cf. Lev. 4:20, 26, 31; 5:10; 16:16, 33-34; Dan. 9:24.
g 3:2. cf. Num. 12:7.

every house is built by someone, but the builder of all things is God. [5]Now Moses surely was faithful in all God's house as a servant, for a witness of things to be spoken later. [6]But Messiah, as Son, is over God's house—and we are His house, if we hold firm to our boldness and what we are proud to hope.

Listen and Obey, or Harden and Fall Away

[7]Therefore, just as the *Ruach ha-Kodesh* says,
"Today if you hear His voice,
[8]do not harden your hearts as in the rebellion,[a]
on the day of testing[b] in the wilderness.
[9]There your fathers put Me to the test,
though they saw My works for forty years.
[10]Therefore I was provoked by this generation,
and I said, 'They always go astray in their heart,
and they have not known My ways.'
[11]As I swore in my wrath,
'They shall not enter My rest.'"[c]

[12]Take care, brothers and sisters, that none of you has an evil heart of unbelief that falls away from the living God. [13]But encourage one another day by day—as long as it is called "Today"—so that none of you may be hardened by the deceitfulness of sin. [14]For we have become partners of Messiah, if we hold our original conviction firm until the end. [15]As it is said,

"Today if you hear His voice,
do not harden your hearts as in the rebellion."[d]

[16]Now which ones heard and rebelled? Indeed, was it not all who came out of Egypt with Moses? [17]And with whom was He provoked for forty years? Was it not with those who sinned, whose bodies fell in the wilderness? [18]And to whom did He swear that they would not enter His rest? Was it not to those who were disobedient? [19]So we see that they were not able to enter in because of lack of trust.

a 3:8. Meribah; cf. Exod. 17:1ff.
b 3:8. Massah; cf. Num. 20:1ff.
c 3:7-11. Ps. 95:7c-11.
d 3:15. Meribah; Ps. 95:7c-8.

4

Make Every Effort to Enter God's Rest

[1]Let us fear then! Though a promise of entering His rest is left open, some of you would seem to have fallen short. [2]For we also have had Good News proclaimed to us, just as they did. But the word they heard did not help them, because they were not unified with those who listened in faith. [3]For we who have trusted are entering into that rest. It is just as God has said,

"So in My wrath I swore,
'They shall never enter My rest,'"[e]

even though His works were finished since the foundation of the world. [4]For somewhere He has spoken about the seventh day in this way: "And God rested on the seventh day from all His works,"[f] [5]and again in this passage:

"They shall never enter My rest."[g]

[6]So then it remains for some to enter into it; yet those who formerly had Good News proclaimed to them did not enter because of disobedience. [7]Again, God appoints a certain day—"Today"—saying through David after so long a time, just as it has been said before,

e 4:3. Ps. 95:11(94:11 LXX).
f 4:4. Gen. 2:2; Exod. 20:11; 31:17.
g 4:5. Ps. 95:11b(94:11b LXX).

"Today, if you hear His voice,
do not harden your hearts."[a]

[8]For if Joshua had given them rest, God would not have spoken of another day later on. [9]So there remains a *Shabbat* rest for the people of God. [10]For the one who has entered God's rest has also ceased from his own work, just as God did from His.

[11]Let us, therefore, make every effort to enter that rest, so that no one may fall through the same pattern of disobedience. [12]For the word of God is living and active and sharper than any two-edged sword—piercing right through to a separation of soul and spirit, joints and marrow, and able to judge the thoughts and intentions of the heart. [13]No creature is hidden from Him, but all are naked and exposed to the eyes of Him to whom we must give account.[b]

Yeshua, Our Compassionate *Kohen Gadol*

[14]Therefore, since we have a great *Kohen Gadol* who has passed through the heavens, *Yeshua Ben-Elohim*, let us hold firmly to our confessed allegiance. [15]For we do not have a *kohen gadol* who is unable sympathize with our weaknesses, but One who has been tempted in all the same ways—yet without sin. [16]Therefore let us draw near to the throne of grace with boldness, so that we may receive mercy and find grace for help in time of need.

5

[1]For every *kohen gadol* taken from among men is appointed to act on behalf of people in matters relating to God,[c] so that he may offer gifts and sacrifices for sins. [2]He is able to empathize with the ignorant and deluded, since he himself also is subject to weakness. [3]For this reason he has to make offerings for sins—just as for the people, so also for himself.[d] [4]And no one takes this honor for himself, but only when he is called by God, as Aaron was.[e]

[5]So also Messiah did not glorify Himself to be made *Kohen Gadol*; rather, it was God who said to Him,

"You are My Son;
today I have become Your Father."[f]

[6]And He says in a different passage,

"You are a *kohen* forever,
according to the order of
Melchizedek."[g]

[7]In the days of His life on earth,[h] *Yeshua* offered up both prayers and pleas, with loud crying and tears, to the One able to save Him from death; and He was heard because of His reverence. [8]Though He was a Son, He learned obedience from what He suffered. [9]And once made perfect, He became the source of eternal salvation to all who obey Him— [10]called by God *Kohen Gadol* "according to the order of Melchizedek."[i]

Moving on to Maturity

[11]About this subject there is much for us to say, and it is hard to explain since you have become sluggish in hearing. [12]For although you ought to be teachers by this time, again you need someone to teach you the basics of God's sayings. You have come to need milk, not solid food. [13]For anyone living on milk is inexperienced with the teaching about

a 4:7. Ps. 95:11.
b 4:13. cf. Job 26:6; 34:21; Ps. 33:13-15.
c 5:1. cf. Exod. 28:1.
d 5:3. cf. Lev. 9:7; 16:6.
e 5:4. cf. Num. 16:40; 18:7; 2 Chr. 26:18.
f 5:5. Ps. 2:7.
g 5:6. Ps. 110:4(109:4 LXX).
h 5:7. Lit. *in the days of His flesh.*
i 5:10. Ps. 110:4(109:4 LXX).

righteousness—he is an infant.[a] 14But solid food is for the mature, who through practice have their senses trained to discern both good and evil.

6

1Therefore leaving the basic teaching of the Messiah, let us move on toward maturity—not laying again a foundation of repentance from dead works and of trust in God, 2of teaching about immersions, laying on of hands, resurrection of the dead, and eternal judgment. 3Now this we will do, if God permits.

4For it is impossible for those who once were enlightened—having tasted of the heavenly gift and become partakers of the *Ruach ha-Kodesh*, 5and having tasted the good word of God and the powers of the *olam ha-ba*, 6and then having fallen away—to renew again to repentance, since they are again crucifying *Ben-Elohim* for themselves and publicly disgracing Him. 7For the earth—having soaked up the rain frequently falling on it—brings forth vegetation[b] useful to those for whom it is farmed; and it shares in God's blessing 8But if it produces thorns and thistles, it is worthless and near to being cursed—its end is to be burned over.[c]

9But even though we speak like this, loved ones, concerning you we are convinced of better things[d]—things coming with salvation. 10For God is not unjust so as to forget your work and the love that you showed for His name, in having served and continuing to serve the *kedoshim*. 11But we long for each of you to show the same eagerness for the certainty of hope to the very end— 12so you will not be sluggish,[e] but imitators of those inheriting the promises through trust and perseverance.

The Promise and the Oath

13Now when God made his promise to Abraham—since He could swear by no one greater, He swore by Himself, 14saying, "Surely I will bless you, and surely I will multiply you."[f] 15And so after waiting patiently, Abraham reached the promise.[g] 16For people swear by someone greater; and the oath, as confirmation, is an end to all their disputing. 17In the same way God, determining to point out more clearly to the heirs of the promise the unchanging nature of His purpose, guaranteed it with an oath. 18So by two unchangeable things, in which it is impossible for God to lie,[h] we who have fled for refuge might have strong encouragement to take hold of the hope set before us. 19We have this hope as an anchor of the soul, both firm and steady—a hope that enters the inner place behind the curtain.[i] 20*Yeshua* has entered there as a forerunner on our behalf, having become *Kohen Gadol* "forever, according to the order of Melchizedek."[j]

7

Melchizedek, a *Kohen* Forever

1For this Melchizedek was king of Salem, *kohen* of God Most High. He met Abraham returning from the defeat of the kings and blessed him,[k] 2and to him Abraham apportioned a tenth of everything. First, by the translation of his name, he is "King of Righteousness"[l]; and then also King of Salem, which is "King of *Shalom*." 3Without father, without mother, without genealogy, having

a 5:14. cf. Isa. 7:15.
b 6:7. cf. Deut. 11:11-15; Gen. 13:10.
c 6:8 cf. Deut. 11:16-17, 26-28; Gen. 19:24-26; Deut. 28:15-68; 30:7.
d 6:9. Deut. 30:1-6.
e 6:12. cf. Heb. 2:1; 4:1-2; 5:11.
f 6:14. Gen. 22:17.
g 6:15. cf. Gen. 2:15.
h 6:18. cf. Num. 23:19.
i 6:19. Heb. *parokhet*; cf. Exod. 26:33; Lev. 16:15; Heb. 9:3.
j 6:20. Ps. 110:4(109:4 LXX); Heb. 5:6, 10.
k 7:1-2. See Gen. 14:17-20.
l 7:2. Heb. *Malki-Tzedek*.

neither beginning of days nor end of life but made like *Ben-Elohim*, he remains a *kohen* for all time.

4Now see how great this man is! Even Abraham the patriarch gave him a tenth out of the plunder. 5Indeed, those sons of Levi who receive the priesthood have, according to *Torah*, a command to collect a tithe from the people[a]—that is, from their kin, although they have come out of the loins of Abraham. 6But this one—who did not have their genealogy—has collected tithes from Abraham and has blessed him, the one holding the promises. 7Now it is beyond dispute that the lesser is blessed by the greater. 8In one case, dying men receive tithes; but in the other, one about whom it is testified that he lives on. 9Through Abraham even Levi, the one receiving tithes, has paid the tithe, so to speak— 10for he was still in his father's loins when Melchizedek met him.

Yeshua, Our *Kohen Gadol* Forever

11Now if perfection was through the Levitical priesthood (for based on it the people had been given the *Torah*[b]), what further need was there for a different *kohen* to arise—designated according to the order of Melchizedek, not according to the order of Aaron? 12For whenever the priesthood is altered, out of necessity an alteration[c] of law also takes place. 13For the one about whom these things are said belongs to another tribe, from which no one has officiated at the altar. 14For it is clear that our Lord has sprung forth[d] from Judah—concerning this tribe, Moses said nothing about *kohanim*. 15And it is even more evident, if another *kohen* arises like Melchizedek— 16one made not by virtue of a *Torah* requirement of physical descent,[e] but by virtue of the power of an indestructible life. 17For it is testified,

> "You are a *kohen* forever,
> according to the order of
> Melchizedek."[f]

18For on the one hand, a former requirement is set aside because of its weakness and ineffectiveness— 19for *Torah* made nothing perfect. But on the other hand, a better hope is introduced, through which we draw near to God.

20Moreover, it was not without a sworn oath. (Others indeed have become *kohanim* without a sworn oath, 21but He with a oath—sworn by the One who said to Him, "*ADONAI* has sworn and will not change His mind, 'You are a *kohen* forever.'"[g]) 22How much more then has *Yeshua* become the guarantee of a better covenant.

23Now on the one hand, many have become *kohanim*, who through death are prevented from continuing in office.[h] 24But on the other hand, the One who does remain forever has a permanent priesthood. 25Therefore He is also able to save completely those who draw near to God through Him, always living to make intercession for them

26For such a *Kohen Gadol* was fitting for us: holy, guiltless, undefiled, separated from sinners, and exalted above the heavens. 27He has no need to offer up sacrifices day by day like those other *kohanim g'dolim*—first for their own sins and then for the sins of the people.[i] For when He offered up Himself, He did this once for all. 28For the *Torah* appoints as *kohanim g'dolim* men who have weakness; but the word of the oath,[j] which came after the *Torah*, appoints a Son—made perfect forever.

a 7:5. cf. Num. 18:21-32.
b 7:11. cf. Exod. 19:5-6; 20ff.
c 7:12; 12:27. Lit. *transposition;* Grk. *metathesis.*
d 7:14. cf. Isa. 11:1.
e 7:16. cf. Exod. 30:30; 32:25-29; Num. 3:9-12.
f 7:17. Ps. 110:4(109:4 LXX).
g 7:21. Ps. 110:4(109:4 LXX).
h 7:23. cf. Exod. 40:15; Num. 25:13; Dan. 6:27(26).
i 7:27. cf. Lev. 6:9-13; 16:11, 15.
j 7:28. cf. Ps. 110:4(109:4 LXX).

8

Yeshua, Mediator of a Better Covenant

[1]Now here is the main point being said. We do have such a *Kohen Gadol*, who has taken His seat at the right hand[a] of the throne of the Majesty in the heavens. [2]He is a priestly attendant of the Holies and the true Tent—which ADONAI set up, not man. [3]For every *kohen gadol* is appointed to offer both gifts and sacrifices, so it is necessary for this One also to have something to offer.[b] [4]Now if He were on earth, He would not be a *kohen* at all, since there are those who offer the gifts according to the *Torah*. [5]They offer service in a replica[c] and foreshadower of the heavenlies—one that is just as Moses was instructed by God when he was about to complete the tabernacle. For He says, "See that you make everything according to the design that was shown to you on the mountain."[d] [6]But now *Yeshua* has obtained a more excellent ministry, insofar as He is the mediator of a better covenant which has been enacted on better promises.

[7]For if that first covenant had been faultless, there would have been no occasion for seeking a second. [8]For finding fault with them, He says,

"Behold, days are coming, says ADONAI,
when I will inaugurate a new covenant
with the house of Israel
and with the house of Judah.
[9]It will not be like the covenant
I made with their fathers
on the day when I took them by the hand
to lead them out of the land of Egypt.
For they did not remain in My covenant,
and I did not care for them, says ADONAI.
[10]For this is the covenant that I will make with the house of Israel
after those days, says ADONAI.
I will put My *Torah* into their mind,
and upon their hearts I will write it.
And I will be their God,
and they shall be My people.[e]
[11]And no more will they teach, each one his fellow citizen
and each one his brother, saying,
'Know ADONAI,'
because all will know Me,
from the least of them to the greatest.
[12]For I will be merciful toward their iniquities,
and their sins I will remember no more."[f]

[13]In saying "new," He has treated the first as old; but what is being made old and aging is close to vanishing.

Messiah Enters the Heavenly Holies

[1]Now even the first covenant had regulations for worship and the earthly sanctuary.[g] [2]For a tent was prepared: in the outer[h] part were the *menorah*, the table, and the presentation of the bread[i]—this is called the Holy Place. [3]Beyond the second curtain[j] was a dwelling called the Holy of Holies.[k] [4]It held a golden altar of incense and the ark of the covenant, completely covered with gold.

a 8:1. cf. Ps. 110:1(109:1 LXX).
b 8:3. cf. Exod. 23:15; 34:20.
c 8:5. cf. Exod. 25:9; 26:30; 27:8; Num. 8:4.
d 8:5. Exod. 25:40.
e 8:10. cf. Jer. 7:22-23.
f 8:8-12. Jer. 31:30-33(31-34); 38:31-34(LXX).
g 9:1ff. cf. Exod. 25:8, 23-29.
h 9:2. Lit. *first*.
i 9:2. cf. Lev. 24:5-9.
j 9:3; 10:20. Heb. *parokhet*.
k 9:3. cf. Exod. 26:31-33; 40:3.

In the ark was a golden jar holding the manna, Aaron's rod that budded, and the tablets of the covenant[a]— [5]and above it, cherubim of glory overshadowing the mercy seat.[b] But it is not now possible to speak in detail about these things.

[6]Now with these things prepared this way, the *kohanim* do continually enter into the outer tent[c] while completing the services; [7]but into the inner,[d] once a year, the *kohen gadol* alone[e]—

and not without blood which he offers for himself and for the unintentional sins[f] of the people. [8]By this the *Ruach ha-Kodesh* makes clear that the way into the Holies has not yet been revealed while the first tent is still standing. [9]It is a symbol for the present time. Accordingly, gifts and sacrifices are being offered that cannot make the worshiper perfect with respect to conscience. [10]These relate only to food and drink and various washings[g]—regulations for the body imposed until a time of setting things straight.

[11]But when Messiah appeared as *Kohen Gadol* of the good things that have now come, passing through the greater and more perfect Tent not made with hands (that is to say not of this creation), [12]He entered into the Holies once for all—not by the blood of goats and calves but by His own blood, having obtained eternal redemption. [13]For if the blood of goats and bulls[h] and the ashes of a heifer sprinkling those who have been defiled[i] sanctify for the cleansing of the flesh, [14]how much more will the blood of Messiah—who through the eternal Spirit offered Himself without blemish to God—cleanse our[j] conscience from dead works to serve the living God?

[15]For this reason He is the mediator of a new covenant,[k] in order that those called may receive the promised eternal inheritance—since a death has taken place that redeems them from violations under the first covenant. [16]For where there is a covenant, the death of the one who made it must be established.[l] [17]For a covenant is secured upon the basis of dead bodies, since it has no strength as long as the one who made it lives. [18]That is why not even the first covenant was inaugurated without blood. [19]For when every commandment had been spoken by Moses to all the people according to the *Torah*, he took the blood of the calves and goats, with water and scarlet wool and hyssop, and he sprinkled both the book itself and all the people. [20]He said, "This is the blood of the covenant which God commanded you."[m] [21]And in the same way, he sprinkled the tabernacle and all the vessels of the ministry with the blood.[n] [22]And nearly everything is purified in blood according to the *Torah*, and apart from the shedding of blood there is no forgiveness.[o]

[23]Therefore it was necessary for the replicas of these heavenly things to be purified with these sacrifices—but the heavenly things themselves with better sacrifices than these. [24]For Messiah did not enter into Holies made with hands—counterparts of the true things—but into heaven itself, now to appear in God's presence on our behalf. [25]And He did not offer Himself again and again—as the *kohen gadol* enters into the Holy of Holies year after year with blood that is not his own. [26]For then He would have needed to suffer again and again from the foundation of the world. But as it is, He has been revealed once and for all at the close of the ages—to put away sin by the sacrifice of Himself. [27]And just as it is

a 9:4. cf. Exod. 25:10-16; 1 Kings 8:7.
b 9:5. cf. Exod. 25:18-19.
c 9:6. Lit. *first tent*, i.e. the Holy Place; cf. Exod. 27:20-21.
d 9:7a. Lit. *second*, i.e. the Holy of Holies; cf. Lev. 16:2, 34.
e 9:7b. cf. Exod. 30:10; Lev. 16:15, 34.
f 9:7c. cf. Num. 15:22, 30.
g 9:10. cf. Lev. 11; Num. 6:3;19:13.
h 9:13a. cf. Lev. 16:14-15.
i 9:13b. cf. Num. 19:9, 17-18.
j 9:14. Some mss. read *your*.

k 9:15. Heb. *brit hadashah*.
l 9:16. cf. Exod. 24:8(LXX); Ps. 50:5(49:5 LXX); Lk. 22:29.
m 9:20. Exod. 24:8.
n 9:21. cf. Exod. 29:12; Lev.8:15.
o 9:22. Lit. *pardon, cancellation, removal;* cf. Mt. 6:12; Mk. 1:4; Lev. 16:26(LXX).

appointed for men to die once, and after
this judgment,[a] 28so also Messiah, was
offered once to bear the sins of many.[b]
He will appear a second time, apart from
sin, to those eagerly awaiting Him for
salvation.[c]

10

Perfect Pardon in the New Covenant

1The *Torah* has a shadow of the good
things to come—not the form itself of
the realities. For this reason it can never,
by means of the same sacrifices they
offer constantly year after year, make
perfect those who draw near. 2Other-
wise, would they not have ceased to be
offered, since the worshipers—cleansed
once and for all—would no longer have
consciousness of sins? 3But in these sacrifices is a reminder of sins year after
year— 4for it is impossible for the blood
of bulls and goats to take away sins.
5So when Messiah comes into the
world, He says,

"Sacrifice and offering You did not
desire,
but a body You prepared for Me.
6In whole burnt offerings and sin offerings You did not delight.
7Then I said, 'Behold, I come to do Your
will, O God
(in the scroll of the book it is written of Me).'"[d]

8After saying above, "Sacrifices and
offerings and whole burnt offerings and
sin offerings You did not desire, nor did
You delight in them" (those which are
offered according to *Torah*), 9then He
said, "Behold, I come to do Your will."
He takes away the first to establish the
second. 10By His will we have been made
holy through the offering of the body of
Messiah *Yeshua* once for all.
11Indeed, every *kohen* stands day by
day serving and offering the same sacrifices again and again, which can never
take away sins.[e] 12But on the other hand,
when this One offered for all time a single sacrifice for sins, He sat down at the
right hand of God— 13waiting from then
on, until His enemies are made a footstool for His feet.[f] 14For by one offering
He has perfected forever those being
made holy. 15The *Ruach ha-Kodesh* also
testifies to us—for after saying,

16"This is the covenant that I will cut
with them:
'After those days,' says ADONAI,
'I will put My *Torah* upon their hearts,
and upon their minds I will write
it,'"[g]

then He says,

17"I will remember their sins and their
lawless deeds no more."[h]

18Now where there is removal of these,
there is no longer an offering for sin.

Let Us Pray Boldly in God's Presence

19Therefore, brothers and sisters, we
have boldness to enter into the Holies
by the blood of *Yeshua*. 20He inaugurated
a new and living way for us through the
curtain—that is, His flesh. 21We also have
a great *Kohen* over God's household.

22So let us draw near with a true heart
in full assurance of faith,
with hearts sprinkled clean from an
evil conscience
and body washed with pure water.

a 9:27. cf. Gen. 3:19, Dan. 12:2.
b 9:28a. cf. Isa. 53:12.
c 9:28b. cf. Mt. 1:21; Rom. 11:26-27.
d 10:5-7, 9. Ps. 40:7-9(6-8); Ps. 39:6-8(LXX); cf. Gen. 22:16-18.
e 10:11. cf. Mic. 6:6-8.
f 10:12-13. cf. Ps. 110:1(109:1 LXX).
g 10:16. Lit. *I will put My laws upon their hearts, and upon their mind I will write them* (Jer. 38:33 LXX); cf. Jer. 31:32(33).
h 10:17. Jer. 31:33(34)(38:34LXX).

23 Let us hold fast the unwavering confession of hope,
for He who promised is faithful.
24 And let us consider how to stir up one another
to love and good deeds.

25 And do not neglect our own meetings, as is the habit of some, but encourage one another—and all the more so as you see the Day[a] approaching.

26 For if we keep on sinning willfully after we have received the knowledge of the truth, there no longer remains a sacrifice for sins, 27 but only a terrifying expectation of judgment and a fury of fire about to devour the enemies of God.[b] 28 Anyone who rejected the *Torah* of Moses dies without compassion on the word of two or three witnesses.[c] 29 How much more severe do you think the punishment will be for the one who has trampled *Ben-Elohim* underfoot, and has regarded as unholy the blood of the covenant by which he was made holy, and has insulted the Spirit of grace? 30 For we know the One who said, "Vengeance is Mine; I will repay," and again, "*ADONAI* will judge His people."[d] 31 It is a terrifying thing to fall into the hands of the living God.

Suffering Perfects *Yeshua's* Followers

32 But remember the former days when, after you were enlightened, you endured a great struggle with sufferings. 33 Sometimes you were publicly exposed to abuses and afflictions, and other times you became partners with those who were treated this way. 34 For you suffered along with the prisoners and joyfully accepted the plundering of your possessions, knowing that you have for yourselves a better and lasting possession. 35 Therefore, do not lose your boldness, which has great reward. 36 For you need perseverance so that, after you have done the will of God, you may receive the promise. 37 For yet

"in a very little while,[e]
the Coming One will come,
and He will not delay.[f]
38 But My righteous one shall live by *emunah*;
and if he shrinks back,
My soul takes no pleasure in him."[g]

39 But we are not among the timid ones on the path to destruction, but among the faithful ones on the path to the preservation of the soul.

11

The Faithful See from Afar

1 Now faith is the substance of things hoped for, the evidence of realities not seen. 2 For by it the elders received commendation. 3 By faith we understand that the universe was created by the word of God, so that what is seen did not come from anything visible.

4 By faith Abel offered God a better sacrifice than Cain. Through faith he was commended as righteous[h] when God approved of his gifts. And through faith he still speaks, although he is dead.

5 By faith Enoch was taken so as not to see death, and he was not found because God took him.[i] For before he was taken, he was commended as pleasing to God. 6 Now without faith it is impossible to please God. For the one who comes to God must believe that He exists and that He is a rewarder of those who seek Him.

7 By faith Noah, when warned about events not yet seen, in holy fear prepared an ark for the safety of his household.

a cf. 1 Cor. 3:13; 1 Thes. 5:4; 2 Pet. 3:18.
b 10:27. cf. Zeph. 1:18; Isa. 26:11(LXX).
c 10:28. cf. Deut. 17:6; 19:15.
d 10:30. Deut. 32:35a, 36a.
e 10:37. Isa. 26:20(LXX).
f 10:37. Hab. 2:3(LXX).
g 10:38. Hab. 2:4(LXX).
h 11:4. cf. Mt. 23:35.
i 11:5. cf. Gen. 5:24(5:24 LXX); Grk. *metathesis*, lit. *transposition*, a change in location.

Through faith he condemned the world
and became an heir of the righteousness
that comes by faith.

8By faith Abraham obeyed when he
was called to go out to a place he was to
receive as an inheritance. He went out,
not knowing where he was going. 9By
faith he migrated to the land of promise as if it were foreign, dwelling in tents
with Isaac and Jacob—fellow heirs of
the same promise. 10For he was waiting
for the city that has foundations, whose
architect and builder is God.

11By faith even Sarah herself received
ability to conceive[a] when she was barren
and past the age, since she considered
the One who had made the promise to
be faithful. 12So from one—and him as
good as dead—were fathered offspring
as numerous as the stars of heaven,
and as uncountable as the sand on the
seashore.[b]

13These all died in faith without receiving the things promised—but they saw
them and welcomed them from afar, and
they confessed that they were strangers and sojourners on the earth.[c] 14For
those who say such things make it clear
that they are seeking a homeland. 15If
indeed they had been thinking about
where they had come from, they would
have had opportunity to return. 16But as
it is, they yearn for a better land—that
is, a heavenly one. Therefore God is not
ashamed to be called their God, for He
has prepared a city for them.

17By faith Abraham, when he was
tested, offered up Isaac. Yes, he who
had received the promises was offering up his one and only son— 18the one
about whom it was said, "Through Isaac
offspring shall be named for you."[d] 19He
reasoned that God was able to raise him
up even from the dead—and in a sense,
he did receive him back from there.

20By faith Isaac blessed Jacob and
Esau, even concerning things to come.
21By faith Jacob, as he was dying, blessed
each of the sons of Joseph, and he
bowed in worship while leaning on the
top of his staff. 22By faith Joseph, when
his end was near, made mention of the
exodus of *B'nei-Israel* and gave instructions about his bones.

23By faith Moses, when he was born,
was hidden for three months by his
parents, because they saw he was an
extraordinary child and they were not
afraid of the king's decree. 24By faith
Moses, when he had grown up, refused
to be called the son of Pharaoh's
daughter. 25Instead he chose to suffer
mistreatment along with the people of
God, rather than to enjoy the passing
pleasures of sin. 26He considered the
disgrace of Messiah[e] as greater riches
than the treasures of Egypt—because
he was looking ahead to the reward. 27By
faith he left Egypt, not fearing the king's
anger—for he persevered as if seeing the
One who is invisible. 28By faith he kept
the Passover and the smearing of the
blood, so that the destroyer of the firstborn would not touch them. 29By faith
they passed through the Red Sea as if on
dry ground. When the Egyptians tried it,
they were swallowed up.

30By faith the walls of Jericho fell
down after they were circled for seven
days. 31By faith Rahab the prostitute did
not perish with those who were disobedient, because she welcomed the spies
with *shalom*.

32And what more shall I say? For time
would fail me if I tell of Gideon, Barak,
Samson, Jephthah, also of David and
Samuel and the prophets. 33By faith they
conquered kingdoms, administered justice, obtained promises, shut the mouths
of lions, 34quenched the power of fire,
escaped the edge of the sword, were
made strong out of weakness, became
mighty in war, and made foreign armies
flee.

a 11:11. cf. Gen. 18:11-14; 21:2. Some mss. add *and she bore a child.*

b 11:12. cf. Gen. 15:5; 22:17; 32:12.

c 11:13. cf. Gen. 23:4; 47:9.

d 11:18. Gen. 21:12(LXX).

e 11:26. cf. Ps. 89:50-51.

[35]Women received their dead raised back to life; and others were tortured, after not accepting release, so they might obtain a better resurrection. [36]Others experienced the trial of mocking and scourging—yes, and even chains and prison.

[37]They were stoned, they were sawed in two, they were murdered with the sword. They went around in sheepskins and goatskins; they were destitute, afflicted, mistreated. [38]The world was not worthy of them! They wandered around in deserts and mountains, caves and holes in the ground. [39]And all these, though commended for their faith, did not receive what was promised—[40]because God had provided something better for us, so that only with us would they reach perfection.

12

Running the Race with Discipline

[1]Therefore, since we have such a great cloud of witnesses surrounding us, let us also get rid of every weight and entangling sin. Let us run with endurance the race set before us, [2]focusing on *Yeshua*, the initiator and perfecter of faith. For the joy set before Him, He endured the cross, disregarding its shame; and He has taken His seat at the right hand of the throne of God.[a] [3]Consider Him who has endured such hostility by sinners against Himself, so that you may not grow weary in your souls and lose heart.

[4]In struggling against sin, you have not yet resisted to the point of bloodshed. [5]Have you forgotten the warning addressed to you as sons?

> "My son, do not take lightly the discipline of *ADONAI*
> or lose heart when you are corrected by Him,
> [6]because *ADONAI* disciplines the one He loves
> and punishes every son He accepts."[b]

[7]It is for discipline that you endure. God is treating you as sons—for what son does a father not discipline? [8]But if you are without discipline—something all have come to share—then you are illegitimate and not sons. [9]Besides, we are used to having human fathers as instructors—and we respected them. Shall we not much more be subject to the Father of spirits and live? [10]Indeed, for a short time they disciplined us as seemed best to them; but He does so for our benefit, so that we may share in His holiness. [11]Now all discipline seems painful at the moment—not joyful. But later it yields the peaceful fruit of righteousness to those who have been trained by it.

[12]Therefore, strengthen the hands that are weak and the knees that are feeble![c] [13]And make straight paths for your feet,[d] so that what is lame will not be pulled out of joint but rather be healed. [14]Pursue *shalom* with everyone, and the holiness without which no one will see the Lord. [15]See to it that no one falls short of the grace of God; and see to it that no bitter root springs up and causes trouble, and by it many be defiled. [16]Also see to it that there is no immoral or godless person—like Esau, who sold his birthright for one meal.[e] [17]For you know that later, when he wanted to inherit the blessing, he was rejected. He found no chance for repentance, though he begged for it with tears.[f]

Entering the Unshakeable Kingdom

[18]For you have not come to a mountain[g] that can be touched, and to a

a 12:2. cf. Ps. 110:1(109:1 LXX).

b 12:6. Prov. 3:11-12.

c 12:12. cf. Isa. 35:3; Job 4:3-4.

d 12:13. cf. Prov. 4:26.

e 12:16. cf. Gen. 25:33-34.

f 12:17. cf. Gen. 27:34-38.

g 12:18. Lit. *something*; cf. Exod. 19:12-18, 20:18-21.

blazing fire, and to darkness and gloom and storm, 19and to the blast of a *shofar*[a] and a voice whose words made those who heard it beg that not another word be spoken to them. 20For they could not bear what was commanded: "If even an animal touches the mountain, it shall be stoned."[b] 21So terrifying was the sight that Moses said, "I am quaking with fear."[c]

22But you have come to Mount Zion—to the city of the living God, the heavenly Jerusalem,[d] and to myriads of angels, a joyous gathering, 23and to the assembly of the firstborn[e] who are written in a scroll in heaven,[f] and to God the Judge of all, and to the spirits of the righteous ones made perfect, 24and to *Yeshua*, the Mediator of a new covenant, and to the sprinkled blood that speaks of something better than the blood of Abel.

25See to it that you do not refuse the One who is speaking! For if they did not escape when they refused the One who was warning them on earth, much less will we escape if we reject the One who warns us from heaven. 26His voice shook the earth then,[g] but now He has promised, saying, "Yet once more I will shake not only the earth, but also the heavens."[h] 27Now this phrase, "Yet once more," shows the removal of those things that are shaken—that is, created things—so that what cannot be shaken may remain.[i] 28Therefore, since we are receiving a kingdom that cannot be shaken, let us show gratitude—through this we may offer worship in a manner pleasing to God, with reverence and awe. 29For our God is a consuming fire.

a 12:19. Grk. *salpigx* (trumpet), Heb. *shofar;* cf. Exod. 19:16(19:16LXX).
b 12:20. Exod. 19:12-13.
c 12:21. Deut. 9:19.
d 12:18, 22. cf. Deut. 12:11.
e 12:23. cf. Exod. 4:22.
f 12:23. cf. Lk. 10:20.
g 12:26a. cf. Exod. 19:18.
h 12:26b. Hag. 2:6.
i 12:27. cf. Isa. 34:4; 54:10; 65:17.

13

Brotherly Love in the Community

1Let brotherly love continue. 2Do not neglect to show hospitality to strangers—for in doing so, some have entertained angels without knowing it. 3Remember the prisoners as if you were fellow prisoners, and those who are mistreated as if you also were suffering bodily. 4Let marriage be held in honor among all and the marriage bed kept undefiled, for God will judge the sexually immoral and adulterers. 5Keep your lifestyle free from the love of money, and be content with what you have. For God Himself has said, "I will never leave you or forsake you,"[j] 6so that with confidence we say,

> "The Lord is my helper; I will not fear.
> What will man do to me?"[k]

7Remember your leaders, who spoke the word of God to you. Consider the outcome of their way of life, and imitate their faith. 8*Yeshua* the Messiah is the same yesterday, today, and forever. 9Do not be carried away by all kinds of strange teachings, for it is good for the heart to be strengthened by grace—not by foods that have not benefited those occupied by them. 10We have an altar from which those serving in the tabernacle have no right to eat. 11For the bodies of those animals—whose blood is brought into the Holies by the *kohen gadol* as an offering for sin—are burned outside the camp.[l] 12Therefore, to make the people holy through His own blood, *Yeshua* also suffered outside the gate. 13So let us go to Him outside the camp, bearing His disgrace. 14For here we have

j 13:5. cf. Deut. 31:6, 8.
k 13:6. Ps. 118:6 (117:6 LXX).
l 13:11. cf. Lev. 16:27 (LXX).

no lasting city, but we seek the one that
is to come. 15Through *Yeshua* then, let us
continually offer up to God a sacrifice of
praise—the fruit of lips giving thanks to
His name. 16Do not neglect doing good
and sharing,[a] for with such sacrifices God
is well pleased.

17Obey your leaders and submit to
them, for they keep watch over your
souls as ones who must give an account.
Let them do this with joy and not with
groaning, for that would be of no benefit
to you.

18Pray for us, for we are convinced
that we have a clear conscience, desiring
to conduct ourselves honorably in all
things. 19I especially urge you to do this,
so that I may be restored to you sooner.

Closing Blessing

20Now may the God of *shalom*,
who brought up from the dead
the great Shepherd of the sheep
by the blood of an everlasting covenant,[b]
our Lord *Yeshua*,
21make you complete in every good thing
to do His will,
accomplishing in us what is pleasing in His sight,
through Messiah *Yeshua*.
To Him be the glory forever and ever. Amen.

Final Greetings

22But I urge you, brothers and sisters,
listen patiently to this word of exhortation,
for in fact I have written to you in
few words. 23Know that our brother
Timothy has been released. If he comes
soon, I will visit you with him.

24Greet all your leaders and all the
kedoshim—those from Italy greet you.

25Grace be with you all.

a 13:16. Heb. *gemilut chasadim* (well-doing; acts of loving-kindness); and Grk. *koinonia* (sharing).

b 13:20. cf. Zech. 9:11 (LXX); Isa. 63:11-14 (LXX); Jer. 32:40(39:40 LXX).

The Letter from Jacob (James)

Introduction

This book often goes by the name "James." The Greek name of the book, however, is not "Demetrios" which translates as "James" but "Iacobos," which translates as "Jacob" or "Ya'akov" in Hebrew. Some say the book was renamed to honor King James for funding in 1611 the English translation widely known as the "Authorized Version."

There are several people named "Jacob" in the New Covenant, but the likely author of this letter is Jacob the brother of *Yeshua*, who probably wrote this letter in the 40s—about the same time period his community hosted the Jerusalem Council (Acts 15). He wrote to Jewish believers in *Yeshua*, as we gather from the address to the "twelve tribes in the Diaspora" (1:1), and the mention of the synagogue (2:2). These may even have been the believers mentioned in Acts 11:19 who were scattered at the time of persecution following Stephen's martyrdom.

Jacob focuses on ethics—how to live out the life of faith. This resonates with the emphasis of many modern Jews for whom ethics is often at the front of the agenda. The difference is that Jacob says that our life flows from our faith in *Yeshua* (2:1). He speaks to such issues as dealing with suffering; handling temptation; treating people fairly rather than playing favorites; showing the reality of one's faith through deeds; and using one's tongue properly (avoiding what modern Judaism calls *lashon ha-ra*, hurtful speech or gossip).

Jacob does not just "lecture" his readers on these things. Reminiscent of the way the book of Proverbs teaches, Jacob uses vivid images. "The one who doubts is like a wave of the sea, blown and tossed by the wind" (1:6). Our tongues are like wild animals that cannot be tamed, like springs of water that have both fresh and salt water (which is never found in nature), like the tiny rudder that can steer a huge ship, like a miniscule spark that manages to burn up an entire forest.

Some wonder if there is a conflict between Jacob and Paul: Paul teaches that we are set right before God, justified by our faith, while Jacob says that this happens from our works (2:24). Actually Paul and Jacob complement each other. God declares us to be righteous because of our faith, while our faith witnesses to others through our deeds. A true faith will show itself in how we live. Paul and Jacob would both be quick to agree to that. We say we have faith in *Yeshua*; now, let's live like it!

A Look Inside Jacob

Greetings (1:1)
Rejoice in Trials (1:2)
Quick to Listen, Slow to Anger (1:19)

Honor the Poor Person (2:1)
Show Faith with Works (2:14)

Dangerous Tongue (3:1)
Gentle Wisdom from Above (3:13)

Resist Pride and Evil (4:1)
If the Lord Wills, We Will (4:13)

Rotten Riches (5:1)
Be Patient for His Coming (5:7)
Praying for the Sick (5:13)

1

Greetings

1Jacob, a slave of God and of the Lord *Yeshua* the Messiah,

To the twelve tribes in the Diaspora: *Shalom*!

Rejoice in Trials

2Consider it all joy, my brothers and sisters,[a] when you encounter various trials, 3knowing that the testing of your faith produces endurance. 4And let endurance have its perfect work, so that you may be perfect and complete, lacking in nothing. 5But if any of you lacks wisdom, let him ask of God,[b] who gives to all without hesitation and without reproach; and it will be given to him. 6But let him ask in faith, without any doubting—for the one who doubts is like a wave of the sea, blown and tossed by the wind. 7For that person must not suppose that he will receive anything from the Lord— 8he is a double-minded man, unstable in all his ways.

9But let the brother in humble circumstances boast in his high position— 10and the rich person in his humble position, because like the flower of the grass he will pass away. 11For the sun arises with a scorching heat and withers the grass, and its flower falls off and the beauty of its appearance is destroyed.[c] So also the rich man in the midst of his pursuits will wither away.

12Happy is the one who endures testing, because when he has stood the test, he will receive the crown of life, which the Lord promised to those who love Him. 13Let no one say when he is tempted, "I am being tempted by God"—for God cannot be tempted by evil, and He himself tempts no one. 14But each one is tempted when he is dragged away and enticed by his own desire. 15Then when desire has conceived, it gives birth to sin; and when sin is full grown, it brings forth death.[d]

16Do not be deceived, my dearly loved brothers and sisters. 17Every good gift and every perfect gift is from above, coming down from the Father of lights, with whom there is no variation or shifting shadow. 18By His will, He brought us forth by the word of truth, so that we might be a kind of firstfruits of all He created.[e]

Quick to Listen, Slow to Anger

19Know this, my dearly loved brothers and sisters: let every person be quick to listen, slow to speak, and slow to anger[f]— 20for human anger doesn't produce the righteousness of God. 21So put away all moral filth and excess of evil and receive with humility the implanted word, which is able to save your souls.

22But be doers of the word, and not hearers only, deluding yourselves. 23For if anyone is a hearer of the word and not a doer, he is like a man who looks at his natural face in a mirror— 24for once he looks at himself and goes away, he immediately forgets what sort of person he was. 25But the one who looks intently into the perfect *Torah*, the *Torah* that gives freedom, and continues in it, not becoming a hearer who forgets but a doer who acts—he shall be blessed in what he does.

26If anyone thinks he is religious and yet does not bridle his tongue[g] but deceives his heart, this person's religion is futile. 27Pure and undefiled religion before *our* God and Father is this: to care for orphans and widows in their distress,[h] and to keep oneself unstained by the world.

a 1:2, 16, 19; 2:1, 5, 14; 3:1, 10, 12; 4:11; 5:7, 10, 12, 19. Or *brethren* (Grk. *adelphoi*); *brothers*, often an audience of males and females.

b 1:5. cf. 1Kings 3:9-12; Prov. 2:3-6.

c 1:11. cf. Isa. 40:7-8.

d 1:15. cf. Ps. 7:14; Isa. 59:4.

e 1:18. cf. Jer. 2:3.

f 1:19. cf. Prov. 10:19; 17:27; 16:32; Eccl. 7:9.

g 1:26. cf. Ps. 39:1; 141:3.

h 1:27. cf. Deut. 14:29; Job 31:16-17; Ps. 146:9; Isa. 1:17, 23

2

Honor the Poor Person

1My brothers and sisters, do not hold the faith of our glorious Lord *Yeshua* the Messiah while showing favoritism.[a] 2For if a man with a gold ring and fine clothes comes into your synagogue, and a poor person in filthy clothes also comes in; 3and you pay special attention to the one wearing the fine clothing and you say, "Sit here in a good place"; and you say to the poor person, "Stand there," or "Sit by my footstool"; 4haven't you made distinctions between yourselves, and become judges with evil thoughts?

5Listen, my dearly loved brothers and sisters. Didn't God choose the poor in this world to be rich in faith and heirs of the Kingdom that He promised to those who love Him? 6But you have dishonored the poor person. Isn't it the rich who oppress you and drag you into court? 7Don't they blaspheme the good name by which you were called? 8If, however, you fulfill the royal law according to the Scripture, "You shall love your neighbor as yourself," you do well. 9But if you show favoritism, you are committing sin and are convicted by the *Torah* as transgressors. 10For whoever keeps the whole *Torah* but stumbles in one point, he has become guilty of all. 11For the one who said, "Do not commit adultery," also said, "Do not commit murder." Now if you do not commit adultery but do commit murder, you have become a transgressor of the *Torah*.[b] 12So speak and act as those who will be judged according to a *Torah* that gives freedom. 13For judgment is merciless to the one who does not show mercy.[c] Mercy triumphs over judgment.

Show Faith with Works

14What good is it, my brothers and sisters, if someone says he has faith, but does not have works? Can such faith save him? 15If a brother or sister is naked and lacks daily food, 2:16 and one of you says to them, "Go in *shalom*, keep warm and well fed," but you do not give them what the body needs, what good is that? 17So also faith, if it does not have works, is dead by itself.

18But someone will say, "You have faith and I have works." Show me your faith without works and I will show you faith by my works. 19You believe that God is one. You do well. The demons also believe—and shudder! 20But do you want to know, you empty person, that faith without works is dead? 21Wasn't Abraham our father proved righteous by works when he offered up Isaac his son on the altar? 22You see that faith worked together with his works, and by the works his faith was made complete. 23The Scripture was fulfilled that says, "And Abraham believed God, and it was credited to him as righteousness"[d]—and he was called God's friend.[e] 24You see that a man is proved righteous by works and not by faith alone. 25And likewise, wasn't Rahab the prostitute also proved righteous by works when she welcomed the messengers and sent them out another way?[f] 26For just as the body without the spirit is dead, so also faith without works is dead.

3

Dangerous Tongue

1Not many of you should become teachers, my brothers and sisters, since you know that we will receive a stricter judgment. 2For we all stumble in many ways. If

a 2:1. Cf. Lev. 19:15; Job 34:19.
b 2:11. Ex. 20:13-14; Deut. 5:17-18.
c 2:13. cf. Prov. 21:13.
d 2:23a. Gen. 15:6; cf. Gal. 3:6.
e 2:23b. cf. Isa. 41:8.
f 2:25. cf. Josh. 2:4ff.

someone does not stumble in speech, he is a perfect man, able to bridle the whole body as well. [3]And if we put bits into the mouths of horses to make them obey us, we guide their whole body as well. [4]See also the ships—though they are so large and are driven by strong winds, they are steered by a very small rudder wherever the will of the pilot directs. [5]So also the tongue is a small member—yet it boasts of great things.[a] See how so small a fire sets a blaze so great a forest! [6]And the tongue is a fire.[b] The tongue is a world of evil placed among our body parts. It pollutes the whole body and sets on fire the course of life—and is set on fire by Gehenna.

[7]For every species of beasts and birds, reptiles and sea creatures, is tamed and has been tamed by mankind. [8]But no human being can tame the tongue. It is a restless evil, full of deadly poison.[c] [9]With it we bless *Adonai* and Father, and with it we curse people, who are made in the image of God.[d] [10]From the same mouth comes blessing and cursing. My brothers and sisters, these things should not be. [11]A spring doesn't pour out fresh and bitter water from the same opening, does it? [12]My brothers and sisters, can a fig tree produce olives, or a vine produce figs? Neither can salt water produce fresh water.

Gentle Wisdom from Above

[13]Who among you is wise and understanding? By his good conduct let him show his deeds in the gentleness of wisdom. [14]But if you have bitter jealousy and selfish ambition in your heart, do not boast and lie against the truth. [15]This is not the wisdom that comes down from above, but is earthly, unspiritual, demonic. [16]For where jealousy and selfish ambition exist, there is disorder and every evil practice. [17]But the wisdom that is from above is first pure, then peaceable, gentle, open to reason, full of mercy and good fruits, impartial, not hypocritical. [18]And the fruit of righteousness is sown in *shalom* by those who make *shalom*.[e]

4

Resist Pride and Evil

[1]Where do quarrels and conflicts among you come from? Don't they come from this, namely your passions that battle within your body parts? [2]You crave and have not. You murder and you envy, yet you cannot get it. You fight and you wage war. You do not have because you do not ask. [3]You ask and do not receive, because you ask with wrong motives so you may spend it on your passions. [4]You adulteresses![f] Don't you know that friendship with the world is enmity with God? Therefore whoever wishes to be a friend of the world makes himself an enemy of God. [5]Or do you think that in vain the Scripture says, "He yearns jealously over the spirit which He made to dwell in us"? [6]But He gives greater grace. Therefore it says,

> "God opposes the proud,
> but gives grace to the humble."[g]

[7]Therefore submit to God. But resist the devil and he will flee from you. [8]Draw near to God, and He will draw near to you. Cleanse your hands, you sinners, and purify your hearts, you double-minded![h] [9]Lament and mourn and weep! Let your laughter be turned into mourning, and your joy into gloom. [10]Humble yourselves in the sight of *Adonai*, and He shall lift you up.[i] [11]Do not speak evil against one another, brothers and sisters. The one

a 3:5. cf. Ps. 12:3-4; Prov. 26:20-21.
b 3:6. cf. Prov. 16:27.
c 3:8. cf. Ps. 140:3.
d 3:9. cf. Gen. 1:26.
e 3:18. cf. Hos. 10:12.
f 4:4. cf. Ezek. 16:32.
g 4:6. Ps. 138:6; Prov. 3:34.
h 4:8. cf. Isa. 1:16; Ps. 24:3-4; Ps. 119:113.
i 4:10. cf. Job 5:11; Ezek. 21:26.

who speaks against a brother or judges his brother, speaks evil against the *Torah* and judges the *Torah*. But if you judge the *Torah*, you are not a doer of the *Torah*, but a judge. 12There is only one lawgiver and judge[a]—the One who is able to save and to destroy. But who are you who judges your neighbor?

If the Lord Wills, We Will

13Come now, you who say, "Today or tomorrow we will go to such and such a town and spend a year there and engage in business and make a profit." 14Yet you do not know what your life will be like tomorrow. What is your life? For you are a vapor that appears for a little while and then vanishes.[b] 15Instead you ought to say, "If the Lord wills, we will live and also do this or that." 16But now you boast in your arrogance. All such boasting is evil. 17Therefore whoever knows the right thing to do and does not do it—for him it is sin.

5

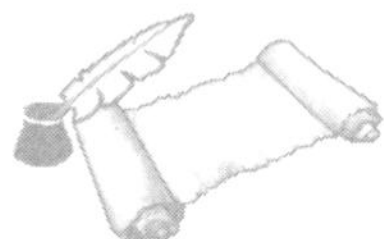

Rotten Riches

1Come now, you rich, weep and wail over the miseries that are coming upon you. 2Your riches have rotted and your clothes have become moth-eaten. 3Your gold and your silver have rusted and their rust will be evidence against you and will eat your flesh like fire. You have stored up treasure in the last days. 4Behold, the wages of the workers who mowed your fields—which you kept back by fraud—are crying out against you. And the cries of the harvesters have reached the ears of the Lord of Hosts.[c] 5You have lived on earth in luxury and self-indulgence. You have fattened your hearts for a day of slaughter.[d] 6You have condemned, you have murdered the righteous person[e]—he does not resist you.

Be Patient for His Coming

7So be patient, brothers and sisters, until the coming of the Lord. See how the farmer waits for the precious fruit of the earth, being patient for it until it receives the early and late rain.[f] 8You also be patient. Strengthen your hearts because the coming of the Lord is near. 9Do not grumble against one another, brothers, so that you may not be judged. Behold, the judge is standing at the doors. 10As an example of suffering and patience, brothers and sisters, take the prophets who spoke in the name of the Lord.

11Behold, we consider blessed those who showed endurance. You have heard of the endurance of Job,[g] and you have seen the outcome of ADONAI—that ADONAI is full of compassion and mercy.[h]

12But above all, my brothers and sisters, do not swear—either by heaven, or by the earth, or by any other oath. But let your "yes" be "yes," and your "no," be "no"—so that you may not fall under judgment.

Praying for the Sick

13Is anyone among you suffering? Let him pray.[i] Is anyone cheerful? Let him sing praises. 14Is anyone among you sick? Let him call for the elders of Messiah's community, and let them pray over him, anointing him with oil in the name of the Lord. 15The prayer of faith will save the one who is sick, and the Lord will raise him up. If he has committed sins, he will be forgiven. 16So confess your offenses to one another and pray for one another so that you may be healed. The effective prayer of a righteous person is very powerful. 17Elijah was a man with a nature like ours, and he prayed earnestly that it

a 4:12. cf. Isa. 33:22.
b 4:14. cf. Prov. 27:1; Job 7:7; Ps. 39:5; 144:4.
c 5:4. Isa. 5:9 (LXX); cf. Lev. 19:13; Deut. 24:15; Jer. 22:13.
d 5:5. cf. Amos 6:1; Jer. 12:3; 25:34.
e Or, *the righteous One*.
f 5:7. cf. Deut. 11:14; Jer. 5:24; Hos. 6:3; Joel 2:23.
g 5:11a. cf. Job 1:21-22.
h 5:11b. cf. Ex. 34:6; Ps. 103:8.
i 5:13. cf. Ps. 50:15.

might not rain. And it did not rain on the
earth for three years and six months.[a]
18He prayed again, and the sky gave rain,
and the earth produced its fruit.
19My brothers and sisters, if any among
you strays from the truth and someone
turns him back, 20let him know that the
one who turns a sinner from the error of
his way shall save a soul from death and
cover a multitude of sins.[b]

---

a 5:17. cf. 1 Kin. 17:1; 18:1
b 5:20. Cf. Prov. 10:12.

The First Letter from Peter

Introduction

Peter, one of *Yeshua's* original twelve disciples, wrote this letter around 62 or 63 CE from Rome, to believers living in what today is Turkey. Eusebius, a historian from the fourth century, believed that the letter addressed an audience of Jewish people living in exile. Jewish people in the Diaspora would relate to being addressed as strangers and sojourners (1:1; 2:11). When Peter, writing from Rome, says that "Babylon" sends greetings (5:13), this covert reference to Rome would seem normal to Jewish people living in scattered communities.

Peter was known as the *shaliach* to the Jewish people, but perhaps that was not his only audience. In 2:12, exactly who should keep their conduct honorable among the Gentiles? Jewish readers in Diaspora who have contact with non-Jewish people? Gentile believers within the communities? Much of Peter's letter does seem to address Gentiles who have joined the believing community—talk about the futile way of life (1:18) and advice to stop past pagan lifestyles (1:14; 4:3-5).

Peter includes Gentiles in the people of God by applying to them the language of the *Tanakh*. His readers in 1:4 have an inheritance; in 1:15 they are called as *kedoshim* to be holy; in 2:9 they are a chosen people, a royal priesthood, a holy nation; in 4:17 they are the family of God. This is not the church "replacing" Israel. It is the enlargement of Israel to now include Gentiles according to God's plan. It is the same idea we find in Paul's letter to the Ephesians (2:12-13).

At the time Peter wrote, these believers were experiencing persecution—if not officially, then certainly in their daily interactions with the pagan world around them. What hope it must have brought them to be included in the promises of God! Peter over and over emphasizes that these promises have come to them through what *Yeshua* has done for them. He has brought blessings through His death (1:19) and resurrection (1:3), and His return will be a time of hope fulfilled (1:7). In fact, *Yeshua's* example in the face of His own sufferings encourages us to do the same

Today's readers can first of all rejoice that God has chosen to expand His kingdom to include non-Jews among His people. Secondly, all believers can take hold of that same "living hope" (1:3) in the face of whatever opposition they encounter.

A Look Inside 1 Peter

Greetings (1:1)
A Message of Living Hope (1:3)
A Call to Be Holy (1:13)

Living Stones (2:1)
Respect and Order (2:13)

Suffering for Doing Good (3:8)

How to Live in the Last Days (4:1)

Shepherds Lead by Example (5:1)
Final Greetings (5:12)

1

Greetings

1Peter, a *shaliach* of Messiah *Yeshua*,

To the sojourners of the Diaspora in Pontus, Galatia, Cappadocia, Asia, and Bithynia—chosen 2according to the foreknowledge of God the Father, set apart by the Spirit for obedience and for sprinkling with the blood[a] of *Yeshua* the Messiah:

May grace and *shalom* be multiplied to you.

A Message of Living Hope

3Blessed be the God and Father of our Lord *Yeshua* the Messiah! In His great mercy He caused us to be born again to a living hope through the resurrection of Messiah *Yeshua* from the dead. 4An incorruptible, undefiled, and unfading inheritance has been reserved in heaven for you. 5By trusting, you are being protected by God's power for a salvation ready to be revealed in the last time. 6You rejoice in this greatly, even though now for a little while, if necessary, you have been distressed by various trials. 7These trials are so that the true metal[b] of your faith (far more valuable than gold, which perishes though refined by fire) may come to light in praise and glory and honor at the revelation of Messiah *Yeshua*. 8Though you have not seen Him, you love Him. And even though you don't see Him now, you trust Him and are filled with a joy that is glorious beyond words, 9receiving the outcome of your faith—the salvation of your souls. 10The prophets, who spoke about the grace that was to be yours, searched for this salvation and investigated carefully. 11They were trying to find out the time and circumstances the Spirit of Messiah within them was indicating, when predicting the sufferings in store for Messiah[c] and the glories to follow. 12It was revealed to them that they were providing these messages not to themselves but to you. These messages have now been announced to you through those who proclaimed the Good News to you by the *Ruach ha-Kodesh*, sent from heaven. Even angels long to catch a glimpse of these things.

A Call to Be Holy

13So brace your minds for action. Keep your balance. And set your hope completely on the grace that will be brought to you at the revelation of *Yeshua* the Messiah. 14Like obedient children, do not be shaped by the cravings you had formerly in your ignorance. 15Instead, just like the Holy One who called you, be holy yourselves also in everything you do. 16For it is written,

"*Kedoshim* you shall be, for I am *kadosh*."[d]

17If you call on Him as Father—the One who judges impartially according to each one's deeds—then live out the time of sojourning in reverent fear.

18You know that you were redeemed from the futile way of life handed down from your ancestors—not with perishable things such as silver or gold, 19but with precious blood like that of a lamb without defect or spot, the blood of Messiah. 20He was chosen before the foundation of the world, but was revealed in these last times for your sake. 21Through Him you are believers in God, who raised Him from the dead and gave Him glory, so that your trust and hope are in God.

22Now that you have purified your souls in obedience to the truth,[e] leading to sincere brotherly love, love one another fervently from a pure heart. 23You have been born again—not from perishable

a 1:2. cf. Exod. 24:3-8.

b 1:7. Lit. *without alloy; mettle, genuineness, proof.*

c 1:11. cf. Lk. 24:26-27.

d 1:16. Lev. 11:44-45; 19:2; 20:7.

e Some mss. insert *through the Spirit.*

seed but imperishable—through the living and enduring word of God. [24]For,

> "All humanity is like grass,
> And all its glory like a wildflower.
> The grass withers, and the flower falls off,
> [25]But the word of the Lord endures forever."[a]

And this is the word that was proclaimed as Good News to you.

2

Living Stones

[1]So get rid of all malice and all deceit and hypocrisy and envy and all *lashon ha-ra*. [2]As newborn babes, long for pure spiritual milk,[b] so that by it you may grow toward salvation— [3]now that you have tasted that the Lord is good.[c] [4]As you come to Him, a living stone[d] rejected by men but chosen by God and precious, [5]you also, as living stones, are being built up as a spiritual house—a holy priesthood to offer up spiritual sacrifices acceptable to God through Messiah *Yeshua*. [6]For it says in Scripture,

> "Behold, I lay in Zion a stone,
> a chosen, precious cornerstone.
> Whoever trusts in Him will never be put to shame."[e]

[7]Now the value is for you who keep trusting; but for those who do not trust,

> "The stone which the builders rejected—
> this One has become the chief cornerstone,"[f]
> [8]and "a stone of stumbling,
> and a rock of offense."[g]

They stumble because they are disobeying the word—to this they were also appointed. [9]But you are a chosen people, a royal priesthood, a holy nation, a people for God's own possession, so that you may proclaim the praises of the One who called you out of darkness into His marvelous light.[h]

> [10]Once you were "not a people,"
> but now you are "God's people."
> You were shown "no mercy,"
> but now you have been shown "mercy."[i]

[11]Loved ones, I urge you as strangers and sojourners to keep away from the fleshly cravings that war against the soul. [12]Keep your conduct honorable among the Gentiles. Then while they speak against you as evildoers, they may—from noticing your good deeds—glorify God in the day of visitation.

Respect and Order

[13]For the Lord's sake, submit yourselves to every human authority—whether to a king as supreme, [14]or to governors sent by him for the punishment of those who do evil and the praise of those who do good. [15]For this is God's will, that you silence the ignorance of foolish men by doing good. [16]Live as free people, but not using your freedom as a cover-up for evil. Rather, live as God's slaves. [17]Honor all people. Love the brotherhood. Fear God. Honor the king.

[18]Slaves, with all respect submit yourselves to your masters—not only to those who are good and gentle, but also to those who are harsh. [19]For this finds favor if, for the sake of conscience toward God, someone endures grief from suffering undeservedly. [20]For what

a 1:24-25a. cf. Isa. 40:6, 8; *the word of our God* in MT, LXX.
b 2:2. Or the pure milk of the word; Grk. *logikos*.
c 2:3. cf. Ps. 34:8(34:8 LXX).
d 2:4. cf. Ps. 118:22; Isa. 28:16.
e 2:6. Isa. 28:16.
f 2:7. Ps. 118:22.
g 2:8. Isa. 8:14.
h 2:9. cf. Exod. 19:5-6; Isa. 42:6
i 2:10. Hos. 1:10; 2:23.

1 Peter 2:4-5

As you come to Him, a living stone rejected by men but chosen by God and precious, you also, as living stones, are being built up as a spiritual house—a holy priesthood to offer up spiritual sacrifices acceptable to God through Messiah Yeshua.

credit is there if, when you sin and get a beating, you endure? But if you endure when you do good and suffer for it, this finds favor with God. 21For you were called to this, because Messiah also suffered for you, leaving you an example so that you might follow in His footsteps:

22"He committed no sin,
nor was any deceit found in His mouth."[a]

23When He was abused, He did not return the abuse.[b] While suffering, He made no threats. Instead, He kept entrusting Himself to the One who judges righteously. 24He Himself bore our sins in His body on the tree, so that we, removed from sins, might live for righteousness. "By His wounds you were healed."[c]

25For you like sheep were going astray,[d]
but now you have returned to the Shepherd and Guardian of your souls.

3

1Likewise, wives, be submitted to your own husbands so that—even if some do not obey the message—by the wives' conduct, without a word they may be won over 2as they observe your pure, reverent conduct.[e] 3Don't let your beauty[f] be external—braiding the hair and wearing gold jewelry or fine clothes.[g] 4Instead let it be in the hidden person of the heart, with the unfading beauty of a gentle and quiet spirit, which in God's sight is very precious. 5For this is the way the holy women, who put their hope in God, used to beautify themselves long ago—being submitted to their own husbands 6just as Sarah obeyed Abraham, calling him lord.[h] You have become her daughters by doing what is good and not fearing intimidation. 7In the same way, husbands, live with your wives in an understanding way. Though they are weaker partners, honor them as equal heirs of the grace of life. In this way, your prayers will not be hindered.

Suffering for Doing Good

8Finally, all of you be harmonious, sympathetic, brotherly, tenderhearted, humble-minded. 9Do not repay evil for evil or insult for insult, but give a blessing instead—it is for this reason your were called, so that you might inherit a blessing.

10For, "The one who loves life,
wanting to see good days,
must keep his tongue from evil
and his lips from speaking deceit.
11He must turn away from evil and do good.
He must seek *shalom* and pursue it.
12For the eyes of *Adonai* are on the righteous
and His ears open to their prayer,
but the face of *Adonai* is against those who do evil."[i]

13Who is going to harm you if you are eager to do good? 14But even if you should suffer for what is right, you are blessed. Do not be afraid or worry about their threats.[j] 15Instead sanctify Messiah as Lord in your hearts. Always be ready to give an answer to anyone who asks you a reason for the hope that is in you, 16yet with humility and reverence—keeping a clear conscience so that, whatever you are accused of, those who abuse you for your good conduct in Messiah may be put to shame. 17For it is better to suffer for doing good (if it is God's will) than for doing evil.

a 2:22. Isa. 53:9.
b 2:23. cf. Isa. 53:7.
c 2:24. Isa. 53:5.
d 2:25. cf. Isa. 53:6; Ps 119:176.
e 3:2. cf. 1 Pet. 1:17; 2:17-18.
f 3:3. Lit. *adornment.*
g 3:3. cf. 1 Tim. 2:9.
h 3:6. cf. Gen. 18:12(LXX *kurios;* MT *adoni*).
i 2:10-12. Ps 34:12-16.
j 2:14. Isa. 8:12-13.

[18]For Messiah once suffered for sins also—the righteous for the unrighteous[a]—in order to bring you to God. He was put to death in the flesh, but made alive by the Spirit. [19]Through the Spirit He also went and preached to the spirits in prison. [20]Long ago they disobeyed while God kept waiting patiently, in the days of Noah as the ark was being built. In that ark a few (that is, eight souls) were brought safely through water. [21]Corresponding to that, immersion now brings you to safety—not the removal of dirt from the flesh, but a pledge to God of a good conscience—through the resurrection of Messiah *Yeshua*. [22]He has gone into heaven and is at the right hand of God, with angels and authorities and powers subjected to Him.

4

How to Live in the Last Days

[1]Therefore, since Messiah suffered in the flesh, arm yourselves also with the same attitude. For the one who has suffered in the flesh is finished with sin. [2]As a result, he lives the rest of his time in the flesh no longer for human desires, but for God's will. [3]For the time that has passed was sufficient for you to carry out the desire of the pagans—living in indecency, lusts, drunken binges, orgies, wild parties, and lawless idolatries. [4]They are surprised that you do not run with them into the same riot of recklessness, and they vilify you. [5]But they will have to give an account to the One who stands ready to judge the living and the dead. [6]For this was the reason the Good News was proclaimed even to those now dead, so that though they are judged in the flesh before humans, they might live in the Spirit before God.

[7]Now the end of all things is near. So be self-controlled and sober-minded for prayer. [8]Above all, keep your love for one another constant, for "love covers a multitude of sins."[b] [9]Be hospitable one to another without grumbling. [10]As each one has received a gift, use it to serve one another, as good stewards of the many-sided grace of God. [11]Whoever speaks, let it be as one speaking the utterances of God. Whoever serves, let it be with the strength that God supplies. So in all things may God be glorified through Messiah *Yeshua*—all glory and power to Him forever and ever! Amen.

[12]Loved ones, do not be surprised at the fiery ordeal taking place among you to test you—as though something strange were happening to you. [13]Instead, rejoice insofar as you share in the sufferings of Messiah, so that at the revelation of His glory you may also rejoice and be glad. [14]If you are insulted for the name of Messiah,[c] you are fortunate, for the Spirit of glory[d] and of God rests on you. [15]For let none of you suffer as a murderer or thief or evildoer or as a troublemaker. [16]But if anyone suffers for following Messiah,[e] let him not be ashamed, but let him glorify God in this name. [17]For the time has come for judgment to begin with the house of God.[f] If judgment begins with us first, what will be the end for those who disobey the Good News of God?

[18]Now, "if it is hard for the righteous to
be saved,
what shall become of the ungodly
and the sinner?"[g]

[19]So then, those who suffer according to God's will—let them trust their souls to a faithful Creator while continuing to do good.

a 3:18. cf. Isa. 53:11-12.

b 4:8. Prov. 10:12.

c 4:14. cf. Ps. 89:50-51.

d 4:14. Many mss. insert here, *and of power.*

e 4:16. Lit. *as a Christian* (Grk. *Christianos*) or *Messianic* (Heb. *M'shichi*); cf. Acts 11:26; 26:28.

f 4:17. cf. Jer. 25:29; Ezek. 9:6; Amos 3:2.

g 4:18. Prov. 11:31 (LXX).

5

Shepherds Lead by Example

[1]Therefore I appeal to the elders among you—as a fellow elder and witness of Messiah's sufferings, and a partaker also of the glory about to be revealed— [2]shepherd God's flock among you. Watch over it not under compulsion but willingly before God, not for dishonest gain but eagerly. [3]Don't lord it over[a] those apportioned to you, but become examples to the flock. [4]When the Chief Shepherd appears, you will receive the unfading crown of glory. [5]Likewise, you younger ones, submit yourselves to the elders. And all of you, clothe yourselves with humility toward one another, for

> "God opposes the proud,
> but gives grace to the humble."[b]

[6]Therefore humble yourselves under the mighty hand of God, so that He may lift you up at the appropriate time. [7]Cast all your worries on Him,[c] for He cares for you. [8]Stay alert! Watch out! Your adversary the devil prowls around like a roaring lion, searching for someone to devour. [9]Stand up against him, firm in your faith, knowing that the same kinds of suffering are being laid upon your brothers and sisters throughout the world. [10]After you have suffered a little while, the God of all grace—who has called you into His eternal glory in Messiah—will Himself restore, support, strengthen, and establish you. [11]All power to Him forever![d] Amen.

Final Greetings

[12]Through Silvanus,[e] whom I consider our faithful brother, I have written to you briefly, encouraging and testifying that this is the true grace of God. Stand firm in it! [13]Messiah's community in Babylon, chosen together with you, sends you greetings. So does my son Mark. [14]Greet one another with a kiss of love.

Shalom to you all who are in Messiah. Amen.

a 5:3. cf. Ezek. 34:4.
b 5:4. Prov. 3:34.
c 5:7. cf. Ps. 55:23(22).
d 5:11. Some mss. read *All glory and power to Him forever and ever*; cf. 1 Pet. 4:11.
e 5:12. Or *Silas*; cf. Acts 15:22ff.

The Second Letter from Peter

Introduction

While 1 Peter focuses on believers who are undergoing persecution—an external problem—Peter's second letter addresses an internal one, namely false teaching. This letter was written shortly before 65 C.E., not long before Peter was killed in Emperor Nero's persecution of Roman believers. Probably he wrote to the same mostly Gentile believers as in 1 Peter.

2 Peter tells us two things about the false teachers. First, they denied the reality of *Yeshua's* return (3:3-4) in judgment. Second, and probably because of this doctrinal error, they led lives of immorality (2:10-20). After all, if *Yeshua* is never coming back and if there is no final judgment, why not just live as we please?

2 Peter 2:19 describes these false teachers as promising freedom while really promoting a form of slavery. This remains relevant today when we consider that there are many people who seek personal freedom by pursuing such goals as wealth, pleasure, or fame apart from God. Without Him, though, it is all too easy to end up enslaved to our ambitions.

But Peter's second letter reminds us that doctrine and behavior are interconnected. What we believe affects how we live, and how we live can affect what we believe—for sometimes people can change their beliefs to justify an improper lifestyle and, on the other hand, living according to Scripture can strengthen our faith.

Peter often encourages his readers to "remember" what he has taught them (1:12-15, 3:1, 5, 8)—a very Jewish concept. In Scripture, when God "remembers" his covenant with Abraham, Isaac, and Jacob (Exodus 2:24), it means that He takes action to deliver His people. At the Passover *Seder* we remember what God has done for our people to encourage us to worship and live for Him. Peter's call for his readers to "remember" certain things and "not forget" others is a call not just to bring certain things to mind, but to actively live a godly life in the hope of *Yeshua's* return.

The return of the Lord is an encouragement to living a godly life now. How do we do that? By following what Peter says in his final verse: growing "in the grace and knowledge of our Lord and Savior *Yeshua* the Messiah."

A Look inside 2 Peter

1

Greetings

[1]Simon Peter, a slave and *shaliach* of Messiah *Yeshua*,

To those who have received a faith equal to ours through the righteousness of our God and Savior, Messiah *Yeshua*:

[2]May grace and *shalom* be multiplied to you in the knowledge of God and of *Yeshua* our Lord.

Qualities for Living Forever

[3]His divine power has given us everything we need for life and godliness, through the knowledge of Him who called us by His own glory and virtue. [4]Through these things He has given us His precious and magnificent promises,[a] so that through them you may become partakers of the divine nature, since you have escaped the corruption that evil desires have brought into the world. [5]Now for this very reason, making every effort, add to your faith virtue; and to virtue, knowledge; [6]and to knowledge, self-control; and to self-control, patience; and to patience, godliness; [7]and to godliness, brotherly love; and to brotherly love, love.[b] [8]For if these qualities are in you and increasing, they keep you from becoming idle and unfruitful in the knowledge of our Lord *Yeshua* the Messiah. [9]But anyone who lacks these qualities is blind—nearsighted because he has forgotten his cleansing from past sins. [10]Therefore, brothers and sisters, make all the more effort to make your calling and election certain—for if you keep doing these things, you will never stumble. [11]For in this way entry into the eternal kingdom of our Lord and Savior, Messiah *Yeshua*, will be richly provided for you.

[12]Therefore I intend to keep reminding you of these things, even though you know them and are well-grounded in the truth that you have. [13]I think it right to stir you up with a reminder, as long as I remain alive in this "tent" of a body[c]—[14]knowing that my death[d] is soon, as our Lord *Yeshua* the Messiah has made clear to me. [15]And I will make every effort for you to always remember these things even after my departure.

Distinguishing True Testimony from Tales

[16]For we did not follow cleverly concocted tales when we made known to you the power and coming of our Lord *Yeshua* the Messiah, but we were eyewitnesses of His majesty. [17]For when He received honor and glory from God the Father, a voice came to Him from the Majestic Glory: "This is My Son, whom I love; with Him I am well pleased!"[e] [18]And we ourselves heard this voice come out of heaven, when we were with Him on the holy mountain.[f] [19]Furthermore, we have the reliable prophetic word. You do well by paying attention to it, as to a lamp shining in a dark place, until the day dawns and the morning star rises in your hearts.[g] [20]Above all understand this: no prophecy of Scripture comes about from a person's own interpretation. [21]For no prophecy was ever brought forth by human will; rather, people spoke from God as they were moved by the *Ruach ha-Kodesh*.[h]

2

False Teachers Condemned

[1]But false prophets also arose among the people,[i] just as there will also be false teachers among you. They will

a 1:4. cf. Josh. 21:4; 1Kings 8:56; Jer. 33:14.
b 1:7. Grk. *philadelphia* (brotherly love); *agape* (love).
c 1:13. cf. 2 Cor. 5:1.
d 1:14. Lit. *the laying aside of my tent.*
e 1:17. Matt. 17:5; (note also Matt. 3:17).
f 1:18. cf. Matt. 17:1, 5; Mk. 9:2-7.
g 1:19. cf. Num. 24:17.
h 1:21. cf. 2 Sam. 23:2; 2 Tim. 3:16.
i 2:1. cf. Deut 13:1-2; Jer. 14:14; Lam. 2:14; Ezek. 13:9; 22:28.

secretly bring in destructive heresies. They will even deny the Master who bought them[a]—bringing swift destruction upon themselves. 2Many will follow their immoral ways, and as a result the way of the truth will be maligned. 3In their greed they will exploit you with false words. Their judgment from long ago is not idle, and their destruction does not slumber.

4For God did not spare angels when they sinned, but threw them into *Sheol*.[b] He put them in chains of gloomy darkness, to be held until the judgment.[c] 5He did not spare the ancient world. He preserved only Noah, a proclaimer of righteousness, along with seven others, when He brought a flood upon the world of the ungodly. 6He devastated the cities of Sodom and Gomorrah, reducing them to ashes[d]—making them an example of what is going to happen to the ungodly. 7He rescued Lot, a righteous man deeply troubled by the shameless immorality of the wicked.[e] 8(For that righteous man, while living among them, was tormented in his righteous soul day after day by lawless deeds he saw and heard.) 9Therefore the Lord certainly knows how to rescue the godly from trials, and how to keep the unrighteous being punished until the Day of Judgment—10especially those who follow after the flesh in its unclean desires and who despise the Lord's authority.[f]

Brazen and arrogant, these people do not tremble while slandering glorious beings; 11yet even angels, though stronger and more powerful, do not bring a slanderous charge against them before the Lord.[g] 12But these people are like irrational animals—creatures of instinct born to be captured and killed. They malign what they don't understand, and in their destruction they will be utterly destroyed. 13They will be paid back for what they have done—evil for evil.[h] They consider carousing in broad daylight a pleasure. They are blots and blemishes, reveling in their deceitful pleasures while feasting together with you. 14They have eyes full of adultery that never stop sinning, enticing unstable souls. They have hearts trained in greed—a cursed brood! 15They have abandoned the straight way. They have gone astray. They have followed the way of Balaam the son of Beor,[i] who loved the wages of wickedness. 16But he received a rebuke for his own wrongdoing. A dumb donkey spoke with a man's voice and put a stop to the prophet's madness.[j]

17These people are springs without water and mists driven by a storm. The gloom of utter darkness has been reserved for them.[k] 18For by mouthing grandiosities that amount to nothing, they entice in sensual fleshly passions those who are barely escaping from those who live in error. 19They promise them freedom while they themselves are slaves of corruption—for a person is a slave to whatever has overcome him. 20For if—after escaping the world's pollutions through the knowledge of our Lord and Savior, *Yeshua* the Messiah—they again become entangled in these things and are overcome, the end for them has become worse than the beginning. 21For it would have been better for them not to have known the way of righteousness, than after learning about it, to turn back from the holy commandment passed on to them.[l] 22What has happened to them confirms the truth of the proverb, "A dog returns to its vomit,"[m] and "A scrubbed pig heads right back into the mud."

a 2:1. cf. 1 Cor. 6:20; 7:23.
b 2:4a. Lit. *hold captive in Tartarus*, the deepest place of Hades or hell.
c 2:4b. cf. Ezek. 26:20; Judah 6.
d 2:6. cf. Gen. 19:24.
e 2:7. cf. Gen. 19:1-2, 16.
f 2:10. Or *lordship*; cf. Judah 8.
g 2:11. cf. Judah 9.
h 2:13. cf. Judah 12.
i 2:15. Lit. *Bosor*, perhaps a wordplay (Heb. *basar* meaning *flesh*); cf. Num. 22:5.
j 2:15-16. cf. Num. 22:21-35.
k 2:17. cf. Judah 13.
l 2:21. cf. Ezek. 18:24.
m 2:22. Prov. 26:11.

3

The Day of the Lord Is Coming

[1]Loved ones, this is now the second letter that I am writing to you. In both I am trying to stir you up by way of a reminder to wholesome thinking— [2]to remember the words previously proclaimed by the holy prophets and the commandment of our Lord and Savior through your *shlichim*.[a] [3]First of all, understand that in the last days, scoffers will come scoffing, following after their own desires[b] [4]and saying, "Where is this promise of His coming?[c] Ever since the fathers died,[d] everything goes on just as it has from the beginning of creation." [5]For in holding to this idea, it escapes their notice that the heavens existed long ago and the earth was formed out of water and through water by the word of God.[e] [6]Through these, the world of that time was destroyed by being flooded with water.[f] [7]But by the same word the present heavens and earth are being reserved for fire—kept until the Day of Judgment and the destruction of ungodly people.[g]

[8]But don't forget this one thing, loved ones, that with the Lord one day is like a thousand years, and a thousand years are like one day.[h] [9]The Lord is not slow in keeping His promise, as some consider slowness.[i] Rather, He is being patient toward you—not wanting anyone to perish, but for all to come to repentance.

[10]But the day of the Lord will come like a thief.[j] On that day the heavens will pass away with a roar, and the elements will melt and disintegrate, and the earth and everything done on it shall be exposed. [11]Since all these things are to be destroyed in this way, what kind of people should you be? Live your lives in holiness and godliness, [12]looking for and hastening the coming of the day of God. In that day the heavens will be dissolved by fire, and the elements will melt in the intense heat.[k] [13]But in keeping with His promise, we look for new heavens and a new earth, where righteousness dwells.[l]

Final Advice

[14]Therefore, loved ones, while you are looking for these things, make every effort to be found in *shalom*, spotless and blameless before Him. [15]Bear in mind that the patience of our Lord means salvation—just as our dearly loved brother Paul also wrote to you with the wisdom given to him. [16]He speaks about these matters in all of his letters. Some things in them are hard to understand, which the ignorant and unstable twist (as they also do with the rest of the Scriptures)—to their own destruction.

[17]Since you already know all this, loved ones, be on your guard so that you are not led astray by the error of the lawless and lose your sure footing. [18]Instead, keep growing in the grace and knowledge of our Lord and Savior *Yeshua* the Messiah. To Him be the glory both now and to the day of eternity! Amen.

a 3:2. cf. Judah 17.
b 3:3. cf. Judah 18.
c 3:4a. cf. Isa. 5:19; Jer. 17:15; Ezek. 11:3; 12:22, 27; Mal. 2:17.
d 3:4b. Lit. *fell asleep*.
e 3:5. cf. Gen. 1:2,6-10; Ps. 24:1-2; 33:6-7; 136:5-6; Prov. 8:24-29.
f 3:6. cf. Gen. 7:11-12
g 3:7. cf. Isa. 66:15-16; Amos 7:4; Zeph. 1:18; Mal. 4:1
h 3:8. cf. Ps. 90:4.
i 3:9. cf. Hab. 2:3.
j Some mss. add *in the night*.

k 3:12. cf. Mic. 1:4.
l 3:13. cf. s. 65:17; 66:22; 32:16; 65:25.

The First Letter from
John

Introduction

These three brief letters were written by the same author as the gospel of John, but at a later time. The recipients are local communities. 1 John does not state the addressee(s) explicitly; 2 John is written to a "lady," which is really a community (reporting greetings from "your sister," another community); while 3 John is sent to one "Gaius." However, all three address growing problems within the body of Messiah which were beginning to gain ground in the Ephesus area (modern Western Turkey), the likely location from and to which these letters were written.

The three letters encourage believers in their faith, urging them to guard against false teachers, who denied that the human *Yeshua* was also divine, that God had really become man, and that their immoral behavior constituted sin. It is hard to pin down one particular group teaching these things, but it could have been an early form of Gnosticism (which believed that matter was evil and that salvation came through secret knowledge), or a heresy called Docetism (which taught that God appeared to take on human flesh but did not truly become man), or another heresy taught by Cerinthus. 1 John warns against this teaching; 2 John advises a community not to welcome teachers peddling false doctrine; while 3 John speaks about a divisive man named Diotrephes, "who loves to be first."

John's letters show how God's Word must always be the test of both teaching and behavior. John especially emphasizes love, faith and obedience, which work out in the lifestyle of believers, in their understanding of *Yeshua*. 1 John in particular remains a beloved classic of the spiritual life, articulating themes of fellowship with God and assurance of forgiveness of sins.

A Look Inside 1 John

God's Manifested Word of Life (1:1)
God's Light Dispels Darkness (1:5)
Cleansing Begins with Confessing (1:8)

Yeshua Atoned for Our Sin (2:1)
Loving God Means Obedience (2:3)
Haters Stumble in Darkness (2:7)
Fellowship with God Conquers Evil (2:12)
The Fleeting World Opposes Eternal God (2:15)
Anointed People Cling to the Anointed One (2:18)
Father and Son Come as One (2:22)
Live in the Anointed One (2:24)
Righteous Children Treasure His Purity (2:29)
Loving Children Emulate His Actions (3:10b)

Yeshua, the Spirit of Truth (4:1)
God's Life-Giving Spirit of Love (4:7)
God's Fulfilling Love (4:17)
Love God—Love God's Family (4:20)

Love God—Live God's Word (5:2)
Believe God's Own Testimony of *Yeshua* (5:6)
Walk Now in Eternal Privileges (5:13)

1

God's Manifested Word of Life

[1]What was from the beginning, what we have heard, what we have seen with our eyes, what we have looked at and touched with our hands, concerning the Word of life—[2]the life was revealed, and we have seen and testify and declare to you the eternal life that was with the Father and was revealed to us. [3]What we have seen and heard we proclaim also to you, so you may have fellowship with us. Indeed, our fellowship is with the Father and His Son, *Yeshua* the Messiah. [4]These things we write so our joy may be full.

God's Light Dispels Darkness

[5]Now this is the message we have heard from Him and announce to you—that God is light and in Him there is no darkness at all. [6]If we say we have fellowship with Him and keep walking in the darkness, we are lying and do not practice the truth.[a] [7]But if we walk in the light as He Himself is in the light, we have fellowship with one another and the blood of His Son *Yeshua* purifies us from all sin.

Cleansing Begins with Confessing

[8]If we say we have no sin, we are deceiving ourselves and the truth is not in us. [9]If we confess our sins, He is faithful and righteous to forgive our sins and purify us from all unrighteousness.[b] [10]If we say we have not sinned, we make Him a liar and His word is not in us.

2

Yeshua Atoned for Our Sin

[1]My children, I am writing these things to you so that you will not sin. But if anyone does sin, we have an Intercessor with the Father—the righteous Messiah *Yeshua*. [2]He is the atonement for our sins, and not only for our sins but also for the whole world.[c]

Loving God Means Obedience

[3]Now we know that we have come to know Him by this—if we keep His commandments. [4]The one who says, "I have come to know Him," and does not keep His commandments is a liar, and the truth is not in him. [5]But whoever keeps His word, in him the love of God is truly made perfect. We know that we are in Him by this— [6]whoever claims to abide in Him must walk just as He walked.

Haters Stumble in Darkness

[7]Loved ones, I am not writing a new commandment for you, but an old commandment—one you had from the beginning. This old commandment is the word you have heard. [8]Yet I am writing a new commandment for you, which is true in Him and in you, because the darkness is fading and the true light is already shining.

[9]The one who says he is in the light and hates his brother is still in the darkness. [10]The one who loves his brother abides in the light, and in him there is no cause for stumbling. [11]But whoever hates his brother[d] is in the darkness and walks in the darkness. He doesn't know where he is going, because the darkness has made his eyes blind.

Fellowship with God Conquers Evil

[12]I am writing to you, children,
because your sins have been forgiven on account of His name.
[13]I am writing to you, fathers,
because you have known the One who is from the beginning.

a 1:6. cf. Prov. 2:12-13; Isa. 9:2; 50:10.
b 1:9. Ps. 32:5; 103:3; Prov. 28:13: Jer. 31:31-32,34.
c 2:2. Lev. 16:30; 17:11; Isa. 53:11-12.
d 2:11. Lev. 19:17.

I am writing to you, young men,
because you have overcome the
evil one.
14 I have written to you, children,
because you have known the
Father.
I have written to you, fathers,
because you have known the One
who is from the beginning.
I have written to you, young men,
because you are strong,
the word of God abides in you,
and you have overcome the evil
one.

The Fleeting World Opposes Eternal God

15 Do not love the world or the things in the world. If anyone loves the world, the love of the Father is not in Him. 16 For everything in the world—the desire of the flesh, the desire of the eyes,[a] and the boasting of life—is not from the Father but from the world. 17 The world is passing away along with its desire, but the one who does the will of God abides forever.

Anointed People Cling to the Anointed One

18 Children, it is the last hour. Just as you heard that the anti-messiah is coming, even now many anti-messiahs have come—by this we know that it is the last hour. 19 They left us, but they didn't really belong to us. If they had belonged to us, they would have remained with us. But they left us so it became clear that none of them belongs to us.

20 But you have an anointing from the Holy One, and you all know. 21 I have not written you because you do not know the truth, but because you do know it, and because no lie is of the truth.

Father and Son Come as One

22 Who is the liar, if not the one who denies that *Yeshua* is the Messiah? This one is the anti-messiah—the one who denies the Father and the Son. 23 No one who denies the Son has the Father; the one who acknowledges the Son also has the Father.

Live in the Anointed One

24 As for you, let what you heard from the beginning remain in you. If what you heard from the beginning remains in you, you also will continue to live in the Son and in the Father. 25 Now this is the promise that He Himself has promised us—eternal life. 26 I have written you these things about those who are trying to mislead you. 27 As for you, the anointing you received from Him remains in you, and you have no need for anyone to teach you. But as His anointing teaches you about all things—and it is true and not a lie—and just as it has taught you, abide in Him. 28 And now, children, abide in Him, so that when He appears we will have confidence and not be ashamed in His presence at His coming.

Righteous Children Treasure His Purity

29 If you know that He is righteous, you also know that everyone who does what is right is born of Him.

3

1 See how glorious a love the Father has given us, that we should be called God's children—and so we are! The reason the world does not know us is that it did not know Him. 2 Loved ones, now we are God's children; and it has not yet been revealed what we will be. But we do know that when it's revealed, we shall be like Him, because we will see Him just as He is. 3 Everyone who has this hope in Him purifies himself, just as He is pure.

a 2:16. cf. Prov. 27:20.

4 Everyone practicing sin also practices lawlessness—indeed, sin is lawlessness. 5 You know that *Yeshua* appeared in order to take away sins, and in Him there is no sin. 6 No one who abides in Him sins; no one who sins has seen Him or known Him. 7 Children, let no one mislead you! The one who practices righteousness is righteous, just as *Yeshua* is righteous. 8 The one who practices sin is of the devil, for the devil has been sinning from the beginning. *Ben-Elohim* appeared for this purpose—to destroy the works of the devil. 9 No one born of God practices sin, because God's seed remains in him. He cannot sin, because he is born of God.

Loving Children Emulate His Actions

10 It is clear who are the children of God and who are the children of the devil by this—anyone who does not act righteously or love his brother is not of God. 11 For this is the message you have heard from the beginning—we should love one another. 12 Do not be like Cain, who was from the evil one and murdered his brother. And why did he murder him? Because his deeds were evil, while his brother's were righteous.[a] 13 Do not be surprised, brothers, if the world hates you.

14 We know that we have passed from death to life, because we love our brothers. The one who does not love remains in death. 15 Everyone who hates his brother is a murderer—and you know that no murderer has eternal life abiding in him. 16 We have come to know love by this—*Yeshua* laid down His life for us, and we also ought to lay down our lives for our brothers. 17 But if someone has material possessions and sees his brother in need and closes his heart against him[b], how does the love of God abide in him? 18 Children, let us not love with word or talk, but in deed and truth!

19 By this we shall know that we are of the truth, and set our heart at rest before Him 20 whenever our heart condemns us. For God is greater than our heart, and knows all things. 21 Loved ones, if our heart does not condemn us, we have confidence before God; 22 and whatever we ask, we receive from Him, because we keep His commandments and do what is pleasing in His sight. 23 Now this is His commandment—that we should believe in the name of His Son, *Yeshua* the Messiah, and love one another, just as He commanded us. 24 The one who keeps His commandments abides in God, and God in him. We know that He abides in us by this—by the Spirit He has given us.

4

Yeshua, the Spirit of Truth

1 Loved ones, do not believe every spirit, but test the spirits to see if they are from God. For many false prophets have gone out into the world.[c] 2 You know the Spirit of God by this—every spirit that acknowledges that Messiah *Yeshua* has come in human flesh is from God, 3 but every spirit that does not acknowledge *Yeshua* is not from God. This is the spirit of the anti-messiah, which you have heard is coming and now is already in the world. 4 You are from God, children, and you have overcome them, because greater is He who is in you than he who is in the world. 5 They are from the world, so they speak from the world and the world listens to them. 6 We are from God; whoever knows God listens to us, but whoever is not from God does not listen to us. By this we know the Spirit of truth and the spirit of error.

God's Life-Giving Spirit of Love

7 Loved ones, let us love one another, for love is from God. Everyone who loves

a 3:12. Gen. 4:8; Prov. 29:10.
b 3:17. Deut. 15:7.
c 4:1. Jer. 14:14; 29:8.

is born of God and knows God. 8The one who does not love does not know God, for God is love. 9The love of God was revealed among us by this—that God sent His one and only Son into the world so that we might live through Him. 10This is love—not that we have loved God, but that He loved us and sent His Son as an atonement for our sins.

11Loved ones, if God so loved us, we also ought to love one another. 12No one has ever seen God.[a] If we love one another, God abides in us and His love is made perfect in us. 13We know that we abide in Him and He in us by this—because He has given us of His Spirit. 14We have seen and testify that the Father has sent His Son as Savior of the world. 15If anyone acknowledges that *Yeshua* is *Ben-Elohim*, God abides in him and he abides in God. 16So we have come to know and trust in the love that God has for us. God is love. Now whoever abides in love abides in God, and God abides in him.

God's Fulfilling Love

17In this way, love is made perfect among us, so that we should have boldness on the Day of Judgment. For just as He is, so also are we in this world. 18There is no fear in love, but perfect love drives out fear. For fear has to do with punishment, and the one who fears has not been made perfect in love. 19We love, because He first loved us.

God's Love—Love God's Family

20If anyone says, "I love God," and hates his brother, he is a liar. For the one who does not love his brother, whom he has seen, cannot love God, whom he has not seen. 21And this commandment we have from Him: that the one who loves God should also love his brother.[b]

a 4:12. Exod. 33:20.
b 4:21. Lev. 19:18.

5

1Everyone who believes that *Yeshua* is the Messiah is born of God, and everyone who loves the Father loves the one born of Him.

Love God—Live God's Word

2We know that we love God's children by this—when we love God and obey His commandments. 3For this is the love of God—that we keep His commandments. And His commandments are not burdensome. 4For everyone born of God overcomes the world. And the victory that has overcome the world is this—our faith. 5Who is it that overcomes the world, if not the one who believes that *Yeshua* is *Ben-Elohim*?

Believe God's Own Testimony of *Yeshua*

6Messiah *Yeshua* is the One who came by water and blood—not by water only, but by water and blood. The Spirit is the One who testifies, because the Spirit is the truth. 7For there are three that testify— 8the Spirit, the water, and the blood—and these three are one.[c] 9If we accept men's testimony, God's testimony is greater—for this it is the testimony that God has given about His Son. 10The one who trusts in *Ben-Elohim* has the testimony in himself; the one who does not trust in God has made Him a liar, because he has not believed in the testimony that God has given about His Son. 11And the testimony is this—that God gave us eternal life, and this life is in His Son. 12The one who has the Son has life; the one who does not have *Ben-Elohim* does not have life.

c 5:8. A few late mss. read: *in heaven, the Father, the Word, and the Holy Spirit, and these three are one. And there are three that bear witness on earth, the Spirit.*

Walk Now in Eternal Privileges

13I wrote these things to you who
believe in the name of *Ben-Elohim*, so
you may know that you have eternal life.
14Now this is the confidence we have
before Him—that if we ask anything
according to His will, He hears us. 15And if
we know that He hears us—whatever we
ask—we know that we have the requests
we have asked from Him. 16If anyone sees
his brother committing a sin not leading
to death, he should ask, and God will give
life to those who commit sin not leading to death. There is a sin leading to
death—I am not saying you should ask
about that.[a] 17All unrighteousness is sin,
but there is sin not leading to death.

18We know that anyone born of God
does not keep on sinning; rather, the
One born of God keeps him safe, and the
evil one cannot touch him. 19We know
that we are of God, and the whole world
lies in the power of the evil one. 20And
we know that *Ben-Elohim* has come and
given us insight, so that we may know
Him who is true—and we are in Him who
is true, in His Son *Yeshua* the Messiah.
This One is the true God and eternal life.

5:21 Children, guard yourselves from
idols.[b]

a 5:16. Num. 15:30; Jer. 7:16.
b 5:21. Some mss. add: *Amen.*

The Second Letter from John

A Look Inside 2 John

God's Truth and Blessings
Abide Forever (1:1)
Lovingly Walk in God's Truth (1:4)
Protect Against Messianic
Pretenders (1:7)
Brotherly Fellowship Is Joyful (1:12)

1

God's Truth and Blessings Abide Forever

1The elder.

To the chosen lady and her children, whom I love in truth—and not I alone, but also all who have come to know the
truth— 2because of the truth that abides in us and will be with us forever:
3Grace, mercy, and *shalom* be with us, from God the Father and from Messiah *Yeshua*, the Father's Son, in truth and love!

Lovingly Walk in God's Truth

4I was overjoyed to find some of your children walking in truth, just as we received as a commandment from the
Father. 5Now I ask you, dear lady, that we love one another. It is not as though I am writing you a new command, but the one we have had from the beginning.[a] 6Now this is love: that we walk according to His commands. This is the commandment—just as you heard from the beginning—that you walk in love.

Protect Against Messianic Pretenders

7For many deceivers have gone out into the world—those who do not acknowledge *Yeshua* as Messiah coming in human flesh. This one is a deceiver and
the anti-messiah. 8Watch yourselves, so you do not lose what we have worked
for but receive a full reward. 9Anyone who goes too far and does not remain in Messiah's teaching does not have God. Anyone who remains in this teaching has
both the Father and the Son. 10If anyone comes to you and does not bring this teaching, do not welcome him into your
home or even give him a greeting. 11For the one greeting him shares in his evil deeds.

Brotherly Fellowship Is Joyful

12Although I have much to write to you, I don't want to do it with paper and ink. But I hope to come to you and speak face to face, so that our joy may be full.
13The children of your chosen sister send you greetings.[b]

a 1:5. Lev. 19:18; 19:34.

b 1:13. Some mss. add: *Amen.*

The Third Letter from John

A Look Inside 3 John

1

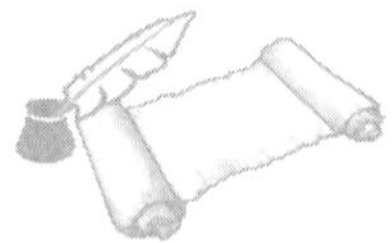

The Joys of Walking Out the Truth

[1]The elder.

To Gaius the loved one, whom I love in truth:

[2]Loved ones, I pray that all may go well with you and that you may be in good health, just as it is well with your soul. [3]For I was overjoyed when some brothers came and testified of the truth in you—how you are walking in truth. [4]I have no greater joy than this—to hear that my children are walking in the truth.

Support Faithful Kingdom Truth Tellers

[5]Loved ones, you are acting faithfully in whatever you do for the brothers and especially for strangers.[a] [6]They have testified to your love before Messiah's community. You will do well to send them on their way in a manner worthy of God. [7]For on behalf of the Name they went out, accepting nothing from the pagans. [8]Therefore we ought to support such people, so we might become co-workers in the truth.

The Lust for Power Condemned

[9]I wrote something to Messiah's community, but Diotrephes, who loves to be first among them, doesn't welcome us. [10]So if I do come, I will call attention to what he is doing—slandering us with wicked words. Not even content with that, he refuses to welcome the brothers, and even forbids those who want to do so— throwing them out of the community!

Do Good Like God Does

[11]Loved ones, do not imitate what is evil but what is good. The one who does good is of God; the one who does evil has not seen God.

Virtue Is Honorable

[12]Demetrius has a good testimony from everyone, even from the truth itself. We also vouch for him—and you know that our testimony is true.

Fellowship Is Desirable

[13]I have much to write you, but I don't want to write to you with ink and pen. [14]But I hope to see you soon, and we will speak face to face.

[15]*Shalom aleichem*. The friends here send their greetings. Greet the friends there by name.

a 5. Lev. 19:34; 25:35.

The Letter from Judah (Jude)

Introduction

Two books in this Bible—Judah and Jacob—have Hebrew names rather than their Greek forms—Jude and James. Because both authors are brothers of *Yeshua* (Matthew 13:55), it seems only fitting to restore a form that more closely matches the Hebrew—*Yehudah* and *Ya'akov*. Some interpret the Gospels as giving evidence that not even *Yeshua's* brothers and sisters understood His deity until following His resurrection (Mark 6:3; John 7:5; Acts 1:14). Yet later, *Yeshua's* brothers travel abroad, spreading the Good News (1 Corinthians 9:5).

Judah is basically concerned with warning against false teachers. Second Peter and Judah both share many thoughts in common, describing the false teachers in similar terms. Both books likely date from the same period in the 60s. It is possible that Judah's readers were Jewish believers, since he quotes not only from the *Tanakh* but even from Jewish sources not found in the Bible.

As in Second Peter, these false teachers are living an ungodly lifestyle, using God's grace as an excuse to live as they pleased. In response, Judah's readers are told to "contend for the faith" (verse 3), employing a word that is used to describe athletes in a contest. As in sports, there is a "defensive" and "offensive" aspect to the life of faith. Defensively, we need to be on guard against false teaching and the behavior that can result from it. Judah compares the false teachers to the unbelieving generation that died in the wilderness after the Exodus, to the angels who sinned (mentioned in Genesis 6), and to the people of Sodom and Gomorrah. In all three cases, it was the behavior of the people that led to their judgment, and their behavior was intertwined with their faith—or lack of faith. As in Second Peter, lifestyle and beliefs are inseparable. And like his brother Jacob, Judah uses colorful metaphors, describing the false teachers as waterless clouds, fruitless, and wild waves (verses 12-13).

Offensively, believers need to "contend," applying the same discipline to their spiritual lives as athletes do in preparing for their events. Judah asks his readers to build themselves up spiritually, to pray, to remain in God's love, and to show mercy to others (verses 20-22).

At the end, Judah's focus is on the power of God to keep all of us from falling, and he ends with a rousing doxology of praise to God and an enthusiastic "Amen!"

A Look inside Judah

Greeting

[1]Judah, a slave of *Yeshua* the Messiah and brother of Jacob,

To those who are called, who are loved in God the Father, and kept safe for *Yeshua* the Messiah:

[2]May mercy and *shalom* and love be multiplied to you!

Contend for the Faith with the Ungodly

[3]Loved ones, though very eager to write to you about our common salvation, I felt it necessary to write to you urging you to continue to contend for the faith that was once for all handed down to the *kedoshim*. [4]For certain people have secretly slipped in—those who from long ago have been marked out for this judgment. They are ungodly people, who pervert the grace of our God into indecency and deny our only Master and Lord, *Yeshua* the Messiah.

[5]Now I wish to remind you—though you have come to know all things —that the Lord,[a] once having saved a people out of the land of Egypt, afterward destroyed those who did not believe. [6]And the angels—who did not keep their own position of authority but deserted their proper place—He has kept in everlasting shackles under gloomy darkness until the judgment of the great Day.[b] [7]In the same way as these angels, Sodom and Gomorrah and the cities around them—having given themselves over to sexual immorality and gone after a different sort of flesh—are displayed as an example, suffering the punishment of eternal fire.[c]

[8]Yet in the same way these people also, by their visionary dreaming, defile the flesh, reject the Lord's authority,[d] and defame glorious beings. [9]But when Michael the archangel, disputing with the devil, was arguing about the body of Moses, he did not dare to render a judgment against him for slander, but said, "May the Lord rebuke you!"[e] [10]But these people slander whatever they do not understand. And whatever they do understand instinctively—like animals without reason—by these things they are destroyed. [11]Woe to them! For they went the way of Cain; they were consumed for pay in Balaam's error; and in Korah's rebellion they have been destroyed.[f]

[12]These people are hidden rocky reefs at your love feasts—shamelessly feasting with you, tending only to themselves.[g] They are waterless clouds, carried along by winds; fruitless trees in late autumn, doubly dead, uprooted; [13]wild waves of the sea, foaming up their own shame;[h] wandering stars, for whom the gloom of utter darkness has been reserved forever.[i]

[14]It was also about these people that Enoch, the seventh generation from Adam, prophesied, saying, "Behold, the Lord came with myriads of His *kedoshim*,[j] [15]to execute judgment against all. He will convict all the ungodly for all their ungodly deeds that they have done in an ungodly way, and for all of the harsh things ungodly sinners have spoken against Him."

[16]These are bellyaching grumblers, following after their own desires. Their mouth speaks grandiose things, showing favoritism for the sake of gain. [17]But you, loved ones, ought to remember the words previously proclaimed by the *shlichim* of our Lord *Yeshua* the Messiah[k]— [18]how they kept telling you, "In the last time there will be scoffers, following after their own ungodly desires."[l] [19]These are the ones who cause divisions—worldly-minded, not having the Spirit.

a 5. Some mss., say *Yeshua*; cf. 1 Cor. 10:4, 9.
b 6. cf. 2 Pet. 2:4.
c 7. cf. Gen. 19:5, 24; Deut. 29:23.
d 8. Or *lordship*; cf. 2 Pet. 2:10.
e 9. cf. Deut. 34:6; Zech. 3:2.
f 11. cf. Gen. 4:3-8; Num. 31:16; Num. 16:1-3.
g 12. cf. 2 Pet. 2:13; 1 Cor. 11:20.
h 13a. cf. Isa. 57:20.
i 13b. cf. 2 Pet. 2:17.
j 14. cf. Gen. 5:24; Deut. 33:2; Dan. 7:10.
k 17. cf. 2 Pet. 3:2.
l 18. cf. 2 Pet. 3:3.

20 But you, loved ones, continue building yourselves up on your most holy
faith, praying in the *Ruach ha-Kodesh*.
21 Keep yourselves in the love of God,
eagerly waiting for the mercy of our Lord
Yeshua the Messiah that leads to eternal
life. 22 And have mercy on those who are
wavering—23 save them by snatching
them out of the fire;[a] but on others have
mercy with fear—hating even the garment defiled by the flesh.

Hymn to God Our Savior

24 Now to the One who is able
to keep you from stumbling,
and to present you blameless
before the presence of His glory
with great joy,
25 to the only God our Savior,
through *Yeshua* the Messiah our
Lord,
be glory, majesty, power, and authority,
before all time,[b] both now and forever. Amen.

---

a 23. cf. Amos 4:11; Zech. 3:2.

b 25. Some mss. omit *Yeshua the Messiah our Lord;* some mss. omit *before all time.*

The Revelation to John

Introduction

The Book of Revelation is an apocalyptic prophecy—a kind of writing found in many of the prophetic books as well as sections of the New Covenant, in which a supernatural revelation is given through fantastic, symbolic visions. Revelation reads like a waking dream—compare the dreams and visions of Daniel, Ezekiel, and Zechariah. Revelation uses these symbols to show that in the end, with the return of Messiah *Yeshua* in fulfillment of the Scriptures, God will be triumphant over all evil in the world. Meanwhile, He is calling His people to stay alert and ready to come out of the world, to be with Him.

Though the author only states that his name is John, many (though not all) scholars are convinced that he is the apostle John who also wrote the fourth gospel and the letters of 1, 2, and 3 John—sharing themes such as the Lamb, the Word and the glory, eternity, and divinity of *Yeshua*. He writes from an island called Patmos, where he was sent into exile at a time of persecution against believers sometime in the late first century. The audience for Revelation included seven communities in the Roman province of Asia, which today is called Asia Minor or Turkey.

The book begins with letters to each of these seven communities, commending them for their faithfulness and rebuking them where they fall short, and encouraging them to continue living for the Lord. The rest of the book consists of symbolic visions and unusual symbols that stir the reader's imagination.

These visions were written to encourage believers to remain faithful in the face of persecution. The message is that God's kingdom will be victorious over all evil in the world. Revelation begins and ends with the promise of *Yeshua*'s return. Through Messiah, God rules over everything that happens—past, present and future. Those who belong to Him (rather than to the world system of Babylon) can rejoice in the glorious wedding feast of the Lamb. Hallelujah!

A Look Inside Revelation

Yeshua's Revelation to John (1:1)
Vision of the Glorious Son of Man (1:12)

Ephesus: Return to Your First Love (2:1)
Smyrna: Do Not Fear
Satan's Testing (2:8)
Pergamum: Beware the Trap
of Balaam (2:12)
Thyatira: Do Not Tolerate Jezebel (2:18)

Sardis: Coming Like a Thief (3:1)
Philadelphia: I Have Loved You (3:7)
Laodicea: Standing at the Door (3:14)

The Heavenly Throne of *ADONAI* (4:1)

A Scroll with Seven Seals (5:1)
Worshiping the Lamb (5:6)

Four Horsemen of the Apocalypse (6:1)

144,000 Marked with a Seal (7:1)
Countless Worshipers Before
the Throne (7:9)

The Seventh Seal and Seven Trumpets
(8:1)

The Angel with a Little Scroll (10:1)

Two Witnesses (11:1)
The Seventh Trumpet (11:15)

Mother, Child, Dragon, and War (12:1)

Two Beasts (13:1)

A Song for the 144,000 (14:1)
Three Angels with Messages (14:6)
Time to Harvest the Earth (14:14)

Song of Moses to the Lamb (15:1)

Seven Bowls of God's Wrath (16:1)

The Vile Prostitute and the Beast (17:1)

Judgment of Babylon (18:1)

Victory Songs in Heaven (19:1)
Wedding of the Lamb (19:6)
Final Battle of this Age (19:11)

The First Resurrection (20:1)
Judgment After 1000 Years (20:7)

A New Heaven and a New Earth (21:1)
The New Jerusalem (21:9)

Yeshua Is Coming (22:6)

1

Yeshua's Revelation to John

1The revelation of *Yeshua* the Messiah, which God gave Him to show to His servants the things that must soon take place. He made it known by sending His angel to His servant John, 2who testified to the word of God and to the testimony of *Yeshua* the Messiah—to everything he saw. 3How fortunate is the one who reads the words of this prophecy, and those who hear and keep what has been written in it—for the time is near.

4John, To Messiah's seven communities in Asia:[a]

Grace to you and *shalom* from Him who is and who was and who is to come, as well as from the seven spirits who are before His throne, 5and from Messiah *Yeshua*, the faithful witness, the firstborn of the dead, and the ruler of the kings of the earth. To Him who loves us and has freed us from our sins by His blood 6and made us a kingdom, *kohanim* to His God and Father—to Him be glory and power forever! Amen!

7"Look, He is coming with the clouds,[b]
  and every eye shall see Him,
  even those who pierced Him.
And all the tribes of the earth
  shall mourn because of Him.[c]
Yes, amen!"

8"I am the Alpha and the Omega,"[d] says *ADONAI Elohim*, "Who is and who was and who is to come, the Almighty!"

9I, John, your brother and fellow partaker with you in the tribulation and kingdom and patient endurance that are in *Yeshua*, was on the island called Patmos because of the word of God and the testimony of *Yeshua*. 10I was in the Spirit on the Day of the Lord,[e] and I heard behind me a loud voice like that of a trumpet, 11saying, "Write what you see in a scroll,[f] and send it to Messiah's seven communities—to Ephesus and to Smyrna and to Pergamum and to Thyatira and to Sardis and to Philadelphia and to Laodicea."

Vision of the Glorious Son of Man

12Then I turned to see the voice that was speaking to me. And when I turned, I saw seven golden menorahs.[g] 13In the midst of the menorahs, I saw One like a Son of Man, clothed in a robe down to His feet, with a golden belt wrapped around His chest.[h] 14His head and His hair were white like wool, white like snow, and His eyes like a flame of fire.[i] 15His feet were like polished bronze refined in a furnace,[j] and His voice was like the roar of rushing waters.[k] 16In His right hand He held seven stars, and out of His mouth came forth a sharp, two-edged sword.[l] His face was like the sun shining at full strength.[m]

17When I saw Him, I fell at His feet like a dead man.[n] But He placed His right hand on me, saying, "Do not be afraid! I am the First and the Last,[o] 18and the One who lives. I was dead, but look—I am alive forever and ever! Moreover, I hold the keys of death and *Sheol*.[p] 19Therefore write down what you have seen, what is, and what will happen after these things. 20As for the mystery of the seven stars that you saw in My right hand, and the seven golden menorahs—the seven stars are the angels of Messiah's seven

a 1:4. The Roman province of Asia, in the western part of Asia Minor (now part of Turkey).
b 1:7a. Dan. 7:13.
c 1:7b. Zech. 12:10-14.
d 1:8. cf. Rev. 21:6; 22:13. cf. Isa. 9:5-6(6-7); 41:4.
e 1:10. cf. Isa. 13:6, 9; Ezek. 30:3; Joel 2:1, 3:4(2:31); Amos 5:18; Obad. 15; Zeph. 1:7, 14; Mal. 4:15.
f 1:11. cf. Isa. 30:8; Jer. 36:2, 4.
g 1:12. cf. Exod. 25:37; 37:23; Zech. 4:2.
h 1:13. cf. Dan 7:13; 10:5; also Ex. 29:5; Lev 8:7.
i 1:14. cf. Isa. 1:18; Dan. 7:9.
j 1:15a. cf. Ezek. 1:7; Dan. 10:6.
k 1:15b. cf. Ps. 93:4; Ezek. 1:24; 43:2.
l 1:16a. cf. Isa. 49:2; Heb. 4:12.
m 1:16b. cf. Exod. 34:29.
n 1:17a. cf. Dan. 8:17-18; 10:9-10, 15.
o 1:17b. cf. Isa. 41:4; 44:6; 48:12.
p 1:18. cf. Job 38:17; Jn. 5:25-27.

communities, and the seven menorahs are the seven communities."

2

Ephesus: Return to Your First Love

[1]To the angel of Messiah's community in Ephesus write: "Thus says the One who holds the seven stars in His right hand, the One who walks in the midst of the seven golden menorahs: [2]I know all about your deeds and your toil and your patient endurance, and that you cannot bear those who are evil. You have tested those who call themselves *shlichim* and are not, and have found them to be liars. [3]You have perseverance and have endured for My name's sake, and you have not grown weary.

[4]"But this I have against you, that you have forsaken your first love.[a] [5]Remember then from where you have fallen. Repent and do the deeds you did at first. If not, I will come to you and remove your menorah from its place—unless you repent.

[6]"Yet you have this going for you, that you hate the deeds of the Nicolaitans, which I also hate. [7]He who has an ear, let him hear what the Spirit is saying to Messiah's communities. To the one who overcomes, I will grant the right to eat from the Tree of Life, which is in the Paradise of God."[b]

Smyrna: Do Not Fear Satan's Testing

[8]To the angel of Messiah's community in Smyrna write: "Thus says the First and Last, who was dead and came to life. [9]I know your tribulation and your poverty (yet you are rich), as well as the slander of those who say they are Jewish and are not, but are a synagogue of satan. [10]Do not fear what you are about to suffer. Behold, the devil is about to throw some of you into prison, so that you may be tested, and you will have tribulation for ten days. Be faithful until death, and I will give you the crown of life.[c] [11]He who has an ear, let him hear what the Spirit is saying to Messiah's communities. The one who overcomes shall never be harmed by the second death."

Pergamum: Beware the Trap of Balaam

[12]To the angel of Messiah's community in Pergamum write: "Thus says the One who has the sharp two-edged sword:[d] [13]I know where you live—where satan's throne is. Yet you continue to hold firm to My name, and you did not deny your faith in Me even in the days of Antipas, My faithful witness, who was killed among you, where satan resides.

[14]"But I have a few things against you. You have some there who hold to the teaching of Balaam, who was teaching Balak to put a stumbling block before *B'nei-Israel*, to eat food sacrificed to idols and to commit sexual immorality.[e] [15]Likewise you also have those who hold to the teaching of the Nicolaitans. [16]Repent then! If not, I will come to you soon and make war against them with the sword of My mouth. [17]He who has an ear, let him hear what the Spirit is saying to Messiah's communities. To the one who overcomes I will give some of the hidden manna,[f] and I will give him a white stone—and written on the stone a new name that no one knows except the one who receives it."[g]

Thyatira: Do Not Tolerate Jezebel

[18]To the angel of Messiah's community in Thyatira write: "Thus says the Son of God, who has eyes like a flame of fire and

a 2:4. cf. Jer. 2:2, 13; Ezek. 16:8, 15.
b 2:7. Heb. *Etz ha-Chaim b'Gan-Eden;* cf. Gen. 2:8-9; 3:22; Prov. 11:30.
c 2:10. cf. Dan. 1:12, 14.
d 2:12. cf. Isa. 49:2.
e 2:14. cf. Num. 25:1-2; 31:16.
f 2:17a. cf. Exod. 16:32-34.
g 2:17b. cf. Isa. 56:5; 62:2.

feet like polished bronze: [19]I know your deeds and your love and faith and service and patient endurance, and that your last deeds are greater than the first.

[20]"But this I have against you, that you tolerate that woman Jezebel,[a] who calls herself a prophetess—yet she is teaching and deceiving My servants to commit sexual immorality and to eat food sacrificed to idols. [21]I gave her time to repent, but she refuses to repent of her immorality. [22]Behold, I will throw her into a sickbed, and those who commit adultery with her into great tribulation—unless they repent of her doings. [23]I will also strike her children with a deadly disease. Then all of Messiah's communities will know that I am the One who searches minds and hearts,[b] and I will give to each of you according to your deeds.

[24]"But to the rest of you in Thyatira, who do not hold to this teaching and have not learned the so-called 'deep things' of satan—I place on you no other burden. [25]Only hold firm to what you have until I come. [26]To the one who overcomes and guards My deeds until the end,

'I will give him authority over the
  nations
  [27]and he shall rule them with an iron
  rod,
as when clay pots are broken into
  pieces.'[c]

[28]Even as I have received from My Father, so I will give him the morning star. [29]He who has an ear, let him hear what the Spirit is saying to Messiah's communities."

3

Sardis: Coming Like a Thief

[1]To the angel of Messiah's community in Sardis write: "Thus says the One having the seven spirits of God and the seven stars: I know your deeds—you have a reputation for being alive, but you are dead. [2]Wake up, and strengthen what remains that was about to die. For I have not found your deeds complete in the sight of My God. [3]So remember what you have received and heard—keep it, and repent. If you will not wake up, I will come like a thief, and you will not know at what hour I will come upon you.

[4]"But still, you have a few people in Sardis who have not stained their clothes. They will walk with Me in white, because they are worthy. [5]The one who overcomes thus will be dressed in white clothes; I will never blot his name out of the Book of Life,[d] and will confess his name before My Father and His angels. [6]He who has an ear, let him hear what the Spirit is saying to Messiah's communities.

Philadelphia: I Have Loved You

[7]To the angel of Messiah's community in Philadelphia write: "Thus says the Holy One, the True One, who has the key of David, who opens and no one will shut, and who shuts and no one opens:[e] [8]I know your deeds. Behold, I have set before you an open door that no one is able to shut—because you have little power, but you have kept My word and have not denied My name. [9]Behold, I will cause those of the synagogue of satan—who say they are Jewish and are not, but lie—behold, I will cause them to come and bow down before your feet,[f] so that they acknowledge that I have loved you!

[10]"Because you have kept My word about patient endurance, I will also keep you from the hour of trial that is coming upon the whole world to test those who dwell on the earth. [11]I am coming soon—hold on to what you have, so that no one will take away your crown. [12]The one who overcomes, I will make him a pillar in the Temple of My God,[g] and he will never leave it. And on him I will write the name of My God and the name of the city of My

a 2:20. cf. 1 Kings 16:31; 21:25.
b 2:23. cf. Ps. 7:9; 26:2; Jer. 11:20; 17:10.
c 2:26-27. cf. Ps. 2:8-9.
d 3:5. cf. Exod. 32:32-33; Ps. 69:28; Dan. 12:1-2.
e 3:7. cf. Isa. 22:22.
f 3:9. cf. Isa. 45:14; 49:23; 60:14.
g 3:12. cf. Jer. 1:18.

God—the New Jerusalem, which comes down out of heaven from My God—and My own new Name. [13]He who has an ear, let him hear what the Spirit is saying to Messiah's communities."

Laodicea: Standing at the Door

[14]To the angel of Messiah's community in Laodicea write: "Thus says the Amen, the Faithful and True Witness, the Originator of God's creation:[a] [15]I know your deeds, that you are neither cold nor hot. Oh, that you were either cold or hot! [16]So because you are lukewarm, and neither cold nor hot, I am about to spew you out of My mouth. [17]For you say, 'I am rich, I have made myself wealthy, and I need nothing.'[b] But you do not know that you are miserable and pitiable and poor and blind and naked. [18]I advise you to buy from Me gold refined by fire so that you may be rich, and white clothes so that you may dress yourself and so the shame of your nakedness will not be revealed, and eye salve to anoint your eyes so that you may see. [19]Those whom I love, I rebuke and discipline. Therefore, be zealous and repent.

[20]Behold, I stand at the door and knock. If anyone hears My voice and opens the door, I will come in to him and will dine with him, and he with Me. [21]To the one who overcomes I will grant the right to sit with Me on My throne, just as I myself have overcame and sat down with My Father on His throne. [22]He who has an ear, let him hear what the Spirit is saying to Messiah's communities."

The Heavenly Throne of *Adonai*

[1]After these things I looked, and behold, there was a door was standing open in heaven.[c] And the first voice, which I had heard speaking with me like a trumpet, said, "Come up here, and I will show you what must take place after these things."

[2]Immediately I was in the Spirit;[d] and behold, a throne was standing in heaven, and One seated on the throne.[e] [3]And the One who was seated was like jasper and carnelian in appearance, and a rainbow around the throne, like an emerald in appearance.[f] [4]Around the throne were twenty-four thrones, and seated on the thrones were twenty-four elders dressed in white clothes with golden crowns on their heads. [5]And out from the throne come flashes of lightning and rumblings and clashes of thunder[g]—and seven torches of fire burning before the throne,[h] which are the seven Spirits of God. [6]And before the throne was something like a sea of glass, like crystal.

In the middle of the throne and around it were four living creatures, full of eyes in front and behind.[i]

[7]The first living creature was like a lion,
the second living creature was like an ox,
the third living creature had a face like a man,
and the fourth living creature was like a flying eagle.[j]

[8]The four living creatures, each having six wings, were full of eyes all around and within.[k] They do not rest day or night, chanting,

"*Kadosh, kadosh, kadosh* Adonai *Elohei-Tzva'ot*,[l]
asher haya v'hoveh v'yavo!
Holy, holy, holy is the Lord God of Hosts,
who was and who is and who is to come!"

a 3:14. cf. Prov. 8:22.
b 3:17. cf. Hos. 12:8; Zech. 11:5.
c 4:1. cf. Ezek. 1:1.
d 4:2. Or *spirit*.
e 4:1. cf. 1 Kings 22:19; Is. 6:1; Ezek. 1:26; Dan. 7:9.
f 4:3. cf. Ezek. 1:28.
g 4:5a; 8:5; 11:19; 16:18. cf. Exod. 19:16.
h 4:5b. cf. Ex. 25:37; Zech. 4:2.
i 4:6. cf. Ezek. 1:5, 18; 10:22.
j 4:7. cf. Ezek. 1:10; 10:14.
k 4:8. cf. Isa. 6:2-3; Ezek. 1:18; 10:12.
l 4:8; 21:22. Grk. *Kurios o Theos o Pantokrator* (Lord God Almighty); cf. Amos 4:13.

[9]And whenever the living creatures give glory and honor and thanks to the One seated on the throne, who lives forever and ever,[a] [10]the twenty-four elders fall down before the One seated on the throne and worship Him who lives forever and ever. And they throw their crowns down before the throne, chanting,

[11]"Worthy are You, our Lord and God,
to receive glory and honor and power,
For You created all things,
and because of Your will they existed and were created!"

5

A Scroll with Seven Seals

[1]And I saw in the right hand of the One seated upon the throne a scroll, written on both the front and the back, sealed with seven seals.[b] [2]I also saw a mighty angel proclaiming with a loud voice, "Who is worthy to open the scroll and to break its seals?" [3]No one in heaven or on the earth or under the earth was able to open the scroll or to look into it. [4]I began to weep loudly because no one was found worthy to open the scroll or to look into it.

[5]Then one of the elders tells me, "Stop weeping! Behold, the Lion of the tribe of Judah,[c] the Root of David,[d] has triumphed—He is worthy to open the scroll and its seven seals."

Worshiping the Lamb

[6]And in the midst of the throne and the four living creatures, and in the midst of the elders, I saw a Lamb standing, as having been slain—having seven horns and seven eyes,[e] which are the seven Spirits of God sent out into all the earth. [7]He came and took the scroll from the right hand of the One seated on the throne. [8]When He had taken the scroll, the four living creatures and the twenty-four elders fell down

before the Lamb, each holding a harp and golden bowls full of incense—which are the prayers of the *kedoshim*.

[9]And they are singing a new song,[f] saying,

"You are worthy to take the scroll
and to open its seals.
For You were slain,
and by Your blood You redeemed for God
those from every tribe and tongue
and people and nation.[g]
[10]You have made them for our God
a kingdom and *kohanim*,
and they shall reign upon the earth."

[11]Then I looked, and I heard the voice of many angels around the throne and the living creatures and the elders—their number was myriads of myriads and thousands of thousands.[h] [12]They were chanting with a loud voice,

"Worthy is the Lamb who was slain,
to receive power and riches
and wisdom and might
and honor and glory and blessing!"

[13]And I heard every creature in heaven and on the earth and under the earth and on the sea and everything in them, responding,

"To the One seated on the throne and to the Lamb
be blessing and honor

a 4:9. cf. Dan. 4:34; 12:7.
b 5:1. cf. Ezek. 2:9-10; Isa. 29:11; Dan. 12:4.
c 5:5a. cf. Gen. 49:9
d 5:5b. cf. Isa. 11:1, 10.
e 5:6. cf. Zech. 3:9; 4:10.
f 5:9a. cf. Ps. 33:3; 40:3; 96:1; 98:1; 149:1; Isa. 42:10.
g 5:9b. cf. Dan. 3:4; 5:19.
h 5:11. cf. Dan. 7:10.

and glory and power forever and
ever!"

14And the four living creatures kept
saying, "Amen!" And the elders fell down
and worshiped.

Four Horsemen of the Apocalypse

1Then I saw when the Lamb opened
one of the seven seals, and I heard one of
the four living creatures say with a voice
like thunder, "Come!"[a] 2I looked, and
behold, there was a white horse.[b] The
one riding on it had a bow, and a crown
was given to him. He went out as a con-
queror so he might conquer.
3When the Lamb opened the second
seal, I heard the second living creature
saying, "Come!" 4Then another horse
came out, fiery red. The one riding on it
was permitted to take peace from the
earth, so that people would slaughter
one another. He was given a great sword.
5When the Lamb opened the third
seal, I heard the third living creature
saying, "Come!" And behold, I saw a
black horse.[c] The one riding on it held a
balance scale in his hand. 6Then I heard
something like a voice in the midst of the
four living creatures saying, "A quart[d] of
wheat for a denarius, and three quarts of
barley for a denarius—but do no harm to
the oil and wine!"[e]
7When the Lamb opened the fourth
seal, I heard the fourth living creature
saying, "Come!" 8Behold, I saw a horse,
pale greenish gray. The name of the one
riding on it was Death, and *Sheol* was following with him. Authority was given to
them over a fourth of the earth, to kill by
sword and by famine and by plague and
by the wild beasts of the earth.[f]
9When the Lamb opened the fifth seal,
I saw under the altar the souls of those
slaughtered[g] for the sake of the word of
God and for the witness they had. 10And
they cried out with a loud voice, saying,
"O Sovereign Master, holy and true, how
long before You judge those who dwell
on the earth and avenge our blood?"
11Then a white robe was given to each
of them, and they were told to rest a
little while longer, until the number of
their fellow servants was complete—
their brothers and sisters who were to
be killed as they had been.
12I saw when the Lamb opened the
sixth seal,

and there was a great earthquake.
The sun became as black as sackcloth
made of goat's hair,
and the full moon became like blood.
13The stars of heaven fell to the earth
like a fig tree drops unripe figs when
shaken by a great wind.
14The heaven ripped apart like a scroll
being rolled up,
and every mountain and island was
moved from their places.

15Then the kings of the earth and the
great men and the military commanders
and the rich and the mighty and everyone—slave and free—hid themselves
in the caves and among the rocks of the
mountains.[h] 16And they tell the mountains and the rocks, "Fall on us, and hide
us[i] from the face of the One seated on
the throne and from the wrath of the
Lamb. 17For the great day of their wrath
has come,[j] and who is able to stand?"

7

144,000 Marked with a Seal

1After this, I saw four angels standing
at the four corners of the earth, holding

a 6:1, 3, 5, 7. Some mss. add *and see.*
b 6:2-3. cf. Zech. 1:8; 6:2-3.
c 6:5. cf. Zech 6:6.
d 6:6. Lit. *choenix;* a day's measure of grain, about a quart.
e 6:6. cf. Ezek. 4:16.
f 6:8. cf. Jer. 15:2-3, 6-7; 29:17-19; Ezek. 5:17; 14:21.
g 6:11. cf. Ex. 29:12; Lev. 4:7.
h 6:15. cf. Isa. 2:10-12, 19, 21.
i 6:16a. cf. Hos. 10:8.
j 6:16b. cf. Isa 13: 9, 13; Ezek. 7:8, 12; Zeph. 1:15, 18.

back the four winds of the earth[a] so that
no wind would blow on the earth or on
the sea or against any tree. 2Then I saw
another angel coming up from the east,[b]
having the seal of the living God. He cried
out with a loud voice to the four angels
who were permitted to harm the earth
and the sea, 3saying, "Do no harm to the
earth or the sea or the trees, until we
have put a seal on the foreheads of the
servants of our God."[c]

4Now I heard the number of those
marked with the seal:

144,000 from every tribe of *B'nei-Israel*—

5 12,000 from the tribe of Judah;
12,000 from the tribe of Reuben;
12,000 from the tribe of Gad;
6 12,000 from the tribe of Asher;
12,000 from the tribe of Naphtali;
12,000 from the tribe of Manasseh;
7 12,000 from the tribe of Simeon;
12,000 from the tribe of Levi;
12,000 from the tribe of Issachar;
8 12,000 from the tribe of Zebulun;
12,000 from the tribe of Joseph;
12,000 from the tribe of Benjamin.

Countless Worshipers Before the Throne

9After these things I looked, and
behold, a vast multitude that no one
could count—from every nation and all
tribes and peoples and tongues—was
standing before the throne and before
the Lamb. They were clothed in white
robes, with palm branches[d] in their
hands 10and crying out with a loud voice,
saying,

"Salvation belongs to our God,
who sits on the throne,
and to the Lamb!"

11And all the angels were standing
around the throne, along with the elders
and the four living creatures; and they
fell on their faces before the throne and
worshiped God, 12saying,

"Amen, blessing and glory
and wisdom and thanksgiving
and honor and power and might
belong to our God forever and ever.
Amen!"

13Then one of the elders answered,
saying to me, "Who are these dressed in
white robes, and where have they come
from?"

14I said to him, "Sir, you know."

Then he said to me,

"These are the ones coming out of the great tribulation.[e]
They have washed their robes and made them white[f]
in the blood of the Lamb.

15For this reason, they are before the
throne of God,
and they serve Him day and night in
His Temple.
The One seated on the throne
will shelter them.[g]
16They shall never again go hungry,
nor thirst anymore;
the sun shall not beat down on
them,
nor any scorching heat.[h]
17For the Lamb in the midst of the
throne
shall shepherd them
and guide them to springs of living
water,
and God shall wipe away every tear
from their eyes."[i]

8

The Seventh Seal and Seven Trumpets

1Now when the Lamb opened the seventh seal, there was silence in heaven for

a 7:1. cf. Isa. 11:12; Ezek. 7:2; Dan. 7:2; Zech. 6:5.
b 7:2. Lit. *rising of the sun.*
c 7:3. cf, Ezek. 9:4, 6.
d 7:9. cf. Lev. 23:40 (Feast of *Sukkot*).
e 7:14a. cf. Dan. 12:1.
f 7:14b. cf. Ps. 51:7; Isa. 1:18; Zech. 3:3-5.
g 7:15. cf. Lev. 26:11; Ezek. 37:27; Jn. 1:14.
h 7:16. cf. Isa. 49:10.
i 7:17. cf. Isa. 25:8.

about half an hour. 2Then I saw the seven angels who stand before God, and seven trumpets[a] were given to them. 3Another angel came and stood at the altar, holding a golden incense burner.[b] He was given much incense to offer up along with the prayers of all the *kedoshim* upon the golden altar before the throne. 4And the smoke of the incense, with the prayers of the *kedoshim*,[c] rose before God from the angel's hand. 5Then the angel took the incense burner and filled it with fire from the altar, and threw it to the earth; and there were clashes of thunder and rumblings and flashes of lightning and earthquakes.[d]

6Then the seven angels holding the seven trumpets prepared to sound them. 7The first trumpeted,[e] and there was hail and fire mixed with blood, and they were thrown upon the earth.[f] A third of the earth burned up, a third of the trees burned up, and all the green grass burned up.

8The second angel trumpeted, and something like a huge mountain[g] ablaze with fire was thrown into the sea. A third of the sea turned into blood, 9a third of the creatures living in the sea died, and a third of the ships were destroyed.

10The third angel trumpeted, and a great star fell from the heavens, burning like a torch. It fell on a third of the rivers and on the springs of water. 11Now the name of the star is Wormwood; and a third of the waters became wormwood, and many people died from the waters that were made bitter.[h]

12The fourth angel trumpeted, and a third of the sun and a third of the moon and a third of the stars were struck, so that a third of them were darkened.[i] A third of the day would not shine, as well as a third of the night.

13Then I looked, and I heard an eagle crying out with a loud voice as it flew high in the sky, saying, "Woe, woe, woe to those who dwell on the earth, because of the remaining blasts of the trumpets the three angels are about to sound!"

9

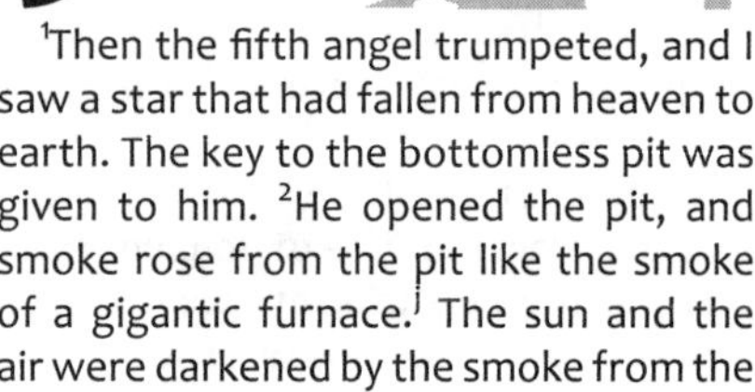

1Then the fifth angel trumpeted, and I saw a star that had fallen from heaven to earth. The key to the bottomless pit was given to him. 2He opened the pit, and smoke rose from the pit like the smoke of a gigantic furnace.[j] The sun and the air were darkened by the smoke from the pit.

3Then from the smoke came locusts upon the earth, and power was given to them like the scorpions have power over the earth.[k] 4They were told to do no harm to the grass of the earth or any green plant or any tree, but only the people who do not have the seal of God on their foreheads.[l] 5And they were permitted not to kill them, but to torment them for five months—and their torment was like the torment of a scorpion when it stings a person. 6In those days, people will seek death but will not find it; they will long to die, but death will flee from them.[m]

7Now the appearance of the locusts was like horses prepared for battle.[n] On their heads were something like crowns of gold, and their faces were like human faces. 8They had hair was like women's hair, and their teeth were like those of lions.[o] 9They had chests like iron breastplates; and the noise of their wings was like the noise of many horse-drawn chariots rushing into battle.[p] 10They have tails like scorpions with stingers; and in

a 8:2, 6, 13. Or *shofars*.
b 8:3. cf. Exod. 30:1-3.
c 8:4. cf. Ps. 141:2.
d 8:5. cf. Exod. 19:16.
e 8:7a, 8, 10, 12; 9:1, 13; 11:15. Or *sounded*; cf. Ps. 98:6.
f 8:7b. cf. Exod. 9:23-26.
g 8:10. cf. Jer. 51:25.
h 8:11. cf. Exod. 7:17-18.
i 9:12. cf. Exod. 10:21-23; Isa. 13:10; Ezek. 32:7; Joel 2:10, 31.
j 9:2. cf. Gen. 19:28; Ex. 19:18.
k 9:3. cf. Exod. 10:12-15.
l 9:4. cf. Ezek. 9:4, 6.
m 9:6. cf. Job 3:21; Jer. 8:3.
n 9:7. cf. Joel 2:4.
o 9:8. cf. Joel 1:6.
p 9:9. cf. Jer. 47:3; Joel 2:5.

their tails is their power to harm people for five months. 11They have as king over them the angel of the abyss. His name in Hebrew is Abaddon, and in Greek he has the name Apollyon.[a]

12The first woe is past. Behold, two woes are still coming after these things.

13The sixth angel trumpeted, and I heard a single voice from the four horns of the golden altar[b] before God. 14It said to the sixth angel, the one holding the trumpet,[c] "Release the four angels who are bound at the great river Euphrates."

15So the four angels—who had been prepared for the hour and day and month and year—were released to kill a third of mankind. 16The number of mounted troops was two hundred million[d]—I heard their number. 17Now here is how I saw the horses and those riding on them: they had breastplates that were fiery red, hyacinth blue, and sulfur yellow. The heads of the horses were as heads of lions, and out of their mouths came fire and smoke and brimstone[e]

18By these three plagues a third of mankind was killed—by the fire and the smoke and the brimstone that came out of their mouths. 19For the power of the horses is in their mouths and in their tails; for their tails are like serpents, having heads by which they inflict injuries.

20But the rest of mankind, those not killed by these plagues, did not repent and turn away from the works of their hands—they would not stop worshiping demons and the idols of gold and silver and stone and wood, which cannot see or hear or walk.[f] 21And they did not repent and turn away from their murders or their sorceries or their sexual immorality or their stealing.

a 9:11. Both names mean *Destroyer*; cf. Job 26:6; 28:22; 31:12; Prov. 15:11.
b 9:13. cf. Ex 30:2-3.
c 9:14. Or *shofar*.
d 9:16. Lit. *two ten thousands of ten thousands* (2 x 10,000 x 10,000).
e 9:17ff; 14:10; 19:20; 20:10; 21:8. Or *sulfur*.
f 9:20. cf. Ps. 115:4-7; 135:15-17; Dan. 5:23.

10

The Angel with a Little Scroll

1Then I saw another powerful angel coming down from heaven, wrapped in a cloud with a rainbow over his head. His face was like the sun and his feet like pillars of fire. 2He had in his hand a little scroll that was open. He set his right foot on the sea and his left foot on the land, 3and he cried out with a loud voice, just as a lion roars. When he cried out, the seven thunders spoke.[g]

4And when the seven thunders had spoken, I was about to write; but I heard a voice from heaven saying, "Seal up what the seven thunders have said. Do not write it down!"[h]

5Then the angel whom I saw standing on the sea and on the land raised his right hand toward heaven 6and swore[i] by the One who lives forever and ever, who created heaven and what is in it, the earth and what is in it, the sea and what is in it, that there would be no more delay.

7But in the days of the voice of the seventh angel—when he is about to trumpet—the mystery of God is completed, just as He declared to His servants the prophets.[j] 8Then the voice that I heard from heaven spoke to me again, saying, "Go, take the scroll that is open in the hand of the angel standing on the sea and on the land."

9So I went to the angel, telling him to give me the little scroll. And he tells me, "Take and eat it. It will be bitter to your stomach, but sweet as honey in your mouth."[k]

10So I took the little scroll from the angel's hand and ate it. It was sweet as honey in my mouth; but when I had swallowed it, my stomach was made bitter.

g 10:3. cf. Ps. 29:3-9.
h 10:4. cf. Dan. 12:4, 9.
i 10:6. cf. Gen. 14:22.
j 10:7. cf. Amos 3:7.
k 10:9. cf. Ezek. 3:1-3.

11 And they tell me, "You must prophesy again about many peoples and nations and tongues and kings."

11

Two Witnesses

1 Then a measuring rod like a staff was given to me, saying, "Get up and measure the Temple of God and the altar, and count those worshiping in it.[a] 2 But do not measure the court outside the Temple—leave it out, because it has been given to the nations, and they shall trample the holy city for forty-two months.[b] 3 And I will grant authority to My two witnesses and they will prophesy for 1,260 days,[c] dressed in sackcloth."

4 These are the two olive trees and the two menorahs that are standing before the Lord of the earth.[d] 5 If anyone wishes to harm them, fire comes out of their mouths and consumes their enemies. If anyone wants to harm them, he must be killed in this way.[e] 6 These two have the power to shut the heavens, so that no rain may fall during the days of their prophesying.[f] And they have power over the waters to turn them into blood, and to strike the earth with every kind of plague as often as they wish.[g]

7 When they have finished their testimony, the beast that rises from the abyss will make war on them, and overcome them and kill them.[h] 8 And their corpses will lie in the open street[i] of the great city that figuratively is called Sodom and Egypt—where also their[j] Lord was crucified. 9 Some from the peoples and tribes and tongues and nations will look at their corpses for three and a half days, not allowing them to be placed into a grave.[k] 10 Those who dwell on the earth will rejoice over them. They will celebrate and send gifts to one another, because these two prophets tormented those who dwell on the earth.

11 But after the three and a half days, the breath of life from God entered them, and they stood up on their feet;[l] and great fear fell on those who were watching them. 12 Then they heard a loud voice from heaven saying to them, "Come up here!" And they went up to heaven in a cloud, while their enemies watched them.[m]

13 At that hour there was a great earthquake, and a tenth of the city collapsed.[n] Seven thousand people were killed in the earthquake, and the rest were terrified and gave glory to the God of heaven.

14 The second woe is past. The third woe is coming soon.

The Seventh Trumpet

15 Then the seventh angel trumpeted, and there were loud voices in heaven saying,

> "The kingdom of this world has
> become
> the kingdom of our Lord and of His
> Anointed One.
> And He shall reign forever and
> ever!"[o]

16 And the twenty-four elders seated on their thrones before God fell on their faces and worshiped God, 17 saying,

> "We thank you, *ADONAI Elohei-Tzva'ot*,[p]
> who is and who was,
> because You have taken Your great
> power
> and begun to reign.

a 11:1. cf. Ezek. 40-42; Zech. 2:1.
b 11:2. cf. Isa. 52:1; Dan. 7:25; 12:7.
c 11:3. cf. Dan. 7:25; 12:7; Zech. 4:2-14.
d 11:4. cf. Zech. 4:3, 11, 14.
e 11:5. cf. 2 Kings 1:10-12; Jer. 5:14.
f 11:6a. cf. 1 Kings 17:1.
g 11:6b. cf. Exod. 7:17-21.
h 11:7. cf. Dan. 7:21.
i 11:8. cf. Isa. 66:24.
j 11:8. Some mss. say *our*.
k 11:9. cf. Ps. 79:2-3.
l 11:11. cf. Gen. 2:7; Ezek. 37:5, 10.
m 11:12. cf. 2 Kings 2:11.
n 11:13. cf. Isa. 29:6; Ezek. 38:19.
o 11:15. cf. Isa. 37:16; Dan. 2:44; 7:14, 27.
p 11:17; 15:3; 16:7. Grk. *Kurie o Theos o Pantokrator* (O Lord God Almighty).

18The nations were enraged,
but Your wrath has come[a]
and the time for the dead to be judged—
to reward Your servants,
the prophets and *kedoshim*,
and those who fear Your name,
the small and the great,
and to destroy the destroyers of the earth."[b]

19Then the Temple of God in heaven was opened, and the Ark of His Covenant appeared in His Temple. And there were flashes of lightning and rumblings and clashes of thunder and an earthquake and heavy hail.[c]

12

Mother, Child, Dragon, and War

1A great sign appeared in heaven: a
woman clothed with the sun, with the
moon under her feet, and on her head
a crown of twelve stars.[d] 2She is pregnant—crying out in birth pains, in agony
to give birth.[e]
3Then another sign appeared in
heaven: a great fiery red dragon that
had seven heads and ten horns, and
seven royal crowns on his heads.[f] 4His
tail sweeps away a third of the stars of
heaven—it hurled them to the earth.[g]
Now the dragon stood before the
woman who was about to give birth, so
that whenever she gave birth he might
devour her child.
5And she gave birth to a son, a male
child, who is to rule all the nations with
an iron rod.[h] And her child was snatched
away to God and to His throne. 6Then the
woman fled into the wilderness, where
she has a place prepared by God so they
might take care of her for 1,260 days.
7And war broke out in heaven, Michael
and his angels making war against the
dragon.[i] The dragon and his angels
fought, 8but they were not strong
enough, and there was no longer any
place for them in heaven. 9And the great
dragon was thrown down—the ancient
serpent, called the devil and satan,
who deceives the whole world.[j] He was
thrown down to the earth, and his angels
were thrown down with him.[k] 10Then I
heard a loud voice in heaven saying,

"Now have come the salvation and the power
and the kingdom of our God
and the authority of His Anointed One,
for the accuser of our brothers and sisters—
the one who accuses them before our God day and night[l]—
has been thrown out.
11They overcame him by the blood of the Lamb
and by the word of their testimony,
and they did not love their lives even in the face of death.
12Therefore rejoice, O heavens,
and you who dwell in them!
Woe to the earth and the sea,
for the devil has come down to you
with great rage,
knowing that his time is short.

13Now when the dragon saw that he
had been thrown to the earth, he stalked
the woman who had given birth to the
male child. 14But the woman was given
two wings of the great eagle,[m] so that
she might fly away from the presence of
the serpent into the wilderness, to the

a 11:18a. cf, Ps. 2:5; 110:5.
b 11:18b. cf. Dan. 7:10; 12:2.
c 11:19. cf. Ex 9:23; 19:16.
d 12:1. cf. Gen 37:9-10.
e 12:2. cf. Isa. 26:17; 66:6-9; Mic. 4:9-10.
f 12:3. cf. Isa. 27:1; Dan. 7:7, 20, 24.
g 12:4. cf. Dan. 8:10.
h 12:5. cf. Isa. 66:7; Ps. 2:9.
i 12:7. cf. Dan. 10:13, 21; 12:1.
j 12:9a. cf. Gen. 3:1.
k 12:9b. cf. Isa. 14:12-15; Dan. 8:10.
l 12:10. cf. Job 1:9-11; Zech. 3:1.
m 12:14a. cf. Exod. 19:4.

place where she is taken care of—for a
time, times, and half a time.[a]
15And from out of his mouth, the serpent spewed water like a river after the
woman, in order to sweep her away with
a flood. 16But the earth came to the aid of
the woman. The earth opened its mouth
and swallowed the river that the dragon
had spewed from his mouth. 17So the
dragon became enraged at the woman
and went off to make war with the rest
of her offspring—those who keep the
commandments of God and hold to the
testimony of *Yeshua*. 18And he stood on
the shore of the sea.

13

Two Beasts

1Then I saw a beast rising out of the
sea,[b] that had ten horns and seven heads.
On his horns were ten royal crowns, and
upon his heads were slanderous names.
2Now the beast that I saw was like a leop-
ard, his feet like a lion's, and his mouth
like a bear's. And the dragon gave him his
power and his throne and great authority. 3One of his heads seemed to have
been slain, but the fatal wound was
healed. The whole earth was amazed
and followed the beast. 4And they worshiped the dragon, because he had given
authority to the beast. They also worshiped the beast, chanting, "Who is like
the beast, and who can make war against
him?"[c]
5The beast was given a mouth utter-
ing great boasts and blasphemies. It
was given authority to act for forty-two
months. 6Then he opened his mouth with
blasphemies against God, to slander His
name and His tabernacle—that is, those
dwelling in heaven. 7He was also permitted to make war against the *kedoshim*
and overcome them, and he was given
authority over every tribe and people
and tongue and nation. 8All who dwell on
the earth shall worship him—everyone
whose name has not been written from
the foundation of the world in the Book
of Life of the Lamb who was slain.

9If anyone has an ear, let him hear.
10If anyone is meant for captivity,
to captivity he goes.
If anyone is to be killed by the sword,
by the sword he must be killed.[d]

Here is the perseverance and faith of
the *kedoshim*.
11Then I saw another beast rising out
of the earth. He had two horns[e] like a
lamb and spoke like a dragon. 12He exercises all the authority of the first beast
before him, and he makes the earth and
all those who dwell in it worship the first
beast, whose fatal wound was healed.
13He performs great signs, even making
fire come down from heaven in the sight
of men.[f] 14And he deceives those who
dwell on the earth through the signs he
is permitted to perform, telling those
who dwell on the earth to make an image
in honor of the beast who has the sword
wound yet lived. 15The second beast was
permitted to give life to the image of
the first beast, so that the image of the
beast could even speak and cause all
who would not worship the image of the
beast to be killed. 16He also causes all—
the small and the great, the rich and the
poor, the free and the slave—to receive
a mark on their right hand or upon their
forehead. 17And so no one can buy or sell
unless he has the mark—either the name
of the beast or the number of his name.
18Here is wisdom: let the one who has
understanding calculate the number of
the beast, for it is a number of a man, and
his number is 666.[g]

a 12:14b. cf. Dan. 7:25; 12:7.
b 13:1. cf. Dan. 7:3.
c 13:4. cf. Exod. 15:11; Isa. 46:5.
d 13:10. cf. Jer. 15:2; 43:11.
e 13:11. cf. Dan. 8:3.
f 13:13. cf. 1 Kings 18:38.
g 13:18. Some mss. say *six hundred sixteen.*

14

A Song for the 144,000

1Then I looked, and behold, the Lamb was standing on Mount Zion,[a] and with Him were 144,000 who had His name and His Father's name written on their foreheads. 2And I heard a voice from heaven like the roar of rushing waters and the booming of loud thunder.[b] The voice I heard was like harpists playing on their harps. 3And they are singing a new song before the throne and before the four living creatures and the elders; and no one is able to learn the song except the 144,000 who had been redeemed from the earth.

4These are the ones who have not defiled themselves with women, for they are virgins.

These are the ones who follow the Lamb wherever He goes.

These have been redeemed from among mankind as firstfruits for God and the Lamb.

5And in their mouth was found no lie—they are blameless.[c]

Three Angels with Messages

6And then I saw another angel flying high in the sky, having a timeless message of good news to proclaim to those who dwell on the earth—to every nation and tribe and tongue and people. 7He said in a loud voice, "Fear God and give Him glory, because the hour of His judgment has come. Worship the One who made heaven and earth and sea and springs of water."

8Another angel, a second one, followed, saying, "Fallen, fallen, is Babylon the great[d]—she who made all nations drink of the wine of the fury of her immorality."

9And another angel, a third one, followed them, saying in a loud voice, "If anyone worships the beast and his image and receives a mark on his forehead or on his hand, 10he shall also drink the wine of God's fury, poured full strength into the cup of His wrath.[e] And he shall be tormented with fire and brimstone[f] before the holy angels and before the Lamb.11The smoke of their torment goes up forever and ever.[g] Those who worship the beast and its image and those who receive the mark of his name have no rest day or night."

12Here is the perseverance of the *kedoshim*—those who keep the commandments of God and the faith of *Yeshua*.

13Then I heard a voice from heaven saying,[h] "Write: How fortunate are the dead—those who die in the Lord from now on!" "Yes," says the Spirit, "that they may rest from their labors, for their deeds follow them."

Time to Harvest the Earth

14Then I looked, and behold, there was a white cloud—and seated on the cloud was one like a son of man.[i] He had a golden crown on His head and a sharp sickle in His hand. 15Then another angel came out of the Temple, crying out with a loud voice to the One seated on the cloud, "Put in your sickle and reap, for the hour to reap has come, because the harvest of the earth is fully ripe." 16So the One seated on the cloud swung his sickle over the earth, and the earth was harvested.[j]

17Then another angel came out of the Temple in heaven, and he also had a sharp sickle. 18Then another angel—the one who has authority over fire—came

a 14:1. cf. Ps. 2:6.
b 14:2. cf. Ezek. 1:24; 43:2.
c 14:5. cf. Zeph. 3:13; Mal. 2:6; some mss. add *before the throne of God.*
d 24:8. cf. Isa. 21:9; Jer. 51:7-8.
e 14:10a. cf. Ps. 75:8; Isa. 51:17; Jer. 25:15-17, 27.
f 14:10b. cf. Gen. 19:24; Ezek. 38:22.
g 14:11. cf. Isa. 34:10.
h 14:13. Some mss. add *to me.*
i 14:14. Or the *Son of Man;* cf. Dan. 7:13-14.
j 14:16. cf. Joel 3:13-14.

out from the altar; and he called out with a loud voice to the one holding the sharp sickle, saying, "Put in your sickle and gather the grape clusters from the vineyard of the earth, because her grapes are ripe." 19So the angel swung his sickle over the earth and gathered the clusters from the vineyard of the earth and threw them into the great winepress of the wrath of God. 20And the winepress was stomped on outside the city, and blood flowed from the winepress as high as a horse's bridle for 1,600 stadia.[a]

15

Song of Moses to the Lamb

1Then I saw another great and wonderful sign in heaven: seven angels who have seven plagues—the last ones, for with them God's wrath is finished. 2And I saw something like a sea of glass mixed with fire, and those who had overcome the beast and his image[b] and the number of his name standing by the sea of glass, holding the harps of God. 3And they are singing the song of Moses[c] the servant of God and the song of the Lamb, saying,

"Great and wonderful are Your deeds,
Adonai Elohei-Tzva'ot![d]
Just and true are Your ways,
O King of the nations![e]
4Who shall not fear and glorify Your name, O Lord?
For You alone are Holy.
All the nations shall come and worship before You,[f]
for Your righteous acts have been revealed!"

a 14:20b. About 200 miles; 1 stade = 607 feet; cf. Isa. 63:1-6.
b Some mss. add *and its mark*.
c 15:3a. cf. Ex. 15:1, 11; Deut. 31:30ff.
d 15:3. Or O Lord God the Almighty; cf. Deut. 32:3-4; Ps. 111:2; 139:14.
e 15:3. Some mss. read *ages*.
f 15:4. cf. Ps. 86:9; Is. 66:23.

5After these things I looked, and the Temple of the Tent of Witness in heaven was opened. 6Out of the Temple came the seven angels having the seven plagues, dressed in pure bright linen and wearing wide gold sashes around their chests.

7Then one of the four living creatures gave the seven angels seven golden bowls full of the wrath of God, who lives forever and ever. 8And the Temple was filled with smoke from the glory of God and from His power.[g] No one was able to enter the Temple until the seven angels' seven plagues were finished.

16

Seven Bowls of God's Wrath

1Then I heard a loud voice from the Temple saying to the seven angels, "Go and pour out on the earth the seven bowls of God's wrath."[h] 2So the first angel went and poured out his bowl on the earth, and foul and painful boils[i] came upon the people having the mark of the beast and worshiping his image. 3Next the second angel poured out his bowl into the sea, and it became blood like that of a corpse; and every living thing in the sea died.[j] 4Then the third angel poured out his bowl into the rivers and the springs of water, and they became blood.[k] 5Then I heard the angel of the waters saying,

"Righteous are You—the Holy One,
who is and who was—
because You have passed these judgments.
6For they have poured out the blood of *kedoshim* and prophets,

g 15:8. cf. Exod. 19:18; 40:34-35; 1 Kings 8:10-11; 2 Chr. 5:13-14; Is. 6:4.
h 16:1. cf. Ps. 79:6; Ezek. 22:31; Zeph. 3:8.
i 16:2. cf. Exod. 9:9-11.
j 16:3. cf. Exod. 7:17-21.
k 16:4. cf. Ps. 78:44.

and You have given them blood to
drink[a]—
they are deserving!"

7Then I heard the altar saying,

"Yes, *ADONAI Elohei-Tzva'ot*,
true and righteous are Your
judgments!"[b]

8The fourth angel poured out his
bowl on the sun, and it was permitted to scorch people with fire. 9People
were scorched with fierce heat, and they
cursed the name of God—the One who
has power over these plagues. But they
did not repent, to give Him glory.

10Then the fifth angel poured out his
bowl on the throne of the beast, and his
kingdom was plunged into darkness.[c]
People gnawed their tongues in pain
11and cursed the God of heaven because
of their pains and their boils. But they did
not repent of their deeds.[d]

12The sixth angel poured out his bowl
over the great river Euphrates; and its
water was dried up, to prepare the way
for the kings from the east. 13Then I
saw—coming from the dragon's mouth
and from the beast's mouth and from the
false prophet's mouth—three unclean
spirits like frogs.[e] 14For they are demonic
spirits performing miraculous signs, who
go out to the kings of the whole world—
to gather them for battle on the great
Day of God the Almighty.[f]

15"Behold, I am coming like a thief! How
fortunate is the one who stays alert and
keeps his clothes on, lest he walk around
naked and they see his shamefulness."

16Then the spirits gathered the kings to
the place called in Hebrew *Har-Megiddo*.[g]

17The seventh angel poured out his
bowl into the air. A loud voice came out
of the Temple[h] from the throne, saying,
"It is done!"[i] 18And there were flashes of
lightning and rumblings and clashes of
thunder and a great earthquake—such
as never happened since mankind has
been on the earth, so mighty was the
quake.[j]

19Then the great city was split into
three parts, and the cities of the nations
collapsed. Babylon the great was remembered before God, to force her to drink
the cup of the wine of His furious wrath.[k]
20Every island fled away, and no mountains were to be found. 21Enormous
hail—about a hundred pounds each[l]—
falls from heaven on the people. And the
people cursed God because of the plague
of hail—so extreme was that plague.[m]

17

The Vile Prostitute and the Beast

1Then one of the seven angels holding
the seven bowls came and spoke with
me, saying, "Come, I will show you the
sentencing of the great prostitute,[n] who
sits on many waters. 2The earth's kings
committed sexual immorality with her,
and those who dwell on the earth got
drunk with the wine of her immorality."

3So he carried me away in the Spirit
into a wilderness, and I saw a woman
sitting on a scarlet beast that was full
of blasphemous names and had seven
heads and ten horns.[o] 4The woman
was clothed in purple and scarlet, and
adorned with gold and precious stones
and pearls.[p] She was holding a golden
cup[q] in her hand full of detestable things
and the filth of her immorality, 5and on

a 16:6. cf. Isa. 49:26.
b 16:8. cf. Ps. 19:9.
c 16:10. cf. Exod. 10:21-22.
d 16:9, 11. cf. Exod. 9:12; 10:20, 27; 11:10.
e 16:13. cf. Exod. 8:6.
f 16:14. cf. Ezek. 30:3; Joel 2:11; Zeph. 1:14.
g 16:16. *Mount Megiddo* or *Armageddon*; cf. 2 Kings 23:29-30; Zech. 12:11.
h 16:17. cf. Isa. 66:6.
i 16:17. cf. Ps. 22:31;
j 16:18. cf. Exod. 19:16-19; Zech. 14:4-5.
k 16:19. cf. Rev. 14:8, 10.
l 16:20l Lit. *weighing a Roman talent.*
m 16:21. cf. Exod. 9:23-24.
n 17:1. cf. Isa. 1:21; Nah. 3:4.
o 17:3. cf. Dan. 7:7,24.
p 17:4a. cf. Ezek. 28:13.
q 17:4b. cf. Jer. 51:7.

her forehead was written a name, a mystery: "Babylon the Great, the mother of prostitutesand the detestable things of the earth."

[6]And I saw the woman drunk with the blood of the *kedoshim* and with the blood of the witnesses of *Yeshua*. When I saw her, I was totally astounded.

[7]But the angel said to me, "Why are you astonished? I will tell you the mystery of the woman and of the beast that carries her, which has the seven heads and ten
horns. [8]The beast that you saw was, and is not, and yet is about to rise up from the abyss and head for destruction. Those who dwell on the earth—whose names have not been written in the Book of Life from the foundation of the world— will be astonished when they see the beast, because he was and is not and is to come.

[9]"This calls for a mind having wisdom. The seven heads are seven mountains on which the woman is seated. They are
also seven kings— [10]five have fallen, one is, the other has not yet come; and when he comes, he must remain a little while.
[11]The beast that was and is not—he himself is the eighth, and is one of the seven,
and is heading for destruction. [12]The ten horns that you saw are ten kings who have not yet received royal power, but receive authority as kings with the
beast for one hour. [13]These kings are of one mind, and they give their power and
authority to the beast. [14]They will make war against the Lamb, and the Lamb will overcome them—because He is Lord of lords and King of kings,[a] and those with Him are called and chosen and faithful."

[15]Then he tells me, "The waters that you saw, where the prostitute is seated, are peoples and multitudes and nations
and tongues. [16]The ten horns that you saw, and the beast—these will hate the prostitute. They will make her desolate and naked,[b] and devour her flesh and
burn her up with fire. [17]For God has put it into their hearts to do His will, and to be of one mind, and to give their royal power to the beast until the words of
God are fulfilled. [18]And the woman that you saw is the great city exercising kingship over the kings of the earth."

a 17:14. cf. Deut. 10:17; Ps. 136:2-3; Dan. 2:47.
b 17:16. cf. Ezek. 16:37, 39; 23:35.

18

Judgment of Babylon

[1]After these things, I saw another angel coming down from heaven, having great authority, and the earth was illuminated by his glory. [2]He cried out with a mighty voice, saying:

"Fallen, fallen is Babylon the great![c]
She has become a lair for demons,
a haunt for every unclean spirit
and for every unclean bird
and for every unclean and detestable beast.[d]
[3]For all the nations have drunk
of the wine of the fury of her immorality.
The kings of the earth have committed sexual immorality with her,
and the merchants of the earth grew rich
off the power of her
self-indulgence."

[4]Then I heard another voice from heaven saying,

"Come out of her, my people,[e]
lest you participate in her sins
and receive her plagues!
[5]For her sins have piled up to heaven,[f]
and God has remembered her crimes.
[6]Pay her back just as she has paid out
and give her back double for her deeds![g]

c 18:2a. cf. Isa. 21:9; Jer. 51:8.
d 18:2b. cf. Isa. 34:11-15; Jer. 50:39; 51:37.
e 18:4. cf. Ex 5:1; 7:16; 8:1, 20; 9:1, 13; 10:3; Jer. 50:8; 51:6, 9, 45.
f 18:5. cf. Jer. 51:9.
g 18:6. cf. Ps. 137:8; Jer. 50:15, 29.

In the cup she has mixed—
mix a double dose for her!
[7]As she has exalted herself and
indulged herself in luxury,
so give her the same measure of
torment and grief!
For in her heart she says,
'I sit as a queen—
I am no widow;
I shall never see grief.'[a]
[8]For this reason her plagues will arrive
in a single day—
death and grief and famine—
and she shall be burned down with
fire.[b]
For mighty is *ADONAI Elohim* who
judges her!

[9]Then the kings of the earth, who committed sexual immorality and indulged in luxury with her shall weep and wail over her when they see the smoke of her burning[c]—[10]standing far off because of the terror of her torment, saying:

"Alas, alas, O great city—
O Babylon, the mighty city!
For in a single hour your judgment
has come!"

[11]And the merchants of the earth weep
and mourn for her,[d] because no one buys
their merchandise anymore— [12]shipments of gold, silver, precious stones, and pearls; fine linen, purple, silk, and scarlet; all kinds of citron wood; all kinds of ivory products; all kinds of products made of costly wood, bronze, iron, and
marble; [13]cinnamon, spice, incense, myrrh, and frankincense; wine, oil, fine flour, and wheat; cattle, sheep, horses, and chariots; and slaves—that is, human souls.

[14]The fruit of your soul's desire has
gone from you,
and all the expensive and beautiful
things are lost to you
—never again will people find
them.

[15]The merchants of these things, who became rich from her, shall stand far off for fear of her torment, weeping and
mourning, [16]saying,

"Alas, alas, O great city—
clothed in fine linen and purple and
scarlet,
adorned with gold and precious
stones and pearls!
[17]For in a single hour so much wealth
has been ruined!"

And every ship captain and passenger, sailors and all who make their living at
sea, stood at a distance [18]and were crying out, seeing the smoke of her burning, saying, 'What city is like the great city?'
[19]And they threw dust on their heads and were crying out, weeping and mourning,

"Alas, alas, O great city—
in her all who had ships at sea
grew rich from her wealth!
For in a single hour has she been
ruined!
[20]Rejoice over her, O heaven,[e]
and you *kedoshim*, *shlichim* and
prophets!
For God has judged her condemnation
of you!"

[21]Then a mighty angel picked up a stone like a great millstone and threw it into the sea,[f] saying:

"So shall Babylon, the great city,
be thrown down with violence,
never to be found again!
[22]And the sound of harpists and musicians,

a 18:7. cf. Isa. 47:7-8; Zeph. 2:15.
b 18:8. cf. Isa. 47:9; Jer. 50:31-32.
c 18:9. cf. Ezek. 26:16-17.
d 18:11. cf. Ezek. 27:27-31.
e 18:20. cf. Jer. 51:48.
f 18:21. cf. Jer. 51:63-64.

flautists and trumpeters,
shall never be heard in you again![a]
And the craftsman of any craft
shall never be found in you again!
And the sound of a mill
shall never be heard in you again!
23And the light of a lamp
shall never shine in you again!
And the voice of the bridegroom and bride
shall never be heard in you again![b]
For your businessmen were the tycoons of the world,
for all the nations were deceived by your sorcery![c]
24And in her was found
the blood of the prophets and *kedoshim*
and all those slaughtered on the earth."

19

Victory Songs in Heaven

1After these things, I heard something like the loud voice of a great multitude in heaven, shouting:

"Hallelujah![d]
Salvation and glory and power
belong to our God.
2For His judgments are true and just.[e]
For He has judged the great prostitute
who corrupted the earth with her whoring,
and has avenged the blood of His servants caused by her hand."[f]

3And a second time they shouted,

"Hallelujah!
The smoke from her goes up forever and ever!"[g]

4Then the twenty-four elders and the four living creatures fell down and worshiped God who is seated on the throne, saying, "Amen! Hallelujah!"[h]

5Then a voice came from the throne, saying:

"Praise our God,
all you His servants and all who fear Him,
both the small and the great!"[i]

Wedding of the Lamb

6Then I heard something like the voice of a great multitude—like the roar of rushing waters[j] or like the rumbling of powerful thunder—saying,

"Hallelujah!
For *Adonai Elohei-Tzva'ot* reigns!
7Let us rejoice and be glad
and give the glory to Him!
For the wedding of the Lamb has come,
and His bride has made herself ready,[k]
8She was given fine linen to wear,
bright and clean!
For the fine linen is
the righteous deeds of the *kedoshim*."

9Then the angel tells me, "Write: How fortunate are those who have been invited to the wedding banquet of the Lamb!" He also tells me, "These are the true words of God."

10Then I fell down at his feet and worshiped him. But he said to me, "See that you do not do that—for I am only a fellow

a 18:22. cf. Isa. 24:8; Ezek. 26:13.
b 18:23a. cf. Jer. 25:10.
c 18:23b. cf. Isa. 23:8; Nah. 3:4.
d 19:1..cf. Ps. 104:35.
e 19:2a. cf. Ps. 19:9.
f 19:2b. cf. Deut. 32:43; 2 Kings 9:7.
g 19:3. cf. Isa. 34:8-10.
h 19:4. cf. Ps. 106:48.
i 19:5. cf. Ps. 115:13; 135:1.
j 19:6. cf. Ezek. 1:24; 43:2.
k 19:7. cf. Ex. 19:14; Ps. 45:13.

servant with you and your brothers and sisters who hold to the testimony of *Yeshua*. Worship God! For the testimony of *Yeshua* is the spirit of prophecy."

Final Battle of this Age

11 Then I saw heaven opened,[a] and behold, a white horse! The One riding on it is called Faithful and True, and He judges and makes war in righteousness. 12 His eyes are like a flame of fire, and many royal crowns are on His head. He has a name written that no one knows except Himself. 13 He is clothed in a robe dipped in blood,[b] and the name by which He is called is "the Word of God."

14 And the armies of heaven, clothed in fine linen, white and clean, were following Him on white horses. 15 From His mouth comes a sharp sword—so that with it He may strike down the nations—and He shall rule them with an iron rod, and He treads the winepress of the furious wrath of *Elohei-Tzva'ot*.[c] 16 On His robe and on His thigh He has a name written, "King of kings, and Lord of lords."[d]

17 Then I saw a single angel standing in the sun, and with a loud voice he cried out to all the birds flying high in the sky, "Come, gather for the great banquet of God—18 to eat the flesh of kings and the flesh of generals and the flesh of mighty men, the flesh of horses and those riding on them, the flesh of all men, both free and slave, both small and great!"[e]

19 Also I saw the beast and the kings of the earth and their armies gathered together to make war against the One who sat on the horse and against His army. 20 Then the beast was captured, and along with him the false prophet who had performed the signs before him by which he deceived those who had received the mark of the beast, as well as those who had worshiped his image. These two were thrown alive into the lake of fire burning with brimstone.[f] 21 The rest were killed with the sword coming out of the mouth of the One riding on the horse. And all the birds gorged themselves with their flesh.

a 19:11. cf. Ezek. 1:1.
b 19:13. cf, Isa. 63:3.
c 19:15. cf. Isa. 49:2; 11:4; Ps 2:9; Isa. 63:3.
d 19:16. cf. Deut. 10:17; Dan. 2:47.
e 19:18. cf. Ezek. 39:17-20.

20

The First Resurrection

1 Then I saw an angel coming down from heaven, holding in his hand the key to the abyss and a great chain. 2 He seized the dragon—the ancient serpent, who is the devil and satan—and bound him for a thousand years.[g] 3 He also threw him into the abyss and locked and sealed it over him, so that he would not deceive the nations any longer, until the thousand years were completed. After these things, he must be released for a short while.

4 Then I saw thrones, and people sat upon them—those to whom authority to judge was given.[h] And I saw the souls of those who had been beheaded because of their testimony for *Yeshua* and because of the word of God. They had not worshiped the beast or his image, nor had they received his mark on their forehead or on their hand. And they came to life[i] and reigned with the Messiah for a thousand years.

5 The rest of the dead did not come to life until the thousand years were completed. This is the first resurrection. 6 How fortunate and holy is the one who has a share in the first resurrection! Over such the second death has no authority, but they shall be *kohanim* of God and the Messiah, and they shall reign with Him for a thousand years.

f 19:20. cf. Isa. 30:33; Dan. 7:11.
g 20:2. cf. Isa. 24:22.
h 20:4. cf. Dan. 7:9; 7:22; Matt. 19:28.
i 20:4b. cf. Isa. 25:8; 26:19; Dan 12:2; Mal. 3:-16-18.

Judgment After 1000 Years

7When the thousand years has ended, satan shall be released from his prison, 8and he shall come out to deceive the nations at the four corners of the earth, Gog and Magog, to gather them for the battle.[a] Their number is like the sand of the sea. 9And they came up on the broad plain of the earth and surrounded the camp of the *kedoshim* and the beloved city—but fire fell from heaven and consumed them.[b]

10And the devil who deceived them was thrown into the lake of fire and brimstone, where the beast and the false prophet are too, and they shall be tortured day and night forever and ever.

11Then I saw a great white throne, and the One seated on it. The earth and heaven fled from His presence, but no place was found for them. 12And I saw the dead—the great and the small—standing before the throne. The books were opened, and another book was opened—the Book of Life. And the dead were judged according to what was written in the books, according to their deeds.[c] 13The sea gave up the dead that were in it, and death and *Sheol* gave up the dead in them. Then they were each judged, each one of them, according to their deeds.

14Then death and *Sheol* were thrown into the lake of fire. This is the second death—the lake of fire. 15And if anyone was not found written in the Book of Life, he was thrown into the lake of fire.

21

A New Heaven and a New Earth

1Then I saw a new heaven and a new earth; for the first heaven and the first earth had passed away, and the sea was no more.[d]

2I also saw the holy city—the New Jerusalem—coming down out of heaven from God, prepared as a bride adorned for her husband.[e] 3I also heard a loud voice from the throne, saying,

"Behold, the dwelling of God is among men,
and He shall tabernacle among them.
They shall be His people,
and God Himself shall be among them and be their God.[f]
4He shall wipe away every tear from their eyes,[g]
and death shall be no more.
Nor shall there be mourning or crying or pain any longer,
for the former things have passed away."

5And the One seated upon the throne said, "Behold, I am making all things new!" Then He said, "Write, for these words are trustworthy and true."

6Then He said to me, "It is done! I am the Alpha and the Omega, the Beginning and the End. To the thirsty I will freely give from the spring of the water of life.[h] 7The one who overcomes shall inherit these things, and I will be his God and he shall be My son.[i] 8But for the cowardly and faithless and detestable and murderers and sexually immoral and sorcerers and idolaters and all liars—their lot is in the lake that burns with fire and brimstone, which is the second death."

The New Jerusalem

9Then came one of the seven angels holding the seven bowls full of the seven final plagues, and he spoke with me,

a 20:8. cf. Ezek. 7:2; 38:2.
b 20:9. cf. Ps. 87:2; Ezek. 38:22; 39:6.
c 12:12. cf. Ex. 32:32; Dan 12:2; Mal. 3:16-18.

d 21:1. cf., Is. 65:17; 66:22.
e 21:2. cf. Is. 61:10.
f 21:3. cf. Lev. 26:11; Ezek. 37:27; Jer. 31:33(38:33 LXX); Zech. 8:8; some mss. omit *and be their God.*
g 21:4. cf. Is. 25:8.
h 21:6. cf. Isa. 55:1; Jn. 7:37-38.
i 21:7. cf. 2 Sam. 7:14; Ps. 89:26-27,

saying, "Come, I will show you the bride, the wife of the Lamb."

[10]Then he carried me away in the Spirit to a great and high mountain,[a] and he showed me the holy city, Jerusalem, coming down out of heaven from God, [11]having the glory of God—her radiance like a most precious stone, like a jasper, sparkling like crystal. [12]She had a great, high wall, with twelve gates, and above the gates twelve angels. On the gates were inscribed the names of the twelve tribes of *B'nei-Israel*— [13]three gates on the east, three gates on the north, three gates on the south, and three gates on the west.[b] [14]And the wall of the city had twelve foundations, and on them the twelve names of the twelve *shlichim* of the Lamb.

[15]The angel speaking with me had a gold measuring rod to measure the city and its gates and walls.[c] [16]The city is laid out as a square—its length the same as its width. He measured the city with the rod—12,000 stadia.[d] Its length and width and height are equal. [17]He also measured its wall—144 cubits by human measurement, which is also an angel's measurement. [18]The material of the city's wall was jasper, while the city was pure gold, clear as glass. [19]The foundations of the city wall were decorated with every kind of precious stone—the first foundation was jasper; the second, sapphire; the third, chalcedony; the fourth, emerald; [20]the fifth, sardonyx; the sixth, carnelian; the seventh, yellow topaz; the eighth; beryl; the ninth, topaz; the tenth, chrysoprase; the eleventh, jacinth; the twelfth, amethyst. [21]And the twelve gates were twelve pearls—each of the gates was from a single pearl. And the street of the city was pure gold, transparent as glass.

[22]I saw no temple in her, for its Temple is *Adonai Elohei-Tzva'ot* and the Lamb. [23]And the city has no need for the sun or the moon to shine on it, for the glory of God lights it up, and its lamp is the Lamb.[e] [24]The nations shall walk by its light, and the kings of the earth bring their glory into it.[f] [25]Its gates shall never be shut by day,[g] for there shall be no night there! [26]And they shall bring into it the glory and honor of the nations. [27]And nothing unholy[h] shall ever enter it, nor anyone doing what is detestable or false,[i] but only those written in the Book of Life.

a 21:10. cf. Ezek. 40:2.
b 2:13. cf. Ezek. 48:31-34.
c 2:25. cf. Ezek. 40:3.
d 2:16. About 1400 miles; 1 *stadia* = 607 feet.

22

[1]Then the angel showed me a river of the water of life—bright as crystal,[j] flowing from the throne of God and of the Lamb [2]down the middle of the city's street. On either side of the river was a tree of life, bearing twelve kinds of fruit, yielding its fruit each month; and the leaves of the tree were for the healing of the nations.[k] [3]No longer will be there be any curse. The throne of God and of the Lamb shall be in the city, and His servants shall serve Him. [4]They shall see His face,[l] and His name shall be on their foreheads.[m] [5]Night shall be no more, and people will have no need for lamplight or sunlight—for *Adonai Elohim* will shine on them.[n] And they shall reign forever and ever!

Yeshua Is Coming

[6]He said to me, "These words are trustworthy and true! *Adonai*, the God of the spirits of the prophets, has sent His angel to show His servants what must happen soon.[o] [7]Behold, I am coming soon!

e 21:23. cf. Isa. 24:23; 30:26; 60:19-20; Zech. 14:6-7;
f 21:24. cf. Isa. 60:3, 5.
g 21:25-26. cf. Isa. 60:11.
h 21:27a. Lit. *common* (Heb. *chol*); cf. Lev. 10:10.
i 21:27. cf. Isa. 52:1; Ezek. 44:9.
j 22:1. cf. Ps. 46:4; Ezek. 47:1; Zech. 14:8.
k 22:2. cf. Gen. 2:9; Ezek. 47:12.
l 22:4a. cf. Exod. 33:11; Ps 17:15; 27:8-10.
m 22:4b. cf. Exod. 39:30.
n 22:5. cf. Isa. 60:19.
o 22:6. cf. Amos 3:7.

Revelation 21:23

And the city has no need for the sun or the moon to shine on it, for the glory of God lights it up, and its lamp is the Lamb.

How fortunate is the one who keeps the
words of the prophecy of this book."
8 I, John, am the one hearing and seeing these things. And when I heard and
saw them, I fell down to worship at the
feet of the angel showing me these
things. 9 But he tells me, "See that you
do not do that! I am a fellow servant with
you and your brothers the prophets and
those keeping the words of this book.
Worship God!"
10 Then he tells me, "Do not seal up the
words of the prophecy of this book, for
the time is near.[a] 11 Let the evildoer still do
evil, and the filthy still be filthy, and the
righteous still do righteousness, and the
holy still be holy.[b] 12 Behold, I am coming
soon, and My reward is with Me, to pay
back each one according to his deeds.
13 "I am the Alpha and the Omega, the
First and the Last, the Beginning and
the End.[c] 14 How fortunate are those
who wash their robes, so that they may
have the right to the Tree of Life[d] and
may enter through the gates into the
city. 15 Outside are the dogs and the sorcerers and the sexually immoral and the
murderers and the idolaters, and everyone who loves and practices falsehood.
16 I, *Yeshua*, have sent My angel to testify
these things to you for My communities.
I am the Root and the Offspring of David,
the Bright and Morning Star."[e]
17 The Spirit and the bride say, "Come!"
And let the one who hears say, "Come!"
Let the one who is thirsty come—let the
one who wishes freely take the water of
life![f] 18 I testify to everyone who hears
the words of the prophecy of this book.
If anyone adds to them, God shall add to
him the plagues that are written in this
book; 19 and if anyone takes away from
the words of the book of this prophecy,
God shall take away his share in the Tree
of Life and the Holy City,[g] which are written in this book.
20 The One giving testimony to these
things says, "Yes! I am coming soon!"
Amen! Come, Lord *Yeshua*![h] 21 May the
grace of the Lord *Yeshua* be with all![i]

---

a 22:10. cf. Dan. 8:26; 12:4.
b 22:11. cf. Dan. 12:10.
c 22:13. cf. Isa. 44:6; 48:12.
d 22:14. cf. Gen. 2:9; 3:22; Prov. 3:18; 11:30.
e 22:16. cf. Isa. 11:1.
f 22:17. cf. Isa. 55:1.
g 21L18-19. cf. Deut. 4:2; 12:32.
h 22:20. Some mss. say *Even so, come, Lord Yeshua.*
i 22:21. Some mss. add *the holy ones* (Heb. *kedoshim*) and *Amen.*

Tree of Life Bible

Glossary

What is the benefit to studying the glossary? Studying the terms in the glossary will help you understand the vocabulary this Bible uses. It also introduces you to terms often used by Jewish believers in Messianic gatherings.

Where can we find the glossary words in the text? At the end of every definition in this glossary you will find chapter and verse references in parentheses. These will show you places where that word is used in context. Looking up those scriptures can be a good way to learn the meanings of these words.

Why are some words *italicized?* In this translation, the italicized words (such as *Elohim*) are transliterated Hebrew. This means we use English letters to represent Hebrew sounds. The transliteration allows you to become familiar with the sounds of spoken Hebrew and may encourage you to learn written Hebrew as well.

How do I say the Hebrew transliterated words? Unlike in English, each vowel sound in Hebrew nearly always has the same sound. Use this chart to help with the pronunciation of the vowels:

a—sounds like the *a* in *father*

e—sounds like the *e* in *sent*

i—sounds like the *i* in *spaghetti*

ei—sounds like the *ey* in *they*

ai—sounds like the ai in *aisle*

u—sounds like the *u* in *truth*

o—sounds like the *o* in *go*

’—sounds like a very short *a* as in *about*

Consonants are like English with these exceptions:

tz—sounds like the *zz* in *pizza*

ch or kh—sounds like the *ch* in *Bach*

Which syllable gets the emphasis in Hebrew? Hebrew words often have their accent on the last part of the word, the opposite of English. But there are many exceptions. Sometimes pronunciation and accents even vary from region to region. So in this glossary we mark the syllable to be accented in **bold**. And while you would read actual Hebrew writing from right to left, read the transliteration from left to right as in English.

Abb*a*—An Aramaic word used as an affectionate and intimate term of address to someone's father. *Yeshua* used it to refer to God as His Father, and believers in *Yeshua* also use it today to address God as Father. In Modern Hebrew, this common name (אבא) means "Dad" or "Daddy." See also Father. (Mark 14:36)

*ADO***NAI** (יהוה)—Hebrew for "LORD." When written in small capitals, it refers to God's personal name *YHWH* as given in the Hebrew Bible. This personal name is God's "covenant name," used when God is relating to the Jewish people in an intimate way. Since its pronunciation is not known, and also out of respect for God's name, Jews traditionally substitute the word *ADONAI*. See also *Elohim* and LORD. (Matthew 1:22; Mark 5:19; Luke 1:5; John 1:23)

*ADO***NAI** *Elo***him** (יהוה אלהים)—Hebrew for "LORD God." This title links Israel's God, the God of the Covenant, with God as Creator of the universe. (Luke 1:32; Revelation 1:8)

ADONAI Elohei-Tzva'ot (יהוה אלהי צבאות)—Hebrew for "LORD God of Hosts" or "LORD God of Heaven's Armies." The Greek equivalent is *Kurios o Theos o Pantokrator*, which is literally "LORD God Almighty" or "LORD God, Ruler over All" (Revelation 4:8; 21:22; cf. Amos 4:13ff.)

ADONAI Tzva'ot (יהוה צבאות)—Hebrew for "LORD of Hosts" or "LORD of Heaven's Armies." The Greek equivalent is *Kurios Sabaoth* (Isaiah 6:3 LXX), but the Septuagint often translates this Hebrew title as *Kurios Pantokrator*, which is literally "LORD Almighty" or "LORD, Ruler over All" (2 Samuel 7:8 LXX). (2 Corinthians 6:18)

Alpha and **O****me**ga—the first and last letters of the Greek alphabet. In the beginning of Revelation, God says while sitting on the throne, "I am the Alpha and the Omega." Yeshua speaks the exact same words at the end of Revelation. These words emphasize continuous existence "from A to Z"—from the beginning to the end of all creation. (Revelation 1:8; 21:6; 22:13)

a**men** (אמן)—At the end of a prayer, this word means, "Let it be so," indicating that the readers or listeners agree with what was just said. At the start of a phrase, it means, "This is a truth you can believe in and live by."

Although everything Yeshua said was true, "amen" adds special emphasis. (Matthew 5:26; Mark 10:15; Luke 23:43; John 10:1)

angel—A supernatural messenger sent by God. (Matthew 1:20; Mark 13:32; Luke 1:11; John 20:12)

a**noin**t—To pour oil on a person or thing. In the *Tanakh*, kings and priests were anointed by the application of oil. The word "Messiah" means "Anointed One." In this case it does not mean that the Messiah had oil put on him, but that God set Him apart for the task of being the Redeemer. See also *Mashiach* and Messiah. (Matthew 6:17; Mark 14:8; Luke 7:46; Luke 14:25 title; John 1:41; John 11:2)

*avo**dah*** (עבודה)—A Hebrew word that means "work," "service," or "worship." It often applies specifically to the work of the *kohanim*, including offering sacrifices and taking care of the Tabernacle and Temple. (Romans 9:4 footnote)

*Bar-**Ab**ba* (בר-אבא)—Aramaic for "Barabbas," meaning "Son of the Father." The name of the prisoner released by Pilate instead of *Yeshua*. (Matthew 27:16-17; Mark 15:7; Luke 23:18; John 18:20)

*Ba**ruch** ha-**ba** b'**shem*** ADO**NAI** (ברוך הבא בשם יהוה)—"Blessed is He who comes in the name of the Lord!" (Psalm 118:26a), Jerusalem's greeting to all pilgrims coming up to celebrate the festivals of Passover, *Shavuot*, and *Sukkot*. (Matthew 21:9; 23:39; Mark 11:9; Luke 13:35)

beelzebul—Originally the name of a Philistine god worshiped in Ekron (spelled **beel**zebub or in Hebrew *baal-ze**vuv***, which means "lord of the flies"). But by the time of *Yeshua*, it had become another name for satan, the prince of demons. (2 Kings 1:2; Matthew 10:25, 12:24-27; Mark 3:22-26; Luke 11:15-19)

*Ben-Avra**ham*** (בן-אברהם)—Hebrew for "Son of Abraham." *Yeshua* is called "Son of David, Son of Abraham." Abraham was promised that he would father a line of kings through the tribe of Judah, which started with David and looked forward to the coming of Messiah. (Matthew 1:1; Luke 3:34 footnote)

*Ben-Da**vid*** (בן-דוד)—One of *Yeshua's* titles, meaning "Son of David." David was promised a dynasty that would never end. This line of kings looked forward to Messiah's everlasting reign. (Matthew 1:1-17; Mark 12:35; Luke 3:31 footnote; Luke 18:38-39)

*Ben El El**yon*** (בן אל עליון)—One of *Yeshua's* titles, meaning "Son of the Most High God." (Mark 5:7; Luke 8:28)

*Ben-Elo**him*** (בן-אלהים)—One of *Yeshua's* titles, meaning "Son of God." In some instances, this title takes the form of *Ben-ha-Elo**him*** (בן-האלהים), "the Son of God." See also Son of Man. (Matthew 4:3; Mark 1:1; Luke 1:35; 3:38; John 11:4)

*Ben-El**yon*** (בן-אליון)—One of *Yeshua's* titles, meaning "Son of the Most High." (Luke 1:32)

*Beso**rah*** (בשורה)—Hebrew for "Gospel" or "Good News." In the Hebrew Scriptures, the Good News is the announcement that *ADONAI* has come to deliver his people and restore Israel from exile. Writers of the New Covenant Scriptures see *Yeshua* as the fulfillment of this proclamation. Their message of Good News tells the story of the life, death, resurrection, and exaltation of *Yeshua*, who is now seated at the right hand of God. (Introduction to Gospel of John)

blasphemy—The profaning of God's name by cursing Him or speaking slander against Him or His Word. The verb is "to blaspheme." (Matthew 12:31; Mark 14:64; John 10:33)

*B'**nei**-Israel* (בני ישראל)—literally, "the sons of Israel" or "the children of Israel," this term is used frequently in the *Tanakh* to represent the entire Jewish nation. (Romans 9:27; Revelation 7:4)

***bra**cha* (ברכה)—a blessing, usually done at a specific time as part of a ritual. A *bracha* acknowledges that God is the Giver of life and good things. (Matthew 14:19; Mark 14:22; Luke 2:28)

Brit Hadashah, also *Brit Chadashah* (ברית חדשה)—Hebrew for "New Covenant." Christians commonly call it the "New Testament." See also covenant.

brit-milah (ברית מילה)—Hebrew for "the covenant of circumcision," (*bris* in Yiddish). The removal of the foreskin of males on the eighth day after birth. Also the ceremony that takes place at that time, signifying the formal entry into the covenant God made with Abraham and his descendants, which included inheriting the land as a permanent possession (Genesis 17:8-14). In English, it is called "circum**ci**sion," and the verb is "to **cir**cumcise." See also circumcision. (Luke 2:21)

brother—from the Greek "adelphos," this term goes beyond blood relationships to refer to a fellow member within Messiah's community. When the plural form refers to a group of both males and females, "adelphoi" is translated as "brethren" or "brothers and sisters." (Matthew 25:40; Acts 11:29; 15:23; 2 Corinthians 13:11; Philippians 4:8)

cen**tu**rion—a Roman military captain in charge of 50-80 soldiers, originally one hundred at full strength. (Matthew 8:5; Mark 15:44; Luke 23:47)

circum**ci**sion—physically the removal of the foreskin (see *brit-milah*), but this term can also apply spiritually to the condition of a person's heart (Deuteronomy 10:16; 30:6; Jeremiah 4:4). Jewish people are sometimes referred to as "those of the circumcision" (Acts 11:1-3; Galatians 2:11-12; Philippians 3:2-6). Paul did not oppose circumcision; in fact, he circumcised Timothy to clarify his status as a Jew (Acts 16:1-4) In contrast, Paul did not circumcise Titus, who was a Gentile (Galatians 2:3-5). (Acts 7:8; Acts 15; Romans 2:25-29)

cohort—A group of 600 Roman soldiers, about one-tenth of a Roman legion. Cohorts mentioned in the New Covenant include the Italian Cohort (Acts 10:1) and the Augustan Cohort (Acts 27:1). (Matthew 27:27; Mark 15:16; Acts 10:1, 21:31, 27:1)

com**mand**ment—An order given by God or by *Yeshua* to His people. According to tradition, the Rabbis have counted 613 commandments in the *Torah*. See also *mitzvah*, the Hebrew term for commandment. (Matthew 5:19; Mark 10:19; Luke 23:56; John 13:34)

commonwealth—a community founded for the common good of its members. Israel enjoys the privileges of being God's nation, called to covenant relationship at Sinai. In Ephesians 2:11-14, Paul tells his Gentile readers that they have joined the commonwealth of Israel as fellow citizens through the reconciling work of *Yeshua*. (Ephesians 2:12)

com**mun**ity—a formal or informal group of people with shared interests or common beliefs. The first use of the Greek term "ekklesia" in the New Covenant occurs on the lips of Yeshua, who says He will build His community on Peter (Matthew 16:18). But this term was first used in the Septuagint when Moses reveals that God told him "gather to Me" the people, that they might hear My words and teach their children (Deuteronomy 4:10 LXX). The emphasis is on people—a holy community "called out" to be "set apart" for God. As Messiah's community expanded globally, new groups gathered and the teaching spread through the *shlichim* and their letters of instruction, which were preserved and passed on to us as part of the New Covenant. Starting from the Hebrew *kahal* (קהל), the Greek word "ekklesia" is also translated as assembly, congregation, or church. (Acts 7:38—Israelites; Romans 16:1; 1 Corinthians 16:19; Philemon 2—local gatherings and house groups; Matthew 18:17; Acts 15:22; 1 Corinthians 11:18—gathering to address community concerns; Acts 5:11; 8:3; 9:31—all believers living in a region; Matthew 16:18; 1 Corinthians 12:28; Ephesians 1:22—Messiah's global community)

covenant—The relationship between God and His people. The Hebrew term is *brit* (ברית). See also *Brit Hada**shah***, Hebrew for the "New Covenant." (Matthew 26:28; Mark 14:24; Luke 1:72)

crucify—A very cruel form of execution practiced by the Romans, reserved for the worst crimes. It involved nailing or binding the criminal's hands and feet to a cross, on which the criminal hung until he died. (Matthew 20:19; Mark 15:20; John 19:10; Acts 2:36; Hebrews 6:6)

Day of the Lord—an expression originally found in the *Tanakh*, referring to a time when God will come to save or deliver some and to judge others (Matthew 24:29-31). In the New Covenant, it is also called by other names, including the "Day of Messiah" (showing that *Yeshua* is Himself divine) or just "the Day." (1 Thessalonians 5:2, 2 Thessalonians 2:2, 2 Peter 3:10—Day of the Lord; 1 Corinthians 1:8—Day of our Lord *Yeshua* the Messiah; 2 Corinthians 1:14—the Day of our Lord *Yeshua*; Philippians 1:10, 2:16—the Day of Messiah; 1 Corinthians 3:13, 1 Thessalonians 5:4, Hebrews 10:25—the Day)

demon—An evil spirit who is an agent of satan. (Matthew 10:8; Mark 1:34; Luke 7:33; John 8:49)

de**nar**ius/plural de**nar**ii—A Roman silver coin, equal to a day's wage. (Matthew 20:2; Mark 6:37; Luke 20:24)

Di**as**pora—The dispersion or scattering of the Jewish people throughout the world. The term is actually Greek; the corresponding Hebrew term is *ga**lut*** (גלות), meaning "exile." (John 7:35)

dis**ci**ple—A student and follower of a teacher, who not only learns the teacher's wisdom, but even more importantly, also models his life on that of the teacher. In Hebrew, a disciple is called a *talmid*, and the plural is *talmidim*. See also talmid. (Matthew 9:10; Mark 3:9; Luke 5:33; John 1:35)

drash (דרש) —A sermon or exposition of Scripture; also an interpretation or explanation. (Matthew 5:1 title; Luke 7:1)

*El El**yon***—see Elyon.

elder—Equivalent to the Hebrew *za**ken*** (זקן)/plural *zekein**im*** (זקנים). Used of leaders within the Jewish community who primarily taught and judged, often in a synagogue setting, and also of similar leaders appointed to oversee Messiah's community. Elders were often—but not always—older men who possessed wisdom. Qualifications for being an elder are listed in 1 Timothy 3:1-7 and Titus 1:6-9. (Matthew 26:3; Acts 14:23; 1 Timothy 4:14; Titus 1:5)

E**loi, **E**loi, **le**ma sa**bach**thani?*—An Aramaic quotation meaning "My God, My God, why have You forsaken Me?" The underlying Hebrew from Psalm 22:2(1) means, "My God, My God, why have You abandoned Me?" The Matthew variation uses "E**li*," the Hebrew form of "My God." (Matthew 27:46; Mark 15:34)

*Elo**him*** (אלהים)—"God" in general terms, or as Creator. Compare with ADONAI, God's "covenant name" used especially in His relationship to the Jewish people. *Elohim* is the plural form of *El* (אל), also found in the Bible occasionally with the same meaning. *Yeshua* is sometimes called Ben-Elohim, the Son of God. (Matthew 4:3; Mark 1:1; Luke 1:35; John 11:4)

*El**yon*** (עליון)—A title for God, meaning "Most High." (Luke 1:35, 76; Acts 7:48). A longer form is *El Elyon* (אל עליון), "God Most High" (Acts 16:17).

emunah (אמונה)—Hebrew for "faith," "trust," or "faithfulness"; the Greek term is "pistis." It is important to stress the integration of heart, mind, soul, and strength when putting your trust in God. (Habakkuk 2:4; Romans 1:17; Galatians 3:11)

en**gaged**—In the first stage of a marriage covenant, usually lasting a year, after which the full marriage would take place and the bride and groom would live together. Engagement, also called "be**troth**al" and in Aramaic ***eru*sin** (ארוסין), in biblical times was much more like a marriage than it is today. It was legally binding and could be broken only by divorce. Sexual intimacy outside of this relationship was considered adultery, punishable by death. (Matthew 1:18; Luke 2:5)

exhor**ta**tion—a strong urging or encouragement with teaching. The range of the Greek word *parakaleo* includes everything from strong urging to softer forms such as requesting, begging, pleading, or even cheerful comforting. (Luke 3:18; Romans 12:8; Hebrews 13:22; 1 Thessalonians 2:12)

Father—God, the King of the universe, in His relation both to *Yeshua* (Matthew 7:21; Mark 8:38; Luke 2:49; John 5:18) and to believers (Matthew 6:9; Mark 11:25; Luke 11:2; John 14:7). Both usages are seen side-by-side in John 20:17. See also *Abba*.

firstfruits—the offering to God of the first part of an agricultural harvest. The Hebrew term is *bikkurim* (בקורים), which pilgrims brought to the Temple from *Shavuot* through *Sukkot*. Until a tithe was offered back to God, the entire crop was considered holy and therefore unavailable for common use. The concept extends to people as well, including the harvest of New Covenant faithful, redeemed by Messiah—the firstfruits from the dead. (Romans 8:23; 11:16; 1 Corinthians 15:20, 23; 16:15; 2 Thessalonians 2:13)

ful**fill**—Accomplish, carry out, or fill full with meaning. The word is found in relation to Scripture or to the words of *Yeshua*, showing that something previously spoken about has now happened. (Matthew 4:14; Mark 14:49; Luke 1:20; John 19:36)

Gali**le**ans—Inhabitants of the Galilee. Judean leaders in Jerusalem tended to look down on the people who lived in Galilee, because they thought they were less sophisticated. (Mark 14:70; Luke 22:59)

Galilee—The northernmost region of Israel, north of Samaria and Judea. *Yeshua* grew up in *Natzeret* and taught in Capernaum and many other towns there. (Matthew 2:22; Mark 1:9; Luke 3:1; John 4:43)

Ge**hen**na—A word for "hell," the place of perpetual misery and suffering after this life. It comes from the Greek "*Ge**en**na*" and the Hebrew "*Gei-Hin**nom***" (גיהנום), which means "the valley of Hinnom." There was actually such a valley by that name near the Temple in Jerusalem. It was used as a garbage dump, and fires were always burning there, making it a suitable picture of life in hell. In Jewish sources, the term is used as the opposite of *Gan-**E**den* (גן-אדן), the Garden of Eden or Paradise. (Matthew 23:33, Mark 9:43)

Gentiles—The term for individuals or people groups who are not Jewish. In Hebrew a common word for Gentiles is *go**yim*** or ***goy**im* (גוים). (Matthew 10:18; Mark 10:33)

glory—The manifestation of God's presence and power, especially in a visible way. The Hebrew word is *kavod* (כבוד). (Daniel 7:13-14; Isaiah 11:10; Matthew 24:30; 25:31; Mark 8:38; Luke 9:31; John 2:11; Romans 8:18; 2 Thessalonians 2:14)

God-fearers—In the first century C.E., this term referred to Gentiles who participated in synagogue services and much of Jewish life, but who did not undergo circumcision. Many of the first Gentiles who came to faith in *Yeshua* were God-fearers. See also proselyte. (Acts 13:16, 26, 43)

grace—Undeserved favor, which God gives to His people. (Mark 7:24 title; Luke 2:40; John 1:16)

Greek—The language spoken in Greece; also a term for people who spoke Greek, including Greek-speaking Jews in or outside of Israel. (Mark 7:26; John 12:20)

ha (ה)—A Hebrew prefix meaning "the." For example, *Yeshua ha-Mashiach* (ישוע המשיח) is "Jesus the Messiah." (See Acts 3:6.) To find a word in a Hebrew dictionary, remove this prefix first.

*Hal**lel*** (הלל)—The series of Psalms 113-118 sung or read at the conclusion of the Passover *seder*. *Hallel* means "praise." (Matthew 26:30; Mark 14:26)

*ha**metz*** or ***ha**metz*, also spelled *chametz* (חמץ)—Leaven, or yeast, which makes bread rise. God commanded Israel not to eat *hametz* during Passover. *Yeshua* teaches that both good and evil spread, the same way *hametz* leavens the whole batch of dough. (Matthew 13:33; 16:6-12; Mark 8:15; Luke 12:1; 13:21)

*Hanuk**kah*** or ***Ha**nukkah*, also spelled *Chanukkah* (חנוכה)—A holiday whose name means "dedication." The Feast of Dedication commemorates the victory of the Maccabees over the armies of Antiochus Epiphanes in 165 BCE and the rededication of the Temple after it had been defiled. (John 10:22)

Hellenist—In the New Covenant, refers to Jews who lived in the Diaspora, or had moved to Israel from the Diaspora, spoke Greek, and were more Greek in their culture than Jewish people brought up in Israel. (Acts 6:1; 9:29; 11:20)

He**ro**dians—A group in ancient Israel that was friendly towards the rule of King Herod and to Rome. (Matthew 22:16; Mark 3:6)

holy—Set apart for God's purposes. God Himself radiates holiness. In Hebrew the term is *ka**dosh*** (קדוש). (Matthew 4:5; Mark 8:38; Luke 1:49; John 17:11)

Holy **Spir**it—See Ruach, Ruach-Elohim, and Ruach ha-Kodesh.

*hoshi**a**-**na*** (הושיעה נא)—"Ho**san**na" in English, a term meaning, "Save now, please," which comes from Psalm 118:25. (Matthew 21:15; Mark 11:9; John 12:13)

im**merse**—To dip the whole body under water as an act of dedication to the Lord or as a profession of faith in *Yeshua*. The word is often seen in other translations as "baptize." The ceremony of dipping is called "immersion" or "baptism." *Yeshua's* cousin was known as John the Immerser (Matthew 3:1; Mark 6:14; Luke 7:20). The Hebrew term for immersion is *te**vi**lah*** (טבילה). (Matthew 28:19; Mark 1:4; Luke 3:3; John 1:26)

inter**cede**—To pray on behalf of another person. The person who prays is called an "inter**ces**sor" or a "**me**diator," meaning someone who comes between God and people in order to help them. (John 17:20 title)

Israel—The name given by God to His chosen people, the Jews. The term refers to the people as a whole, and also to the land where the ten northern tribes lived. In modern times, it refers to the nation established in 1948 as the Jewish homeland. The name in Hebrew is Yisra**el** (ישראל). (Matthew 2:6; Mark 15:32; Luke 7:9; John 1:49)

Je**ru**salem—The royal city from which the kings of Israel ruled and the place where the Holy Temple was located. Sometimes called the "City of Peace," it also refers to the heavenly Jerusalem of the future. Its name in Hebrew is *Yerusha**la**yim* (ירושלים). (Matthew 3:5; Mark 10:32; Luke 9:31; John 2:13)

Jews, **Jew**ish—The Jews are God's chosen people, descended from Abraham, Isaac, and Jacob, with whom He made His covenants. God gave the *Torah* to the Jewish people and promised them the land of Israel. "Jewish" is the word that describes this people or anything that has to do with them, such as holidays and ceremonies. (Matthew 2:2; Mark 7:3; Luke 23:3; John 2:13)

Ju**de**a—The southern part of Israel, south of the Galilee and Samaria. In earlier Jewish history, it was known as the Kingdom of Judah. This region included Jerusalem, where the Temple stood as the center of Jewish religious life. (Matthew 2:1; Mark 13:14; Luke 6:17; John 3:22)

Jud**e**ans—Inhabitants of Judea. The Judean leaders included the ruling priests and *Torah* scholars; the Pharisees; and also the Sadducees, who were in charge of the Temple in *Yeshua's* time. (Matthew 28:15; Mark 1:5; John 5:16)

*Ka**dosh**, ka**dosh**, ka**dosh*** (קדוש קדוש קדוש)

ADO**NAI** *Elo**hei**-Tzva'**ot***, (יהוה אלהי צבאות)

***a**sher ha**ya** v'ho**veh** v'ya**vo**!* (אשר היה והוה ויבוא)—what the four living creatures continually repeat in worship before God, seated on His throne in heaven. The words mean "Holy, holy, holy, is the LORD God of Hosts, who was and who is and who is to come!" (Revelation 4:8)

*kedo**shim*** (קדשים)/singular *ka**dosh*** (קדוש)—Hebrew for "holy." This term describes the people set apart for God, often translated as the "saints" (Greek *hagioi*). In the Torah portion named *Kedoshim*, the people are commanded to be *kedoshim*, for *ADONAI* Himself is *kadosh* (Leviticus 19:1-2). Many letters to Messiah's newly formed communities address Yeshua's followers as the *kedoshim*. (1 Corinthians 1:2; Ephesians 1:1; Philippians 1:1; Colossians 1:2)

Kingdom of God—The reality of God's rulership in our lives now and throughout all the world in the age to come. (Matthew 19:24; Mark 10:14; Luke 6:20; John 3:3)

*ko**hen*** or ***ko**hen* (כהן)/plural *koha**nim*** (כהנים)—A man who offered sacrifices and performed other religious rituals at the Temple in Jerusalem. The *kohanim* were descended from Aaron, the brother of Moses. The priests were mostly from the Sadducee sect of Judaism. See also Levite and Sadducees. (Matthew 8:4; Mark 1:44; Luke 1:5)

ko**hen ga**dol (כהן גדול)/plural *koha**nim** g'do**lim*** (כהנים גדולים)—The high priest who served as head official, the only one to enter the Holy of Holies. Aaron, the brother of Moses, was the first man appointed as kohen gadol. In later times, the kohen gadol was in charge of the Temple and its administration. The *kohen gadol* Caiaphas played a key role in questioning *Yeshua* at His trial. The writer of Hebrews describes *Yeshua* as our great *Kohen Gadol*, who gives us access to God's throne in the heavenly sanctuary. (Matthew 26:57ff; Mark 14:61ff; John 18:19ff; Hebrews 4:14ff.; 10:19-22)

*kor**ban*** (קרבן)—A sacrifice or offering dedicated to God, especially to fulfill a vow. If something was to be dedicated to God, it generally could not be used for other purposes. Some people wrongly used this as an excuse not to provide for their parents in their old age, even though Jewish teaching insisted that the commandment to honor one's father and mother extended to providing for their needs. (Mark 7:11)

*Kri**ot*** (קריות)—A town in the territory of the tribe of Judah, mentioned in Joshua 15:25. The disciple who betrayed *Yeshua* lived in this town. In Greek he is called "**Ju**das Is**ca**riot." His name probably comes from "*Yehu**dah** Ish-Kri**ot***," Hebrew for "Judah, the man from Kriot." (Matthew 10:4; Mark 14:10; Luke 6:16; John 12:4)

la**shon** ha-**ra** (לשון הרע)—Literally "the tongue of evil," Hebrew for gossip or slander. In the spirit of Leviticus 19:16, this behavior is forbidden and its damage to the community is taken very seriously. (2 Corinthians 12:20; 1 Peter 2:1)

last days—also sometimes called the "end of days." The time period that comes at the end of history before the Day of the Lord, the reign of Messiah, and the resurrection of the dead. In the Bible, any time after the Resurrection of *Yeshua* is sometimes called the "last days," or it can refer more specifically to the time just before Messiah returns. It is a phrase found often in the *Tanakh*, as the Hebrew *acha**rit** ha-ya**mim*** (אחרית הימים). (2 Timothy 3:1; Hebrews 1:2; Jacob 5:3).

Levite—Descendants of the tribe of Levi, who served in the Tabernacle and Temple as gatekeepers, musicians, teachers, and assistants to the *kohanim*. The scribes, or *Torah* scholars, came from among the Levites and were the forerunners of the Pharisees. See also scribe, *kohen*, Pharisees, and Sadducees. (John 1:19)

Lord—A title given to *Yeshua* after His resurrection, in recognition of His deity. The Greek term "Kurios" has a wide range of meanings, including "Sir," "Master," and "Lord." Depending on who uses the term and what this person knows about the one being addressed, "Kurios" or "Lord" can indicate various levels of respect—from politely addressing a stranger, boss, or even a king, to recognizing deity worthy of worship. "Kurios" in the Septuagint (the Greek translation of *Tanakh*) refers directly to ADONAI—the LORD, the only God who creates all and rules over all. See also Master and *ADONAI*. (Matthew 15:22; Mark 7:28; Luke 2:11; John 21:7)

Lord's **Sup**per—the ceremony in which we remember Yeshua's atoning death by partaking of bread and wine. Also known as the Lord's Table, Communion, or the Eucharist, and in Hebrew as *Seu**dat** ha-A**don*** (סעודת האדון), it is based on what took place at *Yeshua's* final Passover *Seder*, usually called the "Last Supper." (See Matthew 26:26-29; Mark 14:22-25; Luke 22:17-20; 1 Corinthians 11:23-26)

magi—a name for pagan astrologers who came from the Eastern countries. Magi often served as advisors to a king. Though astrology was forbidden to Israel, the story of the magis gives us a picture of how the coming of Yeshua would affect the Gentile world as well as the Jewish world. (Matthew 2:1)

manna—The bread from heaven that God gave to our people in Exodus 16, as they wandered the desert after being redeemed from slavery in Egypt. The Hebrew term is *man* (מן). (John 6:31)

*Ma**shi**ach* (משיח)—The "Anointed One," called in English the "Messiah," used originally for any priest, prophet, or king on a mission from God. In Greek the word is "Christos," from which we get the English term "Christ." See also Messiah and anoint. (Matthew 26:63; Mark 1:1; John 20:31)

Master—A term of respect, recognizing a teacher's authority. See also Lord. (Matthew 8:21; Mark 11:3; Luke 5:5; John 13:14)

*ma**tzah*** or ***ma**tzah* (מצה)/plural *ma**tzot*** (מצות)—Unleavened bread, which is made without yeast, eaten especially during the feast of Passover. See also *hametz*. (Matthew 26:17; Mark 14:22; Luke 22:19; John 13:26)

Mes**si**ah—A title meaning "Anointed One," often used in speaking of a redeemer sent from God to free His people from exile and oppression. See also anoint and the Hebrew title, *Mashiach*. (Matthew 1:16; Mark 8:29; Luke 2:11; 24:26; John 1:41) *metzo**ra*** (מצרע)—An "infected one" or someone suffering from *tzara'at* or leprosy, such as Simon *ha-Metzora*. See also tzara'at. (Matthew 26:6; Mark 14:3)

mikveh (מקוה)—A place where living water collects, suitable for ritual immersion to wash away impurity. See also immerse. (Matthew 3:13 title)

*mitz**vah*** or ***mitz**vah* (מצוה)/ plural *mitz**vot*** (מצות)—A commandment from God. See also commandment. Another, more modern, meaning is "a good deed." (Matthew 26:10; Mark 14:6; Mark 12:28 title)

nations—See Gentiles. (Matthew 28:19; Mark 13:10; Luke 24:47)

*Na**tze**ret* (נצרת)—Also called "Nazareth" in English, this town is in south central Galilee where *Yeshua* grew up. The name may come from the Hebrew word ***ne**tzer* (נצר), which means "branch." A clan from the line of David founded this town. (Matthew 2:23; Mark 10:47; Luke 1:26; John 1:45-46)

*Natzra**ti*** (נצרתי)—Nazarene, someone from Nazareth. *Yeshua*, who came from Nazareth, was sometimes called *Yeshua ha-Natzrati*. Those who followed Yeshua became known as Natzra**tim** (נצרתים). (Matthew 2:23; 26:71; Luke 18:37; John 18:5, 7; 19:19; Acts 22:8; 24:5)

*o**lam** ha-**ba*** (עולם הבא)—"The world to come" or "the age to come." Following the millennium, it describes a time after the world is perfected under the rulership of Messiah. This term also refers to the afterlife, where the soul passes after death. It can be contrasted with *o**lam** ha-**zeh***, "this world." (Matthew 12:32; Mark 10:30; Luke 18:30; 20:35; Ephesians 1:21; Hebrews 6:5; Revelation 20-21)

pagans—A term used for worshipers of foreign gods or idols. It is different than "Gentiles," which refers to any non-Jews, including followers of *Yeshua*. (Matthew 5:47; Luke 21:24)

*pa**ro**khet* (פרוכת)—The curtain that divided the Holy of Holies from the Holy Place in the Tabernacle and Temple. In modern synagogues, the curtain covering the ark is called a *parokhet*. (footnotes for Matthew 27:51; Mark 15:38; Luke 23:45; Hebrews 6:19; 9:3; 10:20)

Passover—The Jewish festival during which Jews used to journey to the Temple, sacrifice lambs, and eat a special meal commemorating the departure of the Jews from slavery in Egypt. Today it is celebrated at home with a special meal called a *seder*. In Hebrew, this holiday is called *Pesach*. See also *Pesach* and *seder*. (Matthew 26:18; Mark 14:12; Luke 22:7 title; John 13:1)

***Pe**sach* (פסח)—The Hebrew word for "Passover," also for the Passover lamb whose blood on the door caused the angel of death to "pass over" the Israelite homes in Egypt. *Yeshua* is called the Passover Lamb, because His blood saves us from sin and death. (Luke 2:41; John 18:1 title)

Pharisees—One of the sects of Judaism in the first century. The Pharisees had their own views of how exactly to keep *Torah*. They were especially concerned with ritual purity, and (unlike the Sadducees) they believed in the resurrection of the dead. While the Sadducees were more involved with the Temple, the Pharisees were concerned more with home and synagogue life. The Hebrew term is *P'ru**shim*** (פרושים). (Matthew 5:20; Mark 7:3; Luke 7:36; John 4:1)

priest—See *kohen*, Pharisees, and Sadducees.

proselyte—A full convert to Judaism, who underwent immersion in a mikveh and, for men, circumcision. In contrast, the God-fearer did not fulfill all the requirements for full conversion. These criteria probably did not become formalized before the second century C.E. See also *God-fearer*. (Matthew 23:15; Acts 2:11; 6:5)

rabbi—A highly esteemed teacher who trained disciples. The title comes from a Hebrew word (רבי), meaning "My Great One." (Matthew 23:7; Mark 9:5; Luke 12:13; John 4:31)

*Rab**bo**ni* (רבוני)—A title meaning, "My Teacher," "My Master," or "My Lord." It is a variant of "Rabbi." The title is also written as *Rabbuni* in Aramaic and *Rabbouni* in Greek. (Mark 10:51; John 20:16)

***Ra**ca*—Aramaic for "Empty One," probably meaning "empty-headed" or "foolish." The Hebrew word for "empty" is *reik* (ריק). The insult today might be "Airhead!" and in Hebrew *Reika* (ריקא), "good for nothing." (Matthew 5:22)

resur**rec**tion—The act of rising from the dead back to life. The word is also used to refer to the time at the end of history when God will raise the dead. (Matthew 27:53; Mark 12:18; Luke 14:14; John 11:25)

righteous—Morally good, virtuous. See also the Hebrew term *tzaddik* (צדיק). (Matthew 1:19; Mark 6:20; Luke 23:50; John 17:25)

ritual—An established procedure for performing religious acts. (Matthew 15:2; Luke 11:38; John 2:6)

Romans—The people who ruled over the entire Mediterranean world, including Israel, during the time of *Yeshua* (as well as before and after). Their territory was called the "Roman Empire." (Mark 15:1 title; Luke 23:1 title; John 11:48)

***Ru**ach* (רוח)—The Hebrew word for "spirit," "breath," or "wind," equivalent to the Greek "pneuma." *Yeshua* explains wind and Spirit to Nicodemus in John 3:5-8. Scripture frequently refers to the ***Ru**ach ha-**Ko**desh*, the Holy Spirit. (Acts 2:1 title; Acts 10:44 title; Romans 8:1 title)

***Ru**ach ha-**Ko**desh* (רוח הקודש)—The Hebrew name for the Holy Spirit, the Spirit of God. (Matthew 1:20; Mark 1:8; Luke 1:16; John 14:26)

Sadducees—One of the sects of Judaism in the first century. From the Sadducees came most of the priests who officiated in the Temple. In contrast to the Pharisees, they did not believe in the resurrection of the dead. The Hebrew term is *Tz'du**kim*** (צדוקים). See also *kohen* and Pharisees. (Matthew 16:12; Mark 12:18; Luke 20:27)

sal**va**tion—God's saving acts in human history. For Israel, salvation means deliverance from enemies or exile as well as national deliverance from God's judgment, leading to peace and long life in the homeland.

Salvation, with respect to individuals, also refers to deliverance from God's judgment. For *Yeshua's* faithful followers, salvation begins in this life and leads to everlasting life in God's presence in the age to come. See also Savior and *Yeshua*. (Luke 1:77; John 4:22)

Sa**mar**itans—A people descended from a mix of Israelites and other nations that the Assyrians brought to Samaria, as told in 2 Kings 17. The Samaritans practiced an offshoot of Judaism and thought that the Temple in Jerusalem was not a legitimate place to worship. Jewish people and Samaritans did not think well of one other. (Matthew 10:5; Luke 10:33; John 4:9)

San**hed**rin—The highest council of the Jews, exercising legislative and judicial authority. (Matthew 26:59; Mark 15:1; Luke 22:66; John 11:47)

satan or *sa**tan*** (שטן)—The chief fallen angel who opposes God's will on earth. He is the accuser of humanity who tries to undermine God's people and God Himself. The Hebrew name means "adversary." (Matthew 12:26; Mark 1:13; Luke 13:16; John 13:27)

Savior—A title of *Yeshua*, in recognition of His work in making salvation from sin and its consequences possible for all people—both Jewish and Gentile. Also used of God the Father. See also salvation. (Luke 1:47; John 4:42)

Scripture or **Scrip**tures—The Hebrew Bible, known in Hebrew as the *Tanakh*. Christians commonly call it the "Old Testament." Today we use the term "Scripture" to include the New Covenant as well, which was not yet written down in the days of *Yeshua*. See also *Tanakh*. (Matthew 22:29; Mark 12:24; Luke 24:27; John 19:36)

scribe—A *Torah* scholar engaged in interpreting and transmitting the Law, including the task of writing *Torah* scrolls, *mezuzot*, *tefillin*, bills of divorce, and other legal documents. The term in Hebrew is *sofer* (סופר). See also Levites.

***se**der* (סדר)—Literally "order," this term refers to the ceremonial meal commemorating Passover. See also Passover and *Pesach*. (Mark 14:12 title; Luke 22:8; John 13:2)

*Shab***bat** (שבת)—The Sabbath, the seventh day of the week. On this day we are to rest and renew our relationship with our Creator, who also rested on the seventh day. *Shabbat* begins on Friday evening at sundown and ends Saturday evening after three stars appear. (Matthew 12:10; Mark 1:21; Luke 23:56; John 9:14)

*shal***i***ach* (שליח)/plural *shlichim* (שליחים)—A person sent with authority to carry out a mission. This person represents and speaks for the one who commissions him. Other names include apostle, delegate, envoy, emissary, ambassador, and messenger. (Matthew 10:2; Mark 6:30; Luke 22:14; John introduction)

*sha***lom** (שלום)—The Hebrew word for "peace." It also can mean "wholeness" or "well-being." *Shalom* is often used as a greeting ("hello") or as a farewell ("goodbye"). (Matthew 10:13; Mark 9:50; Luke 1:28; John 14:27)

*sha***lom** *alei***chem** or *sha***lom** ***alei****chem* (שלום עליכם)—A greeting that means, "peace be with you all." (John 20:19)

*sham***mash** or **sham***mash* (שמש)/plural *shamma***shim** (שמשים)—A servant, deacon, or attendant who serves in the synagogue or within Messiah's community. The first to be appointed, though not in a formal office, were seven Hellenists in the Jerusalem community, appointed by the Twelve *shlichim* to serve tables and care for the widows (Acts 6:1-6). Qualifications can be found in 1 Timothy. (Romans 16:1; Philippians 1:1; 1 Timothy 3:8-13)

*Shavu***ot** (שבועות)—The Feast of Weeks, sometimes called Pentecost, occurring on the 50th day after Passover. One of the festivals given to Israel in the *Tanakh*, which originally celebrated the harvest but later commemorated the day God gave the *Torah* to Israel. After *Yeshua's* resurrection, the disciples waited for God's gift of the *Ruach ha-Kodesh*, which also came on *Shavuot*. (Acts 2:1, 20:16; 1 Corinthians 16:8)

*She***ol** (שאול)—The Hebrew equivalent of the Greek "Hades," the place where the dead exist. (Matthew 16:18; Luke 16:23)

*shli***chim**—See <u>shaliach</u>.

sho**far* (שופר)—a ram's horn, used in the Bible for summoning armies, calling to repentance, and in other situations. Blasts of various lengths and numbers signified different instructions. Metal trumpets were also used for similar purposes, but exclusively by the *kohanim*. Today, the *shofar* is used on *Rosh ha-Sha**nah and *Yom Kip**pur***, the Jewish High Holy Days. The *shofar* also ushers in the Year of Jubilee. See also trumpet. (Leviticus 25:9-10; Zechariah 9:14; Matthew 24:31; 1 Corinthians 15:52; 1 Thessalonians 4:16-17)

*si**nat** chi**nam*** (שנאת חנם)—hatred without a cause, considered to be a serious violation of Jewish ethics. The Talmud (*Yoma* 9b) attributed the destruction of the Temple in 70 CE to *sinat chinam*. (John 15:25 footnote)

sin offering—the Hebrew term is *hat**ta**t* or *chat**tat*** (חטאת), which means both "sin" (to miss the mark) and "sin offering" (an unblemished sacrifice brought by a person who had inadvertently broken a law that would cut him off from the community). (Romans 8:3; 2 Corinthians 5:21)

sinner—A person who violates the commandments of God. The word can refer to someone who does not act according to God's will, and also (especially in Paul's letters) to all people who are sinners by nature (Matthew 26:45; Mark 2:15; Luke 18:13; John 9:24). Sometimes it refers to people who lived sinfully and had a bad social reputation (Matthew 11:19, Mark 2:15, Luke 19:7).

Son of Man—A name that *Yeshua* commonly uses to refer to Himself. It comes from Daniel 7:13-14, in which the "Son of Man" is given all authority. This name sometimes emphasizes Yeshua's humanity and sometimes His deity. In Hebrew, this title reads *Ben-ha-A**dam*** (בן-האדם). (Matthew 9:6; Mark 9:31; Luke 21:36; John 6:27)

Spirit—The Spirit of God is the One who inspires the prophets, anoints the Messiah and empowers His followers. When not capitalized, the word may describe a person's basic life force or even an evil spirit. See also *Ruach*. (Matthew 3:16; 5:3; 8:16; Mark 1:12; Luke 1:47; John 7:39)

*Suk**kot*** (סוכות)—The Feast of Booths or Tabernacles. This holiday came in the fall at the time of the grape harvest and was a time of great rejoicing. The Hebrew word *suk**kah*** or ***suk**kah* (סוכה) means "booth." *Sukkot* is the plural and can mean either "booths" or the name of this holiday. See also tabernacle. (Matthew 17:4; Mark 9:5; Luke 9:33; John 7:1 title)

syna**gogue**—A place of assembly of Jews for hearing the *Torah*, praying, and worshipping God. There were many synagogues throughout Israel. (Matthew 4:23; Mark 5:22; Luke 4:16; John 9:22)

tabernacle—A temporary dwelling, such as the booths constructed during the Feast of Tabernacles. It is also used in the *Tanakh* of the tent in which God dwelt among the Jewish people in the wilderness and in the land of Israel. When the word is used as a verb, it refers to *Yeshua* coming to dwell among His people, reminding us of the wilderness Tabernacle and also of the Feast of Tabernacles. See also Sukkot. (John 1:14; 7:2)

*tal**mid*** (תלמיד)/plural *talmi**dim*** (תלמידים)—See disciple. (Luke 22:7 title; John 1:35 title)

*Ta**nakh*** (תנ"ך)—The Hebrew Scriptures. This word is an acronym, made up of the first letters of **T**orah (Pentateuch), **N**evi'im (Prophets), and **K**etuvim (Writings). So T + N + K becomes Tanakh. Christians commonly call it the "Old Testament."

*tefil**lin*** or *te**fil**lin* (תפלין)—In English, often called "phylacteries." These are boxes containing Scripture passages, which traditional Jews wrap around the right arm and forehead at weekday morning prayers, in fulfillment of Deuteronomy 6:8. The four Scripture passages contained in them are Exodus 13:1-10, 11-16; Deuteronomy 6:4-9; 11:13-21. (Matthew 23:5)

Temple—The magnificent building in Jerusalem designated by God for sacrifices and worship. It was destroyed in the year 70 CE by the Roman armies. (Matthew 21:12; Mark 11:11; Luke 2:37; John 2:14)

*teshu**vah*** (תשובה)—repentance. The Hebrew term implies "turning" or "returning." When someone repents, he feels sorrowful, stops walking in sinful patterns, changes behaviors, and turns to God. (Acts 2:37 title)

testimony—Evidence given by a witness, who is someone who sees and reports something. Also sometimes called "witness." See also witness. (Matthew 8:4; Mark 14:59; Luke 18:20; John 1:19)

tetrarch—a Roman ruler who ruled part of an area that had been divided in four. That means the entire area would have four tetrarchs, each ruling one part. The word comes from the Greek word for "fourth." (Matthew 14:1; Luke 3:1)

*tik**kun** o**lam*** (תיקון עולם)—Literally, "repair of the world." Today's Jews have extended this classical concept to include the pursuit of social justice and care for the environment. (Luke introduction)

tithe—a portion of income, in the Bible usually agricultural products, which is given to the priests and Levites to provide for their needs. It is based on passages in the *Tanakh* such as Leviticus 27:30. (Matthew 23:23; Luke 18:12)

*To**rah*** or ***To**rah* (תורה)—Literally "instruction," this term can refer to the five books of Moses or more generally to God's commandments. Some Jews distinguish the Written *Torah* from the Oral *Torah*, which was transmitted by oral tradition until being written down at the end of the second century CE. Depending on context, the Greek word "nomos" is usually translated as *Torah* or law in a universal sense. See also commandment. (Matthew 5:17; Mark 1:22; Luke 24:44; John 7:19; Romans 7:1ff.; 1 Corinthians 9:20-21; Galatians 3:21)

trans**fi**gu**ra**tion—a change in form in a way that exalts or glorifies someone. "To transfigure" is the verb form. (Matthew 17:1 title; Mark 9:2 title)

Tree of Life—the tree at the center of the Garden of Eden, the source of eternal life. Scripture points to a future in the New Jerusalem, with access to the Tree of Life. In the meantime, the Torah is a Tree of Life to all who take hold of her. The Hebrew term is *Etz-Chaim* (עץ חיים). (Genesis 2:9; 3:24; Proverbs 3:18; Revelation 2:7; 22:2, 14)

trumpet—a metal horn made of hammered silver, used exclusively by the *kohanim* for occasions such as gathering the people for festivals, giving marching orders, and coronating kings. The Hebrew term is *chatzo**tzrah*** (חצצרה)/plural *chatzo**tzrot*** (חצצרות). See also shofar, or ram's horn, which was used more broadly by the people at large. After the destruction of the Temple, musical instruments were banned and the role of the shofar expanded in religious use. (Numbers 10:1-10; 2 Kings 11:14; 1 Chronicles 15:24, 28; 1 Corinthians 14:8; Psalm 98:6LXX; Revelation 8:2ff.)

Twelve—"the Twelve" refers to *Yeshua's* original twelve disciples listed in Matthew 10:1-4, Mark 3:13-19, and Luke 6:13-16. Matthias replaces Judah from Kriot to maintain the number twelve, symbolic of the twelve tribes of Israel. Additional apostles, or *shlichim*, were later added, including Paul. (Matthew 20:17; Mark 4:10; 1 Corinthians 15:5-9)

*tzad**dik*** or ***tzad**dik* (צדיק)/plural *tzaddi**kim*** (צדיקים)—a righteous person. See also righteous. (Matthew 10:41; 23:29)

*tza**ra'**at* (צרעת)—a general term for skin disease. Though it appears in many translations as "leprosy," it can include that disease as well as various infectious skin afflictions, and even mildew and mold. See also *metzora*. (Matthew 8:2; Mark 1:42; Luke 4:27)

*tzeda**kah*** or *tze**da**kah* (צדקה)—literally, this word means "righteousness," but it also came to mean giving to charity. In modern times, Jewish people often use a *tzedakah box* to give to charity. (Matthew 6:2; Luke 11:41)

tzi**tzit** or **tzi**tzit (ציצית) /plural *tzitzi**yot*** (ציציות)—A fringe that was put on a garment in accordance with Numbers 15:37-41. (Matthew 9:20; 23:5; Mark 6:56)

un**clean**—ritually impure. The Hebrew term is *tamei* (טמא). It was the duty of the *kohanim* to distinguish between *kadosh* (holy) and *chol* (common, mundane, profane, or unholy) and between *tamei* (unclean or ritually impure) and *tahor* (clean or ritually pure) in order to preserve the sanctity and purity that God's presence required (Leviticus 10:10). (Matthew 10:1; Acts 5:16; 8:7—unclean spirits; Acts 10:14, 11:8—unclean food; Acts 10:28—unclean people)

witness—Both the testimony itself and also someone who gives testimony. See also testimony. (Matthew 10:18; Mark 14:63; Luke 24:48; John 1:7)

works—Actions, things one does. In Scripture, these are often actions one does in order to obey God and His Word (Matthew 5:16; John 6:28). Occasionally the word refers to actions that are evil (Luke 11:48; John 7:7). Also, when done by God the Father or *Yeshua*, it refers to their miracles or to acts that demonstrate their power and authority (Matthew 11:2; Mark 6:2; John 9:3).

worship—Reverent honor paid to God, which is right, or to satan or false gods, which is wrong. (See Matthew 4:10; Mark 7:6; Luke 4:7; John 4:22.)

The word can also mean paying homage or bowing down, as when people worshiped *Yeshua* even before they fully understood who He is. (See Matthew 2:11; Mark 15:19, in mockery; John 9:38.) See also *avodah*.

*Ye**shua*** (ישוע)—The Hebrew name of our Messiah, known in English as "Jesus." The name means "salvation." (Matthew 1:21; Mark 6:14; Luke 2:21; John 19:19)

*Yom Shab**bat*** (יום שבת)—Hebrew for "Sabbath day." See also *Shabbat*. (Luke 14:5)

Zion—A mountain in Jerusalem (Mount Zion). The name is more generally used to refer to Jerusalem as a whole or to the land of Israel. In Hebrew it is called *Tzi**yon*** (ציון). (Matthew 21:5; John 12:15)

Israel map 1st Century
Yeshua's Travels
Mediterranean
Sea
1. Up to Jerusalem (John 2:13)
2. To Judea and immersing by
the Jordan at Aenon (John 3:22)
3. Back to Galilee by way of Sh'chem. (John 4:3-42)
4. Rejected in Nazereth. (Luke 4:16)
5. Raising the dead in Nain. (Luke 7:11)
6. Through Galilee to Capernaum. (Mark 1:39)
7. Rejected in Nazereth again. (Matthew 13:54)
8. Back up to Jerusalem. (John 5:1)
9. Crosses Sea of Galilee to the Gadarenes,
stops a storm, heals a demoniac. (Mark 4:35-5:20)
10. On the way to Beitsaida, feeds
5000 families. (Luke 9:10-17)
11. Back across the Sea to Geneseret,
walks on the water. (Matthew 14:22-33)
12. Up to cities of Tyre and Sidon. (Mark 7:24)
13. Down to Sea of Galilee and across to
the towns of Decapolis area. (Mark 7:31)
14. On a mountain at Sea of Galilee, feeds
4000 people. (Matthew 15:29-38)
15. Across to Magdala. (Matthew 15:39)
16. Back to Beitsaida. (Mark 8:22)
17. Up to Caesarea Philippi. (Mark 8:27)
18. A high Mountain, Mt. Hermon (?)
where His glory is seen. Back to
Beitsaida. (Mark 9:2-13)
19. Across to Capernaum. (Mark 9:33)
20. Apostles sent ahead of Him to Samaritan
towns, He follows. (Luke 9:51; [Mark 10:1])
21. Towns of "Judea across the
Yarden". (Mark 10:1)
22. Up to Jerusalem for feasts of
Sukkot & Hanukah. (John 7-10)
23. Withdraws to Aenon. (John 10:40)
24. To Bethany, raises Lazarus. (John 11:1)
25. Withdraws to Ephraim. (John 11:54)
26. To Jericho. (Luke 18:35)
27. Up to Jerusalem for His
final week. (Luke 19:28)
Sidon
Mt. Lebanon
SYRIA
Mt. Hermon
PHOENICIA
Caesarea-
Philippi
Tyre
GAULINITIS
GALILEE
Chorazin
Acco
Capernaum
Beitsaida
Geneseret
Cana
Sea of Galilee
Magdala
Nazereth
Nain
Abila
Gadara
Capitolias
DECAPOLIS
Arbela
Pella
1, 3, 20 & 22
Caesarea
SAMARIA
Gerasa
Aenon
Samaria
(Sabaste)
2 & 23
(from
Judea)
Peniel
Sh'chem
(Sychar)
Shiloh
Gadara
PEREA
Ephraim
Bethel
Yarden
Beitanabris
Philadelphia
Jericho
Julias
Ashdod
(Azotus)
1, 8, 22 & 27
Jerusalem
Besimoth
Ashkelon
Bethlehem
Bethany
Qumran
JUDEA
Gaza
Machaerus
Hebron
Arnon
Dead
Sea
En Gedi

21st Century Israel
Damascus
Sidon
LEBANON
Litani
Mt. Hermon
Leontes
SYRIA
Tel Dan
Tyre
El Kuneitra
Rosh Pina
Rosh ha Nikra
Safed
GOLAN HEIGHTS
Karnaim
Acco
Kineret
Ashtarot
Haifa
GALILEE
Sea of Galilee
Afek
Golan
Nazereth
Afula
Irbid
Megiddo
D'era
Ramot Gilad
Beit-shan
Caesarea
Jenin
Natanya
Tulkarm
Sh'chem
Nablus
Hertziliya
Kfar Sava
Yabok
Tel-Aviv Yaffa
Shiloh
Ez-Zarqa
Mediterranean Sea
Bethel
Rishon L'tzion
Yarden
Bet Nimrah
Amman
Ramallah
Rehovot
Jericho
Ashdod
Jerusalem
Ashkelon
Bethlehem
Gaza
Khan Yunis
Hebron
Dead Sea
Arnon
Raphah
Be'er Sheva
JORDAN
ISRAEL
NEGEV
Tamar
Kadesh Barnea
THE SINAI
EGYPT
Eilat
Aqaba

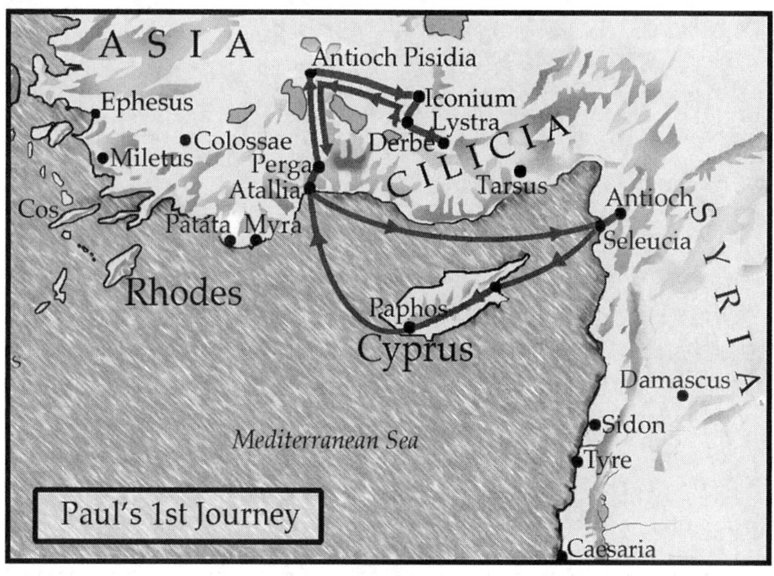
ASIA
Antioch Pisidia
Ephesus
Iconium
Lystra
Colossae
Derbe
Miletus
Perga
CILICIA
Atallia
Tarsus
Cos
Antioch
Patata
Myra
Seleucia
SYRIA
Rhodes
Paphos
Cyprus
Damascus
Sidon
Mediterranean Sea
Tyre
Paul's 1st Journey
Caesaria

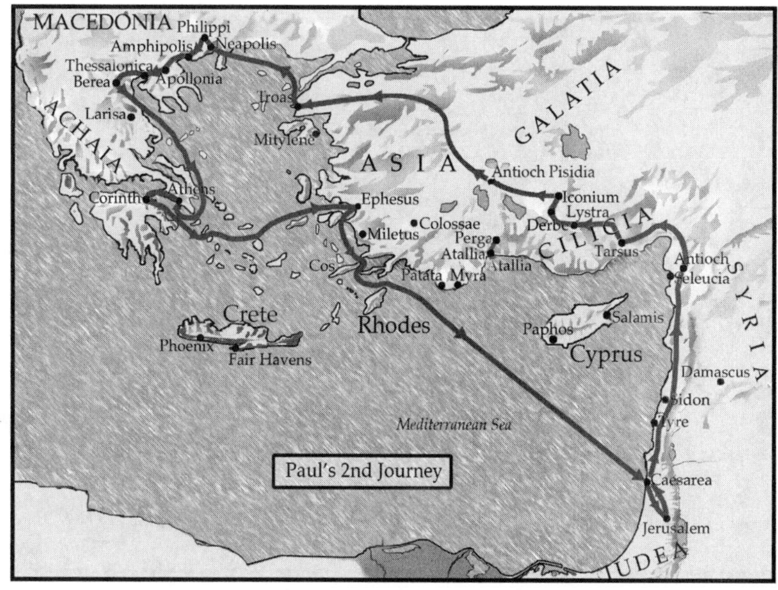
MACEDONIA
Philippi
Amphipolis
Neapolis
Thessalonica
Berea
Apollonia
Troas
GALATIA
Larisa
ACHAIA
Mitylene
ASIA
Antioch Pisidia
Corinth
Athens
Ephesus
Iconium
Lystra
Colossae
Derbe
Miletus
Perga
Atallia
CILICIA
Tarsus
Atallia
Antioch
Seleucia
Cos
Patata
Myra
SYRIA
Crete
Salamis
Rhodes
Paphos
Phoenix
Cyprus
Fair Havens
Damascus
Sidon
Tyre
Mediterranean Sea
Paul's 2nd Journey
Caesarea
Jerusalem
JUDEA

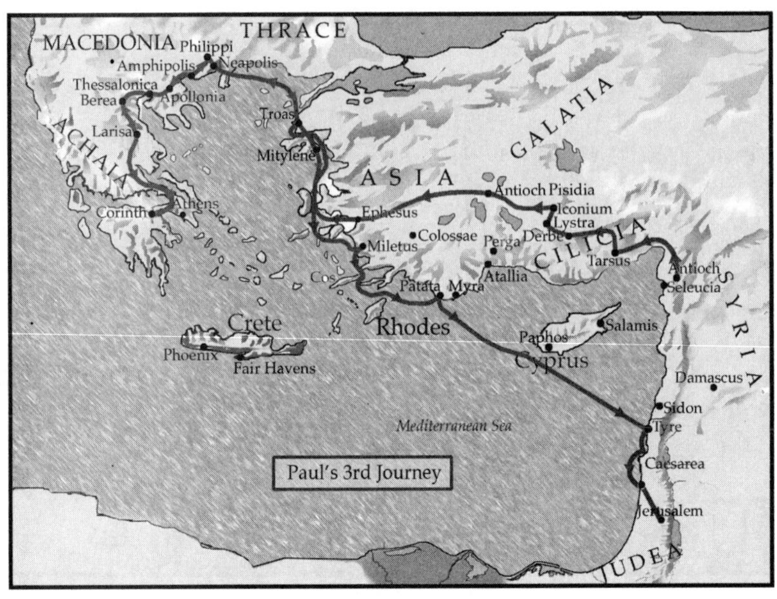
THRACE
MACEDONIA
Philippi
Amphipolis
Neapolis
Thessalonica
Berea
Apollonia
Troas
Larisa
ACHAIA
GALATIA
Mitylene
ASIA
Antioch Pisidia
Iconium
Athens
Corinth
Ephesus
Lystra
Colossae
Perga
Derbe
CILICIA
Miletus
Tarsus
Antioch
Atallia
Cos
Patara
Myra
Seleucia
SYRIA
Salamis
Crete
Rhodes
Paphos
Phoenix
Fair Havens
Cyprus
Damascus
Sidon
Tyre
Mediterranean Sea
Caesarea
Paul's 3rd Journey
Jerusalem
JUDEA

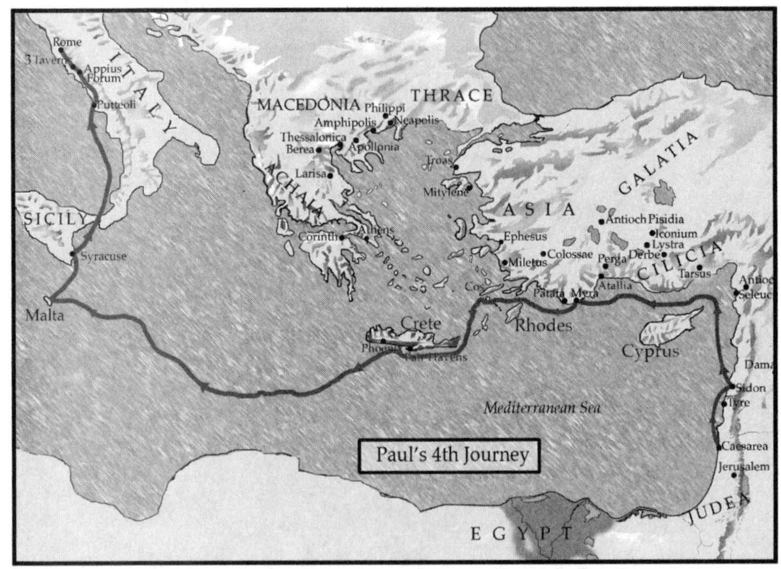
Rome
Appius Forum
ITALY
Putteoli
THRACE
MACEDONIA
Philippi
Amphipolis
Neapolis
Thessalonica
Berea
Apollonia
Troas
Larisa
ACHAIA
Mitylene
GALATIA
SICILY
ASIA
Antioch Pisidia
Iconium
Lystra
Athens
Corinth
Ephesus
Colossae
Perga
Derbe
Syracuse
Miletus
CILICIA
Tarsus
Atallia
Cos
Patara
Myra
Malta
Crete
Rhodes
Cyprus
Sidon
Tyre
Mediterranean Sea
Caesarea
Paul's 4th Journey
Jerusalem
JUDEA
EGYPT

Welcoming the Sabbath

Candlelighting

In traditional Jewish homes, fire may not be ignited after sundown on Friday. A practical activity, the all-important lighting of any flames needed for the next twenty-four hours, developed into one of the most holy times for the Jewish woman—the blessing over the *Shabbat* candles.

Messianic Blessing

ברוך אתה יי אלהינו מלך העולם
אשר קדשנו בדברו
ונתן לנו את ישוע משיחנו
וצונו להיות אור לעולם.

*Ba**ruch** A**tah** Adonai, Elo**hei**nu **Me**lech ha-o**lam**,*
*a**sher** kid'**sha**nu bidva**ro**,*
*v'**na**tan **la**nu et Ye**shu**a M'shi**chei**nu,*
*v'tzi**va**nu l'hi**yot or** l'o**lam**.*

Blessed are You, O Lord our God, King of the Universe,
who has sanctified us with His Word,
and has given us *Yeshua* our Messiah,
and commanded us to be light to the world.

Traditional Blessing

ברוך אתה יי אלהינו מלך העולם
אשר קדשנו במצותיו
וצונו להדליק נר של שבת

*Ba**ruch** A**tah** Adonai, Elo**hei**nu **Me**lech ha-o**lam**,*
*a**sher** kid'**sha**nu b'mitzvo**tav**,*
*v'tzi**va**nu l'had**lik ner** shel Shab**bat**.*

Blessed are You, O Lord our God, King of the Universe,
who has sanctified us with His commandments
and commanded us to light the Sabbath lights.

Blessing the Family

Sons

ישמך אלהים כאפרים וכמנשה.

Y'simcha Elohim k'Efrayim v'chi-M'nasheh.

May God make you like Ephraim and Manasseh.
—Genesis 48:20

Daughters

ישמך אלהים כשרה רבקה רחל ולאה.

Y'simeich Elohim k'Sarah, Rivkah, Rachel, v'Leah.

May God make you like Sarah, Rebecca, Rachel, and Leah.

All

יברכך יי וישמרך
יאר יי פניו אליך ויחנך
ישא יי פניו אליך וישם לך שלום.

Y'varech'cha ADONAI v'yishm'recha;
ya-eir ADONAI panav elecha, vichuneka;
yisa ADONAI panav elecha, v'yasem l'cha shalom.

The LORD bless you and keep you;
the LORD make His face shine upon you, and be gracious to you;
the LORD lift up His countenance upon you, and give you peace.
—Numbers 6:24-26

Wife

אשת חיל מי ימצא ורחק מפנינים מכרה.
בטח בה לב בעלה ושלל לא יחסר.

Eishet chayil mi yimtza, v'rachok mipninim michrah.
Batach bah lev ba'alah v'shalal lo yechsar.

A woman of valor who can find, she is worth far more than precious jewels.
The heart of her husband trusts in her, and he shall have no lack of gain.
—Proverbs 31:10-11

Prayer of Sanctification

We symbolize the joy and holiness of God's day of rest with a cup of wine or grape juice. The *Kiddush*, the "prayer of holiness," reminds us that as those redeemed by the Messiah, we are all called to reflect His holiness.

And there was evening...

ויהי ערב ויהי בקר יום הששי.
ויכלו השמים והארץ וכל צבאם.
ויכל אלהים ביום השביעי מלאכתו אשר עשה
וישבת ביום השביעי מכל מלאכתו אשר עשה
ויברך אלהים את יום השבעי ויקדש אתו
כי בו שבת מכל מלאכתו אשר ברא אלהים לעשות.

__Va__-y'hi __e__rev __va__-y'hi __vo__ker, yom ha-shi__shi__.
Va-y'chu__lu__ ha-sha__ma__yim v'ha-__a__retz v'chol-tzva'__am__.
Va-y'__chal__ Elo__him__ ba-__yom__ ha-shvi'__i__ m'lach__to__ __a__sh__er__ __a__s__ah__,
va-yish__bot__ ba-__yom__ ha-shvi'__i__ mi-kol-m'lach__to__ __a__sh__er__ __a__s__ah__,
va-y'__va__rech Elo__him__ et __yom__ ha-shvi'__i__, va-y'ka__desh__ o__to__,
ki vo sha__vat__ mi-kol-m'lach__to__, __a__sh__er__ ba__ra__ Elo__him__ la'__a__s__ot__.

And there was evening and there was morning, the sixth day.
And the heavens and the earth were completed along with all their host.
And on the seventh day God completed His work, which He had done,
and He rested on the seventh day from all His work which He had done.
And God blessed the seventh day and hallowed it,
because on it He rested from all His work which God had created to do.
—Genesis 1:31b-2:3

Blessing over the Wine

ברוך אתה יי אלהינו מלך העולם
בורא פרי הגפן.

Ba__ruch__ A__tah__ A__DONAI__, Elo__hei__nu __Me__lech ha-o__lam__,
bo__rei__ p'__ri__ ha-__ga__fen.

Blessed are You, O LORD our God, King of the Universe,
who creates the fruit of the vine.

Kiddush (continued)

ברוך אתה יי אלהינו מלך העולם
אשר קדשנו במצותיו ורצה בנו
ושבת קדשו באהבה וברצון הנחילנו
זכרון למעשה בראשית.
כי הוא יום תחלה למקראי קדש
זכר ליציאת מצרים.
כי בנו בחרת ואותנו קדשת מכל העמים.
ושבת קדשך באהבה וברצון הנחלתנו.
ברוך אתה יי מקדש השבת.

*Ba**ruch** A**tah** A**DONAI**, Elo**hei**nu **Me**lech ha-o**lam**,*
*a**sher** kid'**sha**nu b'mitzvo**tav**, v'**ra**tzah **va**nu,*
*v'Shab**bat** kad**sho** b'aha**vah** u-v'ra**tzon** hinchi**la**nu,*
*zika**ron** **l'ma'aseh** v'**rei**sheet.*
*Ki hu **yom** t'**chi**lah l'mi**kra**ei **ko**desh,*
***ze**cher l'tzi**at** Mitz**ra**yim.*
*Ki **va**nu va**char**ta v'o**ta**nu ki**dash**ta mi-kol-ha-a**mim**.*
*V'Shab**bat** kadsh'**cha**, b'aha**vah** u-vra**tzon** hinchal**ta**nu.*
*Ba**ruch** A**tah**, A**DONAI**, m'ka**deish** ha-Shab**bat**.*

Blessed are You, O LORD our God,
who has sanctified us with His commandments and has been pleased with us,
and has given us His holy *Shabbat* as a heritage with love and favor,
as a reminder of the work of creation in the beginning.
For that day is the foremost of our holy called-out times,
a reminder of the exodus from Egypt.
For you have chosen us and sanctified us from among all the nations.
You have given us Your holy *Shabbat* in love and delight as our heritage.
Blessed are You, O LORD, who sanctifies the *Shabbat*.

Blessing over the Bread

ברוך אתה יי אלהינו מלך העולם
המוציא לחם מן הארץ.

*Ba**ruch** A**tah** A**DONAI**, Elo**hei**nu **Me**lech ha-o**lam**,*
*ha-**mo**tzi **le**chem **min** ha-**a**retz*

Blessed are You, O LORD our God, King of the Universe,
who brings forth bread from the earth.

Thanksgiving

Blessing After the Meal

Jewish culture thanks God for the blessing of food both before and after eating.

ברוך אתה יי אלהינו מלך העולם
הזן את העולם כלו בתבו
בחן בחסד וברחמים.
הוא נותן לחם לכל בשר כי לעולם חסדו.
ובתובו הגדול תמיד לא חסר לנו
ואל יחסר לנו מזון לעולם ועד
בעבור שמו הגדול.
כי הוא אל זן ומפרנס לכל ומטיב לכל
ומכין מזון לכל בריתיו אשר ברא.
ברוך אתה יי הזן את הכל.

*Ba**ruch** A**tah** A**DONAI**, Elo**hei**nu **Me**lech ha-o**lam**,*
*ha-**zan** et ha-o**lam** ku**lo** b'tu**vo***
*b'**chein**, b'**che**sed, uv'racha**mim**.*
*Hu no**tein le**chem l'chol-**ba**sar, ki l'o**lam** chas**do**.*
*Uvtu**vo** ha-ga**dol**, ta**mid** lo **cha**sar **la**nu,*
*v'**al** yech**sar la**nu ma**zon** l'o**lam** va-**ed***
*ba-a**vur** sh'**mo** ha-ga**dol**.*
*Ki hu **El** zan umfar**neis** la**kol** u-mei**tiv** la-**kol**,*
*u-mei**chin** ma**zon** l'chol-briyo**tav** a**sher** ba**ra**.*
*Ba**ruch** A**tah** A**DONAI**, ha-**zan** et ha-**kol**.*

Blessed are You, O LORD our God, King of the Universe,
who feeds the whole world in His goodness—
with grace, with kindness, and with mercy.
He gives food to all flesh, for His kindness is everlasting.
Through His great goodness, never have we lacked
and never may we lack food
for the sake of His great Name.
For He is a good God, who feeds and sustains all and does good to all,
and prepares food for all His creatures whom He has created.
Blessed are You, O LORD, who provides food for all.
"You open Your hand and satisfy the desire of every living thing."
—Psalm 145:16

Farewell to *Shabbat*

Havdalah

As Shabbat draws to an end, the aroma of sweet spices lingers as the flame is extinguished until next week.

הנה אל ישועתי אבטח ולא אפחד
כי עזי וזמרת יה יי ויהי לי לישועה.
ושאבתם מים בששון ממעיני הישועה.

*Hi**neh El** yeshua**ti**, ev**tach** v'**lo** ef**chad**.*
***Ki** ozi v'zim**rat Yah** ADONAI **va**-y'hi-**li** lishu**ah**.*
*U-**shav**tem **ma**yim b'sa**son** mi-**ma'ainei** ha-yeshu**ah**.*

Behold, God is my salvation, I will trust and will not be afraid,
for the LORD my God is my strength and my song, He also has become my salvation.
And with joy you shall draw water from the wells of salvation.— Isaiah 12:2-3

ברוך אתה יי אלהינו מלך העולם בורא פרי הגפן.

*Ba**ruch** A**tah** ADONAI, Elo**hei**nu **Me**lech ha-o**lam**, bo**rei** p'**ri** ha-**ga**fen.*

Blessed are You, O LORD our God, King of the Universe, who creates the fruit of the vine.

ברוך אתה יי אלהינו מלך העולם בורא מיני בשמים.

*Ba**ruch** A**tah** ADONAI, Elo**hei**nu **Me**lech ha-o**lam**, bo**rei** mi**nei** v'sa**mim**.*

Blessed are You, O LORD our God, King of the Universe, who creates all kinds of spices.

ברוך אתה יי אלהינו מלך העולם בורא מאורי האש.

*Ba**ruch** A**tah** ADONAI, Elo**hei**nu **Me**lech ha-o**lam**, bo**rei** m'o**rei** ha-**eish**.*

Blessed are You, O LORD our God, King of the Universe, who creates the lights of fire.

ברוך אתה יי אלהינו מלך העולם המבדיל בין קדש לחול.

*Ba**ruch** A**tah** ADONAI, Elo**hei**nu **Me**lech ha-o**lam**, ha-mav**dil** bein **ko**desh l'**chol**.*

Blessed are You, O LORD our God, King of the Universe, who distinguishes between holy and secular.

שבוע טוב
*Sha**vu**a tov*—have a good week!

Messiah's Prayer

אבינו שבשמים יתקדש שמך.
תבוא מלכותך יעשה רצונך
כבשמים כן בארץ.
את לחם חקנו תן לנו היום
וסלח לנו על חטאינו
כפי שסולחים גם אנחנו לחוטאים לנו.
ואל תביאנו לידי נסיון
כי אם חלצנו מן הרע.
כי לך הממלכה והגבורה והתפארת
לעולמי עולמים. אמן.

*A**vi**nu shebasha**ma**yim, yitka**desh** shim**cha**.*
*Ta**vo** mal**chu**t'**cha**, yei'**aseh** r'**tzon**'**cha***
*k'vasha**ma**yim ken ba-**a**retz.*
*Et **le**chem chu**kei**nu ten **la**nu ha-**yom**,*
*u-s'**lach la**nu al chata'**ei**nu*
*k'**fi** she**sol**'**chim gam** a**nach**nu lachot'**im la**nu.*
*V'**al** t'vi'**e**nu li**dei** nisa**yon***
*ki **im** chal**tze**nu **min** ha-**ra**.*
Ki** l'**cha** ha-**mam**la**cha** v'**ha**gvu**rah** v'**ha**tife**ret
*l'**o**l'**mei** ola**mim**. A**men**.*

Our Father in heaven, sanctified be Your name.
Your kingdom come, Your will be done
on earth as it is in heaven.
Give us this day our daily bread.
And forgive us our debts
as we also have forgiven our debtors.
And lead us not into temptation,
but deliver us from the evil one. —Matthew 6:9b-13
For Yours is the kingdom and the power and the glory
forever and ever. Amen.

www.TreeOfLifeBible.org

If you would like to contribute financially to the development of this newly vetted, theologically sound text, you are welcome to learn more about our project and donate online. Rest assured that this text is owned by our not-for-profit corporation and no one will ever be allowed to alter this Biblical text without our written approval.

The ongoing purpose of our corporation is to create and subsidize the distribution of a new Messianic Jewish Version of the Holy Bible to all mankind. All contributions brought in that exceed our need to meet the expenses to complete this new text will go directly to purchasing more bibles to distribute freely to everyone who wants to learn of our Messiah.

Our declaration is that *Yeshua*, Jesus, laid down His life willingly as our eternal offering for sin. We further acknowledge we believe He rose from the dead three days later and sits now at the right hand of God in heaven. We want the whole world to know He is the Son of God.

www.DestinyImage.com

Destiny Image Publishing is our exclusive publisher of this new version and has committed to partnering with us for the duration of this project. When you want to purchase more copies of this book, and the others to follow, go to their website. Help us get this Bible into the hands of everyone you know that needs Messiah! And, be sure to tell your entire social network about us on Facebook and Twitter, too!

The active role of Destiny Image in furthering this project, both financially and professionally, is a blessing for Messianic Jewish believers worldwide. Their commitment to stand with us, to pray for us, to encourage us and to work alongside us is a living example of the brotherly love that changes the world. That is the message of hope and acceptance that *Yeshua's* message is still about!

Behold how good and how pleasant it is for brother's to dwell together in unity. May God's grace and mercy overflow Donald Nori and the entire Destiny Image family, forever in Yeshua's love.

God bless and keep you,

Daniah Greenberg, President
Messianic Jewish Family Bible Project
spreadtheword@messianicfamilybible.org

Tree of Life Bible Fund
PO Box 2183
Syracuse, NY 13220